IN DEFENCE
OF EMMA

'Nineteenth century historians tended to portray Emma as a scheming adventuress who led the naïve hero astray'

Colin White, New letters, page 37.
Published 2005

'[Romney] had known the ecstasy of accomplishment and the tranquil glow of friendship, and basked in the sunshine of one radiant presence.'

George Romney by Sir Herbert Maxwell, page 154
Published 1902

IN DEFENCE
OF EMMA

'Scheming Adventuress'
or
'Radiant Presence' ?

Sylvia K. Robinson

Sylvia K. Robinson

First published in Great Britain in 2016

Copyright © by Sylvia K. Robinson

ISBN 978-1-5262-0407-3

Typeset by Geoff Fisher in 12pt Dante MT
geoff.fisher@yahoo.co.uk

*Printed and bound in Great Britain
by CPI Books (UK) Croydon CRO 4YY*

Dedicated to my family and friends

Contents

List of Illustrations

See plate section

Acknowledgements

MY GRATEFUL THANKS are due to my husband, sons, extended family and many friends for their unwavering support, encouragement and patience throughout the time that I have been immersed in the 18th and early 19th centuries, absorbed in Emma's dramatic life. I am conscious that family and friends have suffered a degree of neglect on my part.

I am deeply indebted to my friend, Christine Hooper, for her valiant effort in typing my very long manuscript for me. Without her steadfast commitment, constructive criticism and advice over a period of five years, this biography would not have been completed.

Special thanks are due to Mrs Anna Tribe, a direct descendant of Emma, for granting access to Emma's bank account, and to Rear Admiral Sir Peter Anson, Bt for permission to access Hamilton's bank account.

Many individuals, specialists in their fields, have generously given up time to assist me: Alex Kidson for guidance on Romney; Jeff Pilkington, Principal Researcher, Archive department at Christie's for assistance on Hamilton's picture sales; Dr Hilary Johnson for editorial assistance; Count Charles de Salis for sharing his extensive knowledge of Napoleon; Michael Nash for information and advice on reference books. To others who have helped in ways too numerous to mention here I extend my sincere thanks.

For finding and supplying information and images in an efficient and friendly manner I owe my thanks to staff at various public institutions: The National Archives; National Maritime Museum; National Portrait Gallery; British Library; National Museum of the Royal Navy; Nelson Museums at Monmouth and Great Yarmouth; Sotheby's; Merton Historical Society; Flintshire Record Office; Victoria and Albert Museum; London Metropolitan Archives and The Goldsmiths' Company.

Every reasonable effort has been made to ensure the accuracy of information contained in this account of Emma's life. Any errors that might be found in the presentation of this information or in my interpretation thereof are entirely my own responsibility.

CHAPTER 1

Obscure Origins

'Few bend at thy bier, unhappy one!
All know thy shame, thy mental suffering none,
All know thy frailties – all thou wast and art!
But thine were faults of circumstance – not heart!'
　　　　　　　　　DR. William Beattie, physician and poet, 1831*

LITTLE IS KNOWN about the childhood and early years of the little girl who became Emma, the wife of Sir William Hamilton and mistress of Admiral Lord Nelson.

No reliable evidence exists to support the many myths, legends and rumours that evolved over time concerning these early years. Repeated uncorroborated stories theorize that she worked for a tradesman in St. James's market; as a parlour-maid and for a 'Lady of Quality'; that she was employed by a Mrs Kelly who provided young escorts to accompany gentlemen to various entertainments such as Ranelagh and Vauxhall Gardens; that her first lover was Captain (later Rear-Admiral) Willet-Payne, whom she had approached to save a cousin from being pressed into naval service. Such unsubstantiated stories led some biographers to accuse Emma of prostitution.

Despite the extraordinary efforts Emma made to *'improve'* herself in the following years, her life was marred by the gossip surrounding these early years. Her reputation never entirely recovered and she often suffered the humiliation of being snubbed by polite society.

Details of Emma's birth are recorded in archives in Flintshire, Wales. Her mother, Mary Kidd, married Henry Lyon on 11 June 1764 at Neston on the Wirral Peninsula, not far from Chester. Emma was born around 26 April 1765 at nearby Ness and her baptism was

---

* Not Nelson's Dr William Beatty.

1

registered, also at Neston, as Emy (Amy or Emly) Lyon on 12 May 1765.

Her father, Henry Lyon, either a local man or possibly from Lancashire, worked in the colliery that opened in 1759 at Ness. He was employed as a blacksmith, making and repairing machinery, tools and horseshoes. Before the opening of the colliery, men in the area would have worked in the agriculture, farming, and fishing industries or as merchant seamen, shipping coal to North Wales and Ireland from the colliery.

Mary, her mother, worked as a dressmaker and in domestic service. Henry Lyon died in June 1765, possibly from consumption, when Emy was barely two months old. Mary and her baby daughter returned to live with the maternal grandmother, Dame Sarah Kidd, who lived in the nearby village of Hawarden in Wales. It appears that Emy's grandfather, Thomas Kidd, who had been a shepherd, had recently died.

Dame Kidd earned a living carting coal in the area, probably supplying the local mansion, Broadlane Hall, owned by the Glynne family. She may also have taken produce from the Hall to market. It has been claimed the little Emy was seen walking alongside the cart, helping to sell the coal.[1] Mary Kidd had a brother, William, and three sisters, whose later married names were Connor, Reynolds and Moore.

Emy was twelve or thirteen years old when she went to work for the Thomas family in Hawarden. Mr Honoratus Leigh Thomas worked in Chester as a surgeon and specialist in smallpox inoculation. Emy was presumably employed to help with the six Thomas children living at home. One of the daughters made a drawing of Emy, an early indication of how beautiful Emma would become.

Mrs Thomas was well-respected in Hawarden and it may be that Emy learned to read and write alongside the other children. Although education was not compulsory at the time, Emy may have attended some classes at the local church. There is no record of a Dame school in Hawarden at that time. Emy seems to have had a happy relationship with Mrs Thomas, who wrote a sympathetic letter to her in 1808 concerning her mother's troublesome family.

Henry Lyon and Mary Kidd both signed their marriage certificate with a mark, signifying illiteracy,[2] and Emy later claimed that her education only began when she was seventeen years old. In years to come, they both proved to be intelligent and capable women. Both were able to write well, albeit with idiosyncratic spelling in Emma's case. Emma learnt to read music and both learnt to speak and write Italian and French. Emma made a valuable contribution to Hamilton's ambassadorial work and her mother managed Nelson's estate at Merton. Had they remained in Hawarden, their futures would most likely have been in domestic service.

Mary decided to go to London, soon sending for Emy to join her, hoping to forge a better life for herself and her daughter. She established herself there under the name of Mrs Cadogan. Later we learn that there may have been a 'Mr Doggin' in her life, a name she upgraded to Cadogan. She found employment for Emy, now known as Emily, with a Dr Budd and his family at Chatham Place, Blackfriars, possibly with an introduction from Mr Thomas. Emily worked with the undermaid, Jane, in the Budd household. The two girls became good friends, a relationship renewed many years later after Jane had realized her ambition to be on the stage, becoming the famous actress, Mrs Jane Powell.

The area known as Covent Garden was not far from Dr Budd's home. In Jane and Emily's time there was a market selling fruit and vegetables in the piazza. The surrounding houses attracted bohemian residents, artists and writers. It is possible that Jane and Emily spent any time off enjoying the atmosphere of the busy market and the excitement of seeing famous actors and actresses around the nearby theatres.

According to legend, the girls pushed their luck too far and stayed out too late one night. Mrs Budd dismissed Emily the following morning. We assume that after this summary dismissal, with little or no money and few possessions, Emily would have gone straight back to her mother for help.

Emily next found employment as a maidservant to Mrs Linley, wife of the composer and joint owner of the Theatre Royal, Drury Lane. Mrs Linley was the wardrobe mistress at the theatre and Emily helped with the cleaning, sorting and care of the costumes. She met the Linleys' beautiful daughter, Elizabeth, a renowned singer, who performed at the theatre. Emily's future interest in acting and singing must have developed while in the Linleys' employment.

The Linleys' second son, eighteen year-old Samuel, a midshipman on HMS *Thunderer*, arrived home in December 1778 desperately ill with a fever. Emily nursed him with great care according to Mrs Linley *'up to the last moment of his decease'.* Distraught and disturbed by Samuel's death and burial on 21 December, Emily left her employment with Mrs Linley.

In the summer of 1779, a Dr James Graham opened the so-called Temple of Health in the Royal Terrace, Adelphi. Dr Graham had studied medicine at Edinburgh University, but was possibly not a fully qualified doctor. His treatments, including the use of electricity and magnetism, were considered eccentric at the time. Unusually, he encouraged open windows, fresh air and personal hygiene.

The house, its fittings and decorations were reputed to have cost £10,000. The ambience was enhanced by music, statuary, paintings and perfumes. The fees were very high and the clientele of ladies and gentlemen of the very highest rank, including Horace Walpole and, it has been claimed, the Prince of Wales.

Dr Graham gave lectures on topics such as *Love and Beauty and their Effects on Human Life* and *The Generation, Increase and Improvement of the Human Race.* Around him during these lectures were young women lightly draped in Grecian style representing Health, Beauty and Wisdom. Emily may have posed in these tableaux.

Dr Graham hoped to appeal to fashionable society with his morally acceptable lectures, albeit tinged with sexual innuendo. Only the rich and famous would have been able to afford his star attraction – the Celestial Bed – claiming to cure infertility, for which he allegedly charged £50 per night, a huge amount at the time, to couples desperate for a child.

The beautiful Emily may have captured the attention of Sir Harry Fetherstonhaugh, a dashing and wealthy twenty-six-year-old, at the Temple of Health when she was just fifteen years old. No doubt Emily was equally impressed by this man about town who in 1774 had inherited his family's estate, Uppark in Sussex, a magnificent house with 800 acres. He had travelled in France and Italy, and was *'very civil and good-humoured'.*[3] Emily agreed to be taken to live 'under his protection' on his estate.

It would not have been considered unusual to be a wealthy man's mistress in those days. Men openly kept mistresses, often flaunting them, and for an impoverished young girl with no chance of an education or profession, it was an option not necessarily frowned upon. Many girls or women living as mistresses might have hoped for marriage or valuable gifts and allowances. Sometimes, when the relationship ended, they might be granted a small pension.

Sir Henry's mother was in residence at Uppark and Emma lived in a cottage on the estate leading a rural lifestyle. Sir Harry taught her to ride and, with youthful exuberance, she became a daredevil horsewoman. She followed the hunt and may have ridden in the private race meetings held on the estate.

Sir Harry, blessed with an income of around £7,000 a year,[4] lived for pleasure. His mother kept the household accounts. His interests included hunting, shooting and country pursuits. He was passionate about horse racing, sometimes riding his horses himself in races at Uppark, Goodwood and Newmarket. He invited many of his London high society gentlemen friends, including the Hon. Charles Greville, to join him in these country pursuits at Uppark. His beautiful young mistress was on hand to sing and dance for his guests after dinner. There is no extant evidence for the oft-repeated legend that she danced naked on the Uppark dining-room table.

Greville, the handsome thirty-two-year-old second son of the Earl of Warwick, was to play a significant role in her life. He was unusual among Sir Harry's friends in that he was a serious-minded, cautious and thoughtful man, interested in the arts and sciences. He had earnest conversations with her warning her of the dangers of her *'madcap'* life.

Emily visited her mother in London during brief periods away from Uppark, calling on Greville at the same time. Concerned about her, Greville gave her some franked envelopes to use should she need to write to him. His concern was well-founded. Before Emily had been at Uppark for a year, she was six months pregnant. Sir Harry dismissed her with barely enough money for her journey home. From a comment Greville made later to Emily, it seems Sir Harry may have doubted that he was the father of the child. Emily always claimed that he *was* the father and in letters exchanged between them thirty years later Sir Harry accepted responsibility.

At the end of the year, in extreme distress, Emily wrote to Greville begging for his help.

CHAPTER 2

Love and Obedience

'What am I but a girl in reall distress … O for God's sake
tell me what is to become on me'
Emma to Greville, January 1782

'… the wild unthinking Emma is a grave thoughtful phylosopher'
Emma to Greville, 22 June 1784

'I truly love you and the thought of your coming home so soon
makes me so happy, I don't know what to do'
Emma to Greville, August 1784

THE HONOURABLE CHARLES Francis Greville was born in December
1749, the second son of the Earl of Warwick. His father died in 1773,
leaving him a mere £100 with which to purchase a mourning ring. His
elder brother succeeded to the earldom, inheriting the family home,
Warwick Castle, and estates.

Charles had a modest income for a man of his standing. He
complained to his uncle, Sir William Hamilton, of *'being only possessed*
of an annuity of £500 a year',[1] an income bequeathed to him by his mother,
Elizabeth, daughter of Lord Archibald Hamilton and sister of Sir William.

Greville was a Member of Parliament for Warwick from 1774-1790,
but MPs were not paid a salary at that time. It was considered an
honour to be elected and they were expected to have private incomes.
He was a Fellow of the Royal Society and a member of the Society of
the Dilettanti. In addition to his interest in mineralogy and the Arts,
Greville was passionate about horticulture. He assisted Sir Joseph
Banks* in setting up the society that became the Royal Horticultural
Society. None of these interests brought in any money.

---

* Sir Joseph Banks, distinguished botanist and President of the Royal Society

Greville supplemented his income by acting as an agent in buying and selling paintings and *'virtu'* (artistic curiosities as collected by connoisseurs) for his uncle and his friends. He began building up what was to become an important collection of minerals worth £13,000 at his death. In his lifelong interest in mineralogy and collecting he found common ground with his uncle, the collector and Envoy Extraordinary to the Court of Naples, Sir William Hamilton.

In such straitened financial circumstances, his only hope was to marry a rich heiress. To present himself as a more substantial person than he actually was to attract this heiress, in 1778 he built a mansion in Portman Square, a new and fashionable area of London, with borrowed capital. His search for a wealthy wife and his hopes of selling the house at a profit after finding her were unsuccessful. He remained living there alone with his 'collection and statues'.

In October 1780, through the auspices of his younger brother, Robert Fulke Greville, he secured a position at the Admiralty with rent-free accommodation in the King's Mews (now the site of Trafalgar Square), [2] though he still spent time in Portman Square. He continued to add to his income by dealing in art, spending hours at the Royal Society and the British Museum and corresponding with his like-minded and sympathetic uncle, Sir William.

Early in 1782 Greville came to the rescue of the desperate sixteen year-old Emily, now six months pregnant. The baby must have been conceived in June 1781, very soon after Emily turned sixteen years old, as 'Little Emma' was born in February or early March 1782. Emily wrote seven letters to Sir Harry, knowing he was in Leicestershire, but received no reply.

In her desperation, Emily may have used one of the franked envelopes Greville had given her to tell him of her plight and that she had returned to Hawarden, probably in December 1781. He must have responded with a note as she sent the following letter to him early in January 1782:

My Dear Grevell Yesterday I did receve your kind letr. It put me in some spirits for believe me I am almost distraktid, I have never hard from Sir H. and he is not at Lechster now I am sure, what shall I dow, good God What shall I dow, I have wrote him 7 letters and no anser, I cant come to town for want of mony, I have not a farthing to bless myself with and I think my frends looks cooly on me, I think so. OG what shall I dow, what shall I dow. O how your letter affected me wen you wished me happiness. OG that I was in your

7

posesion as I was in Sir H. What a happy girl would I have been, girl indead, or what am I but a girl in reall distress, for Gods sake G write the minet you get this and only tell me what I ham to dow, derect some whay. I am almost mad. O for Gods sake tell me what is to become on me. O dear Grevell write to me. Write to me G. Adue and believe yours for ever.

Emily Hart.

Dont tell my mother what distress I am in and dow aford me some comfort.

My age was got out the Reggister and have sent it to My Dear Charles. Once more Adue, once more Adue. O you dear friend.[3]

She enclosed a note that said:

Amy(ly) Daughter of Henry Lyon of Ness by Mary his wife.

Bap: the 12th May 1765.

The above is truly copied from the G. Neston Register by R. Carter, Curate. Neston Dec. 19th. 1781.

In reply to this distraught appeal, the prudent and pedantic Greville wrote Emily a long letter in which he asked if she still loved Sir Harry and whether she might return to live with him. He doubted Sir Harry would take her back and advised her to take a *'steady resolution'*. He tried to be fair and reasonable, but at the same time, made clear his fond feelings for her and expressed his wish that she should now place herself under his care. He ended, most affectionately: *'God bless you my dearest lovely girl, take your determination soon and let me hear from you.'*

Jan 10th. 1782

My dear Emily

I do not make apologies for Sir H's behaviour to you & altho I advised you to deserve his good esteem by your good conduct, I own I never expected better from him, it was your duty to deserve good treatment & it gave me great concern to see you imprudent the first time you came to G: from the country, & as the same conduct was repeated when you was last in town, I began to despair of your happiness, to prove to you that I do not accuse you falsely I only mention 5 guineas, half a guinea for coach, but my Emily, as you seem quite miserable now, I do not mean to give you uneasiness, but comfort, & tell you that I will forget your faults & bad conduct to Sir H. & to myself & will not repent my good humour, if I shall find that you have learnt by experience to value yourself & to endeavor to preserve your Friends by good conduct & affection.

I will now answer your last letter. You tell me you think your Friends look cooly on you, it is therefore time to leave them, but it is necessary for you to decide some points before you come to Town. You are sensible that for the *three next months your situation will not admit of a giddy life if you had wished it, & would therefore be imprudent to come and hunt after new connection, or try to regain the one you gave up as lost, after you have told me that Sir H. gave you barely money to get to your friends, & has never answer'd one letter since, and neither provided for you, nor takes any notice of you; it might appear laughing at you, to advise you to make Sir H. more kind and attentive … You may easily see my Dearest Emily, why it is absolutely necessary for this point to be completely settled <u>before</u> I can move one step. If you love Sir H. you should not give him up & if you can continue with him, it would be ridiculous in me to take care of his girl, who is better able to maintain her, but besides this, my Emily, I would not be troubled with your connexions (excepting your mother) & with Sir H. friends for the universe.*

… & at least if everything fails, if you mean to have my protection I must <u>first</u> know from you <u>that you are clear of every connexion & that you will never take them again without my consent</u>. I shall then be free to dry up the tears of my lovely Emily and to give her comfort, if you do not forfeit my esteem perhaps my Emily may be happy … If you should come to town free from all engagements and take my advice, you will live very retired, <u>till</u> you are brought to bed. You should part with your maid, and take another <u>name</u>, by degrees I would get you a new set of acquaintance, & by keeping your own secret, & nobody about you having it in their power to betray you, I may be expected to see you respected & admired. Thus far relates to yourself, as to the child, Sir H. may be informed of circumstances which may reasonably make him doubt & it is not worth while to make it a subject of altercation, its mother shall obtain it kindness from me & it shall never want.

I inclose you some money, do not throw it away, you may send some presents when you arrive in town, but do not be on the road without some money to <u>spare</u>, in case you should be fatigued & wish to take your time … God bless you my dearest lovely girl, take your determination soon & let me hear from you. Once more Adieu my D. Emily.[4]

Greville, it seems, had been strongly attracted to Emily on his visits to Uppark and during her visits to him in London. She may have flirted with him on these occasions. He is clearly a man who expects unconditional loyalty and faithfulness. She, in turn, considers him a close and good friend. Precisely what Emily had done to deserve the reprimand that she had been 'imprudent' and had behaved badly towards both Sir Harry and Greville, is unknown. Greville refers to '*5 guineas, half a guinea for a coach*', apparently connected with her imprudence. Perhaps Emily had begged this money from either Greville or Sir Harry, then used it to visit other friends?

We can only imagine Emily's reaction to this letter. Whereas Sir Harry had never taken her seriously and had cruelly dismissed her, here was an honourable man declaring his fondness and admiration of her, promising to take care of her, to make sure she is *'respected and admired'*, to accept her mother into his house and to undertake that her baby *'shall never want'*. It must have been with great relief and in high hopes of a happy future that Emily concurred with his terms and conditions.

Leaving her baby with her grandmother, Dame Kidd, Emily arrived in London calling herself Mrs Emma Hart. Greville had suggested she change her name to make a fresh start with new acquaintances unaware of *'her own secret'*. The 'Mrs' was for the sake of propriety.

Greville had taken a house in Edgware Road (near present-day Marble Arch) for Emma, her mother and two maids, with extra space for him to have his own apartment. In those days the area was bordered by fields, distant enough from the centre of London to be a secluded part of his life.

Emma and her mother took up residence there. It appears that Mrs Cadogan had met Charles Greville before he invited Emma to live under his *'protection'*. In her *'distraktid'* letter to Greville Emma had written a postscript *'don't tell my mother what distress I am in'* and Greville mentions her mother in his letter above.

They may have met several times, perhaps when Emma came up to London from Uppark. The ever-cautious Greville would surely not have included Mrs Cadogan in the arrangement without knowing something about her. He must have been aware of her reputation as a capable housekeeper and an excellent cook and seamstress.

Emma's mother's role was to act as cook and housekeeper. She guided, and to an extent restrained her headstrong daughter and in general was reliable and undemanding. She remained by Emma's side for the rest of her life. Both Sir William Hamilton and Lord Nelson became very fond of her.

Greville had 'acquired' a lovely young girl who would be recognized as one of the most beautiful women in Europe. He planned to have portraits of Emma painted by his friend, the artist George Romney, expecting to sell these paintings on, in addition to profiting from the engravings of them that he intended to commission and sell.

The forty-seven year old Romney was an established leading portrait painter of the time, in competition with Sir Joshua Reynolds and Thomas Gainsborough. He had recently taken a lease on no. 24 Cavendish Square (now no. 32), a house containing a large painting studio – 'big enough to entertain a crowd of guests'. Romney had come to London, aged twenty-seven, determined to improve his art, leaving his wife, Molly, and his son, John, behind in Kendal. He had married Molly at the age of twenty-two when she fell pregnant. Soon afterwards, he left to work in York and was an absentee husband and father throughout the marriage until the last few years of his life when he returned to Kendal where Molly, remarkably, cared for him until he died. Romney supported his family throughout the thirty-seven years of his absence.

Already a successful portrait painter, he undertook a two-year study tour in Italy in 1773. There he studied and made copies of works of the great masters including Michelangelo, Raphael, Titian and Correggio. On his return to London he was even more highly regarded, being considered well-travelled and experienced. His clientele came from the higher social strata, among them the Earl of Warwick and his brother, Charles Greville.

Sir Joshua Reynolds was instrumental in establishing the new Royal Academy and was envious of Romney's work. In selecting the foundation members Reynolds had passed over some important artists, including Romney, whom he referred to as 'the man in Cavendish Square'. For his own part, Romney disapproved of the Academy's elitism and preferred to remain independent.

Romney worked at a prodigious pace, sometimes with five or six sittings in one day. He seldom made preliminary drawings, but painted directly onto the canvas, and could produce a portrait in a day. John Wesley said, 'Romney produced more in an hour than Sir Joshua did in ten.' The speed of his brushwork and the fact that his sitters accepted his more spontaneous style meant that his income was considerable, calculated in 1795 to be £3-4,000 per year. Despite his success, Romney suffered extreme mood swings, from joy to gloom, throughout his life.

When Greville introduced Emma to Romney in his studio at 11 a.m. on 12 March 1782, she was just six weeks short of her seventeenth birthday. She was a breath of fresh air for the artist. It was the beginning of a long and very close relationship between artist and model. In Romney's bouts of depression, it was Emma who inspired and reinvigorated him. Their association produced an important contribution to English art.

Romney was entranced by Emma's beauty and grace, delighted by her ability to strike poses and to display a wide range of emotions in her facial expressions. Mrs Cadogan accompanied Emma by carriage to these sittings, certainly initially. We can imagine her sitting quietly in the corner of the studio reading or sewing.

Romney's son, John, described Emma as *'a young female of artless and playful character, of extraordinary Elegance and symmetry of form, of a most beautiful countenance glowing with health and animation',*[5] and wrote that Emma always conducted herself with *'great propriety'.* In his father's dealings with her she was treated with the utmost respect. Perhaps John wanted to quash any rumours that there had been a deeper relationship between his father and Emma.

Romney may have fallen a little in love with Emma but, for her, the relationship was one of father and daughter. She had learnt her lesson and would never have risked her newfound security by betraying Greville.

A biography of Romney by George Paston in 1903 describes Emma:

'It is scarcely necessary to dwell upon the details of her fascinations, since her auburn hair, her brilliant colouring, her perfect mouth and her girlish grace have been immortalized for us by a master hand.'

This biography continues:

'She had exquisite taste and such expressive power as could furnish to an historical painter an inspiring model for the various characters, either delicate or sublime, that he might have occasion to represent. Romney delighted in observing the wonderful command she possessed over her eloquent features and through surprising vicissitudes of her destiny she took a generous pride in serving him as a model; her peculiar force and variations of feeling, countenance, and gesture, inspirited and ennobled the productions of his art.'

Romney's Day Books[6] confirm that he was indeed inspired. The first portrait, later entitled *Nature,* was followed by the full-length figure of *Circe.* Between 1782 and 1786, Emma sat for him over 150 times.

John Romney explains: 'It was a great gratification for her to sit as a model. It amused her, and flattered her vanity. From the peculiarity of her situation she was excluded from society, and the only resources she had were reading, music and sitting for her portrait.'

Emma loved posing for the artist and it offered her the opportunity to dress up in various costumes. We see her posing with a dog, as a spinstress and as classical characters: Circe, St. Cecilia, Cassandra, Iphigenia and many others. With the help of Sir William Hamilton these classical poses later developed into her famous 'Attitudes'.

The hours spent with Romney furthered Emma's education. She opened her heart to her *'friend and more than father'*.

Emma led a quiet life at Edgware Road, trying her best to be *'what Greville pleases'* and *'to manage myself & try to be like Greville'*. She made a few friends, carefully chosen to meet with his approval. The highlights of her life were the days and nights when Greville was at Edgware Road, her visits to Cavendish Square, her music and singing lessons.

Greville occasionally invited his serious-minded friends for dinner. Among them were his younger brother, Robert Greville, equerry to the King, his cousin, Charles Cathcart, and the artist and antiquarian Gavin Hamilton. While they talked, Emma listened. Having had music lessons, perhaps she played the piano and sang for them. Greville later informed Sir William some of his friends had 'made offers for her'.

She learnt that Sir William and Greville were known by affectionate nicknames, Pliny the Elder and Pliny the Younger.* Mrs Cadogan managed the household on £150 p.a. and Emma had a personal allowance of £1 a week. She kept an account book, recording all household expenses, down to the last halfpenny.[7] Devotedly, Greville kept one of these, detailing expenses between 27 October 1784 and 21 February 1785, and Emma's letters until the day he died.

It is clear that living with Greville, Emma was conscious of being thrifty, constrained by his income and his command that there should be no extravagance.

So the months passed, with Emma falling more deeply in love with Greville and *'improving'* all the time. We see in her letters to him in June 1784 that her writing and command of language progressed.

Emma and Mrs Cadogan met Sir William Hamilton for the first time in August 1783. Emma was now a beautiful eighteen-year-old and he was a sprightly fifty-three-year-old, on leave from his home in Naples. Hamilton's wife, Catherine, had died and he had returned

---

* Pliny the Elder was the author of 37 encyclopedic volumes of Natural History. He was killed in the eruption of Vesuvius in 79A.D. His nephew and heir, Pliny the Younger, was an administrator under the Roman Emperor, Trajan.

from Italy to bury her remains in Wales, according to her wishes. He had been granted leave to see to his affairs concerning the extensive estates in Pembrokeshire bequeathed to him by his wife. Hamilton stayed in England for just over a year. Greville was Sir William's favourite nephew and they had much to discuss: their mutual interest in the Arts and Sciences, their respective collections, Hamilton's estates and Greville's financial problems. Hamilton would have met Emma on several occasions during this time.

Sir William had no objection to his nephew keeping a mistress and approved of Greville's determination to see Emma *'respected and admired'*. Emma had, in eighteen months, embraced the lifestyle, etiquette, manners and conventions of distinguished company: Greville, his friends and Romney. Both Greville and Romney had travelled to, and studied in, Italy. Emma was turning from the *'wild unthinking Emma'* into a *'grave thoughtful phylosopher'*, as she soon described herself.

Sir William, a renowned connoisseur of beauty and elegance, was captivated by Emma. He was so impressed with her that he commissioned both Sir Joshua Reynolds and Romney to portray her as a bacchante. He was himself sitting for a portrait by Romney at the time. He had eight appointments at Romney's studio in December 1783. Between January and July 1784 Emma posed for Romney twenty-five times.

Hamilton was attentive to Emma, declared her to be *'better than anything in nature'*, called her *'the Fair tea-maker of Edgeware Row'* and told her she could rely on him if anything happened to Greville. Emma, responding as always to approval and admiration, soon lost her sense of awe of this distinguished gentleman and set out to charm him, calling him 'Uncle Pliny'.

In June 1784, Greville and Hamilton left London to oversee the estates in Wales and to visit relatives in Scotland. It was arranged for Emma and her mother to collect 'Little Emma', as Emma's daughter will be known, from Hawarden for a short holiday. They took lodgings in Parkgate, a seaside resort near her birthplace in Ness, where Emma could bathe in the sea. They hoped that the salt water would be a beneficial treatment for the *'rashes'* on Emma's elbows and knees, (now called psoriasis). This skin condition recurred throughout her life.

By now Emma idolized Greville. She felt indebted to him for

supporting, not only herself, but her mother and daughter too. She wrote to Greville every two or three days. Several of these letters are included here. They are her first letters to Greville since her *'distraktid'* letter of December 1782. She describes her feelings for Greville, her reactions to seeing her daughter, now two and a half years old, her concerns about the expense Greville was incurring by their holiday, her worries about what was to become of Little Emma and about her own health, especially her skin problems.

Chester Saturday Morn

(June 12th. 1784)

My dear Greville

    I have had no letter from you yett which makes me unhappy. I cant go to Abbergelly as it is forty miies & a very uncomfortable place & I am now going to Parkgate as it is the only place beside High lake [Hoylake] I can go to, but I will try to go there. Pray my dear Greville, do write directly & lett it be left at the post office, Parkgate tell calld for. God bless you, write. I have got my poor Emma with me & I have took leave of all my friends. I have took her from a good home & I hope she will prove worthy of your goodness to her & her mother. I should not write now tell I got to Parkgate only I want to hear from you ... My dear Greville dont be angry but I gave me Grandmother 5 guineas for she had laid some out on her & I would not take her away shabbily; but Emma shall pay you.

    Adue, my ever dear Greville & believe me, yours ever truly

Emma Hart

    I will write you on Monday again, My love to Sir W. and say everything that you can. I am low-spirited so excuse me my dear Greville, I wish I was with you. God bless you.[8]

Three days later, on 15 June, Emma writes again:

    ... I am in the house of a Laidy whoes husband is at sea she & her Granmother live together & we board with her at present tell I hear from you. The price is high but they wont lodge any body without boarding and it is comfortable decent & quiet I thought it would not ruin ous tell I could have your oppinion ... I bathe & find the waters very soult; here is a great many Laidys batheing, but I have no society with them as it is best not ... tell me what I am to do with the child for she is a great romp & I can hardly master her. I don't think she is ugly, but I think her greatly improved, she is tall, good eys & brows & all together she will be passible, but she has over grown all her cloaths. I am making & mending all I can for her. Pray my dear Greville do let me come home as soon as you can for I am all most broken hearted being

from you, endead I have no pleasure nor happiness ... Tell Sir W. everything you can & tell him I am sorry our situation prevented me from giving him a kiss but my heart was ready to break but I will give it him & entreat if he will axept it ... Endead my dear Greville, you dont know how much I love you & your behaiver to me wen we parted was so kind, Greville, I dont know what to do, but I will make you amends by my behaiver to you ... so dont think of my faults Greville think of all my good & blot out my bad, for it is all gone & berried never to come again, so good by, my dear Greville, think of nobody but me for I have not a thought but of you & praying for you & for ous to meet again. God bless you & believ me, yours truly & affectionately

Emma Ht.

P.S. Poor Emma gives her duty to you. I bathe her & the people is very civel to ous. I give a guinea & half a week for ous all to gether but you will tell me what to do. God bless you, my dear, dear Greville, I long to see you for endead, I am not happy from you tho I will stay if you like tell a week before you go home, but I must go first. I have had no letter from you & you promised to write to me before I left home. It made me unhappy but I thought you might not have time. God bless you, once more good by.[9]

In her next letter we note that she confesses her maternal feelings for Little Emma:

Parkgate. June 22 1784.

My ever dear Greville

How teadous does the time pass a whay till I hear from you. I think it ages since I saw you & years since I heard from you. Endead, I should be miserable if I did not reccolect on what happy terms we parted, – parted yess, but to meet again with tenfould happiness ... Oh, Greville, when I think on your goodness, your tender kindness, my heart is so full of grattatude that I want words to express it. But I have one happiness in vew which I am determined to practice & that is eveness of temper & steadyness of mind, for endead I have thought so much of your amiable goodness when you have been tried to the utmost that I will, endead I will, manege myself & try to be like Greville – endead I can never be like him ... But mind you Greville, your troo great goodness has brought this at bear, for you dont know what I am. Would you think it Greville – Emma – the wild unthinking Emma is a grave thoughtful phylosopher.

Tis true Greville & I will convince you I am when I see you. But how I am running on – I say nothing abbout this guidy wild girl of mine; what shall we do with her, Greville, she is as wild & as thoughtless as somebody when she was a little girl, so you may gess how that is. Whether you will like it or no

16

there is no telling but one comfort is she is a little afraid of me. Would you believe on satturday whe had a little querel, I mean Emma & me & I did slap her on her hands & when she came to kiss me & make it up I took her on my lap & cried. Now do you blame me or not, pray tell me. Oh Greville, you dont know how I love her, endead, I do, when she comes & looks in my face & calls me mother. Endead, I then am truly a mother for all the mothers feilings rise at once & tels me I am or ought to be a mother, for she has a wright to my protection & she shall have it as long as I can & I will do all in my power to prevent her falling into the errors her poor once miserable mother fell into. But why do I say miserable. Am I not happy abbove any of my sex, at least in my situation, does not Greville love me, or at least like me, does not he protect me, does not he provide for me, is not he a father to my child ... Again, O my dear Greville, the reccolection of past scenes brings tears to my eys, but the are tears of happiness. To think of your goodness is two much. But once for all, Greville, I will be grateful.

  Adue ...

I must not forget to tell you my knees is well as I may say there is hardly a mark & my elbows is much better ... you cant think how soult the watter is & there is a many Laidys bathing here. But, Greville, I am obliged to give a shilling a day for the batheing house & whoman & twopence a day for the dress: it is a great expence & it fretts me wen I think of It ... May God bless you, my dearest Greville & believe me faithfully, affectionatly & truly yours only

Emma Ht.[10]

The following morning, 23 June, Emma added a note indicating her increasing distress at not having heard from Greville:

Thursday Morning.

& no letter from my dear Greville. Why my dearest – what is the reason you dont wright. If you knew my uneaseyness you would. You promised to wright before I left Hawerden & I was much disapointed you did not ... I think if I could but hear from you I should be happy, so make me happy, do pray. Give my dear kind love & compliments to Pliny & tell him I put you under his care & he must be answerable for you to me wen I see him ... say everything you can to him for me & tell him I shall allways think of him with grattude & remember him with pleasure & shall all ways regret loseing is good company ... I am in hopes I shall have a letter to morrow ...' [11]

The next morning, Friday 25 June, waiting yet again for the postman, Emma complains that he has not written and declares her love for him:

With what impatience do I sett down to wright till I see the postman, but *sure I shall have a letter to day. Can you, my dear Greville, no you cant have forgot your poor Emma already ... O Greville, think on me with kindness, think how many happy days, weeks & years, I hope, we may yett pass & think out of some that is past, there as been some little pleasure as well as pain & endead, did you but know how much I love you, you would freily forgive me any former quarels for I now suffer for them & one line from you would make me happy ... for whilst Emma lives, she must be gratefully & ever affectionately yours*

Emma Hart[12]

At last Emma hears from Greville. Her reply on Sunday morning 27 June explains why she had waited so long for this letter:

My dear Greville, I had a letter on Friday from my granmother & she sent me one from you that had been there a fortnight. I am much obligded to you for all the kind things you say to me & tell Sir Will'm I am much obligded to him for saying I looked well. I hope he will allways think so, for I am proud of is good word & I hope I shall never forfeit it, I will at least study to reserve it ... it is now going on a month since I saw you, but I think how happy I shall be to see you again, to thank you for your kindness to my poor Emma & me. She shall thank you Greville, she shall be greatful, she shall be good & make you amends for all the trouble her mother has caused you, but how I am to make you amends God knows, I shall never have it in my power, but Greville, you shall have no cause to complain, I will trye, I will do my utmost & I can only regret that fortune will not put it in my power to make a return for all the kindness & goodness you have shewd me ...[13]

Emma received another letter from Greville in which he criticizes her handwriting. His letter must have mentioned past 'agreaments' concerning Little Emma:

Undated (June or July 1784)

Unkind Greville, yes, I have got your letter but why do you scold me if I wrote scral & ill, it was with thinking with two much kindness on you. You have mad me unhappy by scolding me; how can you when you know my dispotion, when you know it breaks my heart to be scolded & speacily by Greville, but I wont think you meant it ill-natured; tho you have maid me unhappy & if you had killd me, your kindness to my poor Emma would make me forget it for, endead, my Dear Greville, I love you two well to neglect you in any one point, so pray forgive me – & as to your goodness in regard to agreaments, endead, I will come in to all as you propose: I will give her up to you intirely; do what you will with her, I here sollemly say that I will never break from my word. You shall take her, put her there where you propose, lest any quarels, tho I hope there will be none – hope she shall stay whear you propose putting her. Lett what will happen I give her up to you to act as you think proper by her. Take her, Greville & may God reward you for it, tho her Mother cant. All as I desire is that if you will lett me take her home when I go to stay tell you come to see her whilst she is there. Nobody shall see her, tho neither you nor I need be ashamed of her, but if you dont like that, I will give it up, so you see, my Dearest Greville, what confidence I put in you now. Scold me, unkind Greville, how can you do so. Pray wright to me derectly & wright kind. Give my Dear kind love to Sir Willm. say everything from me that you can for endead I love him … It may be some comfort to you peraps to know that my elbows and knees is allmost well & I never was better in my life, so Greville, if you will be happy to see me, you will find me in good health, handsome & fonder & kinder to you than ever … So my dearest cruil Greville, why did you scold me, I would not have scolded you at so great a distance, but I will forgive you & I say again you shall see me every thing you can wish & I will be allways yours ever affectionatly & sincerely.

E.H. Adue[14]

This poignant letter illustrates the difficult choice Emma has to make between Greville and her child. He had obviously reminded her that their agreement did not include Little Emma living at Edgware Road. Sadly, Emma must abandon any hope of keeping her daughter with her: '*I will give her up to you intirely; do what you will with her, I here sollemly say that I will never break from my word.*'

Her unenviable position is indicated by her moving comment: *Take her, Greville & may God reward you for it, tho her Mother cant.*'

In his next letter Greville must have outlined his plan for the little girl to which Emma replied:

Parkgate. July the 3 rd. 1784

I was very happy, my dearest Greville, to hear from you as your other letter vexd me, you scolded me so, but it is over & I forgive you. I am much obliged to you for all the kind things you say to me & I am very happy to think we shall meet soon again, happy, good humerd and chearfull … You dont know, my Dearest Greville, what a pleasure I have to think that poor [Little] Emma will be comfortable & happy & Greville, if she does but turn out well, what a happyness it will be & I hope she will for your sake. I will teach her to pray for you as long as she lives & if she is not grateful and good it wont be my fault … O Greville if her poor mother had ever had the luck & prospect, mearly in haveing a good edducation that she has, what a whoman might she have been, but I wont think. All my happiness now is Greville & to think that he loves me makes recompense for all, for if he did not love me would he be so good, kind & affectionate, No, tis imposible, therefore I will have it so... I must go to diner therefore I will say no more but that I long to see you & dear Sir W. Give my kind, kind love to him, tell him next to you I love him abbove any body & that I wish I was with him to give him a kiss. Dont be affronted Greville, if I was with you I would give you a thousand & you might take as many as you pleased for I long, I mean I long to see you. I sopose you will scold next. Adue. I hope to have a letter from you this next week. We have been a month from home today, Greville, it a great wile. My mother gives her compts. to you and & Sir W & say everything that is kind or will render me dear to him; to more than you can say my heart with gratitude assents & I must ever remain yours ever affectionately & sincerely

E. H.

P.S. ... I bathe Emma & she is very well & grows & her hair will grow very well on her forehead & I dont think her nose will be very snub, her eyes is blue & pretty, but she dont speak through her nose, but she speaks countrified, but she will forget it. We squable sometimes, still, she is fond of me & endead I love her for she is senceble, so much for beauty. Adue. I long to see you.[15]

Emma has taken Greville's scolding – *'if I wrote scral & ill'* – to heart and has made a great improvement in this letter. The content is more thoughtful and composed. Her writing remains a scrawl for the rest of her life.

How strangely prophetic her remarks *'give my kind, kind love to Sir W, tell him next to you I love him above anybody'*.

Emma's letters convey a sense of panic and insecurity while she waits for letters from Greville. She is unsure of his love for her, no doubt dreading the prospect of being abandoned by him. This is not surprising after the way Sir Harry had treated her.

But Greville can be confident that he is the man with whom she is in love. Perhaps a small seed of an idea was planted in his mind when Emma repeatedly says how fond she is of Sir William. Within a few months Greville began a strategy of persuading Sir William to become Emma's new 'protector'.

Emma, her mother and Little Emma returned home to Edgware Road where Emma was ill and anxious for eight days, fearful of Greville's reaction to her bringing Little Emma with her. Her next letter indicates that Greville knew the child was with her and was concerned about the noise and disturbance the little girl could cause.

Edgeware Road. Tuesday August 10, 1784
I received your kind letter last night & my Dearest Greville I <u>want words to</u>
<u>express</u> to you how <u>happy</u> it made me, for I thought I was like a lost sheep &
everybody had forsook me. I was eight days confined to my room, very ill, but
am, thank God, very well now, & a deal better for your kind instructing letter
& I own the justness of your remark. You shall have your appartments to your
self, you shall read, wright or set still just as you pleas, for I shall think my self
happy to be under the seam roof with Greville & do all I can to make it agreable
with out disturbing him in any pursuits that he can follow, to employ him self
in at home or else whare, for your absence has taught me that I ought to think
my self happy if I was within a mile of you, so as I could see the place as
contained you, I should think my self happy abbove my shear, so, my Dear G,
come home & you shall find your home comfortable to receave you, you shall
find me good, kind, gentle & affectionate & every thing you wish me to do I
will do ... Dont think Greville, this the wild fancy of a moments consideration,
it is not. I have thoughraly considered everything in my confinement & <u>I say</u>
<u>nothing now but what I shall practice</u> ... Pray my dearest Greville, do come to
see me as soon as ever you come in to town, for I do so long to see you ... I have
a deal to say to you when I see you. Oh Greville, to think it is nine weeks since
I saw you. I think I shall die with the pleasure of seeing you. Endead, my Dearest
Greville, if you knew how much I think of you, you would love for it, for I am
allways thinking on you, of your goodness, in short Greville, I truly love you &
the thought of your coming home so soon makes me so happy I dont know what
to do. Good by, my ever Dearest Greville, may God preserve & bless you for
ever, pray yours ever affectionately & sencerely
Emma
My kind love to Sir Wm & tell him if he will come soon, I will give him a
thousand <u>kisses,</u> for I do love him a little. Emma is very well & is allways
wondering why you dont come home; she sends her duty to you. Good by, My
Dearest Greville, pray, pray come as soon as you come to town. Good by, God
bless you. O how I long to see you. Adue.[16]

Greville received this adoring letter from his nineteen-year-old
mistress repeatedly declaring how much she loves him and happy to
be submissive and obedient to his needs and wishes. She promises him
peace and quiet in his own apartments.

Emma has accepted that whilst Greville will not have Little Emma
living with them, he will support her and ensure that she receives a
good education.

Greville returned to London on 17 August to find Emma well and busy sitting for Romney, whose Day Book records her twenty-eight sittings with him during August, October, November and December. As usual during September, Romney took his annual holiday at the home of his great friend, the poet William Hayley, at Eartham on the South Downs.

There is no documentary evidence that Romney ever paid Emma for modelling for him. This is surprising since Greville and Hamilton commissioned very few works for themselves; most were sold by Romney to other clients or were still in his studio at the time of his death.

Emma had become the light of Romney's life. When she was around he was happy and inspired, and when she was not, he was depressed. She was to him *'a radiant presence'*.

Greville had found a home for Little Emma and in December she was collected from Edgware Road to be brought up by Mr and Mrs Blackburn in Manchester. The couple had two children of their own and from later evidence it appears that Little Emma lived there comfortably and was known as Emma Carew.

We can only guess how much Emma suffered at parting with her daughter. Having been with her new baby for a mere couple of weeks after the birth, Emma had probably not seen Little Emma until she was collected for the holiday in Parkgate. There are no letters to Greville from either Manchester or Chester until the Parkgate letters.

As far as we know, Emma kept her promise to give her up *'intirely.'* Although Mrs Cadogan travelled to Manchester to see Emma Carew at least twice, (in 1791 and 1801), to check on her well-being and progress, there is no evidence that Emma visited her daughter.

Little Emma had been with her mother and grandmother for nearly six months when what must have been a traumatic separation took place. They had very little choice but to part with her. They could have chosen to return to their insecure lives with limited futures in Hawarden. However, Greville's promise to pay for the little girl's upkeep and education was a major consideration. And Emma was now in love with Greville.

Christmas 1784 at Edgware Road was probably subdued. Greville wrote to his uncle:

'There is not in the parish so tidy a house as ours, it being Christmas Day.'
Emma's daughter faded quietly from the scene.

Emma continued her life in Edgware Road blissfully unaware that, early in 1785, Greville was seriously considering his own future. He had sold his house in Portman Square (at a considerable loss) and decided that his dire financial situation would not allow for his continued relationship with Emma. He believed the only way to improve his finances was to marry an heiress. He hoped for a settled, married life. Marrying Emma was out of the question. However, he was devoted to Emma and concerned about her future. He would never have considered throwing her out as Sir Harry had done. He thought of making her an allowance of £100 a year if he had to leave her without finding her an alternative arrangement.

Meanwhile, Sir William had completed all his business in England and Wales by early September. He had inspected his estates in Wales with Greville and buried his wife in Pembrokeshire. He had renewed his relationship with King George III and Queen Charlotte at Windsor, attended meetings of the Royal Society and spent time with relatives and friends. He arranged for Greville to be his chief agent and overseer of the Welsh estates. Over the years, Greville pressed his uncle to invest heavily in their development.

When Sir William called to say farewell to Emma he found her distraught because Greville was away from London again. He promised his support if Greville should 'die or slight her'. Greville later wrote to his uncle that his words to Emma on this occasion *'had such an effect on her that she regards you as her protector and friend'*.

On 11 September 1784 Sir William set out for Naples, his home for the previous twenty years, looking forward to his life there as ambassador, art collector and volcanologist, but dreading the loneliness of his home, the Palazzo Sessa.

CHAPTER 3

Emma's Transfer from Greville to Hamilton

'I am sensible that I am not a match for so much youth and beauty'
Sir William Hamilton to Greville, 1 June 1785

'You will be able to have an experiment without any risque'
Greville to Sir William Hamilton, 3 December 1785

'I should be glad if I was a little more improved than what I am'
Emma to Sir William Hamilton, 3 December 1785

EMMA WAS IGNORANT of Greville's intention to be freed from her in order to seek a rich wife. She continued with her usual routines, sitting for Romney throughout the year (exact dates are unknown as his Day Book for 1785 has been lost) and trying constantly to please Greville. She was completely unaware that she was about to be passed, like a desirable and unusual work of art, from collector to collector.

As Greville acknowledged, Emma was no fool and would certainly have understood that Hamilton was wealthier and more successful than Greville. Living in a palazzo in sunny Naples with an important and interesting man would have appealed to most women in her situation. However, as future events proved, Emma remained loyal and in love with Greville. Sir William was aware of her feelings, later writing sadly, *'she really loves you when she could only esteem and suffer me'*.

In January 1785 Greville wrote the first of many letters to Hamilton in a campaign to persuade him to take responsibility for Emma. Letters were exchanged between them throughout that year. Six of Greville's excessively long, pompous and egotistic letters are included here (with author's editing). As only one of Hamilton's replies survives, the story is interpreted from Greville's standpoint.

24

Hamilton arrived back in Naples in November 1784 and soon received Greville's first letter:

[January 1785]

Emma is very grateful for your 'remembrance'. Her picture shall be sent by the first ships. [Romney's portrait of Emma as 'Nature'] *She certainly is much improved since she has been with me. She has none of the bad habits which giddiness and inexperience encouraged, & which bad company introduced. She has much pride, & submits to solitude rather than admit of one improper acquaintance. She is naturally elegant & fits herself easily to any situation having quickness & sensibility. I am sure she is attached to me or she would not have refused the offers, which I know to have been great; & such is her spirit that, on the least slight or expression of my being tired or burthened by her I am sure she would not only give up the connection but would not even accept a farthing for future assistance ... If I was independent I should think so little of any other connection that I never would marry. I have not an idea of it at present, but if any proper opportunity offer'd I should be much harassed, not know how to manage, or how to fix Emma to her satisfaction ... I am not quite of an age to retire from bustle & to retire to distress & poverty is worse. I can keep on here creditably this winter ...'*[1]

He wrote again on 10 March 1785 from the King's Mews:

You have not wrote to me this great while. They say here that you are in love. I know you love variety & are a general flirt & of the 60 English, what with widows & young married ladies, an amateur may be caught ... I know your heart is neither calous to friendship nor to beauty ... I am from frequent experience convinced that I can judge for you & you for me, at least suppose cases in which we should think alike ... If you did not chuse a wife, I wish the tea-maker of Edgeware Row was yours, if I could without banishing myself from a visit to Naples. I do not know how to part with what I am not tired with ... She shall never want, & if I decide sooner than I am forced to stop from necessity it will be that I may give her part of my pittance & if I do so it must be by sudden resolution & by putting it out of her power to refuse it; for I know her disinterestedness to be such that she will rather encounter any difficulty than distress me. I should not write to you thus if I did not think you seem'd as partial as I am to her. She would not hear at once of any change, & from no one that was not liked by her. I think I could secure on her near £100 a year... if I could go on I would never make this arrangement, but to be reduced to a standstill & involve myself in distress further than I could extricate myself, & then to be unable to provide for her at all, would make me miserable from thinking myself very unjust to her, & she is too young and handsome to retire into a convent or the country, & is honourable & honest, & can be trusted: after reconciling myself to the necessity, I consider where she could be happy. I know you thought me jealous of your attention to her; I can assure you her conduct entitles her more than ever to my confidence. Judge then, as you know my satisfaction on looking at a modern piece of virtu if I do not think you a second self, in thinking that by placing her within your reach I render a necessity, which would otherwise be heart-breaking, tolerable & even comforting.

Yours ever …[2]

Hamilton's reply is lost, but he must have indicated that he would like Emma to *'do the honours'* in his house. This was clearly considerably more than a disconcerted Greville had expected, for he replied on 5 May:

I have received your letter … If I could have thought that no line could be taken but that of making E. do the honours of your house, I confess I never should have dreamt of it; this is a line so different from what I have practised that I should be among the first to lament that you adopted an unwise plan. I tell you fairly that your expressions of kindness to E & the comfort you promised to her in case anything happened to me, made such an impression on her that she regards you as her protector & friend, & in moments of her thinking of your goodness she related to me your last conversation, & I concluded that your regard to me had been the only reason for your not making present offers. You know that from giddiness & disipation she is prudent & quiet, & that, surrounded with temptations, I have not had any the least reason to complain of her… She has avoided every appearance of giddiness & prides herself on the neatness of her person & on the good order of her house; these are habits both comfortable & convenient to me … If you had given her any of your villas, only making it a decided part that she had a home distinct from your house, whether her visits were frequent or rare, it was immaterial, her home would be distinct, and yet if, as you say, you could not resist taking (her) into your house entirely, you certainly would vary so entirely from my ideas & plan, that I could not follow you … as to running after other men, if once she has taken a line, & is sensible of good intentions towards her, she may be trusted … She is now but 20 … She also finds that a quiet life has restored health & improved her looks. What you say is true that so beautiful a person cannot be long without a protector; there is no doubt about that, but it is not her wish to run the gauntlet … If things remain as they are I shall, to be sure, be much strained in finances. I shall be so whether she remains or not, literally her expenses are trifling; yet when income is very small a trifling expense is felt ... At your age a clean & comfortable woman is not superfluous, but I should rather purchase it than acquire it, unless in every respect a proper party offer'd ...[3]

Greville extols Emma's virtues and reassures his uncle that Emma will cause him no trouble. He is surprised that his uncle intends Emma to live in his main residence and not in *'one of your villas'*. Greville had kept Emma quietly out of the way in Edgware Road, but Sir William had distinctly different ideas.

In the second part of this letter Greville went on to enquire about his possible inheritance of Hamilton's estates.

If his uncle declared him his heir, he could *'obtain the consent of a Lady whose fortune would enable us to live comfortably, & by the future provision which after your death you should settle on us, insure a provision for children if any there should be'*. As he saw it, the problem was that *'suppose a lady of 30,000 was to marry me, the interest of her fortune would not provide equal to her pretensions & also provide a saving for a provision for children'*.

Somewhat astonishingly, he went on to declare: *'I would not wish to have your decision for a less ample fortune, because a less ample fortune would not at present enable me to live comfortably.'*

Hamilton replied on 1 June, addressing the inheritance issue first:

Was I to die this moment my will, which I made in England and left with Hamilton of Lincoln's Inn and brought a copy here, would show that you are the person I esteem most – but I never meant to tell you so as the changes in this life are so various that no one can answer for himself from one moment to another. For example, had I married Lady C. [Lady Clarges whom he had met in Turin] *which might have happened, it must have been a cruel disappointment to you, after having declared you my heir. I only made my will, as every one ought to do, in case of accident, but as I have struggled through many difficulties in life and am now by Lady Hamilton's goodness secured from want, nay have enough to live comfortably shou'd I be dismissed from His Majesty's Service I shou'd not chuse to put anything out of my power ... but was it not for the thought of you profiting on my death ... I should not hesitate in selling the Welsh Estate and purchasing an annuity for my life ...*

Hamilton is concerned for Emma's feelings in the matter and worried about their age difference:

As to E. was I in England and you was to bring your present plan to bear and she wou'd consent to put herself under my protection, I would take her most readily for I really love her and think better of her than of any one in her situation. But, my dear Charles, there is a great difference between her being with you or me, for she really loves you when she could only esteem and suffer me. I see so many difficulties in her coming here, should you be under the necessity of parting with her, that I can never advise it. Tho' a great City, Naples has every defect of a Province and nothing you do is secret. It would be fine fun for the young English Travellers to endeavor to cuckold the old gentleman their Ambassador, and whether they succeeded or not would surely give me uneasiness. My regard for E. is such that if she leaves you and retires in the country, which I suppose she would do was you to marry, I would willingly make her an allowance of £50 a year until your circumstances enable you to provide better for her. I do assure you that when I was in England tho' her exquisite beauty had frequently its effects on me, it would never have come into my head to have proposed a freedom beyond an innocent kiss whilst she belonged to my friend; and I do assure you I should like better to live with you both here and see you happy than to have her all to myself, for I am sensible that I am not a match for so much youth and beauty.[4]

No matter how tempting the offer of Emma, Hamilton seems convinced that Greville's proposal would not be a viable solution. He declares his love for Emma, but is resigned to the fact that Emma is in love with Greville. Despite Greville's assurances Sir William worried that he was *'not a match for so much youth and beauty'*.

Undaunted, Greville tried again, giving more advice to his uncle as to how to handle Emma and proposing that he accompany her part of the way to Naples. He was hopeful of having found a suitably wealthy wife in the youngest daughter of his neighbour, Lord Middleton, with a fortune of around £20,000.

... Now let me say a few words about future plans & Emma. If my letter should produce an offer from them, it is obvious we must part. If there should be no offer, I cannot go to a formal proposal; & I have fully stated that I <u>must</u> vary my plans, & reduce my establishment, which is beyond my means; ... you know that, added to her looks, so cleanly & sweet a creature does not exist, & she is handsomer than when you saw her... As to Englishmen, there is nothing to fear; left to herself, she would conform to your ideas. She has never wished for an improper acquaintance; she has dropt every one she thought I could except against, & those of her own choice have been in a line of prudence & plainness ... if you can find only one or two acquaintances, & let her learn music or drawing, or anything to keep her in order, she will be as happy as if you gave her change of dissipation.

She is no fool, but there is a degree of nature in her, that she has the same pleasure in a retired & confined life as in a more extensive one, & she has no difficulty in confining herself; & yet she has natural gentility & quickness to suit herself to anything, & takes easily any hint that is given with good humor, but I never saw any one so compleatly led by good nature, & I believe she would rather die before she yeilded to ill-treatment. If I could form a plan by which you could have a trial, & could invite her & tell her I ought not to leave England, & that I cannot afford to go on, & state it a kindness to me if she would accept your invitation, she would go with pleasure. She is to be 6 weeks at some bathing place, & when you could write an answer to this and enclose a letter to her, I could manage it, & either by land, by coach to Geneva, & from thence by 'Venturine' forward her, or else by sea ... If there was in this world a person she loved so well as yourself after me, I could not arrange with so much sans froid; & I am sure I would not let her go to you, if any risque of the usual coquetry of the sex being likely either to give uneasiness or appearances ...[5]

Emma and her mother went away for six weeks for Emma to resume her sea-bathing treatment. Greville toured Wales and Cornwall to investigate the commercial prospects of clay and tin. Hamilton explored the volcanic islands in the Gulf of Naples and continued in his ambassadorial duties.

Although busy with all these interests, Hamilton was lonely. In August he confessed to his niece, Mary, that he was *'desolate'*:

'When the court is here I live with their Scn. Majesties, but now they are absent, I pass my time, rather dully, for what is a home without a bosom friend and companion? My books, pictures, music, prospect are certainly something, but the soul to all is wanting.'[6]

It was over three years since his wife, Catherine, had died, one year of which he had spent in England, busy and happy enough. But by August 1785, he had been alone in Naples for almost a year.

In November Greville took up his campaign again:

11 November 1785

... [Emma] goes on so well & is so much more considerate & aimiable than she was when you saw her, & also improved in looks, that I own it is less agreable to part, yet I have no other alternative but to marry or remain a pauper ... I can assure you she would not have a scarcity of offers, she has refused great ones; but I am sure she would prefer a foreign country with you to any other connexion at home, & I would not expose you to any risque ...

During my short stay in town I saw [Gavin] *Hamilton twice; once I called on him & the next brought him to dine with Emma. He says he has not seen*

29

anything like her in G.B., & that she reminds him of a person at Rome whom he admired much, tho' she was deficient in the beauties of the mouth, & that Emma's is both beautiful and uncommon. He has been meditating for a subject; he says he shall not rest untill he has prevail'd on her to sit: you may suppose she was flatter'd, & she told him she put him at once on her list of favourites, because you had spoke of him as a person you regarded, & also because he bore your name ...7

By the beginning of December 1785 it appears that Sir William had been worn down by Greville's persuasive letters and won over to the proposal that he should take over the responsibility of having Emma to live under his protection.

Greville wrote a final letter and, with or without his uncle's absolute agreement, detailed the departure dates and travel plans he had booked for Emma and her mother:

3rd. or 4th. December 1785

My dear Hamilton, as you have fully communicated your sentiments to me, & as you know mine relative to Emma, I shall not enter further on that subject than to explain to you the occasion of your receiving the enclosed [a letter from Emma, quoted below] *and my arrangements & opinion on the occasion ...*

Greville told Sir William that Emma accepted his need to go to Scotland and that although she *'would be very miserable'* during his absence, she had agreed to go to Naples with her mother. Emma had said *'there was not a person in the world she could be happy with,'* than Sir William if Greville was dead, and *'that she should be very happy in learning music & Italian'* provided she was *'under Sir William's roof and protection'*. He continued:

... I would not lead you in any scrape, you know that ... & I declare to you that the little excesses which I have experienced were never devoted to follies, but were given to poor relations in the country, for whose care she professes herself grateful, insomuch that I had only to scold her for not having me supply that demand instead of making herself bare of pocket money.

You will be able to have an experiment without any risque; if it should not turn out as I expect, she will have profited by seeing a little of foreign parts; she will have improved herself & she may come home. I know that you are above acting unkindly to any woman, but particularly to a pretty woman ... I do not see why you should not find some reward for your generosity when I no longer can continue my connexion from the state of my finances ... She has a good constitution, yet it is delicate and I think that her looks improved as well as her health since I considered myself an over-match for her, & as I consider you as my heir-aparent I must add that she is the only woman I ever slept without having ever had any of my senses offended, & a cleanlier, sweeter bedfellow does not exist ... If I have an opportunity I will send her clothes by sea, that she may avoid trouble on the road ... I find that the journey, all expenses included, to Geneva for the 2 will amount to 30gs.

I shall have everything ready for setting out, & have got the refusal of 2 places in the coach which will set out the end of Feb'y, or the beginning of March at furthest ... And now I come to the last part of this subject ... I have never told her story ... I wish, in the case of Emma, that you will use only your discretion, a young person under your protection is all that is necessary ... you will find Emma discrete ... is pleased if she thinks all the world not in her secret ... <u>You</u> must enable me to pay their journey, & you must say to her that you shall be happy to receive her, & hope to make her comfortable at Naples ... She has not a doubt of the pleasure you will have to receive her, and as she will be ready to set out when your answer comes, let Cottier be at Geneva or within reach of Desjeans, at Geneva on the 10th or 15th of March.

Yours ever etc. [8]

Greville, who considered himself 'an over-match' for Emma and his uncle his 'heir-aparent' in possessing her, blatantly assures him that a 'cleanlier, sweeter bedfellow does not exist'. He writes about her as if she were a possession, not a person with private thoughts and feelings. Grateful for Hamilton's generosity in offering to help provide for her he comments: 'I do not see why you should not find some reward for your generosity.' Unknown to Emma, both men expected her to adopt a sexual relationship with her new 'protector' in Naples.

To impress his uncle of Emma's willingness to comply with the arrangement (Hamilton had indicated that he would only agree if Emma was willing), Greville wrote at length about Emma's reaction to his telling her his plan.

He gives the impression that he and Emma had quietly and rationally discussed the situation, but Emma's response to this proposed separation is more likely to have been distress. Greville may have had some difficulty in persuading her to go to Naples. He secured her consent by framing the plan as a great opportunity for her to improve herself further by learning Italian, studying music, and exploring a foreign country.

The first evidence of Emma's generosity towards her family, her grandmother in particular, appears in this letter. Emma had sent some of her own small allowance to her grandmother and she remained generous to her and other relatives throughout her life. Unusual in an age of snobbery, she always acknowledged her impoverished family and refused to be ashamed of them.

Greville offered to forward all Emma's clothes by sea and asked Hamilton to send the money to pay for their journey, which he duly did.

Emma obediently wrote her letter to Sir William to enclose with Greville's:

Edgeware Road

3 December 1785

My Dear Sir William, emboldened by your kindness to me when you was in England, I have a proposal to make that I flatter myself will not be disagreeable to you. Greville,(whom you know I love tenderly) is obliged to go for four or five months in the summer to places that I cannot with propriety attend him to, & I have too great a regard for him to hinder him from pursuing those plans which I think it is right for him to follow; & I know it is necessary for him to keep up his connexions in the world; – and as you was so good as to give me encouragement, I will speak my mind. In the first place, I should be glad if I was a little more improved than what I am, and as Greville is obliged to be absent in the summer he has out of kindness to me offer'd, if you are agreable, for me to go to Naples for 6 or 8 months, and he will at the end of that time fetch me home, and stay a while there when he comes, which I know you will be glad to see him. He therefore proposes for me to sett of the first of March next, as he will sett of then for his extended tour in Scotland, and I could not bear the thought of staying at home by myself when I know If I come to see you, (which will be the greatest pleasure on hearth, Greville excepted) I shall be improving myself and making the time pass agreable; at the same time, he thinks for me to go by the Geneva coach, and if you will let your man that was in England with you meet me there to conduct me to Naples, I shall be glad;and if you will allot me an apartment in your house that I might be under your protection while I am there, and lett Greville occupy those apartments when he comes, you know that <u>must</u> be; but as your house is very large, and you must, from the nature of your office, have business to transact and visitors to see, I shall always keep my own room when you are better engaged or go out, and at other times I hope to have the pleasure of your company and conversation, which will be more agreable to me than anything in Italy. As I have given you an example of sincerity, I hope you will be equally candid and sincere in a speedy answer, as we are confined for time, and no further correspondence will be necessary, as you may depend on me, if you do *approve of it, setting of from London at the time I mentioned in the former part of this letter, and I shall be perfectly happy in any arrangements you will make, as I have full confidence in your kindness and attention to me, and shall long for the time when I can assure you in person how much I am, my dear Sir William, your obliged humble servant, or affectionate Emma, which you like best.*[9]

Emma believes that Greville will come to Naples to *'fetch me home'* at the end of the six or eight months. In asking for her own apartment in Sir William's residence she makes it clear to him that she intends to remain faithful to Greville.

This is how Emma found herself transferred from Greville to Hamilton.

She had been kept in the dark about the contents of the letters passing between Greville and Hamilton over the last year. It was not until 3 December 1785 that Greville told her he must go to Scotland for six to eight months and that she should go to Hamilton in Naples.

For four years Emma had been subservient to Greville. She was no longer *'giddy'* and a *'madcap'* and had made progress in her language, writing and singing skills. Through Greville and Romney she was now familiar with classical education and had gained an appreciation of the arts and sciences. Her innate optimism, good nature, kindness and vivacity flourished when Hamilton offered her the opportunity for her natural personality to develop.

Hamilton's approach to life was very different from that of his nephew. He encouraged her enthusiasm, was amused by a little vulgarity and *'cared not a pin for* [the opinions of] *the great world'.* [10] Emma would enrich his life, as she had done Romney's.

Greville never did find a rich heiress and he died a bachelor. In a letter Lord Nelson wrote to Emma in 1801, he commented, with reference to Greville, *'that other chap did throw away the most precious jewel that God Almighty ever sent on this earth'.*

On 13 March 1786 Emma and Mrs Cadogan set off for Naples, escorted by Gavin Hamilton. The arduous journey overland took six weeks. Gavin Hamilton left the group at Rome and Emma and her mother concluded their journey in Hamilton's own travelling chaise, sent to fetch them.

They arrived at the superbly situated Palazzo Sessa on 26 April 1786, Emma's twenty-first birthday.

CHAPTER 4

Sir William Hamilton – Envoy Extraordinary to the Kingdom of the two Sicilies

'You have a new neighbour coming to you, Mr. William Hamilton ...
He is picture-mad and will ruin himself in virtù-land'
Horace Walpole to the Ambassador in Florence 1764

'... it is the Queen of Naples that actually governs this country'
Hamilton reporting home in 1776

TRAVELLING THROUGH FRANCE, over the Alps, down through northern Italy to Rome and on to Naples, Emma and her mother could not have imagined how different their lives would be from their previous four years in London, cloistered by Greville.

The royal court, Hamilton's homes, the Neapolitan people, their customs and language, the weather and the scenery, the sea and the volcano would be as another world. In London Sir William Hamilton could have given them only a glimpse of the man he was. As yet, they barely knew him.

He had lived the Neapolitan way of life for twenty-two years and was the favourite ambassador of the king and queen. His dedicated cultural interests led him to associate with artists, musicians and writers of many European nationalities. He was known as a connoisseur, an authority on volcanology and for his interest in the natural sciences. He was enthusiastic about swimming, fishing, sailing and hunting.

William Hamilton's parents were both from aristocratic families in Scotland. His father was the seventh son of the third Duke of Hamilton. His mother (the Duke's third wife) was the daughter of the sixth Earl of Abercorn. They married in September 1717. The Duke, hitherto childless and almost sixty years old, remarkably fathered ten children by his new wife before her thirty-sixth birthday. Hamilton's mother became 'Lady of the Bedchamber and Mistress of the Robes' to the Princess of Wales.

William was born in December 1730 and grew up at court alongside the young Prince George, who was seven years his junior. They were always known as 'foster-brothers' and William later benefited by this close connection to the future King George III.

At Westminster School William formed a life-long friendship with Frederick Hervey (later Bishop of Derry and Earl of Bristol, known as the Earl Bishop). They both became renowned collectors of art and virtu.

The Earl Bishop had almost limitless funds with which to indulge his collecting mania. Without this financial advantage Hamilton managed his collections by becoming both collector and dealer. By buying paintings, antiquities and Etruscan vases and selling some, usually at a profit, he was able to build up his remarkable collections.

Hamilton suffered the usual financial constraints by not being the heir to the family fortune. Like his nephew, Charles Greville, he must either marry an heiress or find a well-paid career. For this reason Hamilton understood and sympathized with him. Later, he treated Greville as if he were his own son.

Having joined the Army, aged sixteen, Hamilton acted as General Conway's aide and in his early twenties served as an equerry to George, Prince of Wales until he was twenty-six years old, then for a time, represented Midhurst in Sussex as their (unenthusiastic) Member of Parliament.

Hamilton's mother died in Paris in 1752 and his father died shortly afterwards in 1754.

He resigned his commission when he found his heiress, Catherine Barlow, the daughter of Hugh Barlow, who owned estates in Pembrokeshire.[1] He left these estates to his wife and daughter when he died in 1739. William and Catherine met at the Barlows' London home in Clarges Street. Catherine was twenty years old, accomplished and cultivated, but rather plain-looking. She was introverted, gentle and deeply religious. However, she was acknowledged to be an excellent harpsichord player. Hamilton, now twenty-eight years old, was an accomplished violinist and this mutual interest in music helped their relationship to survive, despite their very different personalities. They married in January 1758.

Hamilton later admitted in a letter to Greville: *'a disagreeable rich devil the Devil himself cou'd not have tempted me to marry, but I have really found a lasting comfort in having married (something against my inclination)*

*a virtuous, good-tempered woman with a little independent fortune to which
we cou'd fly shou'd all other dependencies fail, and live decently without being
obliged to any one.'*[2]

They spent the first six years of marriage living in Pembrokeshire
and London. Catherine's severe asthma suffered in the English winter
weather. Worried about her and dissatisfied with his working life,
Hamilton began searching for an opportunity to live abroad. He heard
that Sir James Gray was about to leave his position as envoy in Naples.

Through his connections with King George III (the Prince of Wales
having succeeded to the throne in 1760) and the Prime Minister,
George Grenville, he secured the position. Hamilton 'kissed hands
with the King' on his appointment on 31 August 1764 as Envoy
Extraordinary to the Kingdom of the Two Sicilies.

Hamilton and Catherine sailed from Marseilles to Naples, arriving
there on 17 November 1764. En route through France he purchased
a hundred bottles of burgundy and spent three hundred pounds on
clothes, an early indication of his liberal approach to expenditure.

Hamilton embraced the Neapolitan lifestyle more successfully than
Catherine. Her health improved, but she was never fully well and
suffered from a nervous disposition.

Horace Walpole wrote: *'His wife is as musical, as he is connoisseur, but
she is dying of an asthma.'*[3] Despite this gloomy prognosis, Catherine
lived for another eighteen years.

In addition to his extensive involvement with the Court, Hamilton
had time to devote to his study of antiquities and art collections.

In a letter to the ambassador in Florence, Walpole wrote: *'You have
a new neighbour coming to you, Mr. William Hamilton … He is picture-mad
and will ruin himself in virtù-land.'*[4]

Hamilton's role in Naples was focused on protecting and increasing
England's trade with the Kingdom. Politically, Naples was
unimportant until the rise of Napoleon many years later. The position
of envoy carried no significant status and only a small salary.
Nevertheless he was always known as 'The Ambassador'.

At the time, Naples was the second largest city on the continent
after Paris and occupied a beautiful location. Their home was the
Palazzo Sessa, originally an 11th century monastery, which Hamilton
rented for around £150 p.a. and where he lived for the next thirty-four
years. The palazzo, situated conveniently close to the royal palace,
was a three-storey building around a courtyard in which the main

apartments had a panoramic view of the bay below and Vesuvius beyond.

Naples lay at the foot of Vesuvius. Hamilton was fascinated by the volcano and became a renowned authority on Pompeii and Herculaneum where, in early excavations of these sites, he purchased his famous collection of Etruscan vases.

His finances fell into the pattern that he followed for the rest of his life. He was almost always in debt, partly due to his private expenditure, but also to the tight-fisted Treasury's lateness in paying his allowances. Worry about debts never inhibited his spending.

As Envoy Extraordinary Hamilton's allowance was £5 per day (£1,825 p.a.) for his expenses. Walpole's prediction proved accurate when, after less than a year in Naples, he owed his London bankers £1,600. He was obliged to beg the government for the higher status of 'Plenipotentiary' that carried an extra £3 per day. He explained that his salary, plus his private fortune (Catherine's income) was insufficient to cover his ambassadorial expenses. In February 1767 his salary was raised to £8 per day (£2,920 p.a.)[5]

King Ferdinand was only thirteen years old when the Hamiltons took up residence in Naples. His father, Charles III of Spain, who had placed Ferdinand on the throne, had appointed an eight-member Council of Regency to rule until his son reached his majority at sixteen.

Hamilton soon established himself on excellent terms with the powerful Prime Minister, Tanucci. He gathered an impressively wide knowledge about the state of Naples and the Kingdom, a valuable asset as his role required him to report back to the Secretary of State every ten days or so for the next thirty-two years.

As Envoy, Hamilton was responsible for the well-being of the English living in Naples and for the stream of 'Grand Tour' English travellers who descended on the city and expected him to entertain them and guide their tours of Pompeii, Herculaneum and Vesuvius. Sometimes tourists stayed at the Palazzo Sessa at Hamilton's expense. Prince Augustus, sixth son of George III, Archduke Maximilian, and the Earl Bishop were among them.

In an early report to the Secretary of State he described the current excavations at Pompeii being carried out under Tanucci's orders: *'Travellers will soon have an opportunity of walking the streets and seeing the houses of this Ancient city (which is infinitely more considerable than Herculaneum).'*[6]

The population of Naples consisted of large numbers of the nobility followed in social standing by thousands of ecclesiastics – priests, monks and nuns. The 'middle classes' were followed by a multitude of the poor, the lowest classes of society, who were known as the 'Lazzaroni' and who were the King's favourites.

Typically, after a fishing trip in the bay and landing his catch, the King would sell the fish to the local people around him and then promptly distribute the money amongst them. They loved him for being one of them and spending time with them. They gave him their loyal support.

After his first meeting with Ferdinand Hamilton wrote: *'He is certainly a most gracious Prince, and the goodness of his heart is conspicuous in his countenance.'*[7]

However, Ferdinand's formal education had been neglected and he was almost illiterate. Lack of social training left him ignorant of court etiquette.

His father, Charles III, concerned that several members of the Spanish royal family had suffered either madness or imbecility, believed that hunting and outdoor exercise was a necessary safeguard against this hereditary affliction developing in his young son. Ferdinand happily complied with this way of life and spent most of his time hunting. He preferred the company of his servants and the Lazzaroni to that of the court and his ministers where his lack of education and his reluctance to exert the authority of his position kept him apart from the normal functions of government.[8]

On becoming King at the age of sixteen he was *'more desirous of becoming his own master to follow his caprices than to govern his Kingdoms or give the least attention to business'*.[9] Hamilton, with his usual tolerance of people's foibles, imperfections and eccentricities, accepted the King as he was and dutifully spent many days and weeks out on hunting trips with the young Ferdinand.

It was an opportunity for him to take some necessary physical exercise and to explore the countryside around Naples. He had to suppress his disgust over the horrific number of animals killed on each outing, all of which the King thoroughly enjoyed, keeping a careful count of the numbers killed and participating in the skinning and carving up of the dead animals.

For Hamilton this hunting was *'carnage rather than sport'*, but he went along with it in the service of his own King. It was an honour that Ferdinand always invited him to the hunt and not the French Minister.

In 1768, eighteen months after becoming king, Ferdinand married Maria Carolina, the sixteen-year-old daughter of Empress Maria Theresa of Austria and sister of Marie Antoinette, Queen of France.

Although it was an arranged marriage, Ferdinand loved Maria Carolina and she tolerated him. Hamilton claimed that the several weeks of royal nuptial celebrations had cost him £1,000 and tried to persuade the government to reimburse him.

The marriage settled into an agreeable arrangement. Ferdinand spent almost all his time out hunting and Maria Carolina loved and took care of her children. During their long marriage, she had eighteen children, many of whom died very young. Having produced a son and heir, she became increasingly interested in the government of the kingdom, which her husband neglected. She insisted on her right to be a member of the Council and became a powerful political force.

By 1778, Maria Carolina was instrumental in replacing the long-serving Tanucci with General John Acton. Between them, Hamilton notified the Secretary of State, they governed the kingdom. Ferdinand matured little over the years and he was happy to allow his wife to take over the responsibilities of government.

The following year, Catherine's mother died, leaving the Pembrokeshire estates to her daughter. They were thus able to live in grander style than Hamilton's salary alone would have allowed and he could afford to add to his collections.

To cheer his wife up after this bereavement, Hamilton took leave and for three months they toured Sicily. He familiarized himself with the other half of the kingdom and explored and climbed Mount Etna. He reported his findings to the Royal Society and wrote to Horace Mann: 'Mount Etna ... is really a most magnificent volcano, Vesuvius appears to me now a mere molehill in comparison.'

Back in Naples they continued to entertain. There were seldom fewer than twelve to dinner and up to sixty on gala occasions.[10] Catherine held her own 'assemblies' on Mondays, when she and other musicians performed. At home, she carried out her duties as the wife of the ambassador admirably but avoided attending court assemblies and functions as much as possible because of her naturally introverted nature and her dislike of the King and Queen. She disdained the eccentricities of behaviour at court and wrote home: 'We live in so

*English a stile that you need not fear any of the Italian ceremonies and
nonsense with us. We enter as little as we can into their stupid Assemblys.'*[11]

If this was a disappointment to Hamilton he did not show it. He
was obliged to spend much of his time with Ferdinand and Maria
Carolina. Catherine accompanied him to concerts and the opera, and
they spent time at Hamilton's three other residences.

Their villa north of Naples at Posillipo (later renamed Villa Emma),
situated on rocks at the edge of the sea, had direct access to the beach.
In the heat of summer they would drive out to the villa in their carriage
and in the cooling sea breezes they could dine, often with friends, read
and relax. Hamilton swam, fished and sailed.

In the winter months of the wild boar season, the court removed
to the royal palace at Caserta, sixteen miles north of Naples.
Hamilton's 'Little Cabin' nearby could house fifty people.[12] Somewhat
run-down, cold in winter, it was used by Hamilton to sleep in after his
days hunting with the King.

A few miles south of Naples, near another royal palace, was his Villa
Angelica at Portici, with splendid views in front of the house and with
the slopes of Vesuvius behind. The villa's extensive gardens were
mostly vineyard. Many guests came to stay here, entertained by
Catherine, Hamilton and other musicians.

Hamilton could observe Vesuvius from Villa Angelica and explored
the volcano with his guide, Bartolomeo, often putting himself in
considerable danger. During the 1767 eruption he and Bartolomeo ran
for their lives when the eruption became far more active than they
had anticipated.

He sent an illustrated, vivid and informative account of his
observations to the Royal Society, to which he had been elected in 1766:

*'I was making my observations upon the lava … when on a sudden, about
noon, I heard a violent noise within the mountain, and at about a quarter of
a mile off the place where I stood, the mountain split and with much noise,
from this new mouth a fountain of liquid fire shot up many feet high, and
then like a torrent, rolled on directly towards us. The earth shook at the same
time that a volley of pumice stones fell thick upon us; in an instant clouds of
black smoak and ashes caused almost a total darkness; the explosions from
the top of the mountain were much louder than any thunder I ever heard, and
the smell of sulphur was very offensive. My guide alarmed took to his heels;
and I must confess that I was not at my ease. I followed close, and we ran near
three miles without stopping; as the earth continued to shake under our feet*

... After having taken breath, as the earth trembled greatly, I thought it prudent to leave the mountain, and return to my Villa, where I found my family in a great alarm, at the continual and violent explosions of the Volcano, which shook our house to its very foundation, the doors and windows swinging upon their hinges.'[13]

The household returned immediately to Naples, calling at the royal palace to warn the royal family to flee. An impenetrable fog, ash, pumice and cinders rained down on Naples, causing panic, rioting and religious ecstasy. Luckily the explosions ceased before bringing disaster upon the city and the community gave thanks in the cathedral.

Despite his successful life as ambassador and his intense interest in the wealth of art and antiquities surrounding him, Hamilton contemplated leaving Naples in 1768.

He hoped to further his career in a more important embassy such as Vienna or Madrid, but his efforts to achieve this ambition were unsuccessful.

He applied for home leave in May 1770. When this was finally granted in May 1771 he packed up his vases, some antiquities and his picture, *Venus disarming Cupid* (believed at the time to be by Correggio) and shipped them home. He hoped to sell these items to help settle some of his debts. His extensive collection included vases, terracottas, specimens of ancient glass, bronzes, ivories, antique gems, gold ornaments and coins.[14]

By June he and Catherine were on their way home.

They were away for nineteen months, one year in England and the remainder travelling there and back. While they were in England Parliament voted £8,400 to purchase the vases and other antiquities for the British Museum.[15] He was very proud to see the Hamilton Collection housed in the museum and much admired.

However, this sale represented a financial loss, taking into account his expenses in producing high quality illustrated portfolios on the vases. The four magnificent portfolios contained hand-coloured illustrations, detailed drawings and measurements depicting the vases. These portfolios inspired Josiah Wedgewood to produce a new range of pottery, copying the style of the Greek and Etruscan art on the vases.

The Correggio did not sell and Hamilton left it with Greville to try to find a buyer at the hoped-for price of £3,000.[16]

In November 1771, the Royal Society presented Hamilton with their

Copley Medal in recognition of his work on volcanoes and in February 1772 he was elected a member of the Society of Antiquaries.

Hamilton sought the recognition of the Order of the Bath, an honour conferred by the King. Limited to thirty-six members, a vacancy only occurred on the death of a member. Hamilton was finally successful on the death of Lord Chandos and was invested on 15 January 1772.

Although one of the main reasons for his visit to England was to raise money to help clear his debts, he was now faced with the expenses incurred in becoming a member of the Order of the Bath; fees for the privilege were £343 and a further £1,034 for his own diamond star and insignia, plus some jewellery for Catherine. The bill for his robes was considerable. This expenditure added a further £2,000 to his debts.[17]

The motto of the Order, *Tria Juncta in Uno*, was later appropriated by Emma in referring to Hamilton, Lord Nelson and herself.

Hamilton and Catherine visited friends and relatives in Warwickshire, (Greville's elder brother, the Earl of Warwick, lived in Warwick Castle), Northamptonshire and Permbrokeshire.

They were on their way home by mid-September. The journey taking almost four months via Geneva, Vienna, Venice, Florence and Rome, they arrived in Naples on 6th January 1773.

By 1774, Hamilton (now Sir William Hamilton) had been in Naples for ten years. He was called *Paesano Nostro* by the King[18] and was his favourite ambassador. His popularity with the King and Queen allowed him to influence them towards England's interests when widespread unrest developed in America, France and Spain. His role in Naples became important to the British Government.

In December he wrote to Greville that he was very short of money and had *'worse than nothing'* with his banker *'owing to the great arrear of the Civil List'*.[19] He urged Greville, then in parliament, to try to have these arrears paid promptly. The negligence of the government in paying Hamilton's allowances naturally caused havoc with his finances.

His appeals for extra allowances incurred by royal celebrations fell on deaf ears. Whereas other diplomats had received special allowances, Hamilton received nothing.

He wrote to the Secretary of State: *'I have no family & can upon extraordinary occasions, or when the Civil List is in Arrear, supply that immediate want by anticipating a portion of my private income as I have done hitherto.'*[20] It seems the government was content to let him use his own money for state affairs.

More visitors descended on the Palazzo Sessa in 1775, including the young Duke of Hamilton, Sir Harry Fetherstonhaugh (who was to have the teenage Emma as his mistress five years later) and Charles Greville, on a second visit to his uncle in Naples. English travellers to Naples arrived in droves. There were usually at least sixty of them in the town, many earning Hamilton's disapproval by their drinking and gaming. Whilst gambling at cards at the palace, where they might be joined by the king, Hamilton felt obliged to take part *'but I played low and my loss was small'.*[21]

Other visitors over the years consisted of a long list of nobility, including Maria Carolina's brothers – Emperor Joseph of Austria, Grand Duke Leopold of Tuscany and Archduke Ferdinand of Milan. Many were shown the sights. No wonder Hamilton wrote, *'My love for Antiquities & natural history have acquired me the Character of the best Cicerone* [guide] *of Naples & its environs which has procured me a great deal of honour to be sure, but attended with some fatigue.'*[22]

Early in 1775, he purchased for £300 a large vase *'far beyond any monument of the kind in Rome',*[23] which Gavin Hamilton had dug up near Hadrian's Villa at Tivoli. He had the vase restored at considerable expense and, through Greville, tried to persuade the British Museum to purchase it for £500. He was disappointed when they were unwilling to pay this price. He had hoped it would add an important piece to his collection in the Museum. Greville later managed to conclude a sale to his brother, the Earl of Warwick. The vase became known as the 'Warwick Vase'.

Hamilton published two exceptionally fine folio volumes entitled *Campi Phlegraei* [Flaming Fields] describing his observations of the volcanoes of Naples and Sicily. Hamilton himself is depicted in some of the specially commissioned dramatic scenes painted by Pietro Fabris.[24] The outstanding quality of these volumes rendered them expensive, over £1,300.[25]

A third volume was added in 1779 after a particularly violent explosion of Versuvius almost buried the town of Ottaiano. *'Had the eruption lasted an hour longer, Ottaiano must have remain'd exactly in the state of Pompeii which was buried under the ashes of Vesuvius just over 1700 years ago with most of its inhabitants ...'*[26]

In January 1776 Hamilton applied for leave to see to his affairs in

Pembrokeshire. Permission was granted more quickly and he and
Catherine were on their way home by the end of May, reaching
England by 20 September. Their intended stay of a few months was
extended to a year in England and six months travelling to and fro.
They visited the Welsh estates and viewed his collection in the British
Museum. Hamilton met Sir Joseph Banks through being elected to the
Society of the Dilettanti. He sat for a portrait by Sir Joshua Reynolds
that portrayed him as a connoisseur, with a vase on his left and
Vesuvius on his right.

After this sojourn in England Catherine was less willing to return
to Naples. She fell ill on the journey and back in Naples by November
1777, she was soon spending much of her time alone. It was the
hunting season again and the court removed to Caserta. Hamilton
was constantly away with the King. He wrote to Greville: '*Ly. H. wou'd
not stay at Naples alone (for without me she kindly says she is being alone),
so that she has led the life of a hermit these two months, as I am out before
daybreak, come home after dark & have just time to dress and go to Court to
play at Biribis with their Sicn* [Sicilian] *Majestys.'*[27]

Catherine was partly to blame for her loneliness. She admitted, '*I
am a bad courtier*'.[28] Although her health improved after returning to
Naples she still suffered from nervous anxiety. Hamilton spoke of her
'nervous disposition'.

During the next couple of years Hamilton was busy, as usual,
purchasing many pictures by Italian artists such as Parmegiano,
Carracci, Cagnacci and one attributed to Leonardo da Vinci (although
he was not convinced of the attribution). Some of these he kept, one
was a gift to Greville and others were for Greville to sell in London.[29]

By 1776, the Minister Tanucci's influence was waning and Hamilton
reported home: '*However the Minister's power is now greatly on the decline
and it is the Queen Of Naples that actually governs this country.'*[30] The
Queen, being passionately anglophile, became his staunchest ally.

Finally, after forty-two years' service, Tanucci was replaced by
General John Acton in 1777, mainly at the Queen's instigation. Acton
was English by birth, though he was born in France. He had served in
both the French and Tuscan navies and arrived in Naples on loan from
the Grand Duke of Tuscany. He was extremely competent and spoke
French and Italian, but was never completely fluent in English. Acton
remained in power throughout Hamilton's remaining career as
Ambassador to Naples.

In 1778 France sided with America in the war against Britain. The American colonies had rebelled and signed the Declaration of Independence on 4 July 1775.

Hamilton passed on information he received that France was planning to attack Ireland. Two days prior to Spain's declaration on 16 June 1779, King Ferdinand leaked information to him that Spain was joining the war. Owing to his long-standing relationship with Ferdinand and Maria Carolina and his privileged position at court, Hamilton succeeded in persuading Naples not to join the war.

In addition to diplomatic duties, Sir William and Catherine led a very varied lifestyle as he described in a letter to Greville in 1780: '*I roll luxuriously in the sea every morning and we dine at our Casino in Pausilipo every day, where it is as cool as it is in England. Spring and Autumn we inhabit our sweet house at Portici which you remember, and in Winter I follow the King to Caserta and the Appenines after wild boars etc.*'

In this same letter he makes an unexpected statement: '*The Queen's affability with musick, of which the King is now passionately fond, makes the evening pass agreeably.*'[31] Catherine, if she attended any of these 'agreeable evenings', could have made a substantial contribution with her excellent piano and harpsichord playing.

During 1781, Catherine's health deteriorated. Hamilton applied for permission to convert the top floor of the Palazzo Sessa into a new apartment so that she could have more light and air in a room with a beautiful view. She enjoyed a summer stay at Villa Angelica where she wrote to Hamilton's niece, Mary: '*we live as English a life as we can make it. In the morning we go out in an open chaise, I work, [needlework] & draw, in the Evening we have musick, afterwards I work & Sir Wm. reads to me.*'[32]

By the beginning of 1782 she was resigned to dying and wrote three letters to Hamilton that he found in her workbox after her death. In these letters she expresses the depth of her love for him (far greater than his for her) and indicates the extent of her dependence on him: '*How shall I express my love & tenderness to you, dearest of earthly blessings! My only attachment to this world has been my love for you, & you are my only regret in leaving it. My heart has followed your footsteps where ever you went, & you have been the source of all my joys ... But all this must have an end − forget & forgive my faults, & remember me with kindness.*' She concludes this letter by addressing the issue of religion over which they did not agree: '*Oh, Lord, bless & convert to thy faith my dear, dear husband & grant that we may live to praise & bless Thee together.*'[33]

In another letter, she describes even more touchingly her love for him and her desolation when he is absent. Poor Catherine knew her strength was declining and in her last letter she appeals to Hamilton to reflect further on religious matters. Hamilton, unaware of the sentiments expressed in these letters, carried on as usual.

In 1782, he had the good fortune to be offered a beautiful vase, one of the most beautiful and famous antiquities he had ever known. James Byres, a dealer in Rome, had purchased what was then called the Barberini Vase from the Barberini family in 1780. It was 10 inches high and made of deep blue glass, covered with mythological scenes worked in white cameo.

Despite being in debt to the tune of £4,000, Hamilton immediately agreed the purchase price of £1,000.[34] The vase was carefully packed up and sent to England where his niece, Mary, acting as his agent, approached the Duchess of Portland, his chosen prospective buyer. The Duchess bought the vase for £3,000 (along with two other smaller antiquities) whereupon it became known as the Portland Vase.

The 'observation tower' on top of the Palazzo Sessa was regrettably not completed in time for Catherine to enjoy. She died on 25 August 1782 at the Villa Angelica of a 'bilious fever' or, as Hamilton described it, she was *'carried off by a putrid fever'.*[35]

She was forty-four.

Catherine had been a loyal companion to Hamilton and he acknowledged his grief in a letter to his sister, the Countess of Warwick: *'In spite of all my Philosophy I am quite unhinged by the cruel separation from an amiable and true friend.'*[36]

Hamilton and Catherine were married for twenty-four years, eighteen of which they had lived in Naples. Catherine left all her estates in Pembrokeshire entirely to him, which provided an annual income of at least £5,000. Her body was embalmed and sent back to England by sea to be buried in the family vault in Slebech Church in Pembrokeshire. She had made Hamilton promise that on his own death, he would be buried beside her.

Hamilton applied for leave to attend to Catherine's burial and to his affairs in Pembrokeshire. In his *'unhinged'* state he threw himself into a frenzy of activity, especially hunting with the King. The King and Queen, knowing he was unhappy at home, kindly invited him to spend the evenings with them. Catherine's death had, however, persuaded him to remain in Naples. In the letter to his sister, he wrote: *'I by no means think of exchanging the office I at present enjoy, not even for one that might be more brilliant & lucrative in appearance – I have weigh'd well every circumstance & I am sure that in the balance of my future happiness the Naples scale preponderates.'*[37]

While he was waiting for leave to be granted, he was distracted from his loneliness by an earthquake in Calabria that devastated the countryside, causing the loss of 40,000 lives. He took his manservant, Cottier, with him and sailed down the coast to investigate. He was away for three weeks and, as usual, compiled a descriptive and comprehensive report for the Royal Society.

Back in Naples on 23 May, he found his permission for leave granted. He left Naples on 27 May, visited galleries in Rome and Florence and continued on via Modena, Mantua, Trento, Bolzano, Innsbruck and Dresden, arriving in London and taking up residence at Nerot's Hotel on King Street in Mayfair during August 1783.

Hamilton's lifestyle, in which his debts were caused mainly through considerable expenditure on entertaining important guests, (both private and on account of ambassadorial duties) and on antiquities, had been well and truly set before Emma and her mother arrived in Naples.

CHAPTER 5

Greville's Deceit and Emma's Love Lost

*'I have ever had a foreboding since I first begun to love you,
that I was not destined to be happy'*
Emma to Greville, 1 August 1786

*[Hamilton] can never be nearer to me than your Uncle
& my sincere freind, he can never be my lover'*
Emma to Greville, 1786

*'I will do as well as I can and hobble in and out of this pleasant
scrape as decently as I can'*
Hamilton to Greville, 1786

THE DAY BEFORE Emma arrived in Naples Hamilton wrote to Greville: *I had an account of the arrival of our friend at Geneva the 27th. of last month (March), so that she may be here in a day or two. The prospect of possessing so delightful an object under my roof certainly causes in me some pleasing sensations, but they are accompanied with some anxious thoughts as to the prudent management of this business; however, I will do as well as I can, and hobble in and out of this pleasant scrape as decently as I can. You may be assured that I will comfort her for the loss of you as well as I am able, but I know, from the small specimen during your absence in London, that I shall have at times many tears to wipe from those charming eyes, & which if shed for any other but yourself, might give me jealousy.*

Now that you have had the resolution of taking this necessary step, you will, I dare say, turn your mind seriously to the improving of your fortune, either by marriage or getting again into employment. You shall hear from me as soon as she arrives ... A short postscript informs Greville that *'the trunk has arrived'*.[1]

Ever the diplomat, accustomed to being polite, charming, tolerant and obliging to all his guests, Hamilton foresaw a difficult situation

approaching that he would need to handle with great care and tact. Naturally looking forward to the company of such a beautiful young woman, but fully aware of her love for Greville ... *'I shall have at times, many tears to wipe from those charming eyes'* and was conscious of the disadvantage of being thirty-five years older than Emma ... *'I will hobble in and out of this pleasant scrape as decently as I can.'*
He faced the situation with some trepidation.

At first Sir William devoted himself to Emma. They breakfasted, dined and supped together, went to the theatre and to the San Carlo opera house and, with Sir Thomas Rumbold, Sir William drove her and Mrs Cadogan along the esplanade in Rumbold's* carriage. He gave her a cashmere shawl, a new dress and some items that had belonged to Lady Hamilton. He found her more beautiful than ever. Sir William was totally smitten.

Not only Sir William was entranced. In Naples, Emma caused a sensation in her English clothes and blue hat. Everyone wanted to meet her. When she went about in her carriage she was noticed and admired, as much for her style and animation as for her beauty. Artists were queuing up to paint her portrait. Soon the people of Naples learnt of her kindness and generosity and admired her even more.

When Georgiana, Duchess of Devonshire, arrived in Naples in 1793, she wrote that Lady Hamilton was *'ador'd here not only for her beauty and her talents but for her charity – they say she assists the poor to ye greatest degree.'*[2]

The Palazzo Sessa, situated on a hilltop near the Royal Palace, must have both amazed and delighted Emma and her mother. The entrance was via a stone staircase opposite the courtyard entrance. On the first floor, along a corridor on the southern side, were three large connecting rooms, decorated with Adam designs and *'furnished in the English taste'*, according to Goethe's description.† Hamilton conducted his official business in these rooms.

The first ante-chamber led through to the library where his secretaries, Smith and Oliver, worked. The adjacent room was Sir William's private study where visitors and guests were received. It contained his collections of antique vases and cameos, specimens of lava, maps and books, and a telescope for viewing Vesuvius. The walls were covered with numerous paintings of every description.

* Sir Thomas Rumbold had been aide-de-camp to Clive at Plassey, India
† Johann Wolfgang Goethe, the renowned German poet

Tischbein, the German artist who had made Naples his home, declared, *'I have never seen a more pleasant room.'* All three rooms had a magnificent view of Vesuvius and the Bay of Naples.

On the western aspect of the building was a suite of four rooms, all with similar views of the sea that became the apartment for Emma and her mother. The suite comprised a large sitting room with a ceiling decorated with gold stars and wreaths. Two similar rooms led to a pretty room with a fireplace. This may have served Mrs Cadogan as a private sitting room when she was not included in embassy functions.

Above the ambassador's reception rooms were a further three rooms, used for special occasions and entertaining guests who had come for pleasure, rather than business. Catherine had held her 'assemblies' here. These were the rooms that could accommodate sixty guests on 'gala occasions'. Diplomats, nobility and friends were entertained, to dine, listen to music and dance in these beautiful rooms.

Sir William's private rooms were above Emma's apartment. Leading off the last of these was the 'observation tower' that Sir William had completed before Emma arrived. This was an unusual circular room occupying the corner position of the building. Half of the circle was a balconied window with a magnificent view of the entire bay. The other half had walls covered with mirrors reflecting the view across the bay, all to stunning effect. Bench seating around the circle provided a place to sit and read and enjoy the sun and the fresh sea air – a peaceful retreat from the busy, narrow streets of Naples down below.

This home served as the British Embassy and Sir William had every right to claim expenses from the government. But these expenses, and his salary, were often late or never paid.

Sir William was known as the *'Cavaliere'* and employed many servants, three of whom were also musicians.

Goethe's description of the Palazzo was written on 22 March 1787: *'The situation and the climate* [of Naples] *are beyond praise; but they are all the resources a foreigner has. Of course, someone with leisure, money and talent could settle down here and live most handsomely. This is what Sir William Hamilton has done in the evening of his days. The rooms in his villa, which he has furnished in the English taste, are charming and the view from the corner room may well be unique. The sea below, Capri opposite, Mount Posilippo to the right, nearby the promenade of the Villa Reale, to the left an old building of the Jesuits, in the distance the coastline from Sorrento to Cape*

Minerva – probably nothing comparable could be found in the whole of Europe and certainly not in the middle of a great city.'[3]

Despite this impressive residence, beautiful surroundings and Sir William's kind attentions and generous gifts, Emma was dejected and forlorn. Four days after her arrival she wrote an anguished letter to Greville:

Naples   April the 30th. 1786

My Dearest Greville

I arrived at this place the 26th. & I should have begun to write sooner but the post does not go out tell to morrow & I dreaded setting down to write for I try to appear chearful before Sr. Wm. as I can & I am sure to cry the moment I think of you, for I feil more & more unhappy at being seperrated from you, & if my total ruin depends on seeing you, I will & must in the end of the sumer, for to live without you is impossible. I love you to that degree that at this time their is not a hardship opon hearth, either of poverty, hunger, cold, death, or even to walk barefooted to Scotland to see you, but what I would undergo. Therefore, my dear, dear Greville, if you do love me, for God sake & for my sake, try all you can to come hear as soon as possible.

You have a true friend in Sr. Wm. and he will be happy to see you & do all he can to make you happy & for me, I will be everything you can wish for. I find it not either a fine horse or a fine coach or a pack of servants or plays or operas can make me happy, it is you that as it in your power, either to make me very happy, or very miserable.

I respect Sr. Wm. I have a great regard for him as the uncle & friend of you & he loves me, Greville, but he can never be anything nearer to me than your Uncle & my sincere freind, he can never be my lover. You do not know how good Sr. Wm. is to me, he is doing every thing he can to make me happy, he as never dined out since I came hear & endead to spake the truth he is never out of my sight, he breakfasts, dines, supes, & is constantly by me, looking in my face, I cant stir a hand, a legg, or a foot but what he is marking as graceful & fine & I am sorry to say it, but he loves me now as much as ever he could Lady Bolingbroke,* endead, I am sorry, for I cant make him happy, I can be civil, oblidging, & I do try to make myself as agreeable as I can to him, but I belong to you, Greville & to you onely will I belong & nobody shall be your heir aparent. You do not know how glad I was to arrive hear the day I did, as it was my Birthday & I was very low spirited. Oh God, that day

---

* Lady Bolingbroke was born Lady Diana Spencer and, after divorcing Lord Bolingbroke, married the Hon. Topham Beauclerc, who died in 1780. She was another of the widows whom Sir William had considered as a marriage prospect.

that you used to smile on me & stay at home & be kind to me, that that day I should be at such a distance, but my comfort is I rely on your promise & September or October I shall see you, but I am quite unhappy at not hearing from you, no letter for me yet Greville, but I must wait with patience. We have had company most every day since I came, some of Sr. Wm.'s freinds. They are all very much pleased with me & poor Sr. Wm. is never so happy as when he is pointing out my beauties to them. He thinks I am grown much more ansome than I was, he does nothing all day but look at me & sigh. Yes, last night we had a little concert, but then I was low, for I wanted you to partake of our amusement.

Sr. Thomas Rumbold: is hear with his son who is dying of a decline ... You cant think what a worthy man he is, he dind with ous & likes me very much & every day as brought is carridge or phaeton, which he as bought hear, & carried me & my mother & Sr. Wm. out & shows ous a deal of civelaties, for you are to understand I have a caridge of Sr. W.'s, a English one painting & new livereys & new coach man, foot man & the same as Mrs. Damer* for of her own, for she did not want to go with us. If I was going about in is carridge they would say I was either is wife or mistress, therefore as I am not or ever can be either, we have made a very good establishment of 4 rooms very pleasant, looking to the sea, our boat comes out today for the first time & we shall begin to bathe in a day or two & we are going for one day or two to Caserta. I was at Pasilipo yesterday, I think it a very pretty place. Sr. W. as given me a camels shawl like my old one. I know you will be pleased to hear that & he as given me a beautiful goun, cost 25 guineas, India painting on wite satin, & several little things of Lady Hamilton's & is going to by me some muslin dresses loose to tye with a sash for the hot weather, made like the turkey dresses, the sleeves tyed in fowlds with ribban & trimed with lace, in short he is all ways contriving what he shall get for me. The people admires my English dresses, but the blue hat, Greville, pleases most. Sr. W. is quite enchanted with it. Oh, how he loves you. He told me he had made is will & left you every thing belonging to him; that made me very happy for your sake. Pray, my dear Greville, do write me word if you want any money. I am affraid I distressed you [caused him financial distress] but I am sure Sr. W. will send you some & I told him he must help you a little now & send some for your jurney hear & he kiss'd me & the tears came into is eyes & told me I might command any thing for he loved us both dearly & oh, how happy shall I be when I can once more see you, my dear, dear Greville. You are every thing that is dear to me on hearth & I hope happier times will soon restore you to

---

* Anne Damer, artist and an old friend of Hamilton's

me for endead I would rather be with you starving, than from you in the greatest splender in the world. I have onely to say I enclose this I wrote yesterday & I will not venture myself now to wright any more for my mind & heart is so torn by different passions that I shall go mad, onely Greville, remember your promise, October. Sr. Wm. says you never mentioned to him about coming to Naples at all, but you know the consequence of your not coming for me. Endead, my dear Greville, I live but on the hope of seeing you & if you do not come hear, lett what will be the consequence, I will come to England. I have had a conversation this morning with Sr. Wm. that has made me mad. He speak half I do not know what to make of it, but Greville, my dear Greville, wright some comfort to me, pray do, if you love me, but onely remember you will never be loved by any body like your affectionate & sincere

   Emma

P.S. Pray, for God sake wright to me & come to me, for Sr. W. shall never by any thing to me but your friend.[4]

It is clear from this letter why Emma is in a bewildered and distressed state. She has not received any letter from Greville – she would certainly have hoped for one on her arrival. In the absence of a letter she was *'very low-spirited'* on her birthday.

After these first few days, Emma suspects that she is expected to become Sir William's mistress: *'I respect Sr. Wm. I have a great regard for him ... he loves me, Greville, but he can never be anything nearer to me than your Uncle and my sincere friend, he can never be my lover.'*

She refers twice to the promise Greville made to her: *'my comfort is I rely on your promise & September or October I shall see you'* and again, *'my mind & heart is so torn by different passions that I shall go mad, onely Greville, remember your promise, October.'* She goes on to say, *'Sr. Wm. says you never mentioned to him about coming to Naples at all'*. No wonder she was *'torn by different passions'*.

This must have come as a great shock to her and she was justifiably angry when she realized that Greville might not come to take her home. When she asked Sir William to send Greville some money for his journey to Naples his eyes had *'filled with tears'* and *'he told me I might command anything for he loved us both dearly'*. Sir William knew that Greville would not be coming to Naples to fetch Emma and believed his growing love for her was unlikely to be reciprocated.

Emma's closing statement became an accurate prophesy: *'but onely remember you will never be loved by any body like your affectionate & sincere Emma.'*

Greville did not reply to this letter, or to the fourteen letters Emma claims to have written. After three months, Emma must finally have registered that Greville had lied to her when he parted from her with love and kisses, and promised to fetch her from Naples in six months' time.

Nevertheless, she wrote another pleading letter to her *Ever Dearest Grevillle* on *22nd. July 1786*:

I am now only writing to beg of you for God sake to send me one letter, if it is onely a farewell. Sure, I have deserved this for the sake of the love you once had for me. Think, Greville, of our former connexion and don't despise me. I have not used you ill in any one thing. I have been from you going for six months [in fact, five months at most] and you have [not] wrote one letter to me – enstead of which I have sent fourteen to you. So pray, let me beg of you, my much-loved Greville, only one line from your dear, dear hands. You dont know how thankful I shall be for it. For if you knew the misery I feel, oh! your heart would not be intirely shut up against; for I love you with the truest affection. Dont lett anybody sett you against me. Some of your friends – your foes, perhaps, I dont know what to stile them – have long wisht me ill. But, Greville, you will never meet with anybody that has a truer affection for you than I have, and I onely wish it was in my power to show what I could do for you. As soon as I know your determination, I shall take my own measures. If I dont hear from you & that you are coming according to promise, I shall be in England by Cristmass at farthest, dont be unhappy at that, I will see you once more for the last time, I find life unsupportable with out you. Oh my heart is intirely broke, then for God sake, my ever dear Greville, do write me some comfort. I dont know what to do, I am now in that state I am incapable of anything. I have a language master [Emma was learning Italian], a singing master, music etc.etc., but what is it for, if it was to amuse you I should be happy, but Greville, what will it avail me. I am poor, helpless and forlorn. I have lived with you 5 years & you have sent me to a strange place & no one prospect, me thinking you was coming to me; instead of which I was told to live, you know how, with Sr. Wm. No, I respect him, but no, never shall he peraps live with me for a little wile like you & send me to England, then what am I to do? what is to become of me? But excuse me, my heart is ful. I tell you, give me one guiney a week for everything, and live with me, and I will be contented. But no more, I will trust to Providence and wherever you go, God bless and preserve you, and may you always be happy![5]

Despite all the excitement and glamour of Naples, and the fuss being made of her, Emma still yearned for Greville, begging him '*to send me one letter, if it is onely farewell'* and declaring *'I love you with the truest affection'*.

The five-month separation had not changed her feelings for Greville, although she could have given in to the temptations of a luxurious lifestyle in Naples with Sir William. She informs Greville *'If I dont hear from you & that you are coming according to your promise'* she will *'be in England by Christmas at farthest'*. She knows now that he has ended his relationship with her: *'I will see you once more for the last time.'*

Although angry with him she begs him for some comfort. She is fearful that if she stays with Sir William, living with him *'you know how'*, he will eventually discard her, as both Sir Harry and Greville had done, and send her back to London with no idea of how or where she would live.

Remarkably, Emma was able to overcome her fears and desperation to continue this letter with news of *'how we go on'* in a friendly manner.

Emma reveals her feelings of insecurity when, in describing events, she appears to boast about her activities and social successes. This may have been to provoke Greville's jealousy. Not surprisingly, Emma was overwhelmed by the attention she attracted since Greville had kept her in such a modest and secluded environment in Edgware Road.

If I have spirits, I will tell you something concerning how we go on, that will make my letter worth paying for. Sr. Wm. wants a picture of me the sise of the Bacante [this was the painting by Romney that he had commissioned in London] *for his new appartments & he will take that picture of me in the black gown at Romneys & I have made the bargain with him that the picture shall be yours if he will pay for it & he will & I have wrote to Romney to send it. Their is two painters now in the house painting me; one picture is finished. It is the size of the Bacante setting in a turbin, a turkish dress, the other is in a black rubin* [Rubens] *hat with fethers, blue silk gown etc. but as soon as these is finished there is two more to paint me & Angelaca* if she comes, & Marchmont is to cut a head of me* [a cameo] *for a ring. I wish Angelaca would come for Prince Draydrixton* [Dietrichstein] *from Veina is here & dines with ous often & he wants a picture of me – he is my cavaliere servente or chechespeo which you like. He is much in love*

---

*Angelica Kauffman, the renowned portrait painter who travelled Europe painting the rich and famous, had arrived in England when she was in her early twenties. Within two years she was elected a founder member of the Royal Academy. Her reputation was made when she was commissioned to paint a portrait of Queen Charlotte.

with me. *I walk in the Villa Reale every night, I have generally two princes, two or 3 nobles, the English Minister & the King, with a crowd beyond ous. The Queen likes me much & desired Prince Draydrixton to walk with me near her, that she may get a sight of me, for the Prince when he is not with ous, he is with the Queen & he does nothing but entertains her with my beauty, the accounts of it etc.etc. But Greville, the King as eyes, he as a heart & I have made an impression on his heart but he told the Prince, Hamilton is my friend & she belongs to his Nephey, for all our friends knows it and the Prince desires his best compliments to you. I must tell you a peice of gallantry of the K. on Sunday. He dined at Pausilipo & he allways comes every Sunday before the Casina in his boat to look at me – we had a small diplomatic party & we was sailing in our boat. The K. directly came up, put his boat of Musick next us & made all the French horns & the wole band play, he took off his hat & sett with his hat on his knees all the wile & when he was going to land, he made his bow & said it was a sin he could not speak English ...*

Emma continues the next day:

I have been to Pompea etc etc and we are going next week round the Islands Corprea, Ischea, Sormenta etc etc. We shall be a whay a little wile, I should feil pleasure in all this if you was heare, but that blessing I have not & so I must make the most of my lot. God bless you, I would write a longer letter but I am going to Paysylipo to diner & I have a conversazyone* to night & a concert. I bathe every day. I have not any irruptions [her skin problem] & what will surprise you I am remarkably fair that everybody says I put on red & wite ... We have had dreadful thunder & lightenen; it fell at the Maltese minister just by our house & burnt is beds & wines etc etc. I have now perswaded Sr. Wm. to put up a conductor to his house; the Lava runs a little but the mountain is very ful & we expect an irruption every day. I must stop or else I should begin & tell you my ideas of the people of Naples, in my next I will.

But Greville, flees, & lice their is milliions. I shall write you an Italian letter soon. God bless you. Make my compliments to your brother & all your friends thats my friends. Pray write to yors ever, with the truist & sincere affection.

Emma

God bless you write, my ever dear, dear Greville.

Emma shows little enthusiasm for the people she meets and the places she visits. '*I should feil pleasure in all this if you was heare, but that blessing I have not & so I must make the most of my lot.*'

---

* This was the custom at the time for friends to gather at a house to take tea and socialise informally

This letter may have crossed with one she finally receives from Greville. Her reply on the 1st August briefly repeats her plaintive longing for him but soon dramatically changes tone. On discovering that Greville had advised her to *'oblige Sir William'*, Emma is furious.

Naples 1st. of August 1786

I have received your letter, my dearest Greville, at last, and you dont know how happy I am at hearing from you, however I may like some parts of your letter, but I wont complain, it is enough I have paper that Greville as wrote on, he as foldet up, he wet the happy wafer, how I envy thee to take the place of Emma's lips, that she would give worlds had she them, to kiss those lips, but if I go on in this whay I shall be incapable of writing. I onely wish that a wafer was my onely rival, but I submit to what God & Greville pleases.

I allways knew, I have ever had a foreboding, since I first begun to love you, that I was not destined to be happy, for their is not a King or prince on hearth that could make me happy without you; so onely consider when I offer to live with you on the hundred a year Sir Wm. will give me, what can you desire, and this from a girl that a King etc, etc, is sighing for.

As to what you write to me to oblige Sr. Wm. I will not answer you for Oh if you knew what pain I feil in reading those lines whare you advise me to W.......[Whore?] nothing can express my rage, I am all madness, Greville, to advise me, you that used to envy my smiles, now with cooll indifferance to advise me to go to bed with him, Sr. Wm. Oh, thats worst of all, but I will not, no I will not rage for if I was with you, I would murder you & myself boath. I will leave of & try to get more strength for I am now very ill with a cold.

I wont look back to what I wrote. I onley say I have had two letters in 6 months nor nothing shall ever do for me but going home to you. If that is not to be, I will except of nothing, I will go to London, their go in to every exess of vice, tell I dye a miserable broken hearted wretch & leave my fate as a warning to young whomin never to be two good, for, now you have made me love you, made me good, you have abandoned me & some violent end shall finish our connexion if it is to finish, but, oh Greville, you cannot, you must not give me up, you have not the heart to do it, you love me I am sure & I am willing to do everything in my power that you shall require of me & what will you have more and I onely say this last time, I will neither beg or pray, do as you like.

No wonder that Emma wrote: *'nothing can express my rage, I am all madness'*. Greville's plan is laid bare. He had *'with cooll indifferance'* advised her to *'to go to bed with him, Sr. Wm'*. Understandably, she raged that if she were near him, she would *'murder you & myself boath'*.

This is her last letter to him on the subject.

Emma's generous nature enabled her to put aside these passionate emotions and continue the letter:

... We have a deal of rain hear & violent winds; the oldest people hear never remember such a sumer, but it is luckey for us. The Queen is very poorly with a cold caught in the Villa Reale & mine is pretty much like it. We dont dine at Passylippo today on account of my cold. We are closely besieged by the K. in a round a bout manner, he comes every Sunday to P... po but we keep the good will of the other party mentioned above & never gives him any encouragement. Prince Draydrixton's our constant friend, he allways enquiries after you, he desires his compliments to you; he speaks English, he says I am a dymond of the first watter & the finest creature on the hearth ... I shall write next post by Sr. Wm. onely I cant let a week go without telling you how happy I am at hearing from you. Pray write as often as you can & come as soon as you can & if you come we shall all go home to England in 2 years & go throug Spain & you will like that. Pary write to me & dont write in the stile of a freind but a lover, for I wont hear a word of a freind , it shall be all love & no friendship.

Sr. Wm. is our freind, but we are lovers. I am glad you have sent me a Blue Hat & gloves; my hat is universaly admired through Naples. God bless you, my dear Greville prays your ever truly and affectionate

Emma Hart

P.S. Pray write for nothing will make me so angry & it is not in your interest to disoblige me, for you dont know the power I have hear, onely I never will be his mistress. If you affront me, I will make him marry me. God bless you for ever.[6]

At the end of the letter Emma reverts to asking Greville to write again *'as often as you can'*. She makes clear that she is no longer prepared to remain in the ignoble position of a mistress, saying, *'I will make him marry me'*. This remark might have shaken Greville's complacency as her marrying his uncle could endanger his promised inheritance.

Greville's continued refusal to write to Emma indicated to her that her desperate letters declaring her love for him and her longing to be with him had no effect on him. He had, however, promised his uncle that he would 'neglect her'. Perhaps when he ignored her final plea, *'I onely say this last time, I will neither beg nor pray'*, she was finally persuaded to give him up. She did not write to him again until August the following year.

Meanwhile Sir William patiently, and with great tact, waited for the situation to resolve itself. In July he had written to his friend, Sir Joseph Banks: '*A beautiful plant called* Emma *has been transplanted here from England & at least has not lost any of its beauty.*'[7] In September he wrote a further comment to him: '*My visitor, for you must know I have* one, *is as handsome as ever & in tolerable spirits considering all – it is a bad job to come from the Nephew to the Uncle but one must make the best of it & I long to see poor Charles out of his difficulties.*'[8]

Emma had been living in the Palazzo Sessa for eight months. For the first three months she had been in an agony of uncertainty about whether Greville loved her and would be coming to fetch her, but she knew the relationship was over when she wrote the letter above. Since then she had neither written to him nor received a reply. Her disappointment and anger gradually abated. She faced facts and regretfully accepted that he was now in the past.

Emma had been fond of Sir William since she first met him due to the respect and admiration he had always shown her. Over the next five months, her feelings developed into love. Not the passionate love she later felt for Lord Nelson, but a love born out of gratitude for all that Sir William had done for her. Hamilton was amusing and had an easy-going attitude to life. Living with him less stressful than it had been with Greville.

Hamilton could have found her tears and tempers a trial but he, too, had been deceived by Greville into believing that Emma was happy to come to him in Naples. However, knowing she could not return to Greville, he maintained his customary tolerance and understanding and persevered with his efforts to help her come to terms with her new situation.

Sympathetic and understanding throughout her months of distress and disappointment over the way Greville had treated her, Sir William had been unfailing in his kindness and generosity. His admiration had grown into love for her and he did everything in his power to cheer her up: encouraged (and paid for) her ambitions in learning music and languages, took her on sight-seeing visits around Naples and to the islands of Capri and Ischia. He kindly suggested that she write to invite Romney and his friend, the poet William Hayley, to visit them in Naples. Sadly, they did not take up this invitation.

In October, Greville and Hamilton had been in contact about what to do if Emma refused to stay in Naples. Hamilton informed his nephew that he was prepared to make Emma an allowance of £100 per year if she returned to England. This was an extremely generous offer. Perhaps he felt guilty about the deception in transferring her to Naples, causing her so much unhappiness.

Greville replied:

Your proposed provision exceeds your promise ... But you have now rendered it possible for her to be respected & comfortable, & if she has not talked herself out of the true view of her situation she will retain the protection & affection of us both. For, after all, consider what a charming creature she would have been if she had been bless'd with the advantages of an early education & had not been spoilt by indulgence of every caprice ... If she will put me on the footing of a friend, which she says I have always assumed, she will write to me fairly of her plans ... but she must not think that I can resume that close connection, and live as I did with her. In the first place I cannot afford it; in the next, it would keep me out of the world, & would ruin me & herself ... the plan I propose is to make Mr. Romney her trustee, & vest your grant in him for her benefit; & I will consider further & write to you when I have form'd my opinion ...[9]

Neither Sir William Hamilton nor Emma needed any more advice from Greville. Emma now had the strength of character to make up her own mind about her future. By December, she had capitulated.

CHAPTER 6

Emma Finds Happiness in Naples

'I am a pretty whoman, and one can't be everything at once;
but now I have my wisdom teeth & will try to be ansome and
reasonable'
Emma to Sir William, 26 December 1786

'Our dear Em goes on now quite as I could wish, improves
daily, & is universally beloved'
Sir William to Greville, 16 February 1787

'Sr William all ready is distractedly in love & indeed I love him
tenderly. He deserves it.'
Emma to Greville, December 1787

WE CANNOT BE sure exactly when Sir William and Emma became lovers. It must have been before the end of December, as nearly four months after Emma's last letter to Greville and eight months after her arrival in Naples, she wrote the following letter to Sir William from Caserta when he was away with the royal hunting party:

Caserta.   December 26th. 1786

Pray don't scold me for writing to you, for endead I can't help it, and I should have been ashamed to have wrote to you without an excuse for doing it, therefore Smith as returned the letter I sent to town, & I told Cottier that I would send it to you or else he might think I was so much in love I could not be 3 days without sending it to you. But lett them think if he will; certain it is I love you & sincerely & indeed I am apprehensive two much for my own quiet, but lett it be. Love as its pleasures & its pains; for instance, yesterday when you went a whay from me, I thought all my heart and soul was torn from me, and my grief was excessive I assure you; to-day I am better, perche [because] the day after to moro is Friday & then I shall have you with me to make up for past pain. I shall have much pleasure and comfort, and my mind tells me you will have much pleasure to come home to me again, and I will setle you & comfort you ... there is nothing I assure you can give me the least comfort tell you come home. I shall receive you with smiles, affection and good humer, & think had I the offer of crowns I would refuse them except you, and I don't care if all the world knows it. If sometimes I am out of humer, forgive me, tell me, put me in a whay to be grateful to you for you kindness to me, and believe me I never will abuse your kindness to me, and in a little time all faults will be corrected. I am a pretty whoman, and one can't be everything at once; but now I have my wisdom teeth I will try to be ansome and reasonable. God bless you, my ever dear friend, etc,etc,ec, and believe me yours and onely yours for ever sincerly.

Do write 3 lines to me, and come home soon.[1]

She had tried so hard to please Greville, and now she is determined to please Hamilton. She refers to her quick temper: '*If sometimes I am out of humer, forgive me ... in a little time all faults will be corrected.*' Due to her unreserved and emotional nature, Emma always expressed her feelings freely and openly. She claimed that Hayley's copy of *The Triumphs of Temper* helped her to control her temper. She knew Greville and Hamilton disliked her tempestuous outbursts. She later wrote to Romney: '*Sir William minds temper more than beauty.*'

Whereas Catherine, Sir William's first wife, could have attended court, but chose not to, Emma, who would have been thrilled by the experience, was excluded as her 'unofficial' position was considered unacceptable. As time passed, she increasingly felt the indignity of her situation.

Hamilton, mindful of her loneliness and boredom through inactivity, may have suggested she return to Naples where she could continue her lessons and enjoy some social life. With Hamilton's encouragement, she returned to the Palazzo Sessa where she entertained friends and was invited out to dine. She described her social life in letters to Sir William, whilst he was obliged to accompany the King on his hunting expeditions:

Naples. January 5th 1787

I shall begin to write to you to night for the post goes of so early in the morning that we are scarce out of bed, and of an evening I am alone after 7 a clock and I feel it a pleasure to wright to you ... I had Hackert, Gatty & Donker last night. Hackert was ful des'd [dressed] going to Skarvonskys [the Russian Ambassador]. Last night, the Duke of Glouster was to be there to some musick, but not the Dutches nor the children ... The French

Ambassador had his house on fire last night; one room was very much on fire, and if they had not got timely assistance it would have gone bad with them.

I have just received your kind letter. I am glad you had such sport. I wish I had been at your post, I should like to see you shoot, tho' I am afraid I should have two much compassion. But I hope you will every day have luck to repay you for the loss of my kisses. God bless you, my dearest dear Sir W. and believe me yours, more than my own or any other person's else, sincerely and affectionately.[2]

A few days later she sent more news:

January 8th. 1787

I do not know how you like this excessive cold weather; but I do think I never felt much colder in Inghilterra; for today it was impossible to keep one's self warm; and I pittied you much, for if you have not a good sport you must be frose with standing still. The ice is lying abbout the streets in Naples, just as it is in London the hardest frosts there is ... I was at Coletalino's today.* She will make a very great likness and very pretty it will be ... Skaveranky gives a dine to-morro to all his musick people, even the harpscord tuner, at Torre-del-Greco. All the Coletalinos go there, and I fancy there will be a fine mess of them altogether, for I don't hear of any body of fashion that is going He has given Hackert†... a hundred guineas a-pece for 2 little pictures, that I should think twenty enough for them, for I am of your opinion, I would pay for good things, but not for bad ones, and the are pretty but not fine painting.

I have Gallunchy from nine to ten, from ten to twelve at the Coletalino's, from twelve to one my lesson, and between 2 and 3 my diner. I dine frequently upstairs, for Gasperino said a fire in that room must be to air it as well ... For if you was to know how kind everybody behaves to me, you would love them.

Tuesday morn: I have just received your kind letter, my dear Sir Wm ... I am sorry you had not any sport. To stay out in the cold yesterday must be enough to kill you. How I wish'd to give you some warm punch, and settle you in my arms all night, to make up for your bad day ...

Adio and believe me, Yours etc.

P.S. I am sorry you don't hear of coming home. But patienzza.[3]

Emma has begun to form opinions on works of art – Hackert's two paintings 'are pretty things but not fine paintings' – and is well-liked by all his servants and friends. She is busy every day, and shows her need to love somebody and to take care of them – 'How I wish'd to give you some warm punch, and settle you in my arms all night.' How happy Sir

---

* Costanza Coltellini, artist, one of four talented sisters who lived with their aunt in Naples.
† Hackert - Court artist.

William must have been to read those words after witnessing her unhappiness, waiting and hoping she might learn to love him.

January 10th. 1787

I had hardly time to thank you for your kind letter of this morning, as I was busy prepairing for to go on my visit to the Convent of S. Romita; and indead I am glad I went, tho' it was a short visit. But tomorrow I dine with them in full assembly. I am quite charmed with Beatrice Acquaviva. Such is the name of the charming whoman I saw today – Oh, Sir William, she is a pretty whoman. She is 29 years old. She took the veil at twenty, and does not repent to this day, though, if I am a judge in physiognomy, her eyes does not look like the eyes of a nun. They are always laughing, and something in them is vastly alluring ... I stopt for one hour with them, and I had all the good things to eat, and I promise you they don't starve themselves ...

She kissed my lips, cheeks and forehead, and every moment exclaimed 'charming fine creature', admired my dress, said I looked like an angel, for I was in clear white dimity and a blue sash. She admired my hat and fine hair, and she said she had heard I was good to the poor, and generous and noble minded ... In short I sat and listened to her and the tears stood in my eyes, I don't know why; but I loved her at that moment ... It is a beautiful house and garden, and the attention of them was very pleasing ... 'Oh, Emma,' she says to me, '... how surprised was I in seeing you tall in statue. We may read your heart in your countenance, your complexion, in short your figure and features is rare, for you are like the marble statues I saw, when I was in the world'. I think she flattered me up, but I was pleased.

Thursday morning: I have just received your kind letter, and I am pleased and content that you should write to me, tho' it is onley one or two lines a day. Be assured I am grateful. I am sorry you had bad sport, and I shall be most happy to see you at home, to warm you with my kisses, and comfort you with my smiles and good humer, and oblige you by my attentions, which will be the constant pleasure of, my Dear Sir William, your truly affectionate, etc[4]

Hamilton's notes to Emma were mostly about the success or failure of his day's hunting. Emma is initially sympathetic, but by her next letter, she is clearly dissatisfied with his letters:

Naples. Sunday night. January [1787]

Endead, my Sir Wm. I am angry. I told you one line would satisfie me, and when I have no other comfort than your letters, you should not so cruely diapoint me; for I am unhappy, and I don't feil right without hearing from you, and I won't forgive you; no, that I won't.

It is a very cold night, and I am just returned from Hart's [Mr Hart, an

English banker]. *He was very civil to me; there was an Abbé and a very genteel man, a friend of Andreas, and an Englishman I did not know; but they was all very polite, and such a profusion of diner that is impossible to describe ... After diner he* [Hart] *fetched an Italian song, that was made of Lady Sophi Ferner fourty years past, and he had translated it to English and would sing it; and when he came to dymond eyes and pearl teeth, he looked at me and bid the others look at me; and he is going to dedicate the English to me ...*

Monday morning: Oh, thank you, my dear Sir William for your letter. Endead, I forgive you and am sorry I scolded you. The wind made me so sleepy that I slept till eight a clock, and was fast asleep when Vinchenzo brought your letter, and I read it in bed, and gave it a good hug. But I wished you had been there. But I gave it a kiss or 2. But I hope you will believe me sencere when I write to you; for endead, everything flows from my heart, and I cannot stop it. I am glad you had some good sport ... Adio, my dear Sir William.[5]

Emma's complaint about Sir William's brief letters prompted him to write more fully and not only about his hunting experiences.

[January 18th. 1787]

Munday morning

Oh, my dearest Sir William, I have just received your dear sweet letter. It has charmed me. I don't know what to say to you to thank you in words kind enough. Oh, how kind! Do you call me your dear friend? Oh, what a happy creature is your Emma! – me that had no friend, no protector, no body that I could trust, and now to be the friend, the Emma, of Sir William Hamilton! ... Think only, my dear Sir William, what I would say to you, if I could express myself, only to thank you a thousand times. Mr. Hart went awhay yesterday with his head turn'd; I sung so well Handell's 3 songs, Picini, Paisiello, etc, that you never saw a man so delighted. He said it was the most extraordinary thing he ever knew. But what struck him was holding on the notes and going from the high to low notes so very neat. He says I shall turn the heads of the English ... Gallucci played solo some of my sofegos and you whold have thought he would have gone mad. He says he had heard a great deal of me. But he never saw or heard of such a whoman before ... and then I made him allmost cry with Handels; and with the comick he could not contain himself, for he says he never saw the tragick and the comick muse blended so happily together ... [Gatty] *he says I am so accomplish'd, so kind, speaks Italian so well, that he sitts 2 hours together and taulks to me. Him and Don Andrea dines with me today ... and the are to come in the evening to hear me sing. Yours etc.*[6]

Hamilton was keen to keep up the Embassy's reputation for music that had been established in Catherine's day. Emma was taught by the very best musicians and was developing a broad repertoire that included not only Handel and other composers favoured by Catherine, but songs by Piccinni, father of Opera Buffa (comic opera, especially Italian). It was her interpretation of this contrasting music that so impressed Hart.

Around this time Emma met the musician, Ferrari. He had been invited by Celeste Coltellini to meet the girl 'whose voice touched everyone's heart and whose beauty outshone that of the Venus de Medici'. Initially sceptical, afterwards he declared she was 'the most beautiful creature he had ever seen' and that her voice, though not fully trained, 'was by nature sonorous, mellow and true'.[7]

Between her 18 January letter and her next letter written three days later, Emma returned to Caserta and, much to her joy, Sir William spent a night at home.

Caserta. Thursday morning [1787]

I can't be happy till I have wrote to you, my dearest Sir William, tho' it is so lately I saw you. But what of that to a person that loves as I do. One hour's absence is a year, and I shall count the hours and moments till Saturday, when I shall find myself once more in your kind dear arms, my dear Sir William, my friend, my All, my earthly Good, every kind of name in one, you are to me eating, drinking and cloathing, my comforter in distress. Then why should I not love you? Endead, I must and ought, whilst life is left in me, or reason to think on you. I believe it is right I should be separated from you sometimes, to make me know myself, for I don't know till you are absent how dear you are to me: and I won't tell you how many tears I shed for you this morning, and even now I can't stop them, for in thinking of you my heart is full.

I have had a long walk since I wrote the other side, and feel better for it. I have had a long lesson, and am going now to have another, for musick quiets my mind, so that I shall study much tell I see you. I can't finish this subject tell I have thanked you, my dearest Sir William, for having given me the means of at least amusing myself a little, if in your absence I can be amused. I owe everything to you, and shall for ever with gratitude remember it. Pray, one little line, if you have time, just that I may kiss your name ... Take care of your dear self, and that is all that's requested from Yours etc.

P.S. I send you a thousand kisses, and remember last night how happy you made me, and I tell you Satturday night I shall be happier in your presence unmixed with thoughts of parting.[8]

Emma is missing Sir William and feeling closer to him but she is still unsettled. She takes long walks and finds that *'music quiets my mind'*. Emma kept her word – *'I owe everything to you, and shall for ever with grattitude remember it'* – until Sir William Hamilton's death.

On 16 February 1787, Sir William wrote to Greville: *'Our dear Em goes on now quite as I could wish, improves daily, & is universally beloved. She is wonderfull, considering her youth and beauty, & I flatter myself that E and her mother are happy to be with me, so that I see my every wish fulfilled.'*[9]

Before Christmas 1786, Sir William and Emma began working on her 'Attitudes', their new concept of theatrical mime performances. Sir William knew of her interest in acting and of her constant desire to be admired, and had seen her posing as classical characters in Romney's studio. Between them they developed her earlier, static poses for Romney into a live mime performance to entertain an audience. He wanted to show off her beauty, grace, and acting ability to friends and visitors. He sought entertaining and challenging activities to occupy her and distract her from her unhappiness over Greville.

Emma portrayed both male and female characters from ancient Greek and Roman myths. Wearing a very simple Grecian style dress and using shawls as her only props, Emma struck different poses, or 'Attitudes'. With her extraordinary ability to adopt various facial expressions, she conveyed a story to the audience. Each pose lasted a few minutes and with swift rearrangements of her hair and shawls, Emma moved seamlessly on to the next 'Attitude' or character. Her performance was an entirely new and original art form.

Goethe had been living in Italy since 1786 and had met Hamilton at Caserta. He was present when Emma performed the 'Attitudes' in March 1787. Goethe's description of Emma's 'Attitudes' is one of the earliest and probably relates to this early performance:

'Sir William Hamilton ... has now, after many years of devotion to the arts and the study of nature, found the acme of these delights in the person of an English girl of twenty with a beautiful face and a perfect figure. He has a Greek costume made for her which becomes her extremely. Dressed in this, she lets down her hair and, with a few shawls, gives so much variety to her poses, gestures, expressions etc. that the spectator can hardly believe his eyes. He sees what thousands of artists would have liked to express realized before him in movements and surprising transformations – standing, kneeling, sitting, reclining, serious, sad, playful, ecstatic, contrite, alluring, threatening,

anxious, one pose follows another without a break. She knows how to arrange the folds of her veil to match each mood, and has a hundred ways of turning it into a head-dress. The old knight idolizes her and is enthusiastic about everything she does. In her he has found all the antiquities, all the profiles of Sicilian coins, even the Apollo Belvedere. This much is certain: as a performance it's like nothing you ever saw before in your life. We have already enjoyed it on two evenings.'[10]

In portraying female characters such as Juno, Niobe, Iphigenia, Cleopatra, and male characters (wearing a white tunic) such as Orestes and Oedipus, Emma was playing to an audience of classically educated people who would recognize portrayals of Gods and mythical characters. Emma was in her element.

Others beside Goethe were impressed by Emma's performances. The artist Elisabeth Vigée Le Brun, who travelled throughout Europe painting the aristocracy and important people, witnessed Emma's 'Attitudes' in Naples and described her impressions: [she has the ability to] *'suddenly change her expression from grief to joy … with shining eyes and flowing hair she appeared perfect as a bacchante; she could then change her expression immediately and appear as sorrowful as the repentant Magdalene … I could have copied her different poses & expressions and filled a gallery with paintings.'*[11]

Emma had similarly inspired Romney when she posed for him during their four-year association in London.

Sir William engaged Vigée Le Brun to paint Emma as a bacchante, dancing with a tambourine. In another portrait Emma is shown reclining on a leopard skin rug. She later wrote: *'I painted Mme. Hart as a baccante, reclining by the side of the sea, holding a cup in her hand. She had a beautiful, very lively face and voluminous tresses of fine chestnut, which could cover her body completely, so she looked wonderful.'*[12]

Emma was now acknowledged as Sir William's consort. She acted as his hostess for functions at the embassy with such natural charm that she won the approval of all the guests, particularly impressing them with her improved Italian, which delighted Sir William. She describes the first full year of her new relationship with Sir William in the very long letter she finally wrote to Greville, over a period of four months from August to December 1787. She was confident enough in herself and her happy relationship with Sir William to regard Greville simply as a friend, although he was not entirely forgiven:

Naples

Agosto 4 (1787)

Altho you never think me worth writing to, yet I cannot so easily forget you and when ever I have had any particular pleasure, I feil as tho I was not right tell I had communicated it to my dearest Greville, for you will ever be dear to me and tho we cannot be to gether, let ous corespond as freinds. I have a happiness in hearing from you and a comfort in communicating my little storeys to you, because I flatter myself that you still love the name of that Emma that was once very dear to you, and, but for unfortunate evels might still have claimed the first place in your affections, and I hope still you will never meet with any person that will use you ill, but never will you meet with the sincere love that I shew'd you, don't expect it for you cannot meet with it ...

We have been to Sorrento on a visit at the Duke Saint de Maitre for ten days. We are just returned, but I never passed a happier ten days, except Edg-re R-d. In the morning we bathed and returned to a fine sumer house where we breakfasted. But first this sumer house is on a rock over the sea that looks over Caprea, Ischea, Procheda, Vesuva, Porticea, Paysilipo, Naples etc. etc. etc. & the sea all before ous, that you have no idea of the beautes of it. From this little Paridise, after breakfast we vewd the lava running down 3 miles of the Vesuvua and every now & then black clouds of smoak rising in to the air, had the most magnificent appearance in the world. I have made some drawings from it, for I am so used to draw now, it is as easey as a.b.c. For when we are at Naples we dine every day at Villa Emma at Paysilipo and I make 2 or 3 drawings. Sir William laughs at me and says I shall rival him with the mountains now. After breakfast I have my singing lesson for Sir Wm. as took a [musician] in to the house but he is one of the best masters in Italia: after my lesson we rode on asses all about the Country, paid visits & dined at 3 and after diner saild about the coast, returned & dress'd for the conversazioni. We had Sir Wm.'s band of muzick with ous ... and I sung generally 2 searrous songs & 2 bufos, the last night I sang fifteen songs, one was a recatitive from a opera at St Carlos, the beginning was Luci belle sio vadoro, the finest thing you ever heard, that for ten minutes after I sung it, their was such a claping that I was obliedged to sing it over again ... in short, I left the people at Sorrento with their heards turned. I left some dying, some crying & some in despair ... But what astonished them, was that I should speak such good Italian ... one asked me if I had left a love at Naples that I left them so soon, I pulld my lip at him, so says, I pray do you take me to be an Italian whoman that as four or five different men to attend her. Look Sir, I am English, I have one cavelere servante & I have brought him with me, pointing to Sir Wm.; but he never spoke a nother word after for before he had been offering him self as cavelere Sevante. He said I was una donna rara.

We are gong up Vesuvua to night, as there is a large eruption, and the lava runs down allmost to Porticea; the mountain looks beautiful. One part their is nothing but cascades of liquid fire ... but I fancy we shall have some very large eruption soon, as large as that of 67 ... Sir Wm. is very fond of me & very kind to me: the house is ful of painters painting me. He as now got nine pictures of me & 2 a painting: Marchant is cutting my head in stone, that is in camea for a ring, there is a nother man modeling me in wax & another in clay. All the artists is come from Rome to study from me that Sir Wm. as fitted up a room that is calld the painting room. Sir Wm. is never a moment from me. He goes no whare without me, he as no diners, but what I can be of the party, no body comes with out the are civil to me; we have allways good company. I now live up stairs in the same apartments where he lives and my old apartments is made the musick rooms whare I have my lessions in the morning & our house at Caserta is fitting up elaganter this year, a room making for my musick and a room fitting up for my master as he goes with ous. Sir Wm. says he loves nothing but me, likes no person to sing but me and takes delight in all I do and all I say so we are happy.

Sunday morning. We was up last night at Vesuvus at twelve a clock and in my life I never saw so fine a sight. [Emma describes the lava running down the mountain setting fire to trees] *so that the mountain looked like one entire mountain of fire ... For me I was inraptured. I could have staid all night there ...*

I left of in a hurry and as not wrote this ten days as we have been on a visit to the Countess Mahoney at Ische 9 days and are just returned from their. We went in a hired vessel & took all Sr Wms. musicians, my harpsichord & master, 4 servants & my maid. I think I never had such a pleasant voyage any where. The Countess came down to the sea shore to meet ous, she took me in her arms & kissd me, thanked Sr Wm. for bringing her the company of so beautiful & lovely whoman. She took ous to her house where there was a full conversazione ... The Countess made me set by her & seemed to have pleasure to distinguish me by every mark of attention & the all allowd the never had seen such a belissima creature in all their life. I spoke Italian to most all, a little French to some that spoke to me in French. The obliged me to sing but I got such applause that for ten minuets you could not hear a word. The Countess gave a great dinner the day after to the noblesse of the place whare I was & in the evening an accadema of musick, where there was others sung, but I gott all the applause again. I sung one little Italian air that the all cried, but one priest that whas their was so in love with me that Sir William was obliged to give him my picture in a snuff box & he carries the snuff box in his breast: this is a priest mind you. So everyday we stayd we had parties of pleasure & the poor Countess cried when we came a whay & I am now setting for a picture for her in a turkish dress, very pretty. I must tell you I have had great offers to be the first whoman in the Italian opera at Madrid where I was to have six thousand pound for 3 years, but I would not engage as I should not like to go into Spain with out I knew people their & I could not speak their language, so I refused it & a nother reason was that Galini as been hear from the opera house at London to engage people & tho I have not been persuaded to make a written engagement, I ceartainly shall sing at the Pantheon & Hanover Square ... Sir William says he will give me leave to sing at Hanover Square on the condition Galini as proposed, which is 2 thousand pounds. Sir William as took my master in to the house & pays him a great price on purpose that he shall not teach any other person ... it is a most extraoirdary thing that my voice is totaly alterd, it is the finest soprana you ever heard, that Sir William shuts his eyes & think one of the Castratos is singing ... Sir William is in raptures with me; he spares neither expence nor pains in any thing ... I have my French master, I have the Queens dancing master 3 times a week, I have 3 lessons in singing a day, morning eight a clock, before dinner & the evening ... & then I give up one hour in the day to reading the Italian ... there is now five painters & 2 modlers at work on me for Sir Wm. & their is a picture going of me to the Empress of Russia, but Sir William as the phaeton at the door after I have had my first singing lesson & dancing & he drives me out for 2 hours & you will say that's right, for as I study a deal, it is right I should have exercise, but last night I did do a thing very extraordinary. We gave yesterday a deplomatic diner, so after diner I gave them a concert, so I sent the coach & my compliments to the Banti who is first whoman at St Carlos & desired her to come & sing at my concert, so she came & their was near sixty people, so after the first quartett I was to sing the first song; at first I was in a little fright before I begun, for she is a famous singer & she placed herself close to me, but when I begun all fear whent a whay & I sung so well that she cried out, just God, what a voice, I would give a great deal for your voice; in short, I met with such aplause that it allmost turned my head ... Poor Sir Wm. was so inraptured with me, for he was afraid I should have been in a great fright and it was of consequence that evening for he wanted to shew me of to some Dutch officers that was there, that is with a sixty gun ship & frigate. The Comodore whoes name is Melvile was so inchanted with me that tho he was to depart the next day, he put it of & gave

me a diner on board that nealy surpasses all description. First Sir Wm. me
& mother went down to the mole ... & the Captain & four more of the first
officers waited to conduct ous to the ship ... we sett down thirty to dine, me
at the head of the table, mistress of the feast, drest all in virgin wite & my
hair in ringlets reaching all most to my heals. I assure you it is so long that I
realy lookd and moved an angel, Sir Wm. said so. That night their was a
great opera at St Carlos in honor of the King of Spains name day ... Well, I
had the finest dress made up on purpose as I had a box near the K & Queen.
My gown was purple sattin, wite sattin petticoat trimd with crape &
spangles, my cap lovely from Paris, all wite fethers ... unfortunately the diner
on board did not finish tell half past five English, then the Comodore & Sir
Wm. would have a nother bottle to drink to the Belle ocche of the loveliest
whoman in the world as the cald me. At least, I wisperd to Sr. Wm. and told
him I should be angry with him if he did not gett up to go as we was to dress
& it was necessary to be at the theatre before the royal party so at last the put
out the boat, so after a salute from the 2 ships of all the guns we arrived on
shoar with the Comodore & five principal officers and in we all crowd in one
coach which is large. We just got in time to the opera, the Comodore went
with ous and the officers came next and attended to my box all the time and
behaved to me as tho I was a Queen.

You must know this letter as been begun abbove 4 months and I have a
wrote a little at a time & I now finish from Caserta where we have been five
weeks. We go to Naples the 28 of this month December and stay the Carnaval
their & then return to this place. I believe we shall have a great erruption soon
for tho we are here 16 miles from Naples yet yesterday the mountain made
such a dreadful noise just like cannons in ones ears. Sir William & me was
yesterday as endead we are every day at the Queens Garden and wilst Mr
Greffer & me ware talking all of a sudin their rose such black collums of smoke
out of Vesuvus attended with such roaring that I was frightened and last night
I went on the leads of our house hear and the throughs was such that I could
see Naples by the light of the fire very plain ...

Last night their was two preists came to our house & Sir William made
me put the shawl over my head & look up & the preist burst in to tears &
kist my feet & said God had sent me a purpose. O propo, now as I have such
a use of shawls & mine is wore out Sir Wm. is quite miserable for I stand in
atitudes with them on me. As you know Mr. Machpherson ask him to give
you one for me, pray do, for mine is wore out ... Thank you for the boxes, I
was enchanted with the hats ... Sir Wm. scolds me for writing so long a letter
... Pray write to me & tell me if I shall sing at the opera or no. We shall be in

London this Spring twelve months: we are going to Rome this spring.
Adio & believe me more your friend than what you are mine.

Emma

I send you a kiss on my name, its more than you deserve ... Pray give my
love to your brother & compliments to Legg, Banks, Tolemach etc. etc. & tell
them to take care of their hearts when I come back; as to you, you will be
utterly undone but Sr Wm. allready is distractedly in love & endead I love
him tenderly. He deserves it. God bless you.[13]

Emma began this letter almost exactly a year since she had last
written to Greville. We note she is still suffering some unhappiness
about their separation: *'Tho we cannot be to gether lett ous corespond as*
friends.'

Emma's remarkably descriptive letters reveal in fascinating detail
the progress she has made in Naples. Her days are busy with singing
and French lessons every day and dancing instruction from the
Queen's dancing master. She spends one hour a day reading Italian
with a tutor and has taken up drawing, which she finds *'as easy as*
a.b.c.'. Both her spoken Italian and her singing have been greatly
admired. She has declined an offer of £6,000 to sing at the Madrid opera
for three years.

She and Sir William spend all his free time together. She reports
that *'he goes no whare without me'* except to court. Buried in her long
description of events is a passing, but significant comment: *'He has no*
diners, but what I can be of the party, no body comes with out the are civil to
me.' Sir William protected her, as far as possible, from being slighted
or treated disrespectfully.

Emma could not be presented at court, but Hamilton told Greville
that the Queen and nobility showed her *'every distant civility'.* In
presenting Emma as his hostess, Hamilton made it clear to the English
contingent living in Naples and Grand Tour visitors that those who
were unwilling to associate with Emma were unwelcome at the
Palazzo Sessa. He was so popular and the embassy was such an
important part of the social and cultural life, that anyone with snobbish
attitudes towards Emma was obliged to put aside their prejudices.

Sir William was delighted with how Emma managed her duties.
She was reverential towards the company they kept and on her best
behaviour, always charming, friendly and discreet. Later she allowed
her more boisterous nature a freer rein. Sir William did not mind. He
loved her for her animated personality and natural manner. They had

spent two happy holidays together: ten days in Sorrento, where Emma said she had *'never been happier, except at Edgeware Road'* and another ten days visiting Countess Mahoney on the island of Ischia.

Emma sat for numerous portraits by various artists. In one portrait for Countess Mahoney, she was shown wearing a Turkish dress (which we will hear about again later). Catherine the Great, Empress of Russia, has requested a portrait of her, no doubt due to reports of Emma's beauty she received from the Russian Ambassador.

An adventurous and appreciative companion for Sir William, Emma's unbounded energy and genuine interest in everything he showed her was in stark contrast to Catherine's quiet, anxious, stay-at-home character. Approaching his fifty-seventh birthday, Sir William must have felt happily reinvigorated by his twenty-two-year-old partner.

Although there is little mention of Mrs Cadogan in letters, it is evident that Sir William accepted her *'countryfied'* speech and manner. She was usually present at dinners, only occasionally absenting herself through choice. Emma certainly never tried to keep her mother apart from any social occasions and Sir William always treated her with respect and affection. We note that Emma's mother had been included in the invitation to dine on board the Commodore's ship.

Emma continued to write to Greville, very often asking him for favours, such as sending shawls or hats and other English items unavailable in Naples, or to send money to her grandmother.

Her letter ended with two more gentle reprimands: *'Adio & believe me more your friend than what you are mine'* and in the postscript, *'I send you a kiss on my name, its more than you deserve'*. Significantly, she adds that Sir William is *'distractedly in love'* with her, adding *'Endead I love him tenderly. He deserves it.'* Emma is enthusiastic about her experiences. She and Sir William had enjoyed a happy and successful year during which their relationship had blossomed.

She told Greville that they would be in London *'this Spring twelve months'*, meaning 1789, but it was not until almost four years later, in 1791, that she and Sir William returned to England for what was to prove a momentous visit for Emma.

While Emma was writing her long letter to Greville, Sir William was also writing to him.

Caserta, December 18th. 1787

We are here as usual, my dear Charles, and I am out almost every day on shooting parties, but I find my house comfortable in the evening with Emma's society. You can have no idea of the improvement she makes daily in every respect – manners, language, and musick particularly. She has now applied closely to singing 5 months, & I have her master (an excellent one) in the house, so that she takes 3 lessons a day; her voice is remarkably fine, & she begins now to have a command over it. She has much expression, & as she applies chiefly to the solfeggia, she will be grounded in musick, & there is no saying what she may be in a year or two; I believe myself of the first rate, & so do the best judges here, who can scarcely believe she has only learnt 5 months. I can assure you her behaviour is such as has acquired her many sensible admirers, and we have a good man society, and all the female nobility, with the Queen at their head, shew her every distant civility. She has wrote a volume for you, but whether she will send it or not I can not tell ...[14]

There is no suggestion in any documents that Emma gave either Greville or Hamilton cause to be jealous. Emma was happy with Sir William and remained loyal. Their relationship did not become complicated until ten years later when Admiral Nelson arrived in Naples.

CHAPTER 7

Emma's Path to Marriage

'Would you think it, [Emma] is preached up by the Queen and nobility as a rare example of virtue.'
Sir William to Greville, 21 September 1790

'I wish to be an example of good conduct and to shew the world that a pretty woman is not allways a fool.'
Emma to Greville, January 1791

'She says it is impossible to continue in her present dubious state, which exposes her to frequent slights and mortification'.
Heneage Legge to Greville, March1791

THE NEXT FOUR years were possibly the happiest of Emma's life. Together she and Sir William led an idyllic and contented life. Their activities and amusements, and Hamilton's work as ambassador were unaffected by the gathering storm in France that would later throw their lives into chaos.

At fifty-eight years old, Hamilton vigorously embraced his life and his many interests, happy to have Emma by his side, sharing his enthusiasm. He was fit and energetic, as yet untroubled by the illnesses that were to weaken him four years later.

Emma was at her most beautiful. She was twenty-three years old, full of energy and optimism. Innumerable sources describe her beauty. She had a flawless strawberries and cream complexion, her auburn hair falling almost to her heels in curls and wisps, or elegantly bound up. Her mouth and blue-grey eyes were the features most commented on, her mouth being compared to the idealized women in ancient Greek sculptures. Hamilton preferred her to wear simple white dresses with coloured sashes that complemented her colouring to perfection. No one who saw her could fail to be impressed by her beauty and grace.

Many who praised Emma for her looks nevertheless despised her *'vulgarity'*. Lady Holland, writing about Lord Bristol (the Earl Bishop) declared: *'Lord Bristol is a great admirer of Lady Hamilton and conjured Sir W. to allow him to call her Emma. That he should admire her beauty and her wonderful attitudes is not singular, but that he should like her society is, as it is impossible to go beyond her in vulgarity and coarseness.'*[1]

Lord Palmerston (the future Prime Minister's father) was more complimentary in his observations: *'She is certainly very handsome and there is a plain good sense and simplicity of character about her which is uncommon and very agreeable.'*[2] Where one person saw *'vulgarity and coarseness'*, another saw *'plain good sense and simplicity of character'*.

Another admirer, the Comte d'Espinchal, on witnessing her 'Attitudes', wrote: *'Mme. Hart, English, superbly tall and with a heavenly figure, has been living for several years with the chevalier Hamilton ... this Mme. Hart, who is one of the most beautiful creatures I have seen, is of obscure origin'* and of her performance, *'You have to have seen her to conceive to what degree this lovely figure enabled us to enjoy the charms of illusion.'*[3]

The remark that Emma is *'superbly tall'* is a seldom-mentioned detail. One author* describes her as almost 5'11" tall. Emma told Sir William in a letter that the nun she had met was surprised she to see her *'tall in stature'*. We gain a strong impression of Emma's stature in Romney's portrait of her as Circe.

Those who found her vulgar and coarse were influenced by the malicious rumours circulating about her *'obscure origins'*. Emma never completely lost her childhood countrified accent and she was often criticized for the manner of her speech. The Earl Bishop, however, was delighted by *'dearest Emma's Dorick dialect'*.

Emma flourished, secure in Hamilton's love for her and in her role as his hostess at the Palazzo Sessa. Her only dissatisfaction with her life at this time was that she was aware of the *'dishonour'* attached to her position. The respectability she sought could only be achieved by marriage to Hamilton.

Sir William, well aware that Emma hoped for marriage, wrote to Greville in May 1789:

Emma often asks, do you love me? ay, but as well as your new apartment? Her conduct is such as to gain universal esteem, & she profits daily in music and language. I endeavour to lose no time in forming her & certainly she would be welcome to share with me, on our present footing, all I have during

* Colin Simpson in 'Emma, The Life of Lady Hamilton'

my life, but I fear her views are beyond what I can bring myself to execute; &
that when her hopes on that point are over, that she will make herself & me
unhappy; but all this is entre nous; if ever a separation should be necessary
for our mutual happiness, I would settle £150 a year on her, & £50 on her
mother, who is a very worthy woman; but all this is only thinking aloud to
you, & foreseeing that the difference of 57 and 22 may produce events; but,
indeed, hitherto her behaviour is irreproachable, but her temper, as you must
know, unequal ... I seriously propose making you a visit next spring, as you
know my affairs require my presence; how we shall manage about Emma is
another question; however, I only trouble myself at present with making her
accomplished, let what may come of it.[4]

Hamilton acknowledges again that the difference in their ages might
cause difficulties in the future, as indeed proved the case.

Sir William took Emma to Rome and bought her a fabulous gift of
diamonds. In a letter to his friend, Sir Joseph Banks, dated 19 August
1788, he confessed: *'She so longed for diamonds that, having an opportunity*
of a good bargain of single stones of a good water & tolerable size, I gave her
at once £500 worth.'

Hamilton's generosity demonstrates how highly he regarded Emma
and his desire to present her suitably attired on formal occasions at
the embassy. However, this gift illustrates his casual attitude to money
as soon afterwards he was complaining bitterly to Greville about falling
into debt.

Emma accompanied Sir William on a trip to Puglia (a southern
Italian province) in the spring of 1789. He had never visited this area
and doubtless hoped to find more treasures for his collections. Despite
the rough conditions of the roads and the uncertain overnight facilities
Emma had insisted on accompanying him. He told Banks *'she is so good*
there is no refusing her'. They travelled many days on foot, transporting
tents and equipment, and camping out overnight. Emma made notes
and perhaps drawings as well.

Sir William reported to Banks: *'Emma says she will write you an*
account of her journey in Magna Grecia, [Puglia] for she has taken notes –
she is as clever as she is beautiful.'[5]

For a month they were close companions in this physically
challenging adventure, away from the pressures of Neapolitan society.

Tired after this expedition, they spent a quiet summer at the Villa
Emma where Emma *'read a great many books'*. When friends came to
dine musical entertainment was provided. One visitor, Lord Herbert,

described the Villa Emma: *'It is built on a small rock and consists of three rooms and a kitchen with a diminutive garden. There are two flights of stairs up to it. When the weather is fine a small terras before the building constitutes the Setting Room with a large Venetian blind over it to guard it from the heat of the sun.'*[6]

Tischbein, the artist, was a frequent visitor. He wrote that *'There is really no more glorious place in the whole world'*.

This blissful existence was interrupted by reports of the storming of the Bastille by the Parisian mob on 14 July 1789. On receiving this news, Hamilton wrote to his Secretary of State on 4 August: *'The news of the late Extraordinary Revolution in France has cast a visible gloom upon the Court'*.[7]

Queen Maria Carolina, Marie Antoinette's sister, correctly feared the worst, as on 5 October King Louis XVI and his Queen, Marie Antoinette, were seized from Versailles, removed to the Tuileries in Paris, and restrained there.

It became vitally important that the port of Naples remained friendly and open to the British fleet. Late in his career, so far spent entirely in the political backwater of Naples, Sir William entered a period of political activity accompanied by great anxiety. Emma proved to be a great help to him.

French refugees arrived in Rome and Naples throughout that year. Hamilton noted: *'The French refugees drop in here apace.'* He, Emma and the court carried on as usual for the time being, although extremely concerned about the events in France.

Hamilton had been busy buying his second collection of vases, reputedly *'larger and more important than the first'*. He now believed the vases to be Greek and not Etruscan, as described in the first collection.

Tischbein helped Hamilton with this collection and with the publication of the Volumes in 1793. He estimated Hamilton had spent about £3,800 on the collection of around 1,500 vases. Hamilton admitted he had also spent about £2,000 on antiquities since his last visit to England, all of which he considered to be investments. Guiltily he wrote to Greville: *'You know it is impossible for me to be without an object whilst I can command a farthing.'*

In addition he had been buying and commissioning many paintings. Walpole had correctly predicted that Hamilton would *'ruin himself in virtu-land'*. Emma would have known little about Sir William's personal finances, but could see his collections piling up on the walls and in the old vaults underneath the Palazzo Sessa. Added to this expenditure was the constant cost of entertaining diplomats, nobility, artists and Neapolitan friends, Grand Tour travellers and friends from England.

It is unlikely that Emma had sight of his letter to Greville before it was sent:

Naples   September 21st. 1790

By degrees I am running into Ross's debt [Ross & Ogilvie, Hamilton's bankers in London] *instead of his being in mine, which he was considerably when I left England. I am determined at any rate to pay all my debts, & one comfort is that I have a sufficient stock in hand to do it. The fitting up of my new apartment* [the observation tower room] *cost me much more than I thought it wou'd – near £4,000. I give Emma £200 a year to keep her & her mother in cloths and washing, and you may imagine every now and then a present of a gown, a ring, a feather, etc., and once indeed she so long'd for diamonds that, having an opportunity of a good bargain of single stones of a good water & tolerable size, I gave her at once £500 worth. She realy deserves everything, & has gained the love of everybody, & wou'd you think it, is preached up by the Queen and nobility as a rare example of virtue. By Aprile's lessons she begins to sing in a capital stile, and has talents for both bravoura, pathetic, & buffo; but, as her voice & expression is so perfect, the pathetic is what I cultivate most, & I am sure in that she will excell any dilettante in England. Her knowledge of musick will surprise you as it does me, for I did not expect her to apply as she has done. She has grown thinner of late, & is the handsomer for it ...*[8]

Late in the year, the Duchess of Argyle arrived with her daughter and son-in-law. Aged fifty-six, in ill health and weak, she had once been the beautiful wife of the Duke of Hamilton, Sir William's cousin. Sir William was delighted when the Duchess looked very favourably on Emma.

Emma, aware of her unacceptable status by the conspicuous absence of some ladies at the Palazzo Sessa, responded to this warm and friendly appreciation and told the Duchess something of her background. Whether the Duchess sympathized with Emma or believed that Sir William and Emma had been secretly married is uncertain, but she allowed her daughter, Lady Charlotte Campbell, to meet Emma.

Lady Elcho, in Naples at the same time as the Duchess, told a friend, 'altho' Sir William's public situation would not permit him to declare it, there is no doubt of his being married to Mrs. H., that he presented her to them on *that ground, & that the behaviour of both parties confirm'd of its being so.'*[9]

Reports of their supposed secret marriage soon spread to England. When his friend, Banks, wrote enquiring about these rumours, Sir William replied on 6 April 1790:

To answer your question fairly, was I in a private station I should have no objection that Emma should share with me le petit bout de vie qui me reste, under the solemn covenant you allude to, as her behaviour in my house has been such for four years as to gain her universal esteem and approbation – but as I have no thoughts of relinquishing my Employment and whilst I am in a public character, I do not look upon myself at liberty to act as I please, and such a step I think wou'd be imprudent and might be attended with disagreeable circumstances ... In the way we live we give no Scandal, she with her Mother and I in my apartment, and we have a good Society. What is to be gained on my side? It is very natural for her to wish it, and to try to make people believe the business done, which I suppose has caused the report in England. I assure you that I approve of her so much that if I had been the person that had made her first go astray, I wou'd glory in giving her a public reparation, and I would do it openly, for indeed she has infinite merit and no Princess cou'd do the honors of her Palace with more care and dignity than she does those of my house; in short she is worthy of anything, and I have and will take care of her in proportion as I feel myself obliged to her. But as to the Solemn League, Amplius Considerandum Est. Now, my Dear Sir, I have more fairly delivered you my Confession than is usually done in this country, of which you may make any discreet use you please. Those who ask out of mere curiosity I shou'd wish to remain in the dark.[10]

Sir William, as King George's representative in Naples, was obliged to secure the King's permission before marrying. In view of his sense of honour and duty to the King it is most unlikely that he would have engaged in a 'secret' marriage.

In Naples, at least, Emma was regarded as a very beautiful and very moral woman. Neapolitans were not known for their morality and Emma's loyalty to Sir William was recognized. He had told Greville that *'she is preached up by the Queen & nobility as a rare example of virtue'*.

In May Hamilton told his niece, Mary Dickenson, that they were postponing their planned visit to England owing to *'the very unsettled state of Europe, which makes it improper for any of his Majesty's Ministers to think of stirring from his post at this moment'*. Here he explains the ongoing problem of his relationship with Emma:

I have deferred my journey until next Year. I do assure you I was truly

sensible of your kindness & affection to me which you shew'd in your last
letter, & which ought to have been answered long ago. Emma read it & wept
over it. I do assure you that her goodness of heart is such, & her conduct has
been such for four years she has resided with me, that I should not hesitate,
was I a private character, to put the law on the side of our Connection. But
as I have experienced that of all Women in the World, the English are the
most difficult to deal with abroad, I fear eternal tracasseries, was she to be
placed above them here, & which must be the case, as a Minister's Wife, in
every Country, takes place of every rank of Nobility.

As it is, many seek Emma's acquaintance, & we have the best company in
Naples at our house. The Duchess of Argyle & that family doat upon Emma,
& really she gains the heart of all who approach her. You would be surprised
at her having learnt so much in 4 years. She is perfect Italian, begins to speak
French tolerably, & sings certainly better than any English woman I ever
heard ...[11]

Not only does Hamilton need the King's permission to marry, he
foresees unpleasant difficulties may arise from Emma's position as his
wife. This would give her precedence over *'every rank of* [visiting]
Nobility', who would strongly object.

The Duchess of Argyle died in London in December. Emma
described her distress in a letter to Greville who was expecting Emma
and Sir William to arrive in London in the spring:

Naples Jany 1791.

I received your obliding letter on Thursday & am sensible of the part you
take in my happiness & welfare ... You may think of my aflictions when I
heard of the Duchess of Argylles death, I never had such a freind as her &
that you will know when I see you & recount to you all the acts of kindness
she shewd to me, for they where two good & numerous to describe in a letter
... You need not be affraid for me in England; we come for a short time & that
time must be occupied in buisiness & to take our last leave. I dont wish to
atract notice, I wish to be an example of good conduct & to shew the world
that a pretty woman is not allways a fool, all my ambition is to make Sir Wm.
happy & you will see he is so. As to our seperating houses, we cant do it or
why should we, you cant think 2 people that as lived five years with all the
domestic happiness thats possible, can separate & those 2 persons that knows
no other comfort but in one anothers comppany, which is the case, I assure
you with ous ... We will let you in to our plans & secretts, Sir William will
lett you know on what a footing we are here. On Monday last we give a concert
& Ball at our hous. I had near four hundred persons, all the foreign ministers

& their wives, all the first ladies of fashion, foreynors and neapolitans, our house was full in every room. I had the Banti, the tenor Casacelli & two others to sing. Sir Wm. dressd me in wite sattin, no coller [colour?] *abbout me but my hair & cheeks ... All the ladies strove to out do one another in dress and jewels, but Sir William said I was the finest jewel amongst them. Every night our house is open to small partys of fifty or sixty men & women. We have musick, tea etc. etc. & we have a great adition lately to our party, we have a new Spanish ambassador & his wife & we as made a great friendship & we are allways together. She is charming ... We shall be with you in the Spring & return heer in Novr. & the next year you may pay ous a visit, we shall be glad to see you. I shall allways esteem you for your relationship to Sir William & haveing been the means of me knowing him. As to Sir W. I confess to you I doat on him nor I never can have any other person but him. This confession will please you I know. I will write more next post.*

Emma[12]

Emma was horrified when Greville advised her that, for the sake of propriety, she and Sir William should live in separate houses while they were in London. She does not mention the matter of a marriage directly, but says, *'we will let you into our plans & secretts'*. If Sir William had agreed to marry her, he wanted to keep it quiet until he had been granted the King's permission.

Accustomed to being snubbed, Emma would have been especially pleased to have the Spanish ambassador's wife as a friend.

A shocking example of the snobbery she suffered appears in a letter that Heneage Legge wrote to his friend, Greville, in March 1791. (Emma had known Legge in London.)

Legge warns Greville that Emma's influence over Sir William *'exceeds all belief'* and that only the King's refusal of permission will protect Hamilton from marrying her, thereby making Emma Greville's aunt. He informs Greville about the rumours of their secret marriage and describes his wife's attitude towards Emma:

... When we came, he [Sir William] *immediately waited upon us with all the kindness & attention that our former acquaintance could dictate, having previously wrote me word while I was at Rome that Emma would be at all times happy to attend Mrs. L. as a nurse, or contribute to her amusement as a companion.*

Mrs. L. is not over-scrupulous in her manners or sentiments beyond the usual forms establish'd by the rules of society in her own country; but, as she was not particularly inform'd of any change in Mrs.H.'s situation, she

had no reason to think her present different from her former line of life, &
therefore could not quite reconcile it to her feelings to accept these offers of
friendship & service, tho' there was no doubt of their being kindly intended.
Mrs. L., therefore, very soon gave it to be understood that she wish'd to
retain her old footing of intimacy with him, but that any other branch of
the family was inadmissible ... The language of both parties, who always
spoke in the plural number – we, us & ours – stagger'd me at first, but soon
made me determine to speak openly to him on the subject, when he assur'd
me what I confess I was most happy to hear, that he was not married: but
flung out some hints of doing justice to her good behaviour, if his public
situation did not forbid him to consider himself an independent man. Her
influence over him exceeds all belief: his attachment exceeds admiration, it
is perfect dotage. She gives everybody to understand that he is now going to
England to sollicit the K's consent to marry her, & that on her return she
shall appear as Ly. H. She says it is impossible to continue in her present
dubious state, which exposes her to frequent slight & mortification; & his
whole thought, happiness & comfort seems so center'd in her presence, that
if she should refuse to return on other terms, I am confident she will gain
her point ...

Her talents & powers of amusing are very wonderfull; her voice is very
fine, but she does not sing with great taste ... her attitudes are beyond
description beautifull and striking, & I think you will find her figure much
improved since you last saw her ... She is much visited here by ladies of the
highest rank, & many of the Corps diplomatique; does the honours if his
house with great attention & desire to please, but wants a little refinement
of manners, ... unless great care is taken to prevent it I am clear she will in
some unguarded hour work upon his empassion'd mind, & effect her design
of becoming your aunt. He tells me he has made ample provision for her, in
which he is certainly right, and with that she ought to be content ...[13]

Sir William had informed Legge that 'Emma would be at all times
happy to attend to Mrs. Legge as a nurse, or contribute to her amusement as
a companion.' But, Mrs. Legge while 'not over-scrupulous about the rules
of society', was nevertheless unwilling to meet Emma.

Any possibility that Emma might refuse to return to Italy with him
if they were not married would certainly have influenced Sir William's
decision to marry her.

Having behaved impeccably for almost five years and having shown
Sir William nothing but devotion, care and admiration, Emma was
justified in insisting on her position being legitimized. Having an innate

sense of justice, he agreed with her. With his usual philosophical disdain for the opinions of others, he decided to marry Emma if he received the King's permission.

In mid-March 1791, almost exactly five years to the day since Emma and her mother had left London for Naples, they all began the journey back to London. Travelling overland via Rome, Florence, Venice and Vienna, they arrived in London in mid-May. They stayed for only three and a half months. Anxious about the uneasy political situation in France and the potential for unrest elsewhere in Europe, Sir William wanted to return to his post in Naples as soon as possible.

Hamilton had been given leave to see to his affairs in Wales. For Emma the main purpose was for him to seek the King's permission to marry her. On meeting Greville again, Emma maintained the same friendly footing that she had adopted in her more recent letters. Sir William had business to discuss with Greville concerning his estates in Wales, and he was much in demand in London at meetings and soirées.

Emma was excited at the prospect of seeing Romney again. Very soon after their arrival, she and Sir William breezed into his studio unannounced, where Emma *'transformed his gloom into sunshine by the alchemy of her beauty, her gay spirits, and her eagerness to serve him as a model'.*[14] Emma was wearing a Turkish costume, most likely the *'Turkish dress and turbin'* she had worn for a portrait in Naples. Romney's joyful reaction was to begin painting her almost immediately. Her first sitting was on 2 June. Between June and September Emma sat for him thirty-five times. She was happy to spend time with Romney whom she regarded as an old friend.

William Hayley (Romney's friend) wrote: *'The fair Emma ... surprised him by an early visit one morning in a Turkish habit, and attended by Sir William Hamilton. Romney had ever treated her with the tenderness of a father, which she acknowledged on this occasion with tears of a lively gratitude, in announcing to him her splendid prospect of being soon married to Sir William, and of attending him to the Court of Naples. The joy of a father, in the brilliant marriage of a favourite daughter, could hardly exceed that of my friend on this occasion.'*[15]

Hayley over-estimated Romney's joy at the news of Emma's marriage. Romney was pleased for her sake, but he was sad to be losing her. His letters to Hayley give us an interesting insight into his feelings and Emma's activities. On 18 June, Emma met the Prince of Wales who promptly commissioned two portraits of her from Romney.

Romney wrote to Hayley on 19 June: ' *At present, and the greatest part of the Summer, I shall be engaged in painting pictures from the divine lady. I cannot give her any other epithet, for I think her superior to all womankind. I have two pictures to paint of her for the Prince of Wales. She says she must see you before she leaves England, which will be in the beginning of September ...* ' [16]

On 7 July, he wrote again: '*I dedicate my time to this charming lady; there is a prospect of her leaving town with Sir William for two or three weeks. They are very much hurried at present, as everything is going on for their speedy marriage, and all the world is following her and talking of her, so that if she had not more good sense than vanity her brain must be turned. The pictures I have begun are Joan of Arc, a Magdalen, and a Bacchante for the Prince of Wales; and another I am to begin as a companion to the Bacchante. I am also to paint a picture of Constance for the Shakespeare Gallery.*'[17]

Emma and Sir William took lodgings in Somerset Street, Sir William happily showing off Emma's talents when they entertained guests. London was agog to see and hear about them. Emma met Sir William's cousin, the Marquis of Abercorn, the Duke of Queensberry and Horace Walpole. Walpole, who had been critical of Emma, was completely won over after he saw her perform at the Duke of Queensberry's: *Oh! but she sings admirably*', he wrote, '*has very fine strong voice; is an excellent Buffa, and an astonishing tragedian; and then her Attitudes are a whole theatre of grace and various expressions*'.[18]

On 8 August, Romney wrote to Hayley expressing a remarkably similar response to Walpole's on her performances:

In my last letter I think I informed you that I was going to dine with Sir William Hamilton and his lady. In the evening of that day there were collected several people of fashion to hear her sing. She performed both in the serious and the comic to admiration, both in singing and in acting; but her Nina surpasses everything I ever saw, and, I believe, as a piece of acting, nothing ever surpassed it. The whole company were in an agony of sorrow. Her acting is simple, grand, terrible, and pathetic. My mind was so much heated that I was for running down to Eartham to fetch you up to see her. But alas! soon after, I thought I discovered an alteration in her conduct to me. A coldness and neglect seemed to have taken the place of her repeated declaration of regard for me. They left town to make many visits in the country. I expect them again the latter end of this week, when my anxiety (for I have suffered much) will be either relieved for increased, as I find her conduct.... You will see everything is in great uncertainty, but it may turn out better than I expect.[19]

Unsettled by Sir William and Emma leaving London to visit relatives and friends, the incredibly sensitive Romney thought he detected a coolness from his *'divine lady'*, which *'nearly broke the painter's heart'*.

Emma had sat for Romney fourteen times in June and sixteen times in July, but there are no sittings recorded from 25 July to 22 August, while Sir William and Emma were away.

Sir William's audience with the King was not until late August. Emma was almost certainly preoccupied and worried about her future. Romney's anxiety increased during this time.

In late July, they visited Mary Dickenson and her husband, John, in Derbyshire. Mary was very kind to Emma, who in turn made a good impression on her husband.

Whilst in Bath Sir William had hoped to present Emma to his old friend the Dowager Lady Spencer, but to avoid meeting Emma, she had left town. He wrote to her informing her of his decision to marry Emma:

A man of 60 intending to marry a beautiful young woman of 24 [actually, Emma was 26] *and whose character at her first outset of life will not bear a severe scrutiny, seems to be a very imprudent step, so it certainly would be 99 times in 100, but I flatter myself I am not deceived in Emma's present character – we have lived together five years and a half, and not a day passes without her having testified her true repentance for the past.* He continues, *she has naturally been subject to frequent mortifications ... her sensibility is so great that her health has been often affected by it. In short, I have at length consented to take off these difficulties, and as the world calls it make an honest woman of her. I do assure your Ladyship that Emma is out of the common line ...*[20]

Lady Spencer's daughter, Georgiana, Duchess of Devonshire, had no such qualms about meeting Emma. She and Lady Elizabeth Foster happened to be in Bath and, hearing about her famous 'Attitudes', had invited her to perform for them the following day. Lady Foster recorded her impressions in her diary:

Having just seen the celebrated Mrs. Hart, who by an extraordinary talent, as Lord Charlemont says, found out a new source of pleasure to mankind, I cannot forbear mentioning the impression which she made upon me. She was introduced last night to the Duchess of Devonshire by Sir W. Hamilton. She appeared to be a very handsome woman, but coarse and vulgar. She sung, and her countenance lightened up – her Buffo songs were inimitable from the expression and vivacity with which they were sung. Her serious singing appeared to me not good – her voice is strong, she is well taught, yet has a forced expression and has neither softness or tenderness ...

This morning she was to show her attitudes. She came, and her appearance was more striking than I can describe, or could have imagined. She was draped exactly like a Grecian statue, her chemise of white muslin was exactly in that form, her sash in the antique manner, her fine black hair flowing over her shoulders. It was a Helena, Cassandra or Andromache, no Grecian or Trojan Princess could have had a more perfect or commanding form. Her attitudes, which she performed with the help alone of two shawls, were varied – every one was perfect – everything she did was just and beautiful. She then sung and acted the mad scene in Nina – this was good, but I think chiefly owing to her beautiful action and attitudes ... In the evening she came again ... She looked very handsome certainly, and she was better draped than the first evening, but her conversation, though perfectly good-natured and unaffected, was uninteresting, and her pronunciation very vulgar ... I must however add, as an excuse for that vulgarity and as a further proof of the superiority of her talents that have burst forth in spite of these disadvantages, that Mrs. Hart was born and lived in the lowest situation until the age of 19, and since that in no higher one than the mistress of Sir W. Hamilton.[21]

In this diary extract Lady Foster repeats untrue stories concerning Emma. We know that Emma had been the mistress of Sir Harry Fetherstonhaugh, owner of the Uppark estate, at the age of fifteen, followed by her long relationship with Charles Greville, second son of the Earl of Warwick before meeting Sir William.

A further scandalous account came from one of Sir William's colleagues, Sir James Bland Burges, an under-Secretary of State in the Foreign Department. Just prior to Sir William and Emma's marriage, he wrote: '*This Mrs. Hart, on her first coming from the country, set out as a common prostitute in Hedge Lane. Being very handsome, she was engaged by the Committee of the Royal Academy to exhibit herself naked as a model for the young Designers. Having continued for some time in this situation, she rose in the Scale of Debauchery, till at length she was taken into keeping by Mr. Charles Greville, who, growing poor, and being desirous of preventing his uncle William Hamilton (from whom he had expectations) from marrying, took her with him to Naples, where Sir William was Minister, and introduced her to him. Sir William grew fond of her, and Mr. Greville was easily prevailed upon to transfer her to him.*'[22]

This wildly inaccurate statement was probably based on similar malicious comments frequently made about Emma, which to some, became the accepted account of her early life. Such opinions influenced many people, including Queen Charlotte and the Dowager Lady Spencer, not to associate with her.

Sir William and Emma visited his fantastically wealthy and eccentric relative, William Beckford. Beckford had built himself a mansion at Fonthill in Wiltshire. Returning from a trip to Paris, he wrote to Hamilton: *'the only glorious object I have set my eyes upon since my arrival in this foggy island is the Breathing Statue you brought over.'*[23]

Continuing on their rounds, Sir William and Emma saw his friends, the Conways, who now lived in Sir William's childhood home, Park Place, near Henley, Walpole at his gothic mansion, Strawberry Hill, and the Duke of Queensberry at his home in Richmond.

By mid-August they were back in London for a few days. Finally, Emma's agony of suspense was over. After his audience with the King, Sir William wrote with the news that he had been granted permission to marry her. Sir William and his 'foster-brother' had enjoyed a friendly meeting, although Queen Charlotte refused to receive Emma at court.

This was a serious blow. It meant that Emma could be Sir William's wife, Lady Hamilton, but in England could not officially hold the title of Ambassadress. Consequently, Emma worried that Queen Maria Carolina would not receive her in Naples.

Before the day of the wedding there were a few more important details to attend to. Hamilton lodged a new will with his London solicitors, making an annual allowance for Emma and Mrs Cadogan, but stating that if he did not have an heir, the estates and all his possessions remained bequeathed to Charles Greville. Hamilton was publicly honoured by being sworn a member of the Privy Council in recognition of his twenty-five years service in Naples.

Emma sat for a portrait by the young Thomas Lawrence who, having heard of her beauty, was determined to paint her. His full-length portrait of her as *La Penserosa* was commissioned by the Marquis of Abercorn, soon to be a witness to the forthcoming marriage.

Mrs Cadogan had travelled north to see her aged mother and on to Manchester to visit Little Emma, now nine years old and known as Emma Carew. She found her granddaughter well and Greville reported that she *'saw her situated to her satisfaction'*.

Despite a busy schedule accompanying Sir William around the

countryside and sitting for Romney, Emma could have found time to visit her daughter. It seems she kept her promise to Greville that she would *'give her up entirely'*. She may have believed that seeing her would only upset the child.

Sir William, now in a hurry to leave London, applied to the Archbishop of Canterbury for permission to be married by Special Licence. He did not want a church wedding and would have preferred a simple ceremony. When the Archbishop refused, the wedding was planned for 6 September at Marylebone Parish Church, no later than 10 o'clock.

Emma had only few days to prepare for her wedding and begin packing for their departure. Nevertheless, she sat for Romney on 22, 23 and 26 August, and again on 4 and 5 September.

On 29 August Romney wrote his last letter to Hayley while Emma was in England:

Cassandra came to town on the 16th. and I did not see her till the 20th., so you may suppose how my feelings must have suffered. She appointed to sit on the 23rd. and has been sitting almost every day since; and means to sit once or twice a day till she leaves London. When she arrived to sit she seemed more friendly than she had been, and I began a picture of her for her mother. I was very successful with it, for it is thought the most beautiful head I have painted of her yet. Now, indeed, I think she is as cordial with me as ever ... Really my mind had suffered so very much, that my health was much affected, and I was afraid I should not have power to have painted any more from her; but since she has assumed her former kindness, my health and spirits are quite recovered. She performed in my house last week, singing and acting before the nobility with most astonishing powers; she is the talk of the whole town, and really surpasses everything, both in singing and acting, that ever appeared. Gallini offered her two thousand pounds a year, and two benefits, if she would engage with him, on which Sir William said pleasantly that he had engaged her for life.[24]

The day of the wedding dawned and a small party gathered at the church. There is no record, but we can safely assume that Mrs Cadogan would have been present, in addition to a few friends, including John Dickenson. It is unlikely that Greville attended. Dr Edward Barry, the Rector of Elsdon, officiated. The witnesses were the Marquis of Abercorn and Mr. Dutens, the Secretary to the English Minister at Turin, whom Sir William and Emma knew well.

In the vestry after the ceremony, mindful of the legal importance of the document, Emma signed her baptismal name, Amy Lyon, in the register that recorded:

The Right Hon'ble Sir Willm. Hamilton of this Parish, widower and Amy Lyons of the same Parish, Spinster, married in this Church by Licence this sixth Day of September in the Year One Thousand Seven Hundred and Ninety One By me, Edw'd Barry, M.D.Clerk.

This marriage was solemnized between us (Wm. Hamilton
                                          (Amy Lyons
In the presence of (Abercorn
                    (L. Dutens
                    (Rector of Elsdon in Northumberland[25]

After the wedding, Sir William and Emma arrived at Romney's studio by 11 a.m. where he continued to work on the portrait of her later called *The Ambassadress*. Romney's day book entry for 6 September records for the first and only time: *Lady Hamilton at 11.*

Romney was so badly affected by Emma's leaving that he had made no appointments until October 16th. At the end of his diary for 1791, on one of the fly-leaves, there is a sad little memorandum in Romney's handwriting: *Sir William H. was married to Emma Sept. 6th. 1791.*[26] Emma's departure for Italy is given as the reason for his subsequent increased melancholy and decline in health.

Sir William and Emma bid Romney an affectionate farewell and Emma, though she corresponded with him, never saw him again.

Two days after the wedding Sir William, Emma and her mother left England for their return journey to Naples.

CHAPTER 8

Emma in her Prime

'Am I Emma Hamilton? It seems impossible I can be so happy'
Emma to Mary Dickenson, 27 September 1791

'My dear, dear husband that has restored peace to my mind ... and what is more, innocence and happiness'
Emma to George Romney, 20 December 1791

'I would not be married to any woman, but yourself on earth, for all the world'
Sir William Hamilton to Emma, 6 January 1792

SIR WILLIAM AND Emma, the new Lady Hamilton, arrived in Paris in time to observe the beginning of the end of King Louis XVI and Queen Marie Antoinette's reign.

The newly formed National Assembly had agreed on a constitution that they presented to the King on 3 September 1791. Lord Palmerston, the father of Queen Victoria's Prime Minister, in Paris since July, had witnessed the deliberations over the new constitution. Through him Sir William and Emma secured an audience with the King and Queen, who, freed from their confinement in the Tuileries, were allowed to hold court three times a week.

On 14 September Hamilton and Emma were present to watch the King accept the new constitution at the Assembly. Palmerston reported: *'The King's speech was short, he spoke very distinctly and audibly but looked distressed and unhappy. The President, who seemed to assume a kind of equality that to me was disgusting, made a long speech to him in answer ... Upon the whole, it seemed to me the last degree of humiliation and had more the air of triumph over a degraded man than a dignified constitutional act.'*[1]

Everyone knew that these were desperately worrying times for the

King and Queen, but no one could have anticipated the horrors that were to come. The Queen would have been pleased to meet the Ambassador for Naples and his wife who were on their way to the court of her sister, Queen Maria Carolina. Marie Antoinette gave Emma a letter to take to Maria Carolina. Although unacceptable at the English court, in Paris Emma was cordially received and entrusted with this important errand.

After spending several days in their company, Lord Palmerston wrote to his wife:

'Sir William and Lady Hamilton are arrived at this hotel and are to stay a few days ... She is very handsome but not elegant ... She seems very good-humoured, very happy and very attentive to him. I am promised an exhibition of her performances that have been much talked of ...'[2]

In a further letter, he added: *'I perfectly agree with everything I have heard in commendation of Lady Hamilton. She is certainly very handsome and there is a plain good sense and simplicity of character about her which is uncommon and very agreeable.'*[3]

Emma was supremely happy. She wrote to Mary Dickenson from Geneva on 27 September:

Dear Madam, a thousand thanks for your kind letter, indeed I feel as if I had not deserved it, but Mr. Dickenson will inform you of the hurry we were in, the last few days we were in England, and believe me, the honour you have done me by corresponding with me, and the pleasure is such that I shall seize every opportunity of shewing my gratitude to you for the happiness your dear and instructive letters give me, and at the same time I hope to profit myself, for having lived five years in Italy and not having had the happiness to have had a dear Mrs. Dickenson to write to me and correct me, I am afraid at first I shall be a dull correspondent, but I hope I shall mend as I go on, and now I am so happy and feel so content, that I shall have a pleasure in writing to you, and believe me before the 6th. September I was always unhappy and discontented with myself: ah Madam, how much do I owe to your dear Uncle. I feel every moment my obligations to him and am always afraid I can never do enough for him since that moment. I say to myself Am I his wife, and I can never separate no more. Am I Emma Hamilton? It seems impossible I can be so happy. Surely no person was ever so happy as I am ... God bless you dear Madam. May you enjoy all the happiness you deserve and believe me your ever obliged your truly grateful and sincere, E. Hamilton.[4]

Sir William received letters of congratulation from friends. Lord Pembroke referred to *'your lovely Lady Hamilton'*. The Earl Bishop wrote on 21 December 1791: *'I congratulate you, my old friend, from the bottom of my heart, upon the fortitude you have shown, & the manly part you have taken in braving the world & securing your own happiness & elegant enjoyments in defiance of them ... nobody mentions your decision but with approbation; no wonder provided that they have ever seen & heard Lady Hamilton; & now I flatter myself you have secured your happyness for life ...'*[5]

Staying briefly in Rome on the way down to Naples, Sir William commissioned Angelica Kauffman, now settled in Rome after fourteen years in England, to paint a portrait of Emma. This highly sought-after artist had earlier written to Sir William: *'How often have I wished ... to see and be acquainted with Mrs. Hart ... and I confess to envy especially all the artists who were so fortunate at least to attempt an imitation of so graceful an object ...'*[6]

Her portrayal of Emma as *The Comic Muse* references her connections with music, comedy and theatre. Emma is shown wearing a cameo portrait of Sir William in recognition of their marriage.

Arriving in Naples on 1 November, Sir William was informed by the Queen that she was happy to receive Emma as she would any *'travelling lady of distinction'*, but could not acknowledge her formally as the ambassadress. This distinction made no difference to Emma and the Queen as they soon became close companions.

Emma's exceptional grace and beauty were often remarked upon, especially after seeing her perform her 'Attitudes'. A 'Grand Tourist,' John Morritt, likened her poses to the figures depicted on Sir William's ancient vases from Herculaneum:

'Her toilet is merely white chemise gown, some shawls and the finest hair in the world, flowing loose over her shoulders. These set off a tall, beautiful figure, and a face that varies forever, and is always lovely. Thus accoutred, with the assistance of one or two Etruscan vases and an urn, she takes almost every attitude of the finest antique figures successively, and varying in a moment the folds of her shawls, the flow of her hair, and her wonderful countenance is at one instant a Sibyl, then a Fury, a Niobe, a Sophonisba drinking poison, a Bacchante drinking wine, dancing and playing the tambourine ... you will be more astonished when I tell you that the change of attitude and countenance, from one to another, is the work of a moment, and that this wonderful variety is always delicately elegant, and entirely studied from the antique designs of vases and the figures of Herculaneum ...'[7]

Emma describes her fascinating new life in Naples in this letter to Romney:

Caserta   December 20 th.1791

I have the pleasure to inform you we arrived safe at Naples. I have been receved with open arms by all the Neopolitans of booth sexes, by all the foreigners of every distinction. I have been presented to the Queen of Naples by her own desire, she as shewn me all sorts of kind and affectionate attentions; in short, I am the happiest woman in the world.

Sir William is fonder of me every day, & I hope I will have no corse to repent of what he as done, for I feel so grateful to him that I think I shall never be able to make him amends for his goodness to me. But why do I tell you this? you know me enough; you was the first dear friend I open'd my heart to, you ought to know me, for you have seen and discours'd with me in my poorer days, you have known me in my poverty and prosperity, and I had no occasion to have lived for years in poverty and distress if I had not felt something of virtue in my mind. Oh, my dear friend, for a time I own through distress my virtue vanquished, but my sense of virtue was not overcome. How gratefull now, then, do I feel to my dear, dear husband that has restored peace to my mind, that has given me honors, rank, and, what is more, innocence and happiness. Rejoice with me, my dear sir, my friend, my more than father, believe me I am still that same Emma you knew me. If I could forget for a moment what I was, I ought to suffer. Command me in anything I can do for you here; believe me, I shall have a real pleasure. Come to Naples, and I will be your model, anything to induce you to come, that I may have an opportunity to show my gratitude to you. Take care of your health for all our sakes. How does the pictures go on? Has the Prince been to you? write to me, I am interested in all that concerns you. God bless you, my dear friend! ... Give my love to Mr Hayly, tell him I shall be glad to see him at Naples. As you was so good to say you would give me the little picture with the black hat, I wish you would unfrill it, and give it to Mr Duten. I have a great regard for him; he took a deal of pains and trouble for me, and I could not do him a greater favour than give him my picture. Do, my dear friend, do me that pleasure, and if there is anything from Naples command me.

We have a many English at Naples, Ladys Malmsbery, Malden, Plymouth, Carnegie, Wright, etc. They are very kind and attentive to me; they all make it a point to be remarkably civil to me. You will be happy at this, as you know what prudes our Ladys are. Tell Hayly I am allways reading his Triumphs of Temper; it was that that made me Lady H., for, God knows, I had for 5 years enough to try my temper, and I am affraid if it had not been for the good example Serena taught me, my girdle would have burst, and if it had I had been undone, for Sir W. minds more temper than beauty. He, therefore, wishes Mr Hayly would come, that he might thank him for his sweet-tempered wife. I swear to

you that I have never been once out of humour since the 6th. of last September.
God bless you.[8]

From her new situation in Naples as Lady Hamilton, Emma might have considered her time with Greville as *'her poorer days'*. Then she had only Greville's £1 a week allowance. Now Emma received a personal allowance from Sir William of £200 a year.

Her comment – *'for a time I own through distress my virtue was vanquished, but my sense of virtue was not overcome'*, could refer to her time as Sir Harry's mistress. Now Sir William had *'restored peace to her mind'* and given her *'innocence and happiness'*. Emma had found it difficult to accept her situation in Naples before her marriage. She had *' for five years enough to try my temper'*.

Obliged to be civil to Emma as the ambassador's wife, many of the English ladies in Naples were nevertheless pleasantly surprised by her conduct. One English lady wrote to Lady Herries: *'I have had Lady Hamilton with me all ye Evening, that is of Jan 14th., we were alone & I am more & more pleased with her.'*[9]

Lady Malmesbury was sufficiently favourably impressed to write: *'She really behaves as well as possible, and quite wonderfully considering her origin and education ... I believe all the English mean to be very civil to her, which is quite right.'*[10]

In January Sir William wrote to Mary:

... the Queen of Naples, informed of all my proceedings, told me she wou'd see my wife tho' she could not acknowledge her as the Wife of the English Minister, & she received her most kindly. Emma very naturally told her whole story & that all her desire was by her future conduct to shew her gratitude to me, and to prove to the world that a young, beautiful woman, tho' of obscure birth, cou'd have noble sentiments and act properly in the great world. In short the Queen of N. is quite fond of her & has taken her under her protection. All the Neapolitan Nobility have been to see her & shew her every atention & the English Ladies who are numerous here this year, are quite fond of her ...[11]

The Queen, and her minister, Sir John Acton, controlled most of the kingdom's political activity. Like Emma, the Queen had a lively personality. Lady Anne Miller wrote:

'Her Majesty is a beautiful woman, she has the finest and most transparent complexion I ever saw; her hair is of that glossy light chestnut I so much admire; it is by no means red; her eyes are large, brilliant, and of a dark blue, her eyebrows exact and darker than her hair; her nose is inclining to the aquiline, her mouth small, her lips very red, (not of the Austrian thickness),

her teeth beautifully white & even, and when she smiles she discovers two dimples, which give a finishing sweetness to her whole countenance, her shape is perfect: she is just plump enough not to appear lean; her neck is long, her deportment easy, her walk majestic, her attitudes and action graceful.'[12]

Similarly, an English midshipman wrote: '... *this energetic woman, whose slender and perfect form seemed to tread on air, while the tender animation of her sparkling eyes expressed a warmth of heart that prompted her (at least in my imagination) to embrace all around her.'*[13]

The Queen and Emma enjoyed one another's company. The Queen was thirty-nine years old and Emma twenty-six when they first met. Emma's humble background, which she had confessed to the Queen, proved of little consequence to Neapolitan society. Maria Carolina was delighted with Emma's charm and natural behaviour. Her cheerful and optimistic outlook helped the Queen in difficult times. Within a year Emma became a great favourite at court.

Sir William described Emma's reception by the King and Queen in a letter to Banks on 27 March 1792:

Lady Hamilton has nothing to do with my public character but their Sicilian Majesties are so good as to receive and treat her as any other travelling Lady of distinction – she has gained the hearts of all even of the Ladies by her humility & proper behaviour, & we shall I dare say, go on well – I will allow with that 99 times out of a hundred such as step as I took would be very imprudent but I knew my way here & here I mean to pass the most of the days that I can have a chance of living. Without a Woman you can have no Society at home & I am sure you will hear from every quarter of the comforts of my house.[14]

Sir William never regretted his marriage, later explaining to Lady Mansfield:

As yet I have no reason to repent of the step which I took contrary to the approbation of the world. The marrying Emma was my own business. I knew what I was doing for as you know I had lived with her for five years before I married ... Look round your circle of <u>prudent well assorted matches</u> in the great world and see how few turn out so well as our seemingly imprudent one ...[15]

Christmas 1791 was spent at Caserta, but on 3 January Sir William was required to accompany the King on a hunting expedition to Persano. Emma insisted that he write to her every day. He happily obliged by sending her fifteen letters between 4 January to 17 January, responding to her daily letters. Seldom quoted, many are included here (with editing)[16] to give an illuminating insight into their relationship. Their mutual regard and happiness is abundantly obvious.

Sir William's love for Emma is charmingly expressed, his letters ending with such phrases as:'*Adieu, my dearest Emma! Yours with my whole soul*', and '*Amuse yourself, my dearest Emma and never doubt of my love.*'

Persano, [Wednesday]

Jan.4, 1792

We arrived here, yesterday, in little more than five hours, and had nearly began with a disagreeable accident, for the King's horse took fright at the guard, and his Majesty and horse were as near down as possible. However, all ended well; and he was as gay as possible, yesterday.

Our first chasse has not succeeded; though there were two wolves, and many wild boars, in the Mena, but the king would direct how we should beat the wood, and began at the wrong end: by which the wolves and boars escaped, and we remained without shooting power. However, ten or twelve boars have been killed ...

The King's face is very long, at this moment; but, I dare say, tomorrow's good sport will shorten it again.

I was sorry, my dear Em. to leave you in affliction: you must harden yourself to such little misfortunes as a temporary parting; but, I cannot blame you for having a good and tender heart. Believe me, you are in thorough possession of all mine, though I will allow it to be rather tough.

Let us study to make one another as comfortable as we can; and 'banish sorrow; till tomorrow' and so on, every day.

You are wise enough to see that line it is proper for you to take: and have, hitherto, followed it most rigorously: and I can assure you, that I have not the least doubt of your continuing in it.

Amuse yourself as well as you can, as I am doing, whilst we are separate; and the best news you can give me is, that you are well and happy ...

Adieu, my dear, dear Emma. I am, with my love to your good mother, yours ever, and faithfully,

W.H.

Persano, Thursday

[Jan. 5th 1792]

We got home early, and I have not yet received your Daily Advertiser.

No sport, again! In the midst of such a quantity of game, they have contrived to carry him far off, where there is none. He has no other comfort, today, than having killed a wild cat; and his face is a yard long.

However, his Majesty has vowed vengeance on the boars tomorrow ... and, I dare say, there will be a terrible slaughter ...

*I have wrote to Mrs. Dickinson [Mary]. I forget whether you have, or
not: if not, pray do it soon; for, you know, she is a good friend of yours ...*

Adieu, my sweet Em. Yours, with all my heart.

W.H.

*Persano, Friday Evening
[Jan. 6th. 1792]*

*... We have been out all day in the rain; I killed none, and the King and
party but few ...*

*You did perfectly right in buying the lamps; and I am glad the Prince
asked to dine with you. I am sure he was comfortably received by you ...*

*The King has declared, he will return to Naples next Saturday se'night;
so you know the worst, my dear Emma. Indeed, I shall embrace you most
cordially; for I would not be married to any woman, but yourself, on earth,
for all the world ...*

Adieu, again! Yours ever,

W.H.

*Persano, Saturday Night,
[January 7th, 1792]*

*... I am glad all goes on so well. I never doubted your gaining every soul
you approach.I am far from being angry at your feeling the loss of me so
much! Nay,I am flattered; but, believe me, the time will soon come, that we
shall meet. Years pass seemingly in an instant; why, then, afraid of a few
days?*

*Upon the whole, we are sociable here; but we go to bed at nine, and get
up at five o'clock. I generally read an hour, to digest my supper, but, indeed,
I live chiefly on bread and butter.*

Adieu, my dear Emma! Ever yours and yours alone.

W.H.

*... The cold and fatigue makes my hand something like yours – which,
by the bye, you neglect rather too much; but, as what you write is good sense,
every body will forgive the scrawl.*

Sunday night, [Jan. 8th, 1792]

*We are come in late; and I have but a moment to tell you we are well,
and I have killed three large boars, a fox, and four woodcocks.*

*Nothing pleases me more, than to hear you do not neglect your singing.
It would be a pity, as you are near the point of perfection.*

Adieu, my dearest Emma! Yours, with my whole soul,

W.H.

Persano, [Monday]
January 10th. [9th.] 1792
Your letter of yesterday, my sweet Em. gave me great pleasure; as I see, all goes on perfectly right for you at Naples.

Your business, and mine, is to be civil to all, and not enter into any party matters. If the Wilkinsons are not content with our civilities, let them help themselves.

We have had a charming day; and most excellent sport ...

Amuse yourself, my dearest Emma, and never doubt of my love.

Yours ever,

W.H.

Persano, [Tuesday] Jan. 10th. 1792
The day has been so thoroughly bad, that we have not been able to stir out; and the King, of course, in bad humour ...

I am glad you have been at the Academy, and in the great world. It is time enough for you to find out, that the only real comfort is to be met with at home; I have been in that secret for some time.

You are, certainly, the most domestic young woman I know; but you are young, and most beautiful; and it would not be natural, if you did not like to shew yourself a little in public.

The effusion of tenderness, with regard to me, in your letter, is very flattering; I know the value of it, and will do all I can to keep it alive. We are now one flesh, and it must be our study to keep that flesh as warm and comfortable as we can. I will do all in my power to please you, and I do not doubt of your doing the same towards me.

Adieu, my dearest Emma! Having nothing interesting to write, and as you insist upon hearing from me every day, you must content yourself with such a stupid letter as this.

Your Ladyship's commands shall always be punctually obeyed by, dear Madam, your Ladyship's most obedient and faithful servant,

W. HAMILTON

Persano, Wednesday
11th. Jan. [1792]
I have just received your letter – and, as I always do – with infinite pleasure.

I hope you received twelve wood-biddies, today; and tomorrow, you will have a wild boar: all left to your discretion.

No talk of returning, yet. We must complete sixteen days shooting, and one day has been lost by bad weather ...

Adieu, my ever dear Emma! We are always in a hurry; though we have, absolutely, nothing to do, but kill, examine, and weigh, wild boars.

I assure you, that I shall rejoice when I can embrace you once more. A picture would not content me; your image is more strongly represented on my heart, than any that could be produced by human art.

Your most affectionate husband,

W.H.

Persano, Thursday night,
[Jan. 12th. 1792]

... I have got your two kind letters. Send for Gasparo; and give your orders, that the servants attend your call: and let him discharge them, if they do not. You are my better half, and may command. Translate this part of the letter to him ...

As to your mother's going with you to the English parties, very well; but, believe me, it will be best for her, and more to her happiness, to stay at home, than go with you to the Neapolitan parties ...

Adieu, my dear Emma! Amuse yourself as well as you can; and believe me, ever, your's alone, with the utmost confidence,

W.H.

Persano, Friday Night
[Jan. 13th, 1792]

... I approve of all you do in my absence; but it would be nonsense, and appear affected, to carry your scruples too far. Divert yourself reasonably. I am sure of your attachment to me, and I shall not easily be made to alter my opinion of you ...

Yours W.H.

Persano, Sunday;
Jan. 15, 1792.

You did admirably, my Dear Em. in not inviting Lady A.H. to dine with the Prince; and still better, in telling her, honestly, the reason. I have always found, that going straight is the best method, though not the way of the world.

You did, also, very well, in asking Madame Skamouski; and not taking upon you to present her, without leave.

In short, consult your own good sense, and do not be in a hurry; and, I am sure, you will always act right ...

The King is very kind to me, and shews every one that he really loves me: and he commends my shooting ... We have much business between this and Saturday: and we are to shoot, Saturday morning, so that we shall arrive late.

What say you to a feet washing, that night? O che Gusto! when your prima ora is over, and all gone.

Adieu, my sweet Emma! Ever yours.

W.H.

Persano, Tuesday Night,
[Jan. 17, 1792]

I told you, my Dear Em, that I expected good sport today! I have killed five boars, and two great ones got off after falling; two bucks; six does; and a hare; fourteen in all.

By the bye, I must tell you, that accept *and* except *are totally different. You always write –* 'I did not except *of the invitation'; when, you know, it should be* 'accept'. *It is, only, for want of giving yourself time to think; but, as this error has been repeated, I thought best to tell you of it …*

We shall be home on Saturday; and indeed, my sweet Emma, I shall be most happy to see you …

Yours, ever, my dear wife,

W.H.

Persano, Wednesday,
[Jan. 18th.1792]

It was not your white and silver, alone, that made you look like an angel, at the Academy. Suppose you had put it on nine parts out of ten of the ladies in company, would any one have appeared angelic?

I will allow, however, that a beautiful woman, feeling herself well dressed, will have a sort of confidence, which will add greatly to the lustre of her eye; but take my word, that, for some years to come, the more simply you dress, the more conspicuous will be your beauty; which, according to my idea, is the most perfect I have yet met with, take it all in all …

I always rejoice when I find you do not neglect your singing. I am, I own, ambitious of producing something extraordinary in you, and it is nearly done.

Adieu! my sweet Em. I rejoice that the time of our re-union is so near –
Saturday night! W.H.

Sir William enjoyed receiving Emma's 'long and interesting' letters and although he says she neglects her handwriting he goes on to say 'but as what you write is good sense, everybody will forgive the scrawl'. Typical of his good taste, he advises Emma that 'the more simply you dress the more conspicuous will be your beauty.'

Emma was happy but the political situation in France created an ever-increasing threat of disruption in their lives. Sir William and the

King and Queen of Naples watched anxiously as events unfolded, concerned about the possible repercussions of the French revolution in Italy.

In January Greville had written to Sir William regarding the transfer to him of responsibility for Little Emma. To Greville's credit, he had paid all this time for her upkeep and education. She was now ten years old. His accounts show that the costs involved were in the region of £60 p.a., a fairly large sum out of Greville's income. He now announced he could no longer afford this expense. Not unreasonably, he expected his uncle to take over, now that Sir William and Emma were married. He gives details of the steps he had taken to charge Sir William's account in London for the payment due and sends a list of the expenses he has allowed for Little Emma's care. His letter concludes:

... I do not mean this necessary step to be concealed from Ly. H. but I should be sorry that she considered it unkindly. You will know better than me that an early decision should be taken about her; Blackburn says she has grown, & that she has been evidently more anxious since Mrs. Cadogan visited her ... I had full confidence in Mrs. Blackburn, & in Mr. B's discretion, & as Mrs Cadogan saw her situated to her satisfaction, I had only to ensure the continuance of her residence with these good people until her plans of life could be settled.

I enclose the account that you may see the particulars of what I have allowed her, which you will continue till her plans are decided on. I cannot have an opinion what the plan should be, but that which is most agreable Ly. H. will be best; & I know that she will consider your attention on this subject as additional proof of your kindness. [17]

Greville's list of payments made to Mr. and Mrs. Blackburn indicate that Little Emma was well provided for, even to the extent of having a piano and music lessons.

Greville suggested that it was now up to Sir William and Emma to decide what plans to make for Little Emma, adding: *'that which is most agreable to Ly. H. will be best.'* Sadly for Little Emma, it was decided that she should remain in the care of the Blackburns rather than be brought over to Naples where she could have been introduced as an adopted child. Sir William was usually kind and generous, but the uncertainty over their future lives in Naples no doubt played a part in the decision not to bring her to Naples.

Emma received a long-awaited reply to her letter from Romney:

No date [1792]

What must you think of my neglect of answering your kind letter? Do not accuse me of ingratitud. I wish I could express myself as I felt at the perusal of it to find your happiness so compleat; May God grant it may remain so till the end of your days. You may be assured that I have the same anxiety that Sir William and yourself should continue to think well of me, and the same desire to do everything in my power that may merit your esteem. I have waited till I could give you some account of the picter of Cassandra and some other of the pictures you were so kind as to let me see. The Cassandra is at last gone to the Shakespeare Gallery. It suits.

The King and Royal Family saw it. I hav never heard from the Prince of Wales until a few days ago Mr. West called and said the Prince desired him to look at the picture for His Royal Hiness. They are near finished. The lively one I have made to suit Calipso.

I am anxious to know what you would wish me to do with the picture with a bonnet as you have not mentioned it in your letter. Mr. Crawford has expressed a great desire of possessing it in preference to the other. I shall wait for your instructions. I sent, as your ladyship required, the picter in black to du Tens ...[18]

Probably due to his fragile mental state, Romney did not take up Emma's invitation to visit Naples where she had promised to be his model – *'anything to induce you to come, that I may have an opportunity to show my gratitude to you'.*

In a further letter, Romney wrote: *'I have had a great number of ladies of figure sitting to me since you left England, but they all fall short of the Spinstress, indeed, it is the sun of my hemisphere and they are but twinkling stars'.*[19]

Married for seven months, Sir William wrote to Horace Walpole, now the Earl of Orford, proudly describing Emma as *'an extraordinary being'*:

Naples April 17th. 1792

... Lady H., who has also had a difficult part to act and has succeeded wonderfully, having gained, by having no pretensions, the thorough approbation of all the English ladies. The Queen of Naples, as you may have heard, was very kind to her on our return, and treats her like any other travelling lady of distinction; in short, we are very comfortably situated here ... You can not imagine how delighted Ly.H. was in having gained your approbation in England. She desires to be kindly remember'd to you. She goes on improving daily, particularly in musick & in the French & Italian languages. She is really an extraordinary being, & most gratefull to me for

having saved her from the precipice into which she had good sense enough to see she must without me have inevitably fallen, and she sees that nothing but a constant good conduct can maintain the respect that is now shown her by every body. It has often been remarked that a reformed rake makes a good husband. <u>*Why not vice versa?*</u>[20]

Despite the troubles in France, English travellers continued to visit Europe, many making their way to Naples. Sir William and Emma were kept busy, but towards the end of the year Sir William suffered his first serious illness. Emma described nursing him in a letter to Greville. She now adopted a formal style of address, 'Dear Sir' or 'My dear Mr. Greville'.

Caserta December 4th. 1792

Dear Sir, I have the pleasure to inform you that Sir William is out of danger & very well considering the illness he as had to battle with. He as been 15 days in bed with a billious fever & I have been almost as ill as him with anxiety, aprehension, & fatige, the last, endeed, the least, of what I have felt & I am now doubly repaid by the dayly progress he makes for the better. Luckily we are at Caserta were his convalescence will have fair play & I am in hopes he will be better than ever he was in his life, for his disorder as been long gathering & was a liver complaint. I need not say to you my dear Mr. Greville what I have suffered, endeed I was almost distracted, from such extreme happiness at once to such misery, that I felt, your good heart may imagine. I was eight days without undressing, eating or sleeping. I have great obligations to the English ladies & Neapolitans, altho we are 16 miles from Naples. Lady Plymouth, Lady Dunmore, Lady Webster & several others sent twice a day & offered to come & stay with me, & the King & Queen sent constantly, morning & evening, the most flattering messages, but all was nothing to me – what cou'd console me for the loss of such a husband, friend & protecter, for surely no happiness is like ours. We live but for one another, but I was to happy, I had imagined I was never more to be unhappy, all is right, I now know myself again & I shall not easily fall in to the same error again, for every moment I feel what I felt when I thought I was loseing him for ever. Pray excuse me, but you who love Sir William may figure to your self my situation at that moment.

I will trouble you with my own affairs as you are so good to enterest yourself about me. You must know I send my grandmother every cristmas, twenty pounds & so I ought, I have 2 hundred a year for nonsense & it wou'd be hard I cou'd not give her twenty pounds when she as so often given me her last shilling. As Sir Wm. is ill I cannot ask him for the order but if you will get the twenty pounds & send it to her you will do me the greatest favour, for if the times passes without hearing from me she may imagine I have forgot her & I wou'd not keep her poor old heart in suspence for the world, & as she as heard of my circumstance (I dont know how) but she is prudent, therefore pray lose no time & Sir Wm. shall send you the order. You know her direction, Mrs. Kidd, Hawerden, Flintshire. Cou'd you not write to her a line from me or send to her & tell her by my order & she may write to you & send me her answer, for I cannot divert myself of my original feelings. It will contribute to my happiness & I am sure you will assist to make me happy, tell her every year she will have twenty pound. The fourth of November last I had a dress on that cost twenty five pounds as it was gala at Court & believe me I felt unhappy all the while I had it on. Excuse the trouble I give you & believe me your sincere

Emma Hamilton.

Sir W as wrote you a few lines.[21]

Emma's distress at the thought of losing Sir William, her 'husband, friend and protecter', is evident. Greatly concerned, the King and Queen had written to her twice a day during his illness.

Despite being 'almost distracted' she remembered to ask Greville to send her grandmother, Mrs Kidd, the twenty pounds she always sent at Christmas, promising that Sir William would reimburse him.

Sir William's health improved enough for him to welcome Lord and Lady Palmerston, when they arrived in Naples just before Christmas. Meeting Emma for the first time in January, Lady Palmerston reported: 'I find her not so beautiful as I expected, but certainly extremely handsome and her figure uncommonly fine. She was well dressed and there is certainly something in her manner very good humoured and a great desire of pleasing. Sir William looks extremely ill ... Her voice is vulgar and she and Sir W. are rather too fond, but upon the whole I think her a very extraordinary woman ...'[22]

After attending a dinner for fifty-three at the Palazzo Sessa, Lady Palmerston reported: 'Lady Hamilton looked extremely handsome and really does the honours uncommonly well. She is extremely obliging, without the appearance of feeling any elevation from the change in her situation. Sir William perfectly idolizes her and I do not wonder he is proud of so magnificent a marble, belonging so entirely to himself.'[23]

On another occasion Lord and Lady Palmerston enjoyed Sir William's hospitality at Caserta where Emma sang accompanied by Sir William's four musicians. After criticizing Emma's singing, Lady

Palmerston commented: *'She is, however, a very extraordinary character, and by her conduct proves how much she merits her great reverse of fortune.'*

She later made an observation that explains the 'vulgarity' of which Emma is often accused: *'Lady H. is to me very surprising, for considering the situation she was in she behaves wonderfully well. Now and then to be sure a little vulgarness pops out, but I think it's more Sir William's fault, who loves a good joke and leads her to enter his stories, which are not of the best kind. She is vastly desirous to please and is very civil and good humoured to all her friends and her attention to Sir William is infinitely amiable ...'*[24]

Life in Naples carried on as usual for the next few months, although clouded by anxiety about the events in France. At this late stage of his life, Sir William's workload increased. He began a period of intense diplomatic activity, working tirelessly to keep Naples, if not with Britain against France, at least neutral and friendly towards Britain.

On 21 September 1792, the National Convention took control of the government of France. The monarchy was brought to an end. By October the King and Queen were imprisoned in the Great Tower, the King separated from his wife and two children. The Convention decided the King should stand trial for treason and he was found guilty almost unanimously.

In discussions about the King's fate, it was suggested that he and his family be exiled to America. However, in the atmosphere of mayhem and hysteria in Paris, amidst daily horrific killings and executions, it was inevitable that the death penalty would be passed on 16 January 1793.

Lady Sutherland wrote to the Duchess of Devonshire: *'They do nothing but arrest, interrogate and guillotine.'*[25]

At the end of January 1793, the news arrived in Naples that Louis XV1 had been publicly guillotined on the 21 January.*

King Ferdinand and Queen Maria Carolina were horrified. Naples went into mourning and the King ordered a Requiem Mass. The entire court attended, except for the representative of the new French Republic, who refused to wear mourning. The Queen's fury over King Louis' execution and her desperate anxiety about the safety of her sister prompted her to write: *'I should like this infamous nation to be cut to pieces, annihilated, dishonoured, reduced to nothing for at least fifty years.'*[26]

Co-operation between Hamilton and the queen became vitally

---

* Robespierre, who had demanded the deaths of both Louis XV1 and Marie Antoinette, was himself executed on 28 July 1794.

important when on 1 February France declared war on Britain. The British fleet needed Naples as a friendly port and the Queen saw that, through Britain, she might protect the monarchy and the Kingdom of the Two Sicilies.

Sir William was given authority to negotiate a treaty with the kingdom, resulting in a treaty of alliance being signed by Sir John Acton and himself on 12 July.[27]By this treaty Britain agreed to maintain a fleet in the Mediterranean to protect Neapolitan merchant ships. Naples agreed to contribute to the fleet, cease all trading with France and not sign a separate peace with France without British permission. It was not until later in the year that Naples became directly involved in the war. French refugees and English travellers continued to arrive in Naples.

In April Georgiana, Duchess of Devonshire, arrived with her mother, Lady Spencer, her sister Harriet and her husband, Lord Ducannon, and the Duke's mistress, Lady Elizabeth Foster (the Earl Bishop's daughter).

The Duke had banished Georgiana from England to give birth to her baby by Charles Grey. She had been travelling in Europe for two years, unhappily awaiting the Duke's permission to return home.

They were to spend considerable time with the ambassador and his new wife, both in Naples and at Caserta, and were frequent guests at the court of the King and Queen, Emma presenting the Duchess to the Queen.

Georgiana and Emma developed a friendship that was renewed when the Hamiltons returned to England. It was on this visit to Naples that Georgiana wrote to her daughter that Emma was *'ador'd here, not only for her beauty and her talents but for her Charity – they say she assists the poor to ye greatest degree'*.

Lady Spencer, who had avoided meeting Emma in England, accepted Sir William's hospitality and was extremely grateful for the attentive nursing Emma and her mother offered to Harriet, who had been ill for months with bronchial pneumonia.

Lady Spencer wrote to Sir William in November 1794: *'My best regards I beg to Lady Hamilton – I often think of the Whist evenings and the Handils Music and Songs at Caserta … hers and Mrs Cadogan's kind care of my poor little girl.'*[28]She was so impressed with Emma that in 1795 she urged Hamilton to ensure that Emma was provided for, should anything happen to him.

The Duke finally summoned Georgiana home and the party left

Naples, except for Lady Spencer and Harriet, who was too weak to travel.

Sir William, pleased Emma was so successful in her role as his wife, wrote to Greville in March:

Emma goes on perfectly to my mind, but she has made our house so agreeable that it is more frequented than ever, & of course, I am at a greater expence. However, I may safely say that no minister was ever more respected than I am here, & the English travellers, as Lord Cholmondley will tell you, feel the benefit of our being so well at this Court, for Emma is now as well with the K. & Q. as I am, & of many parties with them.[29]

On 11 June 1793 he described Emma's progress at court to Banks:

You will be glad to hear as I am sure you must from every quarter of the prudent conduct of Emma. – She knows the value of a good reputation which she is determined to maintain having been compleately recovered. She knows that beauty fades & therefore applies daily to the improvement of her mind. Altho we have had many Ladies of the first rank from England here lately ... the Queen of Naples remarked that Emma's deportment was infinitely superior. She is often with the Queen who really loves her. By coming to Naples at 19 [in fact, Emma was then twenty-one] *she has got the language better than I have in 28 years ...[30]*

The Queen lavished attention on Emma, not only happy with her cheerful attitude and will to please, but also because Emma often acted her liaison with Sir William, especially during the next five years when he was often ill and unable to attend court. Emma nursed him on these occasions and acted as his secretary.

In June, after a busy few months, Emma wrote a long letter to Greville:

Caserta June
2nd. 1793

I shou'd have answerd your kind letter sooner but I have not had time to write to any of my friends these five months, which I am sorry for, as they may accuse me of neglect & ingratitude, which if they do, it will be a wrong accusition, for I literally have been so busy with the English, the Court, my home duties, as to prevent me doing things I had much at heart to do.

For political reasons we have lived eight months at Caserta, that is, making this our constant residence & going twice a week to town to give dinners, balls etc. etc., returning here at 2 or 3 a clock in the morning after the fatige of a dinner of fifty, & ball & supper of 3 hundred, then to dress early in the morning to go to Court to dinner at twelve a clock as the Royal family dine early & they have done Sir Wm. and me the honner to invite us very very often. Our house at Caserta as been like an inn this winter as we have had partys that have come either to see the environs or have been invited to Court. We had the Duchess of Ancaster several days; it is but 3 days since the Devonshire family has left us & we had fifty in familly for four days at Caserta. Tis true we dined every day at Court or at some Casino of the King for you cannot immagine how good our King & Queen as been to the principal English who have been here, particularly to Lord & Ly. Palmerstone, Cholmondlys, Devonshire, Sir G & Lady Webster & I have carried the Ladies to the Queen very often, as she as permitted me to go to her very often in private which I do & the reason why we stay now here, is I have promised the Queen to remain as long as she does, which will be tell the tenth of July. In the evenings I go to her & we are tète á tète 2 or 3 hours; sometimes we sing, yesterday the King & me sung duetts for 3 hours, _it was but bad as he sings like a king_; today the Princess Royal of Sweden comes to Court to take leave of their Majestys. Sir W & me are invited to dinner with her. She is an amiable princess & as lived very much with us; we have given her several dinners, balls etc., etc. for she loves dancing dearly ... the ministers wives are very fond of me as the see I have no pretensions nor do I abuse of her Majestys goodness ... I had been with the Queen the night before _alone en famille_ laughing, singing etc. etc. etc. but at the drawing room I kept my distance and pay'd the Queen as much respect as tho I had never seen her before which pleased her much, but she shewd me great distinction that night & told me several times how much she admired my good conduct. I onely tell you this to shew & convince you I shall never change but allways be simple & natural.

You may imagine how happy my dear, dear Sir William is & I can assure you if ever I had a little teasing caprice it is so intirely gone that neither Sir William or me remembers it & he will tell you the same: endeed you cannot immagine our happiness, it is not to be described, we are not an hour in the day separable, we live more like lovers than husband & wife, _as husbands & wives go nowadays_ ... I study very hard & have made great progress in French & musick & I have had all my songs set for the viola that Sir. Wm. may accompany me which as pleased him much so that we now study together; The English garden is going on very fast, the King & Queen go there every day. Sir. Wm. & me are there every morning at seven a clock, sometimes dine there & allways drink tea, in short, it is Sir Wm.'s favourite child & boath him & me are now studying botany but not to make ourselves pedantical prigs to shew our learning like some of our traveling neigbours, but for our own pleasure. ... Addio. Love me & believe me your sincere friend,

E. Hamilton[31]

Sir William always considered it his duty to take care of the English travellers. It now became particularly important to introduce *'the principle English'* to the King and Queen as these visitors had access to political figures in England. The King and Queen, wishing to strengthen their ties with Britain, were more than willing to meet and entertain those presented to them. Emma often *'carried the Ladies to the Queen'*.

Emma tells Greville that although she was on very relaxed terms with the Queen when they met privately – *'en famille, laughing and singing'* – when she attended court in a formal capacity she *'kept her distance and payed the Queen as much respect as tho I had never seen her before'*.

Since her marriage and acceptance at court, Emma's lifestyle can best be imagined by a brief description of the Royal Palace (Palazzo Reale) at Caserta, built by King Ferdinand's father, the Bourbon King Charles III (when still Charles VII of Naples), to rival the Palace at Versailles. The monumentally large complex, with a façade 245 metres long and five storeys high, contains 1,200 rooms and thirty-four staircases. The magnificent main staircase provides access to the twenty-five royal apartments, decorated and furnished in 18th century style. The complex contains a chapel and a superbly designed royal theatre.

The classically designed surrounding park and gardens are no less spectacular, punctuated by cascades and Baroque fountains. Adjacent to the palace gardens is the English Garden that Hamilton had created for the Queen.*

Considering the scale and splendour of these surroundings, Emma is remarkably matter-of-fact about her close relationship with the Queen and the frequency of their invitations to the royal palace. She takes the elevated company and the regal surroundings in her stride.

On formal occasions Sir William and Emma, in one of her fine dresses and wearing her diamonds, would have ascended the grand staircase to approach the royal apartments. On her private visits Emma enjoyed the company of the royal children. The Queen was a loving mother, spending much time caring for her children. Only seven of her eighteen children survived to adulthood.

In September 1793 Naples was drawn into the war between Britain and France.

Lord Hood, the Commander-in-Chief of the British Mediterranean

---

* The Royal Palace and Park at Caserta are now a Unesco World Heritage site. The description above is taken from Unesco notes.

fleet, was blockading Toulon in support of the Royalists who were holding out against the 'reforms' taking place in Paris. Lord Hood sent Horatio Nelson, aged thirty-five, the Captain of the *Agamemnon*, 64 guns, post-haste to Naples. His instructions were, through Hamilton, to obtain and transport 6,000 Neapolitan troops urgently to Toulon to assist in its defence. Hamilton approached Acton, who immediately granted his request. Nelson was most impressed with Hamilton's success, reputedly saying:

'Sir William, you are a man after my own heart – you do business in my own way'.

Sir William recognized superior qualities in Captain Nelson and invited him to stay at the Palazzo Sessa. King Ferdinand received Nelson enthusiastically. During his four-day stay Nelson dined with the King three times, receiving special recognition by being placed at the King's right hand. The Queen was heavily pregnant with her seventeenth child at the time and did not appear in public.

There was no love-at-first-sight between Nelson and Emma. Nelson spent his time in discussions with Hamilton, Sir John Acton and the King and was grateful for Emma's kind attentions to his stepson, Josiah, who was serving on the *Agamemnon* and had been allowed ashore.

In reciprocation for the hospitality he had received Nelson invited the King to dine on board the *Agamemnon*, along with the Hamiltons and other distinguished English travellers in Naples. The *Agamemnon* not being equipped for such an occasion, Sir William loaned equipment and provided supplies from his own cellars and kitchens.

The Hamiltons and English guests breakfasted on board, but before the King arrived at the appointed time of one o'clock Nelson heard from Sir John Acton that a French man-of-war and three other vessels under her convoy had anchored in Sardinia. Nelson decided to leave immediately to attempt to capture the French man-of-war.

Hurriedly the Hamiltons, guests and all the borrowed equipment were taken ashore. Nelson wrote to his brother, William: *'Unfit as my ship was, I had nothing left for the honour of our Country, but to sail, which I did in the two hours afterwards. It was necessary to show them what an English man-of-war would do.'*[32]

After this brief meeting Nelson and Hamilton corresponded regularly in a friendly manner on business matters. When Nelson wrote to Hamilton in May 1794 from Bastia, he enclosed a brief note for Emma.

Sir William and Emma did not see Nelson again until five years later, by which time he had lost the sight of his right eye and had his right arm amputated. The exhausted and almost unrecognizable hero arrived in Naples a few weeks after the Battle of the Nile.

CHAPTER 9

Emma Becomes Embroiled in Politics

*'Send me some news, political and private for against my will
owing to my situation here, I am got into politicks'*
Emma to Greville, 18 December 1794

*'No person can be so charming as the Queen, she is everything
one can wish, the best mother, wife and friend in the world.'*
Emma to Greville, 18 December 1794

*'I must own to you that I think Italy is in great danger of being
completely plundered and ruin'd.'*
Sir William to Greville, 7 June 1796

ONE MONTH AFTER Nelson's visit, on 16 October 1793, Queen Marie Antoinette followed her husband to the guillotine. On hearing the news, Maria Carolina was distraught. Her hatred of the French became her over-riding passion. She placed a note under a portrait of her sister in her study: *Je poursuiverai ma vengeance jusqu'au tombeau* (I shall pursue revenge until the grave).[1]

Marie Antoinette had endured months of incarceration in the Great Tower. Her husband had been executed and her eight-year-old son forcefully removed from her protection. Later she was taken to the Conciergerie and confined in a damp and sparsely equipped cell. By now she had very few clothes and no personal effects. Her only company was a maid called Rosalie.

In September Marie Antoinette faced two long days of interrogation during which she defended herself against damaging, mostly falsified, accusations. After a further interrogation she was brought before the Revolutionary Tribunal on 14 October. By now her clothes were worn and patched, her hair white and her face gaunt. Only two weeks away from her thirty-eighth birthday, she appeared an old lady.

Despite having no proof of the allegations against her, the jury found her guilty and sentenced her to death on the following day. On the morning of the 16 October, with her hair hacked off and her hands bound, she was taken in a cart to the Place de la Concorde, passing through huge crowds. Every eyewitness agreed that she went to her death with composure.

Ten days earlier, Maria Carolina knowing, or suspecting, the terrible circumstances of her sister's imprisonment and trial had written: *'everything that ends her torture is good'.*

Marie Carolina who gave birth in December to another princess, remained depressed for some months, devastated by the news. Her fears for her own and her family's safety escalated over the next few years, making her increasingly dependent on Sir William and Emma. Through them she gained the support of Britain against France, most importantly through the protection of the British Navy. Confident of this support, she refused to be intimidated, a fighting spirit later admired by Nelson.

She wrote: *'I am not and never shall be on good terms with the French. I shall always regard them as the murderers of my sister and the royal family* [of France], *as the oppressors of all monarchies, as the villains who have seduced and put poniard* [a small, slim dagger] *and poison into the hands of all classes and peoples against legitimate authority, and who have consequently blighted my life.'*[2]

Georgiana, Duchess of Devonshire, a friend of Marie Antoinette, was extremely shocked at the news of her death: *'I cannot express to you the horror I feel. The impression of the Queen's death is constantly before my eyes.'*[3]

Anxiety in Naples was further increased in December when Toulon fell to the French rebels after bombardment by the guns of a young officer named Napoleon Bonaparte. British ships had withdrawn, carrying many royalist refugees to safety, but after only partly succeeding in burning the French ships in the port. The Neapolitan troops obtained by Nelson suffered considerable losses.

The Queen, Emma and Nelson shared a hatred of the French.

In January Hamilton had recovered and was away hunting with the King. The following letter to Emma shows their relationship continuing to flourish. In it he outlines his philosophy about life:

Venasso, Friday 27 January 1794

My Dear Em,

My having grumbled a little, I got a better post today; and have killed two boars and a sow, all enormous...

My study of antiquities, has kept me in constant thought of the perpetual fluctuation of every thing. The whole art is, really, to live all the <u>days</u> of our life; and not, with anxious care, disturb the sweetest hour that life affords – which is the present! Admire the Creator, and all his works, to us incomprehensible; and do all the good you can upon earth; and take the chance of eternity, without dismay ...

The weather is delightful; and, I believe, we shall have done all our business, so as to return on Thursday ...

Adieu, my sweet love! Adieu. Divert yourself – I shall soon be at you again. Yours, ever,

W.H.[4]

Despite his increased workload, Hamilton continued to dedicate attention to his collection of vases. He wrote to Beckford in March 1794: *'Every moment I can steal from business is employed in forwarding my New Publication on the Greek Vases that form my new collection all of which were Under Ground 6 years ago.'*[5] He advanced Tischbein £600 to oversee the production of the second volume, completed in May 1796. He did not offer this second collection to the British Museum, annoyed with them for not buying his Portland Vase.

Hamilton wrote to his friend, the Countess of Lichtenau, hoping she could persuade the King of Prussia to purchase the entire collection: *'... there are more than a thousand vases, and one half of them figured ... on reckoning up my accounts – I must speak frankly – I find that I shall be a loser unless I receive Seven Thousand pounds sterling for this collection ... As respects the Vases, the second collection is far more beautiful and complete than the series in London...'*[6]

Unfortunately, the King of Prussia did not buy the collection and part of it later became a casualty of the war.

Hamilton's financial situation became more and more alarming. His secure and comfortable life began to unravel. Arriving back in Naples in 1791, and after spending over £4,000 on *'Antiquities & Pictures'*, he told his agent in Pembroke that *'having rigged out Her Ladp., to make a proper appearance as my Wife at Naples'* he had about £3,000 left in his account with Ross and Ogilvie. However, this could be in the red if the government were in arrears in paying his salary. They sometimes owed him as much as £4,000.[7]

In 1792, Hamilton was receiving considerably less income from his estates than in Catherine's time. Greville's developments at Milford were swallowing money, though he wrote to his uncle: *'I have set down without mystery everything that you can do for me at present, & in future without diminution of present income.'*[8]

Greville raised a loan of £9,000 at 4% from Hoare's bank, partly to pay off Hamilton's debt of £3,400 to his lawyer in London, the rest for the Milford developments.[9]

The *'diminution of present income'* became a huge concern of Hamilton's. He repeatedly urged Greville to be cautious – *'I am determined not to risk anything that might distress me in the latter part of my life.'* He agreed to the development of an inn and a quay at Milford, but made clear that *'to which two <u>articles I limit all improvements</u>, as realy my expenses increase by everything growing dearer daily'.*[10]

He regarded his estate income as his *'sheet anchor'* against any failure in his other incomes. His fears were realized when, on his return to England, he failed to obtain the pension he felt he deserved from the government.

In July 1795, he calculated: *'I have valuables here that will balance that account* [the debt to his bankers] *if we escape bombardments, earthquakes, invasions & home conspiracies.'*[11]

But his financial situation was indeed to be dramatically affected by several such catastrophies. From now on, Hamilton struggled with his finances and his ill health until his death.

Aside from his serious financial problems, he suffered frequent bouts of illness, one of these occurring after the eruption of Vesuvius in June 1794. He risked his personal safety to observe the phenomenon in order to write his reports for the Royal Society, describing these eruptions as the most violent recorded, except for those in 79 A.D. and 1631.

The shock was felt at the Palace of Caserta, fifteen miles away and even at places over thirty miles from Naples. Hamilton counted fifteen torrents of lava that, by 16 July, had reached the sea, destroying the town of Torre del Greco in passing.

On 17 June he made a dangerous journey in his boat along the coast to see the damage at Torre del Greco and reported: *'I observed that the sea-water was boiling as in a cauldron* [near a] *newly formed promontory, and though I was at least a hundred yards from it observing that the sea smoked near my boat I put my hand into the water, which was literally scalded; by this time my boatman observed that the pitch from the bottom of the boat was melting fast and floating on the surface of the sea, and that the boat began to leak. We therefore retired hastily from this spot and landed at some distance from the hot lava.'*[12]

He was relieved to find that out of a population of about eighteen hundred people no more than fifteen had perished. King Ferdinand offered the people land for a new settlement, but they preferred to stay and rescue whatever they could.

At the end of the month, he thought it safe to attempt yet another ascent of Vesuvius. On this occasion, they did not reach the summit, but after an exhausting day, Hamilton found that the soles of his boots had burnt through, despite an extra thick layer he had added for the climb. He admitted that these expeditions made him ill because he inhaled *'so much sulphurious and mephitic Air'*.

Unaware of these dramatic events, Greville wrote to Emma with good news:

August 18th, 1794

Dear Lady Hamilton,

You will, I am sure, be glad to hear, that a favourable change has been announced to me; and that I am reinstated in the King's household, and honoured with a gold key, as his Vice-Chamberlain – and I hope, in a few days, to be in parliament ...

Friendship has borne me up in the most difficult times; and the general satisfaction which my friends express, on my promotion, renders me very happy at present; and, to make me more so, I have anticipated to my own mind the sincere satisfaction with which you will receive this news.

I should not flatter myself so far, if I was not very sincerely interested in your happiness; and, ever, affectionately yours,

C.F.G.[13]

Emma replied promptly expressing sincere congratulations on his success:

Castellamare, Sepbre 16, 1794

I congratulate you, my dear Mr. Greville, with all my heart on your appointment to the vice chamberlainship. You have well merited it & all your friends must be happy at a change so favourable, not onely for your percuniary circumstances as for the honner of the situation; may you long enjoy it with every happiness that you deserve & I speak from my heart. I don't know a better, honester or more amiable worthy man than yourself & it is a great deal for me to say for what ever I think I am not apt to pay compliments.

My dear Sir William as had the disorder that me & all Naples have had since the eruption, a violent diarea that reduced him to so very low an ebb that I was very much alarmed for him notwithstanding I thought I shou'd have gone with him, but thank God, we are here as happy as possible in the

118

Queens palace, enjoying every comfort & happiness that good health, royall favour & domestick happiness can give us, so much so, the other day, the anniversary of our marriage, Sir Wm told me he loved me better than ever & had never for one moment repented. Think of my feelings in that moment when I cou'd with truth say the same to him ... I never saw Sir William nor never was so happy myself. I tell you this because I know you will rejoice in it ... for the other affair I will write to you fully and as this is a letter of congratulation, nothing shall disturb our happy ideas. I wish you cou'd send me an English riding hat, very fashionable, but I desire you to put it to Sir Wms. Account ...

I am my dear Mr. Grevilles ever sincere & affectionate friend,
Emma Hamilton

P.S. *Mothers love to you; she is the comfort of our lives & is our house keeper. Sir Wm. doats on her.* Give my love to the Col. (his brother – Col. Robert Fulke Greville).[14]*

The widespread dysentery Emma mentions was probably due to water supplies and drainage being damaged by the volcanic eruption. Sir William, now aged sixty-four, was reduced to such a low ebb that Emma and the Queen were alarmed by his condition. The Queen had invited them to stay at her palace at Castellamare to recuperate.

Intriguingly, Emma writes *'for the other affair I will write to you fully.'* We can speculate that the *'other affair'* concerns Little Emma.

The Earl Bishop was again a guest in November, staying with Sir William and Emma both in Naples and at Caserta. In November 1794 a friend, John Denham, had written to Emma informing her that Lord Bristol had told him *'that God Almighty must have been in a glorious mood when he made you'.*[15] Emma *'carried him'* to see the Queen at the royal palace where the Earl Bishop was most impressed with Maria Carolina.

He hoped to interest Sir William in a proposition that Sir William would give up his job (at £3,500 p.a.) in favour of the Earl's son, Lord John Hervey, who had been sacked from his post in Florence, but had nevertheless secured himself a pension of £1,500 p.a. Needless to say, neither Sir William nor the government were in favour of this idea.

During his stay, the Earl Bishop attended a concert arranged by Sir William for Prince Augustus's† entertainment at which the celebrated

---

* Lord Bristol. He was another 'absentee father', spending years on the Continent purchasing works of art for the house he was having built – Ickworth in Suffolk, now a National Trust Property.

† Prince Augustus (sixth son of George 111) spent two years in Naples. Hamilton had been instructed to keep an eye on him.

English opera singer, Mrs Billington, performed. Mrs Billington proved to be a true friend to Emma in her hour of need many years later.

Emma and the eccentric Earl Bishop became good friends. He addressed her – 'my dearest Emma', 'sweet Emma', from 'your affectionate & devoted friend' in his correspondence in 1795. His letters discuss political events in Europe, indicating that she had been present and participated in such discussions with Sir William and the Earl. He clearly regarded her as a woman well versed in current events, not only as a 'beautiful face' (his words):

Naples, Sunday Morning [1795]

I return to you the inclosed, my Dearest Emma, which does equal honour to the excellent head and heart of the writer. I shall begin, for the first time of my life, to have a good opinion of myself, after such honourable testimonials.

In the mean time, I send you an extraordinary piece of news, just written to me from Ratisbon – a courier from the Elector of Mentz, desiring the Empire to make a separate peace with France ... The suburbs of Warsaw taken; the capitulation of the city daily expected. The King of Prussia totally retired beyond Potsdam, and supposed to be at the eve of madness.

Oh! Emma, who'd ever be wise,

If madness be loving of thee.

B.[16]

Later he would write to Sir William, 'I hope to bring a beautiful cabinet to the beautiful Emma , almost as fair as her skin, and as elegant as her form ...'[17]

Sir William and Emma spent most of their time at Caserta. In a letter to Greville, she asks him to send materials and ribbons to make new gowns for court appearances, in accordance with Sir William's concerns that she should be 'rigg'd out... to make a proper appearance as my wife':

Caserta   December
18th. 1794

I have onely time to write you a few lines by the Neapolitan courier who will give you this. He comes back soon so pray send me by him some Ribbands, & fourteen yards of fine muslin work'd for a gownd or fine leno ... & pray pay Hackwoods & put it down to Sir Williams account with his banker, he told me I might, for I have so many occasions to spend my money that my 2 hundred pounds will scarcely do for me a constant attendance at court now once & generally twice a day & I must be well dress'd ... Today we expect the Prince Augustas from Rome, he is to be lodged at the Pallace here & with us in town. Tomorrow we have a great dinner at Court for the Prince. The Queen invited me last night herself. I carried Lord Bristol to her & we pass'd four hours in an inchantment, no person can be so charming as the Queen, she is every thing one can wish, the best mother, wife & friend in the world. I live constantly with her & have done intimately so for 2 years & I have never in all that time seen any thing but goodness & sincerity in her, & if ever you hear any lyes about her contridick them & if you shou'd see a cursed book written by a vile French dog with her character in it dont believe one word. She lent it me last night & I have, by reading the infamous culomny, put myself quite out of humer that so good & virtus a princess shou'd be so infamously described.

Lord Bristol is with us at Caserta; he passes one weak at Naples and one with us; he is very fond of me & very kind, he is very entertaining & dashes at every thing ... We have been here 3 months & remain four or five months longer. We go to Naples every now & then, I ride on horseback. The Queen has had the goodness to supply me with horses, an equery & her own servant in her livery every day, in short, if I was her daughter she cou'd not be kinder to me & I love her with my whole soul.

My dear Sir William is very well & as fond of me as ever... you wou'd be delighted to see how happy we are, no quarelling, nor crossness nor caprices, all nonsense is at an end & every body that sees us are edified by our example of conjugal & domestick felicaty. Will you ever come & see us; you shall be receved with kindness from us boath for we have boath obligations to you for having made us acquainted with each other... Do send me a plan how I cou'd situate Little Emma, poor thing, for I wish it.

E. Hamilton[18]

In asking Greville to let her know how she could 'situate Little Emma, poor thing', Emma seems unaware that Greville and Sir William were corresponding on the matter.

Greville wrote to his uncle on 5 January 1795:

... You mentioned some time ago that the young protégé of Ly. Hamilton should meet your assistance on proper occasion. I told you then I wished you to consult Ly. H. as to what she advised, & that she was too young to be put to anything. Blackburn brought me an account of £29 for her board, etc. which I shall, as before, desire Ross & Ogilvie to pay. I enquired particularly about her; she will not be tall or handsome, but of a good disposition. I had mentioned to Blackburn the impropriety of raising her expectations, & she has no one idea to act or think beyond the quiet & retired life which she passes with Mrs. Blackburn, whose daughters are near her age & are educated with her. I told B. that I conceived something would be decided this Spring ... All this I write because within six months I wish you to consider & decide – both on Ly. H. & on her éleve's account ...[19]

In April the following year Sir William and Emma were ill with 'bilious fever'. The Queen offered to help Emma nurse Sir William. Emma declares that she had been 'near dying'.

During Sir William's absences the Queen became more reliant on Emma as her life-line to England and Emma asks Greville to send her political news, explaining that 'against my will...I am got in to politics'.

Caserta   April 19th.

1795

I write in a hurry as I have a vast deal to do and the Queen as just sent to me that a Courier is to go off for England this afternoon. Poor Sir William as been in bed 8 days with a billious fever and was better but woud get up yesterday which as thrown him back and to day he is not so well, but the doctor who is in the house with me says their is no danger. I am very uneasy and not well myself as I have not been in bed since he was taken ill. He was allways subject to billious attacks, but after this illness I hope he will be better than he as been for some time for the quantity of bile he as discharged these days past is incredible and he is naturaly of a strong healthy constitution. We are going to get good sadle horses as we live much in the country; riding will do him good and is very good for billious complaints ...

My ever dear Queen has been like a mother to me since Sir William as been ill; she writes to me four or five times a day, and offered to come and assist me: this is friendship.

I have seen letters that the King of England is not pleased with this Court and Sir William because they did not leave Castilcical with them.*

Sir W. did all he cou'd and he does not care wether they are pleased or not, as they must be very ungratefull to a minister like him that as done so much to keep up good harmony between the 2 Courts and as done more business in one day than another wou'd have done in ten, owing to the friendly footing he is on here with their Majestys and ministers, so if they are out of humer they may be, but between you and me, I have spoken a great deal to the Queen about the consequence it is to them to have a person of Castilcicalas abilitys and being beloved in England there and I believe he will return from a letter I had from the Queen this morning ... but I can assure you Sir Wm. did all he cou'd to have him kept in England, so don't

* Prince Castelcicala, the Neapolitan Ambassador to London.

let them blame the best and most worthy man living, for they have no minister like him.

I have had Lady Bath with me here 2 days. I carried her to the Queen. She is very shy, but she took a great fancy to me as I put her at her ease and did the honners of a ball for her that she gave at Naples. She envited all the Neapolitan ladies of the first distinction and I was to present them and she took a <u>nervous fit</u> and wou'd not come out of her room for 3 hours. At last I got her out and brought her in to the room between me and Lady Berwick and I carried the ladies who were dancing one by one to her in a corner and she took such a liking that we are very great friends ... Sir Wm. says he wou'd not have her with all her money, however I like her for I think she is a great deal of good about her. You was to have married her I think I heard ...

I had a very bad billious fever this winter, near dying, but it was owing to fatige when Prince Augustus was with us, dancing, supping etc. etc. Send me some news, political & private for against my will <u>owing to my situation here</u> I am got in to politicks and I wish to have news for our dear much loved Queen, whom I adore nor can I live without her, for she is to me a mother, friend & everything. If you could know her as I do how you wou'd adore her, for she is the first woman in the world, her talents are superior to every womans in the world and her heart is the most excellent and strictly good and upright, but you'l say it is because I am so partial but ask every body that knows her. She loves england and attached to our ministry and wishes the continuation of the war as the onely means to ruin that abominable french council ...

> *Ever yours*
> *Emma Hamilton.*[20]

Emma has been accused of exaggerating the importance of her association with the Queen. However, many details emerge in her letters indicating their very close friendship and alliance on political matters.

The Earl Bishop was equally impressed with the Queen. In letters to Emma he described her as 'the invaluable, adorable Queen' and 'our too sensible and inestimable Queen'.

By 1795 Hamilton was growing impatient with all the English visitors:

'Nothing plagues me in the business of a minister but the eternal succession of our travelling countrymen. One would have thought there were such difficulties this year, that few wou'd have arrived at Naples, yet I had 74 at dinner the Queen's birthday & Prince Augustus at their head.'[21]

In a letter to on 16 May 1795 Emma tells Greville that Sir William has recovered his health:

We go tomorrow to Caserta for ten days as the Queen as beg'd to see me & Sir W. as not yet seen their Majestys since his illness; therefore tomorrow we dine at Actons & go to Court in the evening were Sir Wm. will be receved with open arms by all. This air as done him a great deal of good & he is better than he as been for some years. The Queen as offered me to go to her Pallace of Castelamare which I believe we shall in the summer. In short, we are so happy, our situation here is very flattering in the publick character & in private we are models for all husbands & wives ...[22]

Soon even Emma, usually so enthusiastic and optimistic, became tired of the never-ending entertaining and worried about the war reaching Naples. She told Greville on 21 September 1796:

We have not time to write to you as we have been 3 days & nights writing to send by this courier letters of <u>consequence</u> for our government ... I am allmost sick of grandeur. We are tired to death with anxiety & God knows were we shall soon be & what will become of us if things go on as they do now. Sir Wm. is very well, I am not but hope when the cold wether comes on & we go to Caserta, I shall be better. Our house, breakfast, dinner & supper is like a fair & what with attendance on my adorable Queen I have not one moment for writing or any thing comfortable. I however hope soon to get quiet & I then will write you more fully ... Pray do you never think on me ... In haist, ever your sincere

Emma Hamilton

I have now tonight an assembly of 3 hundred waiting.[23]

Emma was working with Sir William on 'letters of consequence' they urgently needed to send to the British government. Her role was copying, and translating, documents to send with Sir William's dispatches. Evidence of this exists in several documents in Italian and French in her handwriting.

She acted as go-between with secret letters and documents from the Queen for Sir William to send to England. In 1798 he kept a document in Emma's handwriting of the secret and additional articles attached to the peace treaty drawn up between Naples and France.[24]

For the first time Emma mentions fears for their safety: 'God knows were we shall soon be & what will become of us if things go on as they do now.'

Hamilton shared her concerns. In March of the previous year he had been aware of increasing threats to the Kingdom of the Two

Sicilies. On 7 June 1796 he warned Greville: '*I must own to you that I think that Italy is in great danger of being completely plundered and ruin'd unless some unforseen accident should operate in its favour, and that very soon ... what a pity that Italy shou'd be robbed of its finest marbles, pictures & bronzes, which you see what has happen'd at Parma will certainly be the case shou'd the French marauders advance.*'[25]

Early in 1796 General Napoleon Bonaparte, now head of the Army in Italy, won several battles against the Austrians in northern Italy. In July, his wife, Josephine, her son, Eugène, and members of the Bonaparte family joined him in a villa just outside Milan, where they remained during 1797. Napoleon began sending famous Italian paintings back to Paris, including some by Correggio and Michelangelo.

During 1796 the Foreign Secretary, Lord Grenville, advised the Neapolitan Ambassador that Naples should negotiate a peace with France because a neutral Naples was of greater benefit to Britain than one occupied by France. The treaty was signed on 10 October.[26] Naples was to remain neutral and allow no more than four ships to enter her ports belonging to any country that was engaged in hostilities against France.

Acton reported to Hamilton that the King and Queen were anxious that the British fleet should remain in the Mediterranean.

Hamilton replied: '*Allow me, my dear Sir, to speak out freely, and I do not do so as the Minister of Great Britain at this Court, but as an impartial Englishman who from very particular circumstances during a Residence of 32 years in this country, is nearly as much attached to it as his native one, and feels equally for the Prosperity, Honor, and Glory of both.*'[27]

To his personal cost, his future actions were based on this loyalty to both countries.

Early in 1797 he explained his ill health to Banks: '*The constant agitation and fatigue of mind which I have undergone for six years past has injured my health very much, and my stomach and bilious complaints are more severel and frequent.*'[28]

In 1797 Corsica was abandoned by Britain after being occupied since 1793. The Pope signed away Romagna, Bologna and Ferrara to France. Austria ceded Belgium and Lombardy to France. By December 1797 Napoleon was back in Paris planning his Egyptian campaign.

The only good news was that in February the British fleet, commanded by Sir John Jervis, defeated the Spanish at the Battle of Cape St. Vincent, during which Nelson played a pivotal role.

Hamilton began to consider retirement and applied to the government for a pension of £2,000 p.a. although he intended to remain in Naples after giving up his post. This seems a reasonable amount in view of his long service record in Naples when compared to the pension of £1,500 p.a. that the young Lord Hervey had been awarded after being sacked from his post. Lord Grenville replied in January 1798 declaring that the Civil List could not allow the pension Hamilton had applied for as it was 'so much beyond the usual proportion of the retreat of Foreign Ministers to their salary'.[29]

The British government was in the midst of a costly war and was increasingly dependent on private banks for loans to finance the war.

In February 1798 the French Directory gave General Berthier orders to march on Rome. He entered the city unopposed. The Pope was banished into exile and a Roman Republic proclaimed.

The French armies had reached the borders of the Kingdom of the Two Sicilies.

King Ferdinand and Queen Maria Carolina, who had feared assassination during revolutionary uprisings in Naples in 1795, faced the prospect of a French invasion of their territories. Maria Carolina had a foreboding that she might meet the same end as her sister, Marie Antoinette. Her hatred of the French and sworn pledge to have revenge for her sister's murder made her even more reliant on Sir William and Emma.

Sir William poured out his worries in a letter to Greville on 28 March 1798:

It is an age since I heard from you, and indeed I have not wrote often to any of my most intimate friends for these last two years that every moment of my time has been taken up with the King's business and often of the most serious nature particularly at the time of the Evacuation of Corsica. As you are in Council and in high office at Court perhaps you will have known what I was about, I have, now that this Court has thought proper to sign a Peace with the French Republic, but little business to do with it, but Sir Gilbert Elliot,* has left me a numerous Colony of French and Corsican Emigres that give me sufficient employment and, to tell you the truth, teaze my heart out always wanting something and never satisfied with the generous protection and support they receive from the King's bounty. However, as the Peace is made I think I may soon without impropriety ask the King's leave to go home

* Sir Gilbert Elliot, Viceroy of Corsica, later Lord Minto, Ambassador in Vienna, and Governor General of India, 1806-1813.

and give a look to my own affairs, and take some arrangement as to my continuing here which I certainly cannot do on my present income as every expense is increased, and from every Foreigner coming well recommended to my house which is well known all over Europe, I am at double expense of any Foreign Minister here, and, <u>entre nous</u>, the Princes of our own Blood Royal that have visited Naples, and H.R.H. who is with us now and has been here many months, is an additional expence. I will dwell no longer on this disagreeable subject but I am determined not to be any way distressed in my latter days – and indeed I begin to find repose necessary and I shall seek it, but I will not give up what I have until I see clearly what I may expect for my long Service and in which I certainly have spent more than all I have ever received from Government, and my own money too.[30]

Sir William knew his financial situation was precarious and that his future incomes from both the government and his estates in Pembrokeshire were uncertain.

He did not know that the British government was acutely anxious about Napoleon's activities or that he and Emma would be embroiled in desperate circumstances before the end of the year.

CHAPTER 10

Nelson

'What has poor Horatio done, who is so weak, that he above all the rest should be sent to rough it out at sea?'
Captain Maurice Suckling to Nelson's father, 1771

'We shall come together as two persons most sincerely attached to each other in friendship'
Nelson to his uncle Captain Suckling regarding his proposed marriage to Fanny Nisbet, 14 November 1795

'I hope you will be able to give me a frigate, to convey the remains of my body to England'
Nelson to St Vincent, 27 July 1797

HORATIO NELSON WAS born in the parsonage house at Burnham Thorpe in Norfolk on 29 September 1758. His father, Edmund Nelson, had been granted the 'livings' of the rectories at Burnham Thorpe, Burnham Ulph and Burnham Norton through his wife's connections to the powerful Walpole family.*

His mother, Catherine, bore eleven children, three of whom died in infancy, leaving Edmund to care for eight children after her early death. Nelson's elder brothers Maurice and William and his sisters Susanna and Catherine (Kitty) played a large part in his life. Horatio, known as Horace in the family, was only nine years old when his mother died.

Ten days later their maternal grandmother died suddenly. These bereavements deeply affected the young Horace, leading him to crave love and approval throughout his life.

Horatio's first sight and smell of the sea was from the north Norfolk

---

* Nelson's maternal great grandmother's eldest brother was Sir Robert Walpole, first Earl of Orford and first British Prime Minister.

coast three miles away. From Holkham Bay he saw the shipping activity up and down the east coast and in the busy little harbour at Burnham Overy Staithe. These sights surely fired his imagination to visualize a life in the wide world beyond his little village, which he later described as 'lonesome'.

Remarkably, this slender little boy, from inauspicious origins in a backwater Norfolk village, succeeded in rising to the heights of immortality simply by his dogged determination and unquenchable thirst for glory.

Horatio and his brother, William, were sent to school in Norwich and a year later, transferred to boarding school in North Walsham, where Horace remained a fee-paying student until 1771.

His mother's two brothers, Maurice and William Suckling, played a significant part in Horatio's life. Maurice pursued a successful naval career while William worked in the Customs Office in London. In 1771 Horatio heard that Captain Maurice Suckling, a childless widower who had enthralled the children with tales of his adventures at sea, had been recalled to service at sea. He begged his older brother, William, to ask their father if his uncle would to take him to sea. It was not uncommon then for boys of twelve years old or even younger to be admitted into the Navy.

Uncle Maurice was surprised and concerned that it was the delicate Horace, not his stronger brother, William, who wanted to go to sea and wrote: *'What has poor Horace done, who is so weak, that he above all the rest should be sent to rough it out at sea? But let him come, and the first time we go into action a cannon ball may knock off his head and provide for him at once.'*[1]

Despite this seemingly callous response, Captain Suckling cared for Horace as though he was his own son for the first six years of his naval career until he passed his lieutenant's examination in April 1777. Perhaps due to his small stature and slight frame, Horace developed a personality and manner of speech that would instantaneously impress everyone who met him.

Horatio Nelson's momentous naval career began on 24 April 1771, when he joined his uncle's ship, HMS *Raisonable*, a 64 gun 'ship of the line,'* lying off Chatham dockyard.

Captain Suckling arranged for Horace to gain experience as a

---

* A ship large enough and powerful enough to join a line of battle. In the post-Napoleonic era, the phrase 'ship of the line' was shortened to Battleship.

seaman by joining a merchant ship on a trip to the West Indies. In the summer of 1771, just before his thirteenth birthday, Horatio set off for Jamaica in the *Mary Ann*. Horace worked hard 'learning the ropes,' and began to learn the seamen's own language. After an absence of nearly a year, the ship arrived home on 17 July 1772. Horatio rejoined his uncle on the *Triumph*.

To give him further experience, Captain Suckling set him to work as a pilot. This skill in shallow waters later served him well in the West Indies, Aboukir Bay, and those off Copenhagen.

Horatio heard about a forthcoming expedition to explore the possibility of finding an open sea passage from the North Pole to the Pacific Ocean. He persisted until given a place on one of the two expedition ships, the *Carcass*. In August the crews were forced on to the ice to haul the ships towards the open sea. Horatio, now sixteen years old, was given charge of a boat and a crew of twelve. The ships broke through the ice to the open sea on 10 August. After this dangerous mission the *Carcass* arrived home safely.

On 27 October Horatio was bound for the East Indies aboard the *Seahorse*, 24 guns, accompanied by the *Salisbury*, 50 guns, commanded by Commodore Sir Edward Hughes. They sailed from Portsmouth on 19 November 1773 and arrived in Madras the following May. Horatio would be away for almost three years. Two fellow midshipmen, Thomas Troubridge and Thomas Hoare, became his lifelong friends.

The East India Company had been trading in the East Indies for almost two hundred years. Nelson learnt to appreciate the importance of British interests in India, knowledge that later influenced his decisions when searching for Napoleon's Armada in the Mediterranean.

The *Seahorse* sailed back and forth around the entire sub-continent of India. Off Madras and Calcutta illness affected the crew. Two men from the *Seahorse* died and twenty more were carried ashore to hospital.

In March 1775, after two months in Madras, the *Seahorse* set sail to carry the 'Honorable Company's' bullion to Bombay. From there, they made a voyage to the Persian Gulf, protecting a convoy of the Company's ships. The round trip back to Madras lasted five months. After cruising off Madras and at anchor in the Madras Roads for two months, he sailed for a final time to Bombay at the end of October via the port of Trincomalee (now in Sri Lanka) and Goa, reaching Bombay on 19 December 1775.

Horatio now fell seriously ill with malaria, an illness that recurred throughout his life. The climate and terrain around the Indian coast resulted in a high mortality rate among Europeans, including those attached to the Navy.

Concerned about the severity of Nelson's illness, Commodore Hughes arranged his return to England aboard the *Dolphin*. On the journey home, feverish, beset with headaches and vomiting, he fell into a deep depression. However, by the time the Dolphin arrived at Spithead five months later, on 31 August 1776, he had recovered his strength. Horatio took his lieutenant's examination and in April he was appointed second lieutenant of the *Lowestoffe*, 32 guns.

Nelson wrote to his brother, William, a few days later (his first extant letter):

Navy Office, April 14th. 1777

Dear Brother,

I passed my Degree as Master of Art [lieutenant's examination] *on the 9th instant and received my Commission the following day, for a fine Frigate of 32 guns. So I am now left in* [the] *world to shift for myself ... I hope I shall bring credit to myself and friends. Am sorry there is no possibility this time of seeing each other but I hope that time will come in a few years ... shall always be glad to hear from you. Believing me to be, dear Brother, your affectionate brother,*

Horatio Nelson[2]

The *Lowestoffe*, under the command of Captain William Locker, sailed from Spithead on 16 May 1777, escorting a convoy to the West Indies where Nelson remained until 24 November 1780. On the Jamaica station, Nelson formed an enduring relationship with Captain Locker and Admiral Sir Peter Parker, the Commander-in-Chief. On Locker's recommendation, Nelson was transferred to the Admiral's flagship, the *Bristol*, 50 guns. He joined as third lieutenant in July 1778 and rose to first lieutenant by September.

On 1 January 1779, Parker gave Nelson command of his first ship, the brig *Badger*, 14 guns, and by September 1779, Nelson was promoted Post Captain of the *Hinchinbroke*, 28 guns.

Cuthbert Collingwood had followed closely in Nelson's footsteps and the two men became lifelong friends. At the home base of the

Jamaica fleet, Port Royal, Sir Peter and Lady Parker often entertained Nelson and Collingwood at their residence.

In January 1780 Nelson was involved in a disastrous attempt to take Fort San Carlos on Lake Nicaragua. Ordered to transport the army to San Juan, Nelson volunteered himself, some boats and crews, to assist in the land expedition.

The expedition, in the aptly named Mosquito Coast, was overwhelmed by torrential rain and tropical illnesses. Malarial fever and dysentery took a heavy toll on the marines and accompanying sailors. Nelson fell ill but, ordered by Parker to transfer to the *Janus*, he was swiftly taken down river. On arrival, exhausted and feverish, he signed off the *Hinchinbroke* to his successor, Collingwood.

Nelson later reported the horrifying details of the mortality rate: *'of two hundred men, [on board the Hinchinbroke]... one hundred and forty-five were buried in mine and Captain Collingwood's time ... not more than ten survived ...'*[3]

Collingwood reported: ... *'the climate was deadly; no constitution could resist its effects.'* The likely cause of this catastrophic death rate was dengue fever.

Too ill to take up his duties on the *Janus*, Nelson was treated with herbal remedies, probably some form of quinine, and later transferred to the care of the Admiral and his wife. Admiral Parker wrote to the Admiralty: *'Captain Nelson is so emaciated and in so bad a state of health that I doubt whether he will live to get home ... His abilities in his profession would be a loss to this Service.'*[4] He was sent home aboard the *Lion*, reaching Spithead on 24 November.

Discharged on 26 November, Nelson went to Bath to recover. For nine months he was on half-pay, struggling to regain his health. He wrote to Captain Locker in January 1781: *'I have been so ill since I have been here, that I was obliged to be carried to and from bed, with the most excrutiating tortures.'*[5] In February he reported: *'My health, Thank God, is very near perfectly restored ...'* Then, in August 1781, he wrote: *'I was commissioned for the Albermarle; and it would almost be supposed, to try my constitution, was kept the whole winter in the North Sea.'*

The ship returned at the end of December and by the 6 April Nelson was ordered to sail for Cork to join a convoy carrying supplies to the British garrison at Quebec. Here Nelson met Alexander Davison for the first time. Davison was eight years older than the twenty-four-year-old Nelson and had made a fortune in Canada acting as a government agent during the American War of Independence. They became close friends.

In Quebec Nelson imagined himself in love with May Simpson, the daughter of the provost-marshal, but was dissuaded by Davison from proposing to her.

In New York he met Rear-Admiral Samuel Hood. With the American war drawing to a close, Hood was ordered to the West Indies with thirteen ships of the line to protect British interests against the French and Spanish. Impressed with Nelson on first meeting, and aware of his knowledge and experience of the West Indies, he arranged for the *Albermarle* to join his fleet.

The fleet was occupied in checking neutral ships and taking occasional 'prizes'. Prize money was by custom shared by the Admiral and the rest of the fleet. News of the peace treaty arrived in Jamaica in April whereupon Hood and his fleet sailed home.*

During his two years as Captain of the *Albermarle*, Nelson had developed his leadership skills to the extent that when the ship was paid off he reported to Locker that *'the whole ship's company offered, if I could get a Ship, to enter for her immediately'*.

Again reduced to half pay, he spent July in London where his illness recurred, before going home to Burnham Thorpe in August 1783. It was twelve years since he had left home as a young boy.

In April 1784, twenty-five years old, he was appointed to the *Boreas*, 28 guns, and ordered to the Leeward Islands station in the West Indies, remaining there for three and a half years. English Harbour in Antigua was the home port, but his most frequent ports of call were St. Kitts and Nevis.

Nelson became involved in several difficult situations. He took a stance against American trading vessels, believing them a threat to British interests. After seizing four American ships he reported, *'writs were taken out against me for £4,000.'* Feelings ran high and he risked arrest if he stepped ashore.

Nelson sent a memorial to the King in June, explaining his position: *'Your Majesty's proclamation prohibiting all Trade with America, to and from the West Indies'* was being *'most shamefully evaded'*[6] by American vessels. In September Lord Sydney replied, *'signifying his Majesty's approbation of my conduct, and orders for the Crown Lawyers to defend me*

---

* In 1783 the United States and Britain signed the Treaty of Paris to end the American War of Independence.

at his expense from all Civil prosecutions'. Claims against him were still being made several years later.

Nelson's only friends on shore were the Commissioner of the Navy, John Moutray and his much younger wife, Mary, at English Harbour. The Moutrays had arrived there as passengers on board Cuthbert Collingwood's ship. Collingwood and Nelson idolized Mary, spending many happy hours at the Moutray's home, Windsor. When the Commissioner's poor health obliged them to return to England Nelson was desolate. In May 1785 he confessed to William: *'This country appears now intolerable, my dear friend being absent. It is barren indeed ... English Harbour I hate the sight of, and Windsor I detest. I once went up the Hill to look at the spot where I spent more happy days than in any one spot in the world ... all was melancholy: the road is covered with thistles; let them grow. I shall never pull one of them up. By this time I hope she is safe in Old England ...'*[7]

Depressed and lonely, Nelson met Frances (Fanny) Nisbet, a young widow who lived with her uncle, Mr Herbert, the President of Nevis, a widower with one daughter, Martha.

On Nelson's third visit to Herbert's charming plantation house, Montpelier, after being shown into the house by a servant, he found Fanny's five-year-old Josiah playing on the floor. The President explained his astonishment: *'Good God, if I did not find that great little man of whom everyone is so afraid, playing in the next room, under the dining table with Mrs. Nisbet's child.'*[8]

Fanny was the daughter of William Woolward, Senior Judge of Nevis, and his wife, Mary, the brother of the President of Nevis. Her mother died when Fanny was two years old and her father died soon after her marriage to his doctor, Josiah Nesbit, in 1779.

Owing to Dr Nesbit's ill health, the newly married couple returned to England where their son, Josiah, was born eleven months later in Salisbury. Within eighteen months the doctor died intestate, leaving Fanny destitute. She appealed for help from her uncle, Herbert, and was invited to return to Nevis and live in his home to act as his hostess. Fanny had been a widow for four years when she and Nelson met. They were both twenty-six years old.

Within weeks Nelson decided that he wanted to marry her. Fanny was cultured and intelligent, but their relationship lacked passion. Nelson writes of his *'love and esteem'* and *'regard'* for her and Fanny seems rather reluctant to consider him a suitable husband.

Throughout his life, Nelson put his ambition for recognition before his desire for wealth. He had amassed very little fortune in the West Indies and was thus obliged to ask his uncle, William Suckling, and Fanny's uncle, Herbert, for financial assistance towards the marriage. He wrote to Fanny:

Boreas, *English Harbour, 11 th. September*

My greatest wish is to be united to you; and the foundation of all conjugal happiness, real love and esteem, is, I trust, what you believe I possess in the strongest degree towards you ... I declare solemnly, that did I not conceive I had the full possession of your heart, no consideration should make me accept your hand. We know that riches do not always insure happiness ... only of this truth be convinced, that I am, your affectionate

Horatio Nelson

P.S. Do I ask too much, when I venture to hope for a line? or otherwise I may venture to suppose my letters may be looked on as troublesome.[9]

He was away in English Harbour for three months (August to October, the hurricane season) but received no letters from Fanny in all that time. However, he persevered. His main concern was how to keep Fanny in the style of life to which she was accustomed in Nevis. Swallowing his pride, he wrote to his uncle, William Suckling:

Boreas, *Nevis, November 14th., 1785*

My dear Sir,

My present attachment is of pretty longstanding; but I was determined to be fixed before I broke this matter to any person. The lady is a Mrs Nisbet, widow of a Dr. Nisbet, who died eighteen months after her marriage, and has left her with a son ... she has been brought up by her mother's brother, Mr. Herbert, President of Nevis ... Her age is twenty-two [actually twenty-six] and ... her mental accomplishments are superior to most people's of either sex; and we shall come together as two persons most sincerely attached to each other from friendship.

... Herbert is very rich and very proud, – he has only one daughter, and this niece, who he looks upon in the same light, if not higher. I have lived at his house, when at Nevis, since June last, and am a great favourite of his. I have told him I am as poor as Job; but he tells me he likes me, and I am descended from a good family ... but he also says ... I can't do much in my lifetime; when I die she shall have twenty thousand pounds; and if my daughter dies before me, she shall possess the major part of my property ...

Thus circumstanced, who can I apply to you but you? ... My future happiness, I give you my honour, is now in your power ... I think Herbert *will be brought to give her two or three hundred a year during his life; and if you will either <u>give me</u> either one hundred a year, for a few years, or a thousand pounds, how happy you will make a couple who will pray for you for ever. Don't disappoint me, or my heart will break …*

Your most affectionate

Horatio Nelson[10]

Nelson was naïve to believe in Herbert's promises, for when he died in 1783, he left Fanny not £20,000, but a mere £4,000.

Nelson told Fanny: *'From my uncle Suckling I have a very kind letter, saying he will do everything in his power to add to my happiness; and if I should want it, that he will give me pecunicary assistance.'*[11]

Fanny seldom wrote to him. In April 1786 he wrote to her from Carlisle Bay:

'My dearest Fanny, I have been looking out anxiously for some time past … making sure of the pleasure of receiving a letter – but it is not to happen …[12]

And on 4 March 1787, *'Never was a poor mortal more disappointed at not receiving a letter.'*[13]

However, Fanny did write suggesting that he stop seizing the American ships attempting to trade with the islands. It was the first warning signal of her timid attitude towards his actions at sea which he found exasperating. He reprimanded her:

Boreas, May 4 th. 1786, Barberous Island

My dearest Fanny,

Had I taken your advice and not seized any Americas, I should now have been with you: but I should have neglected my duty … Duty is the great business of a Sea-officer. All private considerations must give way to it, however painful it is …

Ever with the greatest affection, your

Horatio Nelson[14]

Between May and August the *Boreas* was mainly anchored at Nevis. Spending time together gave their relationship a chance to flourish. In August the *Boreas* sailed to English Harbour for a three months' refit.

A letter from Fanny surprised and delighted him:

Boreas, English Harbour [August 1786]

My dearest Fanny,

What can I say? Nothing, if I speak of the pleasure I felt at receiving your kind and affectionate letter, my thoughts are too big for utterance …[15]

Nevertheless, after fourteen months he still only described his feelings for Fanny as *'esteem and regard'* to William Suckling:

Nevis, July 5th. 1786

I wish I could tell you I was well, but I am far from it. My activity of mind is too much for my puny constitution. I am worn to a skeleton ... you will think it odd if I do not mention Mrs. Nisbet: I can only assure you, that her heart is equal to her head ... My affection for her is fixed upon that solid basis of esteem and regard ...16

And at last, more passionately to Fanny:

Boreas, English Harbour, August 19th. 1786

My dearest Fanny,

My heart yearns to you – it is with you; my mind dwells on nought else but you. Absent from you, I feel no pleasure: it is you, my dearest Fanny, who are everything to me. Without you, I care not for this world; for I have found lately nothing in it but vexation and trouble ... I am alone in the Commanding Officer's house, while my ship is fitting, and from sunset until bed-time I have not a human creature to speak to ... The moment old Boreas is habitable in my cabin, I shall fly to it, to avoid mosquitos and melancholies. Hundreds of the former are now devouring me through all my clothes ...17

Lonely, depressed, plagued by mosquitoes and still anxious about the American ships, Nelson longed to be with Fanny at Nevis.

At the end of 1786 Prince William Henry,* third son of George III, arrived in command of the frigate *Pegasus*. The two men had met in New York in 1782 aboard Admiral Lord Hood's ship, *Barfleur*. The Prince described Nelson's impact on him: *'I was then a Midshipman on board the* Barfleur... *when Captain Nelson of the* Albermarle, *came with his barge alongside, who appeared to be the merest boy of a Captain I ever beheld; and his dress was worthy of attention. He had on a full laced uniform; his lank unpowdered hair was tied in a stiff Hessian tail, of an extraordinary length; the old fashioned flaps of his waistcoat added to the general quaintness of his figure, and produced an appearance which particularly attracted my notice; for I had never seen anything like it before ... My doubts were, however, removed when Lord Hood introduced me to him. There was something irresistibly pleasing in his address and conversation ... that showed he was no common being.'18*

Now, four years later, Nelson was the Prince's commanding officer. They formed a mutually respectful relationship. Nelson described the Prince as *'... a gallant man ... volatile, but always with great good nature'.19*

* The future Duke of Clarence and King William 1V

In his dealings with the Prince, Nelson somehow incurred the displeasure of King George and never regained his favour, despite the spectacular battles he fought and won. The King's attitude can be partly attributed to his mental instability.

In January 1787, looking forward to his wedding, Nelson wrote affectionately to Fanny:

Boreas, *January 13 1787*

I wish I had a fortune to settle on you but I trust I have a good name ... You can marry me only from a sincere affection therefore I ought to make you a good husband and I hope it will turn out that I shall ... you are never absent from my mind in any place or company ... be assured that I am my dearest Fanny ever your most affectionate Horatio Nelson.[20]

Prince William attended their wedding at Herbert's mansion, Montpelier, on 11 March 1787, but reported to Lord Hood: '*Nelson introduced me to his bride ... a pretty and sensible woman and may have a good deal of money if her uncle Mr. Herbert thinks proper. Poor Nelson is head over heels in love ... However, he is more in need of a nurse than a wife. I do not really think he can live long ... I had my Lord the honour of giving her away. He is now in for it. I wish him well and happy and that he may not repent the step he has taken.'* [21]

Nelson wrote to Captain Locker on 21 March: '*I am married to an amiable woman, that far makes amends for everything: indeed till I married her I never knew happiness. And I am morally certain she will continue to make me a happy man for the rest of my days.'*

After one week's honeymoon Nelson was back on duty. On 25 May he sailed from Nevis for the last time to Antigua to make final preparations on board the *Boreas* for the return journey to England.

He returned home in extremely poor health. Fanny chose to sail home on board a merchant ship accompanied by her son, Josiah, uncle Herbert and his daughter, Martha.

The *Boreas* set sail on 4 June, crossed the Atlantic in good weather, arriving at Spithead on 5 July 1787. Nelson then remained ashore, on half-pay, for five and a half frustrating long years.

Nelson and Fanny spent their first Christmas in London with her uncle Herbert at the house he had taken at 5 Cavendish Square. The cold winter and London smog soon affected Fanny. Nelson's brother, William, found a school for Josiah in Norfolk. Nelson wrote to William regarding Josiah:

6 Princes Street, Cavendish Square
January 3rd. 1788

My dear Brother,

I am assured … you will not allow him to do as he pleases; it's mistaken kindness where it happens. I wish him at school to have the same weekly allowance as other boys, and whatever else may be proper for him …

Horatio Nelson [22]

Nelson needed to recuperate from three and a half years' service in the West Indies and he and Fanny went to Bath. He wrote to his old friend Captain Locker, in Kensington:

Bath January 27th. 1788

My dear Sir,

I fear we must at present give [up] all thoughts of living so near London, for Mrs. Nelson's lungs are so much affected by the smoke in London, that I cannot think of placing her in that situation …[23]

He told Locker that he still received claims for damages from American ship owners.

In January Prince William Henry invited Nelson to spend a few days on board his ship *Pegasus*, moored in Plymouth. Nelson reported to Locker: *'I returned from Plymouth three days ago, and found Prince William everything I could wish – respected by all.'*

After three months in Bath, a holiday in Exmouth, and another visit to London in June, Nelson and Fanny travelled to Burnham Thorpe, remaining there for the next five years. Short of money, they were obliged to live with Nelson's father in the parsonage. During this period Nelson *'employed himself with considerable zeal in cultivating his father's garden … he would there often spend the greater part of the day, and dig, as it were, for the purpose of being wearied … when his eyes would admit of It … studying charts, and in writing, or drawing plans.'[24]*

Nelson's half-pay was only £106 p.a. Uncle Suckling gave him £100 p.a. to help out and Uncle Herbert was expected to give Fanny £100 p.a.

Edmund Nelson moved into a cottage at his nearby parish in Burnham Ulf in 1790 to give them some privacy. With Josiah away at school, Fanny had little to occupy her apart from needlework and painting watercolours. Servants were employed both inside and outside the house. It seems from Edmund's letters, that Fanny failed to adapt to Norfolk life, being more used to the climate and the luxury of her uncle's home in the West Indies.

Lonely, often ill, and tied with such a modest income, Fanny regularly retired to her bed for several days. Although Edmund wrote *'she does not openly complain'*, she was clearly unhappy in the bleak Norfolk village.

There were occasional visits to Nelson's relatives, William and Sarah Nelson at Hilborough, Catherine (Kitty) and George Matcham at Barton Hall and Susanna and Thomas Bolton near Norwich. Once a year they visited Lord Walpole at Wolterton, and occasionally visited Mr. Coke at Holkham Hall.[25]

Nelson was desperate to return to naval action.

To Philip Stevens at the Admiralty he wrote:

Barton, near Norwich, Norfolk. August 8th. 1788

Sir,

Having seen by the Gazette a new Board of Admiralty is appointed ... you will be pleased to assure their Lordships of my readiness to serve whenever they may think proper to call for my services. I am, Sir,&c

Horatio Nelson[26]

On 26 August Nelson told Fanny: *'I saw Lord Hood this morning ... He assured me, that ... should any Hostilities take place, I need not fear having a good Ship.'*[27]

At the time he felt that *'There was a prejudice at the Admiralty evidently against me, which I can neither guess at, or in the least account for.'*

Nelson told Prince William that he had *'been disappointed in all my applications'* to Lord Chatham for a ship. The Prince replied expressing his displeasure at Lord Chatham's treatment of him, adding *'should matters between the Countries* [on the continent] *grow serious, you must be employed. Never be alarmed, I will always stand your friend.'*[28]

The Prince, now Duke of Clarence, and Nelson continued to correspond until Nelson's death.

When the Bastille was stormed in Paris on 14 July 1789 Nelson wrote to Locker: *'Is there any idea of our being drawn into a quarrel by these commotions on the Continent?'*[29]

Nelson's hopes of having a child with Fanny faded over the years. He desperately wanted children, but only once admitted his disappointment. In *Sketch of my Life* he wrote: *'In March of this year* [1787] *I married Frances Herbert Nisbet, widow of Dr. Nisbet, of the Island of Nevis; by whom I have no children.'*

His brother, William and sisters Susanna and Kitty, had numerous children between them: William and Sarah had Charlotte and Horatio; his elder sister, Susanna, and Thomas Bolton had six children; his younger sister, Kitty, and George Matcham went on to have fifteen children, four of whom died young. Nelson must have felt his own disappointment keenly.

He was further disappointed when Fanny's Uncle Herbert died in Nevis on 18 January 1793. Their expectations of a *'good deal of money if her uncle thinks proper'* were not to be realised. When Herbert's will was proved in London on 23 March 1793 it contained legacies to members of the family, other than his daughter, Martha. Fanny was not the special favourite Nelson had believed her to be. Before their marriage Nelson had been led to expect a legacy of £20,000 to Fanny and £1,000 to Josiah.

However, Herbert's will states:

'whereas I have hitherto allowed my Neice Frances, the wife of Horatio Nelson also a Captain in his Majesty's Navy the yearly sum of one hundred pounds to and for her own use and benefit and may continue to allow the same during the Term of my natural life after which it is my intention that such an annuity shall cease and instead thereof I give and bequeath unto my said Neice Frances Nelson the sum of THREE THOUSAND POUNDS [author's capitals]... *to be paid within the space of six years next after my death ...'*

A codicil dated 1792 added: *'I give and bequeath to my neice Frances Nelson ONE THOUSAND POUNDS.'* This was to be added to the first bequest. Fanny received £4,000 in total.

Josiah received *'the Sum of FIVE HUNDRED POUNDS to be paid when he is 21 years, with interest paid 5%pa'*, less than he expected.

It emerged that John Herbert had been involved in a long-term relationship with a *'free Mulatto woman named Maria'* by whom he had two sons.

Maria received an annuity of £200 p.a. during the term of her natural life and his sons, John Herbert, in Bristol, received £2,500 and Thomas Herbert of Nevis, received £300. In addition, Sarah Kelly, a niece living in Plymouth, received £2,500. His daughter, Martha, received the *'rents profits and produce'* of his estates and *'all my silverplate, silver utensils, household goods and furniture'*.[30]

On 6 January 1793, Nelson met Lord Chatham in London and was promised his first command of a ship of the line. He wrote joyfully to Fanny:

London 7th. January 1793

Lord Chatham yesterday made many apologies for not having given me a Ship before this time, and said, that if I chose to take a Sixty-four to begin with, I should be appointed to one as soon as she was ready; and that I should as soon as in his power be removed to a Seventy-four... Love to Josiah and believe me

> *Your most affectionate*
> *Horatio Nelson*[31]

His frustration and boredom *'on the beach'* would soon be over.

Seventeen days later the *'commotions on the continent'* took a dramatic turn when King Louis XVI was executed. On 1 February France declared war on England and Holland. Nelson had been appointed to command the *Agamemnon*, 64 guns, which was being prepared for action. She became his favourite ship – 'Agamemnon *sails admirably; we think better than any Ship in the Fleet.'*

There was now the option for Josiah, aged thirteen, to go to sea instead of studying law. Nelson left the decision to Fanny. Taking Herbert's legacies into account, Nelson wrote to Fanny:

> [London] *March 12th. 1793*

My dear Fanny,

Mr. Suckling thinks that it would take our whole income to keep him at the Temple and I suppose we must think of some other walk of life for him. My objection to the Navy now he will be certain of a small fortune is in some measure done away. You must think of this. Would you like to bring him up with you? For if he is to go, he must go with me ... Think about Josiah ...

> *God bless you, yours affectionately*
> *H. Nelson*[32]

Fanny might have felt she had no option, considering their financial position, but to send Josiah to sea with Nelson.

With his appointment to the *Agamemnon*, Nelson reverted to full pay of £245 p.a.* On 15 March, Nelson wrote from Chatham: *' I never was in better health; and I hope you intend a new lease of your life; the not tying up any of the money left you, I consider as a confidence reposed in me, and I shall take care it is not displaced.'*[33]

Nelson and Josiah were established on board *Agamemnon* on 4 April. Nelson told Fanny that he would be going with Lord Hood's fleet to the Mediterranean. Irritated by Fanny's poor packing of his personal effects, he informed her before his departure:

---

* £18.18.0 per 28 day month for the Captain of a 3rd. Rate ship.

'*You forgot to send my things from Mr. Thomas's by the Sheerness boat …I have got a hamper of 3 hams, a breast of bacon, and a face, not being very well packed … the motion of the wagon has rubbed them very much. However, they will do …* 34 And later: *the key of my drawers to the bureau is not come …*'

He urged her to reply to letters from his sisters and to write to his father. When Fanny heard that Nelson would be leaving from Portsmouth, she went to stay with the Matchams, now living at Ringwood in Hampshire.

Nelson wrote from Spithead on 29 April: '*if you and my sister wish to come* [to Portsmouth] *I shall be glad to see you, but do as you like …*' 35

And from Spithead on 6 May: '*I arrived here last night* [after a short cruise to the French coast] *and rather expected to have seen you here … Shall be glad to see you when convenient to Mr. Matcham …*'36

His brief note on 11 May (after he sailed) indicates that Fanny and the Matchams did finally arrive to say goodbye:

St. Helens. Noon Saturday [May 11th. 1793]

My dear Fanny,

I hope you all got home safe you had a fine day. We got out here with the squadron last night and sail at 4 o'clock this afternoon. You shall hear by every opportunity from me. God bless you believe me your most affectionate

Horatio Nelson

He added: *Josiah is in high spirits. You may write to my father that we are gone and pray write Mrs Bolton. I write the names* [of the squadron] *that you may know when any of us come into port. Britannia, Courageux, Colossus, Fortitude, Agamemnon, Lowestoffe, Meleager.*37

Written as Nelson left to fight a war, this letter (devoid of any declarations of love or hopes that he might safely return) indicates that he was not too upset at leaving her.

Nelson and Fanny did not meet again for four years and four months.

Nelson may have already begun to regret his marriage. He was a man of action who sought recognition and glory first and foremost, but longed for a happy home, with children, and the companionship of a wife.

The lack of international wars had denied him the chance of action and Fanny had disappointed his other hopes. By the time he sailed on the *Agamemnon* it seems his marriage to Fanny was simply an affectionate friendship.

During their long separation Fanny lived in Bath with her father-in-law, Edmund, who had taken a house there. She wrote regularly to her husband.

During this long and arduous period of uninterrupted service there were three significant events in which Nelson played a major part: the taking of Corsica from the French, the Battle of Cape St. Vincent off the coast of Spain and the disastrous attack on Santa Cruz on the island of Tenerife.

He wrote to Fanny once or twice a month. One letter written while he was off Toulon on 4 August was unusually affectionate: *'How I long to have a letter from you: next to being with you, it is the greatest pleasure I can receive. The being united to such a good woman, I look back to the happiest period of my life.'*[38]

Three weeks later he wrote to his father:

August 20th off Toulon

My dear Father,

The affairs of France in this Country are worse than ever: the Guillotine is every day employed. A Master of a Ship, whom we spoke from Marseilles, says, there are only two descriptions of people in France – the one drunk and mad; the other, with horror painted in their faces, are absolutely starving; yet nothing brings them to their senses. A Peace with England is what they wish for ... Believe me,

Your most dutiful Son

Horatio Nelson[39]

Lord Hood sent Nelson to Naples to obtain Neapolitan troops. Nelson wrote to Fanny from Naples on 14 September 1793 describing his first meeting with Sir William and Emma Hamilton: *Lady Hamilton has been wonderfully kind and good to Josiah. She is a young woman of amiable manners and who does honour to the station to which she is raised. I am to carry Lord Hood six thousand troops from hence. Remember me to my dear Father, also to Lord and Lady Walpole. Believe me, your most affectionate Husband,*

Horatio Nelson[40]

Lord Hood kept Nelson busy. On 24 September Nelson wrote to his brother, William: *'My dear Brother, I have really been so actively employed, that I have not had time to think of writing letters except to my wife ... my Ship's company are worn out with fatigue. Since the 23rd. April to this day, we have only been twenty days at anchor ...'*[41]

Fanny was anxious about her husband and son. Nelson reassured her: *'I was indeed truly sorry to hear you were not perfectly well. Why should you alarm yourself? I am well, your son is well, and we are as comfortable in every respect as the nature of our service will admit.'*[42]

After the fall of Toulon it became imperative to establish an alternative base for the British fleet in the Mediterranean. Nelson told Fanny on 7 February 1795: *'After the evacuation of Toulon we had no place whatever of our own for the fleet to anchor in.'*[43]

To this end in January 1794 the British forces helped the Corsicans expel the French from the island's forts. In February Hood determined to take Bastia with the naval force only, giving the command of the seamen employed in the batteries to Nelson. In March, during the siege of Bastia, Nelson wrote to Sir William Hamilton informing him of the situation, adding: *'I beg leave to present my most respectful compliments to Lady Hamilton, as does my youngster. I assure you and her Ladyship that I remember with gratitude both your kindnesses to a stranger.'*[44]

Fanny was kept informed of the progress in the attack on Bastia:

April 22nd. 1794 – I have great reason, my dearest Fanny, to be thankful to that Being, who has ever protected me in a most wonderful manner, and in none more so than in my landing here ... it is very hard for my poor seamen, dragging guns up such heights as are scarcely credible ...[45]

By 1 May he was elated at the approaching victory:

My dear Fanny,

I need not, I am certain, say that all my joy is placed in you, I have none separated from you; you are present to my imagination be where I will. I am convinced you feel interested in every action of my life ... Only recollect that a brave man dies but once, a coward all his life long. We cannot escape death; and should it happen to me in this place, remember, it is the will of Him, in whose hands are the issues of life and death ...

Having thus alarmed her, he went on: *'As to my health, it was never better, seldom so well. I have no fears for the Expedition – It will be victory, Bastia will be ours.*[46]

Bastia surrendered on 24 May 1794.

By 20 June, the siege of Calvi had begun. Nelson told Hood: *'the mountain we have to drag the guns up so long and so steep, that the whole of yesterday we were only able to get one gun up, and then we have one mile and a half to drag them ...'*[47]

The *Agamemnon* crews camped on the shore near Calvi. Batteries attacked enemy positions whereupon *'the bastions of the Town opened their fire upon us'*. On 12 July he informed Hood: *'I got a little hurt this morning; not much as you may judge from my writing.'*[48] Stones and gravel flying up from an enemy shot had damaged his right eye.

On 13 July he wrote: *'My eye is better, and I hope not entirely to lose the sight'*,[49] and the next day reported that he was well, *'except my being half blinded by these fellows'*.

On 16 July he wrote to his uncle William Suckling: *'You will be surprised when I say I was wounded in the head by stones from the merlon of our battery. My right eye is cut entirely down; but the Surgeons flatter me I shall not entirely lose my sight of that eye. At present I can distinguish light and dark, but no object... I feel the want of it; but such is the chance of War, it was within a hair's breadth of taking off my head.'*[50]

He made light of his injury in a letter to Fanny on 4 August.

On 10 August, the enemy surrendered.

On arriving at Leghorn he confessed to Fanny:

Off Leghorn   August 18 1794

As it is all past, I may now tell you, that on the 10th July a shot, having hit our battery, the splinters and stones from it struck me with great violence in the face and breast. Although the blow was so severe as to occasion a great flow of blood from my head, yet I most fortunately escaped, having only my right eye nearly deprived of its sight: it was cut down, but is so far recovered, as for me to be able to distinguish light from darkness. As to all the purposes of use, it is gone; however, the blemish is nothing, not to be perceived, unless told ...[51]

The *Agamemnon* remained at Leghorn for one month, undergoing essential repairs.

Nelson, worn out and in pain, lived ashore. He began a relationship with Adelaide Correglia, an opera singer, seeing her whenever the *Agamemnon* was in port over the next two years. Correglia was a useful source of information. He told Sir Gilbert Elliot: '... *one old lady tells me all she knows, which is what we wish.'*

Despite the convention that marriage vows were not respected while serving abroad, some of Nelson's officers were unhappy about his affair. Thomas Freemantle recorded in his diary the following summer: *'Dined with Nelson. Dolly aboard ... he makes himself ridiculous with that woman.'*[52]

Nelson wrote to Hood in October requesting *'that your Lordship will take such measures as you may judge proper that my Sovereign may be informed of my loss of an eye in His Service'*,[53] enclosing two certificates from the Physician to the Fleet and the Surgeon to the Forces. Nelson was awarded an annual pension for his loss.

On 12 October Nelson told Fanny: *'Lord Hood left us yesterday; therefore our hopes of my going Home at present are at an end; however, we must not repine ... I hope you spend the winter cheerfully ...'*[54]

Nelson was impatient with Fanny's repeatedly expressed anxiety. On 31 October, he wrote: *'why you should be so uneasy about me, so as to make yourself ill, I know not ... as to my health, I don't know that I was ever so truly well: I fancy myself grown quite stout ...'*[55]

In January 1795 Nelson wrote: *'much as I shall regret being so long parted from you, still we must look beyond the present day, and two or three more months may make the difference of every comfort, or otherwise, in our income. I hope we have many happy years to live together ...'*[56]

It was more than two years before Fanny saw Nelson again.

Later in January Nelson told her: *'My eye is grown worse, and is in almost total darkness, and very painful at times; but never mind, I can see very well with the other.'*[57]

During 1795 and 1796 Nelson was kept busy in the Gulf of Genoa, when not in a *'general chase of the French fleet'* off Toulon and North Corsica.

His chance of glorious action improved when the highly regarded Admiral Sir John Jervis, the new Commander-in-Chief, arrived. They met on board *Victory*, 100 guns, on 19 January 1796 and formed an immediate rapport. Jervis was impressed with Nelson's assessment of the state of the war in the Mediterranean, his energy and his confidence. Nelson, to his joy, found Sir John *'determined to be active'*.

In April, Nelson was promoted Commodore and on 10 June transferred to the *Captain*, 74 guns. Jervis had used his influence with Lord Spencer, First Lord of the Admiralty, on Nelson's behalf.

In May, he wrote to Fanny: *'It is three years this day that I sailed from Spithead. I believe no person in England would have supposed any ship could have been kept so long abroad or that the war would have lasted.'*[58]

In a letter to her in a letter On 29 May 1796 he commented to her: *'The Dukes of Parma and of Modena have both made treaties with the French, paying large sums of money; and, in their treaties it is specified, that certain pictures are to be delivered, to be sent to Paris. The Palace of the Louvre is to have the finest gallery in the world ...'*[59]

This plundering of Italy's artworks was a grave concern to Sir William Hamilton. He wrote to Greville in June 1796: *'Italy is in great danger of being completely plundered and ruin'd ... what a pity that Italy should be robbed of its finest marbles, pictures and bronzes ...'*

Nelson was occasionally affectionate in his letters to Fanny. On 24 April: *'Rest assured, my dearest Fanny, of my unabated and steady affection'* and on 24 October: *'Assure yourself, my dear Fanny, that my sincere love and affection is by no means weakened.'*

Fanny's replies were full of news, but she often complained about her state of mind and health. In September, Nelson responded: *'I grieve to hear such a bad account of yourself. Cheer up, I shall return safe and sound. The busy and active scene is my delight.'*[60]

France and Spain signed a peace treaty on 19 August 1796. Spain declared war on Great Britain on 11 October. The British government sent orders for Jervis and the fleet to withdraw.

Nelson was bitterly disappointed, telling Fanny on 17 October: *'Much as I shall rejoice to see England, I lament our present orders in sack-cloth and ashes, so dishonourable to the dignity of England, whose Fleets are equal to meet the World in arms; and of all the Fleets I ever saw, I never beheld one in point of officers and men to equal Sir John Jervis's, who is a Commander-in-Chief able to lead them to glory.'*[61]

From October to January 1797 Nelson was engaged in evacuating troops from Bastia Bay, San Fiorenzo Bay and Corsica. All were convoyed to Gibraltar.

He left Gibraltar on 12 February to rejoin Jervis's fleet somewhere between Gibraltar and Cadiz. During one dark and foggy night he found his ship amongst several large Spanish ships. Unnoticed, they sailed quietly through and found Jervis the following day off Cape St. Vincent.

Nelson reported the approaching Spanish fleet to Jervis, who gave orders to prepare for battle. Nelson, who had temporarily been aboard *La Minerve*, 38 guns, transferred back to his own ship, the *Captain*.

The next morning, 14 February, the Spanish fleet appeared over the horizon, an impressive force which included the biggest warship in the world, the *Santissima Trinidad*, 130 guns. When Calder, Captain of the *Victory*, reported to Jervis: *'here are twenty seven sail of the line, Sir John, near double our own!'* Jervis replied: *'Enough, Sir, no more of that, the die is cast and if there are fifty sail of the line, I will go through them.'*[62]

As Nelson had predicted, Jervis was the man to lead them fearlessly into battle.

The British fleet of fifteen sail of the line was heavily outnumbered, but Jervis and Nelson knew that the Spanish ships were undermanned and the crews poorly trained.

The Spanish fleet was sailing in two loose formations. Jervis's plan was to take his fleet in a single line through the middle, separating the two groups. Nelson realized that the Spanish formations were attempting to either join together or to make their escape. Knowing that he was disobeying orders, he ordered Miller, his captain, to haul out of line and to 'take a short cut' to the nearest enemy ships, the tail end of the larger formation that included the *Santissima Trinidad*. Jervis was delighted by his initiative.

After a period of intense battle, when Nelson's ship was so badly damaged that it was incapable of manoeuvre, he ordered Miller to ram the *San Nicholas*, 84 guns, which in turn became entangled with its neighbour the *San Josef*, 112 guns. Nelson and his '*brave fellows*' boarded the *San Nicholas*, secured her surrender and leapt aboard the *San Josef* whose Captain presented Nelson with his sword.* Both Trowbridge and Collingwood had come to his aid. Between them they had taken four ships and severely damaged the *Santissima Trinidad*.

Jervis called off the action at about 5 o'clock in the evening. The remainder of the Spanish fleet ran for port and Jervis withdrew to Lagos. In his account of the battle Nelson reported Jervis's reaction to his efforts: '*the* Victory *passing saluted us with three cheers as did every ship in the fleet. At dusk I went aboard the* Victory, *when the Admiral received me on the quarterdeck and, having embraced me, said he could not sufficiently thank me ...*'[63]

Jervis was created Earl of St. Vincent and awarded a pension of £3,000 a year. Commodore Nelson was invested with the Order of the Bath and in March promoted Rear Admiral of the Blue Squadron. At thirty-eight years old he had finally fulfilled his ambition for recognition and honour.

After the battle Nelson transferred to the *Irresistible*, 74 guns, sending Fanny a brief note on 16 March: '*I am most perfectly well and rich in honour as is Josiah and Hoste. It would not be right to attempt detailing the action as it will come from a much better pen than mine.*'[64]

The official dispatch from Jervis arrived in England on 3 March. It made no mention of Nelson's individual achievements, but in a private letter to the Admiralty Jervis singled out Nelson for praise, along with Troubridge and Collingwood. Nelson wrote his own account of the battle to ensure that his significant part was recognized. It was signed

---

* The fleet awarded this audacious action the famous title- 'Nelson's Patent Bridge for boarding First-Rates'.

and authenticated by Captains Miller and Berry. He sent copies to the Duke of Clarence and Locker, to whom he wrote: '*I send you a short Detail of the transactions of the Captain; and if you approve of it, are at prefect liberty to insert in the newspapers.*'

Fanny would have been aware of her husband's heroism, but she wrote to him with little enthusiasm from Bath on 11 March:

My dearest husband,

Yesterday I received your letter of February 16th., thank God you are well and Josiah. My anxiety was far beyond my powers of expression ... She went on, '*You were universally the subject of conversation*' and that she had heard his '*conduct was above praise*'. She continued with news of Nelson's family and her house-hunting efforts. Without adding any congratulations of her own she remarked: '*I shall not be myself till I hear from you again. What can I attempt to say to you about boarding. You have been most wonderfully protected. You have done desperate actions enough. Now may I, indeed I do beg, that you never board again leave it for the Captains.*'[65]

She repeated her fears for his safety on 20 March: '*I sincerely hope, my dear husband, that all these wonderful and desperate actions – such as boarding Ships – you will leave to others. With the protection of a Supreme Being, you have acquired a character, or name, which all hands agree cannot be greater: therefore rest satisfied ...*'[66]

Nelson received the recognition he craved from all directions, including the King, the Admiralty, Jervis, and Hood. But Fanny woefully failed to understand her husband's over-riding need for action, success and glory.

Unaware of Fanny's reactions Nelson wrote:

Irresistible, Lisbon. February 28th. 1797

My dearest Fanny,

We got up here with our prizes this afternoon. The more I think of our late action the more I am astonished. It absolutely appears a dream. The Santissima Trinidada of four decks lost 500 killed and wounded. Had not Captain been so cut up I would have had her but it is well ... As to myself I assure you I never was better and rich in the praises of every man from the highest to the lowest in the fleet ...[67]

If Nelson was disappointed by Fanny's lack of praise he made no mention of it.

Fanny learnt of their improved financial situation on 14 March. Nelson calculated that his Flag pay and £400 marine pay added to

£1,472 with his agents, Marsh and Creed, amounted to £2,304. He estimated prize money due of not less than £5,000. His pay as Rear Admiral had increased to £638 p.a. and with this came a greater share of prize money. He wrote: *'you will now know how far you can go and that £2,000 can be spared for a home. We cannot be vagabonds any longer.'*

Although Nelson often told Fanny that he would soon be home, he did not apply for leave nor was he recalled.

After four months blockading Cadiz and escorting troops withdrawn from Elba to Gibraltar he joined the *Theseus*, 74 guns, in May and on 14 July set off on a disastrous venture, telling Fanny: *'You must not expect to hear very soon from me as I am going on a little cruise ...'*

Jervis, now Earl of St. Vincent, and Nelson had heard that Spanish merchant ships laden with Mexican silver were on their way to Santa Cruz, Tenerife. When St. Vincent received intelligence that the Spanish ship, *El Principe d'Asturias,* 112 guns, had reached Santa Cruz he decided to attack. Nelson wrote to St. Vincent with his ideas for such an attack, but pointed out that *'All the risk and responsibility must rest with you'*.

St. Vincent's orders to Nelson were to *'proceed with the utmost expedition ... for taking possession of the Santa Cruz, by a sudden and vigorous assault'*.

Nelson set sail on 15 July with a squadron of eight ships on his first independent expedition. The attack failed largely due to poor intelligence about the Spanish defences and the island's natural defences – the mountainous coastal terrain, the sea currents, surf, and wind – proved insurmountable.

The first assault led by Troubridge on 22 July failed and a second direct attack to the Santa Cruz mole, with Nelson leading the forces himself was a disaster. Captain Bowen of the *Tersichore* was killed; the *Fox* cutter sank with the loss of Lt. Gibson and ninety-seven seamen. Nelson stepped ashore brandishing his sword and was struck by a musket ball above the elbow of his right arm. He fell backwards into the boat, bleeding profusely. Josiah saved his life by using his neckerchief as a tourniquet and ordering the crew to row back to the *Theseus*. Nelson managed to climb aboard unaided, but his arm was immediately amputated high above the elbow.

Troubridge and Captain Hood agreed generous terms with Don Gutierrez, the Spanish governor. The British were allowed to sail away, having agreed to no further attacks on the town.

The passage back to Cadiz took three weeks. Nelson was given opium every night to kill the pain. St. Vincent wrote to Fanny:'*He is wounded but not dangerously so ...*'

On 27 July Nelson wrote to St. Vincent, the first letter written with his left hand:

My dear Sir, I am become a burthen to my friends and useless to my Country ... you will perceive my anxiety for the promotion of my son-in-law, Josiah Nisbet. When I leave your command, I become dead to the World ... If from poor Bowen's loss, you think it proper to oblige me, I rest confident that you will do it; the Boy is under obligations to me, but he repaid me by bringing me from the Mole of Santa Cruz.

I hope you will be able to give me a frigate, to convey the remains of my carcass to England. God bless you, my dear Sir, and believe me, your most obliged and faithful,

Horatio Nelson[68]

St. Vincent's reply was kind and encouraging: '*Mortals cannot command success; you and your Companions have certainly deserved It ... I grieve for the loss of your arm, and for the fate of poor Bowen and Gibson, with the other brave men who fell so gallantly.*'[69]

He made Josiah Captain of the *Dolphin* hospital ship.

Nelson played down the loss of his arm to Fanny:

Theseus, at sea, August 3rd. 1797

My dearest Fanny,

I am so confident of your affection, that I feel the pleasure you will receive will be equal, whether my letter is wrote by my right hand or left ... I beg neither you nor my father will think much of this mishap: my mind had long been made up to such an event ...[70]

Exhausted and in pain, Nelson arrived at Spithead aboard the *Seahorse* on 1 September and travelled straight to Bath. His father and Fanny were shocked by his condition. Fanny nursed him devotedly, cleaning his wound and renewing the dressings. Two weeks later they left for London where Nelson sought treatment for his 'stump'. Under the care of a London surgeon, Mr. Cruikshank, his arm healed rapidly. Nelson claimed the expenses and was awarded £135.10.0.

He was invested in the Order of the Bath at St. James' Palace and in November, received the Freedom of the City of London and was presented with a gold box valued at one hundred guineas. He was awarded a pension of £1,000 p.a. for his injuries.

Nelson could now afford to buy his own home. Susanna suggested

'Round Wood', a four-bedroomed house with fifty acres of rich arable land near Ipswich, Suffolk. Nelson completed the purchase for £2,000 on 13 November, but never spent a single night there.

By 11 December he informed Captain Miller: '*I am to have the Vanguard, 74 guns … I am in hopes of joining Lord St. Vincent some time in February …*'

Between Christmas and mid-February 1798, Nelson and Fanny lived in Bath. Nelson took his leave of George III on 14 March. They dined with Lord and Lady Spencer, a great admirer of Nelson. At their first meeting Lady Spencer had written of Nelson:

'*a most uncouth creature … He looks so sickly … and his general appearance was that of an idiot, so much so, that when he spoke, and his wonderful mind broke forth, it was a sort of surprise that riveted my whole attention.*'[71]

This time she reported: '*His attentions to her* [Fanny] *were those of a lover. He … sat by her; apologising to me, by saying he was so little with her, that he would not, voluntarily, lose an instant of her society.*'[72]

Nevertheless Nelson was anxious to return to sea. He joined Captain Edward Berry aboard the *Vanguard* in Portsmouth, hoisted his flag on 29 March, and sailed with a convoy on 9 April after spending fewer than seven months with Fanny.

When he returned, over two years later, their marriage, as far as he was concerned, was over.

CHAPTER 11

Emma and Nelson Reunited after the Battle of the Nile

'Glory is my object and that alone'
Nelson to Fanny, 20 July 1798

'You have now made yourself, my dear Nelson, immortal'
Sir William Hamilton to Nelson, 8 September 1798

*'God, what a victory ! Never, never has there been anything
half so glorious, so compleat.'*
Emma to Nelson, 8 September 1798

IN JANUARY 1798, while Nelson was waiting for the *Vanguard* to complete a refit and assemble a crew, Napoleon had inspected the preparations being made by the French Directory in the Channel ports for an invasion of England.

Napoleon's secretary, Bourrienne, quotes Napoleon in his memoirs: *'I do not want to stay here, there is nothing to do ... I haven't the opportunity for more glory ... It is necessary to go to the Orient. All the great glories come from there ... If the result of an attack on England seems to be doubtful, as I fear, the army of England will become the army of the Orient, and I will go to Egypt.'*[1]

In August 1797 he had written: *'In order to destroy England utterly, we must get possession of Egypt.'*[2]

The British government was unaware that Napoleon had decided an invasion was unlikely to succeed and had abandoned the idea.

Napoleon assembled a Grand Fleet for the conquest of Egypt at Toulon, consisting of 40,000 troops, 300 transports and thirteen ships of the line. The British government knew of this armament, but not its intended destination. Egypt was never seriously considered as a target. It was thought likely to be England, Portugal, Ireland, Naples or Sicily.

After deliberation, the government and the Admiralty decided to send Lord St. Vincent with a British squadron into the Mediterranean. When Nelson joined his fleet off Cadiz on 30 April, St. Vincent wrote to thank Lord Spencer: *'I do assure your Lordship that the arrival of Admiral Nelson has given me new life ... his presence in the Mediterranean is so very essential ...'[3]*

On 2 May St. Vincent received secret orders: *'... the state of affairs rendered it absolutely necessary that the Fleet and Armament at Toulon should be prevented from accomplishing its object.'[4]*

St. Vincent sent Nelson, on board the *Vanguard*, accompanied by the *Orion* (Captain Sir James Saumarez), the *Alexander* (Captain Alexander Ball) and five frigates *'to endeavor to ascertain the real object of preparations being made by the French.'*

Nelson sailed from Gibraltar towards Toulon on 8 May. Napoleon arrived at Toulon on 9 May. The two protagonists were simultaneously taking the stage in the Mediterranean theatre of war, each ignorant of the other's plans. Both Nelson and Napoleon sought 'glory' above all else. Napoleon's aim was to find *'the opportunity for more glory'*. Nelson declared his ambition to Fanny: *'Glory is my object, and that alone.'*

By an extraordinary quirk of fate, Nelson missed the French fleet's departure from Toulon. Nelson's reconnaissance squadron was some distance south of Toulon when a full-blown gale struck, causing immense damage to the ships and the loss of two lives. They were forced to make for Sardinia, arriving on 24 May, the dismasted *Vanguard* having been towed by the *Alexander* for twenty hours. Four days later, with the ships hurriedly repaired, Nelson set sail for Toulon, unaware that the French fleet had departed on 19 May with Napoleon on board the flagship – the towering *L'Orient*, 120 guns.

Further orders had been sent to St. Vincent: *'Having been joined by the Rear Admiral and the Ships above mentioned, your Lordship is to lose no time in detaching from your Fleet a Squadron, consisting of twelve sail of line, and a competent number of Frigates, under the command of some discreet Flag-Officer, into the Mediterranean, with instructions to him to proceed in quest of the said Armament; and on falling in with it, or any other Force belonging to the Enemy, to take or destroy it ...'[5]*

Lord Spencer* wrote privately to St. Vincent: *'... if you determine to send a Detachment, I think it almost unnecessary to suggest to you the propriety of putting it under the command of Sir H. Nelson ...'*

---

* First Lord of the Admiralty and brother of Georgiana, Duchess of Devonshire

Nelson, now Rear Admiral, was the preferred choice to command the squadron.

On 5 June Thomas Masterman Hardy, captain of the 18-gun *Mutine* brig, brought new orders from St. Vincent: Nelson was to rendezvous with Captain Troubridge on board the *Culloden*, with a squadron of ten ships and take command of the entire fleet, now a major fighting force, numbering thirteen ships of the line (all of 74 guns). His captains were to become known as his 'Band of Brothers'.*

Nelson adopted this title from Shakespeare's *Henry V* –

'We few, we happy few, we band of brothers;

For he today that sheds his blood with me

Shall be my brother ...'

His orders were to *'take, sink, burn or destroy'* the French fleet. But first he had to find them. His frantic chase to catch up with the French fleet began.

In May St. Vincent had written to Hamilton promising to aid the threatened Kingdoms, adding a note to Emma: *'... a Knight of superior prowess'* was *'charged with this enterprise, and will soon make his appearance at the head of as gallant a band as ever drew sword or trailed pike.'*[6]

On 17 June, Nelson's squadron anchored in Naples Bay, outside territorial waters because of the peace agreement signed between Naples and France. Nelson sent his second-in-command, Captain Troubridge, ashore to see if Hamilton had any information on sightings of the French fleet. Hamilton had just received Nelson's letter of 12 June:

If the Transfer sloop of war has arrived at Naples you will know that the British fleet is in the Mediterranean and that I have the honour of commanding it ... but I hope we are in good time to save Naples or Sicily from falling into the hands of the Enemy. I beg you will assure the King and Queen of Naples that I will not lose one moment in fighting the French fleet, and that no person can have a more ardent desire of serving them and of fulfilling the orders of the good and great King our Master.

He added: *are the ports of Naples and Sicily open to his Majesty's fleet? Have the Governors orders for our free admission? and for us to be supplied with whatever we want ...?*[7]

Sir John Acton furnished Troubridge with an informal order to all governors of Neapolitan and Sicilian ports to turn a blind eye to British ships taking on water and stores. While Troubridge was ashore, letters were sent out to Nelson from both Sir William and Emma.

* See Appendix 1

On 17 June Nelson received Sir William's first letter and replied:

My dear Sir, your letter by the Boat yesterday did not come to me, but I am just favoured with yours of yesterday. Captain Troubridge will say everything I could put in a ream of paper ... If the Enemy have Malta, it is only as a safe harbour for their Fleet, and Sicily will fall the moment the King's fleet withdraws from the Coast of Sicily: therefore we must have free use of Sicily, to enable us to starve the French in Malta. I need not say more on this very important subject. The King of Naples may now have a part of the glory in destroying these pests of the human race; and the opportunity, once lost may never be regained. God bless you. Depend on my exertions.

I am etc. Horatio Nelson[8]

Emma's letter of 17 June read:

My dear Admiral, – I write in a hurry as Captain T. Carrol stays on Monarch. God bless you, and send you victorious, and that I may see you bring back Buonaparte with you. Pray send Captain Hardy out to us, for I shall have a fever with anxiety. The Queen desires me to say everything that's kind, and bids me say with her whole heart and soul she wishes you victory. God bless you, my dear Sir, I will not say how glad I shall be to see you. Indeed, I cannot describe to you my feelings on your being so near to us. Ever, ever, dear Sir, your affte. and gratefull

Emma Hamilton

Emma sent a second hurried note with a letter from the Queen: 'Dear Sir, I send you a letter I have this moment received from the Queen. Kiss it, and send it back by Bowen, as I am bound not to give any of her letters, Ever yours, Emma.'[9]

Nelson replied:

My dear Lady Hamilton, I have kissed the Queen's letter. Pray say I hope for the honor of kissing her hand when no fears will intervene, assure her Majesty that no person has her felicity more at heart than myself and that the sufferings of her family will be a Tower of Strength on the day of Battle; fear not the event, God is with us. God bless you and Sir William, pray say I cannot stay to answer his letter, Ever yours faithfully, Horatio Nelson[10]

Sir William had been able to advise that the French fleet had been sighted sailing south, heading towards Malta. Nelson immediately set sail in hot pursuit. His stay at Naples was too brief for him to come ashore and Sir William and Emma had not seen him.

When the British fleet disappeared over the horizon, the King and Queen, Sir William and Emma and all of Naples were left in a state of suspense. However, Nelson wrote privately to Sir William:

Vanguard, *at sea*,
18th June 1798

My dear Sir, I would not lose one moment of the breeze, in answering your letter. The best sight (as an Irishman would say) was to see me out of sight; ... I send you an extract of the Admiralty orders to Earl St. Vincent, by which it would appear as determined by the Cabinet to keep a superior Fleet to the enemy in the Mediterranean; for the Admiralty, you know, can give no such orders, but by an order from the Secretary of State. As for what depends on me, I beg, if you think it proper, to tell their Sicilian Majesties, and General Acton, that they may rest assured that I shall not withdraw the King's Fleet, but by positive orders or the impossibility of procuring supplies. I wish them to depend upon me, and they shall not be disappointed ... Pray present my best wishes to Lady Hamilton. Tell her, I hope to be presented to her crowned with laurel or cypress. But God is good, and to Him I do commit myself and our Cause. Ever believe me, my dear Sir, your obliged and faithful

Horatio Nelson[11]

After the storm in May, the five frigates assigned to his fleet never did catch up with him. Since they were the 'eyes' of the fleet he was frustrated and felt disadvantaged in his search for the French fleet. His only source of information was Captain Hardy on the *Mutine*.

Nelson left Naples with Sir William's words in his letter of 9 June still fresh in his mind: *'All Italy Sir looks upon the King's Fleet that you have the honour of Commanding as its Guardian Angel from the Ruin with which it has long been menaced and without which sooner or later it must fall.'*[12] The forthcoming battle would make his name known throughout Europe.

We leave Nelson's desperate attempt to find the French fleet to describe the nerve-wracking situation in which Sir William and Emma found themselves.

Just before Nelson's brief stopover in Naples on 14 June, Sir William made an inventory of his collection of pictures and prints in the fifteen rooms of the Palazzo Sessa. He had built up this outstanding collection over thirty-four years and he considered them to be part of his retirement fund. He was determined not to risk losing his art collection to the French.

Earlier in the year, Hamilton had written to St. Vincent: *'The last message from the French Directory at Paris is exactly the language of our Highwaymen – Deliver your money or I will blow your brains out.'*[13]

The outstanding collection numbered 347 works as listed in his inventory. There were works by almost every renowned artist at the time: Rubens, Canaletto, Leonardo da Vinci, Raphael and Titian. Among the Dutch artists were Van der Velde, Rembrandt, Van Dyck and Frans Hals. Works by English artists were mainly by Sir Joshua Reynolds, George Romney, Sir Godfrey Kneller and Gavin Hamilton, including fourteen portraits of Emma.* [14]

But it was not possible to save it all. During October, November and December, thirteen cases were packed under the direction of 'Sir William's much obliged and obedient humble Servant, James Clarke'. The catalogue of the contents of these cases lists only 213 works.

Another case of paintings from Caserta and five cases of marbles and bronzes were packed in January. His second collection of vases was packed separately, eight cases of which were sent to England, with Nelson's help, on board the warship, Colossus. Sir William's physical and mental strength were further weakened by the emotional stress of saving his art collection.

Fortuitously, not all the cases containing vases were put on board Colossus.

In August, Hamilton wrote to Lord Grenville: 'Altho' I feel myself with all my personal property in danger of being involved in the general ruin of this Country ... I am still happy that I did not profit of the King's gracious leave of absence as my presence here at this moment has been & appears still to be essential to His Majesty's Service, nor will I quit Naples until I can do so with a safe Conscience, let what may be the consequence.' [15]

Sir William had lived with King Ferdinand and Queen Maria Carolina as their favourite ambassador and valued friend for thirty-three years. Emma had lived in Naples for twelve years, for the last seven years as a close companion of the Queen, as a political ally and friend. Both Emma and Sir William were deeply loyal to the King and Queen.

This determined their decision to remain in Naples, rejecting the opportunity to retire and go home, despite the imminent danger to themselves and their property.

Before leaving Naples on 18 June Nelson had decided that the French armament was making for Egypt. He had written to Lord Spencer on 15 June: 'the last account I had of the French Fleet was from a Tunisian Cruizer, who saw them on the 4th., off Trapani, in Sicily, steering

* 3 Romney, 3 Tischbein, 2 Gavin Hamilton, 1 Sir Joshua Reynolds, 2 Vigée le Brun, 1 Angelica Kauffman, and two by lesser artists. There was one portrait of Mrs Cadogan.

to the eastward. If they pass Sicily, I shall believe they are going on their scheme of possessing Alexandria and getting troops to India ...'[16]

On 20 June, the fleet sailed through the Straight of Messina, knowing that Malta had surrendered to the French. Nelson consulted his captains. They agreed with his plan to seek the French at Alexandria. Captain Hardy on the *Mutine* was sent ahead to obtain information from the British Consul there, to whom Nelson wrote: *'I think their object is to possess themselves of some Port in Egypt, and to fix themselves at the head of the Red Sea, in order to get a formidable Army into India; and, in concert with Tippoo Saib, [Sahib] to drive us, if possible, from India ...'*[17]

His two years service in India placed him in this well-informed position, enabling him to make this assessment of Napoleon's plans. However, without his frigates, he lacked reliable information as to the whereabouts of the French fleet.

Believing the French several days sailing ahead of him, Nelson took the fastest possible route to Alexandria. The British and French fleets crossed paths without sighting each other during the night of 21 June. Nelson's fleet arrived at Alexandria on 29 June, a day before the French, who had taken a longer route via Crete.

In a state of intense frustration and acute anxiety at not finding his quarry, Nelson and the fleet turned tail and sailed back to Syracuse in Sicily. From Syracuse, he wrote a brief note to Fanny, now settled at Round Wood:

Vanguard, in Sicily, July 20, 1798

My dearest Fanny,

Except that my health is perfect I have not a word of news to tell you. I have been sent after the French fleet but have not been able to find them to my great mortification or the event I can scarcely doubt.

Since I wrote you a line from off Naples we have been off Malta, to Alexandria in Egypt, Syria into Asia and are returned here without success. However no person will say that it's been for want of activity. I yet live in hopes of meeting these scoundrels but it would have been my delight to have tried Buonaparte on a wind; for he commands the fleet as well as the army.

I hope my dear Fanny that you find everything comfortable where you are. Recollect that I am at no personal expense therefore I hope you will not be sparing of money. Glory is my object and that alone.

God Almighty bless you. Ever your most affectionate

Horatio Nelson

Love to all with you.[18]

The fleet received supplies in Syracuse. Later, Emma claimed that she persuaded Queen Maria Carolina to give orders that the fleet should be granted this favour.

Leaving Syracuse on 25 July and passing the south-west coast of Greece, firm information was received that the French were heading for Alexandria. The burden of expectation on Nelson was immense – the success of his mission to destroy the French fleet was important not only to Britain and Italy, but to all of Europe.

Saumarez, captain of the *Orion*, commented: *'Fortunately I only act here 'en second' but did the chief responsibility rest with me, I fear it would be more than my too irritable nerves would bear.'*[19]

During the long search Nelson frequently invited his captains on board the *Vanguard*, conferring with them and inspiring them with supreme confidence. His informal style contrasted with the more formal system of leadership practised at the time.

Lord Spencer, the Admiralty, the government and the public were becoming increasingly agitated by the lack of news from Nelson. Lord Spencer in particular, had put his reputation on the line by selecting the younger, and less senior, Admiral Nelson to command the fleet.

The British fleet arrived at Alexandria on the morning of 1 August. To their initial disappointment, they found no French ships of the line in the harbour. Fortunately, Captains Hood and Foley discovered seventeen French ships at anchor, in line of battle, in the nearby bay of Aboukir. Napoleon and his army had disembarked and marched towards Cairo.

Nelson immediately gave the signal to prepare for battle, even though darkness would fall in a few hours. It had taken two months to find the French fleet. Nelson was not about to give them the opportunity to escape during the night.

The battle began at 6.30 p.m. and continued throughout the night until 12.45 the following morning, 2 August. Nelson was severely wounded before 8.30 p.m. He was *'struck in the forehead by a langridge shot, or piece of iron, and the skin being cut by it as right angles, it hung down over his face, and as it covered his eye, he was rendered perfectly blind'*.[20]

In intense pain and shock, Nelson believed he had been mortally wounded, but after examination, the ship's surgeon pronounced that he was not in immediate danger. Nevertheless, he was obliged to remain below deck for most of the battle. The full account of the action was written by his Captain, Berry.

The outcome was a sensational victory for the British fleet. Nine line of battle ships were taken. The French set fire to their ship, *Le Timoléon*. The flagship, *L'Orient*, caught fire and exploded in the middle of the night, killing the Commander-in-Chief, Admiral Brueys, who was on board. Indeed, only seventy men of the thousand on board survived. Only two French ships escaped – *Le Guillaume Tell*, 80 guns, and *Le Généreux*, 74 guns, along with two frigates. Another two frigates were burnt and sunk by the French themselves.

It was almost total annihilation of the French fleet. Nelson had fulfilled his orders *'to take, sink, burn or destroy'* the fleet, leaving Napoleon and his army stranded in Egypt.

Nelson had finally achieved his longed-for glory.

However, 'glorious' as these battles were, they were the scene of carnage and tragedy on a colossal scale. Nelson submitted 'Lists of the Killed and Wounded' to St. Vincent: 218 men of the British fleet had been killed, including 16 officers. Among these was George Westcott, Captain of the *Majestic*. Of the 677 wounded, 37 were officers. These included Captains Alexander Ball, Sir James Saumarez and Henry D'E Darby. Nelson did not include his own name among the wounded in the Dispatch.[21]

The French casualties were far greater in number: 5,225 men were *'taken, drowned, burnt and missing'*. 3,105 had been sent on shore, 400 had escaped and 200 were prisoners on board the fleet.

Nevertheless, there was honour and compassion. Boats were sent out during the battle to pick up enemy sailors from the sea. After the battle, arrangements were made for wounded French sailors to be taken ashore and treated by their own surgeons. Troubridge, who had run aground on approaching the French fleet and to his frustration had played no part in the battle, supplied fresh provisions to be served to the sick and wounded ashore.

The scene of death and destruction on the afternoon of 2 August must have been horrific. Despite exhaustion and probably concussed by the blow to his head,* Nelson wrote to his captains:

Vanguard, *off the Mouth of the Nile,*

2nd. day of August, 1798

The Admiral most heartily congratulates the Captains, Officers, Seamen, and Marines of the Squadron he has the honour to command, on the event of

---

* Berry reported to Miller that he believed 'Sir Horatio to be out of danger, though he has been sick'.

the late Action; and he desires they will accept his most sincere and cordial thanks for their very gallant behaviour in this golorious Battle. It must strike forcibly every British Seaman, how superior their conduct is, when in discipline and good order, to the riotous behaviour of the lawless Frenchmen. The Squadron may be assured the Admiral will not fail, with his Dispatches, to represent their truly meritorious conduct in the strongest terms to the Commander-in-Chief.

Horatio Nelson[22]

Nelson reported the battle to St. Vincent, praising his Captains profusely:

Vanguard, of the Mouth of the Nile
3rd. August 1798

My Lord,

Almighty God has blessed his Majesty's arms in the late Battle, by a great Victory over the Fleet of the Enemy, who I attacked at sunset on the 1st. August, off the Mouth of the Nile. The Enemy were moored in a strong Line of Battle for defending the entrance of the Bay, flanked by numerous Gun-boats, four Frigates, and a Battery of Guns and Mortars on an Island in their Van, but nothing could withstand the Squadron your Lordship did me the honour to place under my command.

Their high state of discipline is well known to you, and with the judgement of the Captains, together with their valour, and that of the Officers and Men of every description, it was absolutely irresistible. Could anything from my pen add to the character of the Captains, I would write it with pleasure, but that is impossible.

I have to regret the loss of Captain Westcott of the Majestic, who was killed early in the Action ...

The Ships of the Enemy, all but their two rear Ships, are nearly dismasted: and those two, with two Frigates I am sorry to say, made their escape; nor was it, I assure you, in my power to prevent them ...

The support and assistance I have received from Captain Berry cannot be sufficiently expressed. I was wounded in the head, and obliged to be carried off the deck; but the Service suffered no loss by that event; Captain Berry was fully equal to the important service then going on, and to him I must beg leave to refer you for every information relative to this Victory. He will present you with the Flag of the Second in Command; that of the Commander-in-Chief being burnt in the Orient.

Herewith I transmit you Lists of the Killed and Wounded, and the Lines of Battle of ourselves and the French. I have the honour to be, my Lord, your Lordship's most obedient Servant.

Horatio Nelson[23]

Captain Berry was sent to England in the *Leander* with Nelson's dispatches but was captured on 18 August by none other than the *Généreux*, which had escaped from Aboukir.* Fortunately Captain Capel had been sent with duplicates to proceed overland, via Naples. He reached Naples on 4 September and reported to Nelson: '*I am totally unable to express the joy that appeared in everybody's countenance, and the bursts of applause and acclamations we received. The Queen and Lady Hamilton both fainted: in short, Sir, they all hail you as the Saviour of Europe. A courier sets off tomorrow morning for Vienna, and I accompany him, so that I shall not lose an instant. I have every instruction and assistance from Sir William Hamilton and the other Foreign Ministers, who are all anxious to forward such glorious news.*'[24]

Emma was not alone in fainting in reaction to the exciting news. Captain Capel reported the Queen had fainted and Lord Spencer, when informed of the victory, '*reeled and fainted*' in relief that his choice of Nelson to command was vindicated. Such was the tension caused by the fear of the French.

Sir William and Emma, the King and Queen and all of Naples had waited six weeks for news from Nelson. When news of the victory of the Battle of the Nile (as it came to be known) was received in Naples, the first to write to Nelson were Sir William and Emma. Sir William's letter was written in his usual intelligent ambassadorial style. He expressed his admiration, gratitude and affection:

Naples, September 8th. 1798

It is impossible, my dear Sir Horatio, for any words to express, in any degree, the joy that the account of the glorious and complete Victory you gained over the boasted French Fleet, at the Mouth of the Nile, on the first of August, occasioned at this Court, and in this City. Captain Capel arrived here on Monday last, about one o'clock in the afternoon, and was off the next day, with your Dispatches for our government, and which I hope will be the first authentic account they will receive of the ever-memorable Battle of the Nile – a Battle, I believe of the greatest importance that ever was fought, and the expected good consequences of which are incalculable. History, either ancient or modern, does not record an Action that does more honour to the Heroes that gained that Victory, than the late one of the first of August. You have now completely made yourself, my dear Nelson, <u>immortal</u>.

---

* Berry was wounded in the defensive action against the *Genereux* and suffered severely for several months. The officers and crew of the *Leander* were taken to Trieste where they were released on parole. On his return to England Berry was knighted on 12 December.

God be praised, and may you live long to enjoy the sweet satisfaction of having added such glory to our Country, and most probably, put an end to the confusion and misery in which all Europe would soon have been involved. This Country feels its immediate good effects; and their Sicilian Majesties, their Ministry, and the Nation at large, are truly sensible of it, and loudly acknowledge eternal obligation to your undaunted courage, and steady perseverance.

You may well conceive, my dear Sir, how happy Emma and I are, in the reflection that it is <u>you – Nelson – our bosom friend</u>, who has done such wondrous good, in having humbled these proud robbers and vain boasters ... the King of Naples has just raised 50,000 men more, and has ready 30,000 in tolerable discipline. Italy might be cleared of these ragamuffins in a month's time. They must learn of you. You did not wait for daylight to attack the French Fleet on the first of August, nor for the arrival of your four ships from Alexandria; nor did the Culloden's being on shore prevent your falling on the Enemy directly, like a hawk on its prey. That is the way to do business.

How proud I am of feeling myself an Englishman at this moment! Great Britain alone has truly faced the Enemy in support of the good cause; and Sir Horatio Nelson is the greatest Hero of that Great Britain.

Adieu, my dear and brave friend. Your sincerely attached and humble servant.

William Hamilton[25]

Emma wrote her exuberant response to the victory over several days:

Naples,
September 8,
1798

My dear, dear Sir,

How shall I begin, what shall I say to you. 'Tis impossible I can write, for since last Monday I am delirious with joy, and assure you I have a fevour caused by agitation and pleasure. God, what a victory! Never, never has there been anything half so glorious, so compleat. I fainted when I heard the joyfull news, and fell on my side and am hurt, but well of that. I shou'd feil it a glory to die in such a cause. No, I wou'd not like to die till I see and embrace the Victor of the Nile. How shall I describe to you the transports of Maria Carolina, 'tis not possible. She fainted and kissed her husband, her children, walked about the room, cried, kissed, and embraced every person near her, exclaiming, Oh, brave Nelson, oh, God bless and protect our brave deliverer, oh, Nelson, what do we not owe to *you, oh Victor, Savour of Itali, oh, that my swollen heart cou'd now tell him what we owe to him!*

You may judge, my dear Sir, of the rest, but my head will not permit me to tell you half the rejoicing. The Neapolitans are mad with joy, and if you wos here now, you wou'd be killed with kindness. Sonets on sonets, illuminations, rejoicings; not a French dog dare shew his face. How I glory in the honner of my Country and my Countryman! I walk and tread in the air with pride, feiling I was born in the same land with the victor Nelson and his gallant band.

But no more, I cannot, dare not, trust myself, for I am not well. Little dear Captain Hoste will tell you the rest ... I send you two letters from my adorable queen. One was written to me the day we received the glorious news, the other yesterday. Keep them, as they are in her own handwriting. I have kept copies only, but I feil that you ought to have them. If you had seen our meeting after the battle, but I will keep it all for your arrival. I cou'd not do justice to her feiling nor my own, with writing it; and we are preparing your apartment against you come. I hope it will not be long, for Sir William and I are so impatient to embrace you. I wish you cou'd have seen our house the 3 nights of illumination. 'Tis, 'twas covered with your glorious name. Their were 3 Thousand Lamps, and their should have been 3 millions if we had had time. All the English vie with each other in celebrating this most gallant and ever memorable victory. Sir William is ten years younger since the happy news, and he now only wishes to see his friend to be completely happy. How he glories in you when your name is mentioned. He cannot contain his joy. For God's sake come to Naples soon ... How I felt for poor Troubridge. He must have been so angry on the sandbank, so brave an officer! In short I pity those who were not in the battle. I wou'd have been rather an English powder-monkey, or a swab in that great victory, than an Emperor out of it, but you will be so tired of all this. Write or come soon to Naples, and rejoin your ever sincere and obliged friend,*

Emma Hamilton

The Queen as this moment sent a Dymond Ring to Captain Hoste, six buts of wine, 2 casks for the officers, and every man on board a guinea each. Her letter is in English and comes as from an unknown person, but a well-wisher to our country and an admirer of our gallant Nelson. As war is not yet declared with France, she cou'd not shew herself so openly as she wished, but she as done so much, and rejoiced so very publickly, that all the world sees it. She

---

* Powder monkey – normally a boy employed to carry powder from the magazine to the gun deck.

bids me to say that she longs more to see you than any woman with child can long for anything she may take a fancy to, and she shall be for ever unhappy if you do not come. God bless you my dear, dear friend.

My dress from head to foot is alla Nelson. Ask Hoste. Even my shawl is in Blue with gold anchors all over. My earrings are Nelson's anchors; in short, we are be-Nelsoned all over ... Once more, God bless you. My mother desires her love to you. I am so sorry to write in such a hurry. I am afraid you will not be able to read this scrawl.[26]

Emma's enthusiastic letter to Nelson is matched by many others, notably one from the Queen to Emma:

September 3rd. 1798

My dear Lady,

What happiness, what glory, what consolation for that unmatched, great, and illustrious nation. How obliged and grateful I am to you. I cry, laugh, and embrace my children and husband. The news has quite revived me. I was much oppressed before. What courage! What bravery! to embrace you would be a consolation to me. I shall tomorrow have the joy of seeing your heroes, the defenders of Italy; and if a portrait of Nelson is taken, I will have it in my chamber.

My gratitude is engraven on my heart; vive vive the brave nation and its navy.

I participate in the glory doubly, as being so greatly for our advantage, and also redounding to the fame of the first flag in the world; – hip! hip my dear lady. I am wild with joy; with what pleasure I shall see our heroes this evening. I cannot say that this binds me to your great nation, for I have always been, am, and shall be attached to it; but this augments the gratitude it is so pleasing to feel for people whom you so entirely cherish and esteem. My affectionate compliments to the Chevalier. I embrace you; my children all belonging to me feel as they ought, and are mad with joy. May heaven prosper a nation great, magnanimous, courageous. Surrounded by my beloved family, if it were possible, I would see the brave Nelson, and the victorious squadron, and thank them for their exploits. Adieu, until evening. Do not fail to bring our heroes this evening.[27]

These 'heroes' would be those who brought the news to Naples.

Lady Lavinia Spencer's letter was even more euphoric:

Admiralty, 2nd. October 1798

Captain Capel has just arrived!

Joy, joy, joy to you, brave, gallant, immortalized Nelson! May that great God, whose cause you so valiantly support, protect and bless you to the end of your brilliant Career! Such a race surely never was run. My heart is absolutely bursting with different sensations of joy, of gratitude, of pride, of every emotion that ever warmed the bosom of a British woman, on hearing of her Country's glory – and all produced by you, my dear, my good friend ... This moment the guns are firing, illuminations are preparing, your gallant name is echoed from street to street, and every Briton feels his obligation to you weighing him down ... But I am here come to the end of my paper, luckily for you, or I should gallop on for ever at this rate. I am half mad, and I fear I have written a strange letter, but you'll excuse it. Almighty God protect you! Adieu! How anxious we shall be to hear of your health! Lady Nelson has had an express sent to her.[28]

Some of Fanny's letters are lost and we do not know what her immediate reaction was to her husband's victory. In April she had written, 'As to peace I most ardently wish for it particularly as you will then be satisfied to live quietly at home.'[29]

On 16 July she had written: 'I only write to tell you of my extreme anxiety to hear from you, no one period of the war have I felt more than I do at this moment. I really am so affected that it has enervated me beyond description still I think all will turn out to your most sanguine wishes.'[30]

Fanny's letters were usually restrained and it is unlikely that she wrote in the jubilant language of those quoted above and of the deluge of letters Nelson received, among others, from Lord Spencer, the Lord Chancellor, the Irish Government, Emperor Paul of Russia (who also sent a gold box set with diamonds) the Duke of Clarence, Admirals Howe, Hood and Goodall, his old friends Lady Parker and Captain Locker.

St. Vincent wrote from Cadiz on 27 September: 'My dear Admiral, God be praised, and you and your gallant band rewarded by a grateful Country, for the Greatest Achievement the history of the word can produce. I most sincerely lament the loss of Captain Westcott, and the number of brave Officers and men who have fallen on this signal occasion ... Tell Lady Hamilton I rely on her to administer to your health at Naples, where I have no doubt it will soon be re-established ... Remember me kindly to Troubridge and all your heroes.'[31]

The same day his old friend Collingwood, who had been bitterly disappointed at not being included in Nelson's squadron, wrote from Cadiz: 'My dear Friend,

I cannot express how great my joy is for the complete and glorious Victory you have obtained over the French – the most decisive, and, in its consequence, perhaps the most important to Europe, that was ever won ...'[32]

The fleet remained at Aboukir Bay for almost three weeks. Cleaning up the devastation was a gruelling task when everyone was suffering post-battle trauma. A lieutenant wrote home: *'Since the battle we have been almost killed with fatigue refitting our ships and prizes.'*

In command of these operations and still suffering from his head wound, Nelson had many letters to write, including the following:

To Sir William Hamilton:

Vanguard, *Mouth of the Nile, 8 August 1798*

My dear Sir, Almighty God has made me the happy instrument in destroying the Enemy's Fleet, which I hope will be a blessing to Europe. You will have the goodness to communicate this happy event to all the Courts of Italy, for my head is so indifferent that I can scarcely scrawl this letter ... I hope there will be no difficulty in our getting refitted in Naples. Not more than four or five Sail of the Line will probably come to Naples; the rest will go with the Prizes to Gibraltar ... Your most obliged and affectionate

*Horatio Nelson**

He added on 9 August: *'I have intercepted all Buonaparte's Dispatches going to France. This army is in a scrape and will not get out of it.'*[33]

The following day, in a letter to the Governor of Bombay, he commented:

'Almighty God will in Egypt overthrow these pests of the human race.'[34]

Napoleon was in trouble. He had taken Cairo, which his troops described as *'the vilest and most miserable dog-hole on the face of the earth'*, but with the sinking of the *L'Orient*, had lost his bullion to pay the troops.

On the 13 August Nelson wrote to Fanny:

My dearest Fanny, I am thank God as much better as could be expected, and what I hope will make Europe happy is the certain destruction of the French army. The people of the country are rising against them every hour. Such are the blessed fruits of our conquest. Victory is certainly not a name strong enough for such a scenes as I have passed.

I shall most probably be in England in November but more of this later.

With kindest love to my father and all our friends. Believe me ever your most affectionate husband

Horatio Nelson[35]

Nelson set sail for Naples on 19 August with the *Alexander* and the *Culloden*. But his troubles were not yet over. The ships made slow

---

* Saumarez, in command of six British ships, was sent to Gibraltar with six of the French prizes.

progress in light winds until suddenly hit by a storm on 15 September in which the *Vanguard* suffered severe damage: '*... the foremast went 10 or 12 feet from the deck, two seamen were killed & two lost overboard. Carried away by the topmast.'*

During this voyage Nelson commented on his head wound and health in letters to St. Vincent.

On 10 August: *'My head is ready to split, and I am always so sick: in short, if there be no fracture, my head is severely shaken.'*[36] Later in August he commented: *'My head is so wrong that I cannot write what I wish in such a manner as to please myself.'*[37]

And on 1 September: *'I know I ought to give up for a while, my head is splitting at this moment.'*[38]

He suffered another attack of fever, probably recurring malaria, informing St. Vincent on 21 September: *'I was taken with a fever which has very near done my business: for eighteen hours my life was thought to be past hope; I am now up but very weak both body and mind ... it may please God, that this will be the finish of that fever of anxiety which I have endured from the middle of June ...'*[39]

The symptoms of the Nile wound he describes are similar to concussion – headache, vomiting, feeling stunned or dazed. Concussion can result in changeable behaviour and inappropriate emotional responses. Nowadays Nelson would have been hospitalized, but then he received no such treatment. His irritable behaviour became increasingly noticeable. He thus arrived in Naples in a poor physical and mental state.

On 11 August 1798 he had written to Emma: *'You and Sir William have spoiled me ... I may now be able to shew your ladyship the remains of Horatio Nelson, and I trust my mutilations will not cause me to be less welcome. They are the marks of honour.'*[40]

Fanny, however, heard nothing of his troubles. At sea on 16 September, he wrote claiming his head had healed and he was well, doubtless to protect her from her constant anxiety:

My dearest Fanny, It is hardly possible for me to know where to begin. My head is almost turned by letters already and what am I not to expect when I get on shore. Noise enough to distract me. My head is healed and I am better.

The Kingdom of the Two Sicilies are mad with joy from the throne to the peasant all are alike. From Lady Hamilton's letter the situation of the Queen was truly pitiable. I only hope I shall not have to be witness to a renewal of It ... [41] He then quoted Emma's description of the Queen's reactions.

Damaged by the storm, the *'poor wretched* Vanguard*'* arrived at Naples on 22 September, having been towed the remainder of the journey. Just inside Naples Bay the tow was slipped and *Vanguard* sailed slowly into the harbour. She met with an emotional welcome from the King and Queen, the Princesses, Sir William and Emma, Miss Cornelia Knight, Neapolitan nobility, the Russian Ambassador with his Legation and a joyous crowd on shore.

CHAPTER 12

Dramatic Events in Naples

*'Ten thousand most grateful Thanks are due to your Ladyship for restoring
the health of our valuable friend, Nelson'*
St.Vincent to Emma, 20 October 1798

'Love Sir William and myself for we love you dearly'
Emma to Nelson, 27 October 1798

*'She [Emma] has honoured me by being my Ambassadress to the Queen:
Therefore she has my implicit confidence and is worthy of it.'*
Nelson to St. Vincent, November 1798

*'Things are in such a critical state here, that I desire you will join me
without one moments loss of time ... For God's sake make haste!'*
Nelson to Troubridge, 15 December 1798

IN HER DIARY, Cornelia Knight* described the *Vanguard's* arrival at
Naples:

22 September 1798
*In the evening, went out with Sir William and Lady Hamilton, music etc.
to meet Admiral Nelson, who in the* Vanguard, *with the* Thalia *frigate
(Captain Newhouse), was seen coming in. We went on board, about a league
out to sea, and sailed with him: Soon after us, the King came on board, and
stayed till the anchor was dropped. He embraced the Admiral with the greatest
warmth, and said he wished he could have been in the engagement, and served
under his orders; and that he likewise wished he could have been in England
when the news of the Victory arrived there ... The Admiral came on shore
with us and said it was the first time he had been out of his ship for six months,
except once on board the Lord St. Vincent ... When we landed at the Health
Office, the applause and the crowd of people were beyond description. Admiral*

* Daughter of Rear Admiral Sir Joseph Knight, deceased.

Nelson is little, and not remarkable in his person either way; but he has great animation of countenance, and activity in his appearance; his manners are unaffectedly simple and modest. He lodges at Sir William's who has given him the upper apartment. The whole city is mad with joy ...[1]

Nelson's frequently quoted letter to Fanny vividly describes Emma's emotional arrival on board:

About 25th. September
1798

The poor wretched Vanguard arrived here on the 22nd. of September. I must endeavor to convey to you something of what passed; but if it were so affecting to those who were only united by bonds of friendship, what must it be to my dearest wife, my friend, my everything which is most dear to me in this world? Sir William and Lady Hamilton came out to sea, attended by numerous Boats with emblems, &c., they, my most respectable friends, had really been laid up and seriously ill; first from anxiety, and then from joy. It was imprudently told Lady Hamilton in a moment, and the effect was like a shot; she fell apparently dead, and is not yet perfectly recovered from severe bruises. Alongside came my honoured friends: the scene in the boat appeared terribly affecting; up flew her Ladyship, and exclaiming, O God, is it possible? She fell into my arms more dead than alive. Tears, however, soon set matters to rights; when alongside came the King, [who was given a 21 gun salute]. The scene was, in its way, as affecting. He took me by the hand, calling me his 'Deliverer and Preserver' with every other expression of kindness. In short, all Naples calls me 'Nostra Liberatore' for the scene with the lower Classes was truly affecting. I hope one day to have the pleasure of introducing you to Lady Hamilton. She is one of the very best women in this world. How few could have made the turn she has. She is an honour to her sex and a proof that even reputation may be regained, but I own it requires a great soul. Her kindness with Sir William to me is more than I can express. I am in their house, and I may tell you it required all the kindness of my friends to set me up. Her Ladyship if Josiah was to stay would make something of him and with all his bluntness I am sure he likes Lady Hamilton more than any female. She would fashion him in 6 months in spite of himself. I believe Lady Hamilton intends writing you.

May God Almighty bless you my dearest Fanny and give us in due time a happy meeting. Should the King give me a peerage I believe I scarcely need state the propriety of your going to court. Don't mind the expense. Money is thrash. Again God Almighty bless you.

Ever your most affectionate
Horatio Nelson[2]

We note that Nelson was aware that Emma had suffered a poor reputation in the past that she now, by her 'great soul', had regained.

It was five years since Nelson and the Hamiltons' last meeting in September 1793 and they now insisted that Nelson came ashore to recover at the Palazzo Sessa as their guest. Sir William and Emma would have considered it their duty to care for the injured, exhausted British Admiral. Emma, with her customary compassion and warmth, threw herself into the task with the aid of her mother.

In the beautiful and comfortable Palazzo Sessa, Nelson was given a room with a splendid view of the bay where he could observe his ships at anchor. With Emma and her mother fussing over him and Sir William treating him like a son, his spirits soon revived. After six gruelling months at sea, it was the care he desperately needed.

Nelson wrote to his father at Round Wood:

September 25th. 1798

My dear Father,

I have to thank you for your two affectionate letters from Round-Wood, and if the place and neighbourhood are not so pleasant as could be wished, I trust that my Country will enable me to choose a comfortable resting-place. The Almighty has blessed my exertions for the happiness of mankind, and I am daily receiving the thanks and prayers of Turks and Christians ... The hand of God was visibly pressed on the French: it was not in the power of man to gain such a Victory. In their Sicilian Majesties' thanks and congratulations, are the following lines: History, either ancient or modern, does not record such a Battle. You have saved us, Sir, by this most glorious Action, which, superior to any Battle fought at Sea, has this singular and important consequence – of being to all Europe, I repeat it, of the highest advantage.

The whole letter being in the same strain, is enough to make me vain.

My head is quite healed, and if it were necessary I could not at present leave Italy, who looks up to me as, under God, its Protector. May God Almighty bless you, my dear Father, is the affectionate wish of your dutiful Son,

Horatio Nelson[3]

Nelson knew that Fanny was not happy at Round Wood, where she had lived since 25 May. He had received several letters of complaint from her:

June 25th. 'I have had a visit from Lady Harland. She and Mrs. Boucher are gentlewomen. I have had visits from a few others what are called ladies, but I don't like them ...'[4]

9th. July. 'The Middletons are the only country family who have been attentive ...'⁵

30 July. '... we see nobody – indeed there are no families to visit ...'⁶

Fanny made an effort to redress the complaining tone of her letters in a letter full of local news on 13 August: *'I was determined to see if I could write without tormenting you with my anxieties.'⁷*

However, Nelson's family often visited Fanny and their father. She was busy putting the house into good repair – installing new shutters, mending fences and planting trees. She describes *'particularly fine harvests got in.'*

And on 11 September: *'The newspapers have tormented and almost killed me in regard to the desperate action you have fought with the French fleet.'⁸*

Until Nelson's dispatches arrived in England on 2 October, the newspapers were full of speculation. Lord Spencer, wrote immediately to Fanny when good news of the victory arrived.

Fanny found it difficult to deal with her sudden rise to fame. She wrote in her letter to Lord Hood on 18 October: *'Since my dear Lord, my husband, has gained this victory I have been honoured with the notice of the great of this neighbourhood – truly I don't thank them: they ought to have found their way to the cottage before, that is my way of thinking.'⁹*

The erratic and long-delayed arrival of letters was not the only reason for the impending calamitous breakdown of their relationship. Their lives now took such momentously divergent paths that it proved impossible for them to rekindle the relationship they had prior to their parting in April 1798.

Nelson arrived in Naples a week before his fortieth birthday. Emma was in her prime, a beautiful thirty-three-year-old woman, confident, enthusiastic and excited by Nelson's heroic actions. Sir William, thirty-five years older than Emma, was temporarily rejuvenated by Nelson's astounding victory, but soon became tired and troubled.

He and Emma, in gratitude and with generous abandon, provided a lavish entertainment to celebrate Nelson's birthday on 29 September. He had been ashore for one week when he described this event to Fanny:

1st. to 6th. October 1798

Our time here is actively employed; and between business and what is called pleasure, I am not my own master for five minutes. The continued kind attention of Sir William and Lady Hamilton must ever make you and I love them, and they are deserving the love and admiration of all the world. The

Grand Signior has ordered me a valuable diamond; if it were worth a million, my pleasure would be to see it in your possession. My pride is being your husband, the son of my dear father, and in having Sir William and Lady Hamilton for my friends ... On my birthday, eighty people dined at Sir William Hamilton's, one thousand seven hundred and forty came to a ball, where eight hundred supped ...

Yours ... etc.

Horatio Nelson[10]

Nelson was becoming impatient with the Neapolitans' lack of any sense of urgency towards helping themselves to resist the possible French invasion. He complained to St. Vincent on 30 September: '*I trust, my Lord, in a week we shall all be at sea. I am very unwell and the miserable conduct of his Court is not likely to cool my irritable temper. It is a country of fiddlers, poets, whores and scoundrels.*'[11]

On 4 October he wrote: '*This Country by its system of procrastination will ruin itself. The Queen sees it and thinks as we do.*'[12] At the end of this letter, Nelson confessed the impact of Emma's presence on him: '*I am writing opposite Lady Hamilton, therefore you will not be surprised at the glorious jumble of this letter. Were your Lordship in my place, I much doubt if you could write so well; our hearts and our hands must be all in a flutter: Naples is a dangerous place, and we must keep clear of it.*'[13]

However, his orders required him to remain. Admiralty orders to St. Vincent were relayed to Nelson:

The protection of the Coasts of Sicily, Naples and the Adriatic

Active co-operation with the Austrian and Neapolitan Armies

To cut off all communications between France and Egypt

Blocking-up [i.e. blockading] Malta

Co-operation with the Turkish and Russian Squadrons[14]

His instructions were to give '*the most cordial and unlimited support and protection to His Majesty's allies ... and most carefully to avoid giving to any of them the smallest cause for suspicion, jealousy or offence.*'[15]

Nelson resolved to carry out these orders and the formidable forty-six-year-old Queen Maria Carolina proved his most potent ally. He and Emma were thrown into a working partnership. Her linguistic skills along with her long-standing close relationship with the Queen made her help indispensable. Emma would have been thrilled to be in such an important position. She was able to assist her '*ever dear Queen*' and to take some of the pressure off her tired and ailing husband.

On 15 October Nelson sailed with his squadron for Malta, to make himself *'acquainted with the true state of matters there, to leave a proper Force to blockade the Port'.** Before he left the King and Prince Leopold dined on board. At the King's request, Nelson promised to return in the first week of November.

On 24 October he wrote to Emma from Malta, addressing her as *'my dear Madam'*, describing the situation there and informing her that he intended to be back in Naples at the beginning of November. This was one of the first political letters Nelson wrote to Emma. He informed St. Vincent: *'She has honoured me by being my Ambassadress to the Queen: Therefore she has my implicit confidence, and is worthy of it.'*[16]

It is clear from the exchange of letters between Emma and St. Vincent that she wrote to him at regular intervals. On 18 October he wrote to her from Gibraltar:

My dear Madam,

> The prodigies of the valour performed by your new Chevalier have, I fear, obliterated the memory of your ancient Knight. Nevertheless, I beg your Ladyship will lay me at the feet of the Queen of the Two Sicilies, and assure her Majesty of my profound respect for her person, and that my life is devoted to the defence of it: and, for yourself, accept every kind wish of your Ladyship's truly affection and faithful Knight.

St. Vincent[17]

Two days later he wrote:

My dear Lady Hamilton,

> Ten Thousand most grateful Thanks are due to your Ladyship, for restoring the health of our valuable friend, Nelson, on whose life the fate of the remaining governments in Europe, whose system has not been deranged by these devils, depends. Pray, do not let your fascinating Neapolitan dames approach too near him; for he is made of flesh and blood, and cannot resist their temptations.

> Lady St. Vincent will be transported with your attention to her. I have sent the fan mounts for Lady Nelson and her, by Sir James Saumarez ... I am very much penetrated with the condescension of their Majesties of the Two Sicilies have graciously shewn to me, Through your Ladyship, and I rely on your doing justice to my feelings upon the occasion ... Continue to love me; and rest assured of the most unfeigned and affectionate regard of, my dear Lady Hamilton, your faithful and devoted Knight.

St. Vincent[18]

---

* Malta belonged to the Kingdom of the Two Sicilies, but had been seized by the French, who were now besieged by Nelson's fleet.

While Nelson was away Emma wrote to him over a period of several days, making political comments and giving news of the royal family:

Caserta, October 20th.

My dear Friend,

Oh how we feil our loss! Could you but know how miserable we were for some days, but now hopes of your return revives us ... [Emma tells Nelson that they are at Caserta awaiting the birth of the Princess Royal's baby] *... How we abused Gallo* [the Neapolitan pro-French Minister whom Nelson disliked] *yesterday – how she hates him – he won't reign long, so much the better. Write to me and come soon for you are wanted at Court. All their nodles are not worth yours. Ever ever yours,*

Emma.[19]

October 26th

I must say one more word to you.

We have just had another letter. The Grand Signoir [The Grand Signior of the Ottoman Empire] *has written to the King of England to beg his permission that you may wear the order or feather that he took out of his own turban to decorate you and which is a sign of sovranity. I do not know exactly how many thousand piastres it's worth but unprecedented the present. Vivo il Turco says Emma. If I was King of England I would make you the most noble puissant DUKE NELSON, MARQUIS NILE, EARL ALEXANDER, VISCOUNT PYRAMID, BARON CROCODILE AND PRINCE VICTORY, that posterity might have you in all forms.*

October 27th.

... their arrived here Sunday last 2 couriers, one from London, one from Viena. The first is the comforting news of a fleet to remain in the Meditn, a treaty made of the most flattering kind for Naples, in short everything amicable, friendly and was truly Honerable. T'other from their dear son and daughter [currently ruling Austria] *cold, unfriendly, mistrustfull, frenchified, and saying plainly – help yourselves. How the dear Maria Carolina cried for joy at the one and rage at the other, but Mack is gone to the army prepare to march directly ...*

May you live long long long for the sake of your Country, your King, your family, all Europe, Asia, Affrica and America, and for the scorge of france, but particularly for the happiness of Sir William and self ... I would not be a luke warm friend for the world – I am no ones enemy and unfortunately am difficult and cannot make friendship with all, but the few friends I have, I would die for them and I assure you now, if things take an unfortunate turn here and the Queen dies at her post, I will remain with her ... Thank God the first week of November is near ... Love Sir William and myself for we love you dearly. He is the best husband, friend, I wish I could say father allso, but I should be too happy if I had the blessing of having children, so must be content.

November 2nd.

The Princess not brought to bed – oh dear what can the matter be.[20]

We note Emma's disappointment at not having had any children by Sir William.

Her letters were scrawled at great speed, packed with trivialities, news and serious comments. Nelson loved them, and appreciated her enthusiastic praise.

He wrote to her from Malta: *'Your letters are so interesting, that I am gratified beyond belief at receiving them, and your whole conduct has ever been to me so very much above my deserts that I am absolutely at a loss how to express myself.'*[21]

Nelson's following letter to St.Vincent indicates that he knew Emma wrote regularly to him:

9th. November 1798:

I believe Lady Hamilton has written so fully, and I will answer, so ably, on all subjects, that but little remains for me to say ... her Ladyship's and Sir William's inexpressible goodness to me is not to be told by words; and it ought to stimulate me to the noblest actions, and I feel it will. My mind I know is right, but alas! my body is weak ...'[22]

Nelson arrived back in Naples early in November to learn that he had been created Baron with the title Lord Nelson of the Nile and of Burnham Thorpe. Later in 1799, he listed this award and many other *'presents'* he had received after the Battle of the Nile in his *Sketch of my Life.**

It was a rich haul in monetary value, but for a man far more concerned with honour and recognition than money, the award of a baronetcy from his own country was a disappointment. For their battles Jervis (St. Vincent) had received an earldom and Duncan, a viscountcy. The modest award granted him by the King and Parliament shocked Nelson's family and friends.

In attempting to explain, Spencer wrote to him: *'In congratulating your Lordship on this high distinction, I have particular pleasure in remarking, that it is the highest honour that has ever been conferred on an*

* See Appendix 2.

Officer of your standing in the Service who was not a Commander in Chief.'[23]

In addition Nelson was short-changed in his pension award. He was awarded £2,000 p.a. but not the additional £1,000 p.a. from the Irish government that St. Vincent and Duncan had received.

Nelson felt the injustice, but in his reply to Earl Spencer on 7 December, he did not criticize the award, merely stating that he felt more greatly honoured by continuing to receive the *'unbounded confidence of his King and country.'*

The Princess Royal gave birth early in November. King Ferdinand and Queen Maria Carolina now turned to plans to retake Rome from the French. The Hamiltons and Nelson were involved with these plans, knowing that the British Government was keen to draw Austria into the war. Maria Carolina, as reported by Emma, was enraged because her ruling relatives in Austria were reluctant to be involved beyond sending General Mack to lead the Neapolitan troops.

It was decided that King Ferdinand and Mack would lead the army against the French in Rome, while Nelson transported 5,000 Neapolitan troops to Leghorn. Nelson wrote to Spencer on 13 November: *'Every hour the French are increasing their Italian army, and two new generals are arrived in Rome ... it is aggression, if this Court knows, all the World knows, that the French are collecting an Army to over-run Naples; in a week destroy the Monarchy, plunder, and make it a Republic ... I ventured to tell their Majesties directly that one of the following things must happen to the King, and he had his choice – Either to advance trusting to God for his blessing on a just Cause, to die with l'epeé á la main or to remain quiet and be kicked out of your Kingdom. The King replied he would go on and trust in God ...'*[24]

The same day, he told St. Vincent: *'The King goes to the Army tomorrow; in three days he hopes to march. His Majesty is determined to conquer or die at the head of his Army, which is composed of 30,000 healthy good-looking troops ...'*[25]

Nelson sailed for Leghorn with a squadron on 22 November, reporting to Spencer on the 29th: *'The troops were immediately landed, and possession taken of the Town and the Fortress of Leghorn.'*

Emma had written to him when he left for Leghorn: *'Pray keep your self well for our sakes and do not go on shore at Leghorn. Their is no comfort their for you.'*[26] This appears to indicate that she knew about his liaison with Adelaide Correglia.

In the midst of these dramatic events, Nelson wrote a note to Fanny:

Leghorn, November 29, 1798

My dearest Fanny,

    I brought a cargo of Neapolitan troops and yesterday night took possession of the town and the fortress of Leghorn. I am tolerable and shall sail tomorrow for Naples. As mine is a truly active scene you cannot hope for long letters, but believe me ever with the truest affection, your

Nelson

Kind love to my father and my sister and Mr. Matcham.[27]

Waiting in Naples for news of these critical events, Emma wrote a long letter to Fanny:*

December 2, 1798

    I hope your Ladyship received my former letter with an account of Lord Nelson's arrival and his reception from their Sicilian Majesties and also the congratulations and compliments from this amiable and adorable Queen to your Ladyship, which I was charged with and wrote a month back, but as the posts are very uncertain you may not have received that letter.

    Lord Nelson is gone to Leghorn with the troops of the King of Naples and we expect him soon back. As the King is gone to Rome with his army he urged of my Lord Nelson to be as much at or about Naples as he could, not only to advise and consult with her Majesty (who is regent) for the good of the common cause, but in case of accident to take care of her and her family. Lord Nelson is adored here and looked on as the deliverer of this country. He was not well when first he arrived, but by nursing and asses' milk he went from Naples quite recovered. The King and Queen adore him and if he had been their brother they could not have shown him more respect and attentions. I need not tell your Ladyship how happy Sir William and myself are at having an opportunity of seeing our dear, respectable, brave friend return here with so much honour to himself and glory for his country. We only wanted you [to be here] to be completely happy. Lord Nelson's wound is quite well.

    Josiah is so much improved in every respect. We are all delighted with him. He is an excellent officer and very steady and one of the best hearts in the world ... Sir William desires his kind compliments to your Ladyship and to Lord Nelson's dear respected father. The King is having his picture set with diamonds for his Lordship, and the Queen has ordered a fine set of china with all the battles he has been engaged in and his picture painted on china.

    Josiah desired his duty to you Ladyship and says he will write as soon as he has time but he has been very busy for some time past.

* Emma had already sent Fanny a copy of Cornelia Knight's verses written to celebrate the Battle of the Nile.

May God bless you and yours my dear Madam, and believe me your Ladyship's ever sincere friend and humble servant.

Emma Hamilton

Sir William is in a rage with the ministry for not having made Lord Nelson a viscount, for sure this great and glorious action, greater than any other, ought to have been recompensed more. Hang them I say.[28]

It was a kind and considerate letter, giving Fanny reassuring news about her husband and son. At the time of writing, Emma would have been worried about events taking place. Four days later her life was thrown into chaos.

On 6 December, the French Directory declared war on Naples.

Nelson was back in Naples by 6 December, reporting to St. Vincent: *'... the state of the Country is briefly this: the Army is at Rome, Civita Vecchia taken, but in the Castle of St. Angelo are 500 French troops. The French have 13,000 troops at a strong post in the Roman State, called Castellana. General Mack is gone against them with 20,000: the event in my opinion is doubtful, and on it hangs the immediate fate of Naples. If Mack is defeated, this Country in fourteen days, is lost, for the Emperor [of Austria] has not yet moved his Army, and if the Emperor will not march, this Country has not the power of resisting the French ...'*[29]

As early as 6 October Nelson had informed Earl Spencer: *'... we may be called to save the persons of their Majesties ...'* and had discussed with Sir William and Emma the possibility of having to evacuate the royal family.

Sir William began to pack up his vases and paintings.

King Ferdinand and his army had entered Rome amidst wild cheering from the people. The next day, 30 November, Mack marched his army to attack the French who had retired to Castellana, but his army soon abandoned their General, leaving Ferdinand forced to flee back to Naples.

Nelson wrote to Troubridge, in Leghorn on 9 December: ... *'It is reported, and indeed it is certain, that the Neapolitan Officers and many of their men, are run away even at the sight of the Enemy. As must ever be the case, several brave Officers have fallen. I know not the extent of the disaster, but I believe it is very bad. Keep something very often at Leghorn for I think it very probable that I may be forced to send for you in a hurry...'*[30]

These events were taking place while Napoleon and his army were stranded in Egypt.

On 11 December Nelson wrote to Fanny, avoiding all mention of these dramatic developments:

My dearest Fanny,

You will of course get my letter from Leghorn. I arrived here on the 5th. and the poor Queen has again made me promise not to quit her and her family till brighter prospects appear than do at present. The King is with the army and she is sole regent. She is in fact a <u>Great King</u>. My correspondence has now the additional increase of a Turkish and a Russian admiral which with what I had before takes all my time, but Lady Hamilton's goodness forces me out at noon for an hour. What can I say of her and Sir William's goodness to me. They are in fact with the exception of you and my dear father the dearest friends I have in this world. I live as Sir William's son in the house and my glory is as dear to them as their own. In short I am under such obligations that I can never repay but with my eternal gratitude.

The improvement made in Josiah by Lady Hamilton is wonderful ...

I have not received a scrap of a pen from England since 11th. October. Lord St. Vincent is in no hurry to oblige me now ... Never mind, it is my present intention if matters are in good train to leave the country in March and to be in England in the latter end of May or beginning of June to rest the four months. May God bless you my dear Fanny and my father is the constant prayer of your most affectionate

Nelson[31]

The threat of a French invasion of Naples grew daily. Nelson reported to Spencer on 11 December: *'The Queen has again made me promise not to quit her and her Family till brighter prospects open upon her. She is miserable, we know. None from this house have seen her these three days, but her letters to Lady Hamilton paint the anguish of her soul...'*[32]

Fearing the arrival of the French army, Maria Carolina remembered the fate of her sister, Marie Antoinette.

Three days later Nelson formally informed Sir William of the evacuation plans:

As I have been informed that this Kingdom is invaded by a formidable French Army, I think it my duty to acquaint your Excellency, for the information of the English merchants and others residing at Naples, that the three English transports in this Bay have my directions to receive such effects of the English as they can stow, and that the whole Squadron is ready to receive their persons, should such an event be found necessary as for them to embark.

I have the honour to be &c. Nelson

NB. I need not say that I mean valuable effects, and not household furniture. I also beg leave to recommend that anything sent on board Ship should be done with as little bustle and as much secrecy as possible.[33]

It was Hamilton's duty to arrange the evacuation of the British residents.

This same day, after his disastrous attempt to take Rome, the dejected King Ferdinand arrived back in Naples. The safety of the royal family became paramount. Nelson summoned all available ships from his squadron.

He wrote to Troubridge:

Most secret Naples 15th. December1798

Things are in such a critical state here, that I desire you will join me without one moment's loss of time, leaving the Terpsichore in Leghorn Roads to bring off the Great Duke, should such a measure be necessary. The King is returned here and everything is as bad as possible. For God's sake make haste! Approach the place with caution ... All here join in love and best regards with your faithful friend,

Nelson[34]

He sent instructions to Ball:

Naples, December 15th. 1798

My dear Ball,

I desire you will send me directly the Goliath, and order Foley to come through the Faro of Messina, that he may get information ... the situation in this Country is very critical – nearly all in it are traitors or cowards. God bless you. Keep this secret, except to caution Foley not to approach Naples but with great caution ... Do not send a Neapolitan Ship: There are traitors in the Marine. In short, all is corrupt ...

Nelson[35]

Secrecy in these evacuation plans was essential. There had been revolutionary rumblings in Naples for some time and no one knew how many of the population were loyal to their King and Queen. Rumours of the impending departure of the royal family had to be stifled, especially from the Lazzaroni, the lower classes always loyal to the King, who might have tried to prevent his departure. Naples was indeed now a dangerous place. The royal family had no choice but to escape to their second capital city, Palermo in Sicily.

Sir William was forced to abandon his furniture, beloved antiquities and other possessions in the Palazzo Sessa, the Villa Emma and at Caserta, saving only the vases, pictures and bronzes packed to send to England.

Emma accepted the loss of all their possessions, including most of her clothes, with remarkable calm. She was more concerned for the safety of the King and Queen and their children. In the one remaining week before the evacuation she and her mother worked tirelessly, every night receiving boxes and trunks sent secretly by the Queen to the Palazzo Sessa for transportation to Nelson's ships.

The Queen sent notes to Emma with every delivery of boxes and jewel cases:

'I venture to send you this evening all our Spanish money, both the King's and my own, they are sixty thousand gold ducats. It is all we have, for we have never hoarded, the diamonds of the whole family, both men and women, will arrive tomorrow evening ...'[36]

In a further note she wrote: *'I am in despair of desolation and my tears flow incessantly. The blow, its suddenness has bewildered me, and I do not think I shall recover from it. All my gratitude is devoted to you.'*[37] Another note was signed: *'The most wretched of women, mothers, queens, but your sincere friend.'*[38]

Sir William estimated the value of these gold coins, diamonds and jewels to be two and a half million, sterling.

Nelson worked furiously planning the embarkation for the following day, down to the last detail. He had carried out evacuations of military forces before, but an evacuation of this complexity required all his courage, skill and organizational ability.

He sent Lady Knight a comforting note:

Naples December
20th. 1798

My dear Madam,

Commodore Stone will take care of you. Do not be alarmed, there is in truth no cause for it.

Ever your faithful servant
Nelson[39]

Having had little time to pack their own personal belongings, Sir William, Emma and her mother arranged their own secret departure. An additional distressing aspect of their departure for Sir William was that, bound to secrecy, he could not tell his servants they were leaving Naples. They attended a fête at the Turkish Minister's residence, slipped away early and walked to their pre-arranged departure point to be picked up and rowed out to the *Vanguard* in the dark, leaving their carriage waiting and their servants expecting them home later.

Nelson, meanwhile, made his way through a secret passage to the royal apartments to conduct the royal party to his barge waiting at the quay. They were then rowed out to the *Vanguard* under cover of darkness.

The weather was too rough to set sail on the following day but the *Vanguard* managed to leave at 7 p.m. on Sunday 23 December '*in company with a Neapolitan Ship of the Line, a number of merchant ships and the English transports*'.

On board the *Vanguard* were the royal family, Sir William, Emma and her mother, the Imperial Ambassador and suite, several Neapolitan nobles and their servants and several English gentlemen and merchants. Two thousand more evacuees, including Lady Knight and Cornelia, had been taken aboard other ships.

Next day, the fleet of miscellaneous ships was struck by a violent gale. Nelson wrote that '*it blew harder than I ever experienced since I have been at sea*'. While his full attention was devoted to saving his ship with its precious cargo of people and possessions, (the *Vanguard* lost its topsails, one member of the crew was killed), Emma and her mother, suppressing their own fears and with great courage, selflessly concentrated on helping those around them who were collapsing through sickness and fear.

Emma took care of the Queen and her children in Nelson's cabin. Mrs Cadogan attended the King, whose servants, apart from one man, were incapable of serving him. Once Emma went in search of Sir William and found him in his sleeping quarters, holding a loaded pistol in each hand. He was determined, he explained, to shoot himself rather than go down in a sinking ship '*with the guggle, guggle, guggle, guggle*' of water in his throat.

Further disaster struck the following morning, 25 December, when the Queen's youngest son, six year-old Prince Carlo Alberto, having eaten a good breakfast, was taken ill with convulsions. Emma nursed him throughout the day, but he died in her arms at 7 p.m. The Queen and Emma would not have known the exact cause of his death.*

On this terrifying voyage, the Prince's death must have been almost too much for the Queen and Emma to bear. Maria Carolina doted on her children and Emma knew them all well.†

---

* This may have been an epileptic seizure, although there are seizures caused by diabetes or a heart condition.

† In December 1778 Hamilton had reported the death of a three year old prince whom he described as 'one of the most aimiable and beautiful children I ever beheld'.

After the nightmare voyage, ending with this tragic death, the *Vanguard* reached Palermo and anchored at 2 a.m. Nelson escorted the distressed Queen and the princesses ashore. The Queen was exhausted and too devastated by Prince Albert's death to face a public reception on shore. The King stepped ashore at 9 a.m. to be met by joyous acclamation.

Nelson would have been exhausted and thanking God for saving his ship and its passengers. Hugely relieved, he wrote a note to Emma:

My dear Lady Hamilton

I shall most certainly expect the happiness of seeing you and Sir Wm. & Mrs. Cadogan at dinner, come and let us have as merry an Xt:mas as circumstances will admit. & believe Me Ever Yours Most Truly

Nelson[40]

Presumably, this dinner invitation was deferred to the evening of 26 December, when Sir William and Emma were still on board, as yet unsure of where they might be housed on shore.

CHAPTER 13

Exiles in Palermo

*'Emma goes on perfectly well and plays a very conspicuous part in the
Political line'*
Hamilton to Greville, March 1799

*'I send her [the Queen] every night a messenger to Palermo & she gives me
the orders the same'*
Emma to Greville, 19 July 1799

*'Lord Nelson is here & there & every were, I never saw such zeal &
activity in my life as in this wonderfull man'*
Emma to Greville, 19 July 1799

'The Kingdom of Naples is liberated from thieves and murderers'
Nelson to Fanny, Naples 4 August 1799

FOR THEIR FIRST two nights ashore in Palermo, Sir William and Emma,
both utterly exhausted, were guests of the King and Queen who took
up residence in the Colli Palace. They were soon allocated a summer
villa belonging to the King until Sir William found a residence near the
harbour, the Palazzo Palagonia, which he rented as the British embassy.
Nelson lived there with them whenever he was ashore, sharing expenses.

Many British refugees, including the bankers, Gibbs and Noble, and
Graeffer, the gardener who had created the English garden at Caserta,
were accommodated in the Palazzo. Sir William later wrote of his
'alarmingly costly exile'.

On arrival at Palermo, Nelson sent a full report to St. Vincent
describing the evacuation of Naples and giving Emma full credit for
her contribution and her bravery during the terrifying voyage:

Palermo, December 28th. 1798

My Lord,

On the 22nd. I wrote a line to Commodore Duckworth, telling him, that the Royal Family of the Two Sicilies were safely embarked on board the Vanguard, and requested him to take the first opportunity of acquainting your Lordship of this event. For many days previous to the embarkation it was not difficult to see that such a thing might happen ... from this time, the danger for the personal safety of their Sicilian Majesties was daily increasing, and new treasons were found out, even to the Minister of War. The whole correspondence relative to this important business was carried on with the greatest address by Lady Hamilton and the Queen, who being constantly in the habits of correspondence, no one could suspect. It would have been highly imprudent in either Sir William Hamilton or myself to have gone to Court, as we knew that all our movements were watched ... Lady Hamilton, from this time to the 21st., every night received the jewels of the Royal Family, &c. &c. and such clothes as might be necessary for the very large party to embark, to the amount, I am confident, of full two millions five hundred thousand pounds sterling ... on the 19th. I received a note from General Acton, saying, that the King approved of my plan for their embarkation ... The mob by the 20th. were very unruly, and insisted the Royal Family should not leave Naples; however, they were pacified by the King and Queen speaking to them.

On the 21st., at half-past 8P.M. three barges with myself and Captain Hope, landed at a corner of the Arsenal. I went into the palace and brought out the whole Royal Family, put them into the Boats, and at half-past nine they were all safely on board the Vanguard ... Sir William Hamilton had also directed two Vessels to be hired for the accommodation of the French emigrants, and provisions were supplied from our Victuallers ... on the 23rd., at 7P.M., the Vanguard, Sannite, and Archimedes, with about twenty sail of Vessels left the Bay of Naples; the next day it blew harder than I have ever experienced since I have been at sea. Your Lordship will believe that my anxiety was not lessened by the great charge that was with me, but not a word of uneasiness escaped the lips of any of the Royal Family. On the 25th. at 9A.M. Prince Albert, their Majesties' youngest child, having eat a hearty breakfast, was taken ill, and at 7P.M. died in the arms of Lady Hamilton; and here it is my duty to tell your Lordship the obligations which the whole Royal Family as well as myself are under on this trying occasion to her Ladyship. They necessarily came on board without a bed, nore could the least preparation be made for their reception. Lady Hamilton provided her own beds, linen, &c. and became <u>their slave,</u> for except one man, no person

*belonging to Royalty assisted the Royal Family nor did her Ladyship enter a
bed the whole time they were on board. Good Sir William also made every
sacrifice for the comfort of the august Family embarked with him. I must not
omit to state the kindness of Captain Hardy and every Officer in the
Vanguard, all of whom readily gave their beds for the convenience of the
numerous persons attending the Royal Family ... The Vanguard anchored
at 2A.M. of the 26th. at 5, I attended her Majesty and all the princesses on
shore; her Majesty being so much affected by the death of Prince Albert that
she could not bear to go on shore in a public manner. At 9A.M., his Majesty
went on shore, and was received with the loudest acclamations and apparent
joy. I have the honour to be, &c.*

Nelson[1]

The January weather was unusually cold and snowy. Neither the
Hamiltons' residence nor the Colli Palace had fireplaces, adding to the
discomfort of the evacuees.

On 1 January the Queen wrote: '*There is death in my heart, but in order
not to give offence I have to be at all this* [court receptions]. *The weather is
so perishingly cold and it snows continually, so that all the streets and roofs
are white, which is very extraordinary for Palermo. I have never been so cold
in all my life ...*'[2]

Although determined to regain control of Naples, King Ferdinand
philosophically accepted his situation in Palermo and was content so
long as he could go out hunting. It was beyond Sir William's physical
ability to accompany him. He retired to bed ill for the first three days
and wrote to Greville on 6 January:

'*... from my last dispatch to Lord Grenville, you will hear of the King and
Queen of Naples and all their Royal Family having been obliged to take refuge
on board the Vanguard, and by the contrivance of Lord Nelson and I are safely
lodged in their Palace here with a treasure in jewells and money of not less
than two and a half millions sterling. Emma has had a very principal part in
this delicate business, as she is and has been for several years the real and only
confidential friend of the Queen of Naples ...*'[3]

Emma's letter to Greville vividly describes their experience.

Palermo Jan. 7 1799

*I have onely time to write you one line as Sir William is not sure he can
have a moment to spare today to let you know of our arrival here. We cannot
enter into detail of our being obliged to quit dear Naples. If you are
acquainted with Lords Grenville or Spencer you will know the particulars
from them, know onely the Vanguard Lord Nelson brought ous off with all*

the Royal familly & we arrived here on Christmas day at night after having been near lost, a tempest that Lord Nelson had never seen for thirty years he had been at sea the like; all our sails torn to peices & all the men ready with their axes to cut away the masts & poor I to attend & keep up the spirits of the Queen, the princess Royall, 3 young princesses, a baby six weeks old & two young princes Leopold and Albert, the last, 6 years old, my favourite, taken with convulsions in the midst of the storm & at 7 in the evening of Christmas day expired in my arms, not a soul to help me, as the few women her Majesty brought on board were incapable of helping her or the poor Royal children. The King & prince were below in the ward room with Castelcicala, Belmonte, Grovina, Acton & Sir William, my mother their assisting them, all their attendants being so frighten'd & on their knees praying. The King says my mother is an angel. I have been for twelve nights without once closing my eyes, for 6 nights before the embarkation I sat up at my own house receving all the jewells, money & effects of the Royall familly & from thence conveying them on board the Vanguard, living in fear of being torn to pieces by the tumultuous mob who suspected our departure, but Sir Wm. & I being beloved in the Country saved ous. On the 21st. at ten at night, Lord Nelson, Sir Wm. mother & self went out to pay a visit, sent all our servants a way & ordered them in 2 hours to come with the coach & order's supper at home. When they were gone, we set off, walked to our boat & after 2 hours got to the Vanguard. Lord N. then went with armed boats to a secret passage adjoining to the pallace, got up the dark staircase that goes in to the Queens room and with a dark lantern, cutlasses, pistol etc. etc. brought off every soul, ten in number to the Vanguard at twelve a clock. If we had remained to the next day we should have all been imprisoned, but we remained 2 days in the bay to treat with the Neapolitans but alas with such vile traitors what can you do.

It is not a month since Mack went out with forty thousand men & shamefully to tell those forty thousand have been frightened and beat by about six, eight or ten at the most, nor cou'd the brave unhappy Mack make them fight all the officers bought by the French & all the army naturally corrupt. The gallant Mack is now at Capua fighting it out to the last & I believe coming with the remains of his vile army in to Calabria to protect Sicily, but thank God we have got our brave Lord Nelson, the King & Queen & the Sicilians adore, next to worship him & so they ought for we shou'd not have had this Island but for his glorious victory. He is called here nostro liberatore nostro salvatore.

We have left everything at Naples but the vases & best pictures, 3 houses elegantly furnished, all our horses & 6 or 7 carriages I think is enough for the *vile French for we cou'd not get our things off not to betray the Royal familly & as we were in counsel we were sworn to secrecy, so we are the worst off; all the other ministers have saved all by staying some days after us. Nothing can equal the manner we have been receved here, but dear, dear Naples; we now dare not shew our love for that place for this country is jelous of the other. We cannot at present profit of our leave of absence for we cannot leave the Royal family in their distress. Sir William however says in the Spring we shall leave this as Lord St. Vincent as order'd the ships to carry us down to Gibraltar. God onely knows what yet is to become of us, we are worn out, I am with anxiety & fatige, Sir Wm. as had 3 days a billious attack, but is not well. My dear adorable Queen whom I love better than <u>any person in the world</u>, is allso unwell, <u>we weep together</u> & now that is our onely comfort. Sir William & the King are philosophers, nothing affects them thank God, & we are scolded even for showing proper sensibility. God bless you my dear Sir. Excuse this scrawl & believe me, ever your most oblidged & gratefull*

Emma Hamilton[4]

St. Vincent wrote to Emma on 17 January: *'I shall never cease to admire the magnanimous conduct of your Royal Friend and self, during the late severe Trials at Naples, and during your short voyage to Palermo. The Page of History will be greatly enriched by the introduction of this Scene in it, for the greatness of both your minds, and the firmness and ability, shown in the most critical situation.'*[5]

There was as yet no obvious romantic attachment between Emma and Nelson, other than mutual admiration. They had similar personalities and understanding each other drew them closer together. Both were conscious of their lowly backgrounds and had worked hard to prove themselves. Both consequently always sought attention and recognition. They were generous, to a fault, kind and considerate towards others and both sought to help their own family as much as they could.

Nelson had an opportunity to rest in Palermo after his strenuous and stressful exertions during the previous nine months. He was, however, still in command of his squadron and held himself responsible for the safety of the royal family.

He spent most of the next five months on shore. He masterminded the operations of his squadron, sending orders to those of his Nile captains still with him, confident that they could be relied upon. Keeping in touch with his captains, St. Vincent, Lord Spencer, political figures, other Admirals, consuls and commissioners at various ports around the Mediterranean meant that he spent hours every day writing letters, orders and reports.

'*Here I am writing from morn to eve*', he told St. Vincent.

Nelson warned his brother, William, on 18 January, '*You must excuse short letters*' and said, '*If you get six lines, it is as much as you can expect, for I have more writing than two hands could well get through.*'[6]

St. Vincent wrote him an encouraging note:

...The sensations you must have gone through before and since your departure from Naples, must have been very trying; nevertheless, I trust the greatness of your mind will keep up the body, and that you will not think of abandoning the Royal Family you have by your fitness and address preserved from the fate of their late Royal relations in France ... God bless you my dear Lord, be assured no man loves and esteems you more truly than your very affectionate

St. Vincent[7]

Nelson's orders to continue his command and to support the King and Queen were clearly backed by his Commander-in-Chief. He wrote to Spencer on 7 January: '*... The events which have taken place in the Kingdom of Naples have been so rapid and extraordinary, that it appears a dream. The King, God bless him! is a philosopher; but the great Queen feels sensibly all which has happened. She begs me not to quit Palermo; for that Sir William and Lady Hamilton, and myself, are her only comforts ...*'[8]

The King and Queen, unable to depend on their own army and uncertain of the loyalty of the nobility both in Naples and Palermo, were now dependent on the British for protection. Both Hamilton and Nelson knew they could not leave Palermo until their situation was resolved.

On 2 January Nelson wrote to Fanny: '*it is my intention if I get leave to quit this situation*' and requested she find him a new house: '*I must have a house in London. I should like the one that was Captain Suckling's or one like it. The rooms must be light and airy, but this is supposing my pension is handsome. I wish you to think if Round Wood pleases you, if not, look out for another ... Sir William and Lady Hamilton desire to be kindly remembered to you both and hope to be your sincere friends as they are mine.*'[9]

But, on 17 January, he gave her distressing news about Josiah: '*I wish I could say much to your and my satisfaction about Josiah, but I am sorry to say and with real grief, that he has nothing good about him, he must sooner or later be broke, but I am sure neither you or I can help it, I have done with the subject it is an ungrateful one.*'[10]

The previous August St. Vincent had sent Nelson an extremely critical report on Josiah: *'It would be a breach of friendship to conceal from you that he loves drink and low company, is thoroughly ignorant of all forms of service, inattentive, obstinate, and wrong-headed beyond measure, and had he not been your son-in-law* [the term used at the time for step-son] *must have been annihilated months ago ...'*[11]

Nelson had replied, briefly, in Josiah's defence: *'I am glad to think you are a little mistaken in Nisbet. He is young but I find a great knowledge of the Service in him ... He may have lived too long in Lisbon.'*[12]

Josiah wrote to Nelson in April, promising to mend his ways: *'I have now determined to do everything in my power to deserve the unmerited promotion which you have given me, and hope my endeavours for the future will always meet with your approbation, as you are the only person on earth who has my interest truly at heart...'*[13]

Fanny received a brief update: *'He has sent to say that he is sensible of his youthful follies and that he shall alter his whole conduct. I sincerely wish he may, both for his and your sake.'*[14]

Later that month the French entered Naples where they were met with resistance from the Lazzaroni, who fought hand to hand in the streets until they were overcome. The French set about plundering the palaces, art galleries and museums. On 23 January 1799 the Kingdom of Naples became the Parthenopean Republic. It lasted only five months.

During the month of January Nelson sank into depression. He wrote to Lady Parker on 1 February 1799:

'... My health is such that without a great alteration, I will venture to say a few weeks will send me to that bourne from whence none return; but God's will be done. After the action I had nearly fell into a decline, but at Naples my invaluable friends Sir William and Lady Hamilton nursed and set me up again. I am worse than ever; my spirits have received such a shock that I think they cannot recover it. You who remember me always laughing and gay, would hardly believe the change; but who can see what I have and be well in health? Kingdoms lost and a Royal Family in distress; but they are pleased to place confidence in me, and whilst I live and my services can be useful to them, I shall never leave this country, although I know that nothing but the air of England, and peace and quietness, can perfectly restore me ...'[15]

The same day he commented to St. Vincent: *'... There is no true happiness in this life and in my present state I could quit it with a smile...'*[16]

Nelson assured Captain Ball who was blockading Malta: *'I am very anxious to be with you myself, but I am tied so fast here by their Sicilian Majesties that I cannot move...'*, adding that Sir William had been *'much indisposed'.*[17]

By the end of February he was still preoccupied with thoughts of death when he wrote to Davison: *'Thank you most heartily, my dear Davison, for your letter. Believe me, my only wish is to sink with honour into the grave, and when that shall please God, I shall meet death with a smile. Not that I am insensible to the honours and riches my King and Country have heaped on me, so much more than any Officer could deserve; yet I am ready to quit this world of trouble, and envy none but those in the estate of six feet by two. I am &c*

Nelson[18]*

The numerous exiles in the Palazzo Palagonia were suffering in the bitterly cold weather and from frequent illness. Everyone had been forced to flee Naples saving few possessions. In their unhappiness the British residents took to gambling at cards for an evening's entertainment, as was the custom at the royal palace. Emma is accused of excessive gambling, but it is unlikely that she received money for this from Sir William. Nelson generously passed her small amounts so that she could enjoy a few happy hours in their grim circumstances. He never gambled and he would not have allowed her to squander large amounts.

Emma made friends with Nelson's captains. Alexander Ball wrote to her on 9 February 1799:

My dear Madam,

... I shall have the pleasure of seeing you and Sir William Hamilton in England this summer. How very much I wished to be near you, when you were reading the parliamentary effusions of gratitude and joy for the services Lord Nelson has rendered his country! I would rather be Lord Nelson, than any Duke – or, indeed, any man – in England; and you may guess how very proud I am in having such a friend. Indeed, I feel, that I owe more to him than any man in this world. I have written to Sir William; God bless you both! I remain, with sincere respect and esteem, my dear Madam, your Ladyship's most devoted and obliged humble servant.

Alexander John Ball[19]

The people of Malta were nearing starvation. Emma used her

---

* Nelson and the captains of the Nile fleet had appointed Alexander Davison sole agent to handle the sale of the French ships taken at the Nile and to arrange distribution of the prize money.

influence with the Queen to have money and corn supplied to them. The Emperor of Russia recognized her contribution by awarding her the Order of Malta. She was extremely proud of this award. Alexander Ball was awarded a Knight of the Order of Malta at the same time. Thereafter he called Emma his 'sister.'

Writing to Emma on 23 February, he supports her claim that she helped to obtain corn supplies for the Maltese. '...*We are anxiously waiting for the Maltese deputies to return from Palermo. The inhabitants are critically situated; but, I hope, all will end well. Good news from you will determine it...*'[20]

In March the distressed Sir William received devastating news from Greville that the *Colossus*, the ship carrying some of his precious collection of vases, had foundered off the Scilly Isles. There was little hope of salvaging any of the vases. Added to his other losses at Naples and Caserta, this was a bitter blow. He believed '*all of the best vases in my collection ... The cream of my collection*'[21] were in eight cases on board the *Colossus*.

His friend Sir Gilbert Elliot told his wife: '*It will go far, I think, to break his heart, and I am really most heartily grieved at his loss.*'[22]

All was not entirely lost. Hamilton explained to Greville: '*I have the rest of my vases here on board of a transport, and most of my best pictures and I hope they may get home safe, but if insurance is not too high I shall take that method of saving something at least from the general wreck that has attended my fortune of late ... and I shall be able after all to leave sufficient to Emma and something for my best Friend and those I love best.*'[23]

Sir William believed that he had only a few years left. The task of cheering him up and supporting him in his frailty fell to Emma.

His letter continued: '*...and now Lord Nelson who lives with us and has done so ever since he returned from Egypt says he cannot do without Emma's and my assistance, not having any language but his own. How I shall get out of this scrape I know not, but as I mean to leave him my Secretary as Interpreter and I have made him known to Genl. Acton and the Prince Belmonte who both speak English ... I still hope to be with you some time in June or July...*'

He went on to praise Emma: '*... I need not tell you Emma goes on perfectly well and plays a very conspicuous part in the Political line as she is and has long been the true friend and Confidential one of the Queen of Naples, and is realy of great use to us all...*'

In a further letter to Greville on 8 April, Sir William complains, yet again, of the expenses he is obliged to bear: '...*You may judge, my dear Charles what it is to keep a table for all the poor British emigrants from Naples, who have none, and for all the officers of the fleet, as Lord Nelson lives in the house with us, and all the business, which is immense, is transacted in our house.*'[24]

When he claimed compensation for these expenses on his return home he was disgracefully treated by Grenville and the British government.

His hopes of leaving for England were again postponed: '... *if unfortunately the business should drag on the summer, it not be prudent for me to dash into a London fog at once and I must wait next Spring, and God knows I have little time to lose for I feel old age coming on fast...I love Lord Nelson more and more – his activity is wonderful, and he loves us sincerely.*'[25]

Sir William's current state of mind helps to explain his attitude when Nelson and Emma begin their love affair.

During March Nelson wrote to John Spencer Smith at Constantinople:

Palermo 12th. March 1799

Dear Sir,

I wish very much for two or three very fine India shawls: the price is no object. As I am entirely unacquainted with any person at Constantinople, I take the liberty of requesting the favour of you to ask some of your friends to do me that kindness. The amount I shall pay, with <u>many, many</u> thanks, either in London or any other place, when I know it. In doing this favour you will confer a lasting obligation on,

Nelson[26]

These shawls were intended as a gift for Emma to wear in her 'Attitudes', which she continued to perform in Palermo. As Emma's story unfolds they become heart-rending evidence of her love for him.

At the end of March Nelson received a letter from Davison [dated 7 December] warning him that Fanny intended to join him: '... *I cannot help repeating my sincere regret at your continuation in the Mediterranean ... your valuable better half writes to you ... she is in good health, but very uneasy and anxious, which is not to be wondered at ... She bids me say, that unless you return home in a few months, she will join the Standard at Naples...*'[27]

Fanny may have heard the rumours about Nelson paying undue attention to Emma but, in early December, she was unaware of the dangerous situation in Naples that Nelson was obliged to resolve.

He wrote to her from Palermo on 10 April:

My dear Fanny,

Yesterday brought me your letters of December ... you must not think it possible for me to write even to you as much as I used to do ... You would by February have seen how unpleasant it would have been had you followed any advice, which carried you from England to a wandering sailor. I could, if you had come, only struck my flag and carried you back again, for it would have been impossible to have set up an establishment either at Naples or Palermo. Nothing but the situation of affairs in this country has kept me from England; and if I have the happiness of seeing their Sicilian Majesties safe on their throne again, it is probable I shall yet be home in the summer. Good Sir William, Lady Hamilton and myself, are the mainsprings of the machine, which manage what is going on in this country. We are all bound for England when we can quit our posts with propriety ...

Nelson[28]

He was over-optimistic about an early return to England. He would be involved in the affairs of their Neapolitan Majesties for a further fourteen months.

Events began to move rapidly after an Austro-Russian alliance was formed. Their armies marched into Northern Italy and successfully drove the French back. This encouraged King Ferdinand and Queen Maria Carolina to mount a second campaign to retake Naples. Napoleon at this time was still in North Africa.

They found their leader in Cardinal Ruffo, who had escaped with them from Naples. Ruffo volunteered to raise an army, comprised of Southern Italian rabble, to march on Naples. The King agreed to the enterprise, appointing Ruffo his 'Vicar General'.

At the same time Nelson sent Troubridge with a squadron to blockade Naples. Within days Troubridge had taken the islands in the bay. Nelson informed Spencer on 29 April: *'Since I wrote you last, things have been every day improving in the Kingdom of Naples ... these happy prospects have been brought about, first, by the war of the Emperor [of Austria] secondly, by the wonderful loyalty of the lower order of the people; and lastly, I flatter myself I may say, by the conduct of the English ...'[29]*

A letter from Troubridge and Nelson's reply illustrate the prevailing attitude towards the punishment of those regarded as traitors to their King. Troubridge's letter read:

3rd. April 1799

All the Ponza Islands have the Neapolitan flag flying. Your Lordship never beheld such loyalty; the people are perfectly mad with joy, and are asking for *their beloved Monarch ... If the Nobility were men of principle and of respectability, how easy it would be to get the Neapolitan soldiers and militia to declare for their King. I wish we had a few thousand good English troops, I would have the King of Naples on his throne in forty-eight hours ... If the Navy of the King of Naples had been composed of such men, the people would never have revolted ... I pray your Lordship to send an honest Judge here, to try these miscreants on the spot, that some proper examples may be made ... Pray press the Court to send the Judge by the return of the <u>Perseus</u> as it will be impossible to go on, else; the villains increase so fast on my hands, and the people are calling for justice; eight or ten of them must be hung ...[30]*

Troubridge had arrested a Neapolitan officer and a revolutionary priest, amongst others.

Nelson replied swiftly on 7 April:

... we go to the Queen this evening, where all your letters are already gone, and I have pressed for flour: everything the Islanders want, must and shall be instantly sent. Money, £500, is sent to you ... The universal joy over Palermo for this first success (which I really look upon as the near forerunner of the fate of Naples) is as great as can be wished ... Just come from the Queen and Acton – every provision asked for will begin to be loaded tomorrow. <u>Minerve</u> shall bring the <u>troops</u> and <u>Judge</u>.

Send me word some proper heads are taken off: this alone will comfort me ....

Nelson[31]

The Neapolitan revolution was different from the French revolution in which the nobility either fled or were executed by the rabble. In Naples the common people and the Lazzaroni remained loyal and longed for the King's return. It was the nobility, with some of the intelligentsia, who supported the French in setting up the Parthenopaen Republic.

Early in May Nelson received news from St. Vincent that a French fleet was at sea, attempting to join forces with the Spanish fleet. He immediately gathered together his squadron: four ships from Troubridge and Ball with his line of battleships (leaving the Russian squadron off Malta). Nelson himself was in a quandary whether to join the fleet or stay to protect Sicily. He wrote to St. Vincent from Palermo on 13 May:

'... what a state I am in! If I go, I risk, and more than risk, Sicily, and what is now safe on the Continent ... As I stay, my heart is breaking; and to mend the matter I am seriously unwell ...'[32]

Nelson decided to go.

He left on 19 May and wrote to Emma from the *Vanguard* that evening at 8 o'clock: '*To tell you how dreary and uncomfortable the* Vanguard *appears, is only telling you what it is to go from the pleasantest society to a solitary cell; or, from the dearest friends to no friends. I am now perfectly the* great man *– not a creature near me. From my heart, I wish myself the little man again! You, and good Sir William, have spoiled me for any place but with you. I love Mrs. Cadogan. You cannot conceive what I feel, when I call you all to my remembrance ...*'[33]

The Queen wrote sympathetically to Emma: '*That God accompanies our brave and virtuous Admiral these are my sincerest vows, believe that I lament exceedingly the grief which you have suffered and I will see you with great pleasure tomorrow, try to sleep and rest yourself ... I suffer myself also from the departure of our dear virtuous Admiral.*'[34]

It was a false alarm. Nelson waited in vain near the island of Maritimo, off the western coast of Sicily, for a report or sight of the French fleet. He received welcome news from Emma, in which she had evidently apologized for her handwriting and replied:

My dear Lady Hamilton,

Accept my sincere thanks for your kind letter. Nobody writes so well: therefore, pray, say not you write ill ... I can read, and perfectly understand, every word you write. We drank your and Sir William's health. Troubridge, Louis, Hallowell, and the new Portuguese Captain, dined here. I shall soon be at Palermo for this business must very soon be settled. No one, believe me, is more sensible of your regard, than your obliged and grateful

Nelson[35]

When he heard that the French fleet had made for Toulon he returned to Palermo, arriving on 29 May.

Cornelia Knight reported in her journal that '*a grand dinner was given on the 4th. June 1799, at our minister's and there was a ball at Court in the evening.*'

This was the last dinner Hamilton would give as Ambassador to celebrate the birthday of George III, adding another expense to his mounting debts.

The latest British ship of the line, the *Foudroyant*, 80 guns, was sent out to Nelson in Palermo. On 8 June he transferred his flag from the *Vanguard* to the *Foudroyant*. Nelson was caught in a difficult dilemma. He was receiving reports and orders regarding sightings of the French fleet and at the same time being begged by the King and Queen to proceed to Naples.

News that St. Vincent was ill reached Palermo. In despair, Nelson wrote to him on 12 June:

My dear Lord, our St. Vincent!

What we have suffered in hearing of your illness, and of your return to Mahon! ... If you are sick, I will fag for you; and our dear Lady Hamilton will nurse you with the most affectionate attention. Good Sir William will make you laugh with his wit and inexhaustible pleasantry. We all love you. Come, then, to your sincere friends. Let us get you well... your attached, faithful, and affectionate

Nelson[36]

But his pleas were too late. St. Vincent, too ill to carry on, transferred his command to Vice-Admiral Lord Keith on 16 June and sailed for England on the 23rd. He was worried about leaving Nelson under Keith's command – *'it would revolt his feelings'*. Nelson and Keith did not see eye to eye and had little regard for each other. Keith, a cautious man, had written to his sister on 10 April: '... *The world says he is making himself ridiculous with Lady Hamilton and idling his time at Palermo when he <u>should</u> have been <u>elsewhere</u> ...*'[37] And again on 19 April: '... *a ship from Palermo brings the most wretched account of Sicily – the King despised and insulted by the people ... the Queen, Lady Hamilton and Lord N___n cutting the most absurd figure possible for folly and vanity ...*'[38]

In Palermo certain people were expressing strong criticism of Nelson and the Hamiltons.

Nelson decided to continue his search for the French fleet. Once again he was off the coast of Maritimo – *'anxiously expecting such a reinforcement as may enable me to go in search of the Enemy's fleet, when not one moment shall be lost in bringing them to battle ...'*[39]

Emma wrote to him on 12 June:

I have been with the Queen this evening. She is very miserable, and says, that though the people of Naples are for them in general, <u>yet</u> things will not be brought to that state of quietness and subordination till the Fleet of Lord Nelson appears off Naples. She therefore begs, entreats, and conjures you, my dear Lord, if it is possible, to arrange matters so as to be able to go to Naples. Sir William is writing for General Acton's <u>answer</u>. For God's sake consider it, and do. We will go with you if you come and fetch us. Sir William is ill – I am ill: it will do us good. God bless you.

Ever, ever yours sincerely,

E. Hamilton[40]

Nelson received word that Keith was returning to the *'defenceless state of Minorca'*, while sending Nelson two ships of the line. It was reported that the French fleet might be heading for Naples.

Nelson and his squadron arrived back in Palermo on 20 June where he held a meeting with the King lasting three hours. The following day the *Foudroyant* set sail for Naples with Sir William and Emma on board.

Earlier, Sir William had explained their position to Greville:

'I knew well that if some negotiation was to be necessary between His Majesty, his nobles, and people, no one cou'd go between them with such a probability of success as myself, and they all knew it. Besides, Lord Nelson, for want of languages and experience of this court and country, without Emma and me, wou'd be at the greatest loss every moment. Considering all this, altho' I have rheumatism in my hip, and am tired and worn out almost, I will not abandon their Sicilian Majesties in so very interesting a moment. It will be a glorious circumstance if we can recover Naples without any further aid than that of Great Britain.'[41]

It has been suggested that it was unnecessary for Emma to be on board the *Foudroyant*, implying that she was meddling in state affairs. However, Sir William clearly valued her assistance. More importantly, Emma had instructions from Maria Carolina to act on her behalf. Describing herself as the *'Queens Deputy'*, she sent daily reports to the Queen and received orders by return. Effective communication was possible as the sea journey between Naples and Palermo took only three days.

Before leaving, Hamilton and Nelson visited Lady Knight, who was seriously ill. She begged them to take care of her daughter, Cornelia. Instructions were duly left with Mrs. Cadogan to fetch Cornelia to live at Palazzo Palagonia if her mother died in their absence.

Cornelia wrote in her journal:

'That lady came for me, and I went with her to our minister's, knowing that it was my mother's wish that I should be under her protection; and I must say that there was certainly at the that time no impropriety in living under Lady Hamilton's roof. Her house was the resort of the best company of all nations, and the attentions paid to Lord Nelson appeared perfectly natural. He always spoke of his wife with the greatest affection and respect.'

There was, at this time, clearly no full-blown affair between Nelson and Emma.

The *Foudroyant* arrived in Naples on 25 June, Nelson having been given full powers to act on King Ferdinand's behalf. Cardinal Ruffo, with his volunteer army of 17,000 men, had entered Naples on the 14 June. General Macdonald, in command of the French army, had withdrawn from Naples afraid that he might be cut off from France.

To save further bloodshed and the destruction of Naples by the departing French army, Ruffo had negotiated a truce by which, after their capitulation, those Neapolitans who had defected to the French who wished, might leave in safety on ships for Toulon.

Nelson was horrified that these Republican rebels (who had taken refuge in the Castles of Uovo and Nuovo) were to be allowed to escape unpunished. He considered the terms of the treaty 'infamous'. Ruffo came on board the *Foudroyant* and a long discussion took place between Nelson and himself, with Sir William and Emma acting as interpreters. Nelson failed to convince the Cardinal that the treaty was terminated by the arrival of the British fleet and that, in his opinion, it could not ' *be carried into execution, without the approbation of his Sicilian Majesty.'*

He sent a declaration to the Jacobins in the Castle of Uovo and Nuovo:

'*Rear Admiral Lord Nelson, K.B., Commander of his Brittanic Majesty's Fleet in the Bay of Naples, acquaints the Rebellious Subjects of his Sicilian Majesty in the Castles of Uova and Nuovo that he will not permit them to embark or quit those places. They must surrender themselves to His Majesty's Royal mercy.'*[42]

He sent Troubridge in command of marine forces to besiege the Citadel of St. Elmo.

By 28 June, having relented somewhat, Nelson sent Ruffo a letter:

'*Sir, I am just honoured with Your Eminency's letter; and as His Excellency Sir William Hamilton has wrote you this morning, that I will not on any consideration break the armistice entered into by you, I hope Your Eminency will be satisfied that I am supporting your ideas. I send once more Captains Troubridge and Ball, to arrange with your Eminency everything relative to an attack on St. Elmo ...'*[43]

In addition he sent urgent dispatches to Sir John Acton and the King. Another report was to be delivered to '*Her Sicilian Majesty in person, waiting at that place for her orders, and to return with her Majesty's answers to me at this place.'*

Nelson was urgently seeking endorsement of his decisions and further orders from the King and Queen.

At the end of June, Nelson was faced with responsibility for handling the case of the most significant Neapolitan rebel – Commodore Caracciolo, of the Neapolitan navy. Caracciolo had sailed with the evacuees to Palermo. He felt insulted when the royal party was transported on Nelson's ship rather than on his. In March he had returned to Naples where he decided to serve the Republic, thereby betraying his King and Queen.

The circumstances of Caracciolo's trial and execution caused immense damage to Nelson's reputation. He was subjected in England to strong criticism for his actions in Naples Bay. However, his actions can be judged by reading the letters and orders he wrote at the time.

Having been informed of the details of Caracciolo's treachery, Nelson decided to commit him to trial, having full authority to do so. He sent the following formal order:

To Count Thurn, Commodore and Commander of His Sicilian Majesty's frigate La Minerva.

By Horatio Lord Nelson &c. &c. &c.

Whereas Francisco Caracciolo, a Commodore in the Service of his Sicilian Majesty, has been taken, and stands accused of rebellion against his lawful Sovereign, and for firing at his colours hoisted on board His Frigate the Minerva, *under your command,*

You are therefore, hereby required and directed to assemble five of the senior Officers under your command, yourself presiding, and proceed to inquire whether the crime with which the said Francisco Caracciolo stands charged, can be proved against him, and if the charge is proved, you are to report to me what punishment he ought to suffer.

Given on board the Foudroyant, *Naples Bay*

The 29th. June 1799

Nelson[44]

The court martial took place on board the *Foudroyant*. As Nelson was acting on the King's authority, the *Foudroyant* was, in effect, the seat of government. The Neapolitan naval officers conducting the trial decided that Caracciolo was guilty and sentenced him to death. When this decision was conveyed to Nelson, he wrote the following order to Count Thurn:

Whereas a Board of Naval Officers of his Sicilian Majesty hath been assembled to try Francisco Caracciolo for rebellion against his lawful Sovereign, and for firing at His Sicilian Majesty's Frigate La Minerva; *And whereas the said Board of Naval Officers have found the charge of rebellion fully proved against him, and have sentenced the said Caracciolo to suffer death; You are hereby required and directed to cause the said sentence of death to be carried into execution upon the said Fransisco Caracciolo accordingly, by hanging him at the fore yard-arm of His Sicilian Majesty's Frigate* La Minerva, *under your command, at five o'clock this evening; and to cause him to hang there until sunset, when you will have his body cut down, and thrown into the sea.*

Given on board the Foudroyant, Naples Bay,

The 29th. of June, Nelson[45]

Nelson refused Caracciolo's appeal that he should be shot (as was the custom for men of his rank) rather than suffer the ignominy of death by hanging. He further refused an appeal by both Hamilton and Count Thurn that there should be a stay of execution for twenty-four hours for the *'care of his soul'*.

Nelson's actions appear merciless in this instance. Although he earned the love and respect of his men for the unfailing care and consideration he gave them, he was a strict disciplinarian and believed implicitly in loyalty to his country's sovereign. He would have considered firing on one's own sovereign's ships an unforgiveable treachery.

To understand Nelson's actions we consider Troubridge's attitude to the Neapolitan traitors, in remarks he made in letters to Nelson from the islands in Naples Bay: *'I wish my powers, or ability, would permit my acting more vigorously against the horrid, plundering and treacherous Enemy. His Majesty will, I hope, the moment he regains Naples, make some great examples of his villainous nobles.'*[46]

He further informed Nelson: *'His Majesty has ordered a Court-Martial to try Marshall Yauch; but as there are only four Officers here of the rank qualified to sit, according to Neapolitan laws, I think he cannot legally be tried, until his Majesty sends over three more officers. I should have been happy to have sat on it, and to have directed some of our Captains to have accompanied me: but as we are not in his Sicilian Majesty's service, it would have caused some noise at home, and certainly would not have been legal.'*[47]

Troubridge, under pressure because the number of trials against the rebels was mounting, reported: *'I am really very ill. I must go to bed. This treachery fairly does me up.'*[48]

When a judge attempted to draw Troubridge into supplying a hangman, he refused. Troubridge commented to Nelson: *'I see their drift: they want to make us the principals, and to throw all the odium upon us.'*[49]

Despite Nelson correctly ordering Caracciolo to be tried and executed by Neapolitan officers, his actions certainly caused *'some noise at home'*. He was strongly condemned by some members of Parliament.

Loyal Neapolitans expected the traitors to be punished. Sir William ended his report on Caracciolo's trial and execution to Lord Grenville: *'... [Caracciolo] was condemned and hung up at the yard arm of the Neapolitan Frigate The* Minerva *... at 5 o'clock in the Evening of the same day, where he hung until sunset to the great Satisfaction of His Sicn. Majesties Loyal Subjects Thousands of which came off from Naples in boats with loud applause at so speedy an Act of Justice ...'*[50]

The reputations of both Sir William and Emma also suffered. Malicious stories about Emma were sent home. One story claimed that Nelson and Emma were rowed around the *Minerva* to see Caracciolo hanging from the yard-arm. This was strongly denied by the Hon. William Rushout, later Lord Northwick, who was on board the *Foudroyant* on the day of the execution.

Distressed, Emma reported the event to the Queen, prompting the following reply:

'I have received with infinite gratitude your dear obliging letters; three of Saturday and one of the previous day, together with the list of Jacobins arrested, who are some of the worst villains we have had. I have also noted the sad but merited end of the unfortunate, demented, Caracciolo. I am deeply conscious of all that your excellent heart must have suffered, and this increases my gratitude.'[51]

Before the King arrived in Naples Bay to add his authority to the situation, members of the nobility and intelligentsia, who had supported the French republic, besieged Emma begging for clemency. Many had been friends, and mutual friends of the royal family.

The King was determined to see the rebels punished, while Maria Carolina wavered between ordering punishment and granting forgiveness. She wrote to Nelson:

'I hope that by imposing force by sea, and their being surrounded on all sides, will be sufficient, without shedding blood, to induce them to return to their allegiance, for I would spare even my enemies.'[52]

Cornelia Knight confirms this in her journal:

'The Queen, who has been accused of so much vindictive cruelty, was, to my certain knowledge, the cause of many pardons being granted. And there was one lady in particular whom she saved, who was her declared enemy, and at the head of a revolutionary association.'

Emma had the unenviable task of making lists of those she interviewed and knew to be among the rebels to send to the Queen. Fiercely loyal to the King and Queen, she was torn between her desire to see traitors punished and her abhorrence of any form of cruelty. She tells Greville that she feels *'quite shatter'd'*.

Nelson had less sympathy for the rebels. He wrote to Mrs Cadogan, whom he addressed as *'Signora Madre'* on 17 July:

... I cannot resist the pleasure it will give me to write you a line, especially as I can tell you that Sir William is grown very much better since his embarkation. Our dear Lady is also, I can assure you, perfectly well; but has her time so much taken up with excuses from rebels, Jacobins, and fools, that she is every day most heartily tired. Our conversation is, as often as we are liberated from these teazers, of you and our other friends in the house at Palermo; and I hope we shall very soon return to see you. Till then recollect that we are restoring happiness to the Kingdom of Naples, and doing good to millions ...'53

Midshipman Parsons, on board the flagship, witnessed the agony of the situation:

'Many, very many, of Italy's beauteous daughters, and those of high rank, have I seen prostrate on our deck, imploring protection ... their graceful forms bent with misery – their dark eyes and clasped hands raised to the Father of all for mercy – their clear, olive complexion changing to a sickly hue from anguish of mind ... I grieve to say that wonderful, talented and graceful beauty, Emma Lady Hamilton, did not sympathise in the manner expected from her generous and noble nature'.54

Emma and Sir William had suffered catastrophic losses of property and possessions, and a traumatic departure from their home and lifestyle in Naples. She had little cause to show sympathy, but she would not have sought brutal punishment. It was not in Emma's power to grant pardons. She simply sent lists of names, including pleas for clemency, to Maria Carolina.

But Maria Carolina also sent instructions via Emma that '... *the rebel patriots must lay down their arms and surrender at the discretion of the King. Then, in my opinion, an example should be made of some of the leaders ... the females who have distinguished themselves in the revolution to be treated in the same way and without pity... this is not pleasure but absolutely necessary for, without it, the King could not for six months peacefully govern his people ... I recommend to you, my dear Lady, the greatest firmness, vigour and severity.'55*

However, she sent Emma considerable amounts of money for those in need, 'certain that it will be dispensed appropriately, for I know your heart'.

On shore trials and public executions of both men and women took place under the King's authority. King Ferdinand, Nelson, Sir William and Emma remained on board ship and were spared these horrors.

Sir William was distressed to read names of friends in the lists of those who had been executed. He reported to Greville: 'The trials of the principal Neapolitan rebels having been carried out without intermission ... many of all classes have suffered death by having been beheaded or hang'd; among the latter we have seen with regret the name of Doctor Domenico Grillo, one of the first physicians, botanists and naturalists in Europe.'[56]

The King's revenge was not as bloody as it may appear. Of the rebels who had tried to leave Naples under the armistice agreement, 162 were executed and a further 500 were imprisoned. There were many rebels awaiting trial in Naples. 3,332 Neapolitan Jacobins were freed to sail from Naples into exile.[57] Nevertheless, by virtue of being on board the *Foudroyant* in the bay of Naples at the time, the reputations of Nelson, Sir William and Emma became stained. All three had acted in what they believed to be the best interests of their country, and upheld this belief to the end.

Emma tells her story in a long letter to Greville:

On board the Foudroyant   Bay of Naples   July 19th 1799
Dear Sir,

We have the oppertunity of sending to England & I cannot let pass this good opertunity without thanking you for your kind remembrance in Sir William's letter. Everything goes on wel here, we have got Naples, all the forts & tonight our troops go to Capua. His Majesty is with us on board were he holds his Councils & leves every day. General Acton & Castelcicala with one gentleman of the bed chamber attend his Majesty. Sir Wm. and Lord Nelson with Acton are the Kings Counsellers & you may be assured that the future government will be most just & solid. The King has bought his experience most dearly, but at least he knows his friends from his enimies, he allso knows the defects of his former government & is determined to remedy them for he has great good sense & his misfortunes have made him steady & look in to himself. The Queen is not come, she sent me as her deputy for I am very popular, speak the Neapolitan Language & consider'd with Sir W. the friend of the people ... We arrived before the King 14 days & I had privatly seen all the Loyal party & having the head of the Laseronys, an old friend, he came in the night of our arrival. He told me he had 90 thousand Laseronis ready at the holding up of his finge, but onely twenty with arms. Lord Nelson to whom I enterpreted got a large supply of arms for the rest & they were deposited with this man. In the mean time Calabrease were commiting murders, the bombs we sent in to St. Elmo were returned & the citty in confusion. I sent for this Pali, the head of the Laser's & told him in great confidence that the King wou'd be soon at Naples & that all we required of him was to keep the citty quiet for ten days from that moment. We give him onely one hundred of our marine troops, he with these brave men kept all the town in order ... I have thro him made the Queens party & the people at large have prayd for her to come back & she is now very popular. I send her every night a messanger to Palermo & she gives me the orders the same. I have given audiences to those of her party & settled matters between the nobility & her Majesty. She is not to see on her arrival any of her former evil counsellers, nor the women of fashion alltho Ladys of the bedchamber formerly her friends & companions & who did her dishonner by their desolute life. *All, all* is changed, she has been very unfortunate but she is a great woman & has sense enough to profit of her past unhappiness & will make for the future *'amende honorable'* for the past. In short, if I can judge it may turn out fortunate that the Neapolitans have had a dose of Republicanism but what a glory to our good King to our Country, to ourselves that we, our brave fleet, our great Nelson has had the happiness of restoring the King to his throne, to the Neapolitans their much loved King & being the instrument of giving a future good, solid & just government to the Neapolitans. The measures the King is taking are all to be approved of, the guilty are punished & the faithfull are rewarded. I have not been on shore but once; the King gave us leave to go as far as St. Elmo's to see the effect of the bombs. I saw at a distance our despoil'd house in town & Villa Emma that have been plunder'd & Sir Wm's new appartment, a bomb burst in it but it made me so low-spirited I dont desire to go again. We shall as soon as the government is fix'd return to Palermo & bring back the Royal familly for I foresee not any permanent government tell that event takes place nor wou'd it be politick after the hospitality the King & Queen receved at Palermo to carry them of in a hurry, so you see there is great management required. I am quite worn out for I am enterpreter to Lord Nelson, the King, Queen and altogether feil quite shatter'd but as things go on well that keeps me up. We dine now every day with the King at 12 o'clock, dinner is over by one, his Majesty goes to sleep & we sit down to write in this heat & on board you may guess what we suffer. My mother is at Palermo, but I have an English lady with me who is of use to me in writing & helping to keep papers & things

*in order. We have given the King all the upper cabins, all but one room that
we write in & receve the ladies who come to the King. Sir Wm. & I have an
apartment below in the ward room & as to Lord Nelson he is here & there
& every were, I never saw such a zeal & activity in my life as in this
wonderfull man. My dearest Sir Wm. thank God, is well & of the greatest
use now to the King. We hope Capua will fall in a few days & then we shall
be able to return to Palermo. On Sunday last we had prayers on board, the
King assisted & was much pleased with the order, decency & good behaviour
of the men, the officers etc. etc. Pray write to me. God bless you, my dear Sir
& believe me ever yours most sincerely*

Emma Hamilton

*P.S. It wou'd be a charity to send me some things for in saving all for my
royal & dear friend I lost my little all: never mind.*[58]

The King did not set foot on shore, but gave permission for Sir
William and Emma to take a boat to see the fort at St. Elmo. They
were able to see the *'despoiled'* and *'plundered'* Palazzo Sessa and Villa
Emma in the distance. Distressed and remembering her past happy
life in these homes, Emma reported *'it made me so low-spirited'*. They
did not know that this would be the last time they would see their
much-loved homes.

A celebration dinner was held on board the *Foudroyant* on 1 August,
the anniversary of the Battle of the Nile. Nelson described the event
to Fanny:

Naples 4th. August 1799

My dear Fanny,

*... Thank God all goes on well in Italy, and the Kingdom of Naples is
liberated from thieves and murderers. But still, it has so overthrown the fabric
of a regular Government, that much time and great care are necessary to keep
the Country quiet ... the 1st. August was celebrated here with as much respect
as our situation would admit. The King dined with me; and, when His
Majesty drank my health, a Royal salute of twenty-one guns was fired from
all his Sicilian Majesty's ships of War, and from all the Castles. In the evening
there was a general illumination. Amongst other representations, a large
Vessel was fitted out like a Roman galley; on its oars were fixed lamps, and
in the centre was erected a rostral column with my name: at the stern were
elevated two angels supporting my picture. In short, my dear Fanny, the
beauty of the whole is beyond my powers of description ... This must not make
you think me vain; no, far, very far from it, I relate it more from gratitude
than vanity. I return to Palermo with the King tomorrow and what may then*

be my movements it is impossible to say ... May God bless you all. Pray say, what is true, that I really <u>steal</u> time to write this letter, and my hand is ready to drop ... But ever believe me your affectionate

Nelson[59]

The people of Naples came out in their boats to honour the Hero of the Nile.

The following day Emma reported the conclusion to the affairs of Naples to Greville:

Foudroyant Bay of Naples August 5, 1799

As Sir Wm. wrote to you to day my dear Sir, I will onely say that the Kingdom of Naples is clear. Gaeta & Capua have capitulated & we sail to night for Palermo having been now seven weeks & every thing gone to our wishes. We return with a Kingdom to present to my much loved Queen. I have allso been so happy to succeed in all my comissions & every thing I was charged with. The King is in great spirits. I have receved all the Ladies for him & he calls me his grande Maitresse ... We have had the King on board a month & I have never been able to go once on shore, <u>do you not call that slavery</u>. I believe we shall come here in the Spring. It is necessary, for our pockets & bodys want bracing ...

God bless you & believe me my dear Greville (tis not a crime to call you so) your sincere & affectionate

Emma Hamilton

My mother is at Palermo longing to see her Emma. You cannot think how she is loved & respected by all. She has adopted a mode of living that is charming, she as a good appartment in our house, allways lives with us, dines, etc. etc. onely when she does not like it, for example, great dinners she herself refuses & as allways a friend to dine with her & La Signora Madre dell'Ambasciatrice is known all over Palermo the same as she was at Naples. The Queen has been very kind to her in my absence & went to see her & told her she ought to be proud of her glorious and energick daughter that has done so much in these last suffering months. Their is great preparations <u>for our return</u>, the Queen comes out with all Palermo to meet us, a landing place is made, balls, suppers, illuminations all ready, the Queen has prepared my cloaths, in short, if I have fag'd I am more than repaid. I tell you this that you may see I am not unworthy of having been once in some degree your elevé.

God bless you.[60]

Three days later the *Foudroyant* sailed triumphantly into the harbour at Palermo, where the King received a hero's welcome.

CHAPTER 14

Restoring the Monarchy at Naples

*'The service which you have doubly rendered to me and the
Two Sicilies can never be equalled"*
King Ferdinand to Nelson, January 1799

'I can neither eat nor sleep for thinking of you my dearest love'
Nelson to Emma, 29 January (1800)

*'We are coming home and I am miserable to leave my dearest
friend the Queen'*
Emma to Greville, 25 February 1800

THE QUEEN AND her children came aboard the *Foudroyant* to dine. The joyous celebrations included a twenty-one gun salute, a thanksgiving service, fireworks and illuminations. Nelson, Sir William and Emma were showered with generous gifts.

Maria Carolina gave Emma a diamond necklace with a pendant portrait of the Queen inscribed *Eterna gratitudine* and two coachloads of dresses to compensate her for those she had lost in Naples.[1] Sir William received the King's portrait set in jewels.

He described their generosity to Banks: *'From the Queen, Emma received a bracelet of the Queen's portrait & hair set with diamonds, earrings of pearl & diamonds, an aigrette of her cypher in diamonds, a complete dress of the finest point lace, baskets of gloves, in short just such a present as such a fine woman as Emma, for except for being a little fatter she is as you saw her eight years ago, could desire.'* He himself received *'a thumping yellow diamond set round with Diamonds in a ring'*[2]

The King, having appreciated Emma's help in receiving the Neapolitan ladies and her continuous correspondence with the Queen, presented Emma with his picture richly set with diamonds. Between them they reportedly received gifts to the value of £6,000.

The King rewarded Nelson with the gift of his own gilt-handled, diamond-encrusted sword given to him by his father Charles III of Spain, accompanied by the following letter:

... the service which you have doubly rendered to me and the Two Sicilies, can never be equalled. In the month of August, you were last year, [the Battle of the Nile], *their sole preserver, and also, during the present one, by organising a most judicious defence for those Kingdoms, with an active and imposing force; preserving me and my family, after so many disasters, the possession of both countries ... To your magnanimous Sovereign, my best Ally, to your generous nation, I owe an avowal of my immense gratitude; and rest assured, my Lord, that this gratitude will never cease, but with your affectionate,*

Ferdinando[3]

Sir William informed Lord Grenville that the King *'left a present of Two Thousand Three Hundred Ounces* [of silver] *to be distributed among the Admiral Lord Nelson's servants and the Ship's Company'*. Soon after he created Nelson Duke of Bronte with an estate at the foot of Mount Etna, claimed to be worth £3,000 a year.

Whilst in Naples Bay Nelson heard that the East India Company had voted him £10,000 in recognition of his victory at the Battle of the Nile. Always generous – '*I never regarded money, nor wanted it for my own use'* – he asked Fanny to give his father, brothers and sisters £500 each.

Referring to the plundering of Naples by the French, Nelson wrote to Nepean and Keith, congratulating the Admiralty and his Commander in Chief for the *'entire liberation of the Kingdom of Naples from a band of robbers'*.[4]

In a letter to Davison, written 15 August, he commented: '... [I] *never received one farthing for all the expenses of the Royal Family on board the* Vanguard *and* Foudroyant. *This I expect from the Board of Admiralty, and that they will order me a suitable sum. It has been honour, and not money which I have sought, nor sought in vain ...'*[5]

After seven stressful weeks on board the *Foudroyant* Nelson rested ashore until 4 October.

Having restored the monarchy at Naples, he achieved honour but found himself in trouble with Keith and the Admiralty. Not for the first, or last time, in his life Nelson disobeyed orders. Keith, while defending Minorca (an important base for the British fleet) sent orders to Nelson for ships from his squadron to assist him. Nelson failed to comply. He explained himself in a letter to Keith on 19 July, from Naples:

... I am perfectly aware of the consequences of disobeying the orders of my Commander in Chief; but as I believe the safety of the Kingdom on Naples depends at the moment on my detaining the Squadron, I have no scruple in deciding that it is better to save the Kingdom of Naples and risk Minorca, than to risk the Kingdom of Naples to save Minorca. Your Lordship will, I hope, approve of my decision ...[6]

Although thereby unpopular with Keith, the Admiralty issued only a mild rebuke. He took the precaution of explaining his action to the Duke of Clarence and to Spencer: '*... I have done what I thought right; others may think differently; but it will be my consolation that I have gained a Kingdom, seated a faithful Ally of His Majesty on his throne, and restored happiness to millions ...*'[7]

Spencer neither censured, nor recalled Nelson: '*You have already, my dear Lord, done wonders. What remains for you to do, may not, perhaps be quite so brilliant, but it is no less useful to your country.*'[8]

The government's positive reaction is seen in Lord Grenville's letter to Spencer:

'*... [I] earnestly hope Lord Nelson will not think himself restrained by Lord Keith's orders to go and watch Minorca which nobody is thinking of attacking ... trust there can be no difficulty now in leaving Lord Nelson (as long as his health makes it possible) in the command of the Mediterranean fleet. He is infinitely fitter than Lord Keith (or anyone else I believe) to act with our Allies.*'[9]

Lord Keith took leave in August, leaving Nelson de facto in temporary command of the Mediterranean, but their disagreement caused difficulties for Nelson when Keith returned in January 1800.

Criticism of Sir William and Emma regrettably reached the ears of important people in London.

Charles Lock wrote revengeful and hostile accounts to his father who had connections to Lord Grenville and the Hon. Charles James Fox MP.

Lock, with his wife Cecilia, had been sent out as Consul General to Naples. In Palermo Sir William and Emma found them a house and invited them to dinner. They took an instant dislike to Emma, possibly because Emma hinted that Cecilia might have Jacobin sympathies due to her Irish connections.

Lock's denigration of the Hamiltons began with his letter to his father on 30 June. It contains shocking comments about Emma and Nelson's infatuation with her: *'Sir William and Lady Hamilton embarked with great secrecy for Naples about ten days ago, in the* Foudroyant *which came singly for them off the Harbour with Lord Nelson on board. I underwent a severe mortification in not being invited to accompany Sir William … which I relied on as Sir William had repeatedly promised I should attend him when he went … But for this I may thank that superficial, grasping and vulgar minded woman whose wish to retain her husband in a situation his age and disinclination render him unfit for, has made her use every endeavour to keep me in the dark, and to make it difficult for Sir William to give up his employment at this moment … Sir William has ever showed a forwardness to give me an insight into the politicks of this Court, and of the mode of conducting business, but the unbounded power her Ladyship possesses over him, and Lord Nelson, with her taking the whole drudgery of it upon herself, has easily prevented his intention. The extravagant love of the latter has made him the laughing stock of the whole fleet and the total dereliction of power and the dignity of his diplomatic character, has made the friends of the former* [Sir William] *regret that he retains the title of a situation, of which he has resigned the functions.'*[10]

Lock was obviously incensed by Sir William's lack of attention to him. On another occasion Lock commented: *'His wife is at the bottom of all the mischief. I can paint nothing so black and detestable as that woman.'*[11] Lock's father probably informed Lord Grenville and Charles Fox of these comments. Accusations thus taken to the very highest level damaged the reputations of Nelson, Sir William and Emma.

Lock's attitude influenced his wife, Cecelia, whose mother, the Duchess of Leinster, wrote to her daughter: *'This Lady Hamilton was a Dolly Sir William Hamilton married, and had she been nothing worse it would not have signified, but she is artful, malicious, envious and detracting; has every bad quality and more spiteful to my Cissy than can be conceived.'*[12]

In 1801 Miss Helen Maria Williams, an English authoress living in Naples, *'deeply inbued with Republican values'* published her 'Sketches' on the affairs in Naples during the time the *Foudroyant* was present in the Bay, in which she wrote:

'The judgement of Lord Nelson, in this cruel transaction [Caracciolo's trial and execution] *was influenced and warped by the artful influence of Lady Hamilton, whose devotion to the Royal Family of Naples made her the inmitigable enemy of all rebels to their authority. The trial and execution of Caraccioli were indecently and unjustly accelerated by this wicked siren.'*[13]

However, Nicholas, in his *Dispatches and Letters of Lord Nelson*, states that Miss Williams' *'ignorance and prejudices render her book generally unworthy of credit'*.

The Earl and Countess Lord and Lady Elgin visited Palermo on their way to Constantinople where Elgin had been appointed ambassador.*

Twenty-one-year-old Mary, Lady Elgin, wrote to her mother: *'You never saw anything equal to the fuss the Queen made with Lady H. and Lord Nelson, wherever she moved, was always by her side ... Such a complete old devil as the Queen is, I never met with; she flattered us beyond credibility; to Lord Nelson it was the most fulsome thing possible. I never saw three people made such thorough dupes of as Lady Hamilton, Sir William and Lord Nelson ... It is really humiliating to see Lord Nelson, he seems quite dying and yet as if he had no other thought than her ... Is it not a pity a man who had gained so much credit should fling himself away in this shameful manner?'*[14]

Lady Elgin had heard rumours about Nelson and Emma at Gibraltar and arrived at Palermo already prejudiced against them. She refused the invitation to stay at the Palazzo Palagonia, but could not avoid dining there, afterwards observing: *'I must acknowledge she is pleasant, makes up amazingly... She looked very handsome at dinner, quite in an undress: my father would say, 'there is a fine woman for you, good flesh and blood'. She is indeed a Whapper! and I think her manner very vulgar. He [Lord Nelson] told Elgin privately that he had lived a year in the house with her and that her beauty was nothing in comparison to the goodness of her heart.'*[15]

Lord Elgin commented on Nelson's poor physical health: [he looks] *'very old, has lost his upper teeth, sees ill of one eye, and has a film coming over both of them. He has pains pretty constantly from his late wound in the head. His figure is mean, and, in general his countenance is without animation.'*[16] But he admired Nelson's ' *infinite fire and decision and dismission of difficulties'* on business matters.

Contrary to the derogatory remarks made by Cecilia and Mary, Midshipman Parsons had been in Emma's company for seven weeks on board the *Foudroyant* remembered her as *'an unjustly treated and wonderful woman'* whose *'generosity and good nature was unbounded'* and *'whose heart was of softer materials than to rejoice in the sufferings of the enemies of the court'.*[17]

---

* During this posting Lord Elgin acquired the sculptures from the temples on the Acropolis in Athens. These are the sculptures now known as the 'Elgin Marbles' in the British Museum.

Nelson sent a brief note to Fanny explaining his continued absence: *'The last letter from the King's Minister here, Sir John Acton, is as follows, "My formal demand is, however, to beg of your Lordship to protect the Two Sicilies, with your name and presence, until at last, all Italy is perfectly quiet;" therefore whatever my state of health may be, I cannot move ...'*[18]

When he wrote these letters Nelson was unaware that Napoleon was escaping from Egypt that very same day.

In Cairo Napoleon had heard that things were not going well for France: Italy was lost, the French army were losing battles in Austria and on the Rhine and a financial crisis was provoking unrest in Paris. Concerned, Napoleon decided France was more important than Egypt. He arrived back in Alexandria on 23 August where two French frigates waited in a cove ready to run the English blockade.

He boarded the *Murion* with four of his generals, one admiral, three members of his Arts and Sciences Corps and his stepson, Eugène. Abandoning his army, they stole away. They sailed in secret along the North African coast, showing no lights at night, reaching Frégus in France on 9 October.

Napoleon marched triumphantly to Paris among admiring crowds shouting 'Welcome, our Liberator'. Napoleon and Eugène arrived home on 16 October. By 11 November, he had effected a *coup d'etat* and was made First Consul. On 19 February he installed himself and his wife, Josephine, in apartments at the Tuileries palace last occupied by King Louis XVI and Marie Antoinette.

Nelson, Sir William and Emma, now closely allied, adopted the motto of the Order of Bath, *'Tria juncta in uno'*, worn by both Nelson and Sir William. To Emma, it meant 'One heart in three bodies'.[19] Nelson wrote to Lord Minto in October: *We are the real* tria juncta in uno' and Sir William informed Greville, *'Lord Nelson and I, with Emma, are the* Tria Juncta in Uno.'

In August, medals arrived for Nelson and his Captains, commissioned by Alexander Davison in gratitude for having been appointed prize money agent for ships taken at the Battle of the Nile.

Sir William wrote to Minto in September describing the situation in Palermo:

'Their Majestys have still much to do before the Government of Naples can recover from its late severe shock and they must seriously think of a total reform in that country to ensure a just and lasting one ... The season is so far advanced that I dare not profit of the Goliath that was appointed by

Lord St. Vincent to carry us home, as we should arrive in London probably in the midst of winter and as there is a prospect of this being the last campaign I have determined to defer my return to England until next spring particularly as Lord Nelson is so desirous of a continuance of the assistance he gets from Emma and me, his Lordship as you know not possessing any other language than his own. We have lived together either on shore or on board his ship ever since he returned from Egypt and I do assure your Lordship that the greatest pleasure I have ever had is in having gained the friendship of this great man and been acquainted particularly with the officers of his squadron. I never met with such a set of valuable brave men. I am really now proud of my country. It is the only one that has conducted itself with dignity, firmness and courage at a period that required universal exertion. Mr. Pitt [Prime Minister] has rendered himself immortal … Emma who desires to be most kindly remembered to your Lordship has made a very conspicuous figure of late and was so useful at Naples in the service of their Sicilian Majesties during our late expedition to that capital that she has received magnificent presents from both with their Majesties' pictures diamonds etc. etc.'[20]

Whilst in the Mediterranean Nelson wrote regularly to the Duke of Clarence. In September he received a long letter from the Duke:

Bushy House, August 4th. 1799

Dear Nelson,

It is a long time since I wrote last … I was earnestly engaged in Parliament upon the Slave Trade for several weeks, when I received your first … however, as maritime affairs have taken so strange a turn in the Mediterranean, I think this letter must reach you.

Your first letter, I perceived, was wrote in ill spirits; however, thank God, the Arch-Duke and Suwarrow have brightened up our prospects … Your friend Buonaparte and his Army are no more. I am in great hopes that the formidable expedition from this country, together with the Russians and Swedes, will recover Holland and the Netherlands, and drive the French into their own country. Sure France cannot withstand all these attacks and misfortunes, and tranquillity must at length be restored to Europe. Adieu for the present; write as circumstances arise, and ever believe me, yours sincerely, – William[21]

Towards the end of the year Nelson's letters to Fanny became less frequent.

During their marriage Nelson wrote over two hundred and fifty letters to Fanny. His letters to her were never the passionate declarations of love of his later letters to Emma. Recent letters to

Fanny expressed a dutiful regard for her, but over time he became exasperated by her despondency and indecisiveness.

Writing only once a month, he made the excuse that the volume of his naval correspondence exhausted him and left no time for any personal letters. Letters between them expressed, as always, only 'affection.' From habit, he signed himself 'your affectionate Nelson.' We can discern his withdrawal from her in his letters. By the end of 1799 he had been serving abroad for seven years and had spent only seven months living with Fanny in England, recovering from his arm amputation. During their long periods of enforced separation his feelings for her cooled, but eventually it was her character that alienated him.

In the letters he gives Fanny snippets of news:

11 September: *'I have wrote to you in all ways by sea and land, but short letters, for my time is fully occupied that I never set my foot out of the writing room, except now and then in an evening with Sir William and Lady Hamilton to the palace ...'*

23 September: *'Yesterday brought me your letters of July 28th. and August 3rd. and I thank you for the indulgence you give me of writing short letters ... I am vexed to think the ministers have done nothing for either my good father or my brothers. I feel it very much and at present I believe they cut me off £1000 a year less than either St. Vincent or Duncan ...'*

Port Mahon 15 October: *'... I am in truth most heartily tired of war... I am here and endeavouring to arrange matters for the reducing of Malta. I am fagged out ...'*

Palermo 7 November: *'... I have just received from the Grand Signor a diamond star with a crescent in the centre which I wear above that of the Bath. But these jewels give not money for meat or drink ...'*

Fanny wrote three or four letters every month. She expresses concern about Nelson's health, rather than affection, and makes no mention of the rumours circulating about her husband and Lady Hamilton. Her letters between August and December give an idea of her lifestyle:

Round Wood 18 August: *'... I rejoice in hearing you are well ... Here we are at the Parsonage at Burnham. The Rector [Nelson's brother William] and Mrs. Bolton are with us... The Rector and myself dined at Holkham [Hall] last Thursday, a full public dinner. The Walpoles were there, as usual kind and very attentive to me ...'*

Round Wood 21 October: *'... I long to hear of the arrival of Sir William and Lady Hamilton... I should have such a good opportunity of acknowledging and thanking Sir W. and Lady Hamilton for their attention and kindness to you and my son ...'*

London 13 November: *'... I was ordered to Lisbon by the physician who attends me, he fears the winter will be too much for me. Not knowing whether you would like me going out of the Kingdom I have declined doing it till I have your positive consent and approbation ...'* [Nelson replied advising her against this, describing Lisbon as *'the most dirty place in Europe covered with fog'*]. *'Too much rain and damp weather makes me suffer very much. Round Wood being very cold for our father and myself. I am ordered to spend some months in London ...'*

St. James Street 3 December: *'...we are safely arrived in town a small ready furnished house at 7 guineas per week, consisting of two rooms and a light closet on a floor. Quite large enough for you and my Josiah should you think it right for him to come home ...'*

St. James's Street 10 December: *'... our good father received yesterday from your brother, William, teasing him about no dignitaries for the Nelson family. I must write to the Rector and beg him not to be so tiresome, for truly I am nursing and doing everything I can to make your father comfortable and then he is quite upset by one of these epistles ...'*

She had also written about William in June: *'The various passions that torment the Rector discomposes our good father who has been describing them to me. First of all ambition, pride and a selfish disposition.'*

Nelson's brother, William, was constantly seeking preferment, through Nelson's influence, to a more financially rewarding parish.

St James's Street 26 December: *'Captain Hardy has made us all happy by the flattering accounts he gives us of your health.* I mentioned your letters were written quite out of spirits. He assures me that is owing to the tiresome people you have to deal with ... Captain Hardy told me you be would be gratified if I sent Lady Hamilton anything, therefore I shall send her Ladyship a cap and kerchief such as worn this cold weather ... I am clothed in two suits of flannel and I hope I shall be the better for it. My health is much mended within this month ...'*[22]

Fanny gave her husband details of the life she shared with his father, but her letters lacked the enthusiasm and encouragement he craved and which he received from Sir William and Emma. His hitherto suppressed passions were about to surface in the heady atmosphere in Palermo.

---

* Hardy had returned to England in the *Princess Charlotte*. Sir Edward Berry replaced him as Nelson's flag captain.

Reports of the relationship between Nelson and Emma appeared in the *Times* in November. Oblique references were made to Venus and Cupido, Mark Anthony and Cleopatra and '*Admiral-attitudes*', brazenly referring to the '*Hero and Lady Ham–t-n.*'

In Palermo Nelson's increasing infatuation with Emma was noticed, including presumably, by Sir William. Rumours rebounded around the Mediterranean and further afield. Minto, by then Ambassador in Vienna, commented with more sympathy than most to his wife: '*He does not seem at all conscious of the sort of discredit he has fallen into, or the cause of it, for he writes still not wisely about Lady Hamilton and all that. But it is hard to condemn and use ill a hero, as he is in his own element, for being foolish about a woman who has art enough to make fools of many wiser than an admiral.*'[23]

Emma's beauty, voluptuous figure and sparkling personality had entranced many men over the years. But in her relationship with Sir William she had enlivened his life, cared for him when he was ill and certainly remained faithful to him. He was grateful for her loyalty. He had always recognised that he would be an old man when Emma was still in her prime. Sir William was now almost seventy, Nelson forty-one and Emma thirty-four years old.

When falling in love with Nelson Emma must have known that an affair with him would mean she stood to lose the respectability she had striven so hard to achieve. Sir William had given her security, social standing and recognition for her singing, acting and language skills.

Sir William wrote to Minto on 22 September: '*... I am really so worn out that I should not be surprised if my career should finish at Palermo. The Queen of Naples is also ill and worn out, talking of dying, and what is more extraordinary <u>Emma who looks as well and as blooming as ever, talks of death every day</u>.* [author's emphasis] *I believe it is the heat and scirocco winds that depress us all for Lord Nelson complains too ...*'[24]

Nelson and Emma's low spirits might be linked to their inability to see any future for their relationship. Emma held a deep affection for Sir William and in gratitude for all that he had done for her and for her mother, she was mindful of her promise to care for him. Despite her beauty and charisma and having been propositioned on occasions, she had remained faithful to Greville for five years and to Hamilton for twelve years.

Nelson was a man of honour with a religious conscience – reluctant to cheat on a close friend, whom he respected and admired. It is doubtful that Nelson and Emma would have entered into an intimate relationship behind Sir William's back. When their mutual love and desire became undeniable, they very likely discussed the situation with him.

Sir William believed he had not long to live. Marital relations with Emma had probably ceased due to his age and ill health, but he depended on her for support and companionship.

It seems that, for love of them both, Sir William opted to share Emma with Nelson in a companionable *ménage à trois*. However, the professional consequences for Sir William were damaging since others did not share his philosophical attitude to life.

From Nelson's letters it appears that this agreement was settled towards the end of the year, but he and Emma did not consummate their relationship until January or February the following year.

Troubridge and several other captains were concerned about Nelson's health and his association with Emma. Troubridge, who had known Nelson since they had served together in India, felt strongly enough to write to him on 15 December:

'I see by your Lordship's last letter your Eyes are bad, I beseech, I intreat you do not keep up such horrid hours, you will destroy your constitution. Lady Hamilton is accustomed to it for years, but I saw the bad effects of it in her the other day. She could not keep her eyes open, yawning and uncomfortable all day; the multiplicity of business which your Lordship has to perform must with the total want of rest destroy you, pardon me my Lord it is my sincere esteem for you that makes the mention of it: I know you can have no pleasure sitting up all night at Cards why then sacrifice your health, comfort, purse, ease, everything to the Customs of a Country where your stay cannot be long, I again beg pardon. If you knew my feelings you would I am sure not be displeased with me.'[25]

Nelson replied only that he was having some 'electrical' treatment to improve his sight. Whereupon Troubridge daringly pressed the point even further:

'I trust and hope the Electrifying will restore your sight, pray keep good hours, if you knew what your Friends feel for you I am sure you would cut all Nocturnal partys, the gambling of the people at Palermo is publickly talked of every where. I beseech your Lordship leave off ... Lady Hamilton's Character will suffer, nothing can prevent people from talking, a gambling Woman in the Eye of an Englishman is lost ... you will be surprised when I tell you I hear in all Companys the sums won and lost on a Card in Sir Wm's house ...'[26]

Troubridge had already warned Nelson: '... *Some person about Sir William Hamilton's house sends accounts here, as I have frequently heard things which I knew your Lordship meant to keep secret.*'[27]

An extract from Toubridge's letter to Emma on 14 January suggests that he had raised the subject with her: '*I am duly favoured with your Ladyship's letter of the 8th. inst. & feel most completely happy at your promise to play no more. Be assur'd I have not written to you from any impertinent interference, but from a wish to warn you of the ideas that were going about, which you could not hear of ...*'[28]

Emma took notice of his warnings and the gambling ceased.

It was absurdly claimed that Nelson had lost £12,000. His reputation suffered when Sir William's successor reported to London that Nelson had ruined his health and his fortune gambling in Palermo in Emma's company.

Keith arrived back in the Mediterranean in January, as Commander-in-Chief, on his flagship the *Queen Charlotte* and summoned Nelson to Leghorn. When Nelson arrived there on 20 January the relationship between them was tense. Sir William later wrote to Minto: '... *Entre nous it was an ill judged plan to send Lord Keith out to take command from Lord Nelson whose delicacy you may be sure felt it sensibly, but he had wisdom enough to swallow the bitter pill for the good of the service of his King and Country...*'[29]

After five days at Leghorn, Nelson and the *Foudroyant* set sail for Palermo, accompanied by Keith aboard his flagship. During the eight day voyage Nelson wrote a passionate letter to Emma, his earliest known love letter to her:

Wednesday 29th. January (1800)

'*Separated from all I hold dear in this World what is the use of living if indeed such an existence can be called so ... no separation no time my only beloved Emma can alter my love and affection for you, it is founded on the truest principles of honor, and it only remains for us to regret which I do with the bitterest anguish that there are any obstacles to our being united in the closest ties of this World's rigid rules as we are in those of real love. Continue only to love your faithful Nelson as he loves his Emma, you are my guide I submit to you, let me find all my fond heart hopes and wishes with the risk of my life as I have been faithful to my word never to partake of any amusem[en]t or to sleep on shore.*

Thursday Jany 30th: We have been six days from Leghorn and no prospect of our making a passage to Palermo, to me it is worse than death, I can neither eat nor sleep for thinking of you my dearest love, I never touch even pudding you know the reason, no I would starve sooner, my only hope is to find you have equally kept your promises to me, for I never made you a promise that I did not strictly keep as if made in the presence of heaven, but I rest perfectly confident of the reality of your love and that you would die sooner than be false in the smallest thing to your own faithful Nelson who lives only for his Emma. friday I shall run mad we have had a gale of wind that is nothing but I am 20 leagues farther from you than yesterday noon, was I master notwithstanding the weather I would have been 20 leagues nearer but my Commander In Chief knows not what I feel by absence, last night I did nothing but dream of you altho' I woke 20 times in the night, in one of my dreams I thought I was at a large table you was not present, sitting between a Princess who I detest and another, they both tried to seduce me and the first wanted to take those liberties with me which no woman in this World but yourself ever did, the consequence was I knocked her down and in the moment of bustle you came in and taking me to your embrace whispered I love nothing but you my Nelson, I kissed you fervently and we enjoy'd the height of love, Ah Emma I pour out my soul to you. If you love any thing but me you love those who feel not like your N.

Sunday [2 February] *noon fair wind which makes me a little better in hopes of seeing you to morrow, just 138 miles distant, and I trust to find you like myself, for no love is like mine towards you.'*[30]

Finally Nelson felt able to pour out the passions he had suppressed for so long. The content and language of this letter is in stark contrast to any letter ever written to Fanny, including those soon after their marriage. He expresses with *'bitterest anguish'* the obstacles to their being united by *'this World's rigid rules'*, a reference to the difficulty of obtaining a divorce at the time.

Arriving at Palermo, Keith stayed at the Palazzo Palagonia for eight days. Sir William told Greville: *'... I must own that I am a little tired of keeping open house so long I as have, and which I realy could not do without Emma's doing the honors so well as she does...'*[31]

Despite Emma's best efforts to entertain the Commander-in-Chief, the ungrateful Keith wrote disparagingly about his visit to Palermo: *'I was sick of Palermo and all its allurements and much as I was made up to (their hours are beyond belief) I went to bed at ten...The whole was a scene of fulsome Vanity and Absurdity all the long eight days I was at Palermo.'*[32]

On 12 February Keith sailed for Malta taking Nelson with him. Cruising off Malta Nelson's squadron sighted a small French squadron and gave chase. Six days later he joyfully told Emma he had captured one of the remaining French ships from the Battle of the Nile: '*I have got her – Le Genereux – thank God. Twelve out of Thirteen, only the Guillaume Tell remaining. I am after the others...*'[33]

In Palermo, Emma wrote to Greville:

25th Feb. 1800

Dear Sir,

I recd. your letter by Mr Campbell. He is lodged with u ... He will tell you a little how we go on, as to our domestic happiness. We are more united and comfortable than ever, in spite of the infamous Jacobin papers, jealous of Lord Nelson's glory, and Sir William's and mine. But we do not mind them. Lord N. is a truly virtuous and great man; and because we have been fagging and ruining our health, and sacrificing every comfort in the cause of loyalty, our private characters are to be stabbed in the dark. First, it was said, Sir W. and Lord N. fought; then, that we played, and lost. First, Sir W. and Lord N. live like brothers; next, Lord N. never plays; and this I give you my word of honour. So I beg you will contradict any of these vile reports. Not that Sir W. and Lord N. mind it; and I get scolded by the Queen and all of them for having suffered one day's uneasiness.

Our fleet is off Malta; Lord Nelson has taken Le Genereux, and was after the frigates; so the attempt to relieve Malta has failed.

I have had a letter from the Emperor of Russia, with the Cross of Malta. Sir William has sent his Imperial Majesty's letter to Lord Grenville, to get me permission to wear it. I have rendered some services to the poor Maltese. I got them ten thousand pounds, and sent them corn when they were in distress. The deputies have been lodged at my house; I have been their Ambassadress, so his M. has rewarded me. If the King will give me leave to wear it abroad, it is of use to me. The Q--n is having the order set in diamonds for me; but the one the Emperor sent is gold. I tell you this little history of it that you may be au fait. Ball has it also, but I am the first Englishwoman that ever had it. Sir W. is pleased, so I am happy. We are coming home; and I am miserable to leave my dearest friend, the Q. She cannot be consoled. We have sworn to be back in six months; and I will not quit her till Sir William binds himself to come back. However, I shall have a comfort in seeing some of my old friends; and you in particular. We have also many things to settle ...[34]

A few days later Keith sailed for Genoa, leaving Nelson in charge of the blockade of Malta. But Nelson felt so ill that he soon informed Keith: '*Without some rest I am gone. I must therefore whenever I find the service will admit of it, request your permission to go to my friends at Palermo for a few weeks and leave the command here to Commodore Troubridge. Nothing but necessity obliges me to write this letter.'35*

He also told Emma: *'My head aches dreadfully, and I have none here to give me a moment's comfort.'36*

Nelson was suffering severe chest pains that he believed were heart problems caused by anxiety. He wrote again to Keith: *'My state of health is very precarious. Two days ago I dropped with a pain in my heart, and I am always in a fever ...'37*

Nelson was genuinely unwell, though his symptoms were later thought to be severe indigestion. He remained cruising off Malta until 16 March before returning to Palermo on 24 March.

On his return he sent the *Foudroyant* under Captain Berry back to Malta. During the voyage Berry was fortunate to capture the *Guillaume Tell*. Nelson reported the good news to Nepean at the Admiralty: *'... I have letters from Commodore Troubridge, Captain Dixon and Sir Edward Berry telling me of the capture of the* William Tell *on the morn of the 30th. March, after a gallant defence of three hours ... Thus, owing to my brave friends, is the entire capture and destruction of the French Mediterranean Fleet to be attributed, and my orders from the great Earl of St. Vincent fulfilled ... My task is done, my health is finished, and, probably my retreat for ever fixed ...'38*

Late in January, Sir William had learned via the newspapers that the twenty-nine-year-old Sir Arthur Paget was replacing him. He was unaware that Greville had been campaigning on his behalf with Lord Grenville, begging him to consider: *'... what the percuniary embarrassment of Sr William will be if dismissed without a liberal provision, & what the sentiment of his mind must be if the news of his disgrace & Supercession shall arrive as abruptly to him as it has been communicated to me...'39*

To Greville it seemed that Sir William was to be *'dismissed'* and in *'disgrace'*.

Ignorant of these strong opinions in England Sir William wrote to Nelson on 7 February: *'... I have now not a doubt but we shall have the extreme satisfaction of returning home with our dearest friend Lord Nelson; for your Lordship will have known from Emma, that I have either (after thirty-six years service at this Court) been either kicked up or down out of my post; and Mr Paget, Lord Uxbridge's son, is named Envoy Extraordinary and Plenipotentiary to the King of the Two Sicilies, and is on his way in a Frigate. I have not had the least hint of such an intention from England, public or private; but Lord Grenville has a letter of mine, the beginning of the year 1798, authorising his Lordship to dispose of my place to whom he pleased, if he would ensure me an annuity for life, a clear two thousand pounds sterling – not a nominal pension, as I would rather continue all my life at Naples than retire for less ... I see it gives much uneasiness at this Court, and poor Emma is in the greatest distress. But let me go home and settle my affairs, and she and the Queen may dispose of my old carcass as they please ... Adieu, get yourself well and come to your sincere and hearty friends and let us go home together, but Emma swears she will, like a true Chevr of Malta, make one caravan to Malta before she goes home, that will depend on your Lp.'[40]*

Nelson held a similar view: *'Sir William I think very unhandsomely treated by Ministers they <u>may</u> intend well but should have done well before his removal.'[41]*

Ball, in a letter to a merchant in Malta, described Sir William as '*... the most amiable and accomplished man I know, and his heart is certainly one of the best in the world ...'[42]* At the same time, he confirmed Emma's part in saving the starving Maltese: *'I wish he and her Ladyship would pay me a visit. They are an irreparable loss to me, for I am convinced that but for their influence with their Sicilian Majesties and his ministers the poor Maltese would have starved, and my head would have been sacrificed in their moment of despair.'*

Sir William delayed formally recognising Paget as his successor, not finally taking his official leave of the King and Queen until 22 April 1800. The Queen, having worked closely with Sir William for so many years, was distraught and declared herself *'half dead with grief'* over Hamilton's recall and called his successor *'the fatal Paget'.[43]*

Paget, lodging in the same house as Charles and Cecilia Lock, reported to Grenville that he was poorly received at Palermo: *'It is not to be told the pains that were taken by Lady Hamilton to set the King and Queen and the whole Court against me, even before I arrived ... her Ladyship's language in general has been extremely indiscreet, representing Sir William as an ill-used man ...'[44]*

Nelson was not aware until May that his reputation had been indelibly smeared by accusations made in a speech by Charles Fox, the Leader of the Opposition, in the House of Commons on 3 February 1800:

'I wish the atrocities of which we hear so much, and which I abhor as much as any man, were indeed unexampled. I fear that they do not belong exclusively to the French ... Naples, for instance, has been, among others,

what is called <u>delivered</u>; and yet, if I am rightly informed, it has been stained and polluted by murders so ferocious and by cruelties of every kind so abhorrent, that the heart shudders at the recita l... It is said, that a party of the Republican inhabitants at Naples took shelter in the fortress of Castel del Uovo. They were besieged by a detachment from the Royal Army, to whom they refused to surrender but demanded that a British officer should be brought forward, and to him they capitulated. They made terms with him under the sanction of the British name. It was agreed that their persons and property should be safe and that they should be conveyed to Toulon. They were accordingly put on board a Vessel; but before they sailed, their property was confiscated, numbers of them taken out, thrown into dungeons, and some of them, I understand, notwithstanding the British guarantee, absolutely executed.'[45]

Mr. Fox had obtained some of his information from Charles Lock who had written home privately on 13 July 1799, expecting his father to pass on his comments to Grenville and Fox: *'You will hear with grief the infraction of the articles convented with the Neopolitan Jacobins and of the stab our English honour has received in being employed to decoy these people, who relied on our faith, into the most deplorable situation ... But <u>the sentiment of abhorrence expressed by the whole fleet</u> will I hope exonerate the nation from an imputation so disgraceful and charge it where it should lie, upon the shoulders of <u>one or two</u>.'*[46]

Unable to defend himself as he only heard of Fox's speech three months later, Nelson's part in the events in Naples became the subject of violent controversy.

A furious Nelson wrote immediately to Sir John Acton on 9 May: *'... my health this day is tolerable but has been very indifft: but a broken spirit who can cure. That Scoundrel Mr. Fox has thought it Right to attack my conduct when at Naples & call loudly for an enquiry to wipe off the <u>foul</u> stain on our Nation's honor. I sent you a Copy of my letter to a friend that if the Government have no Objection they may publish it.'*[47]

His letter to Davison read:

Malta, 9th May 1800

My dear Sir

Mr. Fox having, in the House of Commons, in February, made an accusation against somebody, for what he calls a breach of a treaty with Rebels, which has been entered into with a British Officer; and having used language unbecoming either the wisdom of a Senator, or the politeness of a Gentleman, or an Englishman, who ought ever to suppose that His Majesty's

Officers would always act with honour and openness in all their transactions; and as the whole affairs of the Kingdom of Naples were, at the time alluded to, absolutely placed in my hands, it is I who am called upon to explain my conduct and therefore send you my Observations, on the infamous Armistice entered into by the Cardinal; and on his refusal to send in a joint declaration to the French and Rebels, I sent in my Note, and on which the Rebels came out of the Castles, <u>as they ought</u>, and I hope all those who are false to their King and Country will, <u>to be hanged</u>, or otherwise be disposed of, as their Sovereign thought proper. The terms granted by Captain Foote of the Seahorse, at Castel-del-mare, were all strictly complied with, the Rebels having surrendered before my arrival. There has been nothing promised by a British Officer, that His Sicilian Majesty has not complied with, even in disobedience to his orders to the Cardinal. I am &c.

Bronte Nelson of the Nile

Show these papers to Mr. Rose [Secretary to the Treasury] *or some other; and, if thought right, you will put them in the papers.*[48]

This scandal had a critical impact on the reputations of both Nelson and Hamilton, whose finances were particularly affected on his return home. Nelson, though he claimed his spirit was broken, had in his possession a letter from Spencer praising his actions in Naples: '*... the intentions and motives by which all your measures have been governed, have been as pure and good, as their success has been complete...*'[49]

With Hamilton recalled and replaced by Paget, Nelson in his ill-health and dejected state, decided that he would go home. Before leaving he granted Emma's wish to see Malta. It was not just a pleasure cruise for Emma. Nelson would be able to review the siege and take his leave of Ball and Troubridge, two of his Nile captains who had served him faithfully since the day of that battle, contributing so much to his success.

With the Hamiltons and Cornelia Knight on board, the *Foudroyant* left Palermo on 24 April 1800 on a cruise lasting until the end of May. According to Cornelia Knight, they spent two days exploring the ancient city of Syracuse, before joining the blockading squadron off Malta.[50] They were entertained to dinner by Ball and General Graham, stayed in a house prepared for them by Ball near Valetta and visited Troubridge. Emma's 35th birthday was celebrated on 26 April.

Emma became pregnant on this cruise towards the end of April.* A year later Nelson, remembering the cruise, wrote to Emma: '*This*

---

* Nelson and Emma's daughter, Horatia, was born at the end of January,1801.

day twelve months we sailed on our tour to Malta. Ah! Those were happy times: days of ease and nights of pleasure.'[51]

The *'nights of pleasure'* had clearly begun a few weeks earlier, confirmed in a letter he wrote to Emma the following year: '... *Ah! My dear friend, I did remember well the 12th February and also the two months afterwards. I shall never forget them, and never be sorry for the consequences.'*[52]

Spencer wrote to Nelson inviting him to retire from the Mediterranean: *'It is by no means my wish to call you away from service, but having observed that you have been under the necessity of quitting your station off Malta, on account of the state of your health, which I am persuaded you could not have thought of doing without such necessity, it appeared to me much more advisable to come home at once than to be obliged to remain inactive at Palermo ... I trust you will take in good part what I have taken the liberty to write to you as a friend...'*[53]

On the same day, Admiralty orders were sent to Keith, that *'if Lord Nelson's health rendered him incapable of doing his duty, and that should he be desirous of returning to England, he was permitted to do so, and to take his passage in the first ship Lord Keith might have occasion to send home, unless he should prefer returning by land, in which case he was at liberty to strike his Flag in the Mediterranean, and come on shore.'*[54]

Arriving back in Palermo on 1 June they spent eight days preparing to leave. In their absence, the Queen, who had become more and more alienated from the King and his politics, decided to visit her daughter and son-in-law (the Emperor and Empress of Austria). It was arranged that Nelson would transport the Queen, Prince Leopold, three princesses, the future queens of Spain, France and Sardinia, and a large retinue to Leghorn.

Sir William gave a farewell banquet on 5 June. On leaving Palermo he was physically and financially a broken man. He had repeatedly complained that he was *'plagued with bilious attacks and diarrhoa continually owing to the intense heats and damps of this climate'*. It is likely that he suffered from recurring bouts of dysentery.

He owed Gibbs (the banker living at the Palazzo Palagonia) £3,000 and a merchant a further £3,000. He estimated his costs during eighteen months in Palermo as over £13,000. In addition he owed £7,000 to his bankers Ross & Ogilvie in London. He claimed his personal losses for the contents of his houses at Naples to be around £10,000.[55] During the final weeks in Palermo and on the journey home he was obliged to borrow money from Nelson.

Nelson informed Keith that he was transporting the Queen and her party to Leghorn, from where she would proceed overland to Vienna, and requested that he and the Hamiltons be allowed to sail home aboard the *Foudroyant*, claiming his ship badly needed repairs that could only be carried out in England.[56]

Keith, who was finding his command very stressful and who had suffered the loss of his flagship, refused.[57]* Sir William was aware as early as the previous November that they might return overland when he wrote to Minto: '... *Appearances are favourable and that this abominable war may finish with the century, be that as it may, I am grown so old and worn out that I am determined to go home next Spring to get a little repose. If by land we shall certainly not think it out of our way to pay you a visit at Vienna ...*'[58]

The royal party, Nelson, the Hamiltons, Mrs Cadogan and Cornelia Knight sailed from Palermo on 9 July, accompanied by the *Alexander*, the *Princess Charlotte* frigate and the *Santa Doria*. Once again they were caught in a terrible storm during the voyage. Princess Amelie described this event:

'... *Around 3 o'clock the motion increased considerably and the wind blew with unbelievable violence. We found Milady* [Emma] *kneeling on a mattress in the middle of the cabin. Toto* [Princess Antoinette] *cried, ' It's all over, we're dead, we're swamped! Mama* [the Queen] *ordered us all to sit on the floor, pressed against the beds, and this we did, Mama Toto and Ruffo on one side and Milady,* [Prince] *Castelcicala and myself on the other. We were more dead than alive. Nelson came in from time to time to comfort us, saying that there was no danger and that by 7 o'clock we were sure to reach Leghorn. Milady took me in her arms. There was a gust of wind so strong that the vessel dipped under* [water] *three times. Nelson went pale as a sheet and rushed out. Milady began to scream and roll about on the floor. Mama said to us solemnly, 'Command your souls to God' and began to recite aloud a prayer in German ... At five minutes to seven we dropped anchor in the harbour at Leghorn, as Nelson had foretold ...*'[59]

Emma's courage may have failed her due to her pregnancy and, on seeing the colour drain from Nelson's face, she understood the very real danger of their situation. The conditions were so rough in the harbour that they could not go ashore for two days.

---

* Three months earlier, Keith had sent the *Queen Charlotte* out to reconnoitre the Island of Cabrera whilst he remained on shore at Leghorn. Five miles out from Leghorn the ship caught fire and exploded. Only 167 of the 840 men on board survived.

On leaving the *Foudroyant* Maria Carolina gave 2,500 Sicilian crowns to the ship's company, a diamond necklace with the cyphers of all the royal children wound round with their hair to Emma and a gold snuff-box with portraits of the King and Queen set in diamonds to Sir William. Nelson received a portrait of the King with the Queen's initials set in diamonds and emeralds.

Having refused Nelson permission to take the *Foudroyant* to England, Keith suggested that if Nelson and his party proceeded to Minorca they could complete their journey home in the *Seahorse* frigate. Troubrigde, also returning to England, very ill and spitting blood, had offered them passage home in his ship, the *Culloden*, but Nelson declined the offer believing the *Culloden* unsafe.*

Cornelia Knight blamed Emma for the decision that they all return home overland. In a letter to Berry on 2 July she wrote: *'The Queen wishes, if possible, to prosecute her journey. Lady Hamilton cannot bear the thought of going by sea; and, therefore, nothing but impracticability will prevent our going to Vienna ... Lord Nelson is well and keeps up his spirits amazingly. Sir William appears broken, distressed, and harassed.'*[60]

By 16 July she was able to report: *'It is, at length, decided that we go by Land; and I feel all the dangers and difficulties to which we shall be exposed but the die is cast, and go we must. Lord Nelson is going on an expedition he disapproves, and against his own convictions, because he has promised the Queen ... Lady Hamilton ... hates the sea, and wishes to visit the different courts of Germany. Sir William says he shall die by the way, and he looks so ill, that I should not be surprised if he did ...'*[61]

Nelson was adamant that he would see his responsibility for the Queen and her family through to a safe conclusion. On 15 June he wrote to Acton: *'... nothing shall make us quit the Queen and Royal Family until <u>all is safe</u>, and their future plans <u>perfectly</u> and securely settled ...'*[62]

Emma had good reason to prefer to travel home overland. Of the three voyages she had experienced she only enjoyed the cruise to Malta. On both other voyages she had experienced terrifying conditions. She would certainly have felt that her condition would be easier to conceal during an overland journey and it would be safer should any problems arise. A longer journey would give her more

---

* Troubridge's faith in his ships later resulted in tragic consequences. In 1805 he was appointed to command the eastern half of the East Indies station. He went out in the *Blenheim*. In 1807 he left Madras for the Cape in his old and damaged ship. Off Madagascar the ship foundered in a cyclone. Admiral Troubridge and all on board perished.

time to see the Queen in Vienna and to spend with Nelson, postponing the difficulties facing her in London. Sir William had always travelled overland between England and Naples and he would be able to consult doctors on the way if necessary.

The Queen and her party left Leghorn on 15 July to travel across Italy to the port of Ancona on the Adriatic coast. Nelson, Sir William and Emma, Mrs Cadogan and Cornelia followed two days later. The journey home took them almost four months to complete.

CHAPTER 15

Return to England

*'I am sick of hearing of dear Lady Hamilton and am resolved
that you shall give up either her or me'*
Fanny to Nelson in January (?)1801 as reported by Haslewood

*'I have been around the world, and in every corner of it, and
never yet saw your equal'*
Nelson to Emma, 8 February 1801

*'My heart is fit to <u>Burst</u> with greef. Oh, what pain, God only
knows ... I shall go mad with greef.'*
Emma to Sarah Nelson, 27 February 1801 (at Nelson's departure)

THE JOURNEY ACROSS Italy to the port of Ancona was safely completed
in eight days, but not without incident. Cornelia Knight described their
journey in detail to Captain Berry, with whom she had become
friendly in Palermo and on the cruise to Malta:

Ancona 24th. July 1800

*... owing more to good fortune than to prudence, [we] arrived in twenty-six
hours at Florence, after passing within <u>two miles</u> of the French advanced posts.
After a short stay, we proceeded on our way to this place. At Castel San
Giovanni, the coach, in which were Lord Nelson, and Sir William and Lady
Hamilton, was overturned; Sir William and Lady Hamilton were hurt, but
not dangerously. The wheel was repaired, but broke again at Arezzo – the
Queen two days' journey before them, and news of the French Army advancing
rapidly; it was therefore decided that they should proceed, and Mrs. Cadogan
and I remain with the broken carriage, as it was of less consequence we should
be left behind, or taken, than they ...*[1]

Their carriage repaired, Cornelia and Mrs Cadogan caught up with
the others at Ancona. They were transported to Trieste on frigates
belonging to a Russian squadron. Cornelia reports that during the

voyage *'poor Sir William has been so ill, that the physicians had almost given him up ...'* According to Cornelia, Nelson had a bad cold, the *'Queen and thirty-four of her suite have had fevers',* and she herself had been ill.

Having rested for nine days, more travelling brought them to Vienna on the 18 August, where they remained for five weeks.

Soon after arriving they were entertained by Lord and Lady Minto at his impressive ambassadorial residence on the outskirts of Vienna. Lady Minto, delighted to meet Nelson again, wrote to her sister: *'He is just the same as he ever was ... he has the same shock head, and the same honest, simple manners; but he is <u>devoted</u> to Emma; he thinks her quite an <u>angel</u>, and talks of her as such to her face and behind her back; and she leads him about like a keeper with a bear, she must sit by him at dinner to cut his meat, and he carries her pocket-handkerchief ...'*[2]

Minto reported their arrival to Keith:

Vienna, 30 August 1800

Lord Nelson arrived here with Sir W. and Lady Hamilton a few days after the Queen of Naples having been detained at Trieste some time by Sir William's illness. Sir W. has had a relapse here; and altho' he has recovered a little yet he is so feeble and so much reduced that I cannot see how it is possible for him to reach England alive. Lord Nelson has been received here by all ranks with the admiration which his great actions deserve, and notwithstanding the disadvantage under which he presents himself at present to the public eye ...[3]

This public admiration of Nelson began in Trieste and continued at every town and city on their journey. Whenever he appeared in public cheering crowds gathered. On their route through Vienna, Prague, Dresden, Hamburg and finally Cuxhaven, they attended receptions, banquets, balls and concerts. Although she was four months pregnant, Emma performed her 'Attitudes' and sang on several occasions. She concealed her condition by wearing flowing robes and shawls. Sir William's health improved and he enjoyed several fishing expeditions.

They were welcomed in Vienna by Maria Carolina and her daughter, the Empress. Four days later Nelson wrote to Minto: '*... the Queen of Naples has desired anxiously Lady Hamilton to bring you to her this afternoon. The Empress would see us yesterday evening, and we had the noise of five fine healthy children for an hour ...*'[4]

Nelson and Emma sat for portraits by a number of artists; one by Heinrich Fuger is the only portrait depicting Nelson in civilian clothes.

In Vienna they met with Francis Oliver, who had been one of Sir William's secretaries in Naples, and was now employed by Nelson as a secretary and assistant. Oliver, many years later, contributed to Emma's downfall.

Few letters relating to this time by Nelson or the Hamiltons survive. Letters and journals of the people they met describe their experiences. As usual, the opinions expressed vary from maliciously critical to admiring praise.

They left Vienna for a few days to visit Eisenstadt at the invitation of Prince and Princess Esterhazy, who had stayed with Sir William in Naples. They were entertained by concerts given by the Court musician Joseph Haydn. Emma's performance of Haydn's cantata 'Arianna a Naxos' prompted a glowing review in an Hungarian newspaper: [She] 'is a thirty-five- year-old, tall Englishwoman with a very handsome face, who knows well how to demean herself. One of her many rare qualities is her clear strong voice with which, accompanied by the famous Haydn, she filled her audience with such enthusiasm that they almost became ecstatic.'5

A Swedish diplomat, Suerstolpe, thought he had never heard 'anything so heavenly'.

Emma clearly enjoyed this musical interlude. Haydn's biographer wrote: 'In My Lady Hamilton Haydn found a great admirer ... for two days she never left Haydn's side.'6

Sir William was full of admiration for her success. Later in Dresden he was described as '... old, infirm, all admiration of his wife, and never spoke today but to applaud her'.

But James Harris, eldest son of Lord and Lady Malmesbury, present during these four days of celebrations and entertainments, sent harshly critical comments about Emma to his parents:

'Lady Hamilton is without exception the most coarse, ill-mannered, disagreeable woman I ever met with ...'7

There was more criticism of her from the diplomat who had praised her singing:

'Myladi Hamilton, once considered the most beautiful woman in Europe ... wears the Maltese Cross so that she now has all the titles that can impress people ... She is ... the fattest woman I've ever laid eyes on, but with the most beautiful head.'8 He would not have known she was now almost five months pregnant.

Soon after returning to Vienna it was time to take leave of the

Queen. Sir William had written to Greville anticipating this event: '...
*It will be heart-breaking to the Queen of Naples when we go; she has <u>realy</u> no
female friends but her, and Emma has been of infinite use in our late very
critical business. Ld Nelson & I cou'd not have done without her...*[9]

In an emotional parting Maria Carolina gave Emma a letter
addressing her as *'dear dear Emma'* and promising that her affection
and gratitude to *'to my dear friend and sister'* would remain with her
throughout her life. *'To you, I shall never change.'*[10] In addition, she gave
Emma two testimonial letters to take to London, one addressed to the
Queen of England and one to Lady Spencer.

Nelson began to plan ahead for their arrival in England. On 20
September, he wrote to Fanny:

My dear Fanny,

*Since I wrote you from Trieste we have been so continually prepared to set
out that I have not wrote a line till this day. Sir William Hamilton being
recovered we set out tomorrow, and shall be in England the 2nd.week in
October. I have wrote to Davison to take a house or good lodgings for the very
short time I shall be in London, to which I shall instantly proceed and hope
to meet you in the house.*

*You must expect to find me a worn out old man ... May God bless you and
believe me your affectionate*

Bronte Nelson of the Nile[11]

He was over-optimistic as in October they were still in Hamburg.
Since January 1800 he had written very few letters, mostly brief notes,
to Fanny. She did not hear from him again until he arrived at Great
Yarmouth.

The party arrived in Prague on 28 September where Archduke Charles,
a nephew of Maria Carolina's, gave a dinner to celebrate Nelson's 42nd
birthday on the 29th. The following day they set off for Dresden,
travelling by boat on the River Elbe through spectacular scenery.

In Dresden they spent time with the British minister, Hugh Elliott,
Minto's younger brother, and his wife. Their friend, an English widow
Mrs. Melesina St. George, formed a poor opinion of *'the Nelson party'*.

In her journal she wrote scornfully about *'the Tria'*. Her only praise
was for Emma's 'Attitudes', which she witnessed twice. After
describing the performance she wrote: *'It is a beautiful performance,
amusing to the most ignorant, and highly interesting to lovers of art ... It is
remarkable that, though coarse and ungraceful in common life, she becomes
highly graceful, and even beautiful, during this performance.'*[12]

Otherwise she was endlessly critical of Emma and her singing. *'It is also singular that, in spite if the accuracy of her imitation of the finest ancient draperies, her usual dress is tasteless, vulgar, loaded and unbecoming ...*

'I think her bold, daring, vain even to folly, and stamped with the manners of her first situation much more strongly than one would suppose, after having represented Majesty, and lived in good company fifteen years ...

'Her voice is good, and very strong, but she is frequently out of time; her expression strongly marked and various ... She acts her songs, which I think the last degree of bad taste.' [13]

Emma's friendly overtures towards her were contemptuously brushed aside.

Mrs. St. George's disdain extended to the rest of the party: *'Lord Nelson is a little man, without any dignity ...'* , Cornelia was a flatterer who *'... never opens her mouth but to show forth their praise...'* , *'Mrs. Cadogan is – what one might expect.'* [14]

Sir William, though *'old and infirm'*, performed *'feats of activity, hopping round the room on his backbone, his arms, legs, star and ribbon, all flying about in the air'*.

The Electress of Saxony refused to meet Emma *'on account of her former dissolute life'*. Emma was simply told there would be no court while they were in Dresden. Nelson was furious when he was informed that the Elector did not wish to see Emma.

Emma sat for a portrait by the court artist, Johan Heinrich Schmidt. His pastel portrait of her with short, curly hair and wearing her Maltese Cross became Nelson's favourite portrait, which he ever afterwards hung in his cabin, calling her his *'guardian angel'*. Before the journey Emma's lovely long hair had been cut. In the portrait, she is seen wearing a classical high-waisted dress, concealing her pregnancy.

Their boat trip to Hamburg took eleven days. They were disappointed to find that the frigate promised by Hugh Elliot to collect them was not there. In Hamburg Nelson went shopping with Cornelia to buy Fanny a magnificent piece of lace trimming for a court gown. He met the exiled General Dumouriez, who had fallen on hard times, having refused to serve under Napoleon. The General was reluctantly persuaded to accept Nelson's gift of £100.

After waiting nine days in vain for the frigate, they travelled on to Cuxhaven where they took the *King George* mail-packet to Great Yarmouth.

Nelson's expenses on this journey amounted to a small fortune, nearly £3,500. He was covering his own, Sir William's and Cornelia's expenses. Sir William only paid £255, leaving him owing Nelson £1,350, plus the money he owed at Palermo. His total debt to Nelson was £2,276 when they reached London.[15]

At Great Yarmouth on 6 November, Nelson received a joyous welcome from his Norfolk kinsmen. Bells were ringing in the town; the mob unhitched the horses from their carriage and hauled it to the Wrestlers Inn in the town centre, where a military band struck up when the Admiral and Emma appeared on the balcony. The Mayor and Corporation presented him with the freedom of the city and a service of thanksgiving for his safe return was held at Nelson's request.

Nelson had written from Vienna to both Fanny and Davison asking them to arrange a house for him in London *'for his arrival'*. Fanny did not receive her letter until 20 October and wrote to Davison saying she had *'begged my Dear Lord to stop at his own door for a few minutes and I would have everything ready to sett off with him.'*[16] In a further letter sent to both Great Yarmouth and Harwich, she invited the Hamiltons to stay the night at Round Wood.

Nelson replied on the day of his arrival:

Nov. 6th. 1800

My dear Fanny,

We are this moment arriv'd and the post only allows me to say that we shall set off tomorrow noon, and be with you on Saturday, to dinner. I only had time to open one of your letters, my visits are so numerous. May God bless you and my Dear Father, and believe me, ever, your affectionate

Bronte Nelson of the Nile

Sir and Lady Hamilton beg their best regards, and will accept your offer of a bed. Mrs. Cadogan and Miss Knight with all the servants, will proceed to Colchester.[17]

But having heard nothing from him since 20 October, Fanny left for London before his arrival. He arrived with the Hamiltons at Round Wood to find the house empty. Nelson, having for years longed for a home of his own, was deeply disappointed that Fanny was not there to greet them. Angrily he drove away, never to spend a single night in the first home he had ever owned.

They travelled on to spend the night at Colchester. His letter to Fanny on 6 November appeared later re-addressed to Nerot's Hotel, King Street, London.[18]

Nor was a home waiting for him in London. The house Davison

had taken for them at 17 Dover Street was not ready, although they did move in soon afterwards.

Nelson, Sir William and Emma arrived at Nerot's Hotel at 3 p.m. on Sunday 9 November, during the worst thunderstorm in living memory. Waiting in the hotel foyer were Fanny and Nelson's seventy-eight-year-old father, Edmund.

Fanny had not seen her husband for two and a half years, but was forced into a reunion with him in a public place witnessed by Sir William and Emma. She was no doubt nervous, never having never met Sir William and Emma, but aware of the rumours concerning her husband and Emma.

The tense atmosphere was relieved by the sudden arrival of Hamilton's relative, the Duke of Queensberry, who had come from his house in Piccadilly to greet them. Charles Greville had called and left a message.

The *Morning Post* announced their arrival *'in the German travelling carriage of Sir William Hamilton ... Lord Nelson looked extremely well, but in person is very thin: so is Sir William Hamilton: but Lady Hamilton looks charmingly, and is a very fine woman ...'*[19]

At 5 o'clock Nelson, his wife, his father, Sir William and Emma sat down to dinner in the hotel. Sir William's suave manner and diplomatic skills, added to his *'wit and inexhaustible pleasantry'*, smoothed over the difficult situation. Mrs Cadogan and Cornelia had taken rooms at a modest hotel in Albemarle Street.

Nelson had written to Nepean, Secretary to the Admiralty, from Great Yarmouth:

'I beg you will acquaint their Lordships of my arrival here this day, and that my health being perfectly re-established, it is my wish to serve immediately; and I trust that my necessary journey by land from the Mediterranean will not be considered as a wish to be a moment out of active service.'[20]

Nelson was clearly reluctant to remain in England a moment longer than necessary.

The next day, Sir William, Emma and Mrs Cadogan moved into William Beckford's house at 22 Grosvenor Square, temporarily loaned to them.

Disapproval among London society led to the break-up of their friendship with Cornelia. Troubridge, now knighted (at Nelson's request) and promoted Admiral, advised Cornelia to disassociate herself from the *'Tria Juncta in Uno'* as soon as possible to protect her reputation. She wrote in her journal: *'In the evening Sir Thomas Troubridge called upon me ... He advised me to to go to my friend, Mrs. Nepean ... who, on the following day, made me take possession of a room in her house until her children came home for the holidays ...'* [21]

Cornelia declined an invitation to attend a theatre performance with the Hamiltons and the Nelsons. She had, at least, the grace to admit that she found her situation awkward: *'Most of my friends were very urgent with me to drop the acquaintance, but, circumstanced as I had been, I feared the charge of ingratitude, though greatly embarrassed as to what to do, for things became very unpleasant. So much was said about the attachment of Lord Nelson to Lady Hamilton, that it made the matter still worse.'* [22]

Emma was hurt at being suddenly dropped by Cornelia. She wrote furiously in a book Cornelia had given her: *'Given to me by Miss Knight whom I thought good and sincere ... When Lady K. died my poor mother took Miss K. to our house ... We gave shelter to Miss K. for near two years. We brought her free of expense to England. What has she done in return? ... She is dirty illbred ungrateful bad mannered false and deceitful But my Heart takes a noble vengeance. I forgive her.'* [23]

Nelson's anger matched hers. He had taken Cornelia on the *Foudroyant* cruise to Malta and with Sir William had taken care of her in Palermo and on the journey home. Nelson, most unusually using coarse language, later wrote: *'What a Bitch that Miss Knight is.'* [24]

Emma now had to face the hypocritical London society, many of whom were not in a position to condemn her. The newspapers published scandalous cartoons clearly meant to represent Nelson and Emma and debated whether Emma would be received at court.

Doubts about the propriety of associating with Emma were confirmed when Queen Charlotte refused to receive her, as she had done after her marriage to Sir William. He was obliged to attend court without her – a demoralising contrast to their adored position at the Court of Naples.

Nelson was appalled that Sir William was prepared to attend court on his own: *'I would not in Sir William's case have gone to Court without my wife, and such a wife, never to be matched.'* [25]

Sir William, however, could not afford to antagonise the court or the government while he fought to restore his reputation (badly damaged by the reports Lock and Paget had sent home from Palermo), and to rescue his financial situation. His pension, compensation for his personal losses and his ambassadorial expenses had not yet been agreed.

Some friends and relatives accepted Emma as Sir William's wife and turned a blind eye to her relationship with Nelson: the Duke of Queensberry ('Old Q'), the Marquis of Abercorn, a witness to their marriage, Prince Augustus, who had known them in Naples, Lord Palmerston, and Lord Cathcart, another of Sir William's nephews.

However, Lady Frances Harpur, Greville's sister, explained her family's position to Mary Dickenson: *'It was settled by my Brothers and Ld. Cathcart, that it could not be avoided noticing Ly H. without offence to Sr Wm or at least affecting his feelings & He has met with much Vexation & disappointment, as to His Recall* [from Naples] *& is in Weak Health, it was decided on His Acct, Ly H was to be Visited.'*[26]

Lady Frances reported that although Emma was anxious to be accepted by the Hamilton clan and begged permission to call on them, she was herself unwilling to associate with her:

'Sir Wm & Ly H. came to me one Morning, I explained that I could not be in their Society; but hoped He was assured of my affection; He was very kind, laughed and said He knew I was a nun; Would see me some times, said Every one must follow their own Plans ... My brother Warwick visits them ... There is difficulty in inviting them to the castle ... an Occasional Visit, or Eveg may be spent by Ly H. it does not seem desirable or proper for my Nieces to be intimate with Ly H ...'

Sir William accepted the situation philosophically.

Emma now knew that her love for Nelson would cost her the respectability she had gained during her marriage to Sir William.

Lord Palmerston, having called to see them, gave an unusually unbiased assessment of Emma: *'She is grown much larger and her face broader and her features stronger than they were. She was dressed in a white wrapping gown which made her look of very large dimensions, but so completely took away all shape that I cannot judge what her figure would be in common dress. She had a little more conceit and affectation than she had, which is very natural, but she has the same good-humoured manner that she used to have. Her attentions to Sir William do not seem to have relaxed in any degree and they both talk of Lord Nelson in every other sentence. His bust is in the room and Sir William says his friendship and connection with him is the pride and glory of his life.'*[27]

Initially Emma made friendly overtures to Fanny, although she later told Nelson's sister, Sarah, that on their first encounter Fanny's look

1. Sir Harry Fetherstonhaugh (1754 – 1846)
by Pompeo Batoni (1708 – 1787)
at Uppark, West Sussex
© National Trust Images / Prudence Cuming

2. George Romney, *Emma Hart, Lady Hamilton (c 1765 – 1815),
as Circe,* 1782; oil on canvas; 2401 x 1485mm;
Waddesdon, The Rothschild Collection (The National Trust);
Acc.no. 104.1995.
Image © The National Trust, Waddesdon Manor.

3. The Hon. Charles Francis Greville (1749-1809) after
George Romney (1734-1802) Calke Abbey
© National Trust Images

4. George Romney by George Romney oil on canvas, 1784
© National Portrait Gallery, London

5. Sir William Hamilton, (1730 -1803), by George Romney, 1783-1784
7680 x 6510mm. Ailsa Mellon Collection
Image courtesy of the National Gallery of Art,
Washington, D.C.

6a *(above)* Charcoal
drawing of Emma
on a door in the
Palazzo Sessa
by Elizabeth Vigée
Le Brun, 1790
Image courtesy of
Sotheby's

6b *(left)* Mrs
Cadogan, Emma's
mother.
By an unknown
Neapolitan artist
© Trustees of the
National Museum
of the Royal Navy

7. Emma as 'The Ambassadress' by George Romney, 1791
Courtesy of the Blanton Museum of Art,
The University of Texas at Austin.
Bequest of Jack G. Taylor, 1991. Photo: Rick Hall

801   88/1

VAL   5/723.

A
Catalogue

OF

A SELECT PART of the CAPITAL, VALUABLE, and GENUINE

Collection of Pictures,

THE PROPERTY OF

THE RT. HON. SIR W. HAMILTON, K. B.

Purchased by him with great Taste and at a liberal Expence, from several distinguished Cabinets in this Country, and during Thirty-seven Years' Residence as Minister Plenipotentiary at the Court of Naples.

CONSISTING OF THE WORKS OF THE GREAT AND ADMIRED MASTERS IN THE ITALIAN, SPANISH, FRENCH, FLEMISH, AND DUTCH SCHOOLS, VIZ.

Leon. da Vinci,	Schiavoni,	Vernet,
Parmigiano,	Carracci,	Rubens,
Polidoro,	Schidoni,	V Dyck,
Garofalo,	Guido,	Jordaens,
Titian,	Cagnacci,	Teniers,
Giorgione,	L. Giordano,	Berghem,
P. Veronese,	Velasquez,	V de Velde,
Tintoretto,	S. Rosa,	Wouvermans.

Particularly a small Portrait, an exquisite Cabinet Picture, by Leon. da Vinci, formerly in the Collection of the Earl of Arundel, and Lady E. Germaine; a Madona and Child, by Parmegiano; and St. Sebastian, a noble Composition, by V Dyck.

ALSO,

A SMALL, BUT MOST CAPITAL ASSEMBLAGE OF

Antique Bustos, Bas-Reliefs, and other Valuable Marbles,

Particularly a Bust of Nero, in Porphyry; an exquisite Bas-relief of Bacchus, and the Goddess Meta; and an Ægyptian Lion in Basalt.

Which will be Sold by Auction,

BY MR. CHRISTIE,

AT HIS GREAT ROOM, PALL MALL,

On FRIDAY, MARCH 27th, 1801, and following Day,

AT TWELVE o'CLOCK.

N.B. Early in April (together with the remaining Part of the above Collection) will be Sold his truly Valuable Assemblage of Capital and singularly fine Grecian commonly called Hetruscan Vases, and other rare and curious Specimens of Ancient Art, which were saved on the Entry of the French into Naples, and escaped the fatal Effects of the Storm by which Part of this unique Collection was lost, on Board the Colossus Man of War.

The former Part of the above Collection may be Viewed Two Days preceding the Sale, when Catalogues may be had; and timely Notice of the Sale and View of the latter will be given.

(One Shilling, to be returned to Purchasers.)

8. The Catalogue cover of the sale of Hamilton's pictures, 1801
© Christie's Images Limited

9. Horatio Nelson by Sir William Beechey oil on canvas, 1800
© National Portrait Gallery, London

10. Nelson's home, Merton Place.
© National Maritime Museum, Greenwich, London

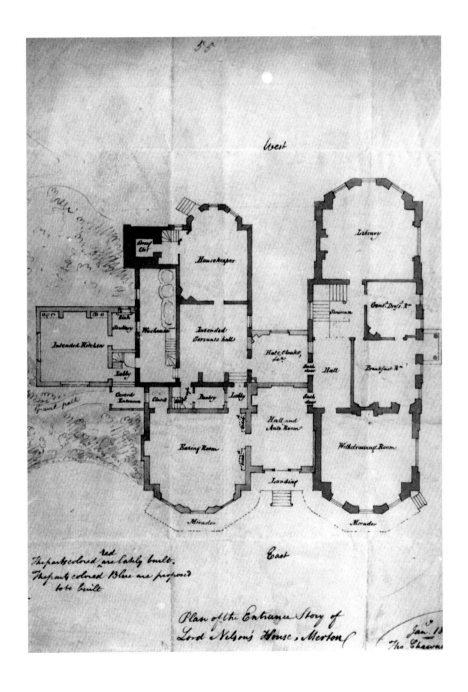

11. 'Plan of the Entrance Story of Lord Nelson's House, Merton'
by Thomas Chawner, January 1805
Picture reproduced by permission of London Borough of Merton

12. Pencil sketch of Nelson by Simon de Koster that Nelson considered
'the most like me'
© National Maritime Museum, Greenwich, London

13. Horatia and her rocking horse at Merton Place
by Thomas Baxter, 1803
© National Maritime Museum, Greenwich, London

Clarges St Janʳ 29ᵗʰ

My dear Respected friend
I have been so ill
so very ill and I am
S͟o͟ ͟B͟r͟o͟k͟e͟n͟ ͟H͟e͟a͟r͟t͟e͟d͟
that I can scarcely hold
my pen to thank you
for your delightful &
consoling letter yet it
is consoling to find a
True & Sincere friend

14. Emma's letter to William Hayley, 29th January 1806

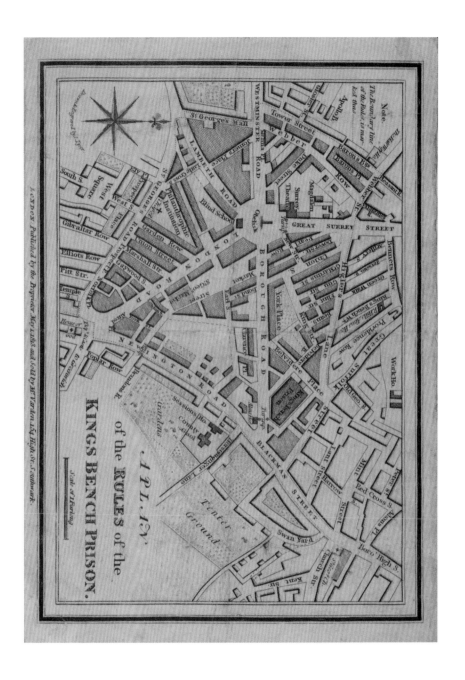

15. The area in London south of the Thames known as *'The Rules'*
© London Metropolitan Archives, City of London

Victory Octr. 19: 1805
Noon Cadiz E S E 16 Leagues

My Dearest beloved Emma the dear
friend of my bosom the Signal has
been made that the Enemys Combined
fleet are coming out of Port, We
have very little Wind so that I have
no hopes of seeing them before tomorrow
May the God of Battles crown my
Endeavours with success at all events
I will take care that my name shall ever
be most dear to you and Horatia both
of whom I love as much as my own
life, and as my last writing before the
battle will be to you so I hope in God that
I shall live to finish my letter after the

16. Nelson's last letter to Emma
© The British Library Board, Egerton 1614, f.125

held an *'antipathy not to be described'*.[28] When Nelson and Fanny moved into 17 Dover Street in mid-November Fanny received a note from Emma addressed to *'Dear Lady Nelson'* apologising for not being able to call on her that day as she was *'not well nor in spirits'*, but hoped for the *'continuance of your friendship, which will be in Sir William and myself for ever lasting to you and your family.'*[29]

Within days Nelson had decided he could not continue with his marriage. Fanny had been dutiful and loyal to Nelson through the years, but had not shown him the love and admiration he needed. His life has progressed to another level – *'He soars in spheres unknown to private stations'* noted his father.[30] Nelson and Fanny were no longer compatible.

We cannot know how they behaved in private, but Nelson did not disguise his irritation with Fanny or his admiration of Emma. He was in emotional turmoil, suffering guilt over his treatment of Fanny and despair at recognising that a legitimately happy future with Emma was impossible. Emma's position was equally tragic, about to give birth to a baby she could not declare as her own, and knowing that the secret must be maintained to protect Nelson's reputation. Apart from Nelson's immediate family, who eventually realised the truth about this child, Emma attempted to keep this secret, at great personal cost, until her dying day.

Future events indicate that Sir William knew about the pregnancy.

Once again Emma was about to become a mother unable to openly acknowledge and love her child. Remembering her comment to Nelson in October 1798 – *'I should be too happy if I had the blessing of having children'*, we can imagine her suffering in her present circumstances.

Nelson was kept away from Fanny and his family by his need to catch up with naval affairs and many other commitments. Not having been in London for so long, there were huge demands on his time. His father wrote to his sister, Catherine (Kitty): *'Your Bro' is so constantly upon the wing that I can but get a short glimpse myself ...'*[31]

Nelson's commitments included paying his respects at the Admiralty, attending the Lord Mayor's Banquet, visiting the Duke of Clarence, attending King George's levee, making his first appearance at the House of Lords, dining with the East India Company and sitting for portraits by Sir William Beechey and John Hoppner. On 8 December, at a public dinner, Simon de Koster made a simple pencil drawing of him, that Nelson later declared *'the most like me.'*[32]

Sir William, at Nelson's insistence, accompanied him to the Lord Mayor's Banquet, an appropriate occasion for the City of London to present Nelson with a magnificent sword, valued at 200 guineas, commemorating his Nile victory. On his way the crowd gathered to see the Lord Mayor's Procession recognised Nelson and, as at Great Yarmouth, some of them joyfully removed the horses from the shafts of his coach and pulled the coach to the banquet at Guildhall.

The following day Nelson and Sir William (as the retiring ambassador to Naples) attended the King's levee where Nelson was distressed to be coolly received by George III.

Collingwood later reported: *'He gave me an account of his reception at Court, which was not very flattering, after having been the adoration of that of Naples. His Majesty merely asked him if he had recovered his health; and then, without waiting for an answer, turned to General ----- and talked to him for nearly half an hour in great good humour ...'[33]*

The King's behaviour may have been because Nelson presented himself wearing his foreign insignia, alongside his British orders, before being granted permission for this favour, or maybe the King was approaching another episode of his 'madness'.

Wounded by his King's apparent ingratitude, Nelson attended a dinner given by Lord Spencer that evening, where Fanny suffered the full brunt of his bad humour. Lady Spencer reported: *'After dinner Lady Nelson, who sat opposite to her husband (by the way he never spoke during dinner and looked blacker than all the devils), perhaps injudiciously, but with a good intention, peeled some walnuts and offered them to him in a glass. As she handed it across the table Nelson pushed it away from him, but so roughly that the glass broke against one of the dishes. There was an awkward pause, and then Lady Nelson burst into tears. When we retired to the drawing room she told me how she was situated.'[34]*

One evening Nelson set out *'in a state of absolute despair and distraction'* to walk alone through the streets of London for many hours:* *'He rambled as far as the city; perambulated Fleet Market, Blackfriars Bridge, etc. and, exhausted with fatigue, as well as over-powered by mental suffering, reached the house of Sir William Hamilton in Grosvenor Square about four in the morning.'[35]*

Sir William and Emma received Nelson sympathetically. Sir William's advice was *'to seek that happiness in his professional pursuits which it seemed unlikely he would ever find at home.'*

* This incident, related by Emma, was described in James Harrison's biography of Nelson.

There were further harrowing evenings for Fanny. Nelson insisted that they entertain the Hamiltons with other guests to dinner at Dover Street. When Emma left the table feeling unwell Nelson rebuked Fanny for not immediately following to attend to her.

All four attended theatre performances at Covent Garden, the Haymarket and Drury Lane, accompanied by Nelson's father and his brother, William. On each of these public appearances the audience greeted Nelson with standing ovations of rapturous applause.

During the performance of *Pizarro* at Drury Lane Fanny fainted and had to be helped from their box by Emma and Nelson's father. Nelson remained seated until the end of the play. The *Morning Herald* reported that *'Her Ladyship however soon became sufficiently recovered to resume her seat and ... remained in the box during the rest of the performance.'*[36]

The play held particular interest for Emma. Jane Powell, with whom Emma had worked during her early days in London at Dr Budd's house, was acting the leading role of Elvira. Mrs Powell was now a famous actress, second only in status to the acclaimed Mrs Siddons. Jane and Emma resumed their friendship and were still in touch years later.

A few days later, Sir William and Emma drove to Stanmore to spend the weekend with Lord Abercorn, accompanied by Nelson and Fanny, who were invited to dinner. This was the last time that Nelson and Fanny appeared together in public.

Emma received a letter from William Beckford, who called her the *'Madonna of the lovely eyes'*[37] and was reputed to be the richest man in England. Sir William, herself, her mother and Nelson were invited to spend Christmas at his magnificent and extraordinary country seat Fonthill Splendens, near Salisbury in Wiltshire. Fanny was not invited. Her humiliation was complete when Nelson accepted the invitation, leaving his wife to spend Christmas in London with his father, his brother William and his wife, Sarah.

They left London on 21 December and did not return until 26 December.

The eccentric Beckford laid on lavish food and wine accompanied by theatrical and musical entertainment for a large party of guests that included local gentry, James Wyatt, his distinguished architect, Benjamin West, President of the Royal Academy, and Madame Banti, Emma's friend from Naples. Emma and Madame Banti sang for the company in the evening.

One evening, after a sumptuous dinner, presented with *'grandeur and originality'*, the company withdrew to the library where *'a collation was presented consisting of various sorts of confectionery served in gold baskets, with spiced wines etc.'*

Emma quietly withdrew. Rows of chairs were arranged in the room beyond and when everyone was seated, *'Lady Hamilton appeared in the character of Agrippina, bearing the ashes of Germanicus in a golden urn ... [she] displayed with truth and energy every gesture, attitude and expression of countenance which could be conceived in Agrippina herself ... the actions of her head, of her hands, and arms in the various positions of the urn; in her manner of presenting it before the Romans, or of holding it up to the Gods in the act of supplication, was most classically graceful ...'*[38]

Despite being eight months pregnant, Emma gave a beautiful performance. The audience was enthralled; some were moved to tears. Benjamin West was so affected that he later painted the scene.

After the dreamlike existence of these few days spent in luxurious and theatrical surroundings, the *Tria* returned to London to face reality: Nelson to spend his last few days at Dover Street and the final break-up with Fanny; Sir William to battle with his desperate financial situation; Emma to face the birth of her baby and Nelson's imminent departure.

Emma found that the Queen would not receive her and therefore neither would large numbers of London society. The newspapers reported on 5 January 1801: *'Lady Hamilton has received no answer whatever to the recommendatory letter which the Queen of Naples wrote to our Queen in her favour, although a Great Personage received it at the Levée from Sir W.H. who was himself the bearer of this courtly epistle to his Royal Consort.'*[39]

On 1 January 1801, Nelson was informed that he was promoted Vice-Admiral of the Blue. Two days later he attended the funeral of his first patron and much-loved mentor, Commodore William Locker and on 9 January Nelson and Fanny signed the documents for the sale of Round Wood. Fanny was never happy there and had often spent long spells in Bath and London. It suited them both to give up the property.

Nelson's solicitor, William Haslewood, probably witnessed the signing of the sale documents. He certainly saw them during the last few days Nelson was in London. Haslewood's account (written many years later) describes the argument between Nelson and Fanny that marked the end of their relationship: *'... I was breakfasting with Lord* and Lady Nelson, at their lodgings in Arlington Street, [actually, Dover Street] and a cheerful conversation was passing on indifferent subjects, when Lord Nelson spoke of something which had been done or said, by 'dear Lady Hamilton', upon which Lady Nelson rose from her chair, and exclaimed, with much vehemence, 'I am sick of hearing of dear Lady Hamilton, and am resolved that you shall give up either her or me.' Lord Nelson, with perfect calmness said – 'Take care, Fanny, what you say. I love you sincerely; but I cannot forget my obligations to Lady Hamilton, or speak of her otherwise than with affection and admiration.' Without one soothing word or gesture, but muttering something about her mind being made up, Lady Nelson left the room, and shortly after drove from the house. They never lived together afterwards. I believe Lord Nelson took a formal leave of her Ladyship before joining the fleet under Sir Hyde Parker …'* Haselwood erroneously stated that Fanny 'never made any apology for her abrupt and ungentle conduct above related, or any overture towards a reconciliation'.[40] In fact Fanny wrote to Nelson in 1801 attempting a reconciliation. Haslewood claimed that Nelson's brother, William, and his sisters, Mrs Bolton and Mrs Matcham and their husbands, 'well knew that the separation was unavoidable on Lord Nelson's part'.[41]

Nelson had known for some time that St. Vincent intended to give him, as his new flagship, the San Josef, 112 guns, the ship he had captured at the Battle of Cape St. Vincent and which he considered the 'the finest ship in the world'. He was ordered to proceed to Plymouth where the San Josef was being prepared for action.

After taking his 'formal leave' of Fanny on 13 January 1801, Nelson left London to take up his command. Some letters were exchanged between them but they never saw each other again.

Nelson's favourite sister, Kitty, defended his conduct to her dying day, saying, 'He had some excuses' and 'she was so very cold'.[42]

Accompanied by his brother, Nelson arrived in Southampton and sent the briefest of notes to Fanny:

Southampton, 13th. January 1801

My dear Fanny,

We are arrived, and heartily tired; and with kindest regards to my father and all the family, believe me your affectionate

Nelson[43]

---

* Haselwood sent this letter to Sir Nicholas Harris Nicolas, editor of the renowned seven volumes of Nelson's Dispatches and Letters, in order to dispel Nicolas's belief that Nelson walked out on Fanny.

He proceeded to Plymouth by coach, writing to Emma the following evening: *'Anxiety for friends left and various workings of my imagination gave me one of those severe pains of the heart, that all the windows were obliged to be put down, the Carriage stop'd, and the perspiration was so strong that I never was wetter, and yet dead with Cold; however it is gone off...'*[44]

These symptoms describe a state of acute anxiety. Nelson was evidently deeply disturbed by his unenviable situation. He had left a desolate Fanny in London, with whom he no longer felt any connection, and his beloved Emma, only two weeks away from giving birth to their baby.

He had arranged with Emma to destroy the letters they wrote to each other. He destroyed all of hers, but thankfully for historians and biographers, she kept all of his. He devised a code to communicate about the forthcoming birth. A fictitious member of his crew, who was presumably illiterate, would communicate through Nelson to his wife. This unsatisfactory arrangement lasted for four months.

Extracts from these letters illustrate his confusing communications:

25 January: *'... I delivered poor Mrs Thompson's note; her friend is truly thankful for her kindness and your goodness ... Poor man! He is very anxious and begs you will, if she is not able, write a line just to comfort him. He appears to me to feel very much her situation; he is so agitated, and will be so for 2 or 3 days, that he says he cannot write, and that I must send his kind love and affectionate regards ...'*[45]

26 January: *'... Mrs Thompson's friend is this moment come into the room. He desires me to thank you for your goodness to his friend. He appears almost as miserable as myself ...'*[46]

28 January: *'... I have this moment seen Mrs Thompson's friend. Poor fellow! He seems very uneasy and melancholy ...'*[47]

Meanwhile, Sir William had found a house to rent at 23 Piccadilly, large enough for them to continue entertaining in their usual style. He paid £1,000 for the lease. From Emma's letter to Greville we know that they had *'left every thing at Naples but the vases & best pictures, 3 houses elegantly furnished, all our horses & 6 or 7 carriages'*. (Sir William later valued these possessions at £10,000). Sir William arranged to sell his *'vases & best pictures'* but meanwhile there was no finance available to furnish and equip the house. Emma was obliged to sell her diamonds in haste, and later claimed she had received a poor price. According to her bank account at Coutts, in January 1800 Emma received £2,000 and in April a further £900, from Cripps & Francillon at 24 Norfolk Street in the Strand. They were *'Jewellers to his Royal Highness the Prince of Wales … the utmost Value given for Diamonds, Pearls & coloured stones'.*

Sir William acknowledged her contribution by making out a legal document by which the furniture and other items purchased by Emma would return to her on his death. Emma replaced her diamonds with cheaper jewellery.

They moved into their new residence in mid-January. Emma had her own suite of rooms and retired there for three days *'with a very bad cold'*, the cover for the birth of her baby on 29 January. This is assumed to be the most likely date, as Nelson received the news on 1 February.

In view of the need for secrecy, it is likely that the resourceful Mrs Cadogan delivered the baby. At the time, babies were usually delivered at home by a professional or amateur midwife. Emma's mother may have had assistance. Nelson sent money *'for those who have been useful to you.'*

Nelson was ecstatic when he heard of the safe arrival of a baby girl. He immediately wrote to Emma: *' I believe poor dear Mrs Thompson's friend will go mad with joy. He cries, prays, and performs all tricks yet dare not shew all or any of his feelings, but he has only me to consult with. He swears he will drink your health this day in a bumper, and damn me if I don't join him in spite of all the doctors in Europe for none regard you with truer affection than myself. You are a dear, good creature, and your kindness and attention to poor Mrs T. stamps you higher than ever in my mind. I cannot write, I am so agitated by this young man at my elbow. I believe he is foolish; he does nothing but rave about you and her …'*[48]

Two days later, he wrote: *'Your good and dear friend, does not think it proper to write with his own hand but he hopes the time may not be far distant when he may be united for ever to the object of his wishes, his only love. He swears before heaven that he will marry you as soon as it is possible, which he fervently prays may be soon. He charges me to say how dear you are to him, and that you must, every opportunity, kiss and bless for him his dear little girl, which he wishes to be called Emma, out of gratitude to our dear, good Lady Hamilton … I have given Lord N. a hundred pounds this morning, for which he will give Lady Hamilton an order on his agents; and I beg that you will distribute it amongst those who have been useful to you on the late occasion …'*[49]

The baby was eventually named Horatia, probably at Emma's request.

Apart from Sir William, Emma and her mother, there were several people employed, and possibly living, in their house: Oliver, Emma's maids Fatima, Julia and Marianne, Sir William's valet, Gaetano, his Neapolitan butler, a French cook and a coachman. Some of these servants must have been aware of Horatia's birth, but news of the birth was not leaked to the newspapers. The *Morning Chronicle* simply reported on 7 February: '*Lady Hamilton did not dine at the Duke of Norfolk's last Sunday, as mentioned in this paper of Monday. We are concerned to find her Ladyship was indisposed.*'

Emma and her mother had only a short time in which to enjoy her new baby. Emma and Horatia were denied the crucial early bonding experience recognised today as so important. Within a few days, Emma delivered Horatia into the care of a Mrs Gibson who lived not far away at Little Titchfield Street. From her written notes to Emma, Mrs Gibson appears to be reasonably well educated. She had a disabled daughter, but there is no record of a husband.

Years later, Mrs Gibson related that Lady Hamilton had arrived in a hackney coach (she would have been recognised in her own coach) carrying a baby carefully concealed in her coat and muff. Lady Hamilton told her that she was acting on behalf of the baby's unknown parents and that absolute discretion was necessary. She would be '*handsomely rewarded*' for her care of the child. Mrs Gibson estimated the baby to be no more than a week old.

Sir William, who we believe knew of the baby's birth, could not agree to her living at 23 Piccadilly, but he must have given permission for Mrs Gibson to bring her to the house to visit Emma when he was out at his numerous society meetings or court appearances.

Mrs Gibson kept some of the notes she received from Emma, making arrangements to visit Horatia or to have her brought to 23 Piccadilly.

The first is dated 7 February 1801: '*Dear Madam – my cold has been so bad I could not go out today but tomorrow will call on you write me by the penny post how the dear little Miss Horatia is – ever your sincere friend E.H.*'[50]

On 11 February she wrote: '*I hope my dear Mrs Gibson that Miss Horatia is well if it is a fine day tomorrow bring her in a coach well wrapet up to see me but let her be well covered getting in and out of the coach come at eleven o'clock.*

> *Your sincere friend*
> *E. Hamilton*[51]

Many years later Hardy described an incident from 1801: ' *When I was in London … I called on Lady Hamilton in Piccadilly. She soon left the room, and presently returned with this child in her arms, saying, 'Look what a pretty baby I have got' but made no observation as to whose it was.'*[52] He did not know at the time that the baby was Nelson's daughter.

Horatia was in Mrs Gibson's care for four and a half years. During this time Emma saw her as often as she could. Nelson's letters indicate how much he doted on his daughter, but he was away at sea much of the time, leaving Emma with the difficult task of caring for Horatia whilst keeping her secret.

Emma received a long letter from Nelson expressing his deep admiration for her:

San Josef, February 8th. 1801

My Dear Lady,

Mr. Davison demands the privilege of carrying back an answer to your kind letter, and I am sure, he will be very punctual in the delivery. I am not in very good spirits; and, except that our country demands all our services and abilities to bring about an honourable peace, nothing should prevent me being the bearer of my own letter. But, my dear friend, I know you are so true and loyal an Englishwoman, that you would hate those who would not stand forth in defence of our King, laws, religion and all that is dear to us. It is your sex that makes us go forth; and seem to tell us – 'None but the brave deserve the fair!' and, if we fall, we still live in the hearts of those females. You are dear to us. It is your sex that rewards us; it is your sex who cherish our memories, and you, my dear, honoured friend, are, believe me, the first, the best of your sex.

I have been the world around, and in every corner of it, and never yet saw your equal, or even one which could be put in comparison with you. You know how to reward virtue, honour, and courage; and never to ask if it is placed in a Prince, Duke, Lord or Peasant: and I hope, one day, to see you in peace before I set out for Bronte, which I am resolved to do … Only tell me how I can be useful to you and Sir William, and believe, nothing could give me more pleasure, being, with the greatest truth, my dear Lady, your most obliged and affectionate friend

Nelson & Bronte[53]*

Nelson was unhappy, unwell and irritable. He had written to Emma in January: '*… My eye is very bad. I have had the physician of the fleet to*

---

* In January Nelson had been granted permission to use his Neapolitan title. For the rest of his life he used the signature above.

examine it. He has directed me not to write ... not to eat anything but the
most simple food; to have green shades for my eyes (will you, my dear friend
make me one or two? Nobody else shall) – and to bath them in cold water every
hour. I fear it is the writing has brought on this complaint. My eye is like
blood, and the film so extended, that I can only see from the corner farthest
from my nose ...'[54]

Fanny received letters from Nelson complaining, yet again, that
items that should have been sent to his ship were damaged or missing:
'All my things are now breaking open for only one key can be found. My
steward says I have no one thing for comfort come ... I have been buying a
few things just to make me <u>un</u>comfortable for in fact I have nothing useful but
two chairs ... I know not where I shall be in a week ...'[55]

The next day he continued: '... Half my wardrobe is left behind ... In
short I find myself without anything comfortable or convenient ... It is now
too late to send half my wardrobe, as I know not what is to become of me, nor
do I care ...'[56]

Nelson's father had left London for Bath and Fanny went to
Brighton. Nelson wrote to her on 3 February: 'My dear Fanny, I received
yesterday your letter from Brighton. It never was my intention to find [fault]
but the fact is I have everything and nothing. If I want a piece of pickle it must
be put in a saucer, if a piece of butter on an earthen plate, but I shall direct
what things I want in future ... Not one thing that Mr Dods sent is but ruined,
large nails drove through the mahogany table and drawers to fasten the
packing cases ... I have six silver bottle stands but not one decanter to fit them,
you told me six of the house ones should be sent. I beg my kindest regards to
Josiah ... and believe me your affectionate

Nelson[57]

The packing and dispatch of Nelson's possessions had been badly
mismanaged. Fanny was either simply inefficient or, understandably,
too distressed. Nelson's unhappiness is clear: ' I know not what is to
become of me, nor do I care.'

Before leaving London he had instructed his agent, Mr Marsh, to
pay £400 into Fanny's account, the first of her quarterly allowances.
Her following unsigned, undated draft letter was probably written at
this time, though it is uncertain whether it was sent to Nelson:

'My dearest husband,

Your generosity and tenderness was never more strongly shown than your
writing to Mr March yesterday morning for the payment of your very
handsome quarterly allowance, which far exceeded my expectation, knowing

your income and had you left it to me, I could not in conscience have said so much.

Accept my warmest, my most affectionate and grateful thanks ... I could say more but my heart is too full. Be assured every wish, every desire of mine is to please the man whose affection constitutes my happiness. God bless my dear husband.'[58]

Nelson had calculated his income at £4,000 p.a. Allowing for having to pay the tax due, he had generously made over nearly half his income to Fanny. In addition she was to be paid the interest due on the £4,000 her uncle Herbert had left her, (Nelson considered this to be her money), making her total income a substantial £1,800 p.a.

Nelson was distancing himself from Fanny while his letters to Emma tell of his admiration and desperate love for her.

Nevertheless, Fanny offered to nurse Nelson when she heard about his eye problems. Her despair is apparent in her letter on 20 February to Davison: '... *My Mind has not yet recovered its Natural calmness – or do I think it ever will – I am now distrustful and fearful of my own shadow ... My anxiety, My fondness for him all rushed forth ... and offered to nurse him and that he should find me the same I had ever been to him faithful, affect* [ionate] *and desirous to do everything I could to please him ... to this letter I have had no reply.'*[59]

She had not yet received a letter Nelson had sent her. He described it to Emma: '*I had a letter from that person in Brighton saying she had heard from my brother that I was ill and offered to come and nurse me but I have sent such an answer that will convince her she would not be received. I am almost afraid you will think I have gone too far, for she must see there is some strong reason but my intentions are in everything to give you satisfaction, therefore do not be angry for the strength of my letter ...'*[60]

Emma received more letters addressed to '*Mrs Thompson to the care of Lady Hamilton.*' Under this clumsy disguise Nelson repeatedly declared his love: '*Your dear friend, my dear and truly beloved Mr T. is almost distracted; he wishes there was peace, or that if your uncle would die, he would instantly come and marry you, for he doats on nothing but you and his child; and, as it is my godchild, I desire you will take great care of it. He has implicit faith in your fidelity, even in conversation with those he dislikes, and that you will be faithful in greater things he has no doubt ...'*[61]

In another letter, he again mentioned marriage:'*Your friend is at my elbow, and enjoins me to assure you that his love for you and your child is, if possible, greater than ever, and that he calls God to witness that he will marry you as soon as possible, and that it will be to his delight to call you his own...'*[62]

Nelson had been transferred to the *St George*, 90guns, and knew that he would soon be sailing with the Baltic fleet under the command of Sir Hyde Parker. In the few weeks before leaving he became almost 'unhinged' by his passionate, but hopeless, love for Emma. The following extracts from his letters reveal his state of mind:

'... *my heart is somehow sunk within me. I long to hear you are well ...*'[63]

'... *I do not think I was ever so miserable as at this moment. I own I sometimes fear you will not be so true to me as I am to you, yet I cannot, will not believe you can be false ... May God send me happiness ...*'[64]

Emma did her best to cheer him up. Nelson thanked her for her numerous letters, sometimes three on the same day. His comments on her letters included:

'*How interesting your letters are! You cannot write too much or be too particular.*'

'*Your letters have made me happy, today.*'

'*Nothing can give me so much pleasure as your truly kind and friendly letters.*'[65]

In his unhappiness, Nelson fantasized that he would one day marry Emma and that they would live in peace on his Bronte estate. Sir William was likely die in the near future, but the situation with Fanny was more complicated. Divorcing her would be almost impossible, and Nelson never mentioned divorce in his letters.*

When Emma told Nelson that the Prince of Wales was invited to 23 Piccadilly to dine and to hear her sing, he was consumed with irrational jealousy. He frantically sent several letters in which he made highly critical, unguarded remarks about the Prince. Emma was extremely unwise not to burn these particular letters as Nelson had instructed her to do.

He wrote from the *St George* in Torbay on 19 February 1801: '*I have received your most affectionate letter, and I feel very much for the unpleasant situation the Prince, or rather Sir William, has unknowingly placed you, for if he knew as much of the P's character as the world does, he would rather let the lowest wretch that walks the streets dine at his table than that unprincipled lyar. I have heard it reported that he has said he would make you his mistress ...*'[66]

---

* Before the mid 19th century the only way of obtaining a divorce that allowed re-marriage was by Private Act of Parliament. Divorce was only granted for adultery and only the wealthy could afford to divorce.

In a further note he confirmed: '*I am so agitated that I can write nothing. I knew it would be so, and you can't help it. Why did you not tell Sir William. Your character will be gone ... I cannot write to Sir William, but he ought to go to the Prince and not suffer your character to be ruined by him. Oh God that I was dead. But I do not, my dearest Emma, blame you, nor do I fear your inconstancy ... I am gone almost mad, but you cannot help it ... He wishes I dare say to have you alone. Don't let him touch; nor yet sitt next you ... God strike him blind if he looks at you – this is high treason, and you may get me hanged by revealing it ...*'[67]

The following day, he relented his outburst: '*Forgive my letter wrote and sent last night, perhaps my head was a little affected. No wonder, it was such an unexpected, such a knock-down blow, such a death. But I will not go on for I shall get out of my sences again ...*'[68]

He finally calmed down when he received an explanation from Sir William:

Piccadilly, February 19th. 1801

My dear Lord,

Whether Emma will be able to write to you today or not is a question, as she has got one of her terrible sick head aches. Among other things that vex her, is that we have been drawn in to be under the absolute necessity of giving a dinner to the Prince of Wales on Sunday next. He asked it himself having expressed his strong desire of hearing Banti's and Emma's voices together. I am well aware of the danger that would attend the Prince's frequenting our house, not that I fear that Emma could ever be induced to act contrary to the prudent conduct she has hitherto pursued, but the world is so ill natured that the worst construction is put upon the most innocent actions.

As this dinner must be, or the Prince will be offended, we shall keep it strictly to the musical part, invite only Banti, her husband, and Taylor and as I wish to shew a civility to Davison I have sent him an invitation ... Emma would really have gone to any lengths to have avoided Sunday's dinner, but I thought it would not be prudent to break with the Prince who really has shown the greatest civility to us when we were last in England and since we returned, and she has at last acquiesced to my opinion ...'[69]

To everyone's relief, the Prince was unable to attend.

Leaving Torbay, Nelson arrived at Spithead (off Portsmouth) on 21 February and on the 23rd obtained leave of absence for three days. He travelled through the night, arriving in London at 7 a.m.

As the Dover Street house was closed up, he put up at Lothian's

Hotel in Albemarle Street, very near to 23 Piccadilly. Emma took him to Mrs Gibson's to meet Horatia for the first time. For years Nelson had longed for a child and he fell in love with his daughter.

His presence in London went unnoticed, although he had appointments at the Admiralty and other business to attend to – notably with Davison, at his house in St. James' Square.

He wrote to Fanny: *'As I am sent for to town on very particular business for a day or two I would not on any account have you come to London but rest quiet where you are. Nor would I have you come to Portsmouth for I never come on shore … I hope Josiah may be able to get a ship now this change of ministers has taken place.* As ever your affectionate Nelson.'*[70]

Having established a friendship with Sarah Nelson, Emma wrote to her in Norfolk. Her letters to Sarah have survived to give us a glimpse into her feelings:

Friday, Noon, February 20th. 1801:

'I have been ill in bed, my dearest Mrs Nelson; I could not take leave of you. My soul was torn in pieces. It is such pain to part with dear friends, and you and I liked each other from the moment we met; our souls were congenial. Not so with 'Tom Tit' [the nickname mocking Fanny's manner of walking, used by Emma and Nelson's family], *for their was an antipathy not to be described … I received letters yesterday from that great <u>adored being</u> what we all love, esteem and admire … How dull <u>my bedroom looks</u> without you. I miss our little friendly chats …'*[71]

24 February: *'My dearest Friend –your dear Brother arrived this morning by seven o'clock. He stays only 3 days … I am in health so-so but spirits to-day excellent. Oh, what a real pleasure Sir William and I have in seeing our great, good, virtuous Nelson. His eye is better. Tom tit does not come to town. She offered to go down, but was refused. She only wanted to go to do mischief to all great JOVE"S relations. 'Tis now shewn, all her ill-treatment and bad <u>heart,</u> JOVE has found it out. Apropos, Lady Nelson is in Brighton yet.'*[72]

The comment *'all her ill-treatment and bad <u>heart</u>'* refers to a situation between Fanny and her son, Josiah, who was in London at the time. It may be that Fanny hoped-for honours for Josiah, but dropped her claims on his behalf to try to gain favour with Nelson. Emma claimed later that Fanny had *'befouled her own nest'.*

Nelson attempted to have Josiah reappointed to the frigate *Thalia* in a last kindness to a stepson he had dearly loved, but who had disappointed him by poor behaviour when in command of the *Thalia*

---

* St. Vincent had succeeded Spencer as First Lord of the Admiralty.

in the Mediterranean. Josiah drank, kept bad company, bullied his crew and was at daggers drawn with his officers.

Nelson had appealed to both Troubridge and Ball for help in correcting Josiah's behaviour. Both had tried, but after a particular incident when Josiah insulted the *Thalia's* master, the circumstances were reported to the Navy Board.

Admiral Duckworth saved Josiah from a court martial and sent him home in October 1800. He was never given another command.

Sarah Nelson heard again from Emma on 25 February: '... *Our dear Nelson is very well in health. Poor fellow, he travelled allmost all night, but you that knows his great, good heart will not be surprised at any act of friendship of his ...'*[73]

On 26 February, after Nelson, Maurice and Troubridge had dined at 23 Piccadilly: '... *We had a pleasant evening and night ... we supped and talked politicks till 2. Oh, my dearest friend, our dear Lord has just come in. He goes off tonight and sails immediately. My heart is fit to Burst with greef. Oh, what pain, God only knows ... I shall go mad with greef. Oh, God only knows what it is to part with such a friend, such a one. We were truly called the 'Tria Juncta in Uno' for Sir William, he and I have but one heart in three bodies.'*[74]

Emma has been accused of ingratiating herself with Nelson's family and destroying their relationship with Fanny, but Nelson had made his own decisions about Fanny, making it difficult for his father, brothers and sisters to associate with her. Emma's friendship with his sisters was genuine. She knew how important they were to Nelson.

Emma would from now on suffer the same agony of separation which Fanny, and all navy wives, endured. She had little to gain and much to lose from her affair with Nelson. They saw very little of each other over the remaining years of his life.

Returning to his ship, the *St George* in Portsmouth, a distraught Nelson wrote to Emma on 27 February: '*Parting from such a friend is literally tearing one's own flesh; but the remembrance will keep our spirits till we meet. My affection is, if possible, stronger than ever for you. And I trust it will keep increasing as long as we both live ...'*[75]

On 1 March he suffered another anxiety attack that he described to Emma: '*After my letter of 8 0'clock this morning went on shore, on board came Oliver, and when he was announced by Hardy, so much anxiety for your safety rushed into my mind that the pain immediately seized my heart which kept increasing for half an hour, that, turning cold, hot, cold &c. I was obliged to send for the surgeon, who gave me something to warm me, for it was deadly chill.'*[76]

Later that day, knowing he would be sailing the next day, Nelson wrote one of his famous love letters to Emma:

'Now, my own dear wife, for such you are in my eyes and in the face of heaven, I can give full scope to my feelings, for I dare say Oliver will faithfully deliver this letter. You know, my dearest Emma, that there is nothing in this world that I would not do for us to live together, and to have our own dear little Child with us. I firmly believe that the Campaign will give us peace, and then we will sett off for Bronte. In twelve hours we shall be across the water and freed from all the nonsense of his friends, or rather pretended ones. Nothing but an event happening to him could prevent my going, and I am sure you will think so, for unless all the matters accord it would bring 100 tongues and slanderous reports if I separated from her (which I would do with pleasure the moment we can be united, I want to see her no more) therefore we must manage till we can quit this country or your uncle dies. I love, I never did love anyone else. I never had a dear pledge of love till you gave me one, and you, thank my God, never gave one to any body else. I think before March is out you will either see us back, or so victorious that we shall insure a glorious issue to our toils. Think what my Emma will feel at seeing a return safe, perhaps with a little more fame, her own dear loving Nelson. Never, if I can help it, will I dine out of my Ship, or go on shore except duty calls me ... You, my beloved Emma, and my country, are the two dearest objects of my fond heart – _a heart susceptible and true_. Only place confidence in me and you never shall be disappointed. I burn all your letters, because it is right for your sake, and I wish you would burn all mine – they can do no good, and will do us both harm if any seizure of them, or the dropping even of one of them, would fill the mouth of the world sooner than we intend. My longing for you, both person and conversation, you may readily imagine. What must be my sensations at the idea of sleeping with you, it setts me on fire, even the thought, and much more the reality. I am sure my love and desires are all to you, and if any woman naked were to come to me, even as I am at this moment from thinking of you, I hope it might rot off if I would touch her even with my hand. No, my heart, my person, and mind is in perfect union of love towards my own dear beloved Emma – the _real bosom_ friend of her, all hers, all Emma's ... My love, my darling angel, my heaven-given wife, the dearest only true wife of her own till death ...'[77]

Emma, Sir William and Greville had not told Nelson about her earlier child, Little Emma, though Emma possibly did tell him later.

Depressed, Nelson wrote to St. Vincent on the same day: '... although, I own, I have met with much more honours and rewards than ever *my most sanguine ideas led me to expect, yet I am so circumstanced that probably this Expedition will be the last service ever performed by your obliged and affectionate friend*

Nelson & Bronte[78]

A concerned St. Vincent replied: '*Be assured, my dear Lord, that every <u>public</u> act of your life has been the subject of my admiration, which I should have sooner declared, but that I was appalled by the last sentence of your letter; for God's sake, do not suffer yourself to be carried away by any sudden impulse ...*'[79]

On 2 March, Nelson sailed from Portsmouth in the *St. George* with his squadron to join Sir Hyde Parker at Yarmouth. The fleet sailed for the Baltic on 12 March, where Nelson would be famously involved in the Battle of Copenhagen.

CHAPTER 16

Nelson's Separation from Fanny and Emma's Purchase of Merton Place

'He certainly as far as I hear is not a happy man'
Susanna Bolton to Fanny, 8 March 1801

'My mind is tranquil and calm, ready and willing to stand in the breach to defend my Country'
Nelson to Emma, 21 March 1801

'I love Nelson's glory, his great and glorious deeds have made on my heart an impression never never to be effaced'
Emma to Sarah, September 1801

'A seaman alone could have given a fine woman full power to <u>chuse</u> & fit up a residence for him without seeing it himself'
Sir William to Nelson, 16 October 1801

ONE WEEK BEFORE sailing from Yarmouth Nelson wrote his last letter to Fanny:

St. George March 4, 1801

Josiah is to have another ship and to go abroad if the Thalia cannot soon be got ready. I have done <u>all</u> for him and he may again as he has often done before wish me to break my neck, and be abetted in it by his friends who are likewise my enemies, but I have done my duty as an honest generous man and I neither want or wish for any body to care what become of me, whether I return or am left in the Baltic, seeing I have done all in my power for you. And if dead you will find I have done the same, therefore my only wish is to be left to myself and wishing you every happiness, believe that I am your affectionate Nelson & Bronte[1]

A shocked Fanny later wrote a comment on the letter: *'This is my Lord Nelson's letter of dismissal, which has so astonished me that I immediately sent it to Mr Maurice Nelson who was sincerely attached to me for his advice, he desired me not to take the least notice of it, as his brother seemed to have forgot himself.*[2]

The same day Nelson wrote a memorandum detailing his financial arrangements for Fanny while he lived:

'Lord Nelson's annual income is about £4000 a year including £200 a year the interest of Lady Nelson's £4000. My plan is to allow Lady Nelson £2000 a year subject to the income tax which as I pay the tax with my own will reduce my net yearly income to £3600.

Lady Nelson to be paid every quarter in advance viz. 1st. January 1801, 1st. April, 1st. July, 1st. October by Messrs. Marsh, Page and Creed £400 each quarter which with interest of the £4000 will amount to £1800 meat money.

Lord Nelson has directed Mr Davison to pay every bill and expense of his and Lady Nelson's to the day of his leaving London.

Nelson

N.B. Lord Nelson gives Lady Nelson the principal of the £4000 mentioned above to be 'at her disposal by will.'[3]

Before he left for the Baltic, Emma wrote a poem to Nelson:

> Silent grief and sad forebodings
> (Lest I ne'er should see him more)
> Fill my heart when gallant Nelson
> Hoists Blue Peter at the fore.
>
> For when duty calls my hero
> To far seas where cannons roar,
> Nelson (love and Emma leaving)
> Hoists Blue Peter at the fore.
>
> Oft he kiss'd my lips at parting
> At every kiss he swore
> Nought could force him from my bosom,
> Save Blue Peter at the fore.
>
> Oh, that I might with my Nelson
> Sail the wide world o'er and o'er,
> Never would I then with sorrow,
> See Blue Peter at the fore.

But (ah me!) his ship's unmooring;
Nelson's last boat sails from shore
Every sail is set and swelling,
And Blue Peter's seen no more.

On his Pendant anxious gazing,
Fill with tears (mine eyes run o'er)
At each change of wind I tremble
While Blue Peter's at the fore.

All the live-long day I wander,
Sighing on the sea-beat-shore:
But my sighs are all unheeded,
When Blue Peter's at the fore.

Emma Hamilton[4]

Emma had expressed her fears for Nelson's safety to Sarah Nelson on 2 March:

'*My dearest Friend,*

Anxiety and heart bleeding for your brother's departure has made me so ill I have not been able to write. I cannot eat or sleep. Oh, may God prosper and bless him … you will have him at Yarmouth in 2 days. Oh how I envy you. Oh God how happy you are to be with that great good virtuous man. My spirits and health is bad indeed …'[5]

Realizing how distraught Emma would be in his absence Nelson wrote to Sarah:

Yarmouth   March 7, 1801

My dear Madam,

I wish you would take a post chaise and go to London and be as near and as much as possible with our dear friend Lady Hamilton who loves and esteems you very much … In doing this favour you shall be at no expense and you will most truly oblige your sincere and affectionate friend

Nelson & Bronte[6]

He wrote asking Davison to pay Sarah £100 as '*she is in London by my desire*'.

Meanwhile Susanna Bolton (Nelson's eldest sister) wrote to Fanny in Brighton. The letter, dated 8 March, confirms that Fanny was not well thought of by Nelson's family (apart from his father): '*Will you excuse what I am going to say? I wish you had continued in town a little* longer, as I <u>have heard</u> my brother regretted he had not a house he could call his own when he returned. Do, whenever you hear he is likely to return, have a house to receive him. If you absent yourself entirely from him, there can never be a reconciliation. Such attention must please him and I am sure will do in the end. Your conduct as he <u>justly</u> says is <u>exemplary</u> in regard to him and he has not an unfeeling heart ... I hope in God one day I shall have the pleasure of seeing you together as happy as ever, he certainly as far as I hear is not a happy man ...'[7]

Her advice was given too late. Nelson's mind was made up and he had 'dismissed' Fanny on 4 March.

Having provided generously for Fanny, his overriding concern was to ensure a safe future for Horatia. In February, he had sent Emma a copy of a draft codicil to his will for her comments. Having bequeathed Emma an income from the Bronte estate and many of his valuable awards, he continued: '...[these awards] to be sold if she pleases and the income to be for her use during her natural life and at her decease it is to be given to a child called _____ in whom I take a very particular interest and as Emma Hamilton is the only person who knows the parents of this female child I rely with the greatest confidence on her unspotted honour and integrity that she will consider the child as mine and be a guardian to it, sheilding it from want and disgrace, and bringing it up as the child of her dear friend Nelson and Bronte ...'[8]

He bequeathed any money he was worth over the sum of £20,000 to Horatia, the interest on this sum to be used for her education until she reached the age of twenty-one.

While drawing up the above documents, Nelson wrote to Emma: '... I have seen, and talked much with Mrs Thompson's friend. The fellow seems to eat all my words, when I talk of her and his child! He says he never can forget your goodness and kind affection to her and his dear, dear child. I have had, you know the felicity of seeing it, and a finer child never was produced by any two persons. It was, in truth, a love-begotten child ...'[9] Writing to Emma when approaching Great Yarmouth Nelson referred again to his bequests:

St. George at Sea March 6th. 1801

How tiresome and alone I feel at not having the pleasure of receiving your dear, kind, friendly and intelligent letters. I literally feel as a fish out of water ... I assure you it gave me great pleasure, instead of pain, the reflection that I was providing for a great friend. I have given you, by will, £3000, and three diamond boxes, & the King of Naples picture in trust, to be at your *disposal, so that it is absolutely your own. By the codicil I have given you the money owing to me by Sir William, likewise in trust … The star I have given you to wear for my sake. You must not think my dearest friend, that this necessary act hastens our departure, but it is a right and proper measure … May the Heavens bless my own dear friend and let me read happy and good news from her. Kiss my dear, dear godchild for me, and be assured I am for ever, ever, ever, your, your, your, more than ever yours, your own, only your &c.* [10]

The same day Nelson drew up a codicil to his will, witnessed by Captains Hardy and Thesiger, outlining Sir William's debts to him which he bequeathed to Emma: *'…nine hundred and twenty seven pounds lent him at Palermo, in January 1799; also the sum of two hundred and fifty five pounds lent him between July and November 1800; also one thousand and ninety-four pounds, being one-half of our expenses from Leghorn to London in 1800, making in the whole the sum of two thousand two hundred and seventy six pounds …'* [11]

On arrival in London Nelson had £16,000 in stocks of various kinds with Marsh & Creed, his Navy Agents. He sold stocks to the value of £6,131.50s. on 26 November 1800, presumably to pay his debts in Palermo and expenses on the journey home, leaving him money to spare for current expenses.

Sir William was hoping to recover money owed to him by the government and the sale of his vases and pictures. He informed Nelson on 19 February: *'… I have fully demonstrated to Lord Grenville and Treasury that £8000 is absolutely necessary for the clearing off my unfunded debt without making up for my [personal] losses. Upon the whole then I do not expect to get more than the net annuity above mentioned [a pension of £2000 p.a.] and the £8000 but unless that is granted I shall indeed have been very ill-used. I hope in my next to be able to inform your Lordship that all has been finally settled. I am busy putting in order the remains of my vases and pictures that you so kindly saved for me on board the Foudroyant and the sale of them will enable me to go on more at my ease and not leave a debt unpaid.'* [12]

Sir William was indeed *'very ill used'*. From his bank records at Coutts we learn that Sir William's hoped-for pension of £2,000 p.a. was not agreed until the following June, eighteen months after his arrival in England.

The Treasury was late in paying his salary for Naples and Palermo, a neglect Sir William had complained about several times before. Even more disgracefully, his pension was to terminate with his death. The

Government made no provision for Emma, who had shared his ambassadorial duties.

His income from his Pembroke estates was estimated by his bankers to be about £1,000 p.a. Greville's expenditure of his uncle's money on a grand plan to develop a large harbour at Milford Haven had drastically reduced Sir William's income. The estate was mortgaged for £13,000.[13]

Sir William, now 71 years old, continued to enjoy his usual lifestyle. Nelson, who helped Sir William draw up a list of his debts, was concerned. Writing to Emma on 10 March:

'What can Sir William mean by wanting you to launch out into expense and extravagance. He that used to think that a little candle-light and iced water would ruin him, to want to set off at £10,000 a year, for a less sum would not afford concerts and the style of living equal to it. Suppose you had set off in this way, what would he not have said ...'[14]

Emma has been unfairly blamed for their *'incorrigible extravagance'*. She enjoyed entertainments, concerts (singing with her friend, Brigida Banti) and dinner parties at 23 Piccadilly, but they were not solely at her instigation. Sir William, returning from a trip to Warwick, found a £400 bill for wine due for payment.

On March 13 Sir William reported cheerfully to Nelson: *'It is quite beyond all expectations that I have found so many of my fine vases; fortunately some cases of the worst were taken on board the Colossus by mistake, when I thought the eight best cases gone.'*[15]

Many cases of important vases had been brought home on the *Foudroyant*. He proposed to sell them at Christie's, who gave notice of this on the catalogue for his picture sale:

'Early in April will be sold his truly valuable ... singularly fine Grecian, called Etruscan vases ... which were saved from Naples and escaped the fatal effects of the storm by which Part of this unique Collection was lost on Board the Colossus Man of War.'[16]

When a collector, Thomas Hope, approached Sir William, he agreed to sell the vases directly to him in order to keep the collection together. An annotation on the Christie's catalogue states: 'SOLD by private contract to Mr HOPE for £5000.' Hamilton had in fact struck a deal with Mr. Hope at £4,000.

Sir William's financial situation was much improved by the sale of pictures at Christie's on 27 and 28 March. The total amount realized was £5,819, on which Christie's commission was due. Among 150 pictures catalogued were works by Leonardo da Vinci, Titian, Tintoretto, Valasquez and Rubens.

Three portraits of Emma were sold:

Lot 28. Mad. le Brun. Head of a Sybil ...

Lot 31. Angelica Kauffman. A muse with a mask in her hand ...

Lot 50. Sir J. Reynolds. His original Bacchante – painted on panel ...

There were no Romney portraits of Emma in this sale.[17]*

Another sale of pictures and drawings on 17 April realized £717. Two further sales at Phillips auctioneers were held on 17 May 1802 and 31 May 1803. In the years 1801, 1802 and 1803, Hamilton's bank account is credited with payments from Phillips & Co. amounting to £2,700.

Nelson's wills drawn up in March indicate that it was highly likely that the British fleet would engage in battle in the Baltic campaign putting all involved at risk of loss of life or limb. The comments in his letters to Emma were alarming: '... *either your Nelson will be safe and Sir Hyde Parker a victor, or your own Nelson will be laid low, in case of the latter I have this day added another codicil to my will ...*'[18]

Having outlined the situation with Denmark in his letter to Emma on 21 March, Nelson extols her virtues:

'Your beauty which I own is beyond that of all other women is still below your understanding ... and both these rare and most extraordinary qualifications are almost eclipsed by your goodness and gentleness of heart ... But your goodness of heart, your amiable qualities, your unbounded Charity, will make you Envied in the world which is to come ... You will not my dear friend at this moment consider these true thoughts of your worth can be with a view of adulation, for it is very possible they may be the last words ever wrote by your old faithful and most attached friend till Death.

Nelson & Bronte

Your heart my friend may feel too much on reading this, pray do not let it, for my mind is tranquil and calm, ready and willing to stand in the breach to defend my Country, and to risk whatever fate may await me in that post of honor, but never mind perhaps I may laughing come back. God's will be done, Amen Amen.'[19]

Nelson's assessment of Emma's qualities as *'rare and extraordinary*

---

* Nelson asked Davison to purchase a portrait of Emma on his behalf. He wrote to Davison on 19 March 1801: 'Have the goodness to pay Mr Christie for me the sum of £300 for a picture, but do you not notice it to anybody'. This is believed to be Vigée le Brun's portrait of Emma as a reclining Ariadne.

qualifications' contradicts numerous other critical reports about her.

The government had decided to respond to the Treaty of Alliance formed by Russia, Sweden and Denmark. Their 'Armed Neutrality' was threatening the superiority of the British fleet in the northern seas, and their ships were interfering with British trade in the area. The purpose of the Baltic expedition was to persuade the Danes to withdraw from the Armed Neutrality by amicable negotiations or by force if necessary.

During the campaign Sir Hyde Parker's caution and indecisiveness gave Nelson the opportunity to display his humanity and inspirational leadership. Again he disobeyed his Commander-in-Chief's orders.

When the Battle of Copenhagen commenced Nelson's twelve line of battle ships, frigates, sloops and bomb vessels sailed into a narrow channel to face a strongly defended line of defence, two miles long, set up by the Danes to protect Copenhagen and its harbour. Nelson had transferred his flag to the *Elephant,* a lighter ship more suitable for shallow waters.

The battle began at five past ten on the morning of 2 April 1801 with heavy firing from both sides. There was loss of life and carnage on a massive scale. Admiral Parker and his squadron were expected to approach from the other end of the channel.

After two and a half hours the Danish defence was weakening, but Nelson's ships had suffered great losses. Several had run aground. At this point, Parker, arriving late and still some distance away, sent the signal for the Action to Cease, which prompted Nelson's now iconic reaction. He disobeyed the order in the manner best described in his report by Colonel Stewart, who commanded the troops embarked and was on board the *Elephant:*

'Lord Nelson, was at this time, as he had been during the whole Action, walking the starboard side of the quarter-deck; sometimes much animated, and at others heroically fine in his observations. A shot through the mainmast knocked a few splinters about us. He observed to me, with a smile, "It is warm work, and this day may be last to any of us at the moment"; and then stopping short at the gangway, he used an expression never to be erased from my memory, and said with emotion, "but mark you, I would not be elsewhere for thousands."

When the signal, No. 39, [to discontinue the engagement] was made, the Signal Lieutenant reported it to him. He continued his walk, and did not appear to take notice of it. The Lieutenant, meeting his Lordship at the next turn asked, "Whether he should repeat it?" Lord Nelson answered, "No, acknowledge it". On the officer returning to the poop, his Lordship called after him, is No. 16 [for close Action] still hoisted? the Lieutenant answering in the affirmative, Lord Nelson said "Mind you keep it so". He now walked the deck considerably agitated, which was always known by his moving the stump of his right arm. After a turn or two, he said to me, in a quick manner, "Do you know what's shown on board of the Commander-in-Chief, No 39?" On asking him what that meant, he answered, "Why, to leave off Action". "Leave off Action!" he repeated, and then added, with a shrug, "Now, damn me if I do". He also observed, I believe, to Captain Foley, "You know, Foley, I have only one eye – I have a right to be blind sometimes," and then with an archness peculiar to his character, putting the glass to his right eye, he exclaimed, "I really do not see the signal." This remarkable signal was, therefore, only acknowledged on board the Elephant, not repeated.'[20]

By 2 p.m. most of the Danish line had ceased firing. At 2.30 p.m. Nelson sent a Flag of Truce on shore. The Prince Regent replied by 'inquiring more minutely into the purport of the message' whereupon Nelson sent the following message ashore:

Elephant 2nd. April 1801

Lord Nelson's object in sending on shore the Flag of Trucee is humanity: he therefore consents that hostilities shall cease till Lord Nelson can take his prisoners out of the Prizes, and he consents to land all the wounded Danes, and to burn or remove his Prizes. Lord Nelson, with humble duty to His Royal Highness, begs leave to say, that he will ever esteem it the greatest victory he ever gained, if this Flag of Truce may be the happy forerunner of a lasting and happy union between my most gracious Sovereign and His Majesty the King of Denmark.

Nelson & Bronte[21]

Nelson and Stewart negotiated with the Crown Prince on shore, during which he was informed that the Tzar of Russia had died. The Crown Prince agreed to an armistice of fourteen weeks and suspension of Danish membership of the Armed Neutrality. On 9 April the agreement was signed and Stewart set off to England with the document.

When news of the victory reached London, the government was greatly relieved. Nelson received congratulations from all quarters including St. Vincent, Lord Spencer, Beckford and the Duke of Clarence.

Sir William and Emma were overjoyed. Sir William wrote one of his entertaining letters to Nelson:

Piccadilly April 16, 1801

What can I say my dear Lord that would convey the smallest idea of what we felt yesterday on receiving the authentic letters confirming your late most glorious victory and read in your own hand that God has not only granted you complete success against the enemies of our country but in the midst of such perils prevented your receiving the smallest scratch. We can only repeat what we knew well and often said before that Nelson <u>was</u>, <u>is</u> and to the <u>last</u> will ever be the <u>first</u>. However, we all agree that when you get safe home once more that you should never more risk your shattered frame … You would have laughed to have seen what I saw yesterday. Emma did not know whether she was on her head or her heels – in such a hurry to tell your great news that she could utter nothing but tears of joy and tenderness. I went to Davison yesterday morning and found him still in bed, having a severe fit of the gout, and with your letter which he had just received, he cried like a child. But what was very extraordinary, assured me that from the instant he had read your letter all pain had left him and that he felt himself able to get up and walk about.

Your brother, Mrs. Nelson and Horace [their son] dined with us – your brother was more extraordinary than ever. He would get up suddenly and cut a caper rubbing his hands, every time that the thought of your fresh laurels came into his head. In short, except myself, and your Lordship knows that I have some phlegm, all the company, which was considerable after dinner – the Duke [old Q.], Lord William [Gordon], Mrs. Este, etc. were mad with joy – but I am sure that no one really rejoiced more at heart than I did. I have lived too long to have ecstasies but with calm reflection I felt for my friend having got to the very summit of glory – the 'Ne Plus Ultra', that he has had another opportunity of rendering to his country the most important service and manifesting again his judgement, his intrepidity and humanity. God bless you my very dear Lord and send you soon home to your friends … Ever your sincerely attached and truly obliged and humble servant

William Hamilton[22]

A letter from Fanny to Nelson exists in draft form. It is not certain that she sent him the letter, but she probably did. If so, he very likely destroyed it. We can imagine her struggling to choose her words carefully:

[April 1801]

My dear Husband,

*   I cannot be silent in the general joy throughout the Kingdom, I must express my thankfulness and happiness it hath pleased God to spare*

your life. All greet you with every testimony of gratitude and praise. This victory is said to surpass Aboukir. What my feelings are your own good heart will tell you. Let me beg, nay intreat you, to believe no wife ever felt greater affection for a husband than I do. And to the best of my knowledge I have invariably done everything you desired. If I have omitted any thing I am sorry for it.

On receiving a letter from our father written in a melancholy and distressing manner, I offered to go to him if I could in the least contribute to ease his mind. By return of post he desired to see me immediately but I was to stop a few days in town to see for a house. I will do everything in my power to alleviate the many infirmities which bear him down.

What more can I do to convince you that I am truly your affectionate wife?[23]

Nelson's father, the Reverend Edmund, who was fond of Fanny, and believed in the sanctity of marriage, gently tried to persuade Nelson to return to his marriage: '... *I have sometimes a hope of receiving you once more surrounded not with public honours alone, but what must add pleasures to every other gratification, a return to domestic joys, the most durable and solid of all others. Be it so. O God.*

Yesterday I received your joyous news, but all things have their alloy, Lady [Nelson] was heavily affected with her personal feelings at not receiving a line from your own hand. In all things may you have a right understanding. Writing is not easy task.'[24]

But Nelson's mind was now 'fixed'. He sent the following instructions to Davison:

St. George
April 23, 1801

My dear Davison,

You will, at a proper time, and before my arrival in England signify to Lady Nelson that I expect, and for which I have made such a very liberal allowance to her, to be left to myself, and without any inquiries from her: for sooner than live the unhappy life I did when I last came to England, I would stay abroad for ever. My mind is fixed as fate: therefore you will send my determination in any way you may judge proper; and believe me ever your obliged and faithful friend,

Nelson & Bronte[25]

Davison could not bring himself to pass on this message. As late as July he wrote to Fanny to tell her Nelson '*is in better health than I had ever reason to expect as he had been extremely ill... A few day's quiet retreat in the country I trust may be of use to him. I hardly need to repeat how happy I should have been to have seen him with you, the happiest. His heart is so pure and so extremely good that I flatter myself he never can be divested of his affection ...'*

Alexander Davison[26]

He meant to be kind, but this would cruelly have raised Fanny's hopes.

On 27 June, Fanny had written to Davison:

'*When I heard on Sunday that my Dear Lord was hourly expected my heart was all thankfulness and pleasure, but a moment's unwelcome and intruding reflection made me truly a miserable and pitiable being. I love him. I would do anything in the world to convince him of my affection. I was truly sensible of my good fortune in having such a Husband. Surely I have angered him. It was done <u>unconsciously</u> and without the least <u>intention</u> I can truly say. My wish, My desire was to please him – And if he will have the goodness to send for me, I will make it my study to obey him in every wish or desire of his – and with cheerfulness – I still hope – He is affectionate and possesses the best of hearts – he will not make me Miserable ... You or no one can tell my feelings in what I have suffered since My Lord left England.'[27]*

Fanny poured out her present suffering and love for Nelson to Davison, but not to her husband.

Both Davison and Susanna Bolton believed that Nelson might return to Fanny. Susanna had written to her on 14 May: '*I suppose by this time, my dear Lady Nelson, you are returned to Bath after your appearance in the Drawing Room which I hope you found as pleasant as you expected ... I thought perhaps you would have stayed in town until my brother arrived,* [back from the Baltic] *but you and my father are better judges than I am what is proper and you are with <u>his</u> father. Keep your spirits up my dear Madam and all will come right again, for tho' he is warm, he has a truly affectionate mind ...'[28]*

Nelson, ill and exhausted after his strenuous physical and mental efforts during the battle had applied for leave. An example of his prodigious exertions was described by Mr Ferguson, Surgeon of the *Elephant*: '*Before the Battle, I could only admire when I saw the first man in the world spend the hours of the day and night in Boats, amidst floating ice, and in the severest weather to mark the path of the buoys'.[29]* He was ready to leave when Colonel Stewart arrived back from London on 4 May with the Admiralty's surprising orders.

Admiral Hyde Parker was recalled and he left on the *Blanche* frigate, a dejected man. Nelson was to take over command and for his first time ever was officially appointed Commander-in-Chief. He remained in the Baltic a further six weeks, during which time the *London Gazette* announced he had been made Viscount.

With Nelson away, Emma needed her friends. Sadly, Romney, with whom she had formed a close relationship, had returned to his home in Kendal only eighteen months before her arrival in London. Since Emma's wedding and departure to Naples, Romney's intermittent bouts of depression grew worse. By 1795, his interest in portrait painting was waning. He wrote to Hayley: *'I am going to decline business'* and spoke of his fear of *'falling into some dreadful melancholy.'* He revived sufficiently to undertake, and complete, his last major commission: *'I shall certainly be happy to execute the picture you mention of Lord Egremont's family. Perhaps it may be my last ...'*[30]

Romney, mentally unwell, determined to build a house for himself in Hampstead. His son, the Rev. John Romney, tried to dissuade him from spending excessive amounts of money on the project. In 1797, Romney travelled up to Cumbria where, to stimulate him, John took him to see the lakes.

Returning to London and having sold his house in Cavendish Square, Romney moved to Hampstead in December 1798. In his twenty-three years in Cavendish Square he had, according to Sir Herbert Maxwell's biography: *'... known the ecstasy of accomplishment and the tranquil glow of friendship, and basked in the sunshine of one radiant presence.'* Emma was certainly the *'radiant presence.'*[31]

Romney had painted around forty vibrant and beautiful major portraits of his beloved Emma.

In January 1799, he made his last visit to Hayley's home at Eartham, staying for a couple of months. He returned to London and saw Hayley for the last time in April. Without announcing his departure, he travelled alone back to Kendal, his health worn down and suffering from depression. Mary, his wife, received him with sympathy and understanding. As his health declined, she undertook to care for him.

When Emma returned to London, Hayley informed Romney that she enquired kindly about him, and asked about a portrait he had painted for her mother. Before Emma left London as Lady Hamilton, Romney had written to Hayley: *'I began a picture of her as a present for her mother. I was very successful with it, for it is thought the most beautiful head I have painted of her yet.'*

Romney now replied to Hayley: 'What you say respecting Lady Hamilton gives me great pleasure indeed. If the picture you mention be at Hampstead, I shall be happy in gratifying her mother with it, and I trust you will take the trouble of conveying it to her in the properest manner.'[32] Hayley duly delivered the portrait to Mrs Cadogan.

Romney wrote again: 'The pleasure I should receive from the sight of the amiable Lady Hamilton would be as salutary as great; yet, I fear, except I should enjoy more strength and better spirits at a better time of the year, I shall never be able to see London again. I feel every day greater need of care and attention, and here I experience them in the highest degree.'[33]

Romney died on 15 November 1802, one month short of his sixty-eighth birthday, sadly without seeing Sir William or Emma again.

In April Mrs Cadogan travelled north to see her family and to visit Little Emma, now nineteen years old. She wrote to Emma:

Chester April 16th. 1801

I have to inform you that I arrived in Chester yesterday, and am happy to say that I left all friends in Hawarden very well. I mean to stop in Chester 2 days, and then go to Liverpool and to stop there two or three days, and then I mean to proceed on my journey to Manchester. I beg you will send me Mrs Blackburn's directions and send me every particular how I am to proceed about the little girl. The next letter you send you must direct to me at Jno. Moore, Moore Street, Liverpool ... Give my kind love to Sir William and accept the same for yourself from your loving and affte. mother, etc.'[34]

Pleading ill-health, Nelson was relieved of his command in the Baltic. On 19 June he sailed for Yarmouth aboard the *Kite* brig, arriving in Yarmouth on 30 June, to the usual joyous reception. He went straight to the hospitals to visit the wounded men sent home from Copenhagen. Nelson spoke to many of the patients and presented every nurse with one guinea.

In London the following day he took rooms at Lothian's Hotel in Albermarle Street, but spent most of his time at 23 Piccadilly. He paid his respects at the Admiralty and went to see Horatia. After eight days in London, Emma arranged a holiday for him. They were joined by William and wife, Sarah, their daughter, Charlotte, Captain Edward Parker (Nelson's protégé), Fatima and other servants. After three days at Burford Bridge near Boxhill, they proceeded to the Bush Inn at Shepperton where Sir William and Nelson enjoyed fishing on the Thames. Nelson visited 'Old Blindy', the blind woman who had lived with his favourite brother, Maurice, for years. Much to Nelson's distress, Maurice had died suddenly in April, while he was in the Baltic. He wrote to Davison: '... *I am sure you will do everything for his poor blind wife ... for such I shall always call her ... I hope he has left her well provided for if not, I beg you will take the trouble to arrange a proper and ample subsistence and I will make it up, it is the only true regard I can pay to his memory he was always good and kind to me ...*'[35] He asked Davison to send her £100 and soon afterwards arranged with him that she should be paid a pension of £200 p.a.

After just three weeks in England, Nelson was summoned to the Admiralty at Whitehall and ordered to take command of a *'Squadron on a Particular Service'*, being assembled to protect the English coast from Orford Ness to Beachy Head. Disturbing information had been received that French troops and flat-bottomed boats were gathering in Le Havre, Dunkirk and Boulogne. It was reported that Napoleon was preparing to visit the troops along the coast. The government and the population were fearful of a possible French invasion.

Nelson left London at 4 a.m. on 27 July and travelled to Sheerness where he hoisted his flag on board the *Unite*. Three days later, he was at Deal where he sent for the *Medusa* in which to cross over to France, where he intended to *'ascertain the possibility of destroying their Vessels in the Harbour of Boulogne'*.[36]

On 9 August he informed the Rt. Hon. Henry Addington (Prime Minister): *'I think I may venture to assure you that the French Army will not embark at Boulogne for the invasion of England; they are suffering this morning from allowing a collection of Craft to be assemble in their Port. Five vessels of different descriptions are sunk on the outside the Pier by our shells; they were all fitted with heavy guns, and full of men.'*[37]

Nelson returned to Harwich and Margate but soon returned to Boulogne for a second attack, on 16 August. This attack, although meticulously planned, was unsuccessful due to the French defensive precautions. Nelson, for the first time, had to report a distressing failure to St. Vincent:

Medusa, *off Boulogne, August 16th 1801*

My dear Lord,

I am sorry to tell you that I have not succeeded in bringing out or destroying the Enemy's Flotilla moored in the mouth of the harbour of Boulogne. The most astonishing bravery was evinced by our Officers and men ... We have lost many brave Officers and men; upwards of 100 killed and *wounded ... the loss has been heavy and the object was great ... No person can be blamed for sending them to the attack but myself; I knew the difficulty of the undertaking, therefore I ventured to ask your opinion. Your kind letter I received half an hour before the attack ... after all this sorrow for me, my health is not improved; my fever is very severe this morning, but believe me ever, my dear Lord, your obliged and affectionate,*

Nelson & Bronte[38]

On 17 August the *Medusa* was back at the Downs. Nelson felt defeat keenly. After attending the funerals of two young midshipmen the Naval Chronicle reported: *'His Lordship was sensibly affected during the funeral, and was seen to shed tears.'*

In his letter to Emma on 18 August, he promised revenge:

'... You ask me, my dear Friend, if I am going on more expeditions? And, even if I was to forfeit your friendship, which is dearer to me than all the world, I can tell you nothing. For, I go out; [if] I see the Enemy, and can get at them, it is my duty: and you would naturally hate me, if I kept back one moment. I long to pay them, for their tricks t'other day, the debt of a drubbing, which, surely, I'll pay: but <u>when,</u> <u>where,</u> or <u>how,</u> it is impossible, your own good sense will tell you, for me or mortal man to say. I shall not act in a rash or hasty manner, that you may rely, and on which I give you my honour.

Nelson & Bronte[39]

When he was given his opportunity for revenge several years later, it cost him his life.

At about the same time that Nelson left London, Sir William left with Greville to visit his Pembroke estates. He sent a cheerful note to Emma:

Burford, 80 miles from London   Saturday night [July 27] 1801

Here we are my dear Emma after a pleasant day's journey. No extraordinary occurrence. Our chaise is good and would have held the famous 'Tria Junta in Uno' very well, but we must submit to the circumstances of the times. Sir Joseph Banks we found in bed with the gout and last night his hot house was robbed of its choicest fruit peaches and nectarines. Amuse yourself as well as you can and you may be assured that I shall return as soon as possible and you shall hear from me often.

Ever yours my dear Emma with the truest affection

William Hamilton

My kindest love to my Lord if he is not gone.[40]

There can be no doubt about Sir William's feelings of pride and affection towards both Emma and Nelson. He was perfectly happy with the *Tria Juncta in Uno*. He kept Emma informed of his activities in further affectionate letters.

William, Susanna and Kitty had never been fond of Fanny. The family history states that Fanny *'had been unsympathetic and often ungracious to them'*. William and Sarah Nelson were the first to take sides with Emma. Soon Susanna and Kitty came to accept Emma for the sake of their brother's happiness and, in time, added their own criticisms of Fanny.

For Nelson's sake, as well as her own, Emma approached his family with her usual friendliness. She wrote William a cheerful letter commenting on a family wedding in Norfolk that she had been unable to attend: *'You go jaunting to Swaffham – well, there is a marriage going on ... I wish I was with you at the fuss – I like to be in a fuss and put the Bride in one – throw the stocking - drink the posset – put them to bed – up and be doing – God will prosper – what an epistle to a Parson! I dare say you will be scandalised. I don't care, I am in a ratle & today I am in a foolish mood ...'*[41]

William replied:

Sunday morning, Sept. 6th. [1801]

My Dear Lady, To be sure you did promise to write to me on Thursday last: and I was very much disappointed at not receiving a letter yesterday, and sent to the Post Office twice, to be certain there was no mistake: and now this morning comes your roguish waggish letter, on a Sunday morning (amidst all my meditations for the good of my parishioners) about love, courtship, marriage, throwing the stocking, going to bed, &c.&c. – quite shocking to a country parson, who can have no idea of such <u>things</u> ... If you was here, you should not laugh at me for nothing. I would give you as good as you brought, at any time ... I don't know how to thank my Brother, for all his goodness to me and mine; my heart overflows, whenever I think of it: but I can't sit down and write a formal letter of thanks; it would be too absurd for <u>me</u> to write, or <u>him</u> to read. He well knows me; and I leave it to your Ladyship (my best and truest friend) to say everything to him, for and from me: it will come best from your lips, and <u>adorned</u> with your eloquence ...'[42]

The same month, Emma sent one of her vividly expressed, outspoken letters to Sarah. After discussing Nelson's situation, she writes a diatribe against Fanny:

'My dear Mrs. Nelson, I have had many letters from my dear Nelson ... <u>My heart says</u> 'Come'; my love of his glory and <u>your husband's cause</u> says, 'stay and let him finish with éclat'. I love Nelson's glory, his great and glorious

deeds have made on my heart an impression <u>never never</u> to be effaced. <u>You</u> and your husband are the only people worthy to be by <u>him beloved</u>. His poor father is unknowing and taken in by a very wicked, bad, artful woman, acting <u>a bad part by so glorious</u> a son. The sin be on their heads. Would your father have seen with patience if she had lived with milord, <u>his own</u> flesh and blood set <u>aside</u> for who? For Nesbit's, the doctor's son, a villain who many times called the glorious Nelson villain, and that he would do for him, yet this boy the --------son would, if this designing woman had had her way, have put you all aside. And <u>your</u> father, Nelson's father, protects this woman and gives the mortal blow to his son. The old man could never hear her till now and now he conspires <u>against the saviour of his country</u> and his darling, who has risen him to such a height of honour, and <u>for whom</u>? A <u>wicked</u> false malicious wretch who rendered his days wretched and his nights miserable; <u>And the father</u> of Nelson says " I will <u>stab</u> my son to the heart" but indeed, he [Nelson] says "my poor father is led now he does not know what he does". But oh! how cruel, how shocking it is and I am afraid the Boltons are not without their share of <u>guilt in this affair</u>. <u>Jealous of you all</u> they have, with the Matchams, pushed this dear old gentleman to act this bad and horrible <u>part</u>, to support a false proud and bad <u>woman</u>, artful and with every bad quality to make wretched those she belongs to ... but let her own wickedness be her punishment. Her sins be on her own head she abandons her own son although a villain! 'Tis a bad bird that befouls its own nest.'[43]

Emma often expressed her emotions in this dramatic style. Greville, Hamilton and Nelson all witnessed her emotional outbursts. In a following letter Nelson writes: '... *you can also thunder forth such a torrent of eloquence, that corruption and infamy would sink before your voice ...*'

Emma was reacting with fury to some incident concerning Fanny and Josiah about which there is no clear information. Whatever the situation was, something had clearly happened as Nelson mentions '*a detestable subject*' in his letter to Emma on 26 September: '... *I had, yesterday, a letter from father; he seems to think that he may do something which I do not like. I suppose, he means, going to Somerset Street.* [Fanny's lodgings]. *Shall I, to an old man, enter upon the detestable subject; it may shorten his days. But, I think, I shall tell him, that I cannot go to Somerset Street to see him. But, I shall not write till I hear your opinion. If I once begin, you know, it will be all out, about her, and her ill-treatment to her son. But you shall decide ...*'[44]

In the absence of both Sir William and Nelson (who was away for three months) Emma was busy. Nelson had asked her to find him a house to purchase so that he would have a home to go to when not on active service.

Having viewed two properties in Chiswick and Turnham Green, Emma found Merton Place in Surrey. The situation and size of the property were perfect. It was seven miles from Whitehall and the Admiralty, only about one hour's carriage drive, and convenient for the road to Portsmouth. The house and garden were situated in one corner of approximately 50 acres of land. Nelson later purchased a further 115 acres. A canal, christened 'The Nile' by Emma, with a substantial stone-clad Italianate bridge over it, ran through the part of the property surrounding the house. This was stocked with fish, a happy circumstance for Sir William. The lawns and walks near the house were *stocked with trees and plants of considerable value'*. Emma had found Nelson his dream home, an idyllic property that she later called Paradise Merton.

Corresponding with Nelson, she arranged the purchase and set about a series of improvements to the house and grounds that continued until his death. Her ability to visualize its potential produced a supremely successful result.

By 1792 the early 18th Century the house had been *'greatly enlarged and improved'* by Sir Richard Hotham. The Particulars of Sale described the property as:

'An elegant and very commodious brick edifice uniformly erected on a pleasing plan and elevation, containing 2 Upper Bed Chambers a very spacious principle Bed Chamber and 2 other principle Bed Chambers and a Water Closet.

2 elegant Drawing Rooms and a most excellent Dining Room of large Dimensions, fitted up with Sienna, Egyptian and White Marble Chimney Pieces, rich India Paper Hangings and correspondent finished; A Breakfast Parlour and small Room; a neat Vestibule and capital principle Staircase.'[45]
In addition there were wine vaults in the basement, attached buildings with bed chambers for servants, a servants hall, store room and laundry, a 'convenient Kitchen with proper connected Offices', a coal vault, wash house and brew house. There was an ice house and a detached building containing a dairy and cool larder.

The sequence of the purchase of Merton Place can be followed through comments in Nelson's letters to Emma:

Deal, August 18th. 1801
'... [I] *hope, my dear Emma, you will be able to find a house suited for my*

comfort. I am sure of being <u>happy</u> by your arrangements.'[46]

Downs, August 31st. 1801

'... I entreat you my dear friend, work hard for me, and get the house and furniture; and I will be happy to lend it to you and Sir William! ... the furniture must be bought with it; and the sooner it is done, the better I shall like it.'[47]

Amazon, September 26, 1801

'... You may rely upon one thing, that I shall like Merton; therefore do not be uneasy on that account. I have that opinion of your taste and judgement, that I do not believe it can fail in pleasing me. We must only consider our means; and, for the rest, I am sure, you will soon make it the prettiest place in the world ... If I can afford to buy the Duck Close, and the field adjoining it would be pleasant; but, I fear, it is not in my power: but, I shall know, when my accounts are settled, at New Years' Day ... Whatever, my dear Emma, you do for my little charge [Horatia] I must be pleased with. Probably she will be lodged at Merton; at least, in the Spring, when she can have the benefit of our walks. It will make the poor mother happy, I am sure. I shall have the child christened when I come up ...'[48]

Amazon. October 8, 1801.

'... your kind letters are arrived. I rejoice that you have got into Merton ...'[49]

Amazon, October 12, 1801

'... I would have every body like your choice; for, I am sure, you have as fine a taste in laying out land, as you have in music ...'[50]

The house and land, plus the furniture mentioned, were purchased from Mrs Greaves for £9,000 with possession promised for 10 October.

Concerned about the delay in the legal proceedings, Emma wrote a forceful letter to the lawyers on 6 October:

As in the agreement Mrs Greves is to give up her house to Lord Nelson the 10th. October, which is Saturday I do not understand why Milords Lawyers cannot settle every thing as the title Deeds are good. Their is nothing more required it is of the greatest consequence that Tuesday or Wednesday milords people shou'd go down & many things are ready order'd to be sent from Portsmouth Deal & other places to Merton their are (coming) now 2 green house plants waiting to be sent & the painters waiting to begin <u>(why not then conclude)</u> Lord Nelson now not in very good health may be in town every moment why not let him have his house. Can the difference be so great between this & Saturday for that day he MUST have it <u>according</u> to AGREEMENT ... let me beg of you then Dear Sir to let the affair be settled directly & you will oblige your Humble Servant

E. Hamilton[51]

Her letter had the required effect as Nelson commented on 8 October, *'I rejoice that you have got into Merton'*. Unaided, Emma handled the legal transaction and organized the arrival of his furniture and other possessions, arranged to get the painters in, and saw to other details, down to the *'2 green house plants'*.

Back from Pembrokeshire and Warwick, Sir William wrote a congratulatory letter to Nelson on 16 October 1801:

'We have now inhabited your Lord's premises some days, and I can now speak with some certainty. I have lived with our dear Emma several years. I know her merit, have a great opinion of the head & heart that God Almighty has been pleased to give her; but a seaman alone could have given a fine woman full power to <u>chuse</u> & fit up a residence for him without seeing it himself. You are in luck, for in my conscience I verily believe that a place so suitable to your views could not have been found, & at so cheap a rate, for if you stay away 3 days longer I do not think you can have any wish but you will find it compleated here, & then the bargain was fortunately struck 3 days before an idea of peace got abroad. Now every estate in this neighbourhood has increased in value, and you might get a thousand pounds tomorrow for your bargain. The proximity to the capital, and the perfect retirement of this place, are, for your Lordship, two points beyond estimation; but the house is so comfortable, the furniture clean & good, & I never saw so many conveniences in so small a compass. You have nothing but to come and enjoy immediately; you have a good mile of pleasant dry walk around your own farm. It would make you laugh to see Emma & her mother fitting up pig-sties and hen-coops, & already the Canal is enlivened with ducks, & the cock is strutting with his hens about the walks. Your Ld's plan as to stocking the Canal with fish is exactly mine. I will answer for it, that in a few months you may a good dish of fish at a moment's warning ...'[52]

We note, with interest, Sir William's comment *'our dear Emma.'* He had used the same expression – *'our dear Em'* - in a letter to Greville from Naples.

Emma's letters to Nelson contained amusing anecdotes about Merton. Her letters were interesting and made him laugh:

Amazon, *October 16th. 1801*

'... the moment I got your letters, off I came, and have read them with real pleasure. They have made me much better, I think; at least I feel so. I admire pigs and poultry. Sheep are certainly most beneficial to eat off grass. Do <u>you</u> get paid for them ... I intend to have a farming book. I am glad to hear you get fish, not very good ones, I fancy ...'[53]

Amazon, *October 17th. 1801*

'... *I shall, you may rely, admire the pig-stye, ducks, fowls &c. for every thing you do, I look upon as perfect ... Sir William's letter has delighted me, with your activity and prudence ...*'[54]

Amazon, *October 19 h. 1801*

'... *I assure you, my dear friend, that I had rather read and hear your little story of a white hen getting into a tree, an anecdote of Fatima, or hear you call – 'Cupidity! Cupidity!'* [Cupidity was a miniature spaniel at Merton], *than any speech I shall hear in parliament; because I know although you can adopt your language and manners to a child, yet that you can also thunder forth such a torrent of eloquence, that corruption and infamy would sink before your voice, in however* <u>exalted</u> *a situation it might be placed ...*'[55]

Amazon, *October 20th. 1801*

'... *How I should laugh, to see you, my dear friend, rowing in a boat; the beautiful Emma rowing a one-armed Admiral in a boat! It will certainly be Caricatured ... Well done, farmer's wife! I'll bet your turkey against Mrs Nelson's; but Sir William and I will decide ...*'[56]

Amazon, *October 21st. 1801*

'...[I] *expect, that all the animals will increase where you are, for I never expect that you will suffer any to be killed ... you are now writing your last letter for Deal; so am I, for Merton, from Deal ... I have much to do, being the last day on board ...*'[57]

Emma, the ambassador's wife, accustomed to frequenting royal palaces, now happily took on the duties of a *'farmer's wife'*. Knowing that Nelson wanted a *'little farm'* to enjoy when he retired and which he believed would bring him extra income, Emma had bought sheep, pigs, chickens, turkeys and ducks on his behalf. In the three months he had been away, she had excelled herself and achieved a small miracle. His *'little farm'* was up and running on his return.

When the preliminaries of peace had been signed with the French republic, which the King called an 'Experimental Peace', Nelson's leave was granted.

Travelling through the night from Deal, Nelson arrived at Merton Place in the early hours of 23 October. When Emma showed him around his extensive new property, an overjoyed Nelson asked: *'Is this too, mine?'*

The deeds were signed on 23 and 24 October. Nelson had managed to raise the £9,000 purchase price. On 15 September he had written to his agents Marsh, Page and Creed: *'I believe I have wrote before sufficient for you to pay to the order of Messrs Booth & Haslewood, six thousand pounds, in part payment of my little farm at Merton ...'*[58] According to the 1801 deeds £2,000 of the original estate was on mortgage. Nelson had written to Davison on 31 August: '*I am after buying a little farm at Merton – the price £9000; I hope to be able to get through it. If I cannot, after all my labour for the Country, get such a place as this, I am resolved to give it all up, and retire for life ...'*[59]

Davison's generous response was to offer a loan to Nelson, who gratefully replied on 14 September: '*My dear Davison, I have to give you ten thousand thanks for your very friendly offer of assisting me in purchasing the Farm. It is true, it will take every farthing I have in the world, and leave me in your debt, and also Tyson's* [his late Secretary] *but I hope in a little time to be able at least to pay my debts ...'*[60]

Nelson began the longest period of leave of his career apart from the five years unemployment, '*on the beach'*, in Norfolk with Fanny. He would spend the happiest eighteen months of his life in his new home.

CHAPTER 17

Happy Days Shared at Merton

'You are to be, recollect, Lady Paramount of all the territories, and all the
waters of Merton and we are all ... to obey your lawful commands'
Nelson to Emma, September 1801

' I care not a pin for the world and am attached to no one as much as you'
Hamilton to Emma, September 1802

' [I] am not blind to your defects, and confess to having many myself;
therefore let us bear and forbear for God's sake'
Hamilton to Emma, October? 1802

'We are all very comfortable and happy'
Emma to Kitty Matchham, 4 January 1803

SIR WILLIAM AND Emma lived at 23 Piccadilly when not staying with
Nelson at Merton, where Sir William shared the expenses. Sir William
maintained the lease on 23 Piccadilly at a cost of around £300 p.a. until
the day he died. He wanted to continue with his interests in London:
attending auction houses, the British Museum, the Royal Society, the
Society of Antiquaries and socialising with his friends, family and
like-minded intellectuals.

Writing to Emma regarding Merton Place, Nelson stipulated: *'You*
shall have the whole arrangement ... To you I may say that my soul is too
big for my purse, but I do earnestly request that all may be mine in the house,
even to a pair of sheets towels etc ... You are to be, recollect, Lady Paramount
of all the territories and all the waters of Merton, and we are all to be your
guests, and to obey all lawful commands.'[1] On 30 September he reminded
her: *'I only entreat again that everything even a book or a cook may be*
mine.'[2]

Nelson, too, had business to attend to in London, including at the

House of Lords where, on 29 October, he took his seat as Viscount Nelson, making his maiden speech on 12 November.[3]

Mrs Gibson kept the notes Emma sent arranging meetings with Horatia, but only thirty-eight of these survive.[4] The majority concern arrangements for Horatia to be brought to 23 Piccadilly. Emma had seen Horatia every week in the first three months after her birth, but less frequently when she was busy with the purchase and setting-up of Merton Place.

Years later Mrs Gibson's daughter, Mary, recalled for Horatia's benefit: *'Horatia remained with the nurse* [Mrs Gibson] *until she was six years old. Lady Hamilton constantly visited her: Lord Nelson was frequently her companion in her visits to her, and often came alone, and played for hours with the infant on the floor, calling her his own child.'*[5]

Emma's relationship with Mrs Gibson was affectionate:

9 October:

My dearest Mrs Gibson, I have sent a person to you to take orders for Miss Thompson pray tell her what you want. I am going out of Town but come back on Tewsday I shall have the pleasure of seeing you I recommend Miss T to your care Write to me at Merton Place near Merton Surry and tell me how you all are milord will be in town soon. Kiss my goddaughter from your affectionate friend   E.Hamilton[6]

On Nelson's first Monday at home he travelled up to London for an appointment at the Admiralty. Emma arranged for him to see Horatia that same day:

October 24th. 1801

'Dear Mrs Gibson, Will you come to Piccadilly with Miss Thompson on Monday at 1 o'clock, not later. I hope my dear god-child is well. Ever yours E. Hamilton.

Another note arranges an outing: *'My dear Mrs Gibson, I hope you are well and Miss Thompson. I will call on you tomorrow, at 1 o'clock to carry you on an airing. Ever yours sincerely E. Hamilton.'*

The following year she arranged a holiday for them in Margate: *'Dear Mrs Gibson, I am glad to fnd you and Miss Thompson well. Let us know how you all go on, and believe me it is a real pleasure to find you are so comfortable. Believe me ever, your sincere friend – E. Hamilton.'*

The Reverend William, Sarah and their children Horace and Charlotte were frequent visitors to Merton. Initially Nelson's sisters, Kitty Matcham and Susanna Bolton, were reluctant to visit, Kitty citing her family and new pregnancy as an excuse. Nelson's situation placed his father in a distressing position. He had written to Nelson from Burnham on 9 October:

My dear Horatio,

Upon the happy return of peace, I may, with a little variation, address you in the words of an apostle and say 'You have fought a good fight, you have finished your military career, with glory, and honour, henceforth, there is laid up for you, much happiness, subject indeed in this present time, to uncertainty … As a public character I could be acquainted only with what was made public respecting you. Now in a private station possibly you may tell me where it is likely your general place of residence may be, so that sometimes we may have mutual happiness in each other … Most likely the winter may be too cold for me to continue here, and I mean to spend it between Bath and London. If Lady Nelson is in a hired house, and by herself, gratitude requires that I should sometimes be with her, if it is likely to be of any comfort to her … I cannot do any public duty nor even walk to the next house, but my dearest son, here is still room enough to give you a warm a joyful and affectionate reception, if you could feel an inclination to look once more at me in Burnham parsonage …

Edmund Nelson[7]

Emma sent a copy of Nelson's reply to Sarah:

Merton Place Saturday [October 17, 1801]

My dearest Friend,

I had letters yesterday from our dear Lord. He has sent me an open letter for me to read and put in the post which I have done this day but I sent you an extract.

'My dear Father, I have received your letter and of which you must be sensible I cannot like for you seem by your conduct to put me in the wrong it is no wonder that they who do not know me and my disposition should. But Nelson soars above them all and time will do that justice to my private character which she has to my public one. I that have given her [Lady Nelson and Josiah] *with her falsity and his £2000 a year and £4000 in money which she calls a poor pittance, and with all that to abandon her son bad as he is and going about defaming me. May God's vengeance strike me dead if I would abandon my children. If he wants reformation, who should reclaim him but the mother? I could say much more but will not out of respect to you, my dear Father, but you know her, therefore I finish.*

On 23 rd. I shall be at Merton with Sir William and Lady Hamilton and them with myself shall be happy, most happy to see you, my dear beloved father, that is your home. My brother and sister, the dear children will soon be with us and happy shall we all be, but more so if you will come ... Ever my dear father's dutiful son, N and B.'

This is an extract what do you think of it? When you and Mr Nelson has read it, pray burn it ... God bless you. In a hurry. Sir William is gone to fetch Charlotte, Viganoni comes so she will have three lessons, 2 today and perhaps 2 tomorrow. Sir William is quite charmed with her. She will have her Italian lesson [which Emma taught her] *and French from Oliver. She shall be early at school on Monday morning and as milord is to arrive on Friday at dinner, she shall be here to receive him and go back to school on Monday early.*

Emma Hamilton[8]

On this same day, Edmund, who felt a duty towards Fanny having lived with her for so long, wrote to Fanny: *'Be assured I still hold fast my integrity, and am ready to join you, whenever you have your servants in the London house as at first thought of. In respect to this business, the opinion of others must rest with themselves, and not make any alteration with us. I have not offended any man and do rely on my children's affection that notwithstanding all that have been said, they will not in my old age forsake me ...'*[9]

In a draft copy of a letter to the Reverend Edmund, dated October 1801, Fanny expresses her concern for Edmund's dilemma having to choose between her and his own children:

My dear Sir,

... The impression your situation has left on my mind is so strong that I cannot delay any longer offering my opinion on the subject of your living with me, which from your conversation makes it impracticable; the deprivation of seeing your children is so cruel, even in thought, it is impossible you can any longer the desire ... [paper cut away] *...*

I am not surprised for I knew that Lord Nelson's friends could not like it. Even supposing his Lordship resided in Italy the offence would be just the same and in my opinion greater. I told Mrs M [Matcham] *at Bath that Lord Nelson would not like your living with me. Oh! my dear Lady Nelson. My brother will thank you in his heart for he knows no one can attend to my father as you do! I had seen the wonderful change pass belief. She had not ...'*[10]

Edmund spent the winter in Bath, as he had done for several years. Fanny had taken a house at 16 Somerset Street in London, but wrote to her father-in-law: *'Be assured at any time I can be of the least use to you, command my services and you shall always find me the same.'*

Letters from both Emma and Nelson persuaded Edmund to visit Merton Place in November. During the 10-day visit he observed his son's happiness and, won over by Emma's charm, established a friendly relationship with her. He wrote to Nelson on 21 December:

'My dear Horatio,

    From an old man you will accept the old fashioned language at the approaching happy season, which is, I wish you a Merry Christmas and a happy New Year. For multiplied favours Lady Hamilton has my respectful thanks ...'[11]

He sent a Christmas blessing to Emma.

To his daughter, Kitty, he reported: *'Your good brother is truly in better health and happier in himself than in good truth I have in any past time observed him to be.'*[12]

On 14 December Emma wrote to Mrs Gibson from Merton Place:

'My dear Mrs Gibson, – If you will take a post-chaise to-morrow <u>Tuesday</u>, and set off at half-past ten o'clock, and bring my god-daughter and your little girl with you, I shall be glad to see you. Tell them to drive you to Merton, and the best way you can come is over Clapham Common. Hire the chaise for the day. You can go back at three o'clock. Do not fail. Ever yours sincerely, E. Hamilton'.[13]

This was Horatia's first visit to her father's home.

On 18 December Fanny wrote her very last letter to Nelson, addressed care of Davison:

To Viscount Nelson and Duke of Bronte, St. James' Square, London.

My dear Husband,

    It is some time since I have written to you. The silence you have imposed is more than my affections will allow me and in this instance I hope you will forgive me in not obeying you. One thing I omitted in my letter of July which I now have to offer for your accommodation, a comfortable warm house. Do, my dear husband, let us live together. I can never be happy til such an event takes place. I assure you again I have but one wish in the world, to please you. Let every thing be buried in oblivion, it will pass away like a dream. I can now only intreat you to believe I am most sincerely and affectionately your wife,

Frances H. Nelson[14]

But Nelson's happiness lay elsewhere, with Emma, Sir William, and his daughter Horatia.

Davison returned the letter to Fanny with a note saying: *'Opened by mistake by Lord Nelson, but not read. A. DAVISON'*

George Matcham had formed a close relationship with Nelson extending beyond friendship and family to include financial and philanthropic matters. After Nelson's death he wrote a sketch of Nelson's life that he had printed privately for the family, in which he sought to exonerate Nelson from what many believed to be his unkind treatment of Fanny. 'G.M.', or 'Mr M' as he was known in the family, describes the marriage:

'Little versed in the mean arts of lesser man, and wholly unacquainted with worldliness, his intercourse with man and womankind was confined. Generous in heart, feeling, and full of sympathy, he would easily have been engaged in friendship, and as readily have been attached in love; but, paired with materials [Fanny] very different from those of which his mind and heart was composed, he early felt the want of that domestic comfort on which he might have rested in the brief hour of peace ... Lauded, admired and sought everywhere but at home, where complaining and reproach formed a sad contrast to the merited reception he met with elsewhere, he naturally turned from the spot, his heart sickened and revolted, and was at last completely estranged.

The connection he formed with a certain lady has been the cause of much blame and much ungrateful calumny. It was certainly in its commencement of a purely platonic kind; nor is it much to be wondered that it afterwards assumed a warmer complexion.

His warm heart eagerly strove to attach itself to some object of primary affection: if Lady Hamilton had not artfully endeavoured to inveigle it, some other female would. Long before Lady H. came to England, he had made up his mind not to remain in this country ... Much pains have been taken to vilify him, the endeavour will be in vain; posterity will do him justice ...'[15]

G.M's youngest son, Nelson Matcham, with remarkable sensitivity, years later added his own account of Emma: '... *The unfortunate Lady, now no more, possessed a devotion to his glory, to his welfare, and to his interest, which knew no bounds, and hesitated at no means to promote these ends. She was moreover, the depository of every secret of his life, as well as the frequent adviser, or rather approver, of his laudibly ambitious projects; and lastly, she was of that cheerful turn which beguiled many a tedious hour, smoothed many a rough moment of melancholy musing, and banished many an unwelcome intrusion of painful remembrance.'*[16]

The Hamiltons, Mrs Cadogan, William, Sarah, Horace and Charlotte arrived at Merton for Nelson's first Christmas in his new home. He was extremely happy to be surrounded by members of his family. Horatia, it appears, was not included on this occasion.

Friendships were established with near neighbours, James Perry, editor and proprietor of the *Morning Chronicle* and the Goldsmid brothers, Abraham, Benjamin and Asher. Nelson and Emma attended the service at the local parish church on the first Sunday after Nelson's arrival, and regularly thereafter, becoming friendly with the vicar, Mr Lancaster. Mr Lancaster's daughter recorded Nelson's generosity: *'I cannot refrain from informing you of his unlimited charity and goodness at Merton. His frequently expressed desire was that none in that place should want, or suffer affliction that he could alleviate; and this I know he did with a most liberal hand, always desiring that it should not be known from whence it came.'*[17]

Sir William and Nelson were both in financial difficulties. Nelson's were largely caused by his unbounded generosity. He had made over £2,000 p.a. to Fanny; set up a pension for 'Old Blindy' of £200 p.a.; paid for Horace's education at Eton; and arranged to send his sister, Susanna, £100 p.a. *'towards the education of her children'*. After deducting taxes and these expenses, he was left with less than £1,000 p.a.

Admirals and captains had their own expenses to pay for extra food, wines and other personal items when they were on active service. Nelson, who often entertained his captains and officers to dinner on board his flagship, complained to Davison in September: *'... the Baltic expedition cost me full £2000. Since I left London it has cost me, for Nelson cannot be like others, near £1000 in six weeks. If I am continued here, ruin to my finances must be the consequence, for everybody knows that Lord Nelson is* <u>amazingly rich</u>*!'*[18]

Nelson's sarcasm is because almost every other Admiral he knew had made a fortune in prize money, including his last commander, Sir Hyde Parker.

The William Nelsons and the Boltons were grateful for his help. William's living at Hilborough brought him £700 p.a. The Boltons relied on a modest income from farming and they had five children – twins Susannah and Kate, Eliza, Anne and Tom.

Only Nelson's sister, Kitty, could be considered comfortably well off. George Matcham and his parents had made *'ample fortunes'* in India and he had an assured income of at least £3,000 p.a.

A generous gift of china to the Matchams prompted G.M. to protest and advise Nelson: *'I am confident my Lord, your income is not, nor ever will be, equal to your generosity.'*[19]

Sir William commented to Emma – *'our Dear Ld. N. is noble, generous, open and liberal to all and I wish to God he could afford it.'*[20]

Only when he received begging letters from strangers did Nelson refuse to help, writing to Emma on 20 October: '... *it is not long ago, a person from Yorkshire desired me to lend him three hundred pounds as he going to set up a school! Are these people mad; or do they take me for quite a fool?*'21

Sir William's money worries continued. Despite selling his pictures and vases for over £10,000 it was not enough to clear all his debts. Merton Place was, in many respects, a paradise for him as well as for Nelson. When the 'Nile' was stocked with fish, he could spend hours enjoying his favourite outdoor pastime. He wrote to Greville on 24 January 1802:

'Knowing as you do the whole of my dispositions I have made after my death, I am sure it is quite unnecessary for me to repeat to you that I expect in cases of necessity every assistance from my Estate in Wales that it is capable of affording – but you will see whether such aid will be further necessary or not. It is but reasonable after having fagged all my life that my last days should pass off comfortably and quietly ...

Nothing at present disturbs me but my debt and the nonsense I am obliged to put up with here, to avoid coming to an explosion, which would be attended with many disagreeable effects, and would totally destroy the comfort of the best man and the best Friend I have in the World. However, I am determined my quiet shall not be disturbed, let the nonsensical World go on as it will.'22

It seems Sir William was becoming irritated by the constant comings and goings of so many people at Merton Place. Nelson enjoyed being surrounded by his family, but their company, particularly the Reverend William, did not necessarily appeal to Sir William.

In January an honorary Doctorate of Divinity was conferred on William Nelson by his university, Cambridge. He now insisted on being called Doctor. Thereafter he was known as '*the Doctor*' or '*the Reverend Doctor*'. He had annoyed Fanny by pressurising her, through Nelson, for 'preferment' and now embroiled Emma in his campaign, pointedly informing her that '*the Deans of Hereford, Exeter, Litchfield, Coventry, York and Winchester are old men*'.

Nelson commented to Emma in October 1801: '*What can Reverend Sir want to be made a Doctor for? He will be laughed at for his pains!*'23

From January to July 1802 Nelson, Sir William and Emma spent most of their time at Merton. Emma wrote to their friend, Captain Bedford, in February: '*Nelson the glorious Nelson is the truly great man in retirement. He seldom goes to town and for that reason he is much desired and sent for ... We are very busy planting, and I am as much amused with pigs and hens as I was at the Court of Naples Ambasadress.'*[24]

Sir William and Nelson often went up to town together, Sir William to his society and British Museum meetings, Nelson for meetings and to visit Davison in St James' Square.

In March Lord Minto arrived for a weekend visit. He had described Emma in 1797: *'Her face is beautiful. She is all Nature, and yet all Art; that is to say her manners are perfectly unpolished, of course very easy, though not with the ease of good breeding, but of a barmaid: excessively good-humoured and wishing to please and be admired by all ages and all sorts of persons that come her way ...'*[25]

After visiting Merton he sent his wife an extremely critical report: *'The whole establishment and way of life is such as to make me angry, as well as melancholy; but I cannot alter it, and I do not think myself obliged or at liberty to quarrel with him for his weakness, though nothing shall ever induce me to give the smallest countenance to Lady Hamilton. She looks ultimately to the chance of marriage, as Sir W. will not be long in her way, and she probably indulges a hope that she will survive Lady Nelson; in the meanwhile she and Sir William and the whole set of them are living with him at his expense. She is in high looks but more immense than ever. She goes on cramming Nelson with trowelfuls of flattery, which he goes on taking as quietly as a child does pap. The love she makes him is not only ridiculous, but disgusting: not only the rooms but the whole house, staircase and all, are covered with nothing but pictures of her and him of all sizes and sorts, and representations of his naval actions, coats of arms, pieces of plate in his honour, the flagstaff of L'Orient etc. – an excess of vanity which counteracts its own purpose. If it was Lady H's house there might be a pretence for it; to make his own a mere looking-glass to view himself all day is bad taste ... She is horrid, but he entertained me in spite of her ...'*[26]

Minto was mistaken. Sir William and Emma were not living with Nelson at his expense. Contrary to Minto's comment that Emma was 'horrid', we have an appreciative opinion of her provided by Midshipman Parsons who called on Nelson at Merton in 1802 to beg for a ship:

'[Emma] entered the study, the most pleasing shape – that of a lovely and graceful woman, and, with her usual fascinating and playful manner, declared 'His lordship must serve me'. His countenance , which, until now, had been a thundercloud, brightened; and Lady Hamilton was the sun that lightened our hemisphere ...'[27]

Nelson knew about Emma's proposals for improvements at Merton, discussed between them in correspondence. He advised her *'not to lay out more than is necessary'*, but allowed her to go ahead.

Emma's interior decoration of the house was influenced by Hamilton's taste in the Palazzo Sessa. The large number of mirrors and glass doors were later described by one of Nelson's servants: *'The house itself was roomy, but not magnificent. Plenty of glass and light seemed to be the predominant taste. Glass doors in front, and a long passage with glass doors opening onto the lawn behind and even plate glass doors to some of the principal rooms threw an abundance of light about the interior.'*[28]

Long-standing friends of Nelson's, besides Minto, disapproved of his relationship with Emma. Troubridge and St.Vincent (who called them *'a pair of sentimental fools'*) never visited Merton. Nelson's own Captain Hardy disapproved and seldom called. Lady Hardy, who knew Fanny well, gave her opinion of Nelson's marriage: *'Lady Nelson was a good, well-disposed woman, surprisingly tiresome and prejudiced, and, though nothing could excuse her husband's conduct towards her, it was not surprising that, used to the gay and unrestrained conversation of Lady Hamilton, he should have been very much bored by his commonplace wife, who however retained to the last the most extraordinary devotion to his Memory and excused even his partiality to her Rival, owning how difficult it must have been to resist her, which I did not myself at all think, but Lord Nelson has never been in clever artful Women's Society and was completely humbugged by Lady Hamilton.'*[29]

The Reverend Edmund died on 26 April. Nelson received the news of his father's decline too late for him to see his father before he died. G. M. arranged for Edmund's body to be taken from Bath to Burnham Thorpe. The Rector was buried in the chancel of Burnham Thorpe church, beside his wife, whom he had survived for thirty-four years. Claiming illness, Nelson did not attend the funeral. He may have dreaded meeting Fanny again.

Sir William was still struggling to bring his financial situation under control. In January he sold some of his diamonds to settle debts with Ragland and Gibbs in Naples, both of whom had begged him to send money for his abandoned servants. They had not been dismissed until November 1801. His account at Coutts was credited in January 1802 with £500 from Phillips & Co, auctioneers, and on 9 March 1802 with a further £600. These credits are probably from the sale of his diamonds.

The new Foreign Secretary, Lord Hawkesbury, treated Sir William shamefully when he attempted to have his pension and debts in Naples and Palermo settled by the Treasury. He tried several times to see Hawkesbury and after his last humiliating visit, went home and wrote to him on 12 June 1802:

My Lord,

I have had the honor of waiting upon your Lordship at your office twice without having had the good fortune of finding your Lordship at leisure to give me an audience. I went again to the office this day at half-past 12 o'clock and sent up a billet to your Lordship entreating a moment's audience and for which I wou'd wait below your Lordship's convenience. After two hours a message came from your Lordship that you was too much engaged to see me this day and desired that I wou'd return some day next week. As my business depended entirely on the notice of your Lordship's office I enquired for either Mr Hammond or Lord Hervey, your Lordship's first Secretaries, and Lord Hervey was so good as to send for me soon after. My business was simply to request that as Lord Grenville had neglected when he went out of office the passing of some of the usual Bills of Extrordinarys due to me as the King's Minister at the Court of Naples, that they might be sent to the Treasury properly authenticated by your Lordship and without which I cannot receive from the Treasury what has long been my due.

I must own, my Lord, feeling my situation as having the honor of being of his Majesty's Privy Council and having served his Majesty at the Court of Naples to the best of my ability for 37 years, that I felt myself humbled by waiting so many hours as I have done in your antechamber, and as I am not sensible of having been wanting in attention or civility to your Lordship (the son of my old and worthy friend Lord Liverpool) when you visited Naples, I hope your Lordship will excuse the Liberty I now take of expressing my feelings and that you will grant the just request I have made to-day to your Lordship through the channel of Lord Hervey.

I have the honor to be

My Lord

Your Lordship's most obt. and most humble servant

William Hamilton[30]

Lord Hawkesbury acted, where Lord Grenville had neglected his claim. His letter to Lord Hawkesbury brought immediate results. On 5 June 1802 Sir William paid, according to his account at Coutts, an amount of £1.5s.6d. as a fee for '*At Exchequer power of Attourney to receive his pension of £2000 p.a*' He had hoped for a pension of £2,000 p.a. clear, but taxes were deducted. This was disappointing but at least his pension had been agreed, though payment was not immediately forthcoming.

On 18 June his account was credited with £630.18s. itemised as '*net of Treasury order for ¼ salary as Late Minister to Naples.*'

His first pension payment of £1,164, for an unspecified period, was credited to his account on 13 August 1802. There followed payments of £446.9s.4d in October, November, and two in January 1803. These payments in quick succession presumably made up for pension payments overdue. It had taken twenty-one months for his pension to be agreed.

More importantly, his account was credited on 19 August with the sum of £6,000 by '*Treasury Compensation*'. This was less than half the amount of £13,222 he had claimed for his '*Bills of Extraordinarys*' i.e. expenses in Naples and Palermo.

The government therefore still owed Sir William substantial amounts of money. The Coutts accounts indicate that Sir William was attempting to settle some of his debts, although they remained considerable on his death.

Sir William, Emma and Nelson planned a visit to Wales to view Hamilton's property at Milford Haven. Nelson's approval of Greville's proposals would have a beneficial influence on Sir William's investment.

Before leaving, an argument blew up between Emma and Sir William. We have Sir William's account of the circumstances of the argument in a letter he wrote from London on 16 July:

'*My dear Emma, It gave me much uneasiness to leave you as I did in a most uncomfortable state but consider you had not had your breakfast and the communication I made you of what passed <u>amicably</u> between Oliver and me did not quite coincide with your Ideas – then came <u>passion humour</u> and <u>nonsence</u>, which it is impossible to combat with reasoning while the passion lasts. There is no being on earth that has a better understanding or better heart than yourself, if you would but give them <u>fair play</u> and keep down the passions that make you see every thing thro' an improper and false medium. I am an old sinner I confess – but I am not the hard hearted man you do not scruple to make me. Your Ladyship is exactly what your old aunt told you, so <u>noble</u>, so <u>generous</u>, so <u>beautifull</u>, that you would give away your A_____ and H thro' your ribs – it is all well and so would I if I could afford it, and our Dear Ld. N. is noble, generous, open and liberal to all and I wish to God he could afford it. In this state you must excuse me if my having lived so long has given me Experience enough that the greatest fortunes will not stand the total want of* *attention to what are called <u>trifling</u> Expenses ... You charge me with having by my Will, left you to poverty and distress, that is by no means my intention. I know your value and mean to do every thing in my power (when I know what I really possess) to prevent that distress, but it is not my fault if by living with a great <u>Queen</u> in <u>intimacy</u> for so many years that your <u>ideas</u> should so far outrun what my means can furnish. Believe me, happiness is in a much <u>narrower</u> compass than most people think. But my Dear Emma let us cut this matter short. I am the old Oak and by God I can not give way to nonsense. Do not then strain the bow too tight ... least the string should break. I love Ld. Nelson. I know <u>the purity of your connection with him</u>. I will do every thing in my power not to disturb the quiet of my best Friend, and his heart God knows is so sensible that a sudden change from his present peace and tranquillity might prove fatal to him.*

We had yesterday a little tiff about Oliver. Ld. N. and I mean as friendly to him as you do, but do not think I am blind, do not think that I am ignorant that besides <u>Sabatini Michele</u> that most <u>ungrateful</u> and <u>impertinent rascall</u>, not to say <u>worse</u> is hidden at Merton. For God's sake as we have cause commune with Ld. Nelson, let us have fair play and do not let your generous and noble way of thinking and acting end in distressing us. I have done now with my Sermon, it comes from my heart which is seldom the case of those that come from the pulpit ...'[31]

The '*little tiff*' between them was evidently about money. It may be that Oliver, who worked for Sir William and Nelson in Piccadilly and Merton, had approached Emma for money. Emma and Oliver had been on friendly terms ever since he had been trusted by Nelson to carry letters to and from Emma, containing intimate details and secrets. Perhaps Emma promised him money, causing Sir William to accuse her of careless financial expenditure. In retaliation, Emma complained about being left in '*poverty and distress*' by Sir William's will. If she knew at that time that he had left her £800 p.a. (£100 of which was for her mother) she may have considered this inadequate compared to the standard of living she and Sir William currently enjoyed and to Fanny's £2,000 p.a. from Nelson.

Sir William added that he was prepared to do anything rather than disturb the fragile equilibrium of his '*best Friend*'.* Sir William concluded his letter:

---

*The reference to Sabatini Michele (who was the brother-in-law of Sir William's long-serving valet, Gaetano Sabatello) concerns his being at Merton, most probably hiding from creditors. It appears Emma may have played a part in helping Sabatini.

*The Duke of Q. chose to dine alone. Ld. Warwick is gone to the Castle, so
I dined at home on <u>pickled salmon, pigeon and peas, cold lamb, and Tart</u> –
GOOD PORT which after every delicacy is most necessary. Would to God I
could enjoy all that is mine and which I know to be superior to what any other
person on Earth possesses, but one can not have eaten one's Cake and have
one's cake. Ponder well my Dear Emma, these lines, let your good sense come
forward – as to me it is perfectly indifferent what may happen!*

I shall be Patience in Purity. Ever yr.

William Hamilton

Nelson decided to purchase an adjoining property of 115 acres from
a Mr Axe for £8,000, partly to protect the privacy of Merton Place. He
borrowed £4,000 from Davison and £4,000 from George Matcham.
Knowing this was his sister's marriage settlement, he arranged with
G.M. to pay interest half-yearly.

The Reverend Doctor and Sarah arrived at Merton to accompany
the party to Wales. Kitty and George, with their young son, George,
were to meet them at Oxford. Nelson informed G.M.: *'The Star Inn,
Oxford, Wednesday the 21st. July. Dinner at 5 o'clock. Dinner for 8. Be so
good as to order it. Need not say for who.'*[32]

In Oxford the following day Nelson received the Freedom of the
City and he and Sir William were awarded honorary degrees by the
university. The Reverend Doctor was awarded an Honorary
Doctorate of Divinity.

Wherever Nelson appeared he was fêted by the local dignitaries and
greeted as the saviour of his country by an adoring public. Having
spent the night at Woodstock, the party arrived, uninvited, at
Blenheim Palace where the Duke of Marlborough refused to see them,
sending a servant with a message offering them cold refreshments in
the park. Humiliated and outraged, even though they had arrived
uninvited, they hastily departed. Sir William and Emma consoled a
distressed Nelson.

They went on to Gloucester where the Matchams left them to
return to Bath. They carried on to Ross, down the river Wye to
Monmouth, and on via Merthyr Tydfil and Carmarthen to Milford,
arriving on 1 August in time to celebrate the fourth anniversary of the
Battle of the Nile.

Greville, had arranged for Nelson to see the natural harbour. For
Hamilton's sake, if not for Greville's, whom he privately disliked,
Nelson praised the harbour, declaring it to be equal to that of

Trincomalee in Ceylon. They attended civic receptions, including a banquet in Nelson's honour. Emma entertained guests singing *Rule Britannia* and *God Save the King*.

The public greeted the party with adulation; some were moved to tears by the sight of Nelson – *'so diminutive, so maimed'*.[33]

The return journey took them via Swansea, Cardiff and Chepstow back to Monmouth by 18 August. They travelled north to Ludlow to stay two days with an old friend of Hamilton's, then to Worcester where Nelson placed a large order for armorial china at the Chamberlain's factory. On the last stage of the journey they travelled to Warwick Castle and finally called to see Lord Spencer at Althorp Park.

Apart from their joint humiliation at Blenheim, Emma had again been subjected to embarrassing rejections, though perhaps Nelson and Sir William kept this from her. The vicar of Carmarthen, happy to pay his respects to Nelson, refused to receive Lady Hamilton. Captain Foley's new wife, Lady Fitzgerald refused at first to have Emma in her house, but was persuaded to receive her.[34]

They arrived back at Merton on 5 September. The six-week tour had been interesting, but exhausting and expensive. Neither Sir William nor Nelson kept a diary of the tour, but Nelson carefully recorded their daily expenses. Despite having enjoyed the hospitality of many friends, their expenses totalled £481.3s.10d., to be shared between them.[35]

They had been away longer than expected. Finding Merton Place *'not fit to receive them'* owing to building works in progress, Emma, Sir William and Nelson went to 23 Piccadilly. Emma wrote to Mrs Gibson on 9 September: *'Dear Mrs Gibson, I shall be glad to see you and Miss Thompson tomorrow, at 23 Piccadilly, at 10 o'clock ...'*[36]

Around this time she arranged for Mrs Gibson to take Horatia to Margate for a holiday. A note to Mrs Gibson reads: *'Mrs Gibson may go to Margate or Ramsgate with Miss Thompson, but not to go with the Hoy, as it is dangerous; and to let Lord N. know where they are and how Miss Thompson is in her health and spirits; and if bathing is necessary to let her bathe.'*[37]

Emma and Sir William went with Nelson to Ramsgate. Emma was keen to bathe in the sea. Her skin problems had possibly been aggravated by the long trip to Wales. She perhaps believed that a rest at the seaside would benefit Sir William. But Sir William was unhappy there and, indicating to Emma that he would rather be in London, she sent him a note:

'As I see it is a pain to you to remain here, let me beg of you to fix your time for going. Weather I dye in Piccadilly or any other spot in England 'tis the same to me, but I remember the time when you wished for tranquillity, but now all visiting and bustle is to your liking. However, I will do what you please, being your affectionate and obedient E.H.'[38]

Sir William replied on the note: *'I neither love bustle nor great company, but I like some employment and diversion. I have but a very short time to live and every moment is precious to me. I am in no hurry, and am exceedingly glad to give every satisfaction to our best friend, our dear Lord Nelson. The question, then, is what we can best do that all may be perfectly satisfied. Sea bathing is usefull to your health: I see it is, and wish you to continue it a little longer; but I must confess that I regret, whilst the season is favourable, that I cannot enjoy my favourite amusement of quiet fishing. I care not a pin for the great world, and am attached to no one so much as to you ...'*[39]

Emma was enjoying her sea bathing. The *Morning Herald* reported: *'She ducks and floats with infinite dexterity, and seems secure against any <u>marine enemy</u>: but as she is young and beautiful she is perhaps in more danger from <u>land sharks</u>!'*[40]

On this occasion there is conspicuously no mention of her being 'immensely fat.'

Emma, possibly accompanied by Nelson, was happy to be able to visit Horatia and Mrs Gibson at nearby Margate. She nevertheless replied to Sir William's note: *'I go when you tell me the coach is ready.'*

Sir William returned the note with the comment: *'This is not a fair answer to a fair confession of mine.'*

The above comments are an example of a typical family disagreement, but we note Sir William's affectionate comment: *'I care not a pin for the world, and am attached to no one so much as to you.'*

Their endearing habit of conducting arguments by writing notes to each other enables us to observe their relationship more intimately.

The improvements being made at Merton must have been completed, or the house at least made habitable, as Sir William gave a dinner party there to celebrate Nelson's 44th birthday on 29th September. Sir William and Emma invited Merton's neighbours Mr Perry and his family, and Abraham Goldsmith and family, to join the party that included Mrs Cadogan and the Reverend Doctor and family.In days spent fishing from the cool banks of the River Thames between Kingston and Hampton, only about five miles from Merton, they enjoyed some peace and quiet. Nelson told Davison in a letter: *'London seems absolutely deserted and so hot and stinking that it is truly detestable …'*[41]

At Merton, Nelson, Sir William, Emma and her mother often entertained guests to dinner and frequently overnight. They included Emma's friends, Mrs Banti and her husband, other Neapolitan friends, Nelson's naval associates, among them his captains, Foley, Fremantle, Hallowell and Ball. Jane Powell, Emma's actress friend, visited. A letter from her to Emma concluded with, *'Please remember me most kindly to your mother and every one at Merton.'*[42]

Nelson, having spent only about eight years in England of his thirty-one years naval service, and in his own home for the first time, was pleased to socialise with his family and friends around his dining table.

Sir William, on the other hand, now seventy-two years old, had had enough of entertaining. He wrote a long letter to Emma setting out their situation:

'I have passed the last forty years of my life in a hurry and bustle that must necessarily attend a public character. I am arrived at the age when some repose is really necessary and I promised myself a quiet home, and although I was sensible, and said so when I married, that I should be superannuated when my wife would be in her full beauty and vigour of youth. That time is arrived, and we must make the best of it for the comfort of both parties. Unfortunately our tastes as to the manner of living are very different. I by no means wish to live in solitary retreat, but to have seldom less than 12 or 14 at table, and those varying continually, is coming back to what was become so irksome to me in Italy during the latter years of my residence in that Country. I have no connections out of my own family. I have no complaint to make, but I feel the whole attention of my wife is given to Lord Nelson and his interest at Merton. I well know the purity of Lord Nelson's friendship for Emma and me, and I know how very uncomfortable it would make his Lordship, our best friend, if a separation should take place, and am therefore determined to do all in my power to prevent such an extremity, which would be <u>essentially detrimental</u> to all parties, but would be more sensibly felt by our dear friend than by us. Provided that our expenses in housekeeping do not encrease beyond measure (of which I see some danger) I am willing to go on upon our present footing; but as I cannot expect to live many years, every moment is precious to me, and I hope I may be allowed sometimes to be my own master, and pass my

time according to my own inclination, either by going [on] my fishing parties to the Thames, or by going to London to attend the Museum, R. Society, the Tuesday Club and Auctions of pictures. I mean to have a light Chariot or post Chaise by the month, that I may make use of it in London and run backwards and forwards to Merton or to Shepperton &c. This is my plan, and we might go on very well, but I am fully determined not to have more of the very silly altercations that happen but too often between us and embitter the present moment exceedingly. If realy we cannot live comfortable together, a <u>wise</u> and <u>well concerted</u> separation is preferable; but I think considering the probability of my not troubling any party long in this world, the best for us all would be for us to bear those ills we have rather than flie to those we know not of. I have fairly stated what I have on my mind. There is not time for nonsence or trifling. I know and admire your talents and many excellent qualities, but am not blind to your defects, and confess to having many myself; therefore let us bear and forbear for God's sake.'[43]

Emma's reply is not recorded but clearly they did agree to *'bear and forbear'* as there is no evidence of any further disagreeable arguments between them during the remaining months of Sir William's life.

He went on his fishing trips, attended his societies and bought his *'light Chariot'*. On 19 November the Herald reported: *'Sir William Hamilton sported an elegant new chariot on Wednesday last for the first time.'*[44] In view of the state of his finances, this was an extravagant purchase.

On 25 October, Nelson wrote to his sister, Kitty: '*... We are all Well and Merton looks even now beautiful. Sir Willm. has been many excursions on the Thames and two days ago brought home more than 60lbs of fish; this has delighted him. All here join in Kind Wishes ...'*[45]

It seems, from Emma's surviving notes to Mrs Gibson that Horatia seldom visited Merton, but she was often summoned to 23 Piccadilly:

7 o'clock, 24th March 1802 [Post-marked]

Lady H. begs Mrs Gibson to come to Piccadilly, No. 23, to-morrow at <u>12 o'clock</u>, and to bring her god-daughter, <u>Miss Thompson, with her</u>'

7o'clock 14th April 1802 [Post-marked]

Dear Mrs Gibson – If you will come in the morning at 12 o'clock, I shall be glad to see you and Miss T. to Piccadilly. Ever yours sincerely, E.H.'

In April, Mrs Gibson and Horatia were invited to Merton:

7o'clock, April 23, 1802 [Post-marked] Lady Hamilton begs Mrs Gibson will come down early to-morrow with her family and Miss Thomson to Merton. She may get a post-chaise and set off at eight in the morning.

Merton, Friday 4 o'clock'[46]

Two unusual notes from Emma and Nelson to Mrs Gibson in November suggest that some information about Horatia had leaked out:

2nd. November, 1802. [Post-marked]

Mrs Gibson is desired to call at 23, Piccadilly, to-morrow, alone, without Miss Thomson, and at ten o'clock. Monday afternoon.'

And from Nelson in a letter post-marked 19 November 1802:

'Mrs Gibson, 9, Little Titchfield Street, Marylebone.

Mrs Gibson is desired on no consideration to answer any questions about Miss Thompson, nor who placed her with Mrs G., as ill-tempered people have talked lies about the child.'[47]

The desire to keep Horatia's true identity a secret was as strong as ever.

William and Sarah's daughter, Charlotte, was now mainly living with Emma. Horace visited during holidays from Eton. In November, Emma describes her busy schedule to Sarah:

'Here we are come up to breakfast this morning. Horace is come with me and we have been out to buy a pair of Boots. He has got a pair big enough I was quite <u>determined on that</u>. Charlotte is not come as today she has 2 principle lessons ... My cold is so bad I can <u>hardly speak</u>. Horace goes to school Sunday, he is got very well and in high spirits. Charlotte and I come to town Monday and Tuesday for my Lord and Sir William are obliged to be in town on business ... Wednesday we return to Merton, dine at Mr Lancaster's [the vicar] were there is a play to be performed. Mrs Bianchi comes Friday after to stay a <u>fortnight</u> with us. Mr Blake I shall have Monday and Tuesday in Town, he is today at Merton, so is Oliver, so Charlotte is kept pretty well to it, so she <u>must</u> be ...'[48]

Oliver and Mr Blake were, with Emma, educating Charlotte. Oliver was now writing most of Nelson's letters for him. Concerned about his eyesight, Nelson consulted his friend, Dr Moseley about his *'good'* eye in October.

Emma received worrying news about her account from Coutts & Co on 21 December:

'Madam – Agreeable to your Ladyship's desire we have the Honor to acquaint you that the present balance of your money in our hands is twelve shillings and eleven pence.'[49] She was obliged to ask Sir William for help. Sir William sent the note with a covering letter to Greville: *'My Lady having left this letter on her Toilet, I supposed necessities were pressing and I have given her an additional credit on Coutts for £130, so that of the £700*

wanting to clear all, having had £120 before, I am to pay £450, if I am not soon paid by the Treasury I am determined to apply to Mr Addington myself, it is most shameful …'[50]

Sir William seems neither shocked, nor angry, about Emma's debts amounting to £700.

Since their return to England he had made Emma a quarterly allowance of £75. During the first six months she did not receive this allowance, but it was made up the following March by a payment of £150. Her allowance in Naples, before their marriage, had been £150 p.a. and after their marriage, £200 p.a. Her allowance now of £300 p.a. is therefore not excessive.

Sir William's letter to Greville continued:

' I am returning today to dinner at Merton. I attended the Council yesterday at R.S. [Royal Society]. Sir Joseph came but was too ill to come upstairs. I went down to him and was glad that I had it in my power to assist him, so I took the Chair at Council and in the Evening. I think of going of on Sunday to stay a day or two at Windsor to have an opportunity of wishing their Majesties a merry Xmas …'

On 23 December, Emma added a note to a letter from Nelson to Kitty.

I hope my Dear Mrs Matcham you will not think me neglectful, but really I have not had anything particularly interesting, & I told our Dear Mr Matcham all I knew … Here we are as happy as Kings & much more so. We have 3 Boltons, 2 Nelsons & only want 2 or 3 Little Matchams to be quite en famille, happy & comfortable, for the greatest of all Joys to our most Excellent Nelson is when he has his sisters or their children with him; for sure no brother was ever so much attached as he is. How I long for the Spring to be happy with you and Mrs Bolton, who has promised to meet you [at Merton]… Our Hero was most Graciously & particularly received by her Majesty when he went with Sir Wm to the Drawing Room. Sir Wm, who is often in private with the R. F. [Royal Family] has had opportunitys of letting them know many truths concerning our incomparable Nelson dont you think he speaks like an angel in the House of Lords? As he must & shall go to Court [on] the Birthday to pay his devoirs to Her Majesty; we shall go for a month to Piccadilly near that time. Lady Mansfield has promised me to take Charge of him & Sir Wm that day, & get them near the K. &c without Crowd. On this condition he goes he says, but dont you think it right? I love him, adore him, his virtues, his Heart, mind, Soul, Courage. His Honour, Glory & happinesswill be ever Dear to his & Yours My Dear Mrs Matcham, ever [your] affectionate friend
Emma Hamilton[51]

Christmas 1802 was a jolly family affair at Merton. Sadly, the rumours spreading about Horatia probably prevented her being there. On 4 January Nelson told G.M. and Kitty, who had been unable to attend due to Kitty's latest pregnancy:

'... *Lady Hamilton gave a little Ball last night to the children; they danced till 3 this morning and are not up yet.'* Emma added: '... *never mind, you will have 18* [children] *like the Queen of Naples. It will be delightful to see you with them all round the table. We have had a Delightful Ball. Charlott outdid herself like an angel she <u>was that</u> night. The little Boltons were Charmed. Tom Bolton is a good Boy & is well behaved & we like him very much. Sir W. is better and gets his appetite. We are all very comfortable and happy ... God bless you all Prays your affectionate* [friend Emma Hamilton].'[52]

This proved to be Sir William's last Christmas. He was feeling better, eating well and surrounded by the warmth of his *'family'* – Emma, Nelson and Mrs Cadogan.

In the winter weather early in the new year his health began to decline. He had celebrated his 73rd birthday on 13 December, but no longer had the reserves to fight an English winter. In February he and Emma gave a *'grand concert'* at 23 Piccadilly. The *Post* reported on 19 February: *'Lady Hamilton had a grand concert a few evenings since at 23 Piccadilly. About 100 fashionable were present, many of whom were amateurs. Her Ladyship sang several bravura songs, and played very difficult concertos on the piano-forte, with such rapidity of execution, as not only astonished but electrified her auditors.'*[53]

It was the last time they hosted such an event.

Sir William attended a meeting of the Dilettante on 6 March at which he offered the Society his *'collection of the original Notes and Drawings relative to the Discoveries in the city of Herculaneum made during the course of the excavations of that City.'* He was too ill to attend the next meeting on 27 March. He wrote to the Society:

'Nothing cou'd have prevented my having the honor of attending at the proposal meeting on Sunday of the Dilettante Society as the fate of a favourite child of mine that I deposited in the hands of the Society will probably be decided [whether to publish the notes and drawings] *– My present State of health & weakness is deplorable and makes it impossible for me to attend ...'*[54]

During the next few days he suffered a sudden collapse. Nelson reported to the Matchams on 2 April 1803:

'Our Poor Dear Sir William is no better today, there is not the smallest hopes of his recovery. Dr Moseley attends, My Lady and Mrs Cadogan nurse

him. He sees all his relations. He feels no pain. There has been a Consultation of Physicians; all advise human aid is now too late. He is going off as an Inch of Candle ... The sorrow and Affliction that reigns in this house is distressing in the Extreme. I lose a friend who has spoke well of me for thirty seven years. We have all paid ample tribute of tears. I think the occasion for a flood is very near at hand ...'[55]

After Sir William made his last amendments to his will at Merton 31 March, Nelson and Emma took him home to 23 Piccadilly. On 1 April Greville arrived. Greville already knew that he was his uncle's main beneficiary but he had another matter to discuss – his own and the Pembroke estates' debts. Greville drew up a memorandum of their discussion that he later used as a sworn statement in proving Hamilton's will. He swore on oath that Sir William told him he was to have the £7,000 treasury stocks that Sir William held. Greville reported that Sir William was still grievously hurt by his treatment by the government and that he would have had more to bequeath to Emma if the Treasury had only honoured its debt to him.

Emma and Mrs Cadogan nursed Sir William day and night for several days. He died in Emma's arms with Nelson holding his hand on the morning of 6 April. Nelson wrote immediately to Davison:

Wednesday, 11o'clock, 6th. April 1803

Our Dear Sir William died at ten minutes past Ten this morning on Lady Hamilton's and my arms, without a Sigh or a Struggle. Poor Lady Hamllton is as you may expect desolate. I hope she will be left properly but I doubt it.[56]

A devastated Emma wrote on a scrap of paper: 'April 6th. Unhappy day for forlorn Emma. Ten minutes past ten dear, blessed Sir William left me.'

Sir William's obituary, published on 7 April, was a complimentary account of his services to his country:

'Sir William was a man of most extraordinary endowments, and his memory will be dear to the literary world by the indefatigable exertions which he made through life to add to our store of knowledge, and of models in the fine arts. His whole life, indeed, was devoted to studies connected with the arts ...' It went on to comment on the splendid hospitality with which he had represented his sovereign, *'his gracious attachment and friendship'* with the King, and his successful career in Naples where he had *'maintained the most perfect harmony between the two Courts'.*

Despite the scandal of Emma's association with Nelson, the writer of the obituary gave a fair account of Emma's contribution to the married life she had shared with Sir William:

'*About twelve years ago, he married Lady Hamilton, and never was a union productive of more perfect felicity. The anxious solicitude, the unwearied attentions, the domestic duties, joined to the uncommon talents and accomplishments of Lady Hamilton, were the sources of the purest happiness to them both, as well as the circle in which they lived. Sir William derived from his Lady, in his last illness, all the consolation of which life was susceptible, and he at length, without a struggle or a sigh, breathed his last breath in her arms.*'[57]

Tichbein, the artist who had known Sir William in Naples, wrote of him: '*... in every respect he was an extraordinary person ... He was a man of the world, who knew how to acquire and enjoy the amenities of life. Not a moment passed him by unused. He was altogether a good, an excellent, a wholly exceptional person.*'[58]

Sir William, Emma's lover, husband, mentor, admirer, and companion for seventeen years was no longer there to sustain her. After his death, Emma's world tragically began to collapse around her.

CHAPTER 18

Sir William Hamilton's Will

SIR WILLIAM WROTE his 'Last Will and Testament', revoking all former wills, on 28 May 1801. Charles Greville and Emma were aware of the contents of this will. Sir William had always let it be known that, in the event that he failed to produce a direct heir, he intended to leave his entire estates to his nephew. For Emma and her mother there was only an annuity of £800 a year.

The repercussions of this will had a profound effect on the remainder of Emma's life, making it necessary to examine Sir William's legacies in detail. A number of important points have been underlined.

The will begins with Sir William's request that he be buried near his first wife, Catherine, as he had promised her: *'This is the last Will and Testament of me, The Right Honorable Sir William Hamilton of Coleby in the County of Pembroke Knight of the Most Honorable Order of the Bath first to fulfill the promise I made to my excellent wife Catherine Lady Hamilton deceased I desire my Body may be deposited near hers in the family vault of the Barlows in Slebech Church in the County of Pembroke and that my funeral may be conducted in as private a manner as decency and propriety will admit.'*

Confirmation that this was carried out as requested is recorded in the Church burial records:

Date April 19th. 1803
Name of Deceased: Sir William Hamilton
Aged: 73 years
Supposed cause of Death: Natural decay
Where buried: Vault in the Chancel

The next stipulation made by Sir William is vitally important as future events indicate that Greville, for whatever reasons, failed to comply. *'... I direct my just Debts and Testamentary expenses and Legacies to be paid and Satisfied out of my Personal Estate and in case my personal Estate shall be insufficient for the payment thereof then I do hereby Charge and make Chargeable in aid thereof all my Manors Hereditaments and Real Estate by me hereinafter given and devised.'*

Sir William's *'personal estate'* proved insufficient to cover all his debts. Some debts remained unpaid, with grave consequences for Emma.

The will continues: *'I give and bequeath unto my Dear Wife Emma, Lady Hamilton the sum of three hundred pounds of Lawful Money of Great Britain to be paid to her immediately after my death and to her mother Mary Cadogan the sum of one hundred pounds of like Lawful Money to be paid to her immediately after my decease ...'*

In due course, Mrs Cadogan received her £100 and, thankfully, Sir William later increased the above bequest to Emma in a codicil to his will.

Greville's bequest follows: *'... And as to all the Residue and Remainder of Monies, stocks, funds and securities Debts Goods and Chattles and all other my Personal Estate and Effects whatsoever and wheresoever from and after the payment of all my Debts, funeral and Testamentary Expenses and Legacies I give and bequeath the [same?] and every part thereof unto my Nephew the Right Honorable Charles Francis Greville second son of the late Francis Earl of Warwick ...'*

Sir William named the executors of his will, outlined the full extent of his estates and gave detailed instructions regarding the payment of his annuity to Emma: *'...I give and devise unto the Most Honorable James Marquis of Abercorn and John Meyrick of Bush in the County of Pembroke their heirs and assigns all my Manors Messauges [dwelling houses] farms, Lands Tenements and Hereditaments ... situate and being in the County of Pembroke Town and County of Haverford West Borough at Carmarthen or elsewhere in the Kingdom of Great Britain ... to the use and intent that the said James Marquis of Abercorn and John Meyrick their Executors and Administrators and Assigns may yearly during the natural life of my said wife Lady Hamilton ... take by and out of the Rents and profits of the said Manors and Hereditaments [one] Annuity or Yearly Rent Charge of eight hundred pounds of Lawful Money of Great Britain clear of all Deductions and to be payable quarterly on the twenty fifth day of March the twenty fourth day of June the twenty ninth of September and the twenty fifth day of December in every year by equal part and the first Quarterly payment thereof to [commence] on such of the said days as shall next happen after my decease ...'*

Emma did not receive the £200 quarterly payments due to her *'clear of all deductions'*, and the first payment was not made until 23 January 1804. Greville deducted government tax due which increased over time as Emma at first received £190 per quarter until March 1805, then £187.17s. until March 1806 and finally £180 quarterly. She received these payments at irregular times, not promptly on the quarterly dates specified by Sir William.

Should Emma marry again, Sir William stipulated that she should still receive her annuity payments: '... *nevertheless to pay the said Annuity or Rent Charge unto my said wife Lady Hamilton and her Assigns during her natural life for her sole and separate use and disposal without being liable to the Debts Contracts forfeiture Dispositions or Engagements of any husband or husbands with whom she my said wife may happen to marry ...*'

In addition to the £100 payable to Mrs Cadogan immediately after his death, Sir William made the following provisions for her: '*...I do hereby declare that the said Annuity or yearly Rent Charge of eight hundred pounds shall be received by my said Wife as well in Confidence that she will during her life provide for her Mother ...*'

In the event of Emma's death before her mother's, Mrs Cadogan was to be provided for:

'*... that the said Mary Cadogan and her Assigns may yearly during her natural life in case she shall survive my said wife Lady Hamilton receive and take by and out of the Rents and profits of the same Manors and Hereditaments one Annuity or yearly Rent Charge of one hundred pounds of Lawful Money of Great Britain clear of all Deductions ...*'

Sir William, who was disappointed in his expectation of a pension of £2,000 p.a. clear of tax deductions, stipulated that both Emma and her mother should receive their annuities clear of all deductions.

The will empowered the executors to take action should Emma not receive her annuity:

'*... I do hereby give to the said Marquis of Abercorn and John Meyrick their Executors* [administrators] *and Assigns in case of non payment of the said Annuity or Yearly Rent Charge of eight hundred pounds by such quarterly payments as aforesaid all such power Right and benefit of Entry and Distress and all other Remedies for Recovering the said Annuity or Yearly Rent Charge of eight hundred pounds and all Arrears Thereof and the Costs and Charges of attending the same ...*'

Many years later payment of Emma's quarterly annuity ceased. The circumstances and consequences of this non-payment will be examined later.

After the '*determination of the Estate*' Sir William named new executors.

'*... The Right Honorable George, Earl of Warwick and Sir John MacPherson of Brompton in the County of Middlesex Baronet their heirs and*

Assigns during the natural life of the said Charles Francis Greville In Trust <u>to support the contingent use and Estates herein after limited from being defeated or destroyed</u> and for that purpose to make Entries and bring Actions as occasion shall require but nevertheless to permit the said Charles Francis Greville and his Assigns during his life to receive and take the Rents and profits of the said Manor and premises to and for his and their own use and benefit …'

On the death of Charles Greville the 'Rents and Profits' passed on to his son or sons in order of seniority and 'priority of birth' with the elder of the male heirs 'always to be preferred'. In '<u>default of such Issue to the use of my Nephew the Honorable Robert Fulk Greville</u>' under the same terms of descent as those which applied to Charles Greville. But only in the case of Robert Greville, in default of male heirs, were any daughters of his entitled to inherit the estates.

After Robert Fulke Greville and any of his heirs, male or female, the next in line were Sir William's nephews, the Right Honorable William Lord Cathcart, followed by the Honorable Archibald Cathcart. The executors remained George Earl of Warwick and Sir John Macpherson.

There is a significant and uncommon declaration in the will whereby Sir William refers to an agreement he made with Greville even before his marriage to Emma: '… *my Will and Mind further is that whereas I sometime since <u>joined with my Nephew the said Charles Francis Greville</u> in a Bond or Obligation to <u>enable him to postpone the payment of several Debts or Sums of money due from him</u> and it being my intention to empower my Nephew to secure <u>the sum of Six hundred pounds immediately</u> upon my said Manors and Hereditaments but to be made payable after my decease as hereinafter mentioned by creating such charge thereon of the said Debts <u>I do hereby direct and declare that it shall and may be lawful to and for my said Nephew Charles Francis Greville at any time or times thereafter as well during my life as after my decease</u> by any Deed or Deeds writing or writings to be Sealed and Delivered by him in the presence of two or more Credible Witnesses and to be with or without power of Revocation and by his last Will and Testament in the writing or any Codicil or Codicils thereof to be by him signed sealed Published and Declared in the presence of and to be attested by three or more Credible Witnesses <u>to charge all my said Manors Messuages Farms Lands Tenements and Hereditaments</u> hereinbefore divised or any part thereof [fairly?] or <u>for the payment of any Sum or Sums of money not exceeding Six thousand pounds</u> of lawful money of Great Britain … <u>subject and without prejudice to the said Annuities or yearly Rent Charges of eight</u>*

hundred pounds and one hundred pounds hereinbefore limited and for securing the same sum or sums not exceeding six thousand pounds with lawful interest ...'

Sir William here set out the manner in which Greville can charge his estate for the payment of an amount *'not exceeding £6000'* and *'without prejudice'* to the £800 and £100 due to Emma and Mrs Cadogan.

A bequest was made to any woman, or women, Charles Greville, Robert Fulke Greville, William Lord Cathcart or Archibald Cathcart might marry: ... *not to exceed the sum of five hundred pounds and four hundred pounds to be made subject and without prejudice'* to the yearly annuities of Emma's eight hundred pounds and Mrs Cadogan's one hundred pounds.

Sir William had taken steps to protect the annual incomes bequeathed to Emma and her mother.

Having covered any eventualities that might arise from the sale of any parts of the estate Sir William finally declared: *'And I do hereby constitute and appoint the said Charles Francis Greville sole Executor of this my last Will and Testament And I do hereby revoke all former Wills by me at any time heretofore made and do publish and declare this to be my Last Will and Testament In Witness whereof I have hereto set my hand and Seal ... this twenty eighth day of May in the year of our Lord One Thousand eight hundred and one.*

Wm Hamilton.'

The will was witnessed by W. Price, Lincolns Inn, Thomas Ward of the same and John Phillips, clerk to Mr Price. The Probate Copy of the above will in the records of the Canterbury Consistory Court bears the date *Merton Surrey March 31st. 1803.*

A week before he died, having given further consideration to his will, Sir William wrote one codicil at Merton dated the same day, 31 March 1803: *'Having heard that there needs no more to make a codicil to a will and to make it valid than that the testator should write it in his own hand and sign on a part of the same will, I do then, feeling myself in a very weak state of health, wish, without making any alteration to my will, to explain a few points. When I made the above written will, I had not purchased £7000 in the stocks 3 per cents and which are now in the hands of Messrs Coutts and Co, my bankers, in the Strand. This stock and whatever money may be found in Coutts hands at my death I bequeath to the Right Hon Charles F. Greville my dear nephew and principal heir. He is well acquainted with all my affairs and will understand my meaning and I dare say act up in every point to what he knows to be my wish. All my old pictures, according to a former agreement, and all I have under the denomination of Vertu, all my drawings and papers are to be given to my said nephew Rt Hon Charles F Greville but, observing in my will that at my death by the will my dear wife Emma would only receive £300 of the £800 I have left her and her mother, as explained in the will. Now, not to leave my dear wife Emma in such confusion at the moment of my death, my will is that my nephew Charles will pay my wife directly £800 out of what I have in the stocks or Coutts hands, and that her annual payments shall go on the same, and as I promised to pay Emma's debts amounting to £700 but have only paid £250, my will is that my nephew, Charles Greville shall pay the remaining £450 from the arrears due to me from the Treasury as the King's Minister at Naples. The copy of Madame Le Brun's picture of Emma in enamel by Bone, I give to my dearest friend Lord Nelson, Duke of Bronte, a very small token of the great regard I have for his Lordship, the most virtuous, loyal and truly brave character I ever met with, God bless him and shame fall on those who not say amen. One little article more and I have done. My noble friend and relation, the Marquis of Douglas and Clysdale, having often expressed a great liking to my famous Amate Tenor, I bequeath to his Lordship the case as it is with the Tenor and Giardine's violin and he may chuse out of my musick any that may suit him. This is also a very small mark of the regard I have for so valuable a friend and relation. All my fire arms I likewise bequeath to my nephew Charles Greville except two guns that are at Merton and which I bequeath to Lord Nelson.*

Merton March 3 1803   Wm Hamilton

In this will and codicil Greville was bequeathed all of Sir William's personal possessions and papers. Not one single personal item is singled out for Emma. Sir William had, over the years, purchased valuable jewellery for her, but she had sold her diamonds (gifts from him and from Queen Maria Carolina) to buy furniture and fittings for 23 Piccadilly.

Concerning his promise to pay the remaining £450 of Emma's debts, Greville took the opportunity to abide by the will's instruction that this £450 should be paid *'from the arrears due to me from the Treasury.'* Sir William may have hoped that the Treasury would pay up soon after his death. In the event, the *'arrears'* were not paid until many years later, by which time Greville had died and the government payout went to Robert Fulke Greville, the next in line to inherit Hamilton's estates. Emma started her life without Sir William with her debt of £450 unpaid.

The codicil confirms Greville's right to the £7,000 stocks and to any money remaining in Sir William's Coutts' account. Sir William had purchased the '£7,000 consolidated 3% [stocks] for the sum of £4,042.10s.' in April or May 1801. These must have been held in a separate account as his Coutts' statements reveal that he received dividends in July 1802 and January 1803.

In fact, on his death, there was no money in his Coutts' account. A credit of £500 is recorded on 10 July 1803 (after his death) to balance and close the account.

Sir William still had an account at his long-standing bankers Ross & Ogilvie through which his estate affairs were conducted. Details of any money in this account at this death are unknown.

On examining Sir William's Death Duties record a further neglect of Emma's dues becomes apparent.

The codicil had stated: '... *my will is that my nephew Charles will pay my wife directly £800 out of what I have in the stocks or Coutts hands and that her annual payments shall go on the same ...*'

Emma's account at Coutts does not show an amount of £800 received '*directly*' or at any time until <u>13 January 1808</u>. Greville may have taken this £800 to be Emma's annual annuity rather than an individual lump sum bequest. Either way, it appears Emma did not receive it. Hamilton's Death Duties record his estate '*Under £10,000*' of which £100 was due to Mrs Cadogan and the '*Residue*' all to the Right Honorable Charles Francis Greville. There is no mention of £800 for Emma.

Clearly, Sir William's finances were in a sorry state at his death, partly due to the government not paying for his ambassadorial expenses at Naples and Palermo.

Blame for Emma's future financial problems must lie in part with Hamilton's will and the execution thereof. Immediately after Hamilton's death, Emma was in dire financial straits.

CHAPTER 19

Emma's Long Separation from Nelson

'Be assured that I am thinking of you every moment.
My heart is full to busting'
Nelson to Emma, 20 May 1803

'But your purse my dear Emma will always be empty.
Your heart is generous beyond your means.'
Nelson to Emma, 26 August 1803

'God only spare him, for my existence hangs by his!'
Emma to Sarah, January, 1804

SHORTLY AFTER SIR William's death, Emma wrote to Greville: *'Lady Hamilton will be glad to know how long Mr. Greville can permit her to remain in the house in Piccadilly, as she must instantly look out for a lodging; and, therefore, it is right for her to know the full extent of time she can remain there. She also begs to know if he will pay her debts, and what she may depend upon; that she may reduce her expenses and establishment immediately.'*[1] Greville gave her until the end of the month.

Nelson had moved out of 23 Piccadilly on the day Sir William died and taken lodgings nearby. Sarah Nelson was summoned to London to comfort and support Emma. Emma's mother had a close and affectionate relationship with Sir William and would have felt his death equally keenly.

Sir William's funeral cortège left Piccadilly on 17 April for his burial in Pembrokeshire, most probably attended by Greville. Nelson, Emma and Mrs. Cadogan remained in London. They kept the proprieties of mourning and Mrs Gibson was informed: *'… Horatia nor anybody can go out till after the funeral, as we are very close and sincere mourners. God bless you.'*[2]

Concerned about Emma's financial situation, both Nelson and

Greville appealed to the government for a proportion of Sir William's pension to be granted to her. Emma wrote to the Prime Minister, The Rt. Hon. Henry Addington:

'Sir, May I trouble you for, and but for a moment, in consequence of my irreparable loss of my ever-honoured Husband. Sir William Hamilton, being no more, I cannot avoid it. I am forced to petition for a portion of his pension, such a portion as in your wisdom and noble nature may be approved, and to be presented to our most Gracious Sovereign as being right. For, Sir, I am most sadly bereaved and I am now placed in circumstances far below those in which the goodness of my dear Sir William allowed me to move for so many years, and below those becoming the relict of such a public minister, who has tried so very long (no less than 36 years) and all his life honoured so very much by the constant friendly kindness of the King and Queen themselves.

And may I mention what is well known to the then Administration at Home how I too strove to do all I could towards the Service of our King and Country. The Fleet itself, I can truly say, could not have got into Sicily but for which I was happily able to do with the Queen of Naples, and thro' her secret instructions so obtained, on which depended the refitting of the Fleet in Sicily and with that all which followed so gloriously at the Nile. These few words, tho' seemingly wrote at large, may not be extravagant at all, they are indeed True. I wish them to be heard only as they can be proved, and being proved may I hope for what I have now desired. Yours etc. etc.'[3]

Emma was justified in claiming a pension as Hamilton's widow. In his final years, it is doubtful Sir William could have carried out his ambassadorial duties without her help.

However, there was no set procedure to receive a pension. Ambassadors could apply on an individual basis upon retirement. The wife of a deceased official could apply, but there was no guarantee they would receive any part of their husband's pension.[4] Addington was reportedly sympathetic to her cause, but with a renewed threat of war with France her appeal was set aside.

The Herald reported on 19 April: '... Lady Hamilton not having been left in independent circumstances, the Minister, it is said, means to recommend to His Majesty to grant a pension to her Ladyship.'[5]

Lord Minto was surprised by the terms of Hamilton's will. He wrote to his wife:

'I have seen Lady Hamilton, who is worse off than I imagined, her jointure being £700 a year, and £100 to Mrs. Cadogan for her life. She told me she had applied to Mr. Addington for a pension, and desired me to promote it in any *way I could, and Lord Nelson coming in, made the same request. I promised to do so ...'*[6]

Emma did not receive any of her annuity payments until nine months after Sir William's death. She received her last allowance of £75 from Sir William on 1 April, five days before he died. This was almost certainly the only money she had at her disposal. Fortunately she was able to improve her position by selling some of the furniture and fittings that she had bought for 23 Piccadilly.

Her bank account shows that she received £514.16s.6d. from Christie's on 12 July, followed by an amount of £1,140.18s.6d. on 14 July, probably also from Christie's. The sale at 23 Piccadilly in June was catalogued by Christie's:

All the elegant
HOUSEHOLD FURNITURE
GLASSES, MIRRORS,
A HARPSICHORD, by B. SHUDI,
Brilliant Cut Chandeliers,
DRAWING ROOM SUITES OF COTTON
In the Eastern Stile.
A CAPITAL SET OF CLAW DINING TABLES,
EXCELLENT CABINET WORK,
And numerous valuable Effects, the Property of the late
Sir William Hamilton, K. B. Dec.
AT HIS LATE MANSION ON THE NORTH SIDE OF
PICCADILLY, OPPOSITE THE GREEN PARK
WHICH
Will be Sold by Auction,
BY MR. CHRISTIE,
ON THE PREMISES
On Monday, June the 20th 1803, and following Day,
AT TWELVE O'CLOCK

The remaining contents were removed to the house Emma took at 11 Clarges Street, a smaller residence, but still comfortable enough for Emma, her mother, and any family who came to stay, along with several servants who occupied light and airy rooms at the top of the house.

Greville found that there was no money left in Hamilton's account at Coutts. Sir William had specified in his codicil that Emma should receive her £800 *'out of what I have in the stocks or Coutts hands'*, and had implied that he trusted Greville to do right by Emma. There was an outstanding debt of £2,000 Sir William owed to Nelson.

Greville claimed his uncle left debts of £5,500, one of which may have been for his new coach, a debt for which Emma was later arrested. To clear these debts Greville presumably had to sell some of the £7,000 in government stocks he had taken such care to ensure that Hamilton left to him.

In May Nelson was warned by the Admiralty to prepare for departure. This was devastating news for Emma. Only one month after losing Sir William, Nelson would soon be leaving to seek out the French fleet yet again. And she was pregnant.

Nelson wrote to St. Vincent on 12 May, hoping he was to have the *Victory*, 100 guns, which had been undergoing repairs and refit for the last three years: *'... if the Victory is ready, or as soon as she is, that I may have her; for all my things, servants, wines &c. &c. are ordered to her, be where she will – even my sheep, poultry, hay, corn and every comfort are ordered to her ...'*[7]

On 16 May Nelson received his commission as Commander-in-Chief of the Mediterranean and two days later war was declared between Britain and France.

Before leaving, Nelson arranged to have Horatia baptized. Mrs Gibson received a note from Emma instructing her to take Horatia to the Marylebone Parish Church where she was *'To give the clergyman a double fee and the same to the Clerk'*,[8] and to bring back a signed certificate of baptism. Emma and Nelson did not attend the ceremony, even though they declared themselves the child's godparents.

The certificate, dated 13 May 1803, records her name and date of birth: *'Horatia Nelson Thompson. B 29 October 1800'*. This date is three months prior to Horatia's actual birth date, possibly their attempt to confuse the circumstances of her birth.

Nelson went to Merton to settle his affairs and wrote to Davison: *'I beg that you will have the goodness to Pay on my account to Emma Lady Hamilton the Sum of One Hundred Pounds on the first day of every month till further orders, the first payment to be made on the first day of June next 1803.'*[9]

Nelson intended these payments to be for the running costs at Merton during his absence, but they do not appear as regular income in Emma's bank account. Perhaps Davison sent the payment round to her in cash from his home in St. James's Square, or simply paid the bills Emma presented to him. Throughout 1803 Nelson repeatedly thanked Davison for his 'kindness to Emma'.

Nelson left London at 4 a.m. on 18 May, sending a brief note to Emma during his journey: 'Cheer up, my dearest Emma, and be assured that I have ever been and ever will be, your most affectionate and faithful Nelson and Bronte.'[10]

Arriving at Portsmouth that day, he informed the Admiralty: 'I arrived here about one o'clock this afternoon, and have hoisted my Flag on board his Majesty's Ship Victory.'[11]

Two days later, he sent a farewell note to Emma: 'You will believe that although I am glad to leave that horrid place Portsmouth, yet the being afloat makes me now feel that we do not tread the same element. I feel from my soul that God is good, and in His due wisdom will unite us, only when you look upon our dear child call to your remembrance all you think that I would say was I present, and be assured that I am thinking of you every moment. My heart is full to bursting. May God Almighty bless & protect you, is the fervent prayer of, my dear beloved Emma, your most faithful, affectionate &c.'[12]

They did not see one another again for two years and three months.

During their long separation they regularly corresponded. Knowing he depended on her cheerful, newsy letters, Emma wrote often. Nelson told Emma in 1804 that he had received hers of 'Sept. 9th, and 29th, October 2, 7, 10, 12, 17th. and November 5th., 8th. to the 24th.' Up to now, he had addressed her as 'My Dear Lady', and 'My Dearest Friend'. Now he called her 'My Dearest Emma' or 'My own dear beloved Emma'.

Nelson sailed for Ushant on 21 May aboard the Victory in company with the Amphion, 32 guns. The following day he wrote to Emma:

May 22nd [1803] Eight o'clock in the morning.

'My dearest Emma,

We are now in site of Ushant and shall see Admiral Cornwallis in an hour. I am not in a little fret, on the idea that he may keep the Victory and turn us all into the Amphion. It will make it truly uncomfortable, but I cannot help myself.

I assure you, my dear Emma, that I feel a thorough conviction that we shall meet again, with honour, riches and in health, and remain together till a good old age. I look at you and My God's Child's picture, but, till I am sure of remaining here, I cannot bring myself to hang them up. Be assured that my attachment, and affectionate, regard is unalterable; nothing can shake it.

And, pray, say so to my dear Mrs T. when you see her. Tell her my love is unbounded, to her and her dear sweet child, and, if she should have more, it will extend to all of them. In short, my dear Emma, say every thing to her which your dear, affectionate, heart and head can think of ... To Mrs Cadogan say every kind thing ...'[13]

He reverted to the subterfuge of referring to *'Mrs Thompson'* to cover the remark *'if she should have more'* which tells us he knew that Emma was pregnant. Emma received two different types of letters from Nelson – those that might be opened and read by the Admiralty were friendly and full of his news, but when he could send his letters privately, he wrote passionately of his love for her and his anguish at being parted from her.

For the rest of 1803, throughout 1804 and until May 1805, Nelson and his fleet remained in the Mediterranean. Having promised Emma that he would be faithful to her, Nelson remained on board ship, never setting foot on shore.

In August he transferred his flag from the *Amphion* to the *Victory*, where he was *'well mounted'* with his Captain Hardy, secretary John Scott, Chaplain the Reverend John Scott (whom Nelson called 'Doctor' Scott), his valet, Chevalier, and other servants.

Emma lived mainly at Clarges Street while Mrs Cadogan was capably managing Nelson's property at Merton, where the country air better suited her health. Emma probably chose to live in London for the sake of propriety and to be nearer to her friends and Horatia. Had she lived openly at Merton it would have been construed as an overt admission of her relationship with Nelson. Hardy had commented after Sir William's death: *'How her Ladyship will manage to live with the Hero of the Nile now, I am at a loss to know, at least in an honourable way.'*[14]

In June Emma visited the Boltons at Cranwich in Norfolk. Being with Susanna and her children distracted her from her grief. The family regarded her as a benefactress, due to her financial generosity and her influence in good taste, elegance and worldly wisdom.

She visited Ramsgate, Margate, Southend and the William Nelsons in Canterbury. Dr Nelson had been gazetted a Prebendary of Canterbury on 24 May 1803. At last he had attained the preferment for which he had solicited Nelson's patronage. The family home was now a pleasant house situated on the north side of the cathedral.

Emma fell into financial difficulties partly because of her

uncontrolled generosity towards Nelson's family, her family and friends. There is ample evidence supporting this generosity.

Charlotte, William and Sarah's daughter, came to live at Clarges Street, where she was looked after and educated at Emma's expense. At other times Emma's cousins, Celicia, Sarah and Mary Connor came to live with her, employed as general assistants and later as governesses to Horatia.

In July Nelson told Emma he had written to Queen Maria Carolina, hoping that the Queen would help her friend:

'My Dearest Emma,

Although I have wrote letters from various places, merely to say 'Here I am' and 'There I am' – yet, as I have no doubt but that they would all be read, it was impossible for me to say more than – 'Here I am, and well' ... I send you copies of the King and Queen's letters. I am vexed, that she did not mention you! I can only account for it, by hers being a political letter.

When I wrote to the Queen, I said – 'I left Lady Hamilton, the eighteenth of May; and so attached to your Majesty, that I am sure she would lay down her life to preserve yours. Your Majesty never had a more sincere, attached, and real friend, than your dear Emma. You will be sorry to hear, that good Sir William did not leave her in such comfortable circumstances as his fortune would have allowed. He has given it amongst his relations. But she will do honour to his memory, although every one else of his friends call loudly against him on that account.'

I trust, my dear Emma, she has wrote you. If she can forget Emma, I hope, God will forgive her. But, you think, that she never will, or can. Now is her time to shew it ...

I have made up my mind, that it is part of the plan of that Corsican Scoundrel, to conquer the kingdom of Naples. He has marched thirteen thousand men into the kingdom, on the Adriatic side; and he will take possession, with as much shadow of right, of Gaeta and Naples ...

I have cautioned General Acton, not to risk the Royal Family too long; but Naples will be conquered, sooner or later, as it may suit Buonaparte's convenience ... I am, you may believe, very anxious to get off Toulon, to join the fleet ... I hope they will come out, and let us settle the matter. You know, I hate being kept in suspense ...'[15]

In the following letter Nelson mentions both Emma's and his own debts.

[July 8th.]

'... You will readily believe, how rejoiced I shall be to get one of your dear,

excellent letters, that I may know everything which has passed in my absence.

I sincerely hope that Mr Booth [a partner in Booth & Haslewood, solicitors] *has settled all your accounts. Never mind, my dear Emma, a few hundred pounds; which is the rigid gripe of the law, not justice, can wrest it from you ...'*

He was aware that Emma was finding it difficult to have her debts of *'a few hundred pounds'* settled by the solicitors. This probably refers to the £450 that Hamilton had promised to pay. *'... I thank God, that you cannot want; (although that is no good reason for its being taken from you) whilst I have sixpence, you shall not want for five pence of it! But, you have bought your experience, that there is no friendship in money concerns; and, your good sense will make you profit of it. I hope the minister has done something for you. But, never mind, we can live on bread and cheese ...'*[16]

Nelson had taken Sir William's valet, Gaetano, back to Naples to see his family. He gave Emma Gaetano's news about Sir William's servants and told her that the Palazzo Sessa was now an hotel.

In August, Nelson wrote several interesting letters to Emma:

Victory, *off Toulon*,

August 1, 1803

[I do not know that you will get this letter]

My Dearest Emma,

Your letter of May 31 ... arrived by the Phoebe *two days ago; and this is the only scrap of a pen which has been received by any person in the fleet since we sailed from England.*

You will readily conceive, my dear Emma, the sensations which the sight and reading even your few lines [occasioned] *... Although you said little, I understood a great deal, and most heartily approve of your plan and society for next winter, and, next spring, I hope to be rich enough to begin the alterations at dear Merton. It will serve to amuse you; and, I am sure, that I shall admire all your alterations, even to planting a gooseberry bush ...*

Hardy is now busy, hanging up your and Horatia's picture ... I want no others to ornament my cabin. I can contemplate them, and find new beauties every day; and I do not want any body else ...

I have great fear, that all Naples will fall into the hands of the French and, if Acton does not take care, Sicily, also. However, I have given my final advice so fully and strongly that, let what will happen, they cannot blame me ...

The King is very much retired. He would not see the French General, St. Cyr, who came to Naples, <u>to settle the contribution for the payment of the French Army</u>.

The Queen was ordered to give him and the French minister a dinner, but the King staid at Belvidere. I think, he will give it up soon; and retire to Sicily, if the French will allow him.

The fleet are ready to come forth; but, they will not come for the sake of fighting me …

With kindest regards to your good mother, and all at Merton, &c.&c.&c., ever yours, most faithfully and affectionately,

Nelson & Bronte[17]

Victory, August 24th. 1803

My Dear Lady Hamilton,

Your friend's godson arrived safe yesterday afternoon; and I shall, you know, always feel too happy in obeying your commands; for, you never ask favours, but for your friends.

In short, in every point of view, from Ambassatrice to the duties of domestic life, I never saw your equal! That elegance of manners; accomplishments; and, above all, your goodness of heart, is unparalleled: and only believe, for ever, and beyond it, your faithful and devoted

Nelson & Bronte[18]

There are two letters written to Emma dated 26 August. The first letter mentions the new extension and other improvements being carried out at Merton:

August 26, 1803. Wrote several days past.

My dearest Emma,

By the Canopus, *Admiral Campbell, I have received all your truly kind and affectionate letters from May 20th.to July 3rd. (with the exception of one, dated May 31st. sent to Naples). This is the first communication I have had with England since we sailed, and all your letters, <u>my dear letters,</u> are so entertaining and which paint so clearly what you are after that they give me either the greatest pleasure or pain, it is the next best thing to being with you. I only desire my dearest Emma, that you will always believe that Nelson's your own, Nelson's <u>alpha</u> & <u>omega</u> is Emma. I cannot alter my affection & love is beyond even this world, nothing can shake it but yourself, and that I will not allow myself to think for a moment is possible. I feel that you are the real friend of my bosom & dearer to me than life and that I am the same to you …*

I rejoice that you have had so pleasant a trip into Norfolk and I hope one day to carry you there by a nearer tie in law, but not in love and affection than at present.

I wish you would never mention that person's name [Fanny?] it works up your anger for no useful purpose, her good or bad character of me or thee no one cares about. This letter will find you at dear Merton where we shall one day meet and be truly happy. I do not think it can be a long War and I believe it will be much shorter than people expect and I shall hope to find the new room built, the grounds laid out neatly, but not expensively, new Piccadilly Gates, Kitchen Garden &c. Only let us have a plan and then all will go on well. It will be a great source of amusement to you and H. shall plant a tree. I dare say she will be very busy. Mrs Nelson or Mrs Bolton &c. will be with you and the time will pass away till I have the inexpressible happiness of arriving at Merton, even the thoughts of it vibrate thro' my nerves for my love for you is as unbounded as the ocean.

I feel all your good mother's kindness and I trust that we shall turn rich by being ecconymists. Spending money to please a pack of people is folly and without thanks. I desire that you will say every kind thing from me to her and make her a present of something in my name ...

I believe Mr Bennett's bill to be correct but it was not intended you should pay that out of the allowance for Merton and how could you afford to send Mrs Bolton 100£ it is impossible out of your income. I wish Mr Addington would give you 500£ a year then you would be better able to give away than at present. But your purse my Dear Emma will always be empty. Your heart is generous beyond your means.

Your good mother is always sure of my sincerest regard, pray tell her so ...[19]

This letter confirms that the £100 per month that Nelson arranged to be paid to Emma was, indeed, 'the allowance for Merton'. Mr. Bennett's bill must have been for building works and therefore should be paid by Davison. Nelson appreciated Emma's gift of £100 to Susanna Bolton, but he was concerned she was being *'generous beyond her means'*.

The second letter on 26 August, a poorly disguised 'Mrs Thompson' letter, was initially published with many words blanked out. The missing words are included here in brackets:

My dearest beloved ...

To say that I think of you by day, night and all day and all night, but too faintly express my feelings of love and affection towards you [the first fruit of] unbounded affection. Our dear, excellent, good [Lady Hamilton] is the only one who knows anything of the matter and she has promised me, when you [are in the straw again] to take every possible care of you, as proof of her never-failing regard for your own dear Nelson. Believe me that I am incapable of wrongdoing you in thought, word or deed. No, not all the wealth of Peru could buy me for one moment: it is all yours and reserved wholly for you, and [you will] *certainly* [be with child] *certainly from the first moment of our happy, dear, enchanting blessed meeting.*

The thoughts of such happiness, my dearest only beloved, makes my blood fly into my head. The call of our Country is a duty which you deservedly in the cool moments of reflection, reprobate was I to abandon, and I should feel so disgraced by seeing you ashamed of me, no longer saying this is the man who is the first to go forth to fight our battles and the last to return, and then all these honors reflect on you. Ah, they will think What a man, What sacrifices has he not made to secure our homes & property's even the society & happy union with the finest and most accomplished woman in the World. As you love how must you feel. My heart is with you, cherish it. I shall, my best beloved return, if it pleases God, a Victor and it shall be my study to transmit an unsullied name. There is no desire of wealth no ambition that could keep me from all my soul holds dear. No it is to save my Country, my Wife in the Eye of God and my children. [...talk with the good Lady Hamilton and she] *will tell you that it is all right, and then only think of our happy meeting.*

Ever for Ever I am yours only even beyond this World.

> *Nelson & Bronte*

Augt. 26th. for Ever for Ever your own Nelson.[20]

On 6 September Nelson added a codicil to his will bequeathing £4,000 to Miss Horatia Nelson Thompson. He sent this to William Haslewood, his solicitor, with the words:

'Private for yourself – and most secret – I send you a Codicil to my Will which you will not communicate to any person breathing.'

In the codicil, Nelson named Lady Hamilton as Horatia's guardian: *'... Knowing she will educate my adopted child in the paths of religion and virtue, and give her accomplishments which so much adorn herself ...'*[21]

He wrote to tell Emma of his bequest:

'I have, my dearest Emma, done what I thank God I have had the power of doing – left £4000 to my dear Horatia, and desire that she may be acknowledged as my adopted daughter, and I have made you her sole guardian; the interest of the money to be paid to you until she is eighteen years of age. I trust, my dearest Friend, that you will (if it should please God to take me out of this world) execute this great charge for me and the dear little innocent, for it would add comforts to my last moments to think that she would be educated in the paths of religion, and receive as far as she is capable, some of those brilliant accomplishments which so much adorn you. You must

not allow your good heart to think that although I have left you this important charge I fancy myself nearer being knocked off by the French Admiral. I believe it will be quite the contrary, that God Almighty will again and again bless our just cause with victory.'22

Emma took this 'great charge' seriously, particularly after Nelson's death when Horatia was old enough to begin her education. Meanwhile Horatia remained with Mrs Gibson. A few extant notes of Emma's to Mrs Gibson indicate that Horatia was taken to Clarges Street and to Merton.

Romford, 40B, August 31, 1803

Dear Mrs Gibson,

I am sorry Miss Thompson has been ill. Pray write and say she continues better. Tell her I shall bring her many pretty things, and she must love her godmother. Write to me and tell me what she says. I hope to see you, Mary, [Mrs Gibson's daughter] *and her after this winter in Town. Ever believe me, yours sincerely, Kiss Horatia often for me. E.H.23*

October 3, 1805

My dear Mrs Gibson, Be so good to bring Miss Thompson on Saturday morning at eleven o'clock, as tomorrow I am engaged. Ever yours most affectionately. E.Hamilton.24

[No date]

Dear Mrs Gibson, I send you fifteen pounds. Give ten to the Doctor and pay yourself, and the other may serve for coach-hire. I am going for today into the country, but shall be glad to see you on Saturday at one o'clock. Ever yours affectionately. E.H.

Kiss my god-child for me.25

[No date]

Dear Mrs Gibson, Will you and Horatia be with me by eleven o'clock to go to Merton. We must defer Mary's visit until next week as the house is full of company. Come by half-past eleven in the morning. Ever yours E. Hamilton.26

On 18 September Emma received welcome news from Nelson: 'The *furniture and linen which was left behind at Palermo and Naples, when you came to England, is, I hope, by this time, safe at Malta. I have desired Mr Noble to unpack, dry them, and send you a list of the contents ... I believe the cases are eighteen in number ...'27*

Nelson was anxious to send Emma a gift 'in return for all your goodness to me and mine!' He sent to Naples for some 'shawls from the King's manufactory' and some 'fine Venetian chains'. Meanwhile, he added: 'I *send you, my dearest Emma, an hundred pounds, which you will dispose of* *as follows: – a <u>present</u> for yourself; and, if you like, a trifle to the servants; something to the poor of Merton; something for Mrs Cadogan, Miss Connor, Charlotte, &c.&c. I only send this as a trifling remembrance of me, whose whole soul is at Merton.'*[28]

One month later Nelson sent another long letter to Emma:

Victory, off Toulon, October 18th 1803

'My dearest Emma,

Your truly kind and affectionate letters, from July 17th to August 24th, all arrived safe …

Believe me, my beloved Emma, that I am truly sensible of all your love and affection, which is reciprocal. You have, from the variety of incidents passing before you, much to tell me; and, besides, you have that happy knack of making every thing you write interesting. Here I am, one day precisely like another; except the difference of a gale of wind, or not …'

Emma was desperate to be with him. She begged Nelson to let her join him at Malta or on board the *Victory* with Charlotte and Horatia. Nelson firmly, but kindly, rejected her desperate appeal:

'… You know, my dear Emma, that I am never well when it blows hard. Therefore, imagine what a cruise off Toulon is; even in summer time, we have a hard gale every week and two days heavy swell. It would kill you and myself to see you. Much less possible to have Charlotte, Horatia &c on board ship. And I that have given orders to carry no women to sea in the Victory to be the first to break them.

And, as to Malta, I may never see it, unless we have an engagement; and, perhaps, not then: for if it is <u>complete</u> I may go home, for three months, to see you: but if you was at Malta, I might absolutely miss you, by leaving the Mediterranean without warning …

Therefore, my dearest beloved Emma, although I should be the happiest of men, to live and die with you, yet my chance of seeing you is much more certain by your remaining at Merton, than wandering where I may never go …

You cannot, I am sure, more ardently long to see me, than I do to be with you; and, if the war goes on, it is my intention to get leave to spend the <u>next winter</u> in England: but I verily believe that, long before that time, we shall have peace …

I know, my own dear Emma, if she will let her reason have fair play, will say I am right; but she is, like Horatia, very angry if she cannot have her own way. Her Nelson is called upon, in the most honourable manner, to defend his country. Absence, to us, is equally painful but, If I had stayed at home, or neglected my duty abroad, would not my Emma have blushed for me? She could never have heard of my praises, and how the country looks up ...

If Mr Addington gives you a pension it is well; but do not let it fret you. Have you not Merton? It is clear – the first purchase [i.e. his mortgage paid]; *and my dear Horatia is provided for: and I hope, one of these days, that you will be my own Duchess of Bronte, and then a fig for them all ... I am glad to find, my dear Emma, that you mean to take Horatia home. Aye! She is like her mother; will have her own way, or kick up a devil of a dust. But you will cure her. I am afraid I should spoil her, for I am sure I would shoot any one who would hurt her ...'*

He continued with news of events in the Mediterranean:

'Naples, I fancy, is in a very bad way, in regard to money. They have not, or pretend not to have, enough to pay their officers; and, I verily believe, if Acton was to give up his place, that it would become a province of France ...'

Finances in Naples were in a deplorable state and Maria Carolina was unable to send money to Emma. His letter ends on a lighter note:

'You ask me, Do you do right to give Charlotte things? I shall only say, my dear Emma, whatever you do in that way, I shall always approve. I only wish I had more power than I have. But somehow my mind was not sharp enough for prize-money ...

I am, ever, for ever, my dearest Emma, your most faithful and affectionate
Nelson & Bronte[29]

Three days later, having told Emma that he wished Horatia *'to be acknowledged as my adopted daughter,'* Nelson wrote to Horatia informing her that he was her father:

MISS HORATIA NELSON THOMPSON

Victory, *off Toulon, October 21st. 1803*

My dear Child,

Receive this first letter from your most affectionate Father. If I live, it will be my pride to see you virtuously brought up; but if it pleases God to call me I trust to himself, in that case I have left dear Lady Hamilton your Guardian. I therefore charge you, my Child, on the value of a Father's blessing, to be obedient and attentive to her kind admonitions and instructions. At this moment I have left you a Codicil, dated 6th. of September 1803, the sum of four thousand pounds sterling, the interest of which is to be paid to Lady Emma Hamilton, your guardian, for your maintenance and education. I shall only say, my dear Child, my God almighty bless you, and make you an ornament to your sex, which I am sure you will be, if you attend to all dear

Lady Hamilton's kind instructions; and be assured that I am my dear Horatia, your most affectionate Father

Nelson & Bronte[30]

Faced with the possibility of being *'knocked off by a French Admiral'* Nelson decided to confirm that he was Horatia's father, without compromising Emma's position. The form of this letter suggests that he intended it to be taken as a legal document. This was the first of two important letters Nelson wrote to Horatia, both of which Emma carefully preserved.* Nelson's family came to accept that Horatia was his daughter and that Emma was her sole guardian.

Emma somehow managed to conceal her pregnancy while she led a social life in Clarges Street. On one occasion she called to see Elizabeth Vigée Le Brun, who wrote in her memoirs:

'She came round to see me, wearing deep mourning with a dense black veil surrounding her. She had her splendid hair cut off to follow the new 'Titus' fashion. I found this Andromache enormous, for she had become terribly fat. She said she was very much to be pitied, that in her husband she had lost a friend and father, and that she would never be consoled.'[31] Her critical comments about Emma being *'terribly fat'* coincided with the secret pregnancy.

The newspapers frequently reported the comings and goings at Clarges Street:

November 19: *'Yesterday the Duke of Queensberry paid a visit to Lady Hamilton in Clarges Street.'*

December 17: *'Mrs Billington and Lady Hamilton are become a <u>duo of musical inseperables</u> and his Grace of Queensberry is admitted about three times a day to make up <u>a terzatto con amore!</u>'*[32]

'Old Q', paid further visits on December 19 and 27.

Sir William, Emma and the Duke had socialized regularly ever since their return from Sicily. He was fond of Emma and demonstrated his generosity towards her a few years later. 'Old Q' was an inveterate flirt and many women, including Emma, wondered whether they would receive bequests from his large fortune on his death.

Emma issued a disclaimer to some of the newspaper reports. The *Morning Post* of 21 December published the following comment: *'We are desired to contradict a paragraph in one of the morning papers relative to Lady Hamilton giving concerts and parties. Her Ladyship lives very retired, and she has been and still continues very unwell, and does not see any company, but a very few near relatives.'*[33]

* See Appendix 3

Nelson's letter to Emma on 7 December includes particularly significant points about his health, his love for Horatia, Emma's pension and his increasing blindness:

'... *I have but one object in mind ... to find the French fleet and to beat them soundly and then all the reward I shall ask is to be allowed to come to England, for this constant wearing of the mind must shake any constitution, but some happy day I doubt not I shall be amply paid ...* [Emma had sent him a watch chain from Horatia] *The watch string came in the right time for the other was very rotten and as it comes from Ha, it is of more value to me than if it was covered with diamonds. She must be grown very much, how I long to hear her prattle. Heavens bless her ... If Mr Addington ever means to give you the pension it is done before this time, if he does not never mind; you have a good house and land at Merton which he cannot take from you, and I do not believe the French will, for although I Hear of their blustering at Boulounge and of Buonapartes being there parading, I can never believe that they can succeed beyond getting a few thousands on Shore to be massacred ...*

Decr 13th. although I have not been ill yet the constant anxiety I have experienced have shook my weak frame and my rings will hardly keep upon my finger, and what grieves me more than all this is that I can perceive a visible (if I may be allowed the expression) loss of sight. A few years must as I have always predicted render me blind; I have often heard that Blind people are cheerful but I think I shall take it to heart, however if I am so fortunate as to gain a great Victory over the Enemy the only favor I shall ask will be for permission to retire, and if the contrary I sincerely pray that I may never live to see it. We must all have an end, but my dearest Emma let us hope the best, my last thoughts will be for you and those we hold most dear but I will have done with this triste subject ...'[34]

The Boltons and Charlotte were at Clarges Street for Christmas. When they left early in January, Horace arrived from Canterbury. Emma wrote to Sarah in January 1804:

'*I have been ill my dearest friend these 8 days, abed with soar Throat, Cold, Cough, but I am better now thank God & the sight of Horace has done me good. The Boltons went yesterday morning. Horace, dear boy, arrived safe at eleven yesterday morning ... Charlotte is taking her dancing lesson, I have one of the best mistresses for her I ever saw – Madamoiselle du Croix...*

I have had more letters from our dear Nelson by the Lisbon mails ... He is all that is tender, good & kind ... I wish you had come, for the idea is took that we shall be invaded, & you must not feel very comfortable, & I, that know your nerves & thoughts of alarm, I feel for you much ... Lady

Aldborough, Lady Elisabeth Halliday & Lady Emily come often to me, so does Lady Stafford, Lady [illegible] *etc.etc.etc., but I live very very retired ...*

My Lord has sent me home my 19 packing-cases from Malta, all safe. He thinks me beautifull allso. God, only spare him, for my existence hangs by his!'[35]

Emma was providing dancing, singing and piano lessons for Charlotte. She happily informed Sarah: *'I never quit her for a moment, my whole time is given up, with pleasure, to this lovely girl.'*

Rumours circulating of a renewed possibility of an invasion by French forces prompted Emma to invite Sarah to London.

In January 1804, Nelson heard that Davison had at long last received his share of the prize money from his lawsuit against St. Vincent. The previous November the Court of the King's Bench had ruled that he was *'entitled to the whole of the Admiral's share of the Prize Money'* for the Battle of the Nile. St. Vincent had been awarded £13,000.[36]

On 13 January he wrote to Davison:

'My dear Davison,

... as I do not hardly know where to begin thanking you, it's almost as well to say nothing. But your kindness to my dear, good Lady Hamilton, is what I shall never forget ... I am sure you felt all which the sincerest friendship could do, that justice had triumphed. This event will put me out of debt, and, I hope build my room at Merton, and leave my income whatever it may be, unclogged ...'[37]

The same day he wrote to Emma concerning his plans for Merton:

Victory, under Majorca,

January 13 th.1804

My own dear beloved Emma,

... I am truly sensible of all your kindness and affectionate regard for me; which, I am sure, is reciprocal, in every respect, from your own Nelson ...

Indeed, if I can help it, I never intend to go out of the ship, but to the shore of Portsmouth; and that will be, if it pleases God, before next Christmas. Indeed I think, long before, if the French will venture to sea.

I send you a letter from the Queen of Naples. They call out, might and main, for our protection; and, God knows, they are sure of me ...

You may safely rely, that I can for ever repeat, with truth, these words – for ever I love you, and only you, my Emma; and, you may be assured, as long as you are the same to me, that you are never absent a moment from my thoughts.

I am glad you are going to Merton; you will live much more comfortable, and much cheaper, than in London: and this spring, if you like to have the house altered, you can do it. But, I fancy, you will soon tire of so much dirt, and the inconvenience will be very great the whole summer.

All I request, if you fix to have it done, that Mr Davison's architect, who drew the plan, may have the inspection; and, he must take care that it does not exceed the estimate ...[38]

Now he had the money to finance the alterations at Merton he suggested Emma could begin the work *'this spring'*, thinking perhaps she would need time to recover after the birth of the new baby.

Emma's busy first three weeks in January were followed by a period of withdrawal from society and letter-writing. Worried, Kitty wrote to her on 31 January, having had no news for some time. Susanna wrote on 3 February asking for news and Kitty wrote a second time a week later, hoping *'illness has not been the occasion of your long silence'*.[39]

Emma probably gave birth during this time. It would tie in because the baby was almost certainly conceived in April 1803.

Nelson had suggested the name Emma. His letter to Emma on 2 April confirms that the baby girl had not survived:

'I have, my dearest beloved Emma, been so uneasy for this last month, desiring most ardently to hear of your well being. Captain Capel brought me your letters sent by the Thisbe from Gibraltar. I opened – opened – found none but December or early in January. I was in such an agitation. At last I found one without a date – which, thank God, told my poor heart that you was recovering but that dear little Emma was no more and that Horatia had been so very ill – it quite upset me. But it was just at bed-time and I had time to reflect, and be thankful to God sparing you and our dear Horatia. I am sure the loss of one – much more both – would have drove [me] mad. I was so agitated as it was, that I was glad it was night and that I could be by myself. Kiss dear Horatia for me and tell her to be a dutiful and good child, and if she is, that we shall always love her ...'[40]

Emma could not give Nelson any details and merely told him that she had recovered. Infant mortality was so common at the time that parents accepted their loss with resignation. Emma had, in fact, been ill for three weeks as she told Sarah in April:

'I have got such a quantity of letters, my dear friend, from my adored Nelson up to the 21st. of January. He is, if it is possible, more kind, more tender than ever ... He has never been out of the Victory, nor does he wish it till he comes home for good. He says he lives and exists only with the fond idea of being happy once again with us. He says I am his Alpha and Omega, the first

thought in the morning and last at night. What exquisite pleasure to be so beloved by so great, so good, so glorious and virtuous a man! I absolutely adore and idolize him ... I have not been out these 3 weeks, so very ill I have been ... I am so agitated I do not know how to write today. I have received such a beautiful watch, and he has sent me a comb and some other things. How good he is to think on every little attention ...'[41]

Perhaps Emma, now nearly thirty-nine years old, had suffered complications during the birth, resulting in the death of the baby and her own ill-health. However, she now had the prospect of over-seeing the alterations to Nelson's house at Merton to distract her.

In his letter on 13 January Nelson had given her the go-ahead for major works at Merton, according to plans already agreed. He warned that Thomas Chawner, *'Davison's architect'*, must take care not to exceed the estimate. His comment that *'the inconvenience will be very great the whole summer'* confirms he was aware of the extent of the alterations. Emma, alone, had not designed the extravagant plans.

Nelson sent further detailed instructions to her on 14 March:

I would not have you lay out more than is necessary at Merton. The rooms, and the new entrance, will take a good deal of money. The entrance by the corner I would certainly have done; a common white gate will do for the present; and one of the cottages, which is in the barn, can be put up as a temporary lodge. The road can be made to a temporary bridge, for that part of the Nile, one day, shall be filled up.

Downing's canvas awning will do for a passage. For the winter, the carriage can be put in the barn; and, giving up Mr Bennett's premises, will save fifty pounds a year: and, another year, we can fit up the coach-house and stables which are in the barn ...

I also beg, as my dear Horatia is to be at Merton, that a strong netting, about three feet high, may be placed round the Nile, that the little thing may not tumble in; and, then, you may have ducks again in it ... I shall be very anxious until I know this is done ...

The expenses of the alterations at Merton you are not to pay from the income. Let it all be put into a separate account, and I will provide a fund for the payment.

All I long for just now, is to hear that you are perfectly recovered; and, then, I care for nothing: all my hopes are, to see you, and be happy, at dear Merton again ...

Ever, my dearest Emma, for ever, I am your most faithful and affectionate
Nelson & Bronte[42]

Overseeing these works was a considerable responsibility for Emma. In the plans drawn up by Thomas Chawner the *'rooms and new entrance'* on the east front of the building were a major two-storey extension which added new rooms and joined together the two sections of the original house. Nelson emphatically decreed that Emma was not to pay for any of this building work. In June he repeated this instruction: *'... I have wrote to Davison to pay every bill relating to the alterations at Merton and that nothing is to be touched on that business from the 100£ a month ...'*[43]

Chawner would have control of the building works and Emma would be in charge of Thomas Cribb, the gardener, and the garden improvements. Emma and Chawner were to be supervised by Davison, who was paying the bills.

Nelson's manager at Bronte, Graeffer, had died in 1802 having achieved little success in his management of the estate. He had spent all of the three years' income on *'fitting up'* a house for himself and his family. There were other debts and Mrs Graeffer was demanding a pension of £200 p.a.

Nelson applied to his banker friend from Palermo, Mr Gibbs, for an assessment of the Bronte situation, but was reluctant to take his initial advice to sell the estate. Gibbs estimated that in three years time the income would be £3,000 p.a. Nelson had laid out money on the estate, but in September, he wrote to the banker, Noble: *'I have never received one farthing from the estate.'*[44]

Nelson had told Emma on 14 March: *'Whilst I am upon the subject of Bronte, I have one word more – and your, dear, kind heart, must not think I shall die one hour the sooner; on the contrary, my mind has been more content ever since I have done: I have left you a part of the rental of Bronte, to be first paid every half year, and in advance. It is but common justice; and, whether Mr Addington gives you any thing or not, you will want it.'*[45]

This bequest of income from the Bronte estate became a contentious issue between Emma and the Reverend Doctor William. Emma received very little of the money bequeathed to her from the estate.

Over the following year Emma and Nelson continued to spend generous amounts of money, both at Merton and in helping their relations. From the *Victory* Nelson later commented to Davison: *'God knows, in my own person, I spend as little money as any man; but you know I love to give away.'*[46]

They were both guilty of '*giving away*' more than they could afford. Emma lavished care and attention on the fifteen-year-old Charlotte, who lived with her, aiming to introduce her into society where she would likely 'make a good match'. Charlotte wrote enthusiastically to her mother: '*My Lady is so kind as to make me acquainted with the first persons, and she is so kind as to make me her everything, which makes me very happy.*'[47]

After Hamilton's death and with Nelson away at sea, Emma became more accepted by society. She informed Charlotte's parents: '*... I have been invited to every party about Town so has Charlotte. We went to the Ladies Concert and to the most Chosen Places to shew we <u>could do so</u>, and your good sense will approve I am sure. Charlotte is so much admired and justly so I think – the Duchess of Devonshire was so civil to Charlotte and told her she wou'd invite her to all her Balls the Walpoles were there every body came up and spoke to me and made so much of us.*'[48]

Emma's generosity towards the Boltons continued, prompting Susanna to write:

'*But indeed I do not like to receive so many presents. Nothing can make me love you better, but so many handsome things as you do for me and mine make me feel uncomfortable. Be assured I have now everything I want, and do not send me more ...*'[49]

Eliza Bolton visited Clarges Street and, with Charlotte, accompanied Emma on holiday to Margate. Emma sent presents to the Bolton girls, enclosing on one occasion two £10 notes to pay for the accounts she had incurred while staying with them. Payments she made to Sarah of £40 in September 1804 and £50 in October 1805 are likely to be for the extra costs incurred by her visits.

In May Emma and Nelson were distressed when Davison was sentenced to a year's imprisonment in the Marshalsea prison in Southwark. He had been tried and convicted of electoral fraud at the elections for two Members of Parliament at Ilchester in Somerset. At the time, Nelson wrote to him: '*I hope in God, my dear Davison, that you will get over these damned prosecutions for the Election. It has, and does, give me very serious uneasiness.*'[50]

Davison's appeal against his sentence failed and he had to serve his term. As wealthier prisoners were allowed to pay for better accommodation, Davison had his own rooms in King's Bench Terrace where he was able to receive visitors. Emma wrote to him: '*I waited all day yesterday my dear Sir for permission to come to you as I was told it would be inconvenient to you having paperers and carpenters with you tell me are you comfortable and when can I see you ...'*[51] She sent Davison cases of honey and maraschino cherries.

When Nelson heard the news, he wrote to Davison immediately: '*By dear Lady H's letter of May 13th. received last night, I received the distressing intelligence of your sentence, at least the confinement but I fear you have likewise a fine to pay ... It has been long hanging over you and the day was sure to arrive. Now the time is passing away and before you receive this letter one quarter of a year will be over, and by the kind attention of your friends time will not hang heavy and even I intend to dine with you in the Xmas holidays ... But joking apart I curse from my heart those who did you such an ill natured turn ...'*[52]

In his letter of 27 June he told Emma: '*I am not surprised at the time poor Davison is to be confined after what passed in Parliament I did not expect so little and I fear he has a heavy fine to pay besides, he would only consult Lord Moira and such clever folks, but an ignoramus like me could only warn him not to touch Boroughs. He has poor fellow been completely duped and who cares not one of these great folks. I most sincerely am sorry for him but a year will soon pass away. Have I not been shut up in a ship without any one comfort he is ashore with his friends round him and even you to go to see him. I would change with him with much pleasure ...'*[53]

In the following months Emma was obliged to appeal to Davison for financial aid, that he duly gave on Nelson's behalf. Acting as Nelson's prize agent and treasurer, he had agreed to let Nelson run up a debt to him. He could afford this service, having amassed a large fortune supplying the government with stores and clothing for the Army and the Navy. He had his own clothing factory and warehouses from which he supplied the barrack office with anything from coal to hay.

If Nelson's £100 per month to Emma was intended to cover costs at Merton it proved to be insufficient. In Nelson's accounts his bills for food alone averaged £65 per week. On his departure the expense of entertaining of his family and friends was reduced, but the costs for the servants were still paid in his absence. These included Mr Cribb, the head gardener, his assistant Hudson, Marianna, an Italian cook, Dame Francis, the housekeeper and Mrs Cummings, the washerwoman. Other servants at various times were Mr White, Francastello, Julia, a second Italian maid, and Emma's Fatima.[54]

There was the additional expense of keeping Horatia with Mrs Gibson. Emma received a note from her:

Tuesday November 7th. 1804

Mrs Gibson's duty to Lady Hamilton, and am happy to inform her Ladyship that Miss Thompson is very well, and desires her love & a kiss to her Ladyship and to her God-papa. I have sent the receipt, and there now remains due up to Novr 5th. 24 pounds two shillings. Your most humble etc.

Receipt

Novr 5th. 1804

RECEIVED of Lady Hamilton the sum of thirty pounds, for lodging and attendance on Miss Thompson. (signed Mary Gibson)[55]

Emma owed Mrs Gibson £54.2s.0d. of which she had only paid £30. The period covered by this bill is not mentioned, but Mrs Gibson would surely not have been able to continue for too long without being paid. Whether Davison reimbursed Emma for these payments is unknown.

Nelson pressed Emma to take Horatia to live with her at Merton, even though he must have realized that the presence a three-year-old child would be difficult to explain. Horatia remained with Mrs Gibson until August 1805.

Emma and Davison developed a mutually affectionate relationship, but a disagreement arose over her proposals for the garden at Merton. He believed her ideas would cost more than Nelson intended. Emma responded to Davison's concerns: *'We do not want a Capability Brown for we refused one that Mr Greville recommended – we have spent little money considering what has been done ... Cribb and myself are the planners and gardners and if you will allow him eight men for 3 months he will be content.'*[56]

Emma and Cribb succeeded in creating a *'beautiful Shrubbery and Walks stocked with Timber and other Trees and Plants of considerable value'.* Apart from the 'Nile' and its bridge, the most notable feature was a walk known as 'Nelson's Quarterdeck' that led to a classical style white pavilion situated on top of a mound, christened 'The Poop'.

Nelson raised hopes of his return on 27 June: *'I shall if it pleases God eat my Christmas dinner at Merton. My health absolutely requires a few months rest even if my services are required again. May God in heaven bless and preserve you my dear Emma ... The French fleet are safe in Toulon. I wish from my heart they were out.'*[57]

In June Emma took Charlotte and Mrs Billington to Canterbury where she and Mrs Billington added their fine voices to the singing of hymns in the Cathedral and Dr Nelson gave a dinner party in their honour. Emma went on to Ramsgate where Horatia joined her.

A worried Nelson wrote on 31 August: '*I am very uneasy at your and Horatia being on the Coast; for you cannot move if the French make the attempt, which, I am told, they have done and been repulsed. Pray God it may be true.*'[58]

Napoleon was elected Emperor on 18 May. Nelson told Emma on 6 June: '*... Nothing new has happened except our hearing the feu-de-joie at Toulon for the declaration of the Emperor. What a capricious Nation those French must be.*'[59]

In July and August the new Emperor was in the area of Boulogne, Dunkirk and Ostende, but he departed Boulogne on 21 August.

On 15 July Emma wrote to Davison: '*I adore Nelson and my only pleasure is thinking on him and his dear return – May God only send him home safe to his Emma. What a sad thing it is to think such a man as him should be entrapped with such an infamous woman as that apoticary's widow ... A woman who has done all she can to ruin, vex and blast his upright Character. Whilst I am free – with talents that he likes, adoring him, that never a woman adored a man as I do my Nelson, loving him beyond all this world, and yet we are both miserable ... <u>patience</u>. God bless you, I shall be most obliged to you to send me a Hundred pounds as I have left all I had with my mother for Merton.*'[60]

Both Emma and Nelson believed Fanny had been spreading derogatory stories about them. Emma set off on 22 July to stay with the Boltons at Cranwich for three weeks. She was kind and generous towards the Bolton children, particularly to Anne, who was a delicate child. Back in London Emma wrote to Davison: '*My jaunt to Norfolk cost me more than that I intended*'. He obliged by giving her some more of Nelson's money. Next, she was off to Cranwich to celebrate Nelson's birthday – '*Now will you do me the favour to send us two bottles of Champagne by the coach to Cranwich, you will make us very happy.*' Once more Davison obliged. He received a letter from Nelson written on 9 August: '*If the new building is finished I shall have a very comfortable house ... I would not have one farthing taken from the hundred pounds a month for any of these improvements; and, as I before wrote to you, I wish to have them in a separate account, that I may know the cost.*'[61] Emma wrote to Davison from Cranwich where she had received a large bundle of Nelson's letters: ' *The <u>thought</u> of seeing him again agitates me and makes me mad with joy, then fear comes across me that he will not come – in short, I am, what with the different feelings that elate and oppress me, not well ... Your Champagne was most excellent and we drank our Hero's Health and yours ...*'[62]

On his birthday Nelson wrote to Emma:

Victory, *September 29th. 1804*

This day, my dearest Emma, which gave me birth I consider as more fortunate than common days as, by my coming into this world, it has brought me so intimately acquainted with you, who my soul holds most dear. I well know you will keep it and have my dear Horatia to my drink my health. Forty six years of toil and trouble! ... by this time, I should think, either my successor has been named or permission is granted me to come home, if so, you will not long receive this letter before I make my appearance, which will make us, I am sure, both truly happy ...[63]

There can be no doubt that Emma was deeply in love with Nelson. When it appeared he might be coming home on leave in October she confessed her love to Davison: '*I am anxious and agitated to see him I never shall be well till I do see him ... I love him, I adore him, my mind and soul is now transported with the thoughts of that blessed ecstatic moment when I shall see him, embrace him. My love is no common love. It may be a sin to love I say it might have been a sin when I was <u>anothers</u> but I had then more merit in trying to suppress it. I am <u>now free</u> and I must sin on and love him more than ever. It is a crime worth going to Hell for.*'[64]

In October Emma wrote again to Davison: '*He is <u>very very</u> anxious to come and I am anxious and agitated to see him. The disappointment would kill me ... For should I not be an ungrateful unfeeling wretch not to pay two fold with love the man that so idolizes me, that adores me. May God only spare Him and send Him safe back. I shall be at Merton till I see Him as He <u>particularly</u> wishes our first meeting should be there ...*'[65]

By November, hopes of Christmas at Merton fading, Nelson wrote:

Victory, *November 23 rd. 1804*

'*... Where is my successor? I am not a little surprised at his not coming. A Spanish War, I thought, would have hastened him ... if they refuse me now, I shall most certainly leave this Country in March or April, for a few months' rest I must have very soon ... my cough is very bad, and my side, where I was struck on the 14th.* February [at the Battle of Cape St. Vincent] *is very much swelled; at times a lump as large as my fist, brought on occasionally by violent coughing, but I hope and believe my lungs are yet safe ...*'[66]

For all Nelson's hopes and assurances that he would soon be home on leave, it was not to be. English frigates captured Spanish treasure ships off Ferrol on the northern coast of Spain.* On 12 December,

---

*To Nelson's distress, this area was deemed to be under the command of Sir John Orde who received a fortune in prize money.

Spain declared war on Britain. There was no possibility of Nelson being granted leave.

Bitterly disappointed, Emma invited all Nelson's relations to Merton for Christmas. The Boltons arrived, William and Sarah remained at Canterbury, but sent Horace to join his sister at Merton. Kitty decided that they would stay in Bath as her family was too large to all descend on Merton.

Nelson and Emma did not meet again for a further eight months.

CHAPTER 20

Twenty-Five Days at Dear, Dear Merton and the Battle of Trafalgar

'I love and revere you beyond this world, as I feel you deserve it of me'
Nelson to Emma, 30 March 1805

'One fortnight of joy and happiness I have had for years of pain'
Emma to Lady Bolton, 6 September 1805

'May God send you victory and home to your Emma,
Horatia and paradise Merton'
Emma to Nelson, 8 October 1805

' I really do feel that the 25 days I was at Merton
was the happiest of my life'
Nelson to Emma, 11 October 1805

THE FATEFUL YEAR of 1805 began with Britain's declaration of war on France on 11 January. Nelson's task in the Mediterranean assumed a greater urgency. After twenty months at sea, tired and ill though he was, he continued his search for the French fleet. Leaving Villeneuve and his squadron under careful observation in Toulon harbour, Nelson scoured the Mediterranean for other French ships.

Emma, along with the entire nation, waited anxiously for news from him. Ever since the previous August when Napoleon was reported to be at Boulogne, an invasion by French forces had been anticipated.

On 6 January Emma received a letter from Davison written from the Marshalsea where Lord Melville had paid him a visit:* *'I had a conversation about yourself, and am sure it will afford you great satisfaction to know how much Lord Melville interests himself in your favour. He tells me*

---

* Viscount Melville was briefly the First Lord of the Admiralty between 1804-1805, and very close to William Pitt, Prime Minister 1804-1806. Neither were successful in obtaining a pension for her.

339

he has spoken to Mr Pitt of the propriety of your having a pension settled on you of £500 per annum, and that he will speak to him again very shortly about it. I asked Lord Melville if I might say as much to you. He immediately said, 'Yes, certainly'. He spoke very handsomely of you, and of your services in favor of this country when in Naples ...'[1]

Emma replied from Clarges Street on 26 January: 'I have been very ill, my Dear Sir, and am in bed with a cold, very bad cold indeed! But the moment I am better, I will call on you. I am invited to dine with Mr Haslewood to-morrow but fear I shall not be able to go ... God bless you! Remember, you will soon be free; and let that cheer you, that you will come out with even more friends than ever. I can only say, I am your ever obliged, and grateful

Emma Hamilton[2]

Emma later wrote to Davison telling him she had heard from Nelson and describing her abject sense of loss: *'I got a letter from my ever dear beloved Nelson last night dated JanY 29 going Thro the Faro of Messina with a brisk wind. He says he is after the French fleet that I shall I couse to glory in Him What ever may be the event & that I am all to Him in this world and God almighty Knows He is all to me I can think of only Him I Live only by His letters in his absence God spare him to us. I have been so low spirited these several days that I know not what to do ...God bless you ever your affectionate*

Emma Hamilton[3]

This may have been Nelson's last letter for some time as his letter of 9 March explains the recent loss of his dispatches and letters:

'I do assure you, My Dearest Emma, that nothing can be more miserable, or unhappy, than your poor Nelson. From the 19th. February we have been beating from Malta to off Palma, where I am now anchored, the wind and sea being so very contrary and bad ... yesterday Captain Layman arrived – to my great surprise – not in his brig, but in a Spanish cartel, he having been wrecked off Cadiz, and lost all the dispatches and letters. You will conceive my disappointment! It is now from November 2d that I have had a line from England. Captain Layman says – he is sure the letters are sunk, never to rise again, but, as they were not thrown overboard until the vessel struck the rock, I have much fear that they may have fallen into the hands of the Dons.

My reports from off Toulon, state the French Fleet as still in Port; but I shall ever be uneasy at not having fallen in with them. I know, my dear Emma, that it is in vain to repine, but my feelings are alive to meeting those fellows, after near two years' hard service. What a time! I could not have thought it possible that I should have been so long absent; unwell, and uncomfortable, in many respects.

However, when I calculate upon the French Fleet's not coming to sea for this summer, I shall certainly go for dear England and a Thousand [times] *dearer Merton. May Heavens bless you, my own Emma!*

I send you a trifle, for a birth-day's gift. I would to God, I could give you more but, I have it not! I get no prize-money worth naming; but if I have the good fortune to meet the French Fleet, I hope they will make amends for all my anxiety, which has been, and is, indescribable.

How is my dear Horatia? I hope you have her under your guardian wing at Merton. May God bless her! ...'[4]

During this time of *'indescribable anxiety'*, Emma, Horatia and Merton were never far from his thoughts:

13 March 1805:

'... You are ever uppermost in my thoughts day or night Calm or full of wind You are never absent from my thoughts ...'

'... remember me to Mrs Cadogan. I am truly sensible of her worth and attention to our interest at Merton ... You cannot imagine how I long to see it but I fear the Kitchen will smell. If so I shall build one separate from the House and make the present one a Servants Hall ...'[5]

16 March:

'The Ship is just parting and I take the last moment to renew my assurances to my Dearest Beloved Emma of my eternal love, affection and adoration. You are ever with me in my Soul, your resemblance is never absent from my mind, and my own dearest Emma I hope very soon that I shall embrace the substantial part of you instead of the Ideal, that will I am sure give us both <u>real pleasure</u> *and* <u>exquisite happiness</u>. *Longing as I do to be with you, yet I am sure under the circumstances in which I am placed you would be the first to say – May Nelson try and get at those french fellows and come with Glory to your own Emma ... Only continue to love me as affectionately as I do you, and we must then be the happiest couple in the world. May God bless you ever prays yours and only your faithful*

Nelson & Bronte[6]

30 March:

'You are sure, my Emma, that I am as anxious to see you as you can be to see me for I love and revere you beyond all this world, because I feel you deserve it of me. Therefore I will say no more upon that subject but shall wait to give you much more efficatious proofs of my love than can be convey'd in a letter. I admire dear Horatia's writing. I think her hand will soon be like her dear Mother's, and if she is but as clever, I shall be content ...'[7]

1 April:

'I am not surprised that we should both think the same about the kitchen; and, if I can afford it, I should like it to be done; but ... we must take care not to get into debt; for then we can neither help any of our relations, and [must] be forever in misery. But of this we [will] talk more, when we walk upon the poop at Merton ...'[8]

4 April:

'... I dare not send a little letter, for what with smoking and cutting all would be read. But let them read this, that I love you beyond any Woman in this World and next our dear Ha. How I long to settle what I intend upon Her and not to leave her to the mercy of any one or even to any foolish thing I may do in my old age ... You will ever glory in your Nelson whether living or dead. I could not exist long in this dreadful suspense, but I am doing what man can do to find them out ...'[9]

In a letter to Davison on 9 March, Nelson concluded: *'... I am sensible of your goodness in paying all my bills for the improvements at Merton, which I will, if I live, or have as much property, repay with many thanks. But I fancy dear Lady Hamilton wants some money to furnish the new part. She will not be extravagant; therefore, if you will let her have the money for it, I shall feel much obliged ...'*[10]

Cruising off Sardinia on 18 April Nelson was informed that the French fleet had left Toulon and were heading for Gibraltar. Nelson had not blockaded Toulon, a tactic he explained in a letter to the Lord Mayor of the city: *'I beg to inform your Lordship, that the port of Toulon has never been blockaded by me, quite the reverse. Every opportunity has been offered the Enemy to put to sea, for it is there we hope to realise the hopes and expectations of our Country, and I trust that they will not be disappointed.'*[11]

A frantic Nelson hastened to catch up with the French fleet, writing despairingly to Ball, in Malta, on 19 April: *'My good fortune seems flown away. I cannot get a fair wind; or even a side wind. Dead foul! – dead foul! But my mind is fully made up what to do when I leave the straights ... I believe this ill luck will go near to kill me; but these are times for exertions, I must not be cast down, whatever I feel ...'*[12]

Poor winds prevented Nelson from reaching Gibraltar until 3 May. He wrote to Emma on 4 May from Tetuan Bay, Morocco, where he was taking on supplies: *'Your poor dear Nelson is, my dearest beloved Emma, very very unwell, after a two years hard fag it has been mortifying the not being able to get at the Enemy. As yet I can get no information about them ... it is now generally believed that they are gone to the West ... You, my own*

Emma, are my first and last thoughts, and to the last moment of my breath they will be occupied in leaving you independent of the World, and all I beg in this World is that you will be a kind and affectionate <u>Father</u> to my <u>dear Daughter Horatia</u>.'[13]

Nelson's personal steward on board the *Victory*, William Chevalier, wrote to Davison (who had recommended him to Nelson): *'... considering the hardships his Lordship undergoes his health is better than could be expected ... in all the bad weather both Night and day that good Man was upon Deck, maimed as he is, sometimes half naked under such heavy rains ...'*[14]

No wonder Nelson regularly complained about his ill-health and exhaustion.

On 9 May, off Cape St. Vincent, Nelson informed Emma: *'My dearest Emma, I think myself a little better, but I can neither drink porter nor eat cheese and that is enough to satisfy me that I am far from well ... My Emma you are everything to me and I love you if possible more than ever. I send you a Bill for £300, £200 of which is for yourself and the other £100 make in little presents from me to those about you.'*[15]

On 11 May, anchored in Lagos Bay, he established that the French fleet was heading for the West Indies. He chased Villeneuve across the Atlantic and by 4 June he and his fleet of eleven ships of the line were anchored in Carlisle Bay, Barbados.

Having been given erroneous information about the whereabouts of Villeneuve's fleet, he missed the chance of bringing the French fleet to battle. After only nine days in the West Indies Nelson hurriedly left Antigua in pursuit of Villeneuve, whom he correctly believed had sailed for Europe.

Although frustrated at not finding Villeneuve's fleet, Nelson considered he had achieved an important goal by following him to the West Indies. He told Emma: *'... However mortified I may individually feel at not fighting them, yet my happy arrival has saved all our West India islands and commerce.'*[16]

Arriving back in Gibraltar on 19 July, Nelson stepped ashore the following day. He noted in his diary: *'I went on Shore for the first time since 16th. of June 1803; and from having my foot out of the Victory, two years, wanting ten days.'*[17] He had kept his promise to Emma to remain faithful to her.

On 22 July, in desperate need of provisions and water, he sailed to Tetuan, where he remained at anchor until 24 July. Ironically, it was during these few days that Sir Robert Calder encountered Villeneuve's returning fleet, making for northern Spain, on 22 July.

Calder took only two enemy ships before fog and nightfall prevented further action. The following day, outnumbered by Villeneuve's fleet, he failed to renew the battle.* Villeneuve withdrew first to Vigo, then to the safety of Ferrol.

The extent of the combined British Channel and Mediterranean fleets under the command of Admiral Cornwallis gave Nelson the opportunity to ask the Admiral for leave. With Cornwallis' permission to take the *Victory* and the *Superb* to Portsmouth, Nelson sailed for England on 25 July.

During the first half of 1805, while Nelson was away, Emma divided her time between Clarges Street and Merton, where her mother was managing the estate. She visited the Boltons at Cranwich, the Reverend Doctor and Sarah at Canterbury, and took holidays at Margate and Southend. Her relationship with Nelson's family was now close and affectionate. Their children spent a great deal of time with Emma, who took pleasure in educating and spoiling them. Both Eliza and Anne Bolton had music lessons with Emma and Mrs Billington at Merton.[18] Susanna had written the previous year: '... *I think I have lost both my daughters, for I hear nothing from them ... You, my dear friend, are too good to them: I hope they are fully sensible of your kindness ...*'[19]

The Nelson family's antipathy towards Fanny was well established by 1804. Kitty wrote to Emma from London: '*My only desire is that we shall not be in the same room and circumstances are now so well understood by our friends that I don't think it likely we shall ever meet her.*'[20]

And later from Bath: '*We were in the same room with Lady N. a few nights since for the first time since she came to Bath. She had then an opportunity of showing her insolence as far as looks could express; so I was told by some friends of mine, she looked as I passed her in that scornful way which could not but be noticed by all that saw her ...*'[21]

Later Lady Bolton added further disparaging remarks from Bath:† Emma was ill during February but was cheered by Nelson's letters from the Mediterranean. She describes her social life at this time in

---

* Calder suffered severe criticism from the government and the nation for his failure to destroy the French fleet when he had the opportunity. Calder demanded a court martial to clear his name.
† Lady Bolton, Susanna's daughter, Catherine, who married her cousin Sir William Bolton. He had been knighted when he stood proxy for Nelson at his Installation of the Knight of the Bath.

a letter to Sarah dated 20 February: *'Depend on this, we shall see our dear Nelson soon and with Glory, fresh glory. Charlotte was at Lady Abercorn's assembly on Monday night after our return from Merton where we had been since Saturday. Tomorrow we go to a great dinner at Lord and Lady Carlton's to meet the Essex's. Friday a small party at Miss Paynes, Lord Levington's sister. Saturday and Sunday, Merton, for we have refused all engagements for those days ... Mrs Matcham is on the point of being confined – how she laughs out her children. Merton is more beautiful, so improved you would not know it again. My Mother has been very ill with an inflammation on her lungs, but she is better ...'[22]*

Lady Bolton wrote to Emma: 'Mr Matcham tells us Merton looked very beautiful. He thought you had made wonderful improvements. I cannot help thinking how delighted Lord Nelson will be with it.'[23]

Emma had overseen substantial improvements at Merton, but there was still much to do to prepare the house for Nelson's return.

On 7 May Nelson wrote to thank Davison: '*... the business of Merton still will call for your kind and friendly attention. The Kitchen I hope will be built before this letter reaches you, and I must trouble you, my friend, to pay the bills; but I hope soon to repay you with many, many kind thanks ...'[24]*

A week later, Nelson congratulated him on his return to his home in St. James' Square.

Nelson now made an important decision. He decided to remove Horatia from Mrs Gibson's care, but was concerned that Mrs Gibson might cause trouble over this. Horatia had lived with Mrs Gibson's family since her birth in January 1801. Nelson wrote to his solicitor, Mr Haslewood:

Victory, May 16th 1805

'It is my desire that Mrs Gibson is given an annuity of twenty pounds a-year, when that she gives up my adopted daughter, Horatia Nelson Thompson, to the guardianship of my dear friend, Lady Emma Hamilton, and promises not to have anything more to do with the child, either directly or indirectly; and I leave my estate chargeable with this annuity.

Nelson & Bronte[25]

The same day he wrote formally to Emma confirming the new arrangement:

Victory, at Sea, May 16th. 1805

My dearest Lady Hamilton,

As it is my desire to take my adopted daughter, Horatia Nelson

Thompson, from under the care of Mrs Gibson, and to place her under your Guardianship, in order that she may be properly educated and brought up, I have, therefore, most earnestly to entreat that you will undertake this charge; and as it is my intention to allow Mrs Gibson, as a free-will offering from myself (she having no claim upon me, having been regularly paid for her care of the child) the sum of twenty pounds a-year, for the term of her natural life; and I mean it should commence when the child is delivered to you. But should Mrs Gibson endeavour, upon any pretence, to keep my adopted daughter any longer in her care, then I do not hold myself bound to give her one farthing; and I shall, most probably, take other measures.

I shall write to Mr Haslewood, upon your telling him that you have received the child, to settle the annuity upon Mrs Gibson; and if you think Miss Connor disposed to be the governess of Horatia, I will make her any allowance for her trouble which you may think proper.

I, again and again, my dearest friend, request your care of my adopted daughter, whom I pray God to bless. I am ever, for ever, my dear Lady Hamilton, your most faithful and affectionate,

Nelson & Bronte[26]

Nelson had asked Emma several times to take Horatia to live at Merton, but she had never done so. Emma and her mother may have considered that with building works in progress at Merton it was an unsuitable environment for a small child. In addition it was up to Nelson to arrange the necessary legal and financial details. Haslewood did not receive his instructions for several weeks and it was August before Horatia moved to Merton.

Despite Mrs Gibson and Horatia's sad parting, Horatia's new lifestyle would be comfortable in the beautiful house and grounds at Merton under the care of Mrs Cadogan and her new governess, Cecilia Connor. Horatia referred to Nelson as her *'dear, dear god-papa'*. She did not know that Emma was her mother or Mrs Cadogan her grandmother.

In June Emma took Charlotte and Eliza Bolton, both regularly staying with her, to see Horace celebrate Eton's three-yearly flag day festival. The event attracted royalty and large crowds.

In July Emma, Mrs Billington, Charlotte and the Bolton girls went to Southend in Essex for a holiday. Charlotte told her mother that Emma was *'very ill with nettle rash'*. The strain of being responsible for two households, added to her anxiety over Nelson, had aggravated her psoriasis.

Her mother wrote to her from Merton on 18 July: *'I shall be very glad to see you to-morrow, and I think you are quite right for going into the country to keep yourself quiet for a while. My dear Emma, Cribb is quite distressed for money, would be glad if you could bring him the £13 he paid, that he paid for the taxes, to pay the mowers. My dear Emma, I have got the baker's and butcher's bills cast up; they come to one hundred pounds, seventeen shillings. God Almighty bless you, my dear Emma, and grant us good news from our dear Lord ...*

Sarah Reynolds [another cousin of Emma's] *thanks you for your goodness to invite her to Sadler's Wells.'*[27]

In need of a rest and beneficial sea-bathing, Emma wrote to Davison on 19 July: *'I am not over rich to go into the Country, alltho' I have reduced my Establishment, perhaps you will assist me a little. The time will now soon come when I shall no longer be a plague to you.'*[28] * Davison dutifully sent her £100. Emma clearly anticipated that Nelson's finances and debts would be sorted out when he returned.

When news of Nelson's imminent arrival was received at the Admiralty an express was sent to Emma at Southend whereupon she left in frantic haste to reach Merton before he arrived. She had told Davison the previous October, when they were expecting Nelson home for Christmas, that *'he particularly wishes our first meeting to be there'.*

The local newspaper reported on 19 August that she had left *'in a chaise and four at five o'clock this morning'*, taking Charlotte with her. Mrs Billington and the *'young ladies of the family party'* remained behind. The coach arrived at Merton in time for Emma to send a note to Nelson.[29]

The *Victory* had anchored at Spithead at 8.30 a.m. on 18 August, but Nelson was not allowed ashore until he had cleared quarantine regulations. He wrote to Emma immediately on arrival:

Victory, *Spithead, 18th August 1805*

I am, my dearest Emma, this moment anchored and as the post will not go out till eight o'clock, and you will not get the letter till eleven or twelve o'clock to-morrow, I have ordered a Post-Office express to tell you of my arrival. I hope we shall be out of quarantine to-morrow, when I shall fly to dear Merton. You must believe all I would say, and fancy what I think; but I suppose this letter will be cut open, smoked and perhaps read. I have not heard from you

---

* At one time Emma had three maids - Julia, Marianna and Fatima. Fatima resided at Merton.

since April by Abbé Campbell. *The boat is waiting, and I must finish. This day two years and three months I left you. God send us a happy meeting as our parting was sorrowful.'*

The following day he wrote again: *'I have this moment got yours of last night from Merton. I shall rejoice to see dear Horatia, Charlotte and Ann and Eliza, and I would not have my Emma's relative go without my seeing her.'*[30]

The identity of the above-mentioned *'Emma's relative'* is uncertain. However, he almost certainly refers to her cousin, Sarah Reynolds, who is mentioned in Mrs Cadogan's recent letter to Emma.

Huge crowds gathered onshore to welcome Nelson home. He was mobbed as he made his way to pay his respects to the Portsmouth Commander-in-Chief and while he waited for a post-chaise at the George Inn. He left at 9 p.m. and arrived at Merton at 6 a.m. on 20 August.

We can only imagine Nelson and Emma's happiness at being reunited, and Nelson's pleasure at seeing the impressive improvements carried out in his absence.

William, Sarah and Horace arrived, soon joined by the Boltons and the Matchams. Susanna replied to a note from Emma: *'Thanks, my dear Lady, for your scrap. It was, indeed, short and sweet, for sweet was the intelligence that my dearest brother was arrived in England. What a Paradise he must think Merton, to say nothing of the Eve it contains. I need not give you joy, for I am sure you have it.'*[31]

Emma wrote to Kitty on 20 August: *'Our Nelson begs his love to you and Mr Matcham, and shall be most happy to see you at Merton and I need not say how glad I shall be to see you in Clarges Street. I shall meet you at Merton. Nelson when he is in town goes to an Hotel* [Gordon's Hotel, Albermarle Street] *The town is wild to see him. What a day of rejoicing was yesterday at Merton. How happy he is to see us all I have not time to say more than God bless you.*

Yours affectionately Emma.[32]

She wrote Kitty a further persuasive note on 22 August: *'We have Room for you all so Come as soon as you can. We shall be happy, most happy. Here are Sir Peter Parker and God knows who, so Nelson has not time to say more than he loves you and shall rejoice to see you. Ever your affectionate, Emma'*

Nelson added a postscript: *'I need not my dear Sister say how happy I shall be to see you and Mr Matcham ... .Ever ... .Your affectionate Brother Nelson & Bronte*[33]

Kitty's little boy, William Alexander, was ill. He died on 27 August, prompting Susanna to write to her from Merton: *'We all feel for your situation, but I write now in the name of Both my Lord & Lady to say they think the sooner you leave such a melancholy scene the better. Therefore let me beg of you to come Imediately, lest you should not be in time to see our Dear Brother. It is very uncertain. He looks remarkably well & you will find him such a kind & affectionate Relation and Friend as seldom is to be met with. Seeing and hearing him will soothe your Griefs ...'*

Emma added: *'My dearest friend pray sett off & Come imediately. Lord Nelson begs his Love to you & Mr Matcham. I can only say you will meet with affectionate Hearts.*

Ever ever your most affectionate
Emma Hamilton[34]

When the Matchams arrived a second dining table was required to accommodate all the children: Charlotte and Horace Nelson, Tom, Eliza and Anne Bolton, George Matcham junior, and of course, little Horatia. Nelson was delighted to be surrounded by all his family. They were all aware that Nelson might not be in England for long. Indeed it was only twenty-five days before he left his beloved Merton Place for the last time.

Lord Minto called at Merton on the first Saturday after Nelson's and reported to his wife:

'... found Nelson just sitting down to dinner, surrounded by a family party of his brother, the Dean, Mrs Nelson and the children of a sister, Lady Hamilton at the head of the table and Mrs Cadogan at the bottom. I had a hearty welcome. He looks remarkably well and full of spirits. His conversation is a cordial in these low times. Lady Hamilton has improved and added to the house and the place remarkably well and without his knowing she was about it. She is a clever being after all. The passion is as hot as ever ...'[35]

Everyone wanted to see Nelson.

On 4 September there was a *'Large company at dinner'*. Later Beckford and the Duke of Clarence, accompanied by Lord Errol, dined at Merton. Numerous visitors called on him in London and at Merton. Towards the end many simply wanted to say goodbye and wish him well. The endless entertaining left very little time for Nelson and Emma to be together on their own.

Emma expressed her distress to Lady Bolton on 4 September:

My dear Friend,

I am again broken-hearted as our dear Nelson is immediately going. It seems as though I have had a fortnight's dream, and am awoke to all the misery of this cruel separation. But what can I do? His powerful arm is of so much consequence to his Country. But I do, no cannot say more. My heart is broken ... God bless you! Ever your affectionate

E. Hamilton[36]

On 6 September Emma wrote to Davison at his home in Northumberland: '... one fortnight of joy & happiness I have had for years of pain here is our Beloved Nelson My Nelson obliged to go again I am Broken hearted as you may imagine When do you Come to town my dear Sir my Beloved Nelson is so delighted with Merton & now he is here 'tis a paradize ...'[37]

After such a long absence Nelson had much business to attend to in London, including meetings at the Admiralty and the Navy office at Somerset House. He called on Marsh, Page and Creed, the Navy agents who handled his naval income, and at Salters, silversmiths, he ordered a child's cutlery set and a silver-gilt cup to be engraved with the inscription, 'To my much-loved Horatia'.

According to George junior's diary, Nelson had a long interview with Pitt, the Prime Minister, who was extremely impressed by his analysis of the political situation and his thoughts on where the French fleet might be heading. Afterwards Pitt asked Nelson to take command of the British fleet being assembled to face the combined fleets of France and Spain, now sheltering in Cadiz harbour. Nelson accepted, despite concern about taking over the command from his old friend, Collingwood, who was stationed off Cadiz.

Wherever he went Nelson was recognized and surrounded by well-wishers. Emma wrote to her friend Mrs Lutwidge on 3 September: * 'He looks very well but he is not strong and again he is asked to go forth for they cannot go on without his powerfull arm. He will not be many days longer with us I believe ... He is adored as he walks the streets, thousands follow him, blessing him and wishing him good luck.'[38]

Lord Minto sent his wife a similar report: 'I met Nelson in a mob in Piccadilly and got hold of his arm, so that I was mobbed too. It is really quite affecting to see the wonder and admiration, and love and respect of the whole world ... It is beyond anything represented in a play or a poem of fame.'[39]

Kitty saw Nelson one day in London. After hearing her concern that he seemed tired and depressed, he replied: 'Ah! Katty, Katty, that Gipsy

---

* Wife of Captain Lutwidge who had taken Nelson on board his ship for the Arctic expedition in 1773.

– reminding her that a gipsy fortune-teller, referring to the present year, had said *'I can see no further.'*[40]

George's diary entry on 16 August comments on Napoleon's threatened invasion of England: *'Bonaparte is arrived at Boulogne, in order as they say to superintend the embarkation of the troops ... All officers and corp are ordered to be in readiness to meet the enemy at a moments notice.'*[41]

Napoleon (that *'Corsican scoundrel'* Nelson had called him) was in Boulogne and the surrounding area throughout August. At Gris Nez, on the 4th, he reviewed an army of 112,000 infantry, followed by reviews of further divisions and the French 'flotilla' nearby. On the 13 August he learned that Villeneuve had sought refuge with his fleet at Ferrol. Towards the end of August he was planning a future operation in Germany. On 3 September Napoleon returned to Malmaison, the private residence purchased by his wife, Josephine.

Nelson received his orders from the Admiralty on 6 September. He wrote to Davison, still in Northumberland:

My dear Davison,

I much fear that I shall not have the pleasure of seeing you before my departure, and to thank you for all your kind attentions ... although I may not be able to pay off [my account] *at this moment, still it would be a satisfaction to me to have it settled ... I hope my absence will not be long, and that I shall soon meet the Combined Fleets, with a force sufficient to do the job well; for half a Victory would but half content me ... But I will do my best; and I hope God Almighty will go with me. I have much to lose, but little to gain; and I go because it's right, and I will serve the Country faithfully.*

Nelson & Bronte[42]

The next day he wrote to Collingwood:

My dear Coll.,

I shall be with you in a very few days, and I hope you will remain Second in Command. You will change the Dreadnought *for* Royal Sovereign, *which I hope you will like. Ever, my dear Collingwood, most faithfully yours*

Nelson & Bronte[43]

The remaining few days flashed by with Nelson attending meetings in London and settling his private affairs. He and Emma attended a private service at their church, taken by Mr Lancaster, witnessed and described the Dowager Lady Spencer: *'... a private Sacrament which Nelson has taken before he embarks ... After the service was over, Nelson took Emma's hand and facing the priest, said 'Emma I have taken the Sacrament with you this day, to prove to the world that our friendship is most pure and innocent, and of this I call God to witness.'*[44]

They exchanged gold rings, a symbol of their belief that, in the eyes of God, they were married.

By 10 September he knew he would leave on 13 September. His belongings were packed and sent down to the *Victory* at Portsmouth. Late in the evening on 11 September an equerry arrived at Merton with the Prince of Wales' request that Nelson call to see him before he left. Nelson was obliged to go to London the following day to pay his respects and take his leave. To gain a few precious hours in his company Emma went with him, remaining at Clarges Street while he went to Carlton House.

The Perrys, Nelson's neighbours, were invited to dine that day. Minto visited and wrote an account to his wife of his last meeting with Nelson: *'I went yesterday to Merton in a great hurry as he, Lord Nelson, said he was to be at home all day, and he dines at half-past three. But I found he had been sent for to Carlton House, and he and Lady Hamilton did not return till half-past five. I stayed till ten at night and took a final leave of him ... Lady Hamilton was in tears all yesterday, could not eat, and hardly drink, and near swooning, and all at table. It is a strange picture. She tells me nothing can be more pure and ardent than this flame.'*[45]

William and Sarah had departed with all the young people. Susanna and the Matchams remained to bid him farewell on his last day.

The next morning Nelson drove to London for his final orders from the Admiralty, returning to spend the evening with Emma and his remaining family. The chaise to take him to Portsmouth was ordered for half-past ten. Horatia had been asleep for hours when Nelson went up to pray beside her cot before departing.

Emma later told Lady Elizabeth Foster that he *'had come back four different times, and the last time he kneeled down and holding up his hand had prayed God to bless her'.*[46]

Emma was too distressed to go out with Nelson to his coach. George Matcham accompanied him and in their final conversation Nelson expressed regret that he had not yet been able to repay the £4,000 George had lent him. G.M. assured him: *'My dear Lord, I have no other wish than to see you return home in safety. As to myself, I am not in want of anything.'*[47]

Aware that he had *'much to lose'* but driven by his unshakeable sense of duty, Nelson composed his thoughts during his journey down to Portsmouth to write the following prayer:

Friday Night; 13th. September

At half-past ten drove from dear Merton, where I left all which I hold dear in this world, to go to serve my King and Country. May the Great God whom I adore enable me to fulfil the expectations of my Country; and if it is His good pleasure that I should return, my thanks will never cease being offered up to the Throne of His Mercy. If it is His good providence to cut short my days upon earth, I bow with the greatest submission, relying that He will protect those so dear to me, that I may leave behind. His will be done. Amen, Amen, Amen.[48]

Arriving at Portsmouth at 6a.m. he gave Mr Lancaster, who was returning to Merton that day, a note to Emma:

6 o'clock, George Inn,

Sept 14th. 1805

My dearest Emma,

I arrived this moment, and Mr Lancaster takes this. His coach is at the door, and only waits for my line. Victory is at St. Helens, and, if possible, shall be at sea this day. God protect you and my dear Horatia, prays, Yours ever

Nelson & Bronte[49]

His diary entry that day reads: *'At six o'clock arrived at Portsmouth, and having arranged all my business, embarked at the Bathing Machines with Mr. Rose and Mr. Canning. At two got on board the Victory at St. Helens, who dined with me, preparing for sea.'*[50]

Nelson tried to avoid the crowds gathered to see him. Leaving the George Inn by the back door, he embarked at the bathing machines rather than the usual place, but soon the crowds gathered again: *'...pressing forward to obtain sight of his face: many were in tears, and many knelt down before him, and blessed him as he passed. England has had so many heroes, but never one who so entirely possessed the love of his fellow-countrymen as Nelson ...'*[51] *

While dining that day Nelson implored his old friend, George Rose (Vice-Pesident of the Board of Trade and Joint Paymaster General) to assist Emma in her quest for a pension. Rose, it transpired, worked tirelessly on her behalf for many years but to no avail.

Three days later Nelson wrote encouragingly to Emma:

* Quoted from Robert Southey's biography of Nelson.

Victory, off Plymouth, September 17th.
Nine o'clock in the morning, Blowing fresh
at W.S.W. dead foul wind.

I sent, my own dearest Emma, a letter to you last night, in a Torbay boat, and gave a man a guinea to put it in the Post-Office. We have had a nasty blowing night, and it looks very dirty ...

I intreat, my dear Emma, that you will cheer up; and we will look forward to many, many happy years, and be surrounded by our children's children. God Almighty can, when he pleases, remove the impediment.

My heart and soul is with you and Horatia.

For ever, ever, I am yours, most devotedly,

Nelson & Bronte[52]

Nelson's diary records on Sunday, September 28th 1805: '*... In the evening joined the Fleet under Vice-Admiral Collingwood. Saw the Enemy's Fleet in Cadiz, amounting to thirty-five or thirty-six Sail of the Line.*'[53]

The next day, his forty-seventh birthday, Nelson invited fifteen officers to dine with him. Captain Codrington wrote to his wife: '*... all of us who did not dine on board the* Victory *yesterday, to go today*'.[54]

Collingwood and Captain Freemantle of the *Neptune*, 98 guns, dined privately with him.

Around 30 September, Nelson wrote to Davison:

Day by day, my dear friend, I am expecting to put to sea – every day, hour and moment; and you may rely that, if it is within the power of man to get at them, that it shall be done; and am sure that all my brethren look to that day as the finish of our laborious cruise. The event no man can say exactly; but I must think, or render great injustice to those under me, that, let the Battle be when it may, it will never have been surpassed. My shattered frame, if I survive that day, will require rest, and that is all I ask for. If I fall on such a glorious occasion, it shall be my pride to take care that my friends shall not blush for me. These things are in the hands of a wise and just Providence, and His will be done! I have got some trifle, thank God, to leave to those I hold most dear, and I have taken care not to neglect it. Do not think I am low-spirited on this account, or fancy anything is to happen to me; quite the contrary, my mind is calm, and I have only to think of destroying our inveterate foe ... Nothing can be finer than the Fleet under my command. Whatever be the event, believe me ever, my dear Davison, your much obliged and sincere friend,

Nelson & Bronte[55]

Nelson wrote again to Davison on 13 October, probably his last letter to him:

My dear Davison,

Many, many thanks for your kind and affectionate note. I should have much rejoiced to see you, but I was called away, and I obeyed. I am vexed you should have had such a fag on my account ... [Davison had travelled through the night to say goodbye to Nelson, but had arrived too late] Some happy day I hope to get at their Fleet, and nothing shall be wanting on my part to give a good account of them.

My dear Lady Hamilton has told me of your kindness, you will do the needful about my accounts, and settle with Mr Chawner for what is going on at Merton. I have not a moment more than to say I am ever most affectionately yours

Nelson & Bronte[56]

Emma sent two letters to Nelson dated 4 and 8 October. Sadly, they arrived too late for him to read. She strove to be cheerful, knowing that Nelson enjoyed and appreciated her letters. Both letters were written at Canterbury, where she was visiting William and Sarah, leaving Horatia at Merton in the care of Mrs Cadogan and her governess, Cecilia.

Canterbury,
October 4th. (1805)

My most dear Nelson,

I forgot to tell you that Lord Sidmouth's son stab'd himself at Worthing about a month ago – that was what H. Adington aluded to ... he is not dead ... Lord Douglas has just call'd; he would have given much to have seen you when you was in England; he looks upon you as the sweetest of all human beings.

The Dr. has invited him to dinner tomorrow. The poor old Duke [Old Q] must have a letter every day from me. I had begun to fret at not having letters from you.

I send you a letter of Miss Connor's for there is much in it about our dear girl, you will like it. I also had one from my mother who doats on her, she says she could not live without her. What a blessing for parents to have such a child, so sweet, altho' so young, so amiable? God spare her to them, and be assured, my life, my soul of your own Emma's fondest affections. You are my all of good. Heavens bless, bless you.

Yours only, yours &c.[57]

With her letter of 4 October, Emma enclosed another written by Cecilia to Charlotte Nelson, and a note written by Horatia. Cecilia's letter describes how well four-year-old Horatia is progressing. The

letter would have delighted Nelson: *'Little Horatia sends a kiss to you &*
Lady H. & her love to all your party. She is looking very well indeed, & is to
me a most delightful companion. We read about twenty times a day, as I do
not wish to confine her long at a time, & she is now learning the names of
the keys on the pianoforte ... She is uncommonly quick, and I dare say will
read tolerably well by the time you see her again. I told her she was invited to
see a ship launched; every morning she asks if it is to be <u>*to-day*</u> *& wanted to*
know if there will be any <u>*firing of guns*</u> *... Horatia has written and indited*
the whole of what is written at the end. She wants to guide my hand as I did
hers, while I write this. My love to my lady.'

Horatia's note to Emma read: *'My dear Lady I thank you for the books.*
I drink out of my Lord's cup every day give my love to him every day when
you write, and a kiss. Miss Connor gave me some kisses when I read my book
well. Oh here three kisses my love to Miss Nelson my dear my Lady I love you
very much. Horatia'[58]

Emma's final letter to Nelson is long and full of news, particularly
about Horatia. In closing she expresses her love for him:

Canterbury, October 8th. 1805

My dearest life, we are just come from church, for I am so fond the Church
Service and the Cannons are so civil; we have every day a fine anthem for me.
Yesterday, Mr, Mrs, and Miss Harrison, Mrs Bridges, Marquis of Douglas,
& General Thornton, and Mr Baker the Member of Parliament dined with
us. The Dr gave a good dinner, and Mariana dressed the macaroni and curry,
so all went off well ... I was obliged to send for Mariana down & my mother
can ill spare her; she gives me such an amiable account of our dearest Horatia.
She now reads very well, and is learning her notes, & French & Italian, &
my mother doats on her. The other day she said at table, 'Mrs Candogging, I
wonder Julia did not run out of the church when she went to be married, for
I should, seeing my squinting husband come in, for my God! how ugly he is,
and how he looks cross-eyed; why, as my lady says, he looks two ways for
Sunday.' Now Julia's husband is the ugliest man you ever saw, but how that
little thing cou'd observe him; but she is clever, is she not, Nelson? We go
tomorrow for 2 days to Ramsgate to see an old friend, poor Lady Dunmore,
who is there, is in great affliction for the loss of her son, Captain John Murry.
Today we dine alone, to eat up the scraps, & drink tea with old Mrs Percy.
Charlotte hates Canterbury, it is <u>*so dull*</u>*; so it is. My dear girl writes every*
day in Miss Connor's letter & I am so pleased with her. My heart is broke
away from her, but I have now had her so long at Merton that my heart cannot
bear to be without her. You will be even fonder of her when you return. She

says, 'I love my dear, dear, godpapa, but Mrs Gibson told me he kill'd all the people, and I was afraid.' Dearest angel she is! Oh, Nelson, how I love her, but how do I idolize you – the dearest husband of my heart, you are all in this world to your Emma. May God send you victory, and home to your <u>Emma, Horatia, and paradise Merton,</u> for when you are there it will be paradise. My own Nelson, may God prosper you & preserve you, for the sake of your affectionate Emma. .

She added a postscript: '... Write often; tell me now you are & how the sea agrees with you, weather it is a bad port to blockade, in short, the smallest trifle that concerns you is so very interesting to your <u>own, faithful Emma</u> ... my compliments to Admiral Louis. God bless you, my own, own Nelson.'[59]

Nelson's following letters to Emma were written during the twenty-one days prior to the Battle of Trafalgar:

Victory, October 1st 1805

My dearest Emma,

It is a relief to me, to take up the pen, and write you a line; for I have had, about four o'clock this morning, one of my dreadful spasms, which has almost enervated me. It is very odd; I was hardly ever better than yesterday. Freemantle stayed with me till eight o'clock, and I slept uncommonly well; but was awoke with this disorder ... However, it is entirely gone off, and I am only quite weak. The good people of England will not believe that rest of body and mind is necessary to me! ... I had been writing seven hours yesterday: perhaps that had some hand in bringing it upon me.

I joined the Fleet late on the evening of the 28th. September, but could not communicate with them until the next morning. I believe my arrival was most welcome, not only to the Commander of the Fleet, but also to every individual in it; and when I came to explain to them the <u>"Nelson touch"</u>, it was like an electric shock.* Some shed tears, all approved – "it was new – it was singular – it was simple!" and from Admiral downwards it was repeated – "it must succeed, if ever they will allow us to get at them! You are, my Lord, surrounded by friends whom you inspire with confidence" ...

May God bless you my dearly beloved Emma. Kiss Horatia for me a Thousand times.[60]

Five days later he wrote again:

'... A decisive stroke on their fleet would make half a peace, and, my dear

---

* The 'Nelson touch' was Nelson's plan to attack the enemy's long line of ships with two columns of his own fleet, approaching them at right angles, in order to break up their superior numbers into three smaller groups. By attacking the middle and rear groups the foremost group would be taken out of the action being unable to turn around in time.

Emma, if I can do that I shall as soon as possible ask to come home and get my rest – at least for the winter ... what greater reward could the country bestow than to let me come to you and Horatia, and dear, dear Merton; and to come to you would be a victory twice gained and the rewards would I know from past experience be beyond what any person except yourself could give.

May God Bless

you my

Dearest Emma

and be assured I am

Yours most faithfully & affectionately

Nelson & Bronte

Kiss Dear Hor. And remember me kindly to all.[61]

He wrote again:

Victory, October 11th 1805

My dearest Emma,

'... *our Battle, I hope will be over long before the summer days. Our friend Sutton is going home for his health ... Ah, my beloved Emma, how I envy Sutton going home; his going to Merton and seeing you and Horatia. I do really feel that the twenty-five days I was at Merton, was the very happiest of my life. Would to God they were to be passed over again, but that time will, I trust, soon come, and many, many more days added to them ...*'[62]

13 October:

I am working like a horse in a mill, but never the nearer finishing my task ... Agamemnon is in sight, and I hope I shall have letters from you, who I hold dearer than any other person in this world, and I shall hope to hear that all our family goes on well, at that dear, dear cottage. Believe all I would say upon this occasion, but letters being in quarantine, may be read, not that I care who knows that I love you most tenderly and affectionately ... Kiss dear Horatia a thousand times for your faithful

Nelson & Bronte[63]

Two days before the battle, knowing it was imminent, Nelson composed his final letters to Emma and Horatia:

Victory, October 19th. 1805, noon

My dearest beloved Emma, the dear friend of my bosom. The signal has been made that the Enemy's Combined Fleet are coming out of Port. We have very little wind, so that I have no hopes of seeing them before tomorrow. May the God of Battles crown my endeavours with success; at all events, I will take care that my name shall ever be most dear to you and Horatia, both of whom I love as much as my own life. And as my last writing before the Battle will

be to you, so I hope in God that I shall live to finish my letter after the Battle.
May Heaven bless you prays your

Nelson & Bronte[64]

Victory, *October 19th. 1805*

My dearest Angel,

I was made happy by the pleasure of receiving your letter of September
19th., and I rejoice to hear that you are so very good a girl, and love my dear
Lady Hamilton, who most dearly loves you. Give her a kiss for me. The
Combined Fleets of the Enemy are now reported to be coming out of Cadiz;
and therefore I answer your letter, my dearest Horatia, to mark to you that
you are ever uppermost in my thoughts. I shall be sure of your prayers for my
safety, conquest and speedy return to dear Merton, and our dearest good Lady
Hamilton. Be a good girl, mind what Miss Connor says to you. Receive, my
dearest Horatia, the affectionate parental blessings of your Father,

Nelson & Bronte[65]

On 20 October, Nelson briefly added details of the Combined Fleets
to Emma's letter above. He ended with *'May the God Almighty give us*
success over these fellows, and enable us to get a Peace.' These were his last
words to her.

These two letters of 19 October were found on Nelson's desk after
the battle. On his return to England Hardy brought them to Emma,
along with her own last two unopened letters.

The Combined Enemy's fleet had put to sea on 19 October. Two
days later they were observed formed in close line of battle off the
coast of Cape Trafalgar. After Nelson's *'laborious cruise'* in search of
them he finally had his chance to *'get at them'*.

At 6.40 a.m. on Monday 21 October the *Victory* signalled *'Prepare for*
Battle' and *'Form the order of Sailing in two columns'*.[66] The *Victory* led
one column and Collingwood in the *Royal Sovereign* the other. Nelson's
fleet of twenty-seven ships of the line was up against the combined
French and Spanish fleets of thirty-three ships of the line, including
three of the biggest ships in the world: the *Santissima Trinidad*, 140
guns, the *Principe de Asturias*, 112 guns, and the *Santa Ana*, 112 guns.
The British fleet was outnumbered by 492 guns.

We can only marvel at the courage, commitment and discipline of
Nelson, his captains and their crews as they sailed agonizingly slowly
into battle – *'the wind was very light from the N.W .... our ships did not*
advance at a greater rate than a mile and a half an hour'.[67]

Nelson retired to his cabin to write a codicil to his will in which he left Emma as a *'Legacy to my King and my Country'*. It was his final attempt to assist Emma in her quest for a government pension:

October the twenty first, one thousand and eight hundred and five, then in sight of the Combined Fleets of France and Spain, distant about ten miles.

Whereas the eminent Services of Emma Hamilton, widow of the Right Honorable Sir William Hamilton, have been of the very greatest service to our King and Country, to my knowledge, without receiving any reward from either our King or Country; – first, that she obtained the King of Spain's letter, in 1796, to his brother, the King of Naples, acquainting him of his intention to declare War against England; from which Letter the Ministry sent out orders to the then Sir John Jervis, to strike a stroke, if opportunity offered, against either the Arsenals of Spain, or her Fleets. That neither of these was done is not the fault of Lady Hamilton. The opportunity might have been offered. Secondly, the British Fleet under my command, could never have returned the second time to Egypt, had not Lady Hamilton's influence with the Queen of Naples caused letters to be wrote to the Governor of Syracuse, that he was to encourage the Fleet being supplied with everything, should they put into any Port in Sicily. We put into Syracuse, and received every supply, went to Egypt, and destroyed the French Fleet. Could I have rewarded these services I would not now call upon my Country; but as that has not been in my power, I leave Emma Lady Hamilton, therefore, a Legacy to my King and Country, that they will give her an ample provision to maintain her rank in life. I also leave to the beneficence of my Country my adopted daughter, Horatia Nelson Thompson; and I desire she will use in future the name of Nelson only. These are the only favours I ask of my King and Country at this moment when I am going to fight their Battle. May God bless my King and Country, and all those who I hold dear. My relations it is needless to mention; they will of course be amply provided for.

Nelson & Bronte

Witness - Henry Blackwood.

    T. M. Hardy.[68]

At 11 a.m. Lieutenant Pasco reported to Nelson's cabin where he *'observed Nelson on his knees. He was then penning that beautiful prayer'.*[69] The cabin having been cleared for action, Nelson was kneeling at his desk.

In his diary, Nelson wrote his last prayer: *'May the Great God, whom I worship, grant to my Country, and for the benefit of Europe in general, a great and glorious Victory and may no misconduct in any one tarnish it; and may humanity after Victory be the predominant feature in the British Fleet.*

For myself, individually, I commit my life to Him who made me, and may his blessing light upon my endeavours for serving my Country faithfully. To Him I resign myself and the just cause which is entrusted to me to defend. Amen, Amen, Amen.'[70]

At 11.35 a.m. Nelson made his famous signal: *'England expects that every man will do his duty'.*[71] Captain Blackwood reported that *'the shout with which it was received throughout the Fleet was truly sublime'.*[72]

Victory's log recorded the action of the day. The following is an abridged account:

8.00 a.m.	light breezes and cloudy ... Enemy's fleet distance 9 or 10 miles
11.30	Enemy began firing
11.40	*Royal Sovereign* commenced firing on the enemy
12.04	*Victory* standing towards the enemy's van with all sails set. Began our fire at the enemy's van. In attempting to pass through their line fell on board the tenth and eleventh ships the Action became general
1.15	Nelson wounded in the shoulder
1.30	*Redoubtable, Téméraire* and another ship had struck. General action continued until 3 p.m. when several of the Enemy's ships around us had struck
4.15	The Spanish Rear-Admiral to windward struck to some of our ships
4.30	When a Victory having been reported to the Right Hon. Lord Viscount Nelson, K.B. and Commander-in-Chief, he died of his wounds.[73]

These simple statements record the dramatic events as they unfolded that historic day.

Nelson and Collingwood led their ships in two columns on a perpendicular line towards two of the most powerful enemy ships. Nelson towards the *Santissima Trinidad*, Collingwood towards the *Santa Ana*. For some considerable time they faced the full firing power of the enemy before being in a position to begin firing themselves.

The *Victory* attempted to break through the line between the *Bucentaure*, 80 guns, and the *Redoubtable*, 74 guns. Nelson's secretary was killed within minutes. His mangled body was thrown overboard by a marine. Nelson enquired, *'Is that poor Scott that is gone?'* When this was confirmed he muttered, *'Poor fellow.'*

The *Bucentaure* and the *Redoubtable* were so close together that Hardy could not get through the line without hitting one of them. He consulted Nelson, who replied, *'I cannot help it. It does not signify which we run on board of. Go on board which you please. Take your choice.'* [74]

Hardy chose the smaller ship and while engaged in firing on both sides, the *Victory* smashed into the *Redoubtable*, whereupon the rigging of both ships became entangled. Fate decreed that her crew were unusually highly trained and motivated by their captain, Jean-Jacques Lucas.

A shot fired from the *Redoubtable* flew between Nelson and Hardy. A splinter ricocheted and struck the buckle of one of Hardy's shoes, prompting Nelson to smile and comment: *'This is too warm work, Hardy, to last long.'* [75]

The *Victory* continued to fire into the lower decks of the *Redoubtable* with devastating effect. Captain Lucas made the surprising decision to order his lower portholes to be closed and, sounding a bugle call, summoned hundreds of men up onto the upper deck. The musketeers and grenadiers threw all their efforts into clearing the *Victory's* upper decks, inflicting colossal damage and multiple injuries, in preparation for boarding her. Nelson and Hardy were pacing a small area of the quarterdeck.

At 1.15 p.m, at the height of the battle, just over one hour after the *Victory* had commenced firing, Nelson was struck by a musket ball fired from high in *Redoubtable's* mizzen top. Hardy saw him collapse onto the deck. A marine, two seamen and Hardy rushed to his aid. With Hardy kneeling beside him, Nelson smiled weakly and said: *'They have done for me at last, Hardy.'* Hardy expressed the hope that the wound was not too severe, but was told: *'My backbone is shot through.'* * As Nelson was carried to the cockpit below (used as an operating theatre during a battle), he insisted on covering his face with his handkerchief so that his departure went unnoticed by the crew.

Nelson knew that his injury would prove fatal and accepted his approaching death. With calm composure he believed his fate to be 'God's will', an attitude he had expressed many times throughout his career. In great pain and having difficulty in breathing, he nevertheless

---

* The musket ball had struck the epaulette on his left shoulder, descended into his thorax fractured his second and third ribs, penetrated the left lobe of his lung, divided a large branch of the pulmonary artery and lodged in his spine between the sixth and seventh dorsal vertebrae.

lucidly communicated his thoughts to those who attended him: Dr William Beatty, the ship's surgeon, Dr Alexander John Scott, the ship's chaplain, and Mr Burke, the purser. William Chevalier and Gaetano Spedillo, Nelson's stewards, supported him in a semi-recumbent posture.

Four times in the agony of his last few hours, Nelson expressed his concern for Emma and Horatia:

To Dr Scott: *'I have to leave Lady Hamilton and my adopted daughter, Horatia, as a legacy to my country.'*

To Hardy: *'Come nearer to me. Pray let my dear Lady Hamilton have my hair and all things belonging to me.'*

To Hardy again later: *'Take care of my dear Lady Hamilton, Hardy. Take care of Lady Hamilton.'*

And finally to Dr Scott: *'Remember that I leave Lady Hamilton and my daughter Horatia as a legacy to my country. Never forget Horatia.'*[76] Towards the end, murmuring with increasing difficulty, Nelson repeated: *'Thank God, I have done my duty.'* He died at 4.30 p.m.

CHAPTER 21

Nelson's Will and Death Duties

NELSON'S WILL IS dated 10 May 1803, to which, over time, he added seven codicils.[1] On 21 October 1805, the day of the Battle of Trafalgar, he added what became known as his final codicil in which he left Emma as a *'Legacy to his King and Country'*.

In this summarized version of the will significant points have been underlined.

Nelson's will begins with directions for his burial:

'This is the Last Will and testament of me Horatio Viscount Nelson of the Nile and of Burnham Thorpe in the County of Norfolk and United Kingdom of Great Britain and Ireland and Duke of Bronte in the Kingdom of Farther Sicily. First in the event that I shall die in England I direct my executors hereinafter named (unless His Majesty shall signify it to be his pleasure that my body shall be interred elsewhere) to cause my body to be interred in the parish church of Burnham Thorpe in the county of Norfolk near the remains of my deceased father and mother and in as private a manner as may be and I direct that the sum of £100 shall be divided amongst the poor of the several parishes of Burnham Thorpe, Sutton and Norton all in the county of Norfolk.'

Nelson then made specific bequests to Emma, his brother and two sisters, and to Alexander Davison and Hardy:

'.... I give and bequeath to Emma Lady Hamilton widow of the right Honorable Sir William Hamilton Knight of the most honorable order of Bath <u>*my diamond star*</u> *as a token of my friendship and regard and I likewise give and bequeath to the said Emma Lady Hamilton* <u>*the silver cup marked E.H.*</u> *which she presented to me.*

Also I give and bequeath to my brother the reverend William Nelson doctor in divinity <u>*the gold box presented to me by the City of London*</u> *also I bequeath to the said William Nelson* <u>*the gold sword presented to me by the Captains who fought with me at the Battle of the Nile.*</u>

Also I give and bequeath to my sister Catherine Matcham_the sword presented to me by the City of London.

Also I give and bequeath to my sister Susannah Bolton the silver cup presented to me by the Turkish company.

Also I give and bequeath to Alexander Davison of St James's Square in the county of Middlesex esquire my Turkish gun scymetar and Canteen

Also I give and bequeath to my late captain and worthy friend Captain Hardy all my telescopes and seaglasses and one hundred pounds in money to be paid three months after my death.'

He left one hundred pounds each to his executors, his brother William Nelson and his solicitor William Haslewood, with instructions to raise a sufficient fund, the interest on which would provide Fanny with an income of a clear yearly sum of one thousand pounds:

'.... all the residue and remainder of my goods chattles and personal estate ... except the household goods and furniture wines plates china linen pictures and prints which shall be in my house at Merton at my decease and also except my diamond sword and jewels hereinafter bequeathed ... to hold them ... upon the trust and for the intents and purposes hereinafter limited expressed ... the trustees shall as soon after as may be after my death convert into money such parts of the same personal estate as shall not consist of money and shall lay out and invest in the purchase of three per cent consolidated bank annuities and also of the money which shall belong to me at my death as by the dividends, interest and income thereof will produce the clear yearly sum of one thousand pounds ... that from time to time during the natural life of Frances Herbert Viscountess Nelson my wife ... the executors ... shall empower the said Viscountess Nelson my wife and her assigns to receive and take the interest and income of the same bank annuities ... and in addition to the sum of four thousand pounds lately given [when he left Fanny] *by me to her and which sum of four thousand pounds it is my will that she shall retain and I direct and declare that the provision made for her by this my will and also the said four thousand pounds shall be accepted and taken by her in lieu and full satisfaction of all dower right ...'*

This was the £4,000 Fanny had inherited from her Uncle Herbert which Nelson had always considered to be *her* money.

In case the annual income from the bank annuities was insufficient, he stipulated that the amount should be made up from Bronte rents:

'... And I also declare and direct that in case the annual income to arise or be produced from the bank annuities to be purchased with the residue of

my personal estate shall be insufficient to answer and pay the sum of one thousand pounds a year then the <u>deficiency shall be answered to the said Viscountess Nelson, my wife, out of the rents issues and profits of my barony town and feud lands and hereditments in Farther Sicily</u> ...'

Fanny was to receive this annual income provided always that:

'... Nothing contained in this my will shall extend or be construed <u>to subject my real estate in England to the payment of the said annuity of one thousand pounds or any part thereof</u>.'

In the event of his own and Fanny's death the one thousand pounds a year was to be divided between William Nelson, Susanna Bolton and Catherine Matcham.

The bequest of £1,000 p.a. to Fanny was to be made *'<u>provided always</u> and in case a pension or pensions to the amount or value of £1000 a year or upwards <u>shall in my lifetime be granted</u> to the said Viscountess Nelson my wife <u>by His Majesty or by Parliament</u> then and in that case the said sum of £1000 a year to be granted to her aforesaid shall be in lieu of the provision hereby made for her and then and in that case <u>the same provision shall cease and be void</u>.'*

In other words, if Fanny was already receiving a government pension of £1,000 p.a. at the time of his death, his own bequest to her of £1,000 p.a. would *'cease and be void'*. Fanny did not receive a government pension <u>in Nelson's lifetime</u> and remained a beneficiary of his provision for her of £1,000 p.a.

<u>After his death</u> at Trafalgar the government granted Fanny, Viscountess Nelson, a pension of £2,000 p.a. She therefore received the very substantial income of £3,000 p.a. for the rest of her life. It is not clear why Nelson thought she might be granted a government pension during his lifetime.

Nelson nominated his brother William and William Haslewood, *'their heirs and assigns to succeed on my death to the duchy of Bronte in the Kingdom of Farther Sicily ... upon under and <u>subject to the trusts and for the intents and purposes hereinafter expressed</u> declared and contained'.*

William was bequeathed the rents and profits of the estate in Sicily, subject to certain *'intents and purposes'* during the term of his natural life. On William's death the estate would be inherited firstly by any son or sons of his, and *'in default of such issue'*, secondly to Susanna and her son or sons, and thirdly to Catherine and her son or sons. The estate remained subject to the trusts, intents and purposes declared in the will.

At any time his heirs and assigns *'at their will and pleasure'* could sell or dispose of any part of the Bronte estate to *'lay out the same in the purchase of any freehold estates held in fee simple and situate in England, Ireland or the principality of Wales'*.

Having dealt with his intentions regarding his estate in Sicily Nelson returned to his personal awards:

'I give and bequeath the diamond hilted sword given to me by his said Sicilian Majesty, the diamond aigrette presented to me by the Grand Signior, my collar of the Order of the Bath, medals of the order of St. Ferdinand and insignia of other awards to the said William Nelson and William Haslewood <u>*in trust that the same maybe held as or in the nature of heirlooms'*</u>.

These items were to be *'taken and enjoyed'* by the person or persons *'for the time being entitled to my real estate in the Kingdom of Farther Sicily or the lands and hereditments purchased and taken in exchange thereof'*.

Finally, his bequest to Emma:

'And I <u>give and devise</u> unto the said <u>Emma Lady Hamilton her heirs and assigns</u> my <u>capital messuage at Merton</u> in the county of Surrey and the outhouses, offices, gardens and pleasure grounds belonging thereto and such and so many and such parts of my grounds farms land tenements and hereditments in the several parishes of Merton, Wimbledon and Mitcham or any of them as together with and including the [?] of the said messuages outhouses offices gardens pleasure grounds shrubbery canal and mote <u>shall not exceed 70 acres as shall be selected by the said Emma Lady Hamilton</u> within 6 months after my decease <u>such selection to be testified by some deed or instruments in writing under her hand and seal</u>.'

Emma was to receive the Merton house and 70 acres free from all debts:

'And I further direct <u>all money due on the security of the same messuage</u> and other hereditaments at my death <u>shall be paid and satisfied out of my personal estate and out of the money arising from the sale of the residue of the said farm</u> under the directions hereinafter contained in exoneration of the said messuage and other hereditments so devised to and for the benefit of the said Emma Lady Hamilton as aforesaid.'

Emma having chosen her seventy acres, his executors were instructed to add the remaining land to his personal estate to provide a fund for payment of his debts:

'And I give and devise unto the said William Nelson and William Haslewood their heirs and assigns <u>all the residue of my lands and grounds</u> in the parishes of Merton Wimbledon and Mitcham aforesaid or so much thereof

as shall be by me sold and conveyed or otherwise disposed of in my lifetime and also in the mean time <u>till selection thereof as aforesaid by the said Emma Lady Hamilton</u> as to such part or parts thereof as are to be or may be selected by the said Emma Lady Hamilton as aforesaid to hold the same unto and to the use of the said William Nelson and William Haslewood ... upon trust that [they and their survivors] *shall <u>as soon as conveniently may be after my decease sell and dispose of the same lands and hereditments</u> either together or in one lot or in parcels and several lots and either by public auction or private contract ...*

And I also direct <u>that the money to arise from the sale of all or any part of my said lands</u> and hereditments hereby directed to be sold shall (after a deduction of all costs and charges attending such sale or sales as aforesaid) <u>be added to and deemed a part of the residue of my personal estate ... in the increase of the primary fund for payment of my debts ...'</u>

Nelson bequeathed the entire contents of his house at Merton to Emma:

'And I give and bequeath <u>all the household furniture implements of a household wines plate</u> [silver plate] *<u>china linen pictures and prints which shall be in and about my house at Merton</u> at my decease and not otherwise disposed of by this my will or any codicil or codicils which I may hereafter make <u>to the said Emma Lady Hamilton for her own use and benefit ...'</u>*

A detailed provision follows for arrangements to be made if one or other of the executors should *'depart this life or be desirous of being discharged from the aforesaid trusts or go to the reside beyond the seas ...'*

The executors were empowered to accept any debts owing to Nelson and to pay any debts claimed against him:

'... that it shall and may be lawful to and for my said trustee or trustees or either of them in his or their discretion to compound any debt or debts owing to or to be owing to my trust estate and to accept part thereof in full payment of the same or to give or allow an enlarged day for the payment thereof ... <u>and to pay any debt which shall be claimed to be due and owing from me</u> in such manner and on such evidence as he or they shall think fit ...'

The will concludes:

... I nominate and appoint the said William Nelson and William Haslewood to be executors in trust of this my last will and testament and I revoke and annul all and every will and wills testament and testaments made by me at any time or times heretofore and declare that this present writing alone contains the whole of my last will and testament. In witness whereof I the said Horatio Viscount Nelson and Duke of Bronte have to the first fourteen

*sheets of my last will and testament contained in fifteen sheets of paper set
my hand and to the fifteenth and last sheet my hand and seal have also affixed
my seal to the top of the first sheet where the several sheets are fastened together
and have executed a duplicate hereof this*

*Tenth day of May in the year of our Lord
one thousand eight hundred and three
Nelson & Bronte*

The will was witnessed and signed by three clerks to Tyler, Booth
and Haslewood, 3 Craven Street, London.

Notably absent from this will of 10 May 1803 were the names of
Horatia and Mrs Cadogan. Nelson later added a bequest to Horatia
(codicil no. 2). Mrs Cadogan remained unmentioned in any codicil.

There are seven codicils written between 10 May 1803 and Nelson's
death. The first was written on 13 May 1803, only three days after the
will outlined above. It contains a significant alteration to the part of
the will that concerns Emma, prompted perhaps by either his brother,
William or his solicitor, Haslewood:

*... whereas in and by my said last will and testament I did <u>give and devise</u>
(among other things) unto Emma Lady Hamilton therein named <u>her heirs and
assigns</u> my capital messuage at Merton in the county of Surrey [etc] ... now <u>I
do hereby revoke and annul the gift</u> and ... in lieu of thereof do give and devise
and dispose of the same in the manner following that is to say <u>I give and devise
unto William Nelson and William Haslewood</u> in my said will named their
heirs and assigns <u>my said capital messuage at Merton</u> [etc.] ... <u>to the use of</u> the
said <u>Emma Lady Hamilton for and during her natural life</u> ... and <u>after the
decease of the said Emma Lady Hamilton to the use of my own right heirs</u>. In
all other respects I ratify and confirm my said last will and testament*

Nelson & Bronte

Whereas in the original will the Merton property was bequeathed
to Emma, her heirs and assigns, she is now only granted <u>the use of the
property during her lifetime</u>.

This underlines Emma's lack of legal status regarding Horatia.
Nelson and Emma had never admitted that Emma was Horatia's
natural mother. Legally, Emma was merely her guardian. Emma
would be unable to bequeath the Merton estate to her daughter. The
codicil stipulated that, in the event of Emma's death, his *'own right
heirs'* should inherit the use of estate.

The second codicil, concerning Horatia, was written on 6 September

1803. I Horatio Viscount Nelson of the Nile ... [etc.] ... Do make and publish a further codicil to the same last will and Testament in manner following that is to say I *give and bequeath to Miss Horatia Nelson Thompson* (who was Baptised on the thirteenth day of May last in the Parish of St Marylebone in the County of Middlesex ...) and who *I acknowledge as my adopted daughter the sum of Four Thousand Pounds Sterling Money of Great Britain* to be paid at the expiration of Six months after my decease or sooner if possible and *I leave my Dearest Friend Emma Lady Hamilton sole guardian of the said Horatia Nelson Thompson* until she shall have arrived at the age of Eighteen years and *the interest of the said four Thousand pounds to be paid to Lady Hamilton for her Education and Maintenance*, this request of Guardianship I earnestly make of Lady Hamilton knowing that She will educate my adopted Child in the Paths of Religion and Virtue and give her those accomplishments which so much adorn herself and I hope make her a fit wife for my Dear Nephew Horatio Nelson who I wish to marry her if he proves worthy in Lady Hamilton's estimation of such a treasure as I am sure she will be.

Further I direct that the legacies of this my codicil as well as those by my last Will and Testament given and bequeathed shall be *paid and discharged from and out of my personal estate only and shall not be charged or chargeable upon my real estates in the United Kingdom* of Great Britain and Ireland and in the Kingdom of Farther Sicily or any or either of them or any part thereof.

In all other respects I ratify and confirm my said last Will and Testament and former codicil. In witness whereof ... [etc.] ... [I] set my hand and seal this sixth day of September in the year of our Lord one Thousand Eight hundred and three.

Nelson & Bronte

Nelson here confirms the instructions in his letter to Haslewood marked 'Private for yourself and most secret'. This letter was proved as the third codicil on 1 December 1805.

Nelson's fourth codicil, leaving Emma an income from his Bronte estates, was written on board the *Victory* on 19 February 1804:

I Horatio Viscount Nelson and Duke of Bronte do hereby *give and bequeath to my Dearest Friend Emma Lady Hamilton* widow of the Right Honorable Sir William Hamilton K. Bth. *the net yearly Sum of Five Hundred pounds* to be paid and considered as a tax upon the Rental of my Estate at Bronte in Sicily *to be paid every Six months the first to be paid in advance* and so continued for and during the term of her natural life, and however I may in *my will have disposed of Bronte. I declare this as a Codicil to my said Will and it is my intent not withstanding any want of legal forms of which I am ignorant that the above net sum should be paid to the said Emma Hamilton as I have wrote.*

Dated on board His Majesty's Ship Victory at Sea this nineteenth day of February, one Thousand Eight Hundred and four.

Nelson & Bronte

Witness our hand the
date as above written.
[Signed by] *TM Hardy Capt. of HMS Victory*
John Scott Secretary

In his own hand Nelson added a note that indicates he was aware that rental income from Bronte was uncertain:

N.B. The aforementioned Sum of five hundred pounds a year to be first paid after the Rent is received.

Nelson & Bronte

In his fifth codicil Nelson remembered the poor blind 'wife' of his dear brother, Maurice, now a widow:

I desire that the Sum of one hundred Pounds Sterling money of Great Britain may be annually paid into the reputed Widow of my brother Maurice Nelson by whatever name she may assume be it S. Nelson or S. Field or any other name, and if I have not the means to pay this Sum exclusive of my other legacys I then trust that my friend Alexander Davison will pay it for me the [same?] every year and to be paid Quarterly as it is paid at present I declare this a Codicil to my Will this seventh day of April one Thousand Eight hundred and four.

Nelson & Bronte

Witness:
[Signatures of] *TM Hardy*
John Scott

While searching the Mediterranean for the French fleet Nelson added a further codicil (number 6) written in his diary, which is not signed by witnesses, but which was later proved on 18 July 1806.

To be added to my Will and Codocils. N & B
I hereby confirm my last Will and Testament bearing a date on or about May 13th. 1803 with the Codocils and confirm anew my legacy to Lady Emma Hamilton and to my adopted Daughter Horatia Nelson Thompson and I

further Give to my Dear Friend Emma Hamilton widow of the Rt Honble Sir Wm. Hamilton K. Bth. the sum of Two Thousand Pounds Sterling and to my Secretary John Scott Esq. the Sum of One hundred Pounds to buy a thing or some token of my remembrance and I request that He will with Capt. Hardy take care of my papers and effects (for my executors) and I give to my friend, the Revd Alexdr John Scott the sum Two hundred Pounds Sterling. Dated on Board the Victory in the Gulph of Palma Sardinia December nineteenth one Thousand Eight hundred and four.

Nelson & Bronte

Codicil number seven was also written in his diary and proved on 18 December 1805.

It simply states:

I give my Dearest Friend Lady Hamilton all the Hay belonging to me at Merton and in Wimbledon Parish. September Eleventh 1805.

Nelson & Bronte

In his final codicil (number 8), written during the morning on the day he died, he left Emma, as a *'Legacy to my King and Country'*. This codicil began: *'October the Twenty first one Thousand Eight hundred and five. There is sight of the Combined fleets of France and Spain distant about Ten Miles.'*

Nelson's will was proved in the Prerogative Court of Canterbury on the Twenty-first day of December 1805.

An extremely interesting account of the financial position after his death is contained in the document drawn up by the Stamp Office entitled *'Legacy duty on Residues of Personal Estate.'*[2]

The Stamp Office calculated the duties due on Nelson's estate from information given by the *'Executor of the deceased, or Trustees of the Real Estate'*. The document lists the total amount of *'Money Received'* by Nelson's estate. The final sum, which included prize money due to him, was probably far in excess of Nelson's expectations. The list of *'Payments out of the Money received as above'* appears to cover all his bequests apart from the Revd Alexdr John Scott, to whom Nelson left the sum of two hundred pounds (codicil number 6).

Unfortunately, although a sum of over £10,000 is listed as payment of debts, the details of these debts are not given.

An unexpected factor appears after the payment of the bequests and debts. There was a 'Residue' of over £12,000.

The *'Money Received'* columns lists the following amounts:*

	£	S	D
Cash in the Tea Trunk	114	6	0
Cash at Bankers	186	13	8
Arrears of rent due at the death of the deceased	100	5	0
[Margin note; 25 Feb. 1806] [details of] Sale of various Bank Stock, East India Stock and Bank annuities	6386	2	6
Carried over	6787	7	2
[Next page] Brought over	6787	7	2
Interest on consols [details given]	219	7	6
	67	10	0
	731	5	0
Cash received for Shares of Prize and Head money due to Testator	31567	11	8
Ditto for Ditto the Battle of Trafalgar	7303	8	2
Ditto further for Shares of Prize and Head money due to Testator	3400	13	6
Cash arising from the REAL Estate by the Will of the deceased, directed to be sold, mortgaged or otherwise disposed of	6863	9	3
Total	**56940**	**12**	**3**

This substantial sum enabled the bequests made by Nelson to be paid, listed as follows:

Payments of the Money received as above

	£	S	D
Charge of obtaining Probate	324	5	4
Funeral expenses	266	8	6
Expenses attending the Executorship and Trusteeship	350	0	0
Debts on simple Contract, Rent and Taxes due at the Death of the Deceased	10289	3	7
Rents and Taxes of Estate ... accrued since his death	133	3	11
For the Purchase of Government or Public Stocks or Funds, transferable at the Bank of England			
On Aug 5 1806 (see note 1 below)	18168	15	0
Ditto Jan 22 1807	1975	0	0

*Amounts listed are in the English currency at the time, of pounds, shillings and pence.

	£	S	D
Ditto Jan 24 1807	501	0	10
Ditto April 28 1807	2108	6	8
Ditto Feb 5 1810	1131	5	0
Percuniary Legacies (see note 2 below)	6600	0	0
Interest of Ditto (if any)	191	5	8
Payments on account of Annuities given by the Will To Mrs Maurice Nelson	429	7	6
To Lady Nelson (...?)	918	15	0
Other Lawful Payments (if any specify the same) Principal sum due to G. Matcham Esq on Mortgage	3685	8	0
Interest thereon at the of Payment (see note 3 below)	167	7	8
Payments on account of Annuities charged by Deed of Testator (see note 4 below)	732	18	3
Total	**47972**	**10**	**11**

Note 1:
An added note applying to this amount is explained in the document as
' 3% Consols ... have been appropriated by
The Exors according to the Directions of
the Will to answer the Payment of an Annuity of
£1000 bequeathed to his Widow the Viscountess Nelson
(The Duty on this Stock will be payable by the Residuary
Legatees after the Death of the said Viscountess Nelson.)'

Note 2:
This amount presumably included the £2,000 bequeathed to Emma, £100 to John Scott and £200 to Revd Alexander John Scott (all in codicil 6); the £4,000 to Horatia (codicil 2); and the
Pecuniary Legacies in Nelson's will of £100 to each of his two executors; £100 to Hardy, and £100 to the poor of Burnham Thorpe.
The above amounts come to a total of £6,700, not £6,600. Perhaps the £100 due to John Scott, his secretary, was not paid as he had been killed at the Battle of Trafalgar. The legacy to the Rev. Alexander John Scott is not mentioned in the death duties document.

Note 3:
The payment to George Matcham settles the debt which Nelson regretted he had not paid when he parted with Mr Matcham at Merton on the night he left to join the *Victory*.

Note 4:
These payments were to Mary Gibson, Mrs Graeffer and Mr Tyson.

The income and expenditure details concluded:

	£	S	D
Total Receipts	56940	12	3
Total Payments	47972	10	11
Balance of Cash in hand carried over	**8968**	**1**	**4**

The next item in the document is titled:

Property now constituting the 'Residue'

	£	S	D
Balance of cash in hand brought over	8968	1	4
3% Consolidated Bank Annuities	6302	1	8
	15270	3	0
Deductions	3107	4	6
Clear residue	**12162**	**18**	**6**

The final deductions of £3,107.4s.6d. covered the Value of Annuities given by the Will to Mrs Maurice Nelson, Mr John Tyson, Mrs Graeffer and Mrs Mary Gibson.

The *'Clear Residue'* of £12,162.18s.6d. was shared equally by William Nelson and his two sisters, Susanna and Catherine, the *'three Residuary Legatees'* named in Nelson's Will. A further document states that William Nelson paid the Duty of £101.7s.1 due on his share of £4,064.6s.2d. on 16 November 1810.

It should be noted that Mr John Tyson (Nelson's secretary after the Battle of the Nile until his return to England) is mentioned as a beneficiary in the above document whereas his name does not appear in Nelson's will. Nelson must, at some time, have given instructions to Haslewood regarding this bequest.

Two further points of interest appear in margin notes:

Attached to the Money received of £731.5s. –, there is a note stating *'exclusive of Lady Nelson'* and *'exclusive also of Miss Horatia, accounted for separately'*.

In the section above listing *'Property now constituting the Residue'*, values are not entered for items bracketed together under the headings:

Household Goods and Furniture

Plate, Linen and China

Books, Prints and Pictures

Wearing Apparel, Jewels, Trinkets and Ornaments of the Person

Wine and other Liquors
Horses and Carriages
Farming Stock and Implements of Husbandry
Handwritten in the margin next to these items is a note that states:
'Specifically bequeathed to Lady Hamilton. Duty paid 3rd. July 1809.'

CHAPTER 22

Emma's Descent into Debt

My heart is broken & my Head consequently weak from the agitations
I suffer ... He that I Loved more than Life is gone'
Emma to Davison, November 1805

'So much courage, virtue and modesty, all united in one individual,
is not to be found again ...'
Queen Maria Carolina, 1805

'I was very happy at Naples, but all seems gone like a dream'
Emma to Hayley, 5 June 1806

EMMA AND SUSANNA received the news of Nelson's death at Merton. Early on 6 November they heard the sound of distant guns in London. Emma, in bed feeling unwell, guessed that they were for *'for some victory in Germany'*. Five minutes later a carriage drew up bringing Captain Whitby bearing a letter from the Admiralty.

Emma's friend, Lady Elizabeth Foster, saw her in London shortly afterwards, and noted Emma's reported reaction: *'I sent to enquire who had arrived. They brought me word, Mr Whitby, from the Admiralty. 'Show him in directly,' I said. He came in with a pale countenance and faint voice said "We have gained a great Victory" – "Never mind your victory" I said "My letters – give me my letters" – Capt Whitby was unable to speak – tears in his eyes and a deathly paleness over his face made me comprehend him. I believe I gave a scream and fell back, and for ten hours after. I could neither speak nor shed a tear ... days have passed on and I know not how they end or begin – nor how I am to bear my future existence ...'*[1]

Emma roused herself to go up to Clarges Street with Susanna, to hear for themselves the details of Nelson's tragic death and glorious victory. Shattered by the news, Emma collapsed into her bed where she remained, grief-stricken, for several weeks. Lady Foster wrote: *'I found her in bed. She had the appearance of a person stunned and scarcely as yet able to comprehend the certainty of her loss. "What shall I do?" and "How can I exist?" were her first words. She then showed me some letters which were lying on the bed – they were from Lord Nelson ...'*

Emma received messages of sympathy from many friends, including Old Q., Hayley, and Goldsmid. The Duke of Clarence particularly enquired after her. Tributes to Nelson were sent to her and printed in the newspapers, none more moving than a letter from Dr Scott to Emma:

'When I think, setting aside his heroism, what an affectionate, fascinating little fellow he was, how dignified and pure his mind, how kind and condescending his manners, I become stupid with grief for what I have lost.'2

Collingwood's dispatches confirming the victory and Nelson's death reached the Admiralty at 1 a.m. on 6 December. Pitt was woken at 3 a.m. and, so distressed at Nelson's death and relief at his victory, could not return to bed. The King was so shocked he was unable to speak for a full five minutes.

George Matcham junior wrote in his diary on 7 November: *'All the ill news confirmed. Admiral Collingwood's letter received. Mama very ill. Received a letter from the Admiralty. Lady Hamilton very ill.'3*

James Perry, Nelson's neighbour, published his tribute in the *Morning Chronicle*, on 7 November: *'Never was a man so formed by gentleness of temper and by an affectionate heart for domestic felicity as the Noble Viscount. He was only truly blest in the bosom of his Family ... It is impossible to conceive a human being of more pure benevolence, and of more active virtue than Lord Nelson.'4*

William and his family arrived in London and rented a house. The Matchams hurried to Merton. Emma and Susanna returned to Merton. Mrs Cadogan told George Rose on 9 November: *'They at this Moment surround her Ladyship's Bed bewailing their sad loss & miserable state.'5*

That same day a grateful King and Parliament granted the Rev Dr William Nelson an earldom, Earl Nelson of Trafalgar and of Merton. His son, Horatio, was created Viscount Merton. 'The Doctor' thus became 'the Earl'.

Unaware of the existence of Nelson's last 'legacy' (Codicil No. 8) written in his diary on the day he died, the family and Emma gathered at Clarges Street to hear Nelson's will and seven codicils.

Nelson's bequests to Emma included Merton Place and its entire contents, 70 acres of land, a £2,000 lump sum, and an income of £500 p.a. from his Bronte estate, in addition to the interest on Horatia's legacy of £4,000 (at 3% about £120 p.a.) to pay for her upbringing and education.

These legacies (plus Emma's annuity from Sir William) appear to leave Emma and Horatia well provided for. However, Merton was very expensive to run and maintain. Emma did not receive the £2,000 lump sum for over a year or any Bronte money for many years.

Had Nelson received all the money due to him before he died (amounting to £34,967, not counting the additional £7,303 prize money for the Battle of Trafalgar) he surely would have left Emma and Horatia a more reliable income. Emma had been in a similar situation on the death of Sir William, who had told Greville that he *'could have had more to bequeath to Emma if the Treasury had only honoured its debt to him'*.

Kitty and George stayed at Merton both to comfort Emma and to see to business affairs in London. Kitty wrote to her son, George, on 17 November, *'If we hear nothing in a few days we shall think of returning home, for here we feel our loss more every day, but it is cruel to mention our going to My Lady at Present. Merton is very dull; quite the reverse to what you knew it ...'*[6]

Emma poured out her feelings of loss and desolation to Davison:

How are you to night my Dear Sir – I have been <u>very ill</u> all Day My Heart Broken & My Head consequently weak form the agitations I suffer – I tell you Truly – I am gone nor do I wish to Live – He that I Loved more than Life He is gone Why then shou'd I Live or wish to Live I Lived but for Him all now is a Dreary prospect before me I never Lamented the Loss of a Kingdom (for I was Queen of Naples) <u>for seven years</u>; nor one sigh ever Escaped me for the Loss I Sustained When I fell from Such a heightth of grateness & Happiness of Naples to misery and wretchedness ... but the Loss of Nelson under this Dreadfull weight of Most wretched Misery that I Suffer I feel & Hope that I shall not be Long after Him – nothing gives me a gleam of Comfort but the Hope that I shall soon follow ... nothing is arrived [from the Victory] which gives the Earl the <u>hungrey</u> fidgets & my indignation rises to See the avaricious workings of Him that ought to feel & love Lady Nelson [Sarah] She does shew Bowels – <u>not the Viscountess</u> [Fanny] she never <u>felt</u> in her life ... but nothing can come to give Comfort to me – in His Grave all my happiness is burried the poor old Duke [Old Q.] has sent ten times to Day & wrote a most affectionate letter to me ...

ever My Dear Sir your afflicted but gratefull Emma.[7] *

---

* This letter sold for £31,070 in the sale of the Alexander Davison collection in 2002 at Sotheby's, London.

Excerpts of Nelson's recent letters were printed in the newspapers. Emma wrote to George Rose strongly denying that she had given the letters to anyone:

Clarges Street, Nov 29th, 1805

I write from my bed, where I have been ever since the fatal sixth of this month, and only rose to be removed from Merton here. I could not write to you, my dear sir, before, but your note requires that I should justify myself.

Believe me then, when I assure you I do not see any one but the family of my dear Nelson. His letters are in the bed with me, and only to the present Earl did I ever read one, and then only a part. It is true he is leaky, but I believe would not willingly tell anything; but I have been told something like some of my letters have been printed in some paper. I never now read a paper and my health and spirits are so bad I cannot enter into a war with vile editors. Of this be assured no one shall ever see a letter of my glorious and dear departed Nelson ...

We learn the extent of Emma's grief in this letter to Rose:

My dear Sir, my heart is broken. Life to me now is not worth having; I lived but for him. His glory I gloried in; it was my pride that he should go forth; and this fatal and last time he went I persuaded him to it. But I cannot go on – my heart and head are gone ... Could you know me you would not think I had such bad policy as to publish any thing at this moment ... Excuse me, but I am ill and nervous, and hurt that those I value should think meanly of me.

When you come to town, pray call on me. I do not know if I shall live in England, as I promised the Queen of Naples to go back to her in case of accident. You will not be able to read this scrawl, but I am very, very ill ... All the family are with me and very kind. The Earl you know; but a man must have great courage to accept the honour of calling himself by that name.

Write me a line to say you have got this and that you believe

Your grateful

Emma Hamilton[8] †

It became impossible for Emma to return to live in Naples after French forces reoccupied the city in 1806 and Napoleon named his brother, Joseph, King of Naples. King Ferdinand and Queen Maria Carolina were again forced into exile in Sicily.

Receiving the news of Nelson's death, the Queen wrote movingly: *'I shall regret him all my life. Twenty vessels* [at Trafalgar] *may increase his*

---

* When Lady Foster saw them lying on Emma's bed they had already appeared in the Morning Chronicle.

† From this time onwards William, the new Earl, signed himself 'NELSON'.

glory, but nothing can console for his loss. So much courage, virtue and modesty, all united in one individual, is not to be found again. For him it is happiness for us a heavy misfortune.'9

Before arriving at Spithead, Hardy wrote to Emma:

Victory, St Helen's, Wednesday night (December 4, 1805)

My dear Lady Hamilton,

I lose not a moment to acquaint you with our arrival and inclose you by Chevalier the last letters written by our most dear and ever to be lamented friend. Be assured my dear Lady Hamilton, that I will do everything that lays in my power to serve you and I trust that you will believe that I am your sincere friend.

T.M. Hardy[10]

No doubt Chevalier gave Emma an account of Nelson's dying hours, during which he had been present.

Emma wrote on her letter from Nelson: 'This letter was found open upon His desk and brought to Lady Hamilton by Captain Hardy. Oh miserable wretched Emma Oh glorious and happy Nelson.'[11]

In Palermo Emma had once begged him to reduce a sailor's punishment. Hardy resented her interference and their relationship had deteriorated. Despite disapproving of her, Hardy was honour bound to carry out Nelson's dying request to 'take care of dear Lady Hamilton'.

Aware of the strained relationship between Hardy and Emma, Captain Blackwood wrote to reassure Emma: '... depend on it that the last words of our Lamented friend will influence his conduct. He desires me, in the most unequivocal manner, to assure you on his good intentions towards you. This I hope will ease your mind.'[12]

The Victory arrived at Spithead on 6 December, bearing Nelson's carefully preserved body. Hardy wrote again to Emma on 8 December regarding Nelson's personal possessions:

Every thing shall be preserved for you that you can wish; and it shall be my constant study to meet your wishes, as it was our ever dear Lord's last request to be kind to you, which I trust, I shall never forget ... I have his hair, lockets, rings, breast-pin, and all your Ladyship's pictures in a box by themselves, and they shall be delivered to no one but yourself ... I beg of you, my dear Lady Hamilton, to keep up your spirits under this most melancholy and trying occasion; and you may be sure of always meeting a most sincere friend in

T.M. Hardy[13]

These possessions, and Nelson's coat (not mentioned above), were delivered to Emma by Captain Blackwood. Lionel Goldsmid described his visit to Clarges Street in his journal:

'... I was a great favourite of Lady Hamilton's and bathed in tears at times as she talked over his virtues and exhibited the various gifts he had made her on different occasions. I was on the bed to aid in passing the rings, shawls, bracelets etc shown to the company of about 15 persons seated in a semi-circle at the foot of the bed ... the very coat in which the dear old Admiral was dressed in the fatal battle and received his death wound was on the outside of the bed – the hole where the bullet passed through stiffened with congealed blood ... '[14]

Hardy's inclusion of Nelson's coat among his personal effects caused trouble between Emma and the Earl. Nelson had instructed Hardy to 'let my dear Lady Hamilton have my hair and all other things belonging to me'. The 'box' containing Nelson's personal effects was opened at Clarges Street with the Earl and, probably, Davison present. Emma did not receive all of Nelson's possessions. The Earl had written to Hardy on 6 December: 'I am very much obliged by your kindness in sending Mr Chevalier to me with the inventory of my poor Brother's effects now on board the Victory. He has my orders to take charge of the whole of them & have them conveyed to London by water ... If there is any Will or Codicil or any paper of that sort intrusted to your care, I will esteem it a favor, if you will send a confidential person without loss of time, to bring it to me, with orders to deliver it to no other person ... '[15]

Hardy sought advice on how to proceed with the Codicil (No. 8). He hurried from Portsmouth to see Rose at his home in Hampshire. Rose decided that the document should be shown to Prime Minister Pitt, and assured Hardy he would so.* Rose immediately informed Emma:

Cuffnells, December 9th 1805

Captain Hardy had the goodness to take the trouble at much inconvenience to himself, to come over here soon after Victory anchored at Spithead, to tell me what passed in the last moments of my late most invaluable friend ... when he manifested a confidence I do would do all in my power to make effectual his last wishes, I shall consider it a sacred duty ... You will learn from the Captain that Lord Nelson ... made an entry in his Pocket Book strongly recommending a remuneration to you for your services to this country ... on which subject he had spoken to me with great earnestness more than once ...[16]

Rose promised to communicate with Pitt at the 'earliest opportunity', but Pitt died unexpectedly on 23 January 1806, before Rose could see

---

* It was not Proved by the Executors as part of Nelson's will until 11 September 1806.

him. Emma's hopes for a positive response to Nelson's dying wish were dashed. Pitt's successor, Lord Grenville, had never been favourably inclined towards Sir William and Emma.

Sir William was badly treated by Grenville regarding the settlement of his pension and expenses claims. Emma wrote to Rose at the time *'... poor Sir William and myself never even got a pat on the back. But, indeed, the cold-hearted Grenville was then in.'* (i.e. as Foreign Secretary).[17]

When the diary arrived in London the Earl was no doubt relieved to find that Nelson's only new codicil left Emma and Horatia to the *'beneficence'* of the King and Country. His own inheritance was unaffected. He took it to Sir William Scott, a legal advisor to the Admiralty, who agreed that it should be shown to the Prime Minister. When Sir William Scott informed Emma of these proceedings, he *'found her in a good deal of Agitation which gradually subsided in conversation'*.

Davison, Nelson's financier, was involved with the two executors dealing with his will. He made a *'true copy from the original'* of the last codicil and sent it to the Prince of Wales who replied:

Brighton, 18 December, 1805

I am extremely obliged to you, my dear Sir, for your confidential letter, which I received this morning. You may be well assured, that did it depend on me, there would not be a wish or desire of our ever to be lamented and much loved friend, as well as adored Hero, that I should not consider as a solemn obligation upon his Friends and Country to fulfil. It is a duty they owe his memory and his matchless and unrivalled excellence. Such are my sentiments, and I hope that there is still in this Country sufficient honour, virtue, and gratitude, to prompt us to ratify and carry into effect the last dying request of our Nelson; and by that means proving, not only to the whole world, but to future ages, that we were worthy of having such a man belonging to us ...

I am, my dear Sir, with the greatest truth, ever very sincerely yours,

George P.[18]

The Prince's hope that there was *'still in this Country sufficient honour, virtue, and gratitude'* to carry out Nelson's *'last dying request'* was never gratified. The King, often mentally unwell, could not be relied on. Emma's expectations rested with Grenville.

On 15 February the Earl took the codicil to *'cold-hearted'* Grenville who retained it until 30 May. In that time, Parliament decided the grants to be given to Nelson's family. To the Earl's advantage Parliament was not distracted by consideration of any obligations to Emma and Horatia.

Emma knew the content of Nelson's codicil from Rose's letter and her meeting with Sir William Scott. The Earl failed to keep Emma fully informed. For many years she believed that he had deliberately suppressed the codicil.

On 11 November King George had approved a state funeral for Nelson. Later, the date chosen was 9 January.

After the Battle of Trafalgar the *Victory* was towed to Gibraltar for essential repairs. When Hardy brough her home to Portsmouth on 6 December Nelson's body was on board, preserved in a large cask filled with brandy.

On 11 December the *Victory* sailed from Portsmouth, Hardy having been ordered to proceed to the Thames estuary. Dr Beatty recommended that the body be examined and on inspection, *'it exhibited a state of perfect preservation'*. He discovered the fatal ball lodged in Nelson's back, and reported on this wound and his death. The remains were embalmed and placed in a lead coffin filled with brandy, camphor and myrrh. Until 21 December the *Victory* was moored in the Thames and the coffin remained in Nelson's cabin.

When the Admiralty ordered the removal of the body, preparations were made on board in readiness for the lying-in-state and burial. The body was removed from its temporary coffin, dressed in *'a shirt, stockings, uniform small-clothes and waistcoat, neck-cloth and nightcap'*, laid in the coffin made from the mast of the *L'Orient*, returned to the lead coffin and sealed up.*

The coffin was taken to a private room at Greenwich Hospital where it remained until it was removed to the Painted Hall for the lying-in-state from 5 to 7 January 1806. Dr Scott, determined to maintain a vigil beside Nelson's body from his death until his interment, attended it constantly in the Painted Hall.

Thousands filed past to pay their last respects. The Prince of Wales and sailors from the *Victory* were allowed private time to say goodbye. Dr Scott wrote to Emma every day. She was dissuaded by Hardy from seeing Nelson's body.

On 8 January the coffin was taken by state barge to the Admiralty at Whitehall in readiness for the procession to St. Paul's Cathedral the

---

* Captain Hallowell had presented the *L'Orient* coffin to Nelson after the Battle of the Nile. On the insistence of his secretary, John Tyson, the *L'Orient* coffin was taken out to the Victory. Nelson inspected this coffin before leaving London. In good humour he had asked for his name to be engraved on the lid, saying, *'I think it highly likely that I may want it on my return'*.

following day. Dr Scott remained at Nelson's side throughout the night.

George junior went to London with his father on 5 January, leaving his mother and sisters at home. Over the next few days they visited Emma several times. George reported: *'Saw Lady H. in bed and low.'* After visiting the Earl who *'talked much of his precedence at the Funeral'*, they called on Haslewood and returned to dine at Clarges Street.

George described the morning of Nelson's funeral:

'Thursday Jan 9th. Rose at 6. Put on full dress. Went to Clarges St. Took up the Boltons. Drove to the Earl's where breakfast was laid out ...were not received at all by the Earl, nor introduced to anybody ... About half past eight the Mourning Coaches came. Lords Merton and Nelson* went in the first, drawn by six horses. My father, Mr. Bolton, Tom [Bolton] and myself in the second ... Went into St. James' Park. Found there a vast number of carriages ... about one arrived at the Horse Guards, where the procession joined by the Prince of Wales and Duke of Clarence ... Poor Mr [Dr] Scott came to our carriage and requested the Heralds to let him go in the same Coach as us. We were happy to receive him. After he had shaken us all heartily by the hand, he said with Tears in his Eyes 'Ah poor Fellow! I remained with him as long as I could and then they turned me away.'[19]

The Earl, Mr Matcham and Mr Bolton, their eldest sons Horace, George and Tom represented the family. Nelson's sisters were not present. Nor were Emma or Fanny.† Emma spent the day at Clarges Street, possibly with Susanna for company. Mr Matcham and George Junior called to see her after the funeral.

The solemn procession moved along the Strand and Fleet Street to St. Paul's. Soldiers lined the streets. The band played the Dead March from Handel's oratorio, *Saul.* The crowds stood silent. Shops were closed.

George junior wrote that when the procession arrived at St. Paul's Cathedral, *'It was the most aweful sight I ever saw.'*

As the Duke of Clarence ascended the steps of St. Paul's, he suddenly stopped, took hold of the colours being carried by some of the *Victory's* sailors, and after speaking with one of them, burst into tears.[20]

Those with tickets had arrived at 7 a.m. when the Cathedral doors were thrown open. They sat quietly until the procession arrived at 1p.m. and the service began.

---

* The Earl and his son Horatio, known as Horace, Viscount Merton. This title was later changed to Viscount Trafalgar.

† It was not customary then for women to attend funerals.

Admiral Sir Peter Parker was Nelson's Chief Mourner. Heading the long list of nobility attending were the Prince of Wales, accompanied by his six brothers: the Royal Dukes of Cambridge, Sussex, Cumberland, Kent, Clarence and York.

Representing the British Navy were numerous admirals, vice-admirals, rear-admirals and over one hundred captains. Of these captains only nine had fought at Trafalgar including Hardy and Bayntun, who bore the Banner of Emblems.* Two colleagues who had played a large part in Nelson's life could not attend. Collingwood was on active service off Cadiz and Troubridge was serving on the East Indian Station.

Seamen from the *Victory* bore the ship's two Union Jacks and the St. George Ensign. The sight of these flags, shot through with holes, torn and shredded, evoked the tragic loss of life during the battle. Before folding and placing these flags on the coffin the seamen spontaneously tore off a part of the Ensign so that they each might each retain a small piece in memory of Nelson.

At 5.33 p.m. the coffin was lowered into its last resting-place in the crypt directly below the great dome of the cathedral to the final chorus 'But his name liveth evermore'.[21]

Next day Emma heard from Mrs. Lutwidge, who, with her husband, had been friends of Nelson and Emma for many years: *'... there has not been a day passed in which my Admiral and self have not thought of you. Our hearts bleed for your sufferings, and, had it been possible to have alleviated your sorrow, dearest Emma, we should not thus long have remained silent; but we could only add our tears to yours for the loss of the greatest hero and best man that ever existed ... Tell me, my beloved Emma, that you will take care of yourself for the sake of the interesting little being consigned to your care, and with such a public testimony of his high sense of those great and good qualities you eminently possess. I own, my dear Emma, I shall have no small curiosity to know who this dear little being is, who is so distinguished ...'*[22]

Curiosity about Horatia was aroused when Nelson's will and codicils were proved on 23 December and published the following day.

In January Hayley wrote to Emma: *'let no sort of trouble depress the native energy of your mind!'*

She replied on 29 January:

---

* Hardy and Samuel Hood, were the only members of Nelson's Nile 'Band of Brothers' present. Trafalgar Captains present were: Hardy, Blackwood, Rotherham, Moorsom, Harvey, Laforey, Bayntun, D.Scott and Durham. Remembered here are Captains John Cooke and George Duff who had also been killed in the battle.

My dear Respected friend,

I have been so ill so very ill and I am <u>So Broken Hearted</u> *that I can scarcely hold my pen to thank you for your delightful and consoling letter yes it is consoling to find a true & sincere friend at this moment when I have lost the most virtuous the truest the bravest & sincerest of friends & to you I am indebted for this glorious man's love and regard for if I had never read you Triumphs of temper I should never have been the wife of Sir William Hamilton nor should I have had an opportunity of cultivating those talents which made the great & immortal Nelson think me worthy of his confidence & which made him say [?] now this last time he went forth to fight his countrys battles "Brave Emma Heroic Emma you encourage me to go forth if there were more Emmas there would be more Nelsons". These last words still I hear, still I feel, and feel proud when I think I was Beloved by Him. To you therefore I owe all my past happiness, but I am now most wretched. I write from bed ... I am very sorry I have promised the Earl Nelson to give him my letters, but none of those in my list, only I beg you to forgive this scrawl, and ever believe me with more gratitude than I can express, your affectionate and grateful*

Emma[23]

Hayley replied immediately with some wise advice: <u>*'As your very sincere friend*</u>*, I should advise you to retain these letters in your own Custody, & not suffer* <u>*even*</u> *me, your old and faithful Friend, to persuade you to impart them to the Public except as some distant day,* <u>*as a legacy to your Country from yourself*</u>*...*[24]

Emma probably gave a few of Nelson's letters to the Earl, but she certainly retained the major collection. She informed Rose that she *'had near 1500 of his letters some of them you shall see but my project is one of these days to have his life written by someone who will do him justice'.*[25]

On 21 January Lord Grenville proclaimed in Parliament: '... *every man must concur in any measure calculated to evince the sense which the Nation entertains of the brilliant and meritorious services of the late Lord Viscount Nelson, and to enable His Majesty so make the most splendid provision for those to whom his honours had devolved.'*[26]

To the avaricious and self-seeking William went the honours Nelson had earned through his *'brilliant and meritorious services'*. The *'splendid provision'* for Nelson's family was not decided until May, but on 1 February the King granted the Lady Viscountess Nelson a net annuity of £2,000 p.a. for the term of her natural life.[27] This, with Nelson's annuity of £1,000 p.a., brought her income to £3000 p.a.

Emma's relationship with William and Sarah began to deteriorate.

Their daughter, Charlotte, who had virtually lived with Emma for three years, was taken home. It seems that the Earl wanted to distance himself from Emma and Horatia.

On 13 February Emma heard from Sarah, her one time good friend, concerning Nelson's coat: *'In point of right there can be no doubt to whom this precious relic belongs, and it certainly is my Lord's most ardent wish as well as my son's who spoke very feelingly on the subject before he left us, to have retain'd it in his possession to be kept as a memorial in Trafalgar House as long as it can hold together. But not with standing all these feelings My Lord is willing, tho' done with a bleeding heart, to part with it to you provided my dear friend you will give us assurances it shall at some future time be restored to the Heir to the Title.'*[28]

There was further trouble for Emma and her mother with the executors, the Earl and Haslewood, over the bills and debts at Merton. Mrs Cadogan disclosed to Emma her mistrust of the executors, whom she rightly believed should pay the debts.

On 13 February she wrote from Merton: *'I will not show them one bill or receipt; I will tell them you have them locked up. Some were as Cribbe [the gardener] has sumed up. I have receipts for thirteen hundred pounds, besides the last forty two. Mrs Cribbe advises me not to show them till you have seen them. On Saturday I shall send Sarah [Reynolds] with them.'*[29]

Emma wrote to Haslewood on 20 March:

Sir,

    Mr Cribb is in want of his money theirfore I shall be glad if you can settle with him

your obedient

Emma Hamilton[30]

On 29 March Mrs Cadogan wrote suggesting that she and Emma take legal advice:

'I have enclosed to you Cribb's account he brought me from Haslewood the other day. Let me know whether you have a copy of the will or not, as I understand the executors are to pay every expence for six months after his death. Pray write me word whether you have employed a lawyer against Haslewood; let me, in particular, for if you have not I will ... I am well informed of the measure of the land your house stands upon, and will not allow the pleasure ground that is taken in, that you have a right to take in what part you like of Linton's farm, and leave out what you like of the Wimbledon estate. Write me every particular that I may not be taken unawares. Don't you think if you was to write to Mr. Goldsmid and let me

know very particularly who I am to apply to ... Pray, my dear Emma, let me know whether you have answered Mr Robert's bill or not ...'[31] *

In March Emma and Horatia went to visit the Boltons in their large farmhouse in Norfolk. Horatia played happily with two-year-old Emma Horatia, Susanna's grandchild by her daughter, Catherine, Lady Bolton. (Emma's godchild, another 'Little Emma') All four of Susanna's daughters were there. Emma recovered her spirits to some extent. When they left, Susanna wrote to Emma: '... when we all met at dinner we were all in tears to see the <u>vacant places</u>, where so lately they had been filled with those so dear to us'.[32]

Susanna and Kitty knew that Horatia was Nelson's daughter and suspected that Emma was her mother. In May, Kitty wrote from Bath: '... God knows nothing can make up to me and mine for our loss. I can only say, God's will be done; but I feel quite heart-broken ... Pray tell her [Horatia] not to forget her aunt Matcham'.[33]

Before Emma and Horatia's second visit to the Boltons in mid-July, Susanna wrote: 'Kiss dear Horatia, and tell her how happy her aunt Bolton will be to see her ...'

The Earl and Countess Nelson expressed no interest in Horatia.

In letters written to Emma for her birthday from her mother and Sarah Reynolds, the strained state of their finances is clear:

Merton, April 26th. 1806

I pray God send you many happy returns of this day. I have sent you a gown of Sarah Reynolds' making. If I had ten thousand pounds to send you this day, I should have been very happy ... I am all over with bricks and dust and stinking paint, being no body but our own family. On Saturday you shall have a menesstra verde and one thing roasted. Mariann will tell you how miserable I have been this week.

My dear Emma, I owe Mariann 4 months' wages, which is two guines; I had it not to give her, and she want shoes and stockings. If you can, give Sarah Connor thirty shillings to pay her washer-woman, as she is indebted to her for three months' washing. I have got her washing down here ... God bless you, my ever dear Emma etc.

Mrs Cadogan enclosed a note from Sarah Reynolds: 'I wish you many happy returns of this day. I should have been very happy had it been in my power to have made you a small present on this day, but not having anything but what my dear aunt and you have been so good as to give me. I wish it had been in my power; I should have been very happy, believe me, my dear Lady

* Emma's Coutts account shows a payment of £52 to Mr F. Roberts on 12 July

Hamilton. *With gratitude and thank you for what you have done for me and my dear father and family. God bless you, dear Lady Hamilton.*'[34]

We note Mrs Cadogan's letter describes building and decorating work still being carried out at Merton.

Parliament finally debated the grants to be made to Nelson's family. On 12 May, William, the Earl, was awarded an hereditary annuity of £5,000 p.a. and £90,000 with which to purchase a suitable house and estate.* Nelson's sisters were awarded a lump sum of £15,000 each.

Grenville had been in possession of Nelson's last codicil since February, but no mention was made of Emma or Horatia. Nelson was naïve in believing his King and Country would give Emma *'an ample provision to maintain her rank in life'* or that Horatia, his *'adopted'* daughter, would receive the *'beneficence'* of his country.

However, one man in Parliament, Mr John Fuller, observed on 19 May (Author's underlinings): *'The Country had, by its liberality to the family of the deceased Hero, evinced the respect and gratitude which were justly due his memory ...'* and he trusted that ... *'neither the magnanimity of that illustrious man, nor the generosity of the Empire, would be forgotten by those who were to receive profits and honours on account of the service which the immortal Nelson had performed'.* And he *'hoped the representative of that family would also shew some degree of generosity, and comply with the wish expressed by the illustrious founder of the family in his last moments.'*[35]

No such generosity either to Emma or to Horatia was forthcoming from the recently ennobled and now extremely wealthy William.

Soon after Grenville returned the last codicil to Haslewood, explaining there was nothing he could do about Nelson's last request, the Earl and family dined with Emma at Clarges Street. Emma accused him of withholding the codicil. Whereupon, she later claimed, he *'threw it to me and said, with a very coarse expression, that I might now do as I pleased with it'.*[36] A violent argument followed and their relationship never recovered.

Fanny contested Nelson's will. In addition to her pension from Nelson, she claimed a right, as his widow, to one third of his personal fortune at the time of his death.[37] However, a large part of Nelson's personal estate had bought government stocks to provide Fanny's *'income'* of £1,000 p.a.

Susanna wrote to Emma: *'I find the Viscountess is going to Law, what for, to enrich that son of hers? For depend upon it she will not gain a sixpence, if so much Income. What a Vindictive Woman she is. Dispute even the last*

* See Appendix 4.

words of the <u>Man</u> *she once* <u>pretended</u> *to* <u>Love</u>. *She has changed her mourning and is off for Cheltenham. I hope it will purge away all her sins.'*[38]

Susanna and Kitty remained hostile towards Fanny. Only the Earl affected any degree of friendship towards her. She had always been bitterly contemptuous of him. While living with Nelson's father she had accused William of *'ambition, pride and a selfish disposition'* and had written other critical comments: *'the roughest mortal that ever lived'*[39] and *'gain gain is his motto'.*[40] During a dinner given by Lord Sidmouth [Addington], after Nelson's death, the Bishop of Chichester was shocked to hear the Earl say to Sarah: *'Never mind the Battle of Trafalgar, for it has made me an Earl and thee a Countess.'*[41]

Emma's financial situation began to descend into the chaos that devastated the rest of her life.

Reckless extravagance has often been suggested as the cause of her difficulties. Some biographers claim that when Nelson returned for his last twenty-five days at Merton, Emma already had debts of between £7,000 and £9,000.

At the time of Hamilton's death, Emma's debts amounted to £450, partly because she did not receive her allowance from Sir William for the first year after their arrival in England. In the two years and four months since, it is unlikely that she could have amassed such debts unless they included Nelson's debts at Merton.

On 8 May 1805 she wrote to Tyson, who had lent money to Nelson in the past: *'First I must tell you what money I had in my banker's hands I have laid out at Merton ... Could you then, my dearest Tyson, either on my account or Lord Nelson's lend me a hundred and fifty pounds?'*[42]

The money *'laid out at Merton'* included the running expenses and fitting out the new rooms, already agreed by Nelson before his death.

Emma may have owed substantial amounts for Merton. In addition, heavy expenditure was incurred during Nelson's last twenty-five days at home. Nelson's family and other guests were wined and dined there almost every day.

Mrs Cadogan had told Emma there were bills amounting to thirteen hundred pounds, plus a further forty-two bills. These expenses, if still unpaid before Nelson's departure, should have been paid by his executors.*

---

* In 1802/3 Nelson and Hamilton scrupulously shared weekly bills for food and some services. The average expenditure was £75 per week, not counting the wages and other expenses arising on the property.

The executors now failed to pay the final building costs at Merton.

Emma told Rose in a following letter: '... *I have incurred heavy expenses in completing what Lord Nelson had left unfinished at Merton so that I am seven thousand pounds in debt, six of which belonged to him and I have paid it with pleasure ...*'[43]

And told Greville in November 1808: '*... Destruction brought on me by* <u>Earl Nelson's</u> *having thrown on me the Bills for finishing Merton ...*'

Nelson had given Davison clear instructions regarding his financial situation at Merton in his letter on 16 September, five weeks before he died: '*... I have requested you to pay Chawner's account for work to be done in his line and what is ordered, viz. the kitchen, ante-room and for altering the dining-room ...*'[44]

A post-script added: '*I have settled Chawner's account for all which has been hitherto done at Merton.*'

On 13 October, eight days before he died, Nelson wrote to Davison: '*You will do the needful about my accounts, and settle with Mr Chawner for what is going on at Merton.*'[45]

When Nelson left England he had settled Mr Chawner's account for the work completed at Merton and asked Davison to pay for the work still in progress. Davison had been responsible for paying Nelson's debts for him, but after Nelson's death this responsibility transferred to the executors.

When neither Davison nor the executors paid for the final works at Merton, Emma was burdened with a huge debt that she could not possibly meet on her income. Indisputably, by Nelson's will, all his debts on the Merton property and all his personal debts should have been paid by his executors. There being a '*Clear residue*', or surplus, of £12,162 in his estate accounts after all his legacies and debts had been attended to, the executors had no excuse for not settling Chawner's bills and other debts arising at Merton. The above £12,162 had been shared by the Earl, Susanna and Kitty.

Adding to Emma's difficulties, Sir William's annuity to her was paid irregularly rather than quarterly. Nor was it clear of tax as Sir William had stipulated. It thus diminished over the years as tax was deducted initially by Charles Greville and later by his brother Robert Fulke Greville.

Bank accounts show that in 1804 she received £190 per quarter, making £760 p.a., not the £800 Sir William had intended. By 1807 this had reduced to £720 p.a. or £180 per quarter, and remained so until her last payment in March 1813. This was a modest income compared to Fanny's £3,000 p.a., the Earl's £5,000 p.a., or Sir William's pension of £2,000 p.a.

Before the end of the year, Emma began to reduce her expenditure.

In May, she began writing to Haslewood asking for advances on Nelson's bequest of £2,000, a bequest she had still not received by December 1806.

Haslewood replied:

Lincolns Inn 31 May 1806

Dear Madam
According to your Ladyship's request, I send below a cheque for one hundred pounds

> *And remain, always, dear Madam,*
> *Your ladyship's mo faithful & obligd sevt*
> *Wm. Haslewood.*

Any tradesman at Merton will Change the cheque.

Messrs Davison & Co Pay the right honble Lady Hamilton or bearer One hundred pounds for Earl Nelson and Wm. Haslewood. 31 May 1806.[46]

Depressed, Emma wrote to Hayley on 5 June:

My dear Hayley,
As I am very low-spirited and very far from well … I was very happy at Naples, but all seems gone like a dream. I am plagued by Lawyers; ill-used by the Government, and distracted by that variety and perplexity of subjects which, as you may suppose, press on me – I pass as much of my time at dear Merton as possible – and I always feel particularly low when I leave it … but I did try and get a victory over myself and seem to be happy altho' miserable … I am your most unhappy, very grateful
> *Emma Hamilton*[47]

About this time Emma's long-lost daughter, Little Emma (Emma Carew), reappeared in her life, evidently in need of money. Emma wrote to Sir Harry, who she had always claimed, was the girl's father:

July 2nd 1806

My dear Sir Harry,
*   If you cannot do what I ask you burn this and say you cannot for I shall attribute your inability to the right cause and be assured I shall not take it ill. I have £2000 coming to me from Earl Nelson but as things are in Chancery it may be Xmas before I receive. If you could lend me £500 be assured it will at this moment be of the greatest use as I am arranging my affairs. You shall surely have it the moment I am paid or when I sell Merton … But I cannot*

bear the idea to have the appearance of begging for a moment as I never did it nor perhaps shall have an occasion to do it again.

Lord St. Vincent is to speak to Mr. Fox and will give testimony of my services. Has professed great friendship for me ... Pray let us meet as th. [though] I had not asked this favour from you. Let me come to Up Park for a few days to speak of old times. Perhaps long before that time I shall have repaid you – indeed I feel at this moment more than I can tell you in asking this favour but let it be as it may I shall never fail.

Your obliged

E.H.

Burn this.

If you do me this favour let me know by a line. E goes tonight but she is taken care of in case of any accident. Pray write that I may not think you angry.[48]

Emma had clearly already been in contact with Sir Harry about Little Emma.

Shortly afterwards she wrote thanking Sir Harry:

Merton. Thursday 6 o'clock

Your letter, my dear Sir Harry, has made me <u>very happy</u> I write from bed very unwell having had a little fever all night. I was agitated yesterday with Ld St. Vincent's kindness. Also last evening with parting for a time from a very amiable naive and <u>good</u>, <u>good</u> hearted person whose health requires air and exercise. Her tears and really sorrow unmanned me for I do not know that I felt more in parting with any friend than I did with her – I shall be in town tomorrow by one. Will you call on me that I may give you my thanks and if you wd let me have it in a letter instead of going to Coutts I shall be obliged to you as it is to pay household as I am giving up. I will give you a note on Coutts. I shall be rich enough one of these days when they do something for me and their debts paid to me but you have this moment made my mind easy, to me that never owed nor probably shall again. It made me completely uneasy and I wish to do all that is comfortable to <u>our</u> friend <u>who be assured</u> in case of accident is provided for and she is gone into the country happy, ever believe me dear Sir Harry your affectionate and grateful

E.H.

Emma enclosed an IOU written to Messrs Coutts: 'Please pay Sir Harry Featherston five hundred pounds nine months after date.'[49]

Sir Harry never presented the IOU to Coutts.

Following her brief reunion with Little Emma, Emma sent a dejected letter to Davison on 4 July:

'I am very unwell, Broken Hearted and going into Norfolk with Lady Bolton. I shall beg of my mother to send you the gun and canteen that our departed angel *left you. I have now a wide world before me, nor any friends although when I was in power many basked in my sunshine. I have done the state <u>no little service</u>, in Nelson's dying moments he gave testimony of my very important services, he recommended me to the King and Country when he was bleeding and dying for that King and Country. All is now over, all forgotten and the poor unhappy forlorn Emma's services also forgotten – but never mind ... I am giving up my home and establishment in Clarges Street and I fear I must give up Merton if the Government do not do anything for me.'*[50]

Emma realized that she could not maintain Clarges Street on her income and that she might have to *'give up'* Merton if she was not granted a government pension. She may have suspected that she could not count on her income from the Bronte estate. Indeed the Earl later claimed that the estate could not afford her annuity.

In August, Oliver, still employed by Emma, introduced her to the writer James Harrison. Oliver persuaded her that Harrison had fallen on hard times and she would be *'saving him from ruin,'* and that she had it in her power to *'alleviate his numerous suffering family'.*

Emma agreed to employ Harrison to write her planned biography of Nelson. Harrison and his *'numerous suffering family'* lived at Merton while he worked on the project.

Emma's finances were thus further stretched. She did not foresee the disastrous consequences of her generosity towards Harrison and his family.

Emma kept control of Nelson's letters, only allowing Harrison sight of those she wished to be included in the biography. However, Harrison (and Oliver?) may have managed to see private letters when she was absent from Merton. There is a strong likelihood that one, or both of them, later blackmailed her.

Harrison's biography was published in 1806, poorly received and condemned by Fanny and St. Vincent.

Distressed and disappointed in her expectations, Emma wrote to Scott from Norfolk:

Cranwich, Sept 17th. 1806

My Dear Friend,

I did not get your letter till the other day, for I have been with Mrs Bolton to visit an old, respectable aunt of my dear Nelson's ... I wish much to see you, consult with you about my affairs. How hard it is, how louch[e] their treatment to me and Horatia. That angel's last wishes are neglected, not to speak of the fraud that was acted to keep back the Codicil. But enough when we meet we will speak about it. God bless you for all your attentions and love *you shewed to our virtuous Nelson and his Dear Remains; but it seems that those that Truly loved him are to be victoms to Hatred, jealousy, and spite, however we have innocence on our sides and we have and had what they that persecute us never had – that was <u>his</u> unbounded love and esteem, his confidence and affection.*

I know well how he valued you and what he wou'd have done for you had he lived. You know the great and virtuous affection he had for me. The love he bore my husband <u>and if I had any influence over him I used it for the good of my country</u>.

Did I ever keep him at home did I not share in his glory <u>even this last fatal victory, it was I bid him</u> [go] forth ... does he not in his last moments do me justice and request at the moment of his glorious death that the King and Nation will do me justice and I have got all his letters and near Eight hundred of the Queen of Naples' letters to shew what I did for my King and country and prettily I am rewarded.

Psha! I am above them. I despise them for thank God I feel that having lived with Honner and glory glory they cannot take from me ... Look at Alexander Davison courting the man he despised, and neglecting now those he used to lick their feet. Dirty vile groveler! But enough till we meet ...

Write to me at Merton, and ever believe me
Your affectionate
Emma Hamilton

Horatia is charming she begs her love to you. She improves Dayly she sends you 100,000,000 Kisses.[51]

Scott was one of the few loyal friends to whom Emma could confess her feelings. She was bitterly disappointed by the government's neglect. She still believed that the Earl was responsible for holding back Nelson's last codicil.

In October Haslewood received a request for a further advance on her £2,000:

London October 14th 1806

My Dear Sir,

I got your letter and Mr Nests [? illegible] & will sign the papers when you please ... You will allso oblige me by letting me have a Hundred pounds on advance of my Two Thousand as I am now in town getting rid of all my establishment.

I beg you to believe me my Dear Sir
Your obliged
E. Hamilton[52]

Also in October, Emma moved to rented rooms in New Bond Street. She wrote to Haslewood again:

136 New Bond St   22 Dec. 1806

Dear Sir

Will you have the goodness to let me have a Hundred pounds you will much oblige your grateful

Emma Hamilton[53]

She received a cheque from Messrs Davison & Co on 23 December 1806. Stressed by her circumstances, Emma wrote the first of her several wills:

I, EMMA HAMILTON, being in sound body and mind, leave this as my last Will and Testament. I beg, as the virtuous and dear Nelson wished me to be buried near him, that, if it is possible, I may be, if it cannot be, then let me be buried at Merton; but if it is possible, let me rest near my ever beloved Nelson. I give to my dear mother, formerly Mary Kidd, then Lions, and after Mary Doggen, or Cadogan, however she may be called, all my property, let it be either in wearing apparel, or furniture, gold, silver, jewels, pictures, wine, and everything in the house at Merton, and seventy acres which the glorious Nelson left me, and two acres and a half which I have bought since, added to it, all of which I give to my dearest mother for her natural life, and after her death, I give all that I have mentioned, Merton and all that belongs to it, inside the house and on the lands, as well as the lands to my dear Horatia Nelson Thomson, or, properly, Horatia Nelson, for her and her children for ever, and if she dies without children, or without a Will, for she can leave it to whom she pleases after she is eighteen years of age, in case then she should die without a Will, I leave it to the heirs of Susannah Bolton, wife of Thomas Bolton, Esq., of Cranwich, Norfolk, on condition that they pay Sarah Reynolds, my cousin, one hundred a-year for her life, and fifty pounds a-year to Cecilia Connor, my cousin; also I beg and leave to my dear Horatia Nelson, that she pays the above yearly pensions to Sarah Reynolds and Cecilia Connor. I do not leave anything to Ann or Mary Ann Connor, the daughter of Michael and Sarah Connor, as she has been a wicked story-telling young woman, and tried to defame her best friends and relations. I leave Horatia Nelson a ward in Chancery, after my mother's death, and I beg my dear friend George Matcham, Esq., of Bath, and his wife, to have the goodness to see after her education, and that she is properly brought up after my mother's death; if they will see to this, Nelson and Emma's spirits will look down on them and bless them. My dearest mother I leave executrix, with full power, if I have not mentioned everything; I mean, that all I am possessed of, pictures, china, plate, coach, everything belonging to me in the house at Merton, and out on the premises, belong to my mother for her natural life, and after, to Horatia Nelson, my ward, she being six years old. She will be six the 29th of this month of October. I beg this to be considered my last Will. - EMMA HAMILTON

October 7th, 1806 [54]

In leaving her property and all her possessions first to her mother, and upon her death to Horatia, Emma seems unaware of Nelson's Codicil No.1. Bequests to her cousins are evidence of the responsibility she felt towards members of her mother's family. Her efforts to maintain their livelihoods were a drain on her income that she could not afford. The full extent of the money she laid out will be seen in a declaration Mrs Connor was obliged to sign in 1808.

Emma's remark about Ann Connor concerns her claiming to be Emma's daughter. Ann may have visited Merton when Little Emma was there and later decided to impersonate her. Emma had written to Susanna and Kitty denying Ann Connor's claims.

The Matchams had purchased Ashfold Lodge in the village of Slaugham, near Horsham in West Sussex with Kitty's government grant. On his way home from purchasing the property G.M. called at Merton, where he reported to Kitty: *'Not withstanding the vast improvements that have taken place since last I saw it, it appeared dull and lonely.'* [55]

During this year Emma suffered the emotions aroused on what would have been Nelson's 49th birthday on 29 September and the first anniversary of his death of 21 October. Struggling to come to terms with her life without him and her alarming financial situation, she appealed to the Earl and Haslewood for help, using language suggesting that she had legal assistance:

Merton, Novr 14, 1806

My Lord,

Having seen with inexpressible pleasure that every wish of the late Lord Nelson regarding the interests of his Family, when only communicated to the gracious Sovereign in whose service he so gloriously fell, has been instantly and Liberally granted by the generous bounty of our King and Country, I am naturally induced to consider as equally certain that the same mode of conveying his last, humble request in favour of the Infant, Horatia Nelson, his adopted daughter, as well as of myself, will be observed with a proportionate degree of attention. I have therefore to require not only on my own behalf, but as Guardian of the said Infant, by virtue of his late Lordship's will, and the CODICIL particularly expressive of that request, that you will have the goodness immediately to assist me in regularly carrying into effect the evident intention of the Testator whose executor you have <u>the honour to be</u>.'[56]

The Earl replied:

Canterbury, November 16, 1806

Dear Lady Hamilton,

No one is more ready and willing to comply with every wish of my Dear and lamented Brother than myself. With regard to what you allude to in your letter of 14th instant – if you will point out what it is you want me to do, either for yourself or the child, I shall be glad to give you every assistance in my power. We expect to be in town about Xmas, and shall hope to see you at our house. Lady Nelson has been in daily expectation of hearing from you. She and Charlotte beg to join in best regards and good wishes with your faithful humble servant,

NELSON[57]

As executor of Nelson's will, he knew Emma had not received her £2,000, nor any of the £500 p.a. Bronte money. He could now have used his influence to press government ministers to act upon Nelson's last codicil, but he offered no further assistance other than allowing her small advances on her £2,000. He had, however, registered Horatia's name as Horatia Nelson in accordance with Nelson's wishes.

Mrs Cadogan made enquiries about Emma's legacy. Haslewood replied in July: 'I am bound to discharge all demands on the estate before anything can be done respecting the legacies'.[58] Apparently 'all demands on the estate' did not include paying for the remaining building works at Merton.

Emma's bank accounts from 1800-1812 neatly balance at the end of each financial year. She must have had to borrow money, probably at exorbitant rates, to pay off some of her mounting debts. Nelson's bequest of the Merton property came encumbered with such huge debts that within three years of his death Emma was obliged to put it up for sale.

Her ill-judged generosity made her precarious financial situation even more unmanageable. While she continued to pursue her claims through St. Vincent and Lord Abercorn and with the unfailing efforts of George Rose, she tried to maintain her mother, her maids and her cousins, Merton and its servants, solely on Sir William's annuity. But this was impossible without a pension from the government or her Bronte annuity.

Emma was unwise not to act on her mother's advice to employ a good lawyer. Nor, it seems, did she attempt to sell some of the contents, or part of the land at Merton, to help in her current predicament. The following November the estimated value of the books, wine, statues, vases and pictures at Merton was estimated at £5,000. Forty acres of the land, situated in the parish of Merton, was valued at £3,500. This excluded the house, gardens and thirty-two acres she hoped to retain.

Emma was reluctant to give up her London connections but the New Bond Street rooms were uncomfortable and inconvenient.

Susanna wrote: '... *I was very much hurt to see you were obliged whether you liked it or not, to mix with their society* [the landlady] *indeed, if they had given you up the front drawing-room entirely and two bed-chambers, you would have been more comfortable.'*[59]

Emma and Horatia spent weekdays in town and weekends at Merton, where Emma continued to entertain.

In August 1807 Kitty invited her to visit Ashfold Lodge. Emma, her mother and Horatia travelled to Ashfold and on to Worthing. George junior's diary records the arrival of the party from Merton: *'Consisting of Lady Hamilton, Lady Bolton, with her sister Anne, Mrs Cadogan, Mrs Bianchi and Miss Horatia Nelson...'*

The Ashfold party joined Emma's friend Mrs. Bianchi, who had taken a house in Worthing.

George (eighteen years old) reported that the young ladies *'were driving themselves in little vehicles drawn by asses'* on the beach. The party enjoyed *' some duets by Lady H. and Mrs B'* and a visit to the theatre. One evening they *'dined en famille and in ye evening went to ye ball, where we danced till 1/2 past 3p.m'*.

They returned to Ashfold and, after a few days, *'the Hamilton party set out for Merton. Her Ladyship first invited me to come to her house on ye 28th October, that being Anne's and Horatia's birthday'*.

It appears she had finally received her £2,000 legacy. Her bank account was credited with £450 on 27 June, £450 on 7 July and £500 on 25 July, making a total of £1,400. After adding the advances she had received and deducting tax paid the total approaches £2,000. Her account ends the year with a credit balance of £3.12s.7d.

Nevertheless, Emma must have had several creditors waiting, with increasing impatience, for payment. During the year June 1807-June 1808, Emma paid off seventy debts, totalling £3,844.

Her income for this year records equally unusual amounts received:

Legacy, as calculated above	£1400
4 annuity payments @£180	£ 720
Exchequer bill	£ 104
From 'her' (unspecified sources)	£1110
Item listed as 'Her Bond' (bank loan)	£ 500
	£3834

Emma now had a much closer relationship with Susanna and Kitty, but wrote to Sarah from Worthing:

[27th August]

Here we are in this delightful place. My dearest Horatia is got well and strong [she was recovering from chickenpox] *and now eats and drinks and sleeps well and* creates universal interest, *altho' Princess Charlotte is here she is left and all come to look at Nelson's angel. She improves in language musick & accomplishments but my heart bleeds to think how proud wou'd her glorious Father have been, he that* lived only for her *whoes last words and thoughts were to her –* she *wou'd* have been every thing, *'tis dreadful to me. However she is my comfort and solace and I act as tho' he cou'd look down and approve and bless Emma for following up his every wish ... You see, my letters are not so gay as they used to be, but my dearest friend, every day my affliction encreases for the loss of my dearest Nelson and Mrs Matcham and I sitt and walk for hours, talking and weeping for him. At this time two years, how happy we were. Every day we think of what we were doing with that angel who appeared amongst us for those happy 25 days. Time only adds to my grief ... My mother who is with* [us] *begs her compliments.*

Ever dear Lady Nelson the miserable

Emma Hamilton[60]

In Worthing Emma heard from Rose that the new Foreign Secretary, George Canning, had been unable to achieve any favourable response to Emma's claims, although he believed them justified. Emma replied:

'I thought Mr Canning would have done me justice for it was not any favour I asked, and I thought the only favour the Saviour of his country begged might have been granted. Although I might not have had any claim for my services his daughter also left desolate and unprovided for. But enough I cannot write with temper.

I must part with Merton although it was the last request he made that I wou'd live and educate Horatia there ... I have had to finish all the buildings he ordered and pay all the bills that he wished to have paid on his return, so that I am seven thousand pounds in debt, six of which belonged to him and I have paid it with pleasure. All I wanted was that I should have had my debts paid, for I lost more than that in property when we served the royal family at Naples, and I thought then that we were helping the good cause ...'[61]

Rose's reply implied that he had taken this as criticism of his efforts. Emma apologised:

'You must have mistaken my letter and my meaning if you could suppose for a moment that I did not feel grateful to you for your kind exertions for me and Horatia ... the King I never though[t] would do anything for me, as he treated dear glorious Nelson ill, and my husband, who had served him thirty-seven years, why should I expect him to help me, but I thought his ministers would have done what was right to the woman who had done so much for her country ... as to dear Horatia, I love her so well and so fondly that be assured every thing shall be done that if he could look down he would approve of. She shall not be a ward in Chancery, nor shall she be left subject to anyone he would have disapproved of. She will go with me and if anything happens to me Mrs. Matcham will be the person, for not to any one of the family beside would I trust her... Excuse this scrawl, for I am so ill at ease and I have fretted myself into a nervous fever and have so much to do that I can scarcely hold my pen.'[62]

George junior joined Tom Bolton at Merton on 24 October for Horatia's birthday: *'... We all went in ye evening to Mr Perry's who was extremely polite to us ... 25th Sunday morning we went to Church and dined at Merton ... great preparations were made for the celebration of little Horatia's birthday ... a large party assembled at dinner ... There was a dance in the evening, which I had the honour of opening with the little Horatia ...'*[63]

Mrs Billington and the vicar, Mr Lancaster, attended the party.

Towards the end of the year, the Prince of Wales with his brothers, the Duke of Clarence and the Duke of Sussex, visited Merton. Emma was accustomed to entertaining royalty and had known the Duke of Sussex, as Prince Augustus, in Naples.*

Susanna was excited and impressed by Emma's royal guests. She wrote:

Cranwich, December 8th

'... How favoured you have been by their Royal Highnesses passing so many days with you. I do not wonder their liking Merton & your society. Did the Prince of Wales spend more than one day with you? Poor Blindy! Had I been

---

* Prince Augustus had spent two years in Naples during which he had, at times, stayed at the Palazzo Sessa and attended many functions there. On one occasion, Sir William and Emma had arranged a concert for his entertainment at which Mrs Billington sang for him.

in her place I should have kept my room the time they were there – at least the Prince ...'[64]

'*Poor Blindy*', Maurice Nelson's 'wife', was staying at Merton when the royal visitors arrived. The Duke of Sussex certainly stayed several days, as George junior noted that on 11 December '*the Duke of Sussex, who was confined in his room with a fever*' at Merton.

This expensive royal visit gave Emma the opportunity to appeal to the Prince of Wales for support in her pension claims and for Horatia to be presented to him. The Prince promised protection of her when he should be in 'a position to act'. It was a promise he did not keep.

CHAPTER 23

Under Threat of Imprisonment

*' You are the only hope I have in this world to assist and protect me in
this moment of unhappiness and distress.'*
Emma to the Duke of Queensberry, 4 September 1808

*'At a moment of desperation, when I thought they neglected me,
Goldsmid and my Citty friends came forward, and they have rescued me
from distruction.'*
Emma to Greville, November, 1808

*'I envy you the entertainment and information of Lady Hamilton's
company. She has I think been very ungratefully treated for her great
publick services.'*
Sir Charles Malet to George Matcham, 1810

THE EARL AND Countess, William and Sarah, suffered a terrible blow
when Horace, their only son and heir, died unexpectedly in January
1808. It was a particular shock for the Earl as the next in line to inherit
the Earldom, the estate and the £5,000 p.a. was Susanna's son, Tom.
Sarah never recovered from the loss of her son.*

Doctors in London were unable to save him from what was later
identified as typhoid fever. He was buried on 25 January at St. Paul's
Cathedral, in a vault near Nelson's tomb.

George junior recorded the sad event: *'... Poor fellow I am truly sorry
for him and his loss is irretrievable to his family ... Poor Ld T ... had been
some time indisposed, but was not supposed in a dangerous state, till a few
days before his death.'*[1]

---

* Such was the Earl's determination to provide an heir himself that after Sarah's death he
married a young widow of twenty-eight when he was seventy years old in 1828. When the
marriage failed to produce any children, Tom Bolton succeeded to the title on William's
death in 1835.

This tragedy helped to repair the relationship between the Earl and his two sisters. Contact was renewed when they all met unexpectedly in Brighton. George's diary records the event on 16 March: *'... By all accounts the meeting was uncommonly cordial, as the N--blem-n received his sisters after an absence of two years with (oh! excess of fraternal affection) a----Grunt ...'*

George junior saw the Earl in London on 22 March: *'Called on the E---l N. He was tolerably civil. Went to ye play with Mrs Bolton and her daughters.'*

Afterwards they called on Emma: *'On arriving at Clarges St. we found ye Duke of Sussex there (a Gentleman of enormous stature) in his Highland dress ... He had been to dine with the Scotch society ...'*

Emma, Horatia, Susanna and her two daughters, Mrs. Peirson and her daughter, all spent a few days at Ashfold. On 10 March Kitty wrote to her: *'... I am delighted to hear of your going to all these great parties; London is certainly the place for your constant residence, where you can enjoy the society of your friends, without the immense expense of entertaining their servants, which you are obliged to do in the country. I hope to hear in your next that Mrs Cadogan is quite recover'd, to whom & to all your party we beg to be kindly remembered, not forgetting my dear Horatia, & accept our sincere good wishes from, My dear Lady Hamilton, your affectionate, etc.'[2]*

Mrs Cadogan had been *'dangerously ill'* the previous April and had accompanied Emma to Ashfold and Worthing in August to recuperate.

In April, Emma decided to sell Merton Place. This raises the question as to whether she had the right to do so. Nelson's codicil no.1 only gave Emma the use of the property *'for and during her lifetime'*. Strictly speaking the property was not hers to sell, although this depends on the law regarding 'settled land' at that time. Debts outstanding on the property meant that it had to be sold and it is likely that Nelson's executors, the Earl and Haslewood, put pressure on Emma to this end.

On 4 April J. Willock of Golden Square valued the house, gardens, farmhouse, barns, stables and outbuildings, with seventy-two acres of land, *'worth the sum of £10,430'* and the furniture and effects in the house, offices, gardens and grounds at £2,500, bringing the value of the entire freehold property and contents to £12,930.[3] This valuation was considerably lower than another calculated later in November. It was a year before Merton was sold.

Mrs Cadogan had been ill on and off for some time. Now Emma's health began to fail.

Concerned, Old Q. offered her the use of his property, Heron House in Richmond, at a nominal rent. The eight-bedroomed house with a garden fronting the Thames provided ample accommodation for Emma, her mother, Horatia and a few servants.

Writing to Emma, George Matcham revealed his opinion of the Earl after the Boltons and the Matchams had applied to him for permission to change their name to Nelson:

'What you have written in respect of the Earl has quite astonished me. I could never have conceiv'd he could have so betray'd Tom Bolton, but it is evident that he is as great an enemy to us as our dear lost friend was our patron. The extinction of the whole family would be a matter of the greatest exultation to him, with the exception of his own dear self and Lady Charlotte. God only knows what his shocking rancour will lead to ... In respect to the change of name, he cannot say it is any personal pride that has made me anxious to assume that of the good & noble Viscount, that I should feel the honour is most true, but I desir'd Mr Haslewood to say that my anxiety was for Mrs. M. and our children to enjoy the honour and the advantage, & that I was very willing to descend to the grave as plain George Matcham; but the man is a rancourous foe to his sisters and their offspring.'[4]

Kitty added a note:

'... If the name of our dearest angel is taken we must all have it, for I will never take one that my good husband is not allowed to have ... Let the family sink or swim together, if equally deserving ...'

Before moving into Heron House Emma and Horatia paid another visit to Norfolk.

In July, while Rose sought the support of Lord Abercorn, Emma, aware of the gravity of her situation, appealed to St. Vincent:

' A strong sense of the deep regard which you have ever shewn, for all that relates to the welfare of our country in general, and consequently to its naval glory in particular; with the tender recollection, how dear you thus rendered yourself to the heart of our immortal and incomparable hero ... I will not arouse the just indignation of your Lordship's great and honourable mind, by reciting the many petty artifices, mean machinations, and basely deceptive tenders of friendship, which hitherto have prevented Lord Nelson's dying request from being duly heard by those to whom it is so peculiarly and pathetically addressed. You, my Lord, cannot be insensible of the value of my public services, since it is to them alone I have been so many years indebted for the proud boast of possessing your friendship.

As the widow of Sir William Hamilton, more than thirty years Ambassador at the Courts of Naples and Palermo, had I never seized the opportunity, or even felt the inclination, to perform any one act of public service, I might still have expected a reasonable pension would be granted, if duly applied for, by the benevolent Monarch whom my husband had so long, so ably, and so faithfully served ...'

Emma pointed out that the widow of Charles Lock, Consul at Palermo for only two years, had been assigned a pension of £800 a year and the widow of Mr Fox had immediately been granted £1,200 a year and his daughter £300 a year. She concluded:

Surely the daughter of Lord Nelson, now Miss Nelson, is not less an object worthy the attention of her King and country, than Miss Willoughby, the daughter of Mr Fox.

I have said, perhaps, more than enough; but the goodness of your Lordship's heart will excuse whatever may flow from mine ...

I shall in a few days, transmit you a printed copy of Lord Nelson's dying request, prefaced by his admirable prayer for his King and country, and accompanied by the Reverend Dr. Scott's attestation ... and relying, with the most unbounded confidence, on your Lordship's judgment, as to what measures may be most advisable to be pursued, for the attainment of objects so important to Miss Nelson, as well as to myself, and so dear to the heart of Britain's greatest naval hero. I am, &c.

Emma Hamilton[5]

Emma firmly believed she was due a pension as Sir William's widow, bearing in mind the support she had given him when he was the ambassador in Naples and Palermo.* Such pensions were not automatically awarded to widows. Emma had *'duly applied for'* a pension, in accordance with the required application.

St. Vincent disapproved of Emma's liaison with Nelson, but nevertheless agreed the government had treated her shabbily. The pension was never granted, despite Nelson's codicil backing her claims.

Many believed this to be an injustice, including Sir Charles Malet, who wrote to G.M.:

'I envy you the entertainment and information of Lady Hamilton's company. She has I think been very ungratefully treated for her great publick services ...'[6]

---

* Sir William kept Emma's transcription of the letter from King Charles of Spain to King Ferdinand, written in Italian, dated 11 August 1795. Two further long and complex letters transcribed by Emma survive, recorded in Morrison 259 and 265: A letter from Spain to the Foreign Minister of Naples dated 31 March 1795 and a letter in French from the Neapolitan Ambassador to Spain to the Queen dated 9 June 1795.

Further evidence appears in a letter from Sir Richard Puleston to Emma in December 1811:

'... I really look on you as a national blessing, and shame fall on those who have so cruelly neglected to recompense your highly eminent services ...'[7]

Rose, hoping he had found a buyer for Merton, wrote to Emma, adding a report on his meeting with Canning:

Old Palace Yard, July 21st. 1808

'I have seen Mr Dawson this morning ... and I find there is now a gentleman from the East Indies about the property at Merton, who is likely to give nearly £13,000 for the house, land & fixtures – exclusive of the furniture, wine & books, the latter I am sure should be packed up and sent to London. From all that passed with Mr Dawson I am led to hope the sale is likely to take place ...

I had an opportunity of a very quiet conversation with Mr Canning on Sunday last, about the paper written by Lord Nelson just before he went into his last action, which has led to further communication on the same subject. I repeat ... that there is a perfect disposition in Mr Canning's mind to give effect to that paper, but the difficulties are, I fear, insurmountable. I can most truly assure you that I have most anxiously and conscientiously discharged all that Lord Nelson could have expected from me if he were now alive, & I am most sincerely grieved that I have failed of success. The point is not absolutely decided, but I should be inexcusable if I were to give you any hope ...'[8]

None of the above appeals succeeded, despite both Rose and Canning agreeing on the justice of her claims. Even Grenville, the following July, admitted to Rose that *'her services deserved reward'*.

The potential sale of Merton Place fell through. An unsuccessful auction of the property followed in June, reported by George junior: *'... going over Westminster Bridge I met Lady Hamilton, who was low on account of ye house at Merton not being sold when put up to auction the day before.'*[9]

The sale of the house being her only means of paying her debts, Emma turned Old Q:

Richmond, September 4th. 1808

My dear Lord and friend, may I hope that you will read this, for you are the only hope I have in this world to assist and protect me, in this moment of unhappiness and distress. To you, therefore, I appeal. I do not wish to have more than what I have. I can live on that at Richmond, only that I may live free from fear – that every debt may be paid. I think, and hope, £15,000 will do for everything. For my sake, for Nelson's sake, for the good I have done my country, purchase it [Merton]; *take it, only giving me the portraits of Sir William, Nelson, and the Queen. All the rest shall go. I shall be free and at liberty. I can live at Richmond on what I have; you will be doing a deed that will make me happy, for lawyers will only involve me every day more and more – debts will increase new debts. You will save me by this act of kindness. The title deeds are all good and ready to deliver up and I wish not for more than what will pay my debts. I beseech you, my dear Duke, to imagine that I only wish for you to do this, not to lose by it; but I see that I am lost, and most miserable, if you do not help me. My mind is made up to live on what I have. If I could but be free from Merton – all paid, and only one hundred pounds in my pocket, you will live to see me blessing you, my mother blessing you, Horatia blessing you. If you would not wish to keep Merton, perhaps it will sell in the spring better – only let me pass my winter without the idea of prison. 'Tis true my imprudence has brought it on me, and villany and ingratitude has helped to involve me, but the sin be on them. Do not let my enemies trample on me; for God's sake then, dear Duke, good friend, think 'tis Nelson who asks you to befriend, etc.*[10]

Understandably, at eighty-four, and however much inclined to help Emma, the Duke of Queensberry had no desire to purchase another property.

Emma's *'imprudence'* continued unabated. Mrs Graeffer had been a guest at Merton for some time; Anne Bolton (who was ill) was being nursed by Mrs Cadogan. Cecilia and Oliver remained employed.

Money-lenders and creditors were pressing for payment. G.M. wrote to his son in November: *'Lady Hamilton has been harassed and grievously insulted by her creditors. Her eyes are open and she seems determined to strike at the root of the evil. Two maids and a foot boy are all her household servants. I hope she will continue to be prudent and feel the comforts of It ...'*[11]

George junior criticized Emma's lifestyle at Richmond after he visited her in October:

'There were some citizens at dinner, but alas! how different was that table now to what I had before been accustomed; where formally elegance presided, vulgarity and grossièreté was now introduced ... A plan of economy has been most laudably laid down by her L----------p but I could have wished that the crowd of obsequeous attendance had been entirely dismissed, instead of being partially diminished.'[12]

Emma's health deteriorated further when she contracted jaundice. She had probably increased her alcohol consumption, weakening a liver already damaged by episodes of amoebic dysentery in Naples. Worried about her health, Emma wrote another Last Will and Testament at Richmond, on 16 October 1808. Her main concerns were as follows:*

... I beg that Merton may be sold, and all debts paid: and, whatever money shall be left after all the debts are paid, I give to my dear mother, and after her death to my dear Horatia Nelson.

I also give all that I am posessed of in this world to my dear mother, Mary Doggin, or Cadogan, for her use, and, after her death, to Horatia Nelson. I give them all my ready money, plate, linen, pictures, wearing apparel, household furniture, trinkets, wine, in short, everything I have in this world to my mother during her life and after her death to me dearest Horatia Nelson ... I beg His Royal Highness the Prince of Wales, as he dearly loved Nelson, that His Royal Highness will protect his child, and be kind to her, for this I beg him, for there is no one I so highly regard as His Royal Highness. Also my good friend the Duke of Queensbury, I beg of him, as Nelson beseeched him to be kind to me, so I commend my dear mother and Horatia to his kind heart ... but if there should be any administration in at my death who have hearts and feelings, I beg they will provide for Horatia Nelson, the child who would have had a father if he had not gone forth to fight his country's battles, therefore she has a claim on them ... I give all my papers, books, lace, and indeed everything to my dear mother and Horatia Nelson. This I declare to be my last Will and Testament, and to do away with all other wills.

Emma Hamilton[13]

Emma's previous will left Merton to her mother and on her death, to Horatia, but now it had to be sold to pay her debts. Emma still possessed 'plate, linen, pictures, wearing apparel, household furniture, trinkets and wine' amounting to a considerable asset.

By November Emma was in imminent danger of being arrested for non-payment to some of her creditors. Merton had not sold. Her neighbour, Abraham Goldsmid, Davison and Rose together devised a means of preventing her arrest. A solicitor, Mr. Dawson, was engaged to draw up a list of her creditors to present to a group of bankers and businessmen assembled to assist her.

Their meeting on 25 November was recorded as follows:

* See Appendix 5 for the full text

At a meeting of the friends of Lady Hamilton, held at the house of
Sir John Perring, Bart., the 25th. Novr., 1808.
Present

Sir John Perring	Mr McClure	Mr Nichol
Mr Davison	Mr Goldsmid	Mr Wilson
Mr Moore	Sir Robert Barclay	Mr Lavie
Mr Gooch		

Mr Dawson attending as Solr. to Lady Hamilton.

Read   A letter from Lady Hamilton addressed to the gentlemen
         attending the Meeting.

Read   A list of debts delivered in by Mr Dawson as obtained by
         advertizement, also a list of additional debts delivered in by Lady
         Hamilton herself, the whole debt estimated at £8,000, exclusive
         £10,000 required to pay off annuities.

Upon consideration of the property possessed by Lady Hamilton the same
was ascertained as follows

Books	£1,500
Wine	2,000
Statues, Vases, China, Pictures	
and other articles of fancy	1,500
Furniture and Fixtures	1,500
House & 32 Acres	7,500
40 Acres	3,500

Taken at a very low rate	£17,500

The above property being independent of her annuities under the
wills of Sir William Hamilton and Lord Nelson, and her claim on
Government.

RESOLVED   That an assignment of the whole of Lady Hamilton's
property be taken, and that the same be made to:

Sir John Perring, Bart.	Richard Wilson, Esq.
Alexander Davison, Esq.	And
Abraham Goldsmid, Esq.	Germain Lavie, Esq.
as Trustees for Sale, etc.	

That in order to afford an immediate relief the following sums be advanced by

Alexander Davison	One thousand pounds
Abm Goldsmid	One thousand pounds
John Gooch	Five hundred pounds

Richd Wilson	Five hundred pounds
Sir Robert Barclay	Five hundred pounds
John Perring	Two hundred pounds

to be secured by the said Trust with interest.

That the money collected by the above advances be applied in payment of all incumbrances absolutely necessary to be immediately discharged.

That all the creditors be applied to to execute the Debt of Trust, and to agree to accept payment out of the Trust Estate.

That pending the Trust Lady Hamilton be allowed to receive her annuities, but in the case of deficiency the same shall be applied in liquidating the balance.

That the Trustees be a Committee to follow up the claim on Government, in which all the friends of Lady Hamilton be requested to co-operate.

That the Trustees do go to market in the most advantageous mode possible, so as not to injure the property by a premature sale.[14]

All those present signed this document.

Several important points should be noted:

Emma had sufficient collateral to cover her borrowings. The valuation of her assets listed above was *'taken at a very low rate'*. Emma had borrowed money against the security of her annuity payments due. In her desperation she had undertaken these loans at extortionate rates of interest resulting in the debt above recorded as £10,000, on top of her 'personal' debts amounting to £8,000.*

The Trust agreed that Emma should be allowed to receive her annuities.

These 'personal' debts amounting to £8,000 included, by her reckoning, £6,000 owing for building works at Merton.

In November Greville reappeared on the scene, having written Emma a *'note'*. She replied with the following:

Sunday Morning.

Dear Sir,

I was on the point of coming to you when I got your note, but I feel sorry to-day I cannot call on you at your house, for I am to meet some of my trustees

---

* An indenture dated 5th. May 1807 between Emma and Francis Gifford of Upavon, a money-lender, was purchased by Wimbledon Museum in 1991. By the indenture, Emma borrowed £1000 and agreed to pay Gifford £100 per quarter for the rest of his natural life. If she was 7 days late on any payment, Gifford was entitled to a further £2000. *(Reprinted from the Trafalgar Chronicle, the Journal of the 1805 Club, 1995).* Had she fallen victim to a confidence trickster?

and my solicitor, at 2 O'Clock, on particular business. As to my dear friend, Mrs Greffer, it was not any favour she wished for herself, for she wou'd not ask one of the King, and I have taken care to give her such letter for the Queen, and beg'd of Her Majesty by the love she bears or once bore to Emma, by all that I have done for her, by the sacred memory of Nelson, by the Charge she has placed in me, that she will be good to Mrs Greffer, whom she allways marked with the Royal Notice. I have given her [the Queen] an account of the Cruel neglect of the present possessor of dear Lord Nelson's honored Titles, Estates and Honours, neglect to me who was the maker of his family and neglect to Mrs Greaffer. But why speak of such people. Let it suffice she sails Thursday and I have done by her as I have done by all that my Glorious Nelson thought I would do if He fell, I have fulfilled and am fulfilling my Duty's daily to his memory.

I will call soon to see you, and inform you of my present prospect of happiness. At the moment of desperation, when I thought they neglected me, Goldsmid and my Citty friends came forward, and they have rescued me from distruction. Distruction brought on my Earl Nelson's having thrown on me all the bills for finishing Merton. Nelson, who attested in his dying moments that I had well served my Country. All these things, and papers of my services and my illtreatment I have laid before my trustees; they are paying my debts. I live in retirement, and the citty are going to bring forward my claims; in short, I have put myself under their protection, and nothing, <u>no power on earth</u> shall make me <u>deviate</u> from my present system ... You will be pleased to hear my mother is well and delighted with my house and small establishment. Horatia is well, and you will, I think, be pleased with her education. Goldsmid has been, and is an angel to me, and his bounty shall never be abused. I hope you will mend as Spring advances, and if you shou'd ever come to Richmond, pray call and see me, and pray believe me, your affectionately,

Emma Hamilton[15]

Neither Emma nor Mrs Graeffer had received the annuities left to them in Nelson's will. Mrs Graeffer chose to return to Palermo, hence Emma's appeal to Maria Carolina on her behalf. Exiled in Sicily, the Queen was unable to help either Emma or Mrs Graeffer.*

Emma recognized Davison's contribution of £1,000 towards

---

* Emma's comment in this letter - *'by the Charge she* [the Queen] *has placed in me'* refers to a subterfuge she resorted to in which she appears to insinuate that Maria Carolina was Horatia's mother - *'Her mother was <u>too great</u> to be mentioned'.* Many years later Horatia commented: *'Poor Lady Hamilton was not a strict adherer to the truth and her statement implying that the Queen of Naples was my mother, was most incredible - had it been so, of course I should have passed as her husband's child'.*

relieving her most pressing debts on 21 December: *'... be assured to my last breathe I shall feel a glory in having had Alexander Davison for my friend as did Nelson to his death Dye Loving & respecting you more than He Did any man living. Relations not Excepted.'*[16]

Battling his own financial difficulties and facing the ruin of his reputation, Davison could offer no further aid other than a temporary loan. On 7 December he was charged in the Court of the King's Bench in Westminster Hall with fraudulently claiming agency commission from the government on goods that he had supplied from his own factories. His explanations were dismissed out of hand. To avoid imprisonment he repaid the government £18,000, the entire amount of commission he had received.* Nevertheless, on 27 April he was sentenced to twenty-one months in Newgate prison.[17]

Imprisonment in Newgate was a thoroughly unpleasant experience, particularly for a man of Davison's standing. Privacy could not be purchased as at the Marshalsea. Between the guilty verdict in February and sentence in April, Davison had been confined in Newgate. Emma wrote him encouraging letters and she and Horatia often visited him.

Determined to maintain her new economy regime, Emma reduced both her staff and her ongoing responsibility for her mother's relations, the Connors and the Reynoldses. She had a document drawn up late in December that her aunt, Mrs Connor, was obliged to sign:

Mrs. Connor voluntarily acknowledges, that she and her children have been generously supported for many years by the bounty of Lady Hamilton, who has expended, on her account, as she believes, little less that Two Thousand Pounds, and still kindly protects them: and Mrs. Connor farther declares, that all the reports to Lady Hamilton of reflections on her Lady-ship, by Mrs. Connor; such as having sold the bed from under her, and the like scandalous aspersions are totally false and unjustly intended to prejudice Lady Hamilton against her, to whom she the said Mrs. Connor now protests she can never be sufficiently grateful. To Mrs. Cadogan too, Mrs. Connor hereby acknowledges she is likewise indebted for the most kind and generous assistances.

Signed by Mrs. Connor, this 29th. Decr.1808 in the presence of
Jane West
Elizth. Harrison
Sarah Connor[18]

---

* In 1809 he partially recovered his financial situation when, to avoid damaging publicity, the government settled a debt of £11,000 owing to him by the Prince of Wales.

Emma had, belatedly, realized that she could not afford to support her relations.

A letter to Emma from Mrs Thomas, the widow of her first employer in Hawarden, provides further evidence of Emma's generosity towards her various cousins: ... *'I am truly sorry that you have so much trouble with your relations, and the ungrateful return your care and generosity meets with, is indeed enough to turn your heart against them. However, ungrateful as they are, your own generous heart cannot see them in want, and it is a pity that your great generosity towards them shou'd be so ill-placed ...'*[19]

Aware of her calamitous situation and of the ominous threat of imprisonment, she wrote to Rose: *'This want of success* [in her pension claims] *has been more unfortunate for me, as I have incurred very heavy expenses in completing what Lord Nelson had left unfinished at Merton and I have found it impossible to sell the place. From these circumstances I have been reduced to a situation the most painful and distressing that can be conceived, and should have been actually confined in prison if a few friends from the attachment to the memory of Lord Nelson had not intervened to prevent it, under whose kind protection alone I am enabled to exist ...'*[20]

In March she wrote to Sir William Scott: *... I have suffered much, but I hope yet all will be right. I feel it a comfort that in my splendour I did good. I served my country and many basqued in my sunshine. But my only ambition now is that I shall fulfill Nelson's last request, take care of his Horatia, make my mother comfortable, pay everyone what is their due, act honourably and right and be esteemed by good and sensible men. Do you, my dear sir, think well of and love your ever grateful and affectionate*

Emma Hamilton.[21]

Over the next few years, Emma suffered the loss of several significant people in her life. Her optimism alternated with despair and depression.*

The first of these losses was Greville, who died at his home in Paddington, on 23 April 1809, a few days before his 60th birthday. Other than paying Emma Sir William's annuity, he had not given her any financial assistance, despite having the benefit of Sir William's estates, art works, books and other collections for years. Greville, dying

---

* Troubridge had died in 1807 when his ship went down in a storm on his way home from India. Sir Alexander Ball, Knighted in 1801, died in October 1809. Honoured by the Maltese, where he had been Governor since 1802. Vice-Admiral Lord Cuthbert Collingwood, died in March 1810, on his way home from his long period of service in the Mediterranean after the Battle of Trafalgar.

intestate, left nothing to Emma. His executors sold his collection of minerals to the British Museum for £13,727. In accordance with Hamilton's will, his estates passed to Greville's younger brother, the Hon. Robert Fulke Greville.

Kind Old Q, realizing that there might be a delay before Emma received her annuity payment from Robert Greville, contacted Coutts & Co., who made a note on Emma's account on 29 June: *'As Lady Hamilton experiences some inconveniency from the delay in the payment of her Jointure which has taken place in consequence of the death of Mr Greville, to pay her drafts to the extent of the £180 for a quarter due at Midsummer last charging them as usual to her account for which he* [the Duke of Queensbury] *promises to be answerable if we should not receive the Jointure for that period – if we do receive it – it will of course replace the overpayment and he requests that Lady Hamilton may not be informed of his interference upon this occasion.'*[22]

In April, Abraham Goldsmid purchased Merton Place and some of the contents for nearly £13,000. Fabulously wealthy, he owned a mansion in St. James' Square in addition to his country home near Merton.

On 23 April, Susanna wrote to Emma: *'I am glad to hear Goldsmid has purchased Merton rather than any stranger. You, I hope, will feel more easy now it is gone ...'*[23]

Emma, her mother and Horatia now lived quietly at Richmond for the rest of the year. Largely blaming the Earl for her debts, Emma nevertheless wrote to Sarah soon after the meeting with her *'Citty friends'*: *'... Horatia improves in beauty, talents and virtue every day. She is a glorious child, cou'd He have lived to see her – alas that wou'd have been too much happiness ... I have been living in the Citty with Alderman and Lady Perrin[g] this week. Horatia had a great dinner given to her on her birthday, the Lord Mayor drank her health and she was put on the table after dinner and she made a speech which made them all cry. Their is more hospitality in the Citty than anywhere ...'*[24]

Early in June Christie's held a three-day sale of some of the contents from Merton:

A Catalogue of
The Very Choice & Extremely Valuable
Library of Books
of
Antiquities & Prints

Marbles & Bronzes
A few articles of Ornamental Furniture
PICTURES
Drawings & Prints framed & glazed
The property of the late
Sir William Hamilton K.B.
and the
Rt. Hon. Lord Viscount Nelson
deceased
Removed from his Lordship's late Villa
at Merton.

The sale realized £1,907 but Christie's have no record of who received this payment. Some of the items sold had belonged to Nelson and Emma should have received part of the proceeds in accordance with Nelson's will. No credit of any amount from Christie's appears in Emma's bank account between June and December 1809. Robert Greville may have received the entire amount (since Greville had died) but unless he gave cash directly to Emma for those items, yet again, she did not receive money due to her.

Susanna and Kitty invited Emma and Horatia to visit. Kitty wrote in May: *'We shall be happy to see Madomlle Roulach* [Horatia's new French governess.] *and any part of your family; we beg Mrs Cadogan will come with you. Be assur'd we shall be at all times delighted to have you here and accommodate you to the best in our power. Mr M. and the girls beg to join me in every affectionate wish to you ... P.S. Pray kiss Horatia for us; I hope she has not forgot her aunt Matcham.'*[25]

Susanna and her daughter Anne wrote repeatedly. Emma seldom replied. Anne wrote on 26 July: *'My mother and myself have been anxiously expecting to hear from you this last month; fear you are not well, or have quite forgot your friends at Cranwich ...'*

Emma and Horatia had been ill, but this would not be the only reason Emma did not visit. She was suffering from jaundice and probably depressed. She had no money for travelling expenses and she had previously sent money to cover the extra expense incurred by their visits.

Anne wrote again in August: *'... I was extremely sorry to hear poor Horatia has been so unwell. My mother sends her love and hopes that you will come into Norfolk as you promised, as perhaps the change of air may be good for Horatia ... Hope you will write quite soon and tell us Horatia is quite well, and what has been the matter with her ...'*[26]

Susanna wrote: 'How sorry I am for our dear Horatia. Give my love to her, I shall be most happy to see her and you too, before the summer leaves ...'

By 29 September Susanna urged Emma to go to Cranwich: '... where you will be most cordially received. Tell Horatia we shall be most happy to keep her birthday and Anne's together this year. How long it is since we had the pleasure of hearing from you'.[27]

And again two weeks later: 'What can be the reason my dear Lady, that we have not heard from you. I was in hopes that you would have fixed your time for coming into Norfolk. I long to see you; why not keep the birthdays together?'[28]

Emma's decline in health and finances meant that, for the first time in many years, she and Horatia did not visit the Boltons in Norfolk, despite Susanna's warm-hearted plea, 'I long to see you.'

Towards the end of the year Emma, Horatia and Mrs Cadogan moved to furnished lodgings in Albermarle Street.

Emma's accounts at Coutts for this period, 30 June to 24 November, illustrate her perilous financial situation. Having received her annuity on 25 March, she was nine shillings overdrawn on 24 June. The annuity due in June was not received until 10 August when Emma had only ninepence in her account. Her expenditure on itemized bills for this period was £283. She had paid £100 cash into her account (from an unspecified source) against which she had made two withdrawals of £50. Her next annuity was received in November, but she was left with only £77 when they returned to London. Emma's accounts do not indicate extravagance, but any cash transactions would not show up. She may have received cash payments from the sale of hay at Merton, bequeathed to her by Nelson.

Even under a more frugal regime, there was no money left to clear any outstanding debts, to visit Norfolk or to holiday at the seaside.

Emma had endured a very difficult year in 1809. There was yet worse to come in 1810.

Passing through London Lady Bolton and her daughter attempted to visit Emma in her Albermarle Street lodgings. She wrote to Emma on 3 January: 'I cannot describe my disappointment at calling at No 36 Albermarle Street and finding they did not know you. I then tried at No 44 the Hotel, but they said they knew no such person ...'[29]

Mrs Cadogan died suddenly on 14 January 1810. The precise cause of her death is unknown although she had suffered from bronchitis in the previous two years. Emma had once written that she was 'very ill with an inflammation on her lungs'.

Emma was devastated by the loss of her mother. Mrs Cadogan had been her stalwart support ever since they had moved into Greville's house in Edgeware Road together. For twenty-eight years she had been her dependable companion, offering unwavering love and support. For Horatia, now aged nine, it was another significant bereavement.

Over a year later Emma wrote: *'I have lost the Best of Mothers, my wounded Heart, my Comfort all buried with her. I can not now feel any pleasure but that of thinking and speaking of her.'*[30]

Mrs Cadogan was buried in a vault in the church on Paddington Green, near the home they had shared with Greville. Two large amounts of £100 and £80 were withdrawn from Emma's account on 17 & 18 January, presumably to pay for the funeral and burial expenses.

Sir Harry and Emma were now on friendly terms. He sent her baskets of game and wrote on the very day her mother died:

Up Park Thursday

[14 January 1810]

'It gives me the greatest pleasure to receive a more favourable account from you, and I trust you will soon be relieved from all that load of anxiety you have had so much of lately, & which no one so little deserves ... Pray take care of yourself. Endeavour to obtain rest which you have been so long without, & make use of all the resources of a strong mind & a happy disposition. I generally stay here till the end of March, and shall hardly be in town before my usual time. Be assured I shall lose no time in seeing you, which I wish much to do ... Tho' I lament that there should be such a reason for your quitting Richmond ... at all events I shall stand a better chance of seeing more of you ... Pray let me hear from you occasionally ...'[31]

Sir Harry, an extremely wealthy man, did not offer her any further financial aid. Perhaps he, like the Boltons and the Matchams, was unaware of the severity of her financial position.

On hearing of Mrs Cadogan's death, Susanna wrote on 27 January: *'... Do pray cause to be written only one line to say how your health is – miserable I know you must be. Dear Blessed Saint, was she not a mother to us all. How I wish I was near you, but that is impossible. I am afraid I shall never get so far from home again, but I know you have many friends around you. My dear Friend, endeavour to support yourself under this very severe trial, for the sake of dear Horatia. What can she do without you and many other friends amongst whom I rank myself. Do pray come as the spring gets milder. Every one hear will endeavour to soothe you...'*[32]

Despite Susanna's deteriorating health, she repeated her invitations in April and May.

Soon after her mother's death, Emma and Horatia moved to lodgings at 76 Piccadilly where she was closer to friends. Old Q. lived at 138 Piccadilly and her friend, Lady Elizabeth Foster, (now Duchess of Devonshire) was living at the Duke of Devonshire's mansion, Devonshire House.* Sir Harry wrote again in February, promising to visit her, asking how she spent her time and whether she still had her *'young éléves'* with her.

Her *'young éléves'* were no longer with her. There is one reference of Emma and Charlotte going to a concert together. Otherwise Charlotte is notably absent.†

Living so close to Old Q., Emma probably visited him regularly. He had admired and socially accepted her from the time she first arrived in England, before her marriage to Sir William.

In July Old Q. stepped forward once again to help. He transferred £2,500 from his Coutts account into hers, ensuring that this money was to pay her outstanding bills by adding a note to Mr Coutts: *'Lady Hamilton is not to touch a shilling of the money on any account whatsoever'*.

Abraham Goldsmid agreed to pay the bills on her behalf.

Emma's account shows the receipt of the £2,500 on 24 July and the payment of £2,500.5s.0d. to Abraham Goldsmid that same day. The money paid some of the more urgent creditors, but did not free Emma from the anxiety of all her debts.

In summary, Emma's *'Citty Friends'* had calculated her debts at £18,000. She had sold Merton, with some of the contents, for nearly £13,000 which left a deficit of £5,000, to which should be added the loans from the *'Citty Friends'*, making her debt at this time £8,700. Old Q.'s £2,500 now reduced this amount to £6,200. Had she received the £6,000 owed for improvements at Merton she would have been almost free of debt, assuming she had been living within her means.

---

* Lady Foster had been the Duke's mistress for more than twenty years. Georgiana, Duchess of Devonshire, died in 1806. Lady Elizabeth Foster and the Duke of Devonshire were married on 19 October 1809. After the Duke's death in 1812 she lived at Devonshire House until 1816 when she moved to Rome.

† On 3 July this year Charlotte married the Hon. Samuel Hood, later 2nd. Viscount Baron Bridport, whom she had first met at Merton. The ceremony took place at St Marylebone church. There is no evidence that Emma was invited to the wedding. If she was not, it was a cruel exclusion on the part of the Earl and Sarah, considering all the years of care Emma had devoted to their daughter. Emma later accuses Charlotte of ingratitude.

Early in September Emma and Horatia visited Ashfold.

Sarah Connor, who was sharing Emma's apartments and running errands for her, realised that Emma had paid two months' rent before moving into the apartments and wrote to Emma at Ashfold warning her that, although Sarah herself was leaving, the landlady intended to continue charging as if they were both there.

A week later Sarah wrote again: *'Your last two letters I got, and thank you for them, I found the codicils and took them to Lord Herdley* [Eardley] *but did not see him. It is now 3 o'clock and no Mr Goldsmid is come, nor do I look for him now today, so when I shall get to you, God knows. Their's one excuse for him – the clerk told me the other day that it was feared he should lose a large sum of money. It would not ruin him has he was so rich, but that the amount was so large. I hope it may turn out better than he expects. He is a good man; its a pity he should suffer ...'*[33]

Abraham Goldsmid committed suicide by shooting himself in his garden at Morden Hall on 28 September, after a colossal financial failure in the City, prompting a claim by the East India Company for payment of £350,000 by 28 September. His brother, Asher, inherited Merton Place.

In recent years Abraham Goldsmid had done all he could to help Emma. His death would have been a huge shock and caused her great distress.

Around this time, Emma received a letter of farewell from Emma Carew (Little Emma), which she carefully preserved:

Sunday morning (1810)

Mrs Denis's mention of your name and the conversation she had with you, have revived ideas in my mind which an absence of four years has not been able to efface. It might have been happy for me to have forgotten the past, and to have began a new life with new ideas; but for my misfortune, my memory traces back circumstances which have taught me too much, yet not quite all I could have wished to have known – with you that resides, and ample reasons, no doubt, you have for not imparting them to me. Had you felt yourself at liberty so to have done, I might have become reconciled to my former situation and have been relieved from the painful employment I now pursue. It was necessary as I then stood, for I had nothing to support me but the affection I bore you; on the other hand, doubts and fears by turns oppressed me, and I determined to rely on my own efforts rather than submit to abject dependence, without a permanent name or acknowledged parents. That I should have taken such a step shews, at least, that I have a mind misfortune has not subdued. That I should persevere in it is what I owe to myself and to you, for it shall never be said that I avail myself of your partiality or my own inclination, unless my claim on you is greater than you have hitherto acknowledged. But the time may come when the same reasons may cease to operate, and then, with a heart filled with tenderness and affection, will I shew you both my duty and attachment. In the meantime, should Mrs Denis's zeal and kindness not have over-rated your expressions respecting me, and that you should really wish to see me, I may be believed in saying that such a meeting would be one of the happiest moments of my life, but for the reflection that it may also be the last, as I leave England in a few days, and may, perhaps, never return to it again. I remain etc. '34

It was four years since Emma Carew had last appeared at Merton. Her letter indicates that she believes Emma to be her mother, but has never been given confirmation. Even with Hamilton and Nelson gone, Emma still felt unable to acknowledge her first daughter. The time and opportunity never did arise for her *'reasons'* for this to *'cease to operate'*. Emma deprived herself of the *'tenderness and affection'* and the *'duty and attachment'* Little Emma was prepared to give her. Emma would surely have replied, but there is no record of this or evidence that she made any further appeal to Sir Harry on Little Emma's behalf.

At the end of the year Emma suffered yet another loss. Old Q. died just before Christmas, aged eighty-five. He left Emma a legacy of £500 p.a, but his will, complicated by numerous codicils, was contested. Emma never received his legacy.

On Christmas Day, 1810, Susanna repeated her invitation to visit them: *'... we shall be truly happy to see you as soon as you can conveniently leave town, which I hope will be as soon after the funeral as you can; it will change the scene at any rate & we will endeavor to make Cranwich as cheerful as we can ...'* '35

With the deaths of Greville, Mrs Cadogan, Abraham Goldsmid and Old Q., and with Davison in prison, Emma was left to fend for herself. Kitty's husband, George, was the only close contact who might have given helpful advice had Emma taken him into her confidence.

For the next two years, Emma and Horatia led a semi-withdrawn life, attempting to avoid the incessant pressure from creditors. They finally settled in what proved to be their last home in England at 150 Bond Street. (Now No. 147). Emma arranged the premises with what remained of her possessions. The catalogue of a future sale of her possessions from these premises included: Bedsteads with Chintz hangings, excellent Bedding, Sofas, Chairs, Footstools, Bookcases, Mahogony Breakfast Tables, Carpets, splendid china Dinner, Desert, and Sandwich Sets and Horatia's piano. There were numerous books, a few paintings, and other sentimental personal effects.

Ill and with forlorn hopes of any financial improvement, it is very likely that Emma sank into depression. She seldom wrote to Susanna, Kitty or other friends.

Her hopes were temporarily raised when George III suffered a relapse that was judged to be permanent and the Prince of Wales became Regent on 5 February 1811. Although he may have dined with her in Bond Street her pension claim did not progress.*

Early in 1811 Lord Mansfield, one of Robert Greville's executors, wrote to advise Emma that there might be some delay in the payment of her annuities. He suggested that she avoid spending her annuity payment before it arrived. He clearly had no idea of the serious financial difficulties caused by the late payments.

Mr Coutts seems to have made allowances for the irregular payments. On 20 February 1811, for instance, Emma's account was credited with £180 with a further credit of £180 on 11 May. By 24 June Emma's balance stood at twopence. She did not receive a further annuity until 15 October, a double payment of £360. Her next credit did not appear until 7 March the following year, almost five months later, followed by another six-month gap until £359 was credited in September.

Emma was obliged to appeal to G.M. for a loan. He replied:

April 15th. 1811

It is very fortunate that you applied to me at this instant; had you applied five days ago, I had not a hundred to lend, but having received seven hundred pounds three days ago since to be invested in the funds for Mrs M. & the children, Mrs M has consented to withold one hundred pounds of that sum for you. I know you will repay it as soon as you can, but do not mention my having lent you any money. I wish not the trustees to be acquainted with It ...'[36]

In May Emma raised loans from Carlo Rovedino, one of her Neapolitan opera singer friends who had been entertained at Merton and at Richmond. She signed two promissory notes to him on 13 and 14 May for £150 each.[37]

So ignorant was Susanna of Emma's financial problems that in September she wondered if Emma could send a 'loan' of £100 to a member of the Nelson family who had fallen into debt.

---

* King George III died deaf, blind and deluded in 1820.

Major Lockhart Gordon, critical of Emma and Nelson in Palermo, came across Emma, Cecilia and *'some half-dozen children'* including Horatia, in Greenwich Park. It was Emma's 46th birthday and she was taking the children to celebrate at the Ship Inn. He gave an unflattering description of her in his Personal Memoirs:

'Age and circumstance had made sad ravages in her formerly splendid countenance; but the eye, though less brilliant, was still beautiful and that fascinating mouth from which sculptors had modelled yet retained its expression. The lovely hair which was wont to hang over her polished forehead was now tucked under a huge cap, or perhaps it had become gray – be that as it may, it no longer served as an ornament ... She was humiliated to find that I, who had beheld her in all her glory, surrounded by royalty, should now see an old woman, divested of all her charms, and reduced to comparative poverty ... She dropped her veil and I observed her eyes filled with tears. Alas, those were happy days, never to return ...'[38]

He noted that her clothes were sombre and shabby – *'The only part of it that denoted a person above the rank was a cashmere shawl'*. This was one of the shawls Nelson had given Emma that she wore until she died.

Emma and Horatia made their last visit to the Boltons at Cranwich in July. The Boltons, wanting a larger home, moved to Bradenham Hall, near Swaffham in November.

On 3 September, after over eight years' delay, the government finally paid Sir William's claim for his ambassadorial expenses in Naples and Palermo. The £8,268 was paid, not to Emma, but to Robert Fulke Greville.[39] What was a windfall to him would have been a life-saving amount to Emma, had he shared it with her.

Judging by her Coutts account, Emma did not receive payment for the debts of £450 that Sir William had stipulated that his nephew Charles Greville should pay Emma out of the government's compensation award when it arrived. The executors of Hamilton's will did not ensure that she received it.

On 4 September, Emma wrote a new will, properly signed and witnessed by Thomas Coxe and William Haslewood. It is a long document revealing her love for Horatia and concern for her future security:

September the fourth 1811

I, Emma Hamilton of 150 Bond Street London Widow of the Right Honourable Sir William Hamilton formerly Minister at the Court of Naples being in sound mind and body Do give to my Dearly beloved Horatia Nelson daughter of the Great and Glorious Nelson all that I shall be possessed of at my Death money jewells pictures wine furniture books wearing apparel silver gold-plated or silver-gilt utensils of every sort I may have in my house or houses or of any other persons' houses at my Death any marbles bronzes busts plaster of Paris or in short every thing that belonged to me I give to my best beloved Horatia Nelson all my table linen Laces ornaments in short everything that I have I give to Her any money either in the house or at my bankers all Debts that may be owing to me I beg that she may have I give to Horatia Nelson all silver with inscription with Viscount Nelson's name on or His arms I give to Her wou'd to God it was more for her sake I do appoint George Matcham, Esq of Ashfold Lodge in the County of Sussex and the Right Honble. George Rose of Old Palace Yard Westminster my Executors and I leave them Guardians to my dear Horatia Nelson and I do most Earnestly Entreat of them to be the Protectors and Guardians and to be Fathers to the Daughter of the Great and Glorious Nelson and it is my wish that H.R. Highness the Prince Regent or if before my Death he shall become King, that He will provide for the said Horatia in such a manner that she may live as becomes the daughter of such a man as her victorious Father was and as His Royal Highness often promised me that he wou'd have me Remunerated when he had it in his power for the services that I have rendered to my King and Country and as I have never been Remunerated nor ever received one sixpence from Government let me on my knees beg of His Royal Highness to provide for the said Horatia Nelson the only child of the Great and Glorious Nelson and I beg after my Death that a copy of this my last Will and Testament may be sent to His Royal Highness the Prince Regent or if he is King it may be sent to His Majesty for His High worth Honour & probity and the Friendship which he had for Nelson will induce Him to protect His Child for me H.R.H always shewed me the greatest kindness and for the sake of Sir William Hamilton whom His R. Highness so highly honored that He will provide for the orphan Horatia when my head is laid low She will want protection theirfore to God Almighty to His R. Highness and to my Executors do I most earnestly recommend Her on my knees blessing Her and praying for Her that she may be happy virtas good and amiable and that she may remember all the kind instructions and good advice I have given her & may she be what her Great and immortal Father wished Her to be brought up with virtue honor religion and rectitude Amen Amen Amen I do hereby annul all wills made by me formerly and I beg that this may be considered as my Last Will and Testament written with my own Hand this September the fourth 1811,

Emma Hamilton.

Emma wisely chose George Matcham and George Rose as her executors and guardians of Horatia. George Matcham would in time honourably carry out her wishes.

An important point should be noted: '... *I give to her any money either in the house or at my bankers all Debts that may be owing to me ...*' By these '*debts owing*' to her, Emma would mean the money the Earl has not yet paid to her from the Bronte estate.

Below Emma's signature is written in a different hand: '*Not to be registered by Order of the Judge. RCC*'.

This annotation is not dated and is followed in Emma's handwriting by:

I beg to be Buried near my Dearest mother in Padington Church as I cannot be buried in the [illegible] near my Dear & Lamented virtuous Great Nelson whoes glory victory Honor & happiness I feel proud to say I did contribute to as he in Dying ... [illegible] ... & as our friendship was pure virtuas & strictly Honorable I glory in our Exalted friendship – I am sorry to say that I should have had it in my power to have left His Daughter more if I had not unthinkingly been the Dupe of the present Earl Nelson and His wife son & ingratefull daughter Lady Charlotte Hood whom I educated & nourished in my [illegible] cloathed fed and tried to Educate but alas with all the Hundreds of pounds nay thousands I may say she had a bad cold Heart & [illegible] the Earl Nelson & His wife & daughter knows that Viscount Nelson was Horatia's Father I say nothing of Her mother my oath was pledged & she is of too High a Rank & her life too dear for me to betray However ill He has requited me for my pains <u>risks</u> and Tryals for Her – if ever she shall Hear of my Death she may shed a tear & say she has to Death proved my friend & kept my secret as she [promised?] & risked all for me on many occasions – I beg this my Last Will & Testament may be Registered in Doctors Commons and that my Executors may see it done

Emma Hamilton

Emma declares her friendship with Nelson was '*pure, virtuas, and strickly Honorable*', echoing Nelson's similar portrayal of their relationship, further muddying the waters as to the identity of Horatia's mother. In the last muddled lines it is not clear who had proved her friend and '*kept her secret*'.

Emma continues with a plea to Maria Carolina: '*Her Majesty the Queen of Naples will I hope be of use to my Dear Horatia Nelson as the Dear and Great Nelson loved her Majesty & Dominions theirfore to His Daughter she will I hope remit something for she has many many obigations to me in allso having contributed to serving Her & all Her children – but I hope now Her Heart will feil & Her Soul have some compassion on the Dear Child of her Saviour & protector which Nelson was to Her and Her Kingdoms.*

Signed Emma Hamilton

Emma goes on:

If I shall have any money in the Funds or Landed property at my Death I give to the said Horatia Nelson all and every thing belonging to me and if she shall dye before she shall be able to make her will I give all that I have bequeathed to her to the Daughters of Mr. John & Amy Moore my late Aunt and Uncle and now living in Moore Street Liverpool and I pray to God to bless them but I hope my Dear Horatia will live to be happy and marry well and I hope that she will make Her will as soon as I am Dead for I do absolutely give her all I have I still hope Mr. Matcham and Mr. Rose will see to the educating of Horatia and that she may live with Mrs. Matcham's family till she is disposed to some worthy man in marriage I forgot to mention that I also give Horatia all my china glass crockery ware of every sort that I have ...

Emma Hamilton

Signed sealed published and declared by Emma Hamilton as her last will and testament in the presence of Thomas Coxe A.M. – William Haslewood of FitzRoy Square, Middlesex.[40]

In using the phrase *'If I shall have any money'* did Emma have a sense of foreboding that she might have nothing to leave to Horatia?

Emma was invited to the dinner given at Guildhall on Lord Mayor's Day, probably the last grand occasion she attended. A Mrs Dolland noted in her diary on 9 November: *'... There were more women of fashion than usual; upon the whole it was grand and well conducted ... I was sorry to see* Lady Hamilton *and Signora Storace* [an opera singer] *there. Women of that character should not be introduced to dazzle the citizen's wives and daughters ...'*[41]

In December Emma heard again from Sir Harry. Unaware of her circumstances, he assumed she was enjoying life in London:

Sunday [December 1811]

'*I hope you received my last envoi in due time for the purpose ... You have been a long while silent, which I regret, as I am always happy to hear what is doing & where you are ... I conclude you are now fixed in London for what is called the season, and enjoying the society of a few you like ... I suppose you see a good deal of the Duchess of Devonshire ... I shall expect the pleasure of a billet now and then ...'*[42]

Emma and Horatia made their last visit to Norfolk for the wedding of Susanna's daughter, Eliza, to her cousin Harry Girdlestone, on 27 December in the West Bradenham church, near the Boltons' new home, Bradenham Hall. Emma was the guest of honour and chief witness of the marriage.

During 1812, there were no visits to the Boltons or the Matchams, despite repeated invitations. Emma made few public appearances. She withdrew from society in fear of being discovered by her creditors. When anyone called at her door there was no reply.

She continued her efforts to pay various individuals. Between February and October, she paid Mr Hicks £40, Mr McGowren £100, Mr Robinson £82, Mr Giblett £95 and Mr Goodwin £75, most likely suppliers of normal household requirements, rather than moneylenders. Her personal withdrawals of cash were minimal.

In July, reduced to *'comparative poverty'* but not yet impoverished, she accepted the invitation to attend a party given for the Prince of Wales, now the Prince Regent. The poet Samuel Rogers records meeting her there and hearing her sing. Perhaps she attended this party hoping for an opportunity to ask the Prince of Wales, once more, for help.

Thomas de Quincey, a friend of Coleridge,* met Emma in London around now and heard her recite Lady Macbeth's sleepwalking scene. He wrote: *'Nelson's Lady Hamilton ... had Medea's beauty and Medea's powers of enchantment'* and that she was *'the most effectively brilliant woman he ever saw'*.[43]

Emma still had the power to entrance with her beauty, her voice and her acting ability.

The Matchams wrote repeatedly asking her to visit. Kitty wrote on August 6: *'We are looking forward with great pleasure to our annual meeting at Ashfold and hope the time is now drawing very near when we shall talk over the occurrences of the year ...'*[44]

Kitty received no reply and concerned, wrote again on 8 September: *'We have been anxiously expecting to have a line from you every day, & begin to be fearful it is indisposition which prevents your writing ... I am desired to request one line, letting us know how you are & when we may expect to have the pleasure of seeing yourself and Horatia here.'*[45]

Kitty's fears were correct. Emma was suffering an acute attack of jaundice.

James Perry, their Merton neighbour, visited Emma and Horatia in

* Coleridge had been Alexander Ball's secretary in Malta.

Bond Street to celebrate Horatia's birthday in October. It is possible that Emma was too afraid to take Horatia out for a more joyful celebration.

Emma's situation was now extremely serious. Creditors lay in wait to accost her in Bond Street. Sending many of her papers and treasured possessions on ahead, she fled with Horatia to Fulham to take refuge with her old friend, Mrs Billington. She and Horatia spent Christmas 1812 in hiding with Mrs Billington and her husband.

CHAPTER 24

Emma and Horatia Confined to 'Living Within the Rules'

'I am alone and feel forlorn in this world'
Emma to Lord Sidmouth, 7 February 1813

*'I ask not alms, I ask not anything but right,
and to know weather I am to receive my due or not.'*
Emma to Earl Nelson, 29 April 1814

AFTER CHRISTMAS EMMA voluntarily submitted herself to 'Living within the Rules', an area in Southwark, south of the Thames, controlled by the King's Bench Prison and reserved for debtors. Debtors living there could not be approached by their creditors.

Fearful of returning to Bond Street and of suffering a public arrest but unable to encroach on Mrs Billington's hospitality indefinitely, Emma probably sought the protection of 'The Rules' to give herself time to pay her most aggressively demanding creditors.

She began to sell her treasured possessions. Desperate to raise money, in January, she sold the enamel miniature left her by Sir William, for £200 to Davison, who had been released from prison early in 1811.

Emma, Horatia and Miss Wheatley (who had replaced Cecilia) found accommodation in what was known as a 'sponging-house' at 12 Temple Place on the east side of Surrey Street (now Blackfriars Road). For the privilege of 'Living within the Rules', rather than in the King's Bench Prison itself, Emma paid a daily rent of 4s. 6d. plus other dues to the prison Marshall.

Debtors living Within the Rules were allowed to walk around within a prescribed area of about three square miles. They could attend church services in the chapel of the Magdalen Hospital opposite 12 Temple Place. Any taverns and places selling 'Spiritous Liquors' were prohibited.

On 3 January Emma wrote to James Perry:

12 Temple Place, January 3rd. 1813

Will you have the goodness to see my old Dame Francis,* as you was so good to say to me once at any time for the present existing and unhappy circumstances you wou'd befriend me, & if you could, at your convenience, call on me to aid me by your advice as before? My friends come to town to-morrow for the season, when I must see what can be done, so that I shall not remain here, for I am so truly unhappy and wretched, & have been ill ever since I had the pleasure of seeing you on dear Horatia's birthday that I have not had either spirits or energy to write to you. You that loved Sir William & Nelson, & feel that I have deserved from my country some tribute of remuneration, will aid by your counsel your ever affectionate and grateful

Emma Hamilton[1]

Kitty wrote to Emma at Bond Street on 1 January, unaware of her situation. The letter was presumably collected and brought to Emma by Miss Wheatley.

'We are sorry to find our dear Horatia has had the whooping-cough so severely; but I trust the worst is over. The best thing you can do is to change air. Come down to us, where you will be quiet and, I hope, happy ... Do my dear Lady, let us hear from you soon; we are anxious to know how our dear little girl is, to whom we all beg our love, and not forgetting to wish her and you many many happy returns of the season, likewise our best wishes to Miss Weatley. I am glad to find you are bringing your affairs to a conclusion, I need not say that none of your friends will rejoice more than we shall to hear that they turn out to your satisfaction.'[2]

At last Emma confessed to Kitty.

Kitty immediately replied, offering to take Horatia to live at Ashfold and to supply Emma with potatoes and other produce from their farm:

Monday night, January 25th 1813

'Your letter has made us very uneasy respecting the health of our dear Horatia. God grant she is still doing well; this is very severe weather, and we have nothing but coughing all over the house. My good man is far from well; his cough is very bad. Do give our best love to our dear girl, and tell her we hope, as soon as the doctors will allow her to change the air, her uncle will go in the coach as far as Reigate, take a postchaise from thence, which will give our horses time to rest, and she will be at Ashfold Lodge before dark. I need not say, my dear Lady, what happiness it would be to us to see you with her,

---

* Dame Francis had been one of Emma's servants for many years. Asher Goldsmid had retained her and her husband as caretakers at Merton Place.

but if you cannot manage to come, we will endeavour to supply your place. You know she is one of our children, & while we have a loaf for them she shall share it, & with it our best affections ... The potatoes are at the Elephant & Castle, directed to you, & to be left till called for ... Do send as soon as you receive this; as soon as the frost is gone, more shall be sent. We shall be glad to get a line from you; our anxiety is great about both. May God bless you is our prayer.[3]

Emma did not allow Horatia to go to Kitty. She loved her dearly and was determined to keep her promise to *'fulfill Nelson's last request, to take care of his Horatia'*.

James Perry solicited the help of a Merton neighbour, the wealthy Alderman Joshua Smith.*

Between them, and presumably with the £200 from Davison, Emma's release was secured early in March and she returned to 150 Bond Street.

The previous December (and with the help of a Mr. Russell, recommended to her by James Perry), Emma had written two 'Memorials' appealing directly to King George III and HRH the Prince Regent. They are long documents, abridged here.

The first undated Memorial of four pages to the King began:

'The Memorial of Dame Emma Hamilton, widow of his Excellency, the late Sir William Hamilton, K.B. your Majesty's most faithful Ambassador at the Court of Naples.

Humbly sheweth,

That her late husband, Sir William Hamilton, in his liberal and munificent discharge of his honourable duties of that elevated situation, to which he was exalted by the goodness of your most gracious Majesty, had so considerably encumbered his private fortune that he was incapable of making a sufficient provision for your Majesty's Memorialist to maintain, after his decease, the rank to which he had indulgently raised her, and which it was her constant study as much as possible to merit, by anxiously entering into all her husband's zealous and enlarged views of diplomatic devotion to the true interests of our dear country, and the beloved Sovereign who had thus benignantly vouchsafed to honour him...'

The document put forward the important contributions Emma had made whilst living in Naples and Palermo:

– that through her *'confidential friendship'* with the Queen of Naples she had obtained the King of Spain's letter to the King of Naples in

---

* President of the Southwark borough council, and Mayor of the City of London in 1810.

which he had expressed his *'intention to declare war against England'*. This important document she had given to Sir William who had *'immediately transmitted it to your Majesty's Ministers'*.

– that through the Queen she had obtained a *'secret order for the victualling and watering'* of Nelson's fleet at Syracuse, (contrary to the Kingdom's declared neutrality) enabling him to proceed to Alexandria and the Battle of the Nile.*

– that during the blockade of Malta she had secured supplies for the *'distressed natives'* and thereby prevented *'that important fortress from fatally falling under the entire domination of the French'*, for which service the Emperor of all the Russia's had awarded her the Petit Croix of the Order of Malta.

– that she had endeavoured to *'merit the regard of her King and country'* by using her influence to benefit the *'Royal British Navy.*

The document concluded:

'That the solemn recognition of such services, by that immortal man, the late Lord Viscount Nelson, and his pathetic call for their kind remuneration, at the moment when he was about to commence his last and fatal conflict with the enemies of his King and country, in whose battle, at the moment of victory, he so gloriously fell, bequeathing to the generosity of your Majesty and his country the future fortunes of your humble Memorialist, must afford an everlasting proof that she is not altogether unworthy of being enabled, by the condescending bounty of your Majesty, with the generous concurrence of her country, to maintain that rank and dignity which she derived from the affections of a beloved husband, and which, it is humbly presumed, your Majesty's Memorialist has not, in any single instance, ever disgraced or abused ...'[4]

The King was ill and no attention was ever paid to this petition.

In her Memorial to the Prince Regent, consisting of twenty-three pages, Emma described in detail all her services from the time of her marriage to Sir William Hamilton in September 1791. Once again she accused the Earl of withholding Nelson's codicil, *'afraid that I should be provided for in the sum that Parliament was expected to grant to uphold the hero's name and family'*.

The Memorial concluded with Emma asking for remuneration and

---

* This fact has been regularly addressed in an attempt to verify her claim. The author, Walter Sichel, having studied available evidence, believed that Nelson knew that Emma and the Queen had secretly (without informing Hamilton and Acton) arranged for the *'victualling and watering'* to be supplied to his fleet in Syracuse. Failing this arrangement Nelson would have had to sail to Majorca for supplies, losing valuable time.

explaining that her personal losses in Naples and Palermo forced her to do so:

'Time has gone on. Thinking that my case could not be overlook'd, I have felt easy; had the curtail'd provision left me by Sir William, under the conviction of its being an ample one by the country, has diminish'd without a semblance of extravagance, and now find myself in embarrassments that imperiously press on me to look for remuneration for those services, expenditures, and losses, that I have recited ... In that expectation being liberally realised I can have nothing but implicit confidence, as our august Prince was well acquainted with it by Lord Nelson himself, and fully coincided in its justice.

I may, however, without fear of exaggeration affirm that my private funds in monies expended and losses sustained, have suffer'd a diminution of full £20,000. Had I hoarded these sums that I must be permitted to say, I generously expended for the honor and advantage of the country, I might at this hour have a competence independent of any remuneration for the services I have quoted, and which I have no doubt the country would wish me to enjoy.'5

The *Times* reported:

*'Lady Hamilton has published a narrative of the services she rendered to her country, by her influence with the Queen of Naples, while resident with her husband, the late Sir William Hamilton at that Court; the cost of which, and the losses sustained by her in the accomplishment of these services, she states at not less than £20,000. Her Ladyship says she is embarrassed, and wishes for remuneration.'6 ***

In her Memorial to the Prince Regent, Emma added:

'I also appeal to Messrs Canning and Rose, to state if, on behalf of Government, they had not reassured his Lordship on their taking leave of him on board the Victory at Portsmouth, the 14th Sept., 1805, <u>on his last sailing</u>, 'that the promises made by Mr Pitt in my favour should be fully realized.'

George Canning, then Treasurer of the Navy, and George Rose had dined with Nelson on his last night in England and both were annoyed by Emma's comment in the published memorial.

Rose wrote to Emma on 18 February:

Dear Madam,

I had a letter from Mr Canning last night ... It is incumbent on me, therefore, to state to you that Mr Canning was not a party to the conversation

---

* Later Emma claims to have used some of her own money on one occasion to send provisions to Sir John Jervis (St. Vincent) and on another for the corn supplies sent to the starving population at Malta.

between Lord Nelson and me, and could not have heard a syllable of it ... It is not merely to state that, however, that I now trouble you, but to apprise you that your recollection is not correct as to what I told you passed between me and Lord Nelson at the time ... I did not know you were now bringing your claim forward again, till I received Mr Canning's letter.'[7]

Emma replied on 4 March that she would have sent Rose a copy of her memorial if she had not been so ill and added: *'... a kind friend of mine has told me that the reason my claims have not been remunerated was owing to a most infamous falsehood raised against my honor and that of the brave and virtuous Nelson, which is false, and it shall be made known, for I will appeal to a generous public, who will not let a woman who has served her country with the zeal I have, be left to starve and insult.'*[8]

Two days later Rose wrote his last letter to Emma:

Dear Madam,

I return the copies of your memorial, etc. ... in doing which it is impossible for me to avoid expressing my very deep regret at your having referred to Mr Canning and myself for assurances having been given to Lord Nelson, on board the Victory, *'that the promises made by Mr Pitt in your favour should be fully realized', because the accuracy of that cannot be supported by either of us. In a letter I wrote you a fortnight ago, I reminded you of what did pass in my last interview with Lord Nelson ... and I must lament that your statement was not conformable to that.*[9]

Emma had earlier written to Lord Sidmouth, (ex P.M. Addington):

150 Bond Street, February 7, 1813

MY LORD, – I had a letter written to your Lordship with a copy of my memorial and narrative to H.R.H. the Prince Regent, when to my surprise I saw the letter published in the newspapers, which very much disconcerted my way of proceeding; my desire being that of laying my case before H.R.H., the Ministers, your Lordship, and a select few of the chief nobles and gentlemen of Parliament, who are noted for attention to public business ... I am sure of your Lordship's potent protection as far as you will see it deserving.

My story is told truly as the circumstances rose to my memory. And with a safe conscience I can say, whatever is omitted I believe to be to my own disadvantage, as all my actions were guided by a Heart and Soul devoted like your Lordship's own to our dear, dear Country.... Forgive me this intrusion, but Nelson loved you, and I am alone and feel forlorn in this world, and his spirit, if it cou'd look down, would bless you for your kindness and attention to his last wishes in the moment of death and victory to your Lordship's ever obliged and most gratefull,

Emma Hamilton[10]

Lord Sidmouth, (who had admired Nelson), was given the disagreeable task of informing Emma that her appeal had been rejected:

Whitehall, March 6th 1813

Madam,

It is very painful to me, to acquaint your Ladyship, that after a full communication, with Lord Liverpool [the Prime Minister], *on the subject of your memorial to his Royal Highness, the Prince Regent, I am unable to encourage your hopes, that the object of it can be accomplished. His Lordship sincerely regrets the embarrassment which you have described, but upon comparing them with representations now before him of difficulty and distress, in many other quarters, and upon review of the circumstances with which they are attended, he finds it impossible so to administer the scanty means of relief and assistance, which, under the authority of the Prince Regent, are at his disposal, as to satisfy his own sense of justice to others, and at the same time give effect to your Ladyship's application.*

I have the honour to be, Madam,

Your Ladyship's obedient humble servant,

SIDMOUTH.[11]

After hours spent working on these memorials the reply was a bitter disappointment to Emma.

It seems that none of her friends or contacts were willing or able to help her. Davison had written to Emma while she was preparing her memorials:

... I sincerely pray that you may speedily be extricated from every embarrassment and difficulty and that the Nation will ultimately do justice to you by granting you the pension which you so many years have been led to expect – and which in my humble opinion your claims so full entitle you to – I feel for your situation, as much as any one – but who is there, on Earth, that has suffered equally with myself? Could my wishes avail, you would soon very quickly be relieved from every unpleasant sensation – remember me to Horatia, and am, as I have ever been, your faithful servant

Alex Davison[12]

Alderman Smith was one of the few who assisted her, becoming her generous benefactor.

By now, Emma would surely have been in a distressed state. She has lost all three of the most important people in her life: Hamilton, Nelson and her mother. They had given her stability, love and encouragement. The Earl and his family now chose not to associate with her. Her creditors, aware of the failure of her appeal to the Prince

Regent and the government, would now begin to pursue their claims even more vigorously.

In her desperation and loneliness, Emma was too weakened to deal with a difficult daughter. Horatia, approaching adolescence, was suffering her own difficulties, and tensions between them boiled over when Horatia began to behave badly. Emma appealed to Mr Russell for support in correcting her wayward daughter. Horatia was obliged to write to him:

My dear Friend, Thanks for your valuable letter I hope it will correct me of such behaviour and trust me dear Mr Russell I know my error and with my dear Mothers goodness to me (which after such conduct I did not deserve) correct a fault which would be detestable to every one if ever again (which I hope will never happen) I by any means do wrong I will read your friendly letter and then I shall do wright again

And believe

Dear Mr Russell

Yours affectionately and Greatfully

Horatia Nelson.[13]

Horatia's efforts to correct her bad behaviour were short-lived. Just as Emma and Sir William had written notes to each other while living together, Emma now wrote to Horatia expressing the feelings of a mother towards a troubled and troublesome daughter:

April 18th (Easter Sunday) 1813

Listen to a kind, good mother, who has ever been to you affectionate, truly kind, and who has neither spared pains nor expense to make you the most amiable and accomplish'd of your sex. Ah, Horatia! if you had grown up as I wish'd you, what a joy, what a comfort might you have been to me! for I have been constant to you, and willingly pleased for every manifestation you shew'd to learn and profitt of my lessons, and I have ever been most willing to overlook injuries. But now 'tis for myself I speak & write. Look into yourself well, correct yourself of your errors, your caprices, your nonsensical follies, for by your inattention you have forfeited all claims to my future kindness. I have weathered many a storm for your sake, but these frequent blows have kill'd me. Listen, then, from a mother who speaks from the dead! Reform your conduct, or you will be detested by all the world, & when you shall no longer have my fostering arm to sheild you, whoe betide you! you will sink to nothing. Be good, be honourable, tell not falsehoods, be not capricious, follow the advice of the mother whom I shall place you in at school, for a governess must act as mother. I grieve & lament to see the increasing strength of your turbulent passions; I weep & pray you may not be totally lost; my fervent prayers are offered up to God for you; I hope you will yet become sensible of your eternal welfare. I shall go join your father & my blessed mother, & may you on your death-bed have as little to reproach yourself as your once affectionate mother has, for I can glorify, & say I was a good child. Can Horatia Nelson say so? I am unhappy to say you CANNOT. No answer to this? I shall tomorrow look out for a school, for your sake & to save you, that you may bless the memory of an injured mother.

P.S. Look on me now as gone from this world.[14]

What had Horatia done to be reprimanded in this manner by Emma? She may have been rebellious, ungrateful and rude – all now accepted as normal teenage behaviour. She was clearly too young to appreciate the dreadful stress that Emma was suffering.

Both Horatia and Emma refer to Emma as Horatia's *'mother'*. Although Emma declares herself to be Horatia's mother no less than four times, she also mentions *'a governess must act as a mother'*. Publically, Emma remained Horatia's 'guardian'. Years later, Horatia would still not accept that Emma was her mother.

Despite Emma's evident love for Horatia, their relationship became more fraught. Mrs Cadogan was no longer there to restrain Emma's temper. Horatia like her mother, exhibited bouts of temper. Approaching adolescence and having led an unsettled life since her father's death, she and Emma reacted to each other with emotional outbursts.

Having been refused a government pension and her incomes from Hamilton and Nelson being unreliable, Emma knew that she was close to financial disaster.

The final page of Emma's account at Coutts inexplicably closes on 30 March 1813. There are no records for the remaining fifteen months that she lived in England. Either the account lapsed after March 1813 when no further annuities were paid in, or the final pages of the account were removed from Coutts at a later date. The former is the most likely as Emma later wrote to Robert Fulke Greville saying her *'jointure of eight hundred pounds a year has now been for a long time accumulating'*.

Emma received all annuities due for the years 1810, 1811 and 1812, albeit irregularly paid and usually late. The very last receipt of £180 is credited on 30 March 1813.

During the first three months of 1813 Emma withdrew £223.15s.

for her own use and paid Mr (Alderman?) Smith £136.5s. Her account closed with her last withdrawal of £130 on 30 March, leaving the account balanced to the penny.

Later letters between Emma and Robert Greville indicate that from now on Emma's only income was Horatia's interest on Nelson's bequest, which was apparently paid.

In May Emma sold her silver and plate, possibly to Alderman Smith. He had earlier purchased, from Richmond, furniture and other items including Nelson's coat, Emma's most treasured possession, for £400. Emma had never handed Nelson's coat over to the Earl, possibly reasoning that, since his son and heir had died, he did not deserve to have it.* Alderman Smith probably purchased the above items to put into storage on her behalf and as security against other financial 'loans'.

Anne Bolton wrote to Emma on 4 May informing her that her mother's health had declined: '... *her complaint is extreme weakness indeed she has hardly any strength left ... God only knows how long she may continue with us'.*[15] But Emma was too depressed and anxious herself to respond to this news.

The Matchams tried several times to see Emma and Horatia in May. Kitty wrote to Emma on 19 May: *'We were truly mortified to find you from home the three times we called ... I am afraid we must go to Bradenham to see my dear sister, if she makes a point of seeing us ... I much fear she will never recover; but we must look forward with hope ... God bless you, dear Horatia, and believe us at all times, yours affectionately etc.'*[16]

By June, Emma could no longer avoid her creditors or satisfy their demands for payment. On 28 June, she was publicly arrested. After a court appearance, she returned to 12 Temple Place, taking Horatia and only clothes and a few belongings with her.

Just over a week later, on 8 July, the contents of her last home at 150 New Bond Street were put up for sale by auction by order of the Sheriff of Middlesex. The catalogue of Emma's last remaining possessions is a poignant reminder of the lifestyle she had once enjoyed with Hamilton and Nelson.

On hearing that the auction would take place while she was confined in 12 Temple Place, Emma had no opportunity to remove any treasured items. Her only hope of retaining any of these personal

---

* In 1845 Nelson's coat was purchased by Prince Albert for the nation from Alderman Smith's widow. It was presented to Greenwich Hospital and is now in the National Maritime Museum.

effects against a time when she might be released lay with Alderman Smith. Once again, he purchased a number of items before the sale, possibly after discussions with Emma. Her possessions were listed as follows in 'A Catalogue of the Elegant HOUSEHOLD FURNITURE, The property of a Lady of Distinction, on the premises, No. 150 New Bond Street, On Thursday, July 8, 1813.'[17]

Some items have names pencilled in the margin next to the item sold. Several are marked to 'JJS' (Alderman Smith) and several to 'Salter', Emma's friend John Salter, the jeweller. Davison, too, may have purchased items before the sale.

Items purchased by John Salter were:

A 7 feet 4-post patent bedstead, mahogany feet pillars, lath bottom, rich chinz furniture, lined and fringed, and japanned cornices – £25

A set of mahogany bed steps – £3

A mahogany chest of drawers, with secretaire and wardrobe over – £6.16s.6d.

A pair of gilt 2 light branches – £1

A gentleman's portrait, framed and glazed, and a bust of Lord Nelson – £1.10s.0d.

Two bronze busts, and brackets – 13 shillings

A mahogany Canterbury – £2

A bedstead, a hair squab, 4 cushions and cotton cases – £9.9s.0d.

A music stool, a stand, and 2 Ottomans – £1.12s.0d.

La Belle Assemblee, 2 volumes – 14 shillings

Analyze Deniontra, 2 toms (tomes) – 9 shillings

Items purchased by Alderman Smith were:

Two large trunks and 2 sea chests – £1.10s.0d.

A Canterbury – £2.2s.0d.

A mahogany brass bound celleret and a wine cooler – £2

Six ebonized chairs, cane seats – £2.14s.0d.

An etwee [etui] case, a pocket glass, silver mounted, 2 spoons, 2 earrings, 2 bracelets, and a miniature – £1.15s.0d.

A mahogany frame reading chair, cane back, sides, and seat, and 2 cushions in morocco cases – £6.6s.0d.

Six ebonized chairs, cane seats, and 2 with elbows – £4.4s.0d.

Seven tin dish-covers, a tin rosateur, and bottle jack – £1.9s.0d.

Were these items purchased for themselves, or did they purchase some to give to Emma in 12 Temple Place, or to keep in store for her future use?

The catalogue lists four extremely important items that sold for high prices to unknown buyers:

A gold box set with pearls with an enamel from Vernet – £58

A ditto set with brilliants, with a portrait of His Majesty – £49

A very fine ditto, with antique drawings – £34

A watch set with diamonds – £30

Two sentimental items sold and not indicated as being bought by John Salter or Alderman Smith are of significant importance. One is listed as *'The freedom of the City of Oxford, and gold box, as presented to Lord Nelson in the year 1802'*, sold for £20; the other *'The order of merit in gold, and a star'*, sold for £12. Was this Emma's 'Cross of Malta'?

The heart-breaking record of Emma's losses, down to the last frying pan, is abridged here.*

FRONT ATTIC:

A wool mattress in a white case, a large deal chest, three blankets, a counterpane, and a pair of sheets

BACK ATTIC:

Two dumb bells, a small tool chest, a high basket, some mahogany pillars and a trunk

SECOND FLOOR:

Bed Room:

A high wire fender, set of fire irons, a hearth rug, a feather bed, 3 down pillows, four large blankets, a Japan chiffonier, a Grecian couch, hair squab and bolster, plus five various mahogany chest-of-drawers (This must have been her own bedroom as it contained the 7-foot bed bought by Salter.)

Front Room:

A handsome satin wood writing table, a 2-flap mahogany dining table, two sets of French window curtains and 2 painted blinds (sold for £1), a capital mahogany secretaire and bookcase, glazed doors and brass astringal, a time piece, a chimney ornament and a pianoforte by Tomkinson.

FIRST FLOOR:

Front Room:

A pair of capital bronze figures 2 lights each, a mahogany frame sofa, a handsome mahogany breakfast table on pillar and claw, a Kidderminster carpet, a pier glass 28x18 in a gilt frame, three bronze busts (sold for £1)

* See Appendix 6.

PAINTINGS:
Europa and the Bull, fine, Titian, a quantity of coloured prints and drawings, a print framed and glazed the *Victory of the Nile*, a snuff box made from the mast of the *L'Orient* man of war, the portrait of the late Sir William Hamilton, K.B. enamelled on china from the original painting by Sir W. Beachey.

CHINA:
An elegant Dinner Service, comprising 184 pieces
A Dessert Set to match comprising 41 pieces
A breakfast set comprising 70 pieces
A white and gold tea and coffee set comprising 50 pieces

GLASS:
Several items including: eight decanters, 8 goblets, 3 hock glasses, 3 wine ditto, a water jug, 5 cut goblets, 12 wine glasses and 15 finger glasses

DRAWING ROOM:
A handsome steel register stove, a pair of light ormulu candlebras, a pair of Georgian mahogany card tables, a Japanned sofa, a sofa in cotton case, the elegant chinz pattern cotton window curtains, an easy chair, a mahogany frame reading chair and a Brussels carpet planned to room 27 feet x 16 feet 8.

BOOKS:
There is an extremely long list of books, very few of which sold. 72 itemized books, many in sets of several volumes and six lots of 50 books each. The listed books cover Emma's interest in music, history, art, poetry, costume and travel. The last six lots in the book collection are listed as *' a quantity of music books'*. A pencilled note next to these 6 lots bracketed together reads *'Horatia'*. Either someone purchased these on her behalf with her (own) money or the auctioneer set them aside for her.

The sale ends with a short list of items in the Hall, Kitchen and Pantry. The kitchen contained a poker, tea-kettle, a frying-pan, various other cooking and serving pans and a 77 piece set *'part of a blue and white dinner service'* that must have been for Emma's and Horatia's daily use.

The very last items are in the Pantry: A deal table, a chair, a fender, a glass, a piece of baize, a mahogany knife tray, 2 Japan ditto and a rattle.

The total amount raised by the sale was £687. Very few items remained unsold.

The catastrophic result of this sale was that Emma and Horatia now had no home, no furniture, no china, glass, pictures or books. Horatia's piano had been sold. Nor did Emma have any income if she was not receiving her annuity payments from Robert Greville.

Who could, and should, have helped her? The Earl and Sarah in particular, other members of Nelson's extended family, the Duke of Clarence and the Duke of Sussex, Lady Elizabeth Foster, now the Duchess of Devonshire, Sir Harry, St. Vincent, other long-standing friends in the political and naval world and Emma's own friends, such as Mrs Billington.

Some of Nelson's captains had died and others were serving abroad. Lord Minto was away in India, where he was Governor General of Bengal. He arrived home in May 1814 and died a month later. Hardy, who would certainly have remembered Nelson's last words to him: *'Take care of my dear Lady Hamilton, Hardy, take care of poor Lady Hamilton. Kiss me, Hardy ... God bless you, Hardy',*[18] had left England for the North American station, shortly after Nelson's funeral. He was briefly in England in 1809, when Emma was already in difficulties.*

In 1812, he contacted Emma to ask about Horatia. He had never believed that Nelson was the father of the child. Her answer is recorded: Received 7th. October 1812, from Lady Hamilton: *My dear Sir Thomas, Let me only say to you that which is true. Horatia is our dear Nelson's daughter. May God bless you! Emma Hamilton.*[19]

Everyone was aware of Emma's situation from newspaper reports. They knew how much Nelson had loved her, and for his sake, might have assisted Emma and his daughter.

The blows that rained down on Emma continued mercilessly. Resettled at 12 Temple Place she received the news that her loyal friend, Susanna, had died on 13 July at Bradenham Hall, aged 58. Susanna was buried at her father's old church at Burnham Thorpe.

Emma tried to put on a brave front, attempting to live as normally as possible while confined 'Within the Rules'. She was determined to celebrate, as always, Nelson's Nile Victory on 1 August. She wrote to Sir Thomas Lewis (MP) on 31 July:

12 Temple Place, Saturday 31st July
My dear Sir Thomas, Will you come to-morrow to meet our good pope

---

* He remained abroad until 1809. On his return he was posted to Lisbon. From August 1812, he was again stationed in North America, returning to England in June 1815, when he was knighted.

[Abbé Campbell, one of her friends] *and Mr Tegart* [her doctor]. *It is the first of Agust do come, it is a day to me glorious, for I largely contributed to its success and at the same time it gives me pain and grief thinking on the Dear lamented Chief who so bravely won the day and if you come we will drink to his Immortal Memory. He cou'd never have thought that his Child and My self should pass the anniversary of that victorious day were we shall pass it, but I shall be with a few sincere and valuable friends, all Hearts of Gold, not Pinchback and that will be consoling to the afflicted heart of your Faithful Friend.*

Emma Hamilton[20]

Merton and Richmond friends visited them. Emma taught Horatia Italian and French and hired a piano for her at 15/- a month. The Matchams wrote regularly, receiving few replies. Horatia visited Alderman Smith's home to play with his two little girls and, when Emma became ill, she was allowed to take carriage rides in the area. They attended church services at the Magdalen Hospital, a home for reformed prostitutes, where the girls were known for their beautiful singing.

The weeks passed by until Emma arranged a birthday celebration for Horatia on 29 October. She described the party to her friend Mrs Lambert:

My ever dear Mrs Lambert,

Your dear kind letter gave me great pleasure & that this day week I shall have the pleasure of your company to stay with me for a few days is beyond my power of utterance. Yesterday, my dear Horatia's birthday, His Royal Highness [the Duke of Sussex] *dined with me, Mrs B* [Billington?], *Mr Perry of the* Morning Chronicle, *Col. O'Kelly & in the evening Col. Smith – we were very merry, I wished for you. Storace* [the opera singer] *called today for the first time. I am so much better you will be surprised to see me. Abbé Campbell in a letter today from Devonshire begs his love to you, His Royal Highness begs his compliment s...Horatia's love, love, love. She is attentive to her studies and behaves very* [well? Illegible]

Your affectionate and grateful

Emma Hamilton[21]

This birthday celebration may not have been to Horatia's liking. The day after the party Horatia had another bout of rebellion and Emma wrote her a strongly worded letter:

October 31st 1813

'Horatia; – Your conduct is so bad, your falsehoods so dreadfull, your cruel treatment to me such that I cannot live under these afflicting circumstances;

my poor heart is broken. If my poor mother was living to take my part, broken as I am with greif and ill-health, I should be happy to breathe my last in her arms. I thank you for what you have done today. You have helped me on nearer to God, and may God forgive you. In two days all will be arranged for your future establishment, and on Tuesday at 12, Col and Mrs Smith, Trickey [her lawyer] Mr & Mrs Denis, Dr Norton will be here to hear all. Every servant shall be put on their oath, for I shall send for Nany at Richmond – Mr Slop, Mrs Sice, Anne Deane – and get letters from the Boltons and Matchams to confront you, & tell the truth if I have used you ill; but the all-seeing eye of God know my innocence. It is therefore my command that you do not speak to me till Tuesday, & if to-day you do speak to me, I will that moment let Col & Mrs Clive into all your barbarous scenes on my person, life and honour.'[22]

We will never know exactly what Horatia said or did to provoke this letter.* Emma's statement that Horatia should *'tell the truth if I have used you badly'* indicates that Horatia accused her of ill-treatment. The threat of a new arrangement for Horatia's *'future establishment'* is never mentioned again.

The Matchams sent Horatia a present, a new hat, and some family news. One of the Matcham's daughters, (probably Catherine), wrote to Emma:

November 21st 1813

Mama only received your letter dated 23rd. October yesterday, which I hope will account to you for my not writing before. We have sent Horatia two or three letters since the date of yours, which must have made it appear still more extraordinary, but we were most happy to find you are better and can take an airing in the carriage. Mama has not been at all well for some time, but we hope in a short time to see her regain her usual spirits and strength. You know this is not the most pleasant time of year, and the loss we have all had in one of the best of aunts cannot so soon be forgot ... It is always a pleasure to hear from you and Horatia, to whom all her cousins unite in kind remembrances ... Papa, I believe wrote an account of us all in the box which contained Horatia's hat, which we were happy to hear she liked.

Mama would have written to you, but is unable at present ... We shall not see you this winter-time I suppose, but at any rate write soon & believe me, etc.'

G.M. attached a note to Emma:

Novr 21st, 1813

---

* Nelson had written to Emma in October 1803 - *'Aye! She is like her mother, will have her own way, or kick up a devil of a dust'.*

Pray let us know the Carrier's name of the wagon which passes your house. We will supply you with potatoes all the winter, and send you a turkey by the first opportunity. If you find it impossible to pay us a visit, Mrs M. and I shall be tempted to go to Temple Place before the close of the winter and pass a day with you. We have always been sensible of the ingratitude you have met with, but is it not better to be wholly freed from any attention of that man, who is insensible to everything but what immediately appertains to his own interest? Write as soon as ever you can, and give directions for anything our farm can supply, etc.[23]

There is no evidence that such a visit took place. Kitty was unwell and a hard winter followed. Once again G.M. condemns the Earl's behaviour towards Emma.

The Matchams and Haslewood became friends after Haslewood and his family moved to a house nearby, Slaugham Park. Did they at this time, knowing the appalling circumstances Emma and Horatia were in, put any pressure on the Earl to pay Emma her Bronte money or even to personally contribute towards their well-being? If they did, the Earl made no response.

The promised turkey arrived in December in time for Emma and Horatia to celebrate Christmas. A small, but good-humoured party sat down to dinner, described by one of the guests, Sir William Dillon, a friend of Emma's in Nelson's day:

'I found a letter from Lady Hamilton inviting me to dine with her. Three years had elapsed since I had seen her ... Upon my arrival her Ladyship greeted me most sincerely. "How did you know I was in Town?" I demanded. She acquainted me that a friend who had seen me at the Admiralty had told her, and that she was highly delighted to shake me again by the hand. I noticed a splendid display of plate on the table, and covers laid for four, but made no enquiries who the guests were ...

While we were thus occupied, I was surprised by the entrance into the room of H.R.H. the Duke of Sussex, Soon afterwards Mrs B. [Billington] made her appearance. The Prince was all kindness, and wondered I had not been to see him ...

The dinner being served, the conversation turned in another direction. I had to do the honours – carve etc. The first course went off on complete order, and I could not help thinking that rather too much luxury had been produced. H.R.H. did not expect such an entertainment from the lady who received him. However, there was a sad falling off in the second course, and a great deficiency in attendance, as also of knives and forks. I had to carve a good-sized bird, but had not been supplied with the necessary impliments. Time passed on, but no servant made his appearance. At last Lady H. said: "Why don't you cut up that bird?" I told her I was in want of a knife and fork." 'Oh!" she said, "'you must not be particular here". "Very well my lady," I rejoined." 'I did not like to commit myself in the presence of H.R.H. but since you desire it, I will soon divide the object before me. Besides, you are aware that, as a Midshipmen, I learnt how to use my fingers!" Then, looking round, I found what I wanted, and soon had the bird in pieces. My reply produced some hearty laughter, and the repast terminated very merrily. After a sociable and agreeable entertainment, I took my leave of the company.'[24]

Emma must have borrowed the 'splendid display of plate on the table' either from neighbours or possibly Alderman Smith. This was probably the last time she entertained in the style of the dinners she had hosted during her life with Hamilton and Nelson.

Severe cold weather began in December 1813, the temperature remaining below zero until the end of January 1814. Snowfalls were heavy and frequent. The Thames froze and the last of the Frost Fairs was held between Blackfriars and London Bridge early in February.

Emma fell ill and remained virtually bed-ridden for the first three months of the new year.

News of Napoleon's abdication in Paris and the end of the war in Europe reached London on 12 April. The city celebrated joyously with illuminations, banquets, parties and processions.

On 21 April, in the midst of this patriotic rejoicing, Nelson's letters to Emma were anonymously published in two small volumes: *The Letters of Lord Nelson to Lady Hamilton*. Emma did not at first realize that Nelson's letters, containing his jealous and abusive remarks about the, then, Prince of Wales were included in the publication.* She responded with a letter to James Perry the following day:

12 Temple Place, April 22nd. 1814

To my great surprise I saw yesterday in the Herald *that Lord Nelson's letters to me were published. I have not seen the book, but I give you my honour that I know nothing of these letters. I have been now nine months in Temple Place, & allmost all the time I have been very ill with a bilious complaint, brought on by fretting and anxiety, & lately I have kept my bed for near twelve weeks, nor have I seen any person except Dr. Watson & Mr. Tegart, who*

---

* The Letters of Lord Nelson to Lady Hamilton with a supplement of interesting Letters by Distinguished Characters in Two Volumes. London. Printed by MacDonald and Son, Smithfield. For Thomas Lovewell & Co Staines House, Barbican.

have attended me with kindness & attention, & to whoes care I owe my life. About four years ago my house in Dover Street was on fire, & I was going into Sussex for 3 months, & I left part of my papers in a case with a person to whom I thought I cou'd depend on. Weather this person has made use of any of these papers, or weather they are the invention of a vile, mercenary wretch, I know not, but you will oblige me much by contradicting these falsehoods, and you much gratify your gratefull, Emma Hamilton

P.S. ... I am now suffering for having been too generous, for I might have been rich if I had only thought of myself & not of my country. I have now given all up to pay my debts, not having ever received one farthing from Government, neither as the widow of a minister who served 37 years, and for the last ten years my indefatigable pains and the procuring of the letters for the supplying of the fleet before the glorious Battle of the Nile ... Yet all this has hitherto been neglected, nor have my great and glorious friend's wishes in the moment of death & victory been listened to. God bless you, my dear sir, my heart is too full to say more.[25]

By *'I know nothing of these letters,'* Emma indicated she knew nothing of how they came to be published.

Friends and advisors warned her that, with the publication of Nelson's comments, she had lost any hope of help from the Prince Regent. Emma had not destroyed Nelson's letters to her although he had instructed her to do so, but in keeping these particular letters she had brought destruction down upon herself.

G.M. wrote to Emma [April 1814]:

'We are all anxious, my dear Lady Hamilton, to see you at Ashfold. The summons to Mrs. M. and myself to escort you and dear Horatia to this place would be most grateful to us. You have heard of the Earl's conduct; he has been as inimical to the whole family as his present means allowed. But, I have no doubt, the principal train of his thoughts are directed to injure as much as possible those who were loved by his brother, the good & noble Lord. When our house is free of visitors, Mr. [George jnr.] M. & myself purpose going as far as your house, and staying with you a few hours. We shall not go into London, our only object will be to see you & talk over our future destination. The dear beautiful Ashfold is offered for sale ... You will consely infer that we seek another country. We do; but where, I cannot determine till I have some conversation with my travelled friends. Write us frequently. I offer a joint wish that we may all settle abroad in some city, town, or village, etc.'[26]

Perhaps this letter gave Emma the idea to move to France.* Having

*The Matchams did not sell Ashfold Lodge or move abroad until 1818.

forfeited any hope of assistance from the Prince Regent or the Dukes of Clarence and Sussex, all of whom were themselves heavily in debt, Emma was obliged to appeal to the Earl for some of her Bronte money, that she claims she had never received:

> 12 Temple Place in the Rules of the Kings Bench
> April 29th 1814

My Lord,

It cannot be more disagreeable to you to receive a letter from me than it is for me to write to you but as I will not have anything to say or do with Lawyers without I am compell'd to it I shall be glad to know from your Lordship weather the first half year of the Bronte pension which my ever dear lamented Friend the glorious & virtuous Nelson left in his will I was to receive & which I never have received I shall be glad to know how it is to be settled, as nor from my present situation which has been brought on not by any crime but by having been too generous to the ungratefull, and I rather glory in being the injured and not the injurer, and to us every sixpence is of the utmost consequence to me, on account of Horatia Nelson's education the beloved Child of dear Nelson. I do not in the midst of poverty neglect her Education which is such as will suit the rank in life which she will yet hold in society & which her great father wish'd her to move in. I ask not alms, I ask not anything but right, and to know weather I am to receive my due or not.

Believe me, my Lord, yours,

Emma Hamilton[27]

The Earl, having ignored Emma since her letter in 1806 asking for help, sent her £225, after deducting £25 tax due. This payment arrived on 5 May. James Perry and Alderman Smith raised a small sum for her in the city and probably added contributions themselves, which, with the £225, paid off her *'just creditors'*. Alderman Smith obtained her discharge from Lord Ellenborough, the Chief Justice of the King's Bench.

Emma refused to pay the sums demanded by the unscrupulous annuitants who had duped her into paying exorbitant interest rates in her desperation as she tried to sell Merton Place.

Emma and Horatia were allowed to leave Temple Place almost a year to the day of being confined to 'The Rules'. On their last day in England, 2 July, they made their way across London Bridge along the Thames to the Tower where, to avoid possible interception and arrest, they boarded a small vessel, the *Little Tom*, to take them across to France. Emma had only £50 in her pocket out of which she had to pay their fares.

CHAPTER 25

Despair, Destitution and Death

'If my dear Horatia was provided for I should dye happy ...
How I would bless them that enabled me to do it!'
Emma to Sir William Scott, from Calais, 12 September 1814

'If there is humanity still left in British hearts, they will not suffer us to die
with famine in a foreign country.'
Emma to Lord Sidmouth, from Calais, 7 October 1814

THREE DAYS LATER, after a rough crossing, they landed in Calais where Emma initially took refuge in the smart Hotel Dessein, while she made her plans. She may have hoped to make influential contacts there.

Her arrival in France, aged forty-nine, accompanied by her thirteen-year-old daughter, contrasted sharply with her arrival twenty-three years before, when, as the new Lady Hamilton, she was presented to Queen Marie Antoinette.

In Calais the fresh air, good food and sense of freedom exhilarated Emma. She wrote an optimistic letter to George Rose:

Hotel Dessin [Dessein] Calais, July 4th

We arrived here safe, dear Sir, after three days' sickness at sea, as for precaution we embarked at the Tower. Mr. Smith got me the discharge from Lord Ellenborough.

I then begged Mr. Smith to withdraw his bail, for I would have died in prison rather than that good man should have suffered for me, and I managed so well with Horatia alone that I was at Calais before any new writs could be issued against me. I feel so much better, from the change of climate, food, air, large rooms and liberty, that there is a chance I may live to see Horatia brought up. I am looking for a lodging. I have an excellent Frenchwoman who is good at everything for Horatia and myself, and my old dame [Francis] who is coming will be my establishment. Near me is an English lady, who has resided here for twenty-five years, who has a day school, but not for eating and sleeping. At eight in the morning I take Horatia; fetch her at one; at three we dine, and then in the evening, we walk. She learns everything – piano, harp, languages grammatically. She knows French and Italian well, but she will improve. Not any girls but those of the first families go there. Last evening we walked two miles to a fête champetre pour les bourgois. Everybody is pleased with Horatia, The General and his good old wife are very good to us, but our little world of happiness is in ourselves. If, my dear Sir, Lord Sidmouth would do something for Horatia, so that I can be enabled to give her an education and also for her dress it would ease me, and make me very happy. Surely he owes this to Nelson. For God's sake, do try for me, for you do not know how limited [I am] I have left everything to be sold for the creditors, who do not deserve anything, for I have been the victim of artful mercenary wretches, and my too great liberality and open heart has been the dupe of villains. To you, Sir, I trust, for my dearest Horatia, to exert yourself for her, and that will be an easy passport for me.[1]*

Emma has accepted that Rose can no longer achieve anything on her behalf and simply asks him 'to exert himself' for some remuneration for Horatia.

Two days later, 6 July, Emma still excited by her freedom, wrote her last letter to Davison:

'... the air & exercise & liberty has done more good than all the calomel in the world ... who would vegetate in fog and vapour when they can live cheaper & better & breathe pure air in another country. England has never done anything for me ... Horatia is at her lessons but begs her love to you she is charming and grown since you saw her in vile Banco Regio [she] speaks such good French she was taken for a French girl ...*

Education goes on, for I would sooner starve than her fine and beautiful mind should not be cultivated and made rich with Honer, virtue and Rectitude and accomplishments, such as her Glorious Father wished her to have ... Vile Banco Regio –truly a fit place for Lady Hamilton, the Representative of the Queen of England for many years, with Honor & Respect, and the assistant and co-operator for the good of their country with glorious Nelson and all-so for Nelson's only Child, his flesh & Blood – fye on them ...'[2]

Some letters to and from Emma were opened and detained at the Calais Post Office.[3] If Emma was unaware of this, she probably presumed that the recipients of her letters chose not to reply. Two or three letters were addressed to Alderman Smith. The first written in August announced: *'I am got into a farmhouse 2 miles from Calais and live Comfortably'*, the second, in September, refers to the publication of her letters from Nelson: *'I have beg'd of Sir Wm. Scott to speak to you and the Lord Chancellor to lay an injunction on the scoundrels Harrison and Lovel* [Lovewell – the publisher] *for the stolen letters and let me beg of you not to let one letter be taken from your House. Mr Dorrott has so enraged me against those villains that I can only say when I am more calm I will write fully ...'*

After a brief stay in a cheaper hotel, Quillac's, 'Old Dame Francis' arrived and they moved into the farmhouse near Calais.

From there Emma wrote to Sir William Scott. We learn of her hopes and fears, and that despite previous claims of her love of luxury, she was, it seems, contented with a simple lifestyle:

Common of St. Peter's, two miles
from Calais.
Sept. 12 1814

But pray direct for me, if you do me so much honour and happiness as to write, chez Dessin, Calais.

Many thanks, my dear Sir William, for your kind letter. If my dear Horatia was provided for I should dye happy, and if I could only now be enabled to make her more comfortable and finish her education, oh God how I would bless them that enabled me to do it! She allready reads, writes, and speaks Italian, French and English, and I am teaching her German and Spanish. Music she knows but all must yet be cultivated to perfection, and then our own language, geography, arithmetic, etc. etc. she knows. We read English, Roman and Grecian History, but it is a great fatigue to me, as I have been eight months ill and am now in a state of convalescence. I must be very quiet.

I have been at this farmhouse six weeks, a fine garden, common, large rooms ... I have an ass for Horatia, as she wants, now she is fourteen, exercise. I go in a cart for my health. The Jaundice is leaving me, but my Broken Heart does not leave me. I have seen enough of grandeur not to regret it, but comfort and what would make Horatia and myself live like gentlewomen would be all I wish, and to live to see her well settled in the world but my dear Sir William, without a pound in my pocket what can I do? the 21st. of Oct. fatal day, I shall have some, I wrote to Davison to ask the Earl to let me have my Bronte pension quarterly instead of half yearly and the Earl refused, saying he was too poor, although I got the good and great Lord Nelson that estate by means of the Queen [of Naples]. *I set out from town ten weeks or more ago with not quite fifty pounds, paying our passage also out of it; think then of the situation of Nelson's Child, and Lady Hamilton who so much contributed to the Battle of the Nile, paid often and often out of my own pocket at Naples for to send*

*to Sir John Jervis provisions and also of Palermo for corn to save Malta, indeed
I have been ill used. Lord Sidmouth is a good man and Lord Liverpool is also
an upright Minister, pray and if ever Sir William Hamilton's and Lord
Nelson's services were deserving ask them to aid me. Think what I must feel
who was used to give God only knows, and now to ask! Earl and Countess
Nelson lived with me seven years, I educated Lady Charlotte and paid at Eton
for Trafalgar. I made Lord Nelson write the letter to Lord Sidmouth for the
Prebendary of Canterbury, which his Lordship kindly gave him. They have
never given the dear Horatia a frock or a sixpence.*

*We have excellent beef, mutton, and veal at five pence a pound, chickens
a shilling for two, partridges five pence of two, and turbot per pair half a
crown. Bread very cheap, milk from the cows on our Common like cream, two
quarts for four sous. All our mornings are given up to studys, we walk and
dine at two, go in my cart, she on her donkey, every body very kind to us.
Every Wednesday there is a dance, where all the persons of Rank and there
daughters dance, a mile from this place. We pay 3 pence for going in.*

*Horatia is adored, she dances all those dances, and speaks french like a
french girl. She is good, virtuous and religious. We go to the Church of St.
Peter's and read our prayers in French, for they are exactly like our own.*[4]

Emma is clearly not well, '*convalescing*' after eight months illness in
London and still suffering from '*the Jaundice*'.

Although Sir William Scott was a friend of the Earl, Emma criticizes
the Earl and Sarah – '*they have never given the dear Horatia a frock or a
sixpence*'. The Earl and Countess had not lived with her '*for seven years*'
although they had been frequent visitors, sometimes staying for several
weeks. Emma had certainly educated Lady Charlotte to a high standard
and kept her, at her own expense, both in London and at Merton.

Emma is now '*without a pound*' in her pocket.

She still has the strength to fight the newspaper allegations being
made against her:

Village of St. Pierre, Near Calais
September 14, 1814

Mr. Editor, I was surprised to observe that the Morning Herald, *with
other newpapers, had published that I fled from my bail. This is false; and I
had had Ellenborough's discharge. Mr. Alderman Smith, who became my
bail, never lost a shilling by me. I have left in England [all] which I possessed
to pay my creditors, retaining only that sufficient for Horatia and myself to
subsist upon at a farm-house. My innocence, I trust, will support me against
all the calumnies that have been raised against me. I have taken an oath and*

confirmed it the altar that I know nothing of those infamous publications that are imputed to me. Many letters were stolen from me by that scoundrel, whose family I had in charity so long supported. I never once saw or knew of them. That base man is capable of forging any handwriting; and I am told that he has obtained money from the [Prince of Wales] *by his impositions. Sir W. Hamilton, Lord N., and myself were too much attached to his* [Royal Highness] *ever to speak or think ill of him. If I had the means I wou'd prosecute the wretches who have thus traduced me. I entreat you to contradict the falsehood concerning my bail, and also the other malicious reports I have alluded to in this letter, which will much oblige the much injured*

*Emma Hamilton*⁵

Once again Emma denies being responsible for the publication of the letters, but it was widely believed that she had sold Nelson's letters, considered a despicable action by those wishing to preserve Nelson's reputation. In another letter to Sir William Scott she wrote:

*'I again before God declare I know nothing of the publication of these letters'*⁶

Further distressing news reached Emma when Queen Maria Carolina died on 8 September, aged 62, having spent her last three years in Vienna.*

Nine days after her letter to Sir William Scott, Emma wrote to Robert Greville:

Common of St. Pierre, 2 miles from Calais

21st. September [1814]

You know that my jointure of eight hundred pounds a year has been now for a long time accumulating. If I was to die, I should have left that money away, for the annuitants have no right to have it, nor can they claim it, for I was most dreadfully imposed upon for my good nature, in being bail for a person whom I thought honorable. When I came away I came with honor, as Mr. Alderman Smith can inform you, but mine own innocence keeps me up, and I despise all false accusations and aspersions. I have given up everything to pay just debts, but annuitants never will. Now, sir, let me entreat you to send me a hundred pounds, for I understand you have the money. I live very quiet in a farm house, and my health is now quite established. Let me, sir, beg this favour to your,

Emma Hamilton

---

* After the royal family fled for the second time from Naples to Sicily in 1806, Maria Carolina had quarrelled with the then British Ambassador who persuaded King Ferdinand to banish her from Sicily in 1811. Ever since Emma and the Queen parted in 1800 they had continued to correspond up until 1809.

P.S. – Sir Wm. Scott writes me there is some hopes to my irresistible claims – such are his words. The best meat here five pence a pound, 2 quarts of new milk 2 pence, fowls 13 pence, a couple of ducks the same. We bought 2 fine turkeys for four shillings, an excellent turbot for half-a-crown, fresh from the sea, partridges five pence the couple, good Bourdeaux wine, white & red for fiveteen pence the bottle, but there are some for ten sous, halfpence.

Ld. Cathcart past 3 days ago. Horatia improving in person & education every day. She speaks French like a French girl, Italian, German, English, &c.[7]

Robert Greville replied within a week:

Gt. Cumberland Street,
Oxford St. Septr. 27th., 1814.

Madam, – Your letter of Septr. 21st. I received only by yesterday's post, & I reply to it without delay. It is now some time since the regular payments from me of your annuity of eight hundred pounds a year were very unexpectedly interrupted by a notice addressed to me by professional persons, & on the ground that you had made over the greater part of the same for percuniary considerations received by you, & in consequence warning me not to continue the payts. of your annuity otherwise than to them in the extent of these claims.

Not hearing from you in the long intermediate time which followed respect & your not receiving your paymts. as usual, I could scarce doubt the unpleasant statements I had received. Still, I have demurred making any payts. when called on, and under existing circumstances I must not venture to make payments in any direction until this mysterious business is made clear to me, and whereby my acts by legal authority may be rendered perfectly secure to me.

This done, of course I shall pay arrears & continue all future payments whenever they shall be due, with the same precision & punctuality as has hitherto always been maintained & which were attended to to the day, until they were thus interrupted. But now my own security requires that I should clearly know how this mysterious business actually stands, e'er I shall deem it prudent or safe for me to stir a step in a case where I am resolved not to act on doubtful respects, I remain, Madam,

Your obedient humble servant,
Robert F. Greville[8]

When Emma left England with only £50 in her pocket, she would have been anticipating living quietly, supporting herself and Horatia, on Sir William's annuity. Robert Greville's letter, above, admitted that he had not paid her annuity for *'some time'*, having received notices claiming that Emma had *'made over the greater part of the same'* in exchange for *'percuniary considerations'*, and that until he had cleared up this *'mysterious business'*, he was unable to pay her any further annuities. Did he have the legal right to stop paying her annuities? Without having any instructions to do so from Emma or her solicitor? Despite the claims from remaining annuitants, he could have sent Emma at least some of her annuity from Sir William.

She had only asked for one hundred pounds.

Judging by Emma's sudden decline over the next few weeks, Robert Greville's letter was the final blow that she was mentally unable to withstand. Stripped of all her possessions, apart from the few she and Horatia had brought with them on the channel crossing, she was finally broken down by the confirmation that she now had no income with which to support herself and her daughter.

On 7 October, Emma wrote her final letter to Lord Sidmouth, appealing for help:

Common of St. Pierre October 7th 1814

My Lord,

It is with the utmost anguish & regret I write to you. Sir William Scott was so kind knowing my services to my country to speak to your Lordship on behalf of myself and Horatia, the daughter of the Glorious and virtuous Nelson, if there is Humanity still left in British Hearts, they will not suffer us to die with famine in a foreign Country. For God's sake then send us some relief. Let Horatia, who will be fourteen on 29th October finish her education, let her be provided for. At present we have not a shilling in our pockets, altho' I spent all I had on the family of Earl Nelson. He never takes notice of <u>his brother's child</u>, altho' <u>he knows well</u> she is his child. I will not teaze your Lordship any more, only to say if Horatia will be provided for, & believe my Lord your grateful

Emma Hamilton

My direction is chez Desin⁹

There is no record of Lord Sidmouth's reply.

This letter is possibly the last she ever wrote. Emma's prime concern is that Horatia should be provided for and able to complete her education. She had made the same plea in her letter to Sir William Scott a month earlier.

Emma had informed Sir William Scott on 12 September she was *'without a pound in my pocket'*. Now, on 7 October she writes *'we have not a shilling in our pockets'*. The £50, minus their fares, had lasted for three months.

How horrified Nelson, the country's great, glorious and Immortal Hero, would have been to see his country and his brother allow his beloved Emma and Horatia to sink into the destitution they now suffered.

There are no further letters to the Matchams, the Boltons, Alderman Smith or Robert Greville. Emma had always maintained that she would not beg.

She could no longer afford even their farmhouse lodgings. She and Horatia returned to Calais where she took two rooms in a house in the Rue Francaise. They were left completely alone when Dame Francis returned to England. There was no money to pay her wages, or her keep.

Emma was forced to pawn some of her few remaining possessions. Some trinkets, a dress, a watch, a gold pin and an Indian shawl, one of her treasured gifts from Nelson, were exchanged for a modest return.[10]

Days after arriving at the cramped and cold lodgings, Emma took to her bed. Horatia shared her room, her bed in an alcove. Emma was too ill, exhausted and totally broken down to appeal for help from any quarter. Horatia took it upon herself to write appeals to the Earl for an advance on her annuity and to a friend, most likely either Alderman Smith or Mrs. Billington.

The friend sent £20, the Earl sent £10.

The Earl's mean and ungrateful behaviour towards Emma and his brother's daughter cannot be too strongly condemned. The Earl had not withheld Nelson's last codicil, but nor had he put any pressure on the government on her behalf. It is difficult to assess with any certainty if, and when, Emma was ever paid any of her Bronte legacy, apart from the £225 just prior to her leaving England. It is doubtful that the Earl paid all the debts due at Merton on Nelson's death despite the £12,162 'residue' in Nelson's death duties account. Emma and Horatia never received any of this.

Emma had no friends or contacts in Calais. As an ex-ambassadress she may have told Horatia to seek help, if necessary, from the English Consul in Calais.

Ill and feeling hopeless and abandoned, Emma began drinking heavily, probably seeking oblivion and relief from pain. The Consul, ironically a Mr Henry Cadogan, later presented an account to Mr. Matcham and Mr. Haslewood for money he had lent her, plus her wine and spirits bill, amounting to £77*, for which he was reimbursed.[11]

Horatia recalled, many years later:

'Latterly she was scarcely sensible, I imagine that her illness originally began by being bled whilst labouring under an attack of jaundice whilst she lived at Richmond. From that time she was never well, and added to this, the baneful habit she had of taking spirits to a fearful degree, brought on water on the chest.'[12]

After a very cold winter, Emma was extremely ill, suffering from jaundice and the attendant symptoms of depression and dropsy, as well as the effects of alcohol abuse and probably broncho-pneumonia, described by Horatia as *'water on the chest'*. No doctor seems to have been called. Horatia was too inexperienced to deal with the situation. In any case, there was no money to pay for a doctor. Mr Cadogan may not have been aware of how ill Emma was towards the end.

Emma died at 1 p.m. on 15 January 1815, three months before her 50th birthday.

A priest was called to administer the last rites. In her *'scarcely sensible'* state it is likely that Emma was unconscious during the final prayers and proceedings. Horatia never reported any last words her mother may have spoken, although she later described Emma's last tragic days:

' She died in January 1815, and was buried in the burying ground attached to the town. That was a sad miserable time to me. The service was read over the body by a Roman Catholic priest who attended her at her request during her illness. Lady H. had, ever since she had been in Calais, professed herself as Catholic.

Latterly her mind became so irritable by drinking that I had written to Mr Matcham, and he had desired that I would lose no time in getting some respectable person to take me over and that I was to come to them, where I should always find a home. After her death, as soon as he heard of it, he came to Dover to fetch me.

With all Lady H.'s faults – and she had <u>many</u> – she had many fine qualities, which, had she been placed early in better hands, would have made her a very superior woman. It is but justice on my part to say that through <u>all her</u> difficulties she <u>invariably</u> till the last few months, expended on my education, etc., the whole of the <u>interest</u> of the sum left me by Lord Nelson, and which was left entirely in her control.'[13]

* See Appendix 7.

Nobody came to fetch Horatia from Calais or to help Emma in what proved to be her terminal illness. To her credit, Horatia stayed with Emma to the bitter end.

The authorities in Calais recorded Emma's death:

'A.D. 1815, Janvier 15, Dame Emma Lyons, agée de 51 ans, née à Lancashire, à Angleterre, domicilée à Calais, fille de Henri Lyons, et de Marie Kidd, Veuve de William Hamilton, est decéde le 15 Janvier, 1815, à une heure après midi au domecile du Sieur Damy, Rue Francaise.'[14]

When her death was announced in the *Morning Post* on 25 January, Robert Greville sought confirmation from the Calais authorities. He received a reply from the Maire de Calais stating that she had died on 15 January. He also received a letter from Mr John Jones, Lincoln's Inn, dated 26 January:

'I have received information this morning, upon which I can rely, that Lady Hamilton is certainly dead, and was buried on Friday last. I understand that she died in extreme poverty.'[15]

Did Robert Greville suffer any pangs of guilt and remorse over not sending Emma the £100 she had begged for? Perhaps he and the Earl each thought the other was sending her money when, in fact, they had left her penniless.

The Justice of the Peace in Calais made an inventory of Emma's effects. At the time of her death she had clothing and effects valued at 228 francs, plus fifteen francs in a box. The equivalent of just over £9 at the time.[16]

Her funeral on 21 January was arranged by Henry Cadogan. He recorded his expenses:

'Funeral expenses of the late Lady Emma Hamilton, as paid by me, Henry Cadogan, at Calais in France, Janry, 1815: An oak coffin, casked, church expenses, priests, candles, burial-ground, men sitting up, dressing the body, spirits &c. &c ... £28.10s.0d.'[17]

Emma's body was laid to rest *'in the burial ground attached to the town'* and not, as she had requested in her last will, near her mother in the church on Paddington Green. Her grave was marked by a wooden cross, which was later replaced by a headstone. This disappeared when the cemetery fell into disuse not long afterwards.

It was not the Earl, who should have arranged for her body to be returned to England or, at least, taken responsibility for her funeral, but the faithful Alderman Smith who reimbursed Henry Cadogan:

Rec'd, Febry 4th, 1815, of J.J. Smith, Esq., the sum of twenty-eight pounds ten shillings, being the amount of funeral expenses for the late Lady Emma Hamilton, at Calais, in France, as paid by me.

(Signed) Henry Cadogan[18]

It may have been Henry Cadogan who informed the English ships in the harbour of Emma's death. A procession followed the coffin from the church to the grave consisting of *'many captains whose vessels were at that time in the harbour'. The Gentleman's Magazine* reported in March that *'all the English gentlemen in Calais and its vicinity, to the number of fifty'* attended the funeral.[19]

They honoured Emma in memory of Nelson.

> *... I've seen the poet – painter – sculptor's gaze*
> *Speak, with rapt glance, their eloquence of praise:*
> *I've seen thee, as a gem in royal halls,*
> *Stoop like presiding angel from the walls,*
> *And only less than worshipp'd! Yet 'tis come*
> *To this! when all but slander's voice is dumb;*
> *And they who gazed upon thy living face,*
> *Can hardly find thy mortal resting-place.*[20] *

* Concluding lines from Dr William Beattie's poem.

Appendices

APPENDIX 1

Nelson's flagship, *Vanguard*, Captain Edward Berry:

Culloden	T. Troubridge
Theseus	R. W. Miller
Alexander	Alexander J. Ball
Minotaur	Thomas Louis
Swiftsure	Benjamin Hallowell
Audacious	David Gould
Defence	John Peyton
Zealous	Samuel Hood
Orion	Sir James Saumarez
Goliath	Thomas Foley
Majestic	George B. Westcott
Bellerophon	Henry D'E Darby

APPENDIX 2

Nelson's Awards after the Battle of the Nile:

From my own most gracious Sovereign, a Peerage of Great Britain and a gold medal.

From the Parliament of Great Britain, for my life and two next heirs, £2000 per annum.

From the Parliament of Ireland not known, but supposed the same as given to St. Vincent and Duncan, £1000 per annum.

From the Honourable East India Company, £10,000 (Nelson shared a large part of this with his family)

From Alexander Davison 'Esq., a gold medal

City of London, a sword

The Captains who served under my orders in the Battle of the Nile, a Sword
The Grand Signor, a Diamond Aigrette, or Plume of Triumph' valued at
£2000.

The Grand Signor's mother, a box set with diamonds, valued at £1000

Emperor of Russia, a Box set with diamonds, and a most elegant Letter - £2500

King of the Sicilies, a Sword, richly ornamented with diamonds, and a most
elegant and Kind Letter, £5000; and the Dukedom of Bronté, with an Estate
supposed worth £3000 per annum

King of Sardinia, a Box set with diamonds, and a most elegant Letter, £1200

APPENDIX 3

Emma entrusted these letters to her friend, Georgiana, Duchess of
Devonshire, to take care of for Horatia.
In 1815, while Horatia was living with the Matcham family, G.M.
received a letter from Mr Coutts informing him that he had letters
entrusted to him by the Duchess of Devonshire. When she was going
abroad the Duchess of Devonshire, considering them of too much
value to leave with her papers, placed them in the care of Mr Coutts
in a packet labelled *'To the particular care of Lady Hamilton.'* [Nicolas,
7, p.380]

APPENDIX 4

The Earl did not purchase a property until 1814 when he acquired
Stanlynch, near Salisbury in Wiltshire. The house was renamed
Trafalgar House. He received a further £10,000 Government grant for
renovations. On his death in 1835 Thomas Bolton inherited the
property. When Thomas died less than a year later, his twelve-year
old son, Horatio inherited the estate.

APPENDIX 5

Emma's 1808 Will:

This I declare to be my last Will and Testament, October 16th. 1808.

If I can be buried in St. Paul's, I should be very happy to be near the glorious Nelson, whom I loved and admired, and as once Sir William, Nelson and myself had agreed we should all be buried near each other. If the King had [not] granted him a public funeral, this would have been, that three persons who were so much attached to each other from virtue and friendship should have been laid in one grave when they quitted this ill-natured slanderous world. But 'tis past, and in heaven I hope we shall meet. If I am not permitted to be buried in St. Paul's, let me be put where I shall be near my dear mother, when she is called from this ungrateful world. But I hope she will live, and be a mother to Nelson's child, Horatia. I beg that Merton may be sold, and all debts paid: and, whatever money shall be left after all the debts are paid, I give to my dear mother, and after her death to my dear Horatia Nelson. I also give all that I am possessed of in this world to my dear mother, Mary Doggin, or Cadogan, for her use, and, after her death, to Horatia Nelson. I give them all my ready money, plate, linen, pictures, wearing apparel, household furniture, trinkets, wine, in short, everything I have in this world to my mother during her life, and after her death to my dearest Horatia Nelson. I hope Mr George Rose will be my executor, and take care of my dear mother and Horatia, and if he should not be living, I hope his eldest son will do me this last favour to see justice done to Nelson's daughter, and also I beg His Royal Highness the Prince of Wales, as he dearly loved Nelson, that His Royal Highness will protect his child, and be kind to her; for this I beg of him, for there is no one that I so highly regard as His Royal Highness. Also my good friend the Duke of Queensbury, I beg of him, as Nelson beseeched him to be kind to me, so I commend my dear mother and Horatia to his kind heart. I have done my King and country some service, but as they were ungrateful enough to neglect the request of the virtuous Nelson in providing for me, I do not expect they will do anything for his child; but if there should be any administration in at my death who have hearts and feelings, I beg they will provide for Horatia Nelson, the child who would have had a father if he had not gone forth to fight his country's battles, therefore she has a claim on them. I declare before God, and as I hope to see Nelson in heaven, that Ann Connor, who goes by the name of Carew and tells many falsehoods that she is my daughter, but from what motive, I know not, I declare that she is the eldest daughter of my mother's sister Sarah Connor, and that I have the mother and six children to keep, all of them, except two, having turned out bad. I therefore beg of my mother to be kind to the two good ones, Sarah and Cecilia. This family having by their extravagance almost ruined me, I have nothing to leave them, and I pray to God to turn Ann Connor, alias Carew's heart. I forgive her, but as there is madness in the Connor family, I hope it is only the effect of this disorder that may have induced this bad young woman to have persecuted me by her slander and falsehood. I give all my papers, books, lace, and indeed, everything to my dear mother and Horatia Nelson. This I declare to be my last Will and Testament, and to do away with all other wills.

Emma Hamilton

APPENDIX 6

The following is an abridged version of 'A Catalogue of the Elegant HOUSEHOLD FURNITURE, The property of a Lady of Distinction, on the premises, No. 150 New Bond Street, On Thursday, July 8, 1813.'
(Room by room, which, in addition, gives an indication of the accommodation at 150 Bond Street):

FRONT ATTIC:
A wool mattress in a white case, a large deal chest, three blankets, a counterpane, and a pair of sheets

BACK ATTIC:
Two dumb bells, a small tool chest, a high basket, some mahogany pillars and a trunk

SECOND FLOOR:
Bed Room:
A high wire fender, set of fire irons, a hearth rug, a feather bed, 3 down pillows, four large blankets, a Japan chiffonier, a Grecian couch, hair squab and bolster, plus five various mahogany chest-of-drawers. (This must have been her own bedroom as it contained the 7 foot bed bought by Salter.)

Front Room:
A handsome satin wood writing table, a 2-flap mahogany dining table, two sets of French window curtains and 2 painted blinds (sold for £1), a capital mahogany secretaire and bookcase, glazed doors and brass astringal, a time piece, a chimney ornament and a piano forte by Tomkinson.

FIRST FLOOR:
Front Room:
A pair of capital bronze figures 2 lights each, a mahogany frame sofa, a handsome mahogany breakfast table on pillar and claw, a Kidderminster carpet, a pier glass 28x18 in a gilt frame, three bronze busts (sold for £1)

PAINTINGS:
Europa and the Bull, fine, Titian, a quantity of coloured prints and drawings, a print framed and glazed the Victory of the Nile, a snuff box made from the mast of the L'Orient man of war, the portrait of the late Sir William Hamilton, K.B. enamelled on china from the original painting by Sir W. Beachey.

CHINA:
An elegant Dinner Service, comprising 184 pieces
A Desert Set to match comprising 41 pieces
A breakfast set comprising 70 pieces
A white and gold tea and coffee set comprising 50 pieces

GLASS:
Several items including: eight decanters, 8 goblets, 3 hock glasses, 3 wine ditto, a water jug, 5 cut goblets, 12 wine glasses and 15 finger glasses

DRAWING ROOM:
A handsome steel register stove, a pair of light ormulu candlebras, a pair of Georgian mahogany card tables, a Japanned sofa, a sofa in cotton case, the elegant chinz pattern cotton window curtains, with continued draperies lined and fringed, an easy chair, a mahogany frame reading chair and a Brussels carpet planned to room 27 feet x 16 feet

BOOKS:
There is an extremely long list of books, very few of which sold. 72

itemized books, many in sets of several volumes and six lots of 50 books each. The listed books cover Emma's interest in music, history, art, poetry, costume and travel. Of note are: Vitari Vite De Pittori (Lives of the Painters), Doomsday Book, 2 volumes, Johnson's dictionary and Johnson's life, Gibbon's Roman Empire, 8 volumes of Shakespeare, Hayley's Life of Romney and one book entitled Lady Hamilton's Attitudes. The last six lots in the book collection are listed as *'a quantity of music books'*.

The sale ends with a short list of items in the Hall, Kitchen and Pantry. The kitchen contained a poker, tea-kettle, a frying-pan, various other cooking and serving pans and a 77 piece set *'part of a blue and white dinner service'* that must have been for Emma's and Horatia's daily use. The very last items are in the Pantry: A deal table, a chair, a fender, a glass, a piece of baize, a mahogany knife tray, 2 Japan ditto and a rattle.

APPENDIX 7

Henry Cadogan's wife sent a bill to Haslewood for money lent to Emma, added to which were the costs of retrieving Emma's possessions from the pawnbrokers for Horatia:

Mr. Cadogan's bill	£77.0.0
Paid woman for duplicates	£4.10.0
Necklace and trinkets from the Pawnbrokers	£16.5.0
Paid Jeweller for watches, gold pin, & necklace	£15.0.0
Paid for an Indian Shawl, silk dress, one long silk shawl, several small do, two gowns & basket	
	<u>£3.5.0</u>
	£116.0.0

The Eyre-Matcham's account of Emma's last days states:

'Although she had recourse to raising money from pawn-brokers, Lady Hamilton never experienced actual want.'

This is substantiated with a reference: *'Nelson, by G.Lathom Brown, pp 417-418.*

He calculates that the yearly interest of the money and property left to her at over £2000. Her poverty was the result of sheer extravagance.' [Eyre-Matcham, page 277]

Bibliography

PRIMARY SOURCES

National Archives, Kew, London
National Maritime Museum, Greenwich, London
Nelson Museum, Monmouth, Wales
Nelson Museum, Great Yarmouth, Norfolk
Coutts Bank, London
House of Commons Library, Westminster
London Metropolitan Archives
Bank of England, London
Merton Historical Society
Christie's Auctioneers, London
Sotheby's Auctioneers, London
The British Library, St Pancras, London
The Goldsmiths' Company, London

SECONDARY SOURCES

Adkins, Roy, *Nelson's Trafalgar, The Battle that Changed the World* (2005)
Allen, Joseph, *Life of Nelson* (1852)
Jaffé, Patricia, *Lady Hamilton in relation to the art of her time* (1972)
Catalogue of the Exhibition at the Iveagh Bequest, Kenwood Arts Council of Great Britain and Greater London Council
Baily, J.T. Herbert, *Emma, Lady Hamilton* (1905)
Beatty, William M.D., *Authentic Narrative of the Death of Lord Nelson* (London1807)
Bennett, Geoffrey, *Nelson, The Commander* (1972)
Beresford, Rear-Admiral Lord Charles C.B. M.P. and Wilson, H.W., *Nelson and His Times* Printed by Eyre & Spottiswoode (date?)
Bishop, Edward, *Emma, Lady Hamilton* (1969)
Bowen, Marjorie, *Patriotic Lady* (1970)
Bradford, Ernle, *Nelson: The Essential Hero* (1977)

Broadley, A.M. & Bartelot, M.A., *Nelson's Hardy, His Life, Letters and Friends* (1909)

Bryant, Sir Arthur, *Nelson* (1970)

Clayton,Tim & Craig, Phil, *Trafalgar The men, the battle, the storm* (2004)

Coleman, Terry, *Nelson* (2001)

Colvin, John, *Decisive Battles* (2003)

Cordingly, David, *Billy Ruffian, The Bellerophon and the Downfall of Napoleon* (2003)

Cronin, Vincent, *Napoleon* (1971)

Cross, David A., A Striking Likeness (2000)

Danby, Frank, *Nelson's Legacy. Lady Hamilton: Her Story & Tragedy* (1915)

Deane, Anthony, *Nelson's Favourite, HMS Agamemnon at War 1781-1809* (1996)

Delaforce, Patrick, *Nelson's First Love, Fanny's Story* (1988)

Downer, Martyn, *Nelson's Purse* (2004)

Eyre-Matcham, M., *The Nelsons of Burnham Thorpe* (1911)

Foreman, Amanda [1], *The Duchess* (1998)

Foreman, Amanda [2], Georgiana's World. Georgiana, Duchess of Devonshire (2001)

Forester, C.S., *Nelson* (1929)

Fothergill, Brian [1], *Sir William Hamilton, Envoy extraordinary* (1969, 2005)

Fothergill, Brian [2], *The Mitred Earl, An Eighteenth-Century Eccentric* (1974)

Fraser, Antonia, *Marie Antoinette, The Journey* (2001)

Fraser, Flora, *Beloved Emma, The Life of Emma, Lady Hamilton* (1986

Furneaux, Rupert (Gen. ed. Ludovic Kennedy), *The Seven Years War* (1973)

Gardiner,Robert (ed.), *The Campaign of Trafalgar 1803-1805* (1997)

Gérin, Winifred, *Horatia Nelson, A Treasure house of the Nelson Family* (1981)

Gill,Edward, *Nelson and the Hamiltons on Tour* (1987)

Godden, Angelica [1], *The Sweetness of Life, a biography of Elizabeth Vigée Le Brun* (1997)

Godden, Angelica [2], *Miss Angel, The Art and World of Angelica Kauffman Eighteenth Century Icon* (2006)

Goodwin, Peter, *Nelson's Men O'War, The Illustrated Story of Life in Nelson's Navy* (2003)

Goodwin, Peter, *HMS Victory, Admiral Nelson's Warship at Trafalgar, Pocket Manual 1805* (2015)

Gore, John, *Nelson's Hardy and his wife* (1935)

Gower, Lord Ronald Sutherland, *George Romney* (1904)

Hadlow, Janice, *The Strangest Family* (2014)

Hardwick, Mollie, *Emma, Lady Hamilton, A Study* (1969)

Harvey, Robert, *Mavericks, The Maverick Genius of Great Military Leaders* (2008)

Hague, William, *William Pitt The Younger* (2004)

Hibbert, Christopher, *Nelson, A Personal History* (1994)

Hore, Peter, *Nelson's Band of Brothers, Lives & Memorials* (2015)

Hough, Richard, *Nelson, A Biography* (1980)

Hansard, House of Commons (1806)

Howarth, David, *Trafalgar, The Nelson Touch* (1969)

Howarth, David & Howarth, Stephen, *Nelson, The Immortal Memory* (1988)

Hudson, Gilbert, (ed), *Nelson's Last Diary, September 13-October 21, 1805* (London 1917)

Hudson, Roger (ed.), *Nelson and Emma* (1994)

Kennedy, Ludovic, *Nelson and his Captains* (1951)

Kerr, Admiral Mark C.B., M.V.O., *The Sailor's Nelson* (1932)

Kidson, Alex, *George Romney 1734-1802* (2002)

King, Dean with Hattendore, John B. (eds.), *Every Man will do his Duty* (1997)

Knight, Miss Cornelia, *The Autobiography* (1861)

Knight, Roger, *The Pursuit of Victory* (2005)

Laing, Margaret, *Josephine & Napoleon* (1973)

Lambert, Andrew, *Nelson, Britannia's God of War* (2004)

Laughton, John Knox, *Nelson* (1895)

Lavery, Brian, *Horatio Lord Nelson* (2003) The British Library Historic Lives

Lever, Evelyne, *Marie Antoinette, The Last Queen of France* (2000)

Lloyd, Christopher, *Nelson and Sea Power* (1973)

Lofts, Norah, *Emma Hamilton* (1978)

Lovewell, Thomas & Co Publisher of *The Letters of Lord Nelson to Lady Hamilton;*

With a supplement of Interesting letters by Distinguished characters (Anonymous)

McGowan, Alan, *HMS Victory, Her Construction, Career and Restoration* (1999)

Macauley, Thomas Babington (Ed. Joseph Hamburger), *Napoleon and the Restoration of the   Bourbons (1977)*

Maxwell, Sir Herbert, *George Romney, The Makers of British Art* (1902)

Maynard, C., *A Nelson Companion, A Guide to the Royal Navy of Jack Aubrey (2003)*

Meade-Fetherstonhaugh, Margaret & Warner, Oliver, *Uppark and its people (1988)*

Merton Historical Society, *A History of Lord Nelson's Merton Place* (1998)

Morrison, Alfred, *The Collection of Autograph Letters, The Hamilton-Nelson Papers,*
Volumes 1 and 2. (1894)

Morriss, Roger, Lavery, Brian and Deuchar, Stephen (ed.) Van Der Merwe, Pieter, *Nelson,   An Illustrated History* (1995) National Maritime Museum

Morriss, Roger, *Nelson, The Life and letters of a hero* (1996)

Naish, G.P.B., *Nelson's Letters to his wife and other documents 1785-1831* (1958)

Nicolson, Nigel, *Napoleon 1812* (1985)

Nicolas, Sir Nicholas Harris, *The Dispatches and Letters of Vice Admiral Lord Viscount Nelson, Seven Volumes (London1845)*

Oman, Carola [1], *Nelson* (1947)

Oman, Carola [2], *Napoleon's Viceroy, Eugène de Beauharnais* (1966)

Paston, George, *George Romney, Little book on Art (1903)*

Pettigrew, T.J., *Memoirs of the Life of Vice-Admiral Lord Viscount Nelson* (1849)

Pocock, Tom [1], *Horatio Nelson* (1987)

Pocock, Tom [2], *Remember Nelson, The Life of Captain Sir William Hoste* (1977)

Pocock, Tom [3], *Nelson's Women* (1999)

Rathbone, Philip, *Paradise Merton, The Story of Nelson and the Hamiltons at Merton Place (1973)*

Rodger, N.A.M., *The Command of the Ocean, A Naval History of Britain (1649-1815) (2004)*

Ross, David, *Nelson, Britain's Greatest Naval Commander* (2005)

Russell, Jack, *Nelson and the Hamiltons* (1969)

Sichel, Walter, *Emma Lady Hamilton* (1907)

Simpson, Colin, *Emma, The Life of Lady Hamilton* (1983)

Smith, Timothy Wilson, *Napoleon* (2007)

Sotheby's Catalogue [1], Nelson: The Alexander Davison Collection, London 21 October 2002

Sotheby's Catalogue [2], English Literature and History 17 December 2009

Southey, Robert, *The Life of Nelson* (1887)

Spencer, Countess, Althorp, A short history of Althorp and the Spencer Family (1982)

Stephens, H. Morse, *Revolutionary Europe (1789-1815)* (1897)

Sugden, John [1], *Nelson, A Dream of Glory* (2004)

Sugden, John [2], *Nelson, The Sword of Albion* (2012)

Terraine, John, *Trafalgar* (1976)

Tours, Hugh, *The Life and Letters of Emma Hamilton* (1963)

Trevelyan, George Macaulay, O.M., *British History in the Nineteenth Century and After (1782-1919)* (1937)

Walder, David, *Nelson* (1978)

Walker, Richard, *The Nelson Portraits* (1998)

Warner, Oliver, [1] *A Portrait of Lord Nelson* (1958)

Warner, Oliver, [2], Emma Hamilton and Sir William (1960)

Warner, Oliver, [3], *Nelson's Battles* (1965)

Warwick, Peter, *Here was Paradise - a description of Merton Place* (1995) Reprinted from the Newsletter of the 1805 Club

Wheatcroft, Andrew, *The Habsburgs* (1995)

White, Colin (ed.)[1], *Nelson, The New Letters* (2005)

White, Colin (ed.) [2], *The Nelson Companion* (1995)

Wickson, Robert, *Nelson's Love Letters to Lady Hamilton* (2005)

Williams, Kate, *England's Mistress, The Infamous Life of Emma Hamilton* (2006)

NOVELS

Foxwell, Nigel	*Emma Expects*	(1987)
Hearn, Miranda	*Nelson's Daughter, A novel*	(2005)
Prole, Lozania	*Our Dearest Emma*	(1949)
Sontag, Susan	*The Volcano Lover*	(1992)

Notes on Sources

*The Letters of Lord Nelson to Lady Hamilton, Volumes 1 and 2. Anonymous. Published by Thomas Lovewell & Co, 1814. Letters from these volumes will be given below under the name Lovewell.

** Morrison, volumes one and two, are followed by the Manuscript number.

Chapter 1. Obscure origins
1. Hardwick, p.5
2. Sichel, p.40
3. Meade-Fetherstonhaugh, p.48
4. Fraser, p.10

Chapter 2. Love and obedience
1. Morrison, 1,138
2. Williams, p.81
3. Morrison, 1, 113
4. Ibid. 1, 114
5. Sichel, p.62
6. Romney's Day Books – Hugh Tours, Appendix
7. Morrison, Appendix A
8. Morrison, 1,124
9. Ibid. 1, 125
10. Ibid. 1, 126
11. Ibid. 1, 126
12. Ibid. 1, 126
13. Ibid. 1 126
14. Ibid. 1, 127
15. Ibid. 1, 128
16. Ibid. 1, 129

Chapter 3. Emma's transfer from Greville to Hamilton
1. Morrison, 1, 134
2. Ibid. 1, 136
3. Ibid. 1, 137
4. Fothergill [1], p.163

5. Morrison, 1, 138
6. Constantine, p.140
7. Morrison, 1, 139
8. Ibid, p.142
9. Ibid, p.143
10. Tours, 198 and Fraser, p.264

Chapter 4. Sir William Hamilton – Envoy Extraordinary to the Kingdom of the Two Sicilies
1. Fothergill[1], p.25
2. Morrison, 1, 95
3. Constantine, p.17
4. Constantine, p.17
5. Ibid, p.30
6. Ibid, p.30
7. Fothergill [1], p.34
8. Ibid, p.34
9. Ibid, p.43
10. Fothergill [1], p.113
11. Constantine, p.27
12. Fraser, p.98
13. Constantine, p.37
14. Ibid, p.64 and Fothergill [1], p.51
15. Constantine, p.65
16. Ibid. p.64
17. Ibid. p.66
18. Ibid. p.71
19. Morrison, 1, 40
20. Constantine, p.87
21. Morrison, 1, 52
22. Constantine, p.83
23. Fothergill [1], p.113
24. Ibid, p.111
25. Morrison, 1, 71
26. Constantine, p.79
27. Ibid, p.97
28. Ibid, p.97
29. Fothergill [1], p.114
30. Ibid, p.106

31. Morrison, 1, 92
32. Constantine, p.109
33. Morrison, 1, 117
34. Constantine, p.127
35. Ibid, p.114
36. Ibid, p.116
37. Ibid, p.116

Chapter 5. Greville's deceit and Emma's love lost
1. Morrison, 1, 149
2. Fraser, p.177
3. Fothergill [1], p.180
4. Morrison, 1, 150
5. Ibid, 1, 152
6. Ibid, 1, 153
7. Hardwick, p.25 and Fraser, p.86
8. Fraser, p.92
9. Morrison, 1, 154

Chapter 6. Emma finds happiness in Naples
1. Morrison, 1, 157
2. Ibid, 1, 158
3. Ibid, 1 159
4. Ibid, 1, 160
5. Ibid, 1, 162
6. Ibid, 1, 163
7. Fraser, p.108
8. Morrison, 1, 164
9. Ibid, 1, 165
10. Fothergill [1], 179 and Fraser, p.115
11. Williams, p.140
12. Ibid, 135
13. Morrison, 1, 168
14. Ibid, 1,171

Chapter 7. Emma's path to marriage
1. Fothergill, [2] p.115
2. Fraser, p.162
3. Ibid. p.142
4. Morrison, 1, 177
5. Fothergill [1], p.185
6. Jaffé, p. 33
7. Constantine, p. 172
8. Morrison, 1, 185
9. Fraser, p.139

10. Ibid. p.140
11. Ibid. p.141
12. Morrison, 1, 189
13. Ibid. I, 190
14. Paston, p.117
15. Fraser, p.152
16. Paston, p.119
17. Ibid. p.120
18. Fothergill [1], p. 195
19. Paston, p.121
20. Fraser, p.149
21. Tours, p. 89
22. Fothergill [1], p.168
23. Constantine, p.179
24. Paston, p.122
25. Tours, p.93
26. Ward and Roberts, Romney Catalogue Raisonné

Chapter 8. Emma in her prime
1. Constantine, p.184
2. Fraser, p.161
3. Constantine, p.184
4. Fraser, p.163
5. Morrison, I, 200
6. Goodden [2], p.214
7. Ibid, p.213
8, Morrison, 1, 199
9. Fraser, p.166
10. Ibid. p.167
11. Ibid. p.166
12. Tours, p.64
13. Knight, p.157
14. Tours, p.95
15. Hibbert, p.91
16. Lovewell, volume 2, Supplement
17. Morrison, 1, 201
18. Ibid. I, 210
19. Cross, p.124
20. Morrison, I, 208
21. Ibid, 1, 215
22. Fraser, p.173
23. Ibid. p.173-4
24. Ibid. p.174
25. Foreman, p.278
26. Fraser, p.176
27. Constantine, p.190

28. Vincent, p.294
29. Morrison, 1, 220 and Tours, p.101
30. Tours, p.101
31. Morrison, 1, 221
32. Hibbert, p.92 and Nicolas, 1, 328

Chapter 9. Emma becomes embroiled in politics
1. Tours, p.104
2. Sugden [2], p.146
3. Foreman, p.279
4. Lovewell, volume 2, Supplement
5. Constantine, p.198
6. Fothergill [1], p.227
7. Constantine, p.202-203
8. Morrison, 1, 204 and Constantine, p.202
9. Ibid. Morrison and Constantine
10. Constantine, p.203
11. Morrison, 1,267
12. Fothergill [1], p.217
13. Lovewell, volume 1
14. Morrison, 1, 246 and Tours, p.106
15. Morrison, 1, 248
16. Lovewell, volume 1
17. Fothergill [2], p.215
18. Morrison, 1, 250
19. Ibid. 1, 252
20. Ibid. 1, 263
21. Constantine, p.205
22. Morrison, 1, 264
23. Ibid. 1, 287
24. Fothergill [1], p.225
25. Jaffé, p.56
26. Constantine, p.212
27. Fothergill [1], p.224
28. Ibid. p.228
29. Constantine, p.207
30. Fothergill [1], p.229

Chapter 10. Nelson
1. Vincent, p.16
2. Nicolas, 1, p.21
3. Ibid. p.8-9, footnote
4. Vincent, p.41
5. Nicolas, 1, p.36
6. Ibid. p.134

7. Ibid. p.131
8. Vincent, p.68
9. Naish, p.19 and Nicolas, 1, p.139
10. Nicolas, 1, p.144
11. Ibid. p.155
12. Ibid. p.166
13. Naish, p.49
14. Nicolas, 1, p.167 and Naish, p.31
15. Nicolas, 1, 193
16. Ibid. p.186
17. Ibid. p.187
18. Vincent, p.48 and Pocock [1], p.58
19. Nicolas, 1, p.203
20. Naish, p.41
21. Vincent, p.81
22. Nicolas, 1, p.265
23. Ibid. p.266
24. Ibid. p.278
25. Ibid. p.278, footnote
26. Ibid p.276
27. Ibid. p.276
28. Ibid. p.294, footnote
29. Knight, p.125
30. National Archives, Prob/11/1230
31. Naish, p.72
32. Ibid. p.73
33. Ibid. p.74
34. Ibid. p.76
35. Ibid. p.78
36. Ibid. p.79
37. Ibid. p.80
38. Ibid. p.85
39. Nicolas, 1, p.319
40. Naish, p.90 and Nicolas, 1, p.326
41. Nicolas, 1, p. p.327
42. Nicolas, 1, p.333 and Naish, p.93
43. Naish, p.196
44. Nicolas, 1, p.379
45. Ibid. p.385
46. Ibid. p.390
47. Ibid. p.412
48. Ibid. p.436
49. Ibid. p.437
50. Ibid. p.441
51. Ibid. p.484
52. Pocock [1], p.125
53. Nicolas, 1, p.492

54. Ibid. p.494
55. Ibid. p.497
56. Nicolas, 2, p.1
57. Ibid. p.3
58. Naish, p.291
59. Nicolas, 2, p.173
60. Naish, p.304
61. Nicolas, 2, p.290
62. Pocock [1], p.129
63. Ibid. p.131
64. Naish, p.314
65. Nicolas, 2, p.358, footnote
66. Naish, 352
67. Nicolas, 2, p.358
68. Ibid. p.434
69. Vincent, p.217
70. Nicolas, 2, p.436
71. Knight, p.259
72. Naish, p.381

Chapter 11. Emma and Nelson reunited after the Battle of the Nile

1. Memoirs of Bourrienne, Napoleon's secretary, 1829
2. Cronin, p.144
3. Nicolas, 3, p.11
4. Ibid. p.24
5. Ibid. p.24
6. Sugden [2], p.62
7. Nicolas, 3, p.28
8. Ibid. p.32
9. Tours, p.17
10. Ibid. p.117
11. Nicolas, 3, p.33
12. Vincent, p.251
13. Constantine, p.214
14. Fothergill [1], p.231-232 and Appendix, p.330
15. Constantine, p.216
16. Nicolas, 3, p.31
17. Ibid. p.37
18. Naish, p.398
19. Knight, p.286
20. Nicolas, 3, p.55
21. Ibid, p.54-55
22. Ibid. p.61
23. Ibid. p.56

24. Ibid. p.71
25. Ibid. p.71
26. Tours, p.120, Russell p.38 and Vincent, p.284
27. Pettigrew, vol.1, p.140
28. Nicolas, 3, p.74
29. Naish, p.423
30. Ibid. p.439
31. Nicolas, 3, p.84
32. Ibid. p.87
33. Ibid. p.93
34. Ibid. p.96
35. Ibid. p.96
36. Ibid. p.100
37. Ibid. p.108
38. Ibid, p.113
39. Ibid. p.128
40. Jaffé, p.57
41. Naish, p.399

Chapter 12. Dramatic events in Naples

1. Tours, p.122
2. Nicolas, 3, p.130 and Tours, p.123
3. Nicolas, 3, p.131
4. Naish, p.436
5. Ibid. p.436
6. Ibid. p.443
7. Ibid. p.445
8. Ibid. p.448
9. Ibid. p.458
10. Nicolas, 3, p138
11. Ibid. p.138
12. Ibid. p.144
13. Ibid. p.144
14. Ibid. p.143
15. Ibid. p.144
16. Vincent, p.302
17. Lovewell, vol.1, supplement.
18. Lovewell, vol.1, supplement
19. Russell, p.47
20. Ibid. p.47
21. Ibid. p.49
22. Nicolas, 3, p.167
23. Ibid. p.75
24. Ibid. p.70
25. Ibid. p.166

26. Russell, p.52
27. Naish, p.478
28. Ibid. p.461
29. Nicolas, 3, p.183
30. Ibid. p. 189
31. Naish, p.418-419
32. Nicolas, 3, p.195
33. Ibid. p.200
34. Ibid. p.202
35. Ibid. p.201
36. Fothergill [1], p.253
37. Ibid. p.253
38. Ibid. p.254
39. Tours, p.127
40. Russell, p.59

Chapter 13. Exiles in Palermo
1. Nicolas, 3, p. 210-213
2. Tours, p.132
3. Ibid. p.132
4. Ibid. p.130-131
5. Knight, p.313
6. Nicolas, 3, p.235
7. Ibid. p.215
8. Ibid. p.224
9. Naish, p.479
10. Ibid. p.480
11. Russell, p.37
12. Ibid. p.38
13. Ibid. p.71
14. ibid. p.71
15. Nicolas, 3, p.248
16. Ibid. p.239
17. Ibid. p.247
18. Ibid. p.272
19. Lovewell, volume 1.
20. Lovewell, volume 1.
21.Constantine, p.224
22. Fothergill [1], p.263
23. Ibid. p.264
24. Morrison, 2, 381 and Russell, p.69
25. Ibid. Morrison and Russell
26. Nicolas, 3, p.291
27. Vincent, p.306
28. Naish, p.482
29. Nicolas, 3, p.340
30. Ibid. p.316-317

31. Ibid. p.317-318
32. Ibid. p.361
33, Ibid. p.361
34. Russell, p.73
35. Nicolas, 3, p.363
36. Ibid. p.379
37. Russell, p.68
38. Ibid. p.68
39. Nicolas, 3, p.380
40. Ibid. p.491
41. Morrison, 2, 384 and Fothergill [1], p.268
42. Nicolas, 3, p.386
43. Ibid. p.394
44. Ibid. p.398
45. Ibid. p.398
46. Ibid. p.360
47. Ibid. p.360
48. Ibid. p.358
49. Ibid. p.358
50. Constantine, p.238
51. Russell, p.83
52. Fothergill [1], p.269
53. Tours, p.138
54. Pocock [1], p.204
55. Ibid. p.201
56. Ibid. p.204
57. Vincent, p. 332
58. Tours, p.139
59. Nicolas, 3, p.434
60. Tours, p.140-141

Chapter 14. Restoring the monarchy at Naples
1. Tours, p.143
2. Russell, p.93
3. Nicolas, 3, p.438
4. Nicolas, 3, p.429
5. Nicolas, 3, p.441
6. Ibid. p.415
7. Ibid. p.409
8. Vincent, p.326
9. Ibid. p.327
10. Russell, p.77-78
11. Ibid. p.89
12. ibid. p.99
13. Nicolas, 3, p.504

14. Fothergill [1], p.285
15. Fraser, p.240
16. Knight, p.334
17. Sugden [2], p.261
18. Nicolas, 3, p.460
19. Nicolas, 7, p.393, Nicolas, 4, p.63,
    Pocock [1], p.209
20. Naish, p.513
21. Nicolas, 4, p.24
22. Naish, p.489 to 543. Letters
    between Nelson and Fanny.
23. Naish, p.475
24. Ibid. p.515
25. Russell, p.104
26. Ibid. p.104.
27. Howarth & Howarth, p.223
28. Russell, p.105
29. Naish, p.521
30. Vincent, p.345
31. Russell, p.109
32. Ibid. p.110
33. Ibid. p.110
34. Tours, p.146-147
35. Nicolas, 4, p.191
36. Ibid. p.190
37. Ibid. p.196
38. Ibid. p.218
39. Constantine, p.245
40. Nicolas, 4, p.185-186
41. White [1], p.238
42. Sugden [2], p.305
43. Oman [1], p.334 and 339
44. Fraser, p.244
45. Nicolas, 3, p. 509-510
46. Oman [1], p.317
47. White [1], p.238
48. Nicolas, 4, p.232
49. Ibid. p.115, footnote
50. Knight, Cornelia, vol. 1, p.147
51. Knight, p.339
52. Sugden [2], p.313
53. Nicolas, 4, p.242 and Hibbert, p.205
54. Nicolas, 4, p.242 and Naish, p.525
55. Sugden [2], p.292, Constantine,
    p.244 and Fothergill [1], p.304
56. Nicolas, 4, p.242
57. Ibid. p.211, notes

58. Naish, p.515
59. Sugden [2], p.332-333
60. Nicolas, 4, p.263 and Tours, p.149
61. Nicolas, 4, p.263 and Tours, p.151
62. Nicolas, 4, p.251

Chapter 15. Return to England

1. Nicolas, 4, p.264
2. Tours, p.153 and Knight, p.342
3. Tours, p.154 and Naish, p.526
4. Nicolas, 4, p.265
5. Vincent, p.378 and Fraser, p.256
6. Vincent, p.378
7. Knight, p.342
8. Fraser, p.255
9. Morrison, 2, 405 and Russell, p.88
10. Oman [1], p.349
11. Naish, p.496
12. Tours, p.156
13. Ibid. p.157
14. Ibid. p.156
15. Morrison, 2, pages 404 and 405
16. Knight, p.345
17. Tours, p.160
18. Naish, p.496
19. Russell, p.143
20. Nicolas, 4, p.267
21. Knight, Cornelia, p.158
22. Ibid. p.162
23. Hibbert, p.227 and Constantine,
    p.254
24. Hibbert, p.227, Sugden [2], p.375
    and Wickson, p.46
25. Hibbert, p.232
26. Constantine, p.255
27. Nicolas, 7, p.393 and Fothergill [1],
    p.303
28. Oman [1], p.359
29. Hardwick, p.73
30. Eyre-Matcham, p. 169
31. Ibid. p.181
32. Walker, p.129
33. Nicolas, 4, p.278
34. Coleman, p.239
35. Oman [1], p.361
36. Tours, p.165
37. Fraser, p.265

38. Tours, p.169
39. Ibid, p.166 and Naish, p.572
40. Nicolas, 7, p.392
41. Ibid. p. 392
42. Eyre-Matcham, p.153
43. Naish, p.573
44. Russell, p.159
45. Wickson, p.25
46. Ibid. p.21
47. Ibid. p.22
48. Russell, p.165 and Fraser, p.270
49. Russell, p.166
50. Nicolas, 7, p.372
51. Ibid. p.372
52. Ibid. p.386
53. Nicolas, 4, p.284
54. Wickson, p.22
55. Naish, p.618
56. Ibid. p.618
57. Ibid. p.619
58. Ibid. p.588 and Oman [1], p.366
59. Knight, p.357
60. Naish, p.563
61. Tours, p.173
62. Ibid. p.175
63. Wickson, p.21
64. Tours, p.172
65. Wickson, p. 20 and 32
66. Morrison, 2, 524
67. Ibid. 518
68. Ibid, 521
69. Naish, p.576
70. Ibid. p.620 and Gérin, 21
71. Gérin, p.19
72. Ibid. p.21
73. Ibid. p.22
74. Ibid, p.22
75. Wickson, p.28
76. Ibid. p.29
77. Ibid. p.30
78. Nicolas, 4, p.291
79. Ibid, p.291

Chapter 16. Nelson's separation from Fanny and Emma's Purchase of Merton Place

1. Naish, p.580
2. Ibid, p.580
3. Ibid. p.580
4. Morrison, 2, 572 and Russell, p.185-186
5. Naish, p.579
6. Ibid. p.581
7. Russell, p.189
8. Naish, p.574
9. Wickson, p.32
10. Ibid. p.34
11. Tours, p.178
12. Naish, p.576
13. Russell, p.150
14. Ibid. p.183 and Fraser, p.274
15. Fothergill [1], p.312
16. Christie's Catalogue, London
17. Ibid.
18. Russell, p.190
19. Ibid. p.191
20. Nicolas, 4, p.308-309
21. Ibid. p.316
22. Naish, p.584
23. Ibid. p.585
24. Ibid. p.596
25. Ibid. p.586
26. Ibid. p.588
27. Knight, p.400
28. Naish, p.587
29. Nicolas, 4, p.312
30. Maxwell, p.146
31. Ibid. p.154
32. Ibid. p.158
33. Ibid. p.158
34. Morrison, 2, 563 and Tours, p.180
35. Nicolas, 4, p.378
36. Ibid. p.433
37. Ibid. p.438
38. Ibid. p.464
39. Ibid. p.473
40. Naish, p.589
41. Hardwick, p.106
42. Lovewell, volume 1, supplement
43. Naish, p.592
44. Wickson, p.41
45. Merton Historical Society, p.33
46. Wickson. p.37
47. Ibid. p.39

48. Ibid. p.41
49. Ibid. p.42
50. Ibid. p.44
51. Tours, p.185
52. Ibid. p.106
53. Wickson, p.47
54. Ibid. p.49
55. Ibid. p.51
56. Ibid. p.55
57. Ibid. p.56
58. Tours, p.183
59. Nicolas, 4, p.481
60. Ibid. p.489

Chapter 17. Happy days shared at Merton

1. Oman [1], p.421
2. Gérin, p.33
3. Nicolas, 4, p.520
4. Nicolas, 7, p.371
5. Ibid. p.370
6. Ibid. p.371-375
7. Naish, p.594
8. Ibid. p.595
9. Ibid. p.595
10. Ibid. p.593
11. Gérin, p.44
12. Naish, p.596
13. Nicolas, 7, p.375
14. Naish, p.596
15. Eyre-Matcham, p.286
16. Ibid. p.286
17. Gérin, p.44
18. Vincent, p.454 and Nicolas, 4, p.489
19. Vincent, p.474
20. Russell, p.262
21. Wickson, p.55
22. Russell, p.256 and Oman [1], p.430
23. Wickson, p.44
24. Russell, p.276
25. Fothergill [1], p.220
26. Hibbert, p.293, Oman [1], p.434 and Gérin, p.45
27. Vincent, p.427
28. Gérin, p.38 and Merton History Society
29. Vincent, p.352

30. Fothergill [1], p.318
31. Russell, p.262
32. Eyre-Matcham, p.201
33. Constantine, p.274
34. Ibid. p.275
35. Morrison, 2, Appendix C, p.401 and Tours, p.283
36. Nicolas, 7, p.376
37. Ibid. p.376
38. Morrison, 2, 679, Russell, p.270 and Tours, p.198
39. Morrison, 2, 680 and Tours, p.198
40. Russell, p.270
41. Ibid. p.270
42. Tours, p.200
43. Morrison, 2, 684, Tours, p.199 and Fothergill [1], p.321
44. Constantine, p.279 and Russell, p.275
45. Eyre-Matcham, p.203
46. Nicolas, 7, 375-376
47. Ibid. p.376
48. Russell, p.275
49. Ibid. p.277
50. Ibid. p.277 and Morrison, 2, 694
51. Eyre-Matcham, p.204
52. Ibid. p.206
53. Russell, p.208
54. Constantine, p.280
55. Eyre-Matcham, p.206
56. Russell, p.283
57. Ibid. p.283
58. Constantine, p.156

Chapter 18. Sir William Hamilton's Will.

1. National Archives, PROB/11/1390
   Pembrokeshire Record Office,
   SLEBECH HPR/30/75
   National Archives, IR/26/74

Chapter 19. Emma's long separation from Nelson

1. Tours, p.202 and Lovewell, volume 1, Supplement
2. Nicolas, 7, p.377
3. Russell, p.285

4. National Archives by letter
5. Russell, p.285
6. Ibid. p.285
7. Nicolas, 5, p.64
8. Nicolas, 7, p.377
9. Hibbert, p.321
10. Tours, p.204
11. Nicolas, 5, p.66
12. Wickson, p.57
13. Ibid. p.58
14. Russell, p.286
15. Nicolas, 5, p.117
16. Wickson, p.61
17. Nicolas, 5, p.149
18. Ibid. p.175
19. National Maritime Museum, CRK/19/33
20. Ibid. CRK//19/34
21. Nicolas, 7, p.380
22. Gérin, p.67
23. Nicolas, 7, p.381
24. Ibid. p.381
25. Ibid. p.382
26. Ibid. p.382
27. Nicolas, 5, p.206
28. Wickson, p.70
29. Ibid. p.72
30. Nicolas, 7, p.380
31. Hibbert, p.21
32. Russell, p.297
33. Ibid. p.297
34. Eyre-Matcham, p.210
35. Hardwick, p.162-163
36. Nicolas, 5, p.370
37. Ibid. p.370
38. Wickson, p.76
39. Hardwick, p.165
40. Wickson, p.81
41. Hardwick, p.167
42. Nicolas, 5, p.440
43. Transcript from Nelson Museum, Great Yarmouth
44. Knight, p.425
45. Wickson, p.77
46. Nicolas, 6, p.307
47. Hardwick, p.173
48. Gérin, p.74
49. Morrison, 2, 791 and Vincent, p.528
50. Nicolas, 5, p.143
51. Downer, p.266
52. Ibid. p.264
53. Transcript from Nelson Museum, Great Yarmouth
54. Hardwick, p.147
55. Tours, p.208
56. Russell, p.307 and Downer, p.268
57. Transcript from Nelson Museum, Great Yarmouth
58. Nicolas, 6, p.182
59. Nicolas, 6, p.49
60. Russell, p.309
61. Nicolas, 6, p.148
62. Russell, p.315
63. Nicolas, 6, p.205
64. Hardwick, p.179
65. Downer, p.270
66. Nicolas, 6, p.278

Chapter 20. Twenty-five days at dear, dear Merton and the Battle of Trafalgar

1. Tours, p.211
2. Ibid. p.211
3. Sotheby's [1], p.152
4. Nicolas, 6, p.149
5. White [1], p.48
6. Russell, p.32 and White [1], p.49
7. Knight, p.488
8. Wickson, p.105
9. Russell, p.326
10. Nicolas, 6, p.355
11. Russell, p.311
12. Nicolas, 6, p.410
13. Russell, p.327
14. Sotheby's [1], p.151
15. Russell, p.327
16. Ibid. p.330
17. Nicolas, 6, p.475
18. Sichel, p.416
19. Morrison, 2, 797 and Tours, p.210
20. Morisson, 2, 798 and Russell, p.319
21. Morrison, 2, 806 and Russell, p.321
22. Russell, p.325
23. Ibid. p.329

24. Nicolas, 6, p.427
25. Ibid. p.441
26. Ibid. p.441
27. Morrison, 2, 821 and Tours, p.213
28. Russell, p.331
29. Ibid. p.333
30. Gérin, p.89
31. Ibid. p.89
32. Eyre-Matcham, p.226
33. Ibid. p.227
34. Ibid. p.227
35. Oman [1], p.513 and Tours, p.214
36. Nicolas, 7, p.28
37. Sotheby's [1], p.155
38. Knight, p.497
39. Ibid. p.497 and Oman [1], p.517
40. Eyre-Matcham, p.233
41. Ibid. p.226
42. Nicolas, 7, p.30
43. Ibid. p.32
44. Fraser, p.306
45. Gérin, p.99
46. Ibid. p.100
47. Oman [1], p.524
48. Nicolas, 7, p.33
49. Gérin, p.101
50. Nicolas, 7, p.35
51. Ibid. p.35
52. Ibid. p.40
53. Ibid. p.53
54. Oman [1], p.530
55. Nicolas, 7, p.55
56. Ibid, p.118
57. Morrison, 2, 844
58. Gérin, p.102 and Sichel, p.425
59. Morrison, 2, 844
60. Nicolas, 7, p.60
61. Russell, p.343 and Nelson and his times
62. Nicolas, 7, p.385
63. Ibid. p.385
64. Ibid. p.132
65. Ibid. p.132
66. Ibid. p.137
67. Ibid. p.151
68. Ibid. p.140
69. Ibid. p.140
70. Ibid. p.139
71. Ibid. p.146
72. Ibid. p.149
73. Ibid. p.153
74. Ibid. p.157
75. Ibid. p.157
76. Beatty, M.D., William, Authentic Narrative of the Death of Lord Nelson

Chapter 21. Nelson's Will and Codicils
1. Will and Codicils – National Archives PROB/1//22 and Nicolas, 7, ccxx1
2. Stamp Office, Death Duties – National Archives IR/59/1
3. Nelson's Diary 13 September 1805-15 October 1805 – National Archives PROB/1/22

Chapter 22. Emma's descent into debt
1. Tours, p.220
2. Downer, p.274 and Sugden [2], p.841
3. Eyre-Matcham, p.238
4. Russell, p.350
5. Knight, p.536 and Tours, p.221
6. Gérin, p.107
7. Sotheby's [1] p.175
8. Russell, p.351 and Gérin, p.108
9. Sugden [2], p.837
10. Gérin, p.110
11. Morrison, 2, 269, footnote
12. Gérin, p.110
13. Ibid. p.111
14. Tours, p.221
15. Gérin, p.111
16. Ibid. p.113
17. Fraser, p.292
18. Nicolas, 7, p.310
19. Eyre-Matcham, p.247
20. Nicolas, 7, p.310
21. Ibid. p. 412-417
22. Gérin, p.125
23. Sotheby's [2]

24. Hardwick, p.223
25. Hardwick, p.221
26. Nicolas, 7, p.316
27. Ibid. p.329
28. Hibbert, p.380, notes
29. Morrison, 2, 865
30. Nelson Museum, Monmouth, E225
31. Morrison, 2, 870
32. Ibid. 873
33. Ibid. 877
34. Ibid. 874
35. Nicolas, 7, p.334.
36. Oman [1], p.567
37. Russell, p.353
38. Morrison, 2, 882
39. Naish, p.528
40. Sotheby's, p.195
41. Hardwick, p.202
42. Sichel, p.512
43. Hardwick, p.230
44. Nicolas, 7, p.39
45. Ibid. p.118
46. Nelson Museum, Monmouth, E228
47. Sichel, p.505 and Hardwick, p.225
48. Hardwick, p.217
49. Ibid. p.218
50. Russell, p.354 and Fraser, p.322
51. Nicolas, 7, p.394-395 and Nelson
    Museum, Great Yarmouth
52. Nelson Museum, Monmouth, E232
53. Ibid. E220
54. Nicolas, 7, p.387
55. Eyre-Matcham, p.255
56. Sichel, p.505 and Tours, p.226
57. Ibid. Sichel and Tours
58. Knight, p.536
59. Gérin, p.140
60. Ibid. p.143 and Hardwick, p.229
61. Hardwick, p.230
62. Ibid. p.231
63. Eyre-Matcham, p.260-261
64. Morrison, 2, 932 and Tours, p.228

Chapter 23. Under threat of imprisonment

1. Eyre-Matcham, p.262
2. Morrison, 2, 937 and Tours, p.228
3. Morrison, 2, 938 and Sichel, p.444,
   footnote
4. Morrison, 2, 943
5. Ibid. 949
6. Eyre-Matcham, p.271
7. Morrison, 2, 1032
8. Tours, p.230
9. Eyre-Matcham, p.266
10. Morrison, 2, 951 and Gérin, p.160
11. Eyre-Matcham, p.267
12. Ibid. p.266
13. Morrison, 2,959 and Tours, p.232
14. Morrison, 2, 961
15. Sichel, p.507 and Tours, p.233
16. Sotheby's [1], p.203
17. Downer, p.349-350
18. Gérin, p.168
19. Morrison, 2, 930
20. Sichel, p.446
21. Ibid. p.524
22. Tours, p.236
23. Morrison, 2, 965 and Sichel, p.449,
    footnote
24. Hardwick, p.238
25. Morrison, 2, 969 and Gérin, p.169
26. Morrison, 2, 978
27. Ibid. 981
28. Ibid. 982
29. Gérin, p.171
30. Hardwick, p.246
31. Morrison, 2, 989 and Tours, p.238
32. Morrison, 2, 991 and Gérin, p.173
33. Morrison, 2, 1001 and Tours, p.241
34. Ibid. 1003
35. Tours, p.243
36. Morrison, 2, 1021 and Tours, p.245
37. Morrison, 2, 1018, 1019 and Sichel,
    p.456
38. Fraser, p.336
39. Knight, p.423
40. National Archives, PROB/1/25
41. Hardwick, p.257, footnote
42. Morrison, 2, 1030
43. Hardwick, p.253
44. Gérin, p.182
45. Ibid. p.182

Chapter 24. Emma and Horatia confined to 'Living within the Rules'
1. Morrison, 2, 1042
2. Ibid. 1041
3. Ibid. 1044
4. Ibid. 1045
5. Ibid. 1046
6. Hardwick, p.265
7. Gérin, p.185
8. Ibid. p.185
9. Ibid. p.185
10. Sichel, p.482
11. Gérin, p.186
12. Downer, p.312
13. Gérin, p.187
14. Morrison, 2, 1047
15. Ibid. 941 and Gérin, p.190
16. Morrison, 2, 1049
17. National Maritime Museum, ID PBB 7683 and 749.1
18. Nicolas, 7, p.251 and Dr Beatty
19. Nicolas, 7, p.386
20. Gérin, p. 193
21. Hardwick, 269-270
22. Morrison, 2, 1051
23. Ibid. 1052
24. Tours, p.253 and Fraser, p.347
25. Morrison, 2, 1054 and Tours, p.254-255
26. Morrison, 2, 1053
27. Russell, p.360, Hardwick, p.277 and Gérin, p.199

12. Nicolas, 7, p.395 and Gérin, p.208
13. Tours, p.258
14. Ibid. p.259
15. Morrison, 2, 1060
16. Pettigrew, 2, p.636
17. Morrison, 2, p1062
18. Ibid. 1064
19. Hardwick, p.286
20. Sichel, p.475

Chapter 25. Despair, destitution and death
1. Gerin, p.201-202 and Sichel, p.467
2. Downer, p.313 and Russell, p.361
3. Eyre-Matcham, p.277
4. Hardwick, p.281 and Sichel, p.510
5. Sichel, p.511 and Gérin, p.206
6. Sichel, p.462
7. Morrison, 2, 1055
8. Morrison, p.370 footnote and Gérin, p.205
9. Gérin, p.204
10. Eyre-Matcham, p.279
11. Ibid. p.279

Index

British fleet in, 145–46
Calvi (Corsica), siege of, 145
Coutts Bank, 248, 268, 292, 301, 394, 418, 438
Cripps & Francillon, 248

D

Damer, Anne, 52
Davison, Alexander, 132–33, 364
   Emma, correspondence & friendship with, 335, 336, 337, 339–40, 347, 350, 379, 394–95, 436, 451
   financial support for Emma, 334
   imprisonment of, 414
   Merton Place, loan to purchase from, 282
   Nelson, Horatio, correspondence with, 195, 197, 213, 266n, 270-71, 329, 334, 351, 354–55
   Nesbit, Fanny, correspondence with, 270-71, 287
   Prince of Wales, correspondence with, 383
   prosecution, for electoral fraud, 333–34
Dickenson, Mary, 81, 87
   Emma, correspondence with, 93
   Hamilton, Sir William, correspondence with, 96
Dilettanti, Society of, 6, 303
Dillon, Sir William, 446–47
Dutens, Louis, 90, 91, 95

E

Earl Bishop (Lord Bristol), 35, 77, 121
   Emma, correspondence with, 120
   Hamilton, Sir William, correspondence with, 93–94
   Naples, visit to, 119–20
East India Company, 130, 213, 266n
Egypt
   Alexandria, British fleet's arrival, 161
   Bonaparte, Napoleon, attempt to
      conquer, 154
   Nelson, Horatio, pursuit of French fleet to, 159–60
   Nile, Battle of the, 161–63
Elcho, Lady, 80–81
Elgin, Lord & Lady, 216
Ellenborough, Lord, 449
Elliot, Sir Gilbert *see* Minto, Lord
Espinchal, Comte d', 77
Esterhazy, Prince and Princess, 236

F

Fabris, Pietro, 43, 45
Ferdinand, King of Naples, 37, 107, 380
   background & interests of, 38
   Maria Carolina, marriage to, 39
   Naples, evacuation from, 184–87
   Palermo, evacuation to, 189–90, 193
   rebels, treatment of, 206, 207
   Rome, re-taking of from the French, 180
Fetherstonhaugh, Sir Harry, 4–5, 43, 55
   Emma, correspondence with, 393-94, 419, 427
   'Little Emma', 4–5, 393-94, 419, 427
Fitzgerald, Lady, 297
Foster, Lady Elizabeth, 87–88, 352, 377, 420
   Naples, visit to, 108
Foudroyant (ship), 200
   Berry, Captain Edward, command of, 226
   Malta, sail to, 229
   Naples, return to, 202
Fox, Charles, 227–29
France
   Bonaparte, Napoleon, control of, 217
   Boulogne, attacks on, 274
   Britain, conflict with, 142, 144–47, 316, 338, 342-43
   French Revolution (1789), 79, 92